ANTOINE BUSNOYS

ANTOINE BUSNOYS

METHOD, MEANING, AND CONTEXT
IN LATE MEDIEVAL MUSIC

ぞ❦❦ぞ

EDITED BY
PAULA HIGGINS

CLARENDON PRESS · OXFORD

*This book has been printed digitally and produced in a standard specification
in order to ensure its continuing availability*

OXFORD
UNIVERSITY PRESS

Great Clarendon Street, Oxford OX2 6DP

Oxford University Press is a department of the University of Oxford.
It furthers the University's objective of excellence in research, scholarship,
and education by publishing worldwide in

Oxford New York

Auckland Cape Town Dar es Salaam Hong Kong Karachi
Kuala Lumpur Madrid Melbourne Mexico City Nairobi
New Delhi Shanghai Taipei Toronto
With offices in
Argentina Austria Brazil Chile Czech Republic France Greece
Guatemala Hungary Italy Japan South Korea Poland Portugal
Singapore Switzerland Thailand Turkey Ukraine Vietnam

Oxford is a registered trade mark of Oxford University Press
in the UK and in certain other countries

Published in the United States
by Oxford University Press Inc., New York

ISBN 0-19-816406-8

Cover illustration: Busnoys, *Bel acueil.* Yale University, Beinecke Rare Book and Manuscript Library,
MS91 ('Mellon Chansonnier'), fol. 1ˇ.

CPI Antony Rowe, Eastbourne

Acknowledgements

THE essays in this volume began life as papers delivered at the Busnoys conference held on 8–11 November 1992 at the University of Notre Dame, and I should like to thank a number of individuals from that institution who helped make that event possible: Ethan Haimo, Chair of the Music Department, for encouraging the idea and for releasing funds from the Alice Tully Endowment for the Fine Arts to engage two world-class vocal groups for the occasion; Jennifer Warlick and Robert Burke, of the Institute for Scholarship in the Liberal Arts, for assistance with obtaining conference funding; Howard Hanson of the Graduate School, Mr Adrian King, a Notre Dame alumnus from Philadelphia, and the Institute for Scholarship in the Liberal Arts, for financial support crucial to the editing and final production of the volume.

I am also grateful to the National Endowment for the Humanities for generous financial support that enabled the conference to be conducted on a much larger scale than would otherwise have been possible; to Leeman L. Perkins for his invaluable help with planning the conference programme and for gently prodding me to submit the ultimately successful NEH Conference Grant application; to Pomerium and The Orlando Consort for their unforgettable concerts of Busnoys's music, and particularly to the latter for spontaneously performing musical examples during papers, for attending the conference sessions, and for the infectious air of enthusiasm and good spirit they contributed to the ongoing co-operation between scholars and performers; to Murray Steib for expertly producing the musical examples; and to Mary Alice Mohr and Carolyn Tobolski for their competent research assistance.

The volume would never have materialized without the support of several individuals from Oxford University Press, in particular Bruce Phillips, who believed in the project from its inception and steadfastly encouraged its completion; Helen Peres da Costa, who expertly guided the manuscript and proofs through all stages of the exceedingly complicated production process; and Leofranc Holford-Strevens, who generously offered his unparalleled linguistic expertise towards the refinement of virtually all the translations in the volume. Bonnie Blackburn, over the many months of editing and pre-production, answered endless queries and offered invaluable advice; her impeccable attention to detail in the copy-editing of the manuscript, as well as the index, has contributed significantly to the final product. I must also thank Elizabeth Aubrey and Bernhold Schmid for their help in obtaining photographs from libraries in Paris and Munich. And no expression of gratitude could repay the immense debt I owe to all the contributors for their unfailing enthusiasm from the outset and for their good-natured co-operation in meeting even the most unreasonable deadlines.

Finally, I owe special thanks to Rob Wegman, whose abiding friendship supported me during the most crucial phases of editing and preparing the volume for production; to Michael Long, Marsha Dubrow, Donna Jackson, Alex Blachly, Tina Muxfeldt, Mary Frandsen, and Rebecca Higgins who were always there to offer encouragement, advice, and good humour during the tough patches in the long process; and, most of all, to Teodoro and Jesse Giuliani for their loving patience and understanding.

P.H.

Wolfson College, Oxford
May 1995

South Bend, Indiana
September 1999

Contents

PART II. INTERTEXTUAL, CONTEXTUAL, AND HERMENEUTIC APPROACHES TO LATE MEDIEVAL MUSICAL CULTURE

PART III. ISSUES OF AUTHORSHIP, ATTRIBUTION, AND ANONYMITY IN ARCHIVAL AND MUSICAL SOURCES

PART IV. READING THE THEORISTS ON COMPOSITIONAL PROCEDURES AND CHANGING STYLES

PART V. BUSNOYS'S LEGACY

x   *Contents*

List of Illustrations

List of Tables

List of Music Examples

List of Complete Editions of Pieces

Abbreviations

Busnoys LTW	Antoine Busnoys, *Collected Works: The Latin-Texted Works*, ed. Richard Taruskin (Monuments of Music in the Renaissance, 5; New York, 1990)
Census-Catalogue	*Census-Catalogue of Manuscript Sources of Polyphonic Music 1400–1550*, 5 vols. (American Institute of Musicology, 1979–88)
CMM	Corpus mensurabilis musicae
CSM	Corpus scriptorum de musica
EMH	*Early Music History: Studies in Medieval and Early Modern Music*
JAMS	*Journal of the American Musicological Society*
LU	*Liber usualis*
ML	*Music and Letters*
MSD	Musicological Studies and Documents
New Grove	*The New Grove Dictionary of Music and Musicians*, ed. Stanley Sadie (London, 1980)
TVNM	*Tijdschrift van de Vereniging voor Nederlandse Muziekgeschiedenis*

Archival Sources

BAR	Brussels, Archives générales du Royaume
LADN	Lille, Archives départementales du Nord
PAN	Paris, Archives nationales
PADV	Poitiers, Archives départementales de la Vienne

Sigla of Manuscripts (* = poetry source)

Aosta	Aosta, Biblioteca del Seminario Maggiore, MS A¹ D19
Aug 142a	Augsburg, Staats- und Stadtbibliothek, MS 2° 142a
Barc 454	Barcelona, Biblioteca Central, MS 454
Bas F.X.1–4	Basle, Öffentliche Bibliothek der Universität, MS F. X. 1–4
Bas F.X.10	Basle, Öffentliche Bibliothek der Universität, MS F. X. 10
Ber 78.C.28	Berlin, Staatsbibliothek zu Berlin—Preußischer Kulturbesitz, Kupferstichkabinett, MS 78. C. 28
Ber 40021	Berlin, Staatsbibliothek zu Berlin—Preußischer Kulturbesitz, MS Mus. 40021

Bol Q15	Bologna, Civico Museo Bibliografico Musicale, MS Q 15
Bol Q16	Bologna, Civico Museo Bibliografico Musicale, MS Q 16
Bol Q17	Bologna, Civico Museo Bibliografico Musicale, MS Q 17
Bol Q18	Bologna, Civico Museo Bibliografico Musicale, MS Q 18
Br 215–16	Brussels, Bibliothèque royale, MSS 215–216
Br 5557	Brussels, Bibliothèque royale, MS 5557
Br 6428	Brussels, Bibliothèque royale, MS 6428
Br IV.90	Brussels, Bibliothèque royale, MS IV. 90 (cf. Tournai 94)
Cam R.2.71	Cambridge, Trinity College Library, MS R. 2. 71
Cape	Cape Town, South African Public Library, MS Grey 3. b. 12
Cas	Rome, Biblioteca Casanatense, MS 2856 ('Casanatense Chansonnier')
CG XIII.27	Vatican City, Biblioteca Apostolica Vaticana, MS Cappella Giulia XIII. 27
Chigi	Vatican City, Biblioteca Apostolica Vaticana, MS Chigi C. VIII. 234 ('Chigi Codex')
Cop	Copenhagen, Det Kongelige Bibliotek, MS Thott 291, 8° ('Copenhagen Chansonnier')
Cop 1848	Copenhagen, Det Kongelige Bibliotek, MS Ny kongelige Samling 1848, 2°
Cord	Paris, Bibliothèque nationale, fonds Rothschild, MS 2973 ('Chansonnier Cordiforme')
Cort 96	Cortona, Biblioteca Comunale, MS 96
CS 14	Vatican City, Biblioteca Apostolica Vaticana, MS Cappella Sistina 14
CS 15	Vatican City, Biblioteca Apostolica Vaticana, MS Cappella Sistina 15
CS 42	Vatican City, Biblioteca Apostolica Vaticana, MS Cappella Sistina 42
CS 51	Vatican City, Biblioteca Apostolica Vaticana, MS Cappella Sistina 51
CS 63	Vatican City, Biblioteca Apostolica Vaticana, MS Cappella Sistina 63
Dij	Dijon, Bibliothèque municipale, MS 517 ('Dijon Chansonnier')
*Dres	Dresden, formerly Sekundogenitur-Bibliothek, MS Quart 117 ('Ms. du prince Jean de Saxe') (lost)
EscA	Real Monasterio de San Lorenzo del Escorial, Biblioteca y Archivo de Música, MS V.III.24

EscB	Real Monasterio de San Lorenzo del Escorial, Biblioteca y Archivo de Música, MS IV.a.24
FC 2439	Florence, Biblioteca del Conservatorio di Musica Luigi Cherubini, MS Basevi 2439 ('Basevi Codex')
FC 2442	Florence, Biblioteca del Conservatorio di Musica Luigi Cherubini, MS Basevi 2442 ('Strozzi Chansonnier')
Fl 27	Florence, Biblioteca Nazionale Centrale, MS Panciatichi 27
Fl 107bis	Florence, Biblioteca Nazionale Centrale, MS Magliabecchi XIX. 107bis
Fl 121	Florence, Biblioteca Nazionale Centrale, MS Magliabecchi XIX. 121
Fl 164–7	Florence, Biblioteca Nazionale Centrale, MS Magliabecchi XIX. 164–167
Fl 176	Florence, Biblioteca Nazionale Centrale, MS Magliabecchi XIX. 176
Fl 178	Florence, Biblioteca Nazionale Centrale, MS Magliabecchi XIX. 178
Fl 229	Florence, Biblioteca Nazionale Centrale, MS Banco Rari 229 (olim Magliabecchi XIX. 59)
FR 2356	Florence, Biblioteca Riccardiana, MS 2356
FR 2794	Florence, Biblioteca Riccardiana, MS 2794
Fr VII 20	Frankfurt am Main, Stadt- und Universitätsbibliothek, Fragm. lat. VII 20
Glog	Cracow, Biblioteka Jagiellońska, Berlin MS 40098 ('Glogauer Liederbuch')
Lab	Washington, DC, Library of Congress, Music Division, MS M2.1.L25 Case ('Laborde Chansonnier')
Leipzig 1494	Leipzig, Universitätsbibliothek, MS 1494 ('Apel Codex')
*Lille 402	Lille, Bibliothèque municipale, MS 308 (*olim* 402)
Linz 529	Linz, Bundesstaatliche Studienbibliothek, MS 529
*Lo 380	London, British Library, MS Lansdowne 380
*Lo 16439	London, British Library, Add. MS 16439
Lo 31922	London, British Library, Add. MS 31922
Lo 35087	London, British Library, Add. MS 35087
Lucca 184	Lucca, Archivio di Stato, Biblioteca Manoscritti, MS 184 ('Lucca Codex' or 'Mancini Codex')
Lucca 238	Lucca, Archivio di Stato, Biblioteca Manoscritti, MS 238
Mel	New Haven, Yale University, Beinecke Library for Rare Books and Manuscripts, MS 91 ('Mellon Chansonnier')

MC 871	Montecassino, Biblioteca dell'Abbazia, MS 871 (*olim* 871N)
Mi 2268	Milan, Archivio della Veneranda Fabbrica del Duomo, Sezione Musicale, Librone 2 (*olim* 2268)
Mi 2269	Milan, Archivio della Veneranda Fabbrica del Duomo, Sezione Musicale, Librone 1 (*olim* 2269)
Mod α.M.1.13	Modena, Biblioteca Estense e Universitaria, MS α.M.1.13 (Lat. 456)
ModB	Modena, Biblioteca Estense e Universitaria, MS α.X.1.11
Mont 823	Montserrat, Biblioteca del Monestir, MS 823
Mun 328–331	Munich, Universitätsbibliothek, MSS 8° 328–331
Mun 3154	Munich, Bayerische Staatsbibliothek, Musiksammlung, Musica MS 3154 (= Maier, no. 42) ('Chorbuch des Nikolaus Leopold')
Namur	Namur, Archives du Royaume, town account-books
Nap VI E 40	Naples, Biblioteca Nazionale, MS VI E 40
Niv	Paris, Bibliothèque nationale, Département de la Musique, Rés. Vmc. 57 ('Chansonnier Nivelle de La Chaussée')
*Ox Taylor	Oxford, Taylor Institution, MS 8° F 3
Par 676	Paris, Bibliothèque nationale, Département de la Musique, Fonds du Conservatoire, Rés. Vm⁷ 676
Par 1597	Paris, Bibliothèque nationale, MS f. fr. 1597 ('Lorraine Chansonnier')
*Par 1719	Paris, Bibliothèque nationale, MS f. fr. 1719
*Par 1722	Paris, Bibliothèque nationale, MS f. fr. 1722
Par 2245	Paris, Bibliothèque nationale, MS f. fr. 2245
*Par 2798	Paris, Bibliothèque nationale, fonds Rothschild, MS 2798
Par 4379	Paris, Bibliothèque nationale, MS n. acq. fr. 4379 (cf. Sev)
*Par 7559	Paris, Bibliothèque nationale, MS n. acq. fr. 7559
*Par 9223	Paris, Bibliothèque nationale, MS f. fr. 9223
*Par 15771	Paris, Bibliothèque nationale, MS nouv. acq. fr. 15771
Par 16664	Paris, Bibliothèque nationale, MS f. lat. 16664
Pav	Pavia, Biblioteca Universitaria, MS Aldini 362
Per 431	Perugia, Biblioteca Comunale Augusta, MS 431 (*olim* G. 20)
Pix	Paris, Bibliothèque nationale, MS f. fr. 15123 ('Pixérécourt Chansonnier')
Porto	Oporto, Biblioteca Pública Municipal, MS 714
Reg C120	Regensburg, Bischöfliche Zentralbibliothek, MS C 120 ('Pernner Codex')

*Roh	Berlin, Staatsbibliothek zu Berlin—Preußischer Kulturbesitz, Kupferstichkabinett, MS 78 B 17 (formerly Hamilton) ('Rohan Chansonnier')
Sched	Munich, Bayerische Staatsbibliothek, MS Germ. mon. 810 (*olim* Mus. 3232; Cim. 351a) ('Schedelsches Liederbuch')
Seg	Segovia, Archivo Capitular de la Catedral, MS s.s.
Sev	Seville, Catedral Metropolitana, Biblioteca Capitular y Colombina, MS 5-1-43 (cf. Par 4379)
SG 461	St Gallen, Stiftsbibliothek, MS 461 ('Sicher Liederbuch')
SG 462	St Gallen, Stiftsbibliothek, MS 462 ('Heer Liederbuch')
SG 463	St Gallen, Stiftsbibliothek, MS 463
SM 26	Vatican City, Biblioteca Apostolica Vaticana, MS Santa Maria Maggiore 26 (*olim* JJ.III.4)
SP B80	Vatican City, Biblioteca Apostolica Vaticana, MS San Pietro B 80
Spec	Hradec Králové, Krajské Muzeum, Knihovna, MS II A 7 ('Speciálník Codex')
Tournai 94	Tournai, Bibliothèque de la Ville, MS 94 (cf. Brus IV.90)
Tar 3	Tarazona, Archivo Capitular de la Catedral, MS 3
Tr 88	Trent, Museo Provinciale d'Arte, Castello del Buon Consiglio, MS 1375 (*olim* 88)
Tr 89	Trent, Museo Provinciale d'Arte, Castello del Buon Consiglio, MS 1376 (*olim* 89)
Tr 90	Trent, Museo Provinciale d'Arte, Castello del Buon Consiglio, MS 1377 (*olim* 90)
Tr 91	Trent, Museo Provinciale d'Arte, Castello del Buon Consiglio, MS 1378 (*olim* 91)
Tr 93	Trent, Museo Diocesano, MS BL
Tur I.27	Turin, Biblioteca Nazionale Universitaria, MS Riserva musicale I. 27
Urb 1411	Vatican City, Biblioteca Apostolica Vaticana, MS Urb. lat. 1411
Vat 11953	Vatican City, Biblioteca Apostolica Vaticana, MS Vat. lat. 11953
Ver 755	Verona, Biblioteca Capitolare, MS DCCLV
Ver 757	Verona, Biblioteca Capitolare, MS DCCLVII
Ver 759	Verona, Biblioteca Capitolare, MS DCCLIX
Vienna 18746	Vienna, Österreichische Nationalbibliothek, Musiksammlung, MS Mus. 18746
Vienna 18810	Vienna, Österreichische Nationalbibliothek, Musiksammlung, MS Mus. 18810

Wolf	Wolfenbüttel, Herzog August Bibliothek, MS Guelf. 287 extrav. ('Wolfenbüttel Chansonnier')
Wolf 78	Wolfenbüttel, Herzog August Bibliothek, MS 78 Quodlibetica 4°
Wolffheim	Washington, DC, Library of Congress, MS M2.1 M6 Case ('Wolffheim Fragment')
Zwi 78/2	Zwickau, Ratsschulbibliothek, MS LXXVIII, 2
Zwi 78/3	Zwickau, Ratsschulbibliothek, MS LXXVIII, 3

Printed Books (* = poetry source)

Canti B	*Canti B. Numero cinquanta* (Venice: Ottaviano Petrucci, RISM 1502²)
Canti C	*Canti C. Numero cento cinquanta* (Venice: Ottaviano Petrucci, RISM 1504³)
*Chasse	*La Chasse et le départ d'amours* (Paris: Antoine Vérard, 1509)
Egenolff	[*Lieder zu 3 & 4 Stimmen*] (Frankfurt am Main: Christian Egenolff; RISM [*c*.1535]¹⁵)
*Fabri	Pierre Fabri, *Le grant et vray art de pleine rhetorique* (Rouen, 1522)
*Fleur	*La Fleur de toute joyeuseté* (Paris: [Jean Bonfons], n.d.)
*Jard	*Le Jardin de plaisance et la fleur de rethoricque* (Paris: Antoine Vérard, *c*.1501)
Odh	*Harmonice musices Odhecaton A* (Venice: Ottaviano Petrucci, RISM 1501)

Instrumental Tablatures

+Ber 40026	Berlin, Staatsbibliothek zu Berlin—Preußischer Kulturbesitz, MS Mus. 40026 ('Kleber Orgeltabulatur')
+SG 530	St Gallen, Stiftsbibliothek, MS 530 ('Sicher Orgeltabulatur')
+Spinacino i	Francesco Spinacino, *Intabulatura de lauto libro primo* (Venice: Ottaviano Petrucci, RISM 1507⁵)
+Spinacino ii	Francesco Spinacino, *Intabulatura de lauto libro secundo* (Venice: Ottaviano Petrucci, RISM 1507⁶)
+Thibault	Paris, Bibliothèque nationale, MS s.s. (*olim* collection of G. Thibault)

1

INTRODUCTION

Celebrating Transgression and Excess: Busnoys and the Boundaries of Late Medieval Culture

❧✻ ✻❧

PAULA HIGGINS

> *J*e ne puis vivre ainsy tousjours
> *A*u mains que j'aye en mes dolours
> *Q*uelque confort
> *U*ne seulle heure, ou mains ou fort;
> *E*t tous les jours
> *L*éaument serviray Amours
> *J*usqu'a la mort . . .[1]

(I can't live like this any longer unless I have some comfort for my pain; just one hour, or less—or more; and every day I'll serve the god of love faithfully unto death.)

WHEN Antoine Busnoys penned the poem containing the lines above, he embedded in them an acrostic yielding the name of a woman: one 'Jaqueljne d'Aqvevjle' (Jacqueline d'Hacqueville).[2] In so doing he broke the cardinal rule of courtly love: a commitment to absolute secrecy. Beyond betraying the name of a lady in the kind of ludic *tour de force* typical of the composer's works, the poem itself transgresses the boundaries of

---

I wish to thank Rob Wegman for his thoughtful response to the penultimate draft of this essay.

[1] Antoine Busnoys, *Je ne puis vivre ainsi toujours*. For an edition see Leeman L. Perkins and Howard W. Garey (eds.), *The Mellon Chansonnier* (New Haven, 1979), no. 12.

[2] For editions of the texts of the four Hacqueville songs see Paula Higgins, 'Parisian Nobles, a Scottish Princess, and the Woman's Voice in Late Medieval Song', *EMH* 10 (1991), 145–200; and Leeman L. Perkins, 'Antoine Busnois and the d'Hacqueville Connection', in Mary Beth Winn (ed.), *Musique naturelle et musique artificielle: In memoriam Gustav Reese = Le Moyen français*, 5 (1979), 49–64.

polite courtly love discourse: the scarcely veiled sexual innuendo of the phrase 'just one hour—or less or more' and the obscene *double entendre* on the word 'confort' ('con fort'). Following a direct address to the lady, in which the male persona instructs her to 'pay close attention to this poem' (lest she miss the acrostic?), he reverts to his tortured, brooding *monologue intérieur*: because of the lady's indifference, he is 'wasting away', 'walking in a hundred circles', 'staying up all night', and 'drowning in tears'. The hyperbolic rhetoric of this poem portrays a compelling persona at once impatient, desperate, passionate, dramatic, and fraught with lovesickness, that is, 'somatic symptoms of psychological breakdown caused by intense, erotic passion'.[3] Blurring the boundaries between poet and persona, Busnoys himself seems to leap off the page.

The musical profile of *Je ne puis vivre* matches in every respect the clever skill with which Busnoys incorporated textual games into the poem. George Perle singled out the piece as 'a special repository for exceptional details, including a long sequence involving all the parts, *Stimmtausch*, and ostinato passage in the bass, and the clearly defined tonality of C major', and considered it typical of 'the wonderful subtlety and ingenuity of his rhythmic ideas, probably unsurpassed in the history of music'.[4] Busnoys wrote at least three other songs concealing the name of the same woman, one of them involving an even more blatant verbal pun on her name and ingenious musical puzzle wherein the superius functions simultaneously as a three-part canon at the unison and the independent upper voice of a conventional three-voice song.[5] As others have noted, the 'specificity, originality, and intensity' of literary and musical expression apparent in the Hacqueville songs suggests a preoccupation with the female subject that almost surely exceeded the bounds of literary convention.[6]

---

[3] The language of the poem bears striking similarities to somatic symptoms of lovesickness (wasting, confusion, insomnia, sighs, and tears) as understood by medieval medicine. See Mary Frances Wack, *Lovesickness in the Middle Ages: The* Viaticum *and its Commentaries* (Philadelphia, 1990), 146–62, esp. 151 and 158. Arguing that lovesickness was a 'social and psychological response to historical contradictions in aristocratic culture', Wack amasses substantial evidence from medieval medical treatises to show that lovesickness was not 'simply a literary posture, a game of poetic conventions', but 'as "real" for medieval physicians as melancholy, headache, baldness, and scalp lice' (p. 149).

[4] George Perle, 'The Chansons of Antoine Busnois', *Music Review*, 11 (1950), 89–97 at 94. For another discussion of the piece see Paula Marie Higgins, 'Antoine Busnois and Musical Culture in Late Fifteenth-Century France and Burgundy' (Ph.D. diss., Princeton University, 1987), 35–43.

[5] *Ha que ville et abominable*. In Dijon 517, the earliest source of the song, two Latin rubrics draw attention to the dual function of the upper voice-part. Both versions of the song are edited in *A Florentine Chansonnier from the Time of Lorenzo the Magnificent: Florence, Biblioteca Nazionale Centrale MS Banco Rari 229*, ed. Howard Mayer Brown (Monuments of Renaissance Music, 7; Chicago, 1983), nos. 197 and 197a.

[6] Perkins, 'Antoine Busnois', was the first to pursue this line of thought with respect to the Hacqueville songs. In my 'Parisian Nobles', 147–8, I took it further in examining the problem that 'personal poetry' has traditionally posed to literary critics, who are generally inclined to dismiss it altogether as a category of literary analysis. I adopt the criteria of 'specificity, originality, and intensity' put forth by Edward Lowinsky who attempted to reconcile the divergent viewpoints on autobiographical readings of late medieval poetry in his article 'Jan van Eyck's *Tymotheus*: Sculptor or Musician? With an Investigation of the Autobiographic Strain in French Poetry from Rutebeuf to Villon', *Studi musicali*, 13 (1984), 33–105, esp. 68. See also below, n. 22.

In a sense, the creative 'attitude' of Busnoys's Hacqueville songs seems entirely consistent with that of the composer of the motet *Anthoni usque limina*, who concealed his own name in the text itself, wrote a clever verbal canon to ensure the reader would not miss it, and constructed the piece in symmetrical halves corresponding to the numerical cipher of his own name; and of the 'unworthy musician of the count of Charolais' who, while cloaking his name in the protective shroud of the conventional medieval humility topos, declared himself as the author of the ostentatiously virtuosic motet *In hydraulis* and as the musical 'offspring' (*propago*) of its dedicatee, Johannes Ockeghem, 'the reincarnation of Orpheus'.[7]

The unparalleled artistic self-consciousness manifested in each of these works compels one to ask, what kind of character was this Antoine de Busnes, *dit* Busnoys? First and foremost, perhaps, a man whose foregrounding of himself as the composer of *Anthoni* and *In hydraulis* betrays an overweening concern with constructing himself as an *auctor*; second, a man whose thematizing of creative genealogy and signs of an absolute past (Pythagoras, Orpheus, Greek-flavoured musical terms) manifests a certain anxiety about legitimation;[8] and third, a man whose description of himself as the metaphorical 'son' of a composer he allegorizes as the most gifted musician in Greek mythology clearly indicates that he had a fairly high opinion of himself. That is not, of course, to suggest that such a seemingly arrogant self-assessment was necessarily unwarranted. Indeed, everything we know about Busnoys, which is not a great deal, confirms that his contemporaries regarded him as a truly exceptional man and consistently invoked superlatives to describe him.[9] Tinctoris considered Busnoys and Ockeghem as 'the most outstanding and most famous professors of the art of music',[10] 'the most excellent of all the composers I have ever heard',[11] and whose music was 'worthy of the immortal gods'.[12] Adam of Fulda singled out Busnoys, along with Dufay, as 'the most learned' composers of his generation.[13] Pietro Aron called Busnoys 'a great man and an excellent musician'.[14] Even those, like Tinctoris and

---

[7] For editions of both pieces see *Busnoys LTW*, nos. 8 and 10.

[8] For an excellent study treating the thematizing of genealogy in the works of Rabelais see Carla Freccero, *Father Figures: Genealogy and Narrative Structure in Rabelais* (Ithaca, NY, and London, 1991).

[9] A summary of the following theoretical citations may be found in Higgins, 'Antoine Busnois', 13–21.

[10] 'Praestantissimis ac celeberrimis artis musicae professoribus'. Johannes Tinctoris, *Liber de natura et proprietate tonorum*, in *Opera theoretica*, ed. Albert Seay, 2 vols. (CSM 22; Rome, 1975), i. 65.

[11] 'Okeghem, Busnois, Regis, et Caron, omnium quos audiverim in compositione praestantissimi'. Tinctoris, *Proportionale*, ibid. iia. 10.

[12] 'Quorum omnium omnia fere opera tantam suavitudinem redolent ut, mea quidem sententia, non modo hominibus heroibusque verum etiam *Diis immortalibus dignissima censenda sint*' (emphasis added). Tinctoris, *Liber de arte contrapuncti*, ibid. ii. 12. For a recent interpretation of this passage in the context of late medieval aesthetics see Rob C. Wegman, 'Sense and Sensibility in Late Medieval Music: Thoughts on Aesthetics and "Authenticity" ', *Early Music*, 23 (1995), 299–312.

[13] Adam of Fulda, *Musica*, in *Scriptores ecclesiastici de musica sacra*, ed. Martin Gerbert, 3 vols. (St Blasien, 1784; repr. Hildesheim, 1963), iii. 341.

[14] Pietro Aron, *Toscanello in Music*, trans. Peter Bergquist, 2 vols. (Colorado College Music Press Translations, 4; Colorado Springs, 1970), i. 55.

Adrian Petit Coclico, who occasionally felt moved to criticize rather than praise his musical practice, described it in terms of transgression and excess. Defending the logic behind a fine point of mensural notation, Tinctoris complains 'Busnoys *alone* disagrees'.[15] Consigning Busnoys to his pejorative category of musical 'mathematicians', Coclico laments 'when they hope to spread their invented art widely and make it more outstanding, they rather defile and obscure it. In teaching precepts and speculation they have specialized excessively and, in accumulating a multitude of symbols and other things, they have introduced many difficulties'.[16]

Equally compelling testimony to Busnoys's somewhat exceptional character is a contemporaneous document which described him in 1465 as a 'very serious and famous man', 'exceptionally expert in music and poetry' who would 'best teach the choirboys'.[17] More alarming, and even more suggestive of an extravagant personality prone to physical and emotional excess, is an earlier document of 1461 which recounts a rather ignominious incident in which Busnoys, together with a number of cohorts, allegedly beat up a priest to the point of bloodshed—not once, but on five separate occasions—actions for which he was subsequently excommunicated. To add insult to injury, he then proceeded, in open defiance of canon law, to celebrate Mass in his state of anathema.[18] Whatever the sordid circumstances and penal consequences of Busnoys's crime, they do not seem to have unduly impeded his subsequent career or tainted his posthumous reputation.[19] Thereafter he went on to become master of the choirboys at Saint-Martin of Tours and Saint-Hilaire-le-Grand in Poitiers, two of the most renowned churches in Christendom, and subsequently entered the service of the Burgundian court under Charles the Bold, then the most magnificant musical establishment in western Europe.[20] His music survives in more than fifty manuscripts and prints of the fifteenth and sixteenth centuries whose provenances extend from England to Hungary. In 1494 an Italian trombone-player arranged a now-lost Busnoys motet, dedicated it to the doge of Venice, and dispatched it as a gift to the duke of Mantua, boasting that 'all of Venice wished to hear no other'.[21] Posthumous legend (whatever its truth value) acknowledged Busnoys

---

[15] On Tinctoris's criticisms of Busnoys's mensural practice see Rob C. Wegman, 'Mensural Intertextuality' (below, Ch. 8).

[16] Adrian Petit Coclico, *Musical Compendium (Compendium Musices)*, trans. Albert Seay (Colorado College Music Press Translations, 5; Colorado Springs, 1973), 8.

[17] See Paula Higgins, 'Musical Politics in Late Medieval Poitiers', (below, Ch. 7).

[18] Pamela F. Starr, 'Rome as the Centre of the Universe: Papal Grace and Musical Patronage', *EMH* 11 (1992), 223–62 at 249–56 and 260.

[19] See Higgins, 'Musical Politics'.

[20] For Busnoys as *magister puerorum* at Saint-Martin of Tours and Saint-Hilaire-le-Grand in Poitiers see Higgins, 'Musical Politics'; on Busnoys's career at the Burgundian court see ead., '*In hydraulis* Revisited: New Light on the Career of Antoine Busnois', *JAMS* 36 (1986), 36–86.

[21] For the text and translation of the document, as well as relevant bibliography, see Higgins, 'Antoine Busnois', 9–11 and n. 7.

as the progenitor of the *L'homme armé* mass tradition; and he was without question the composer most imitated and emulated by his younger contemporaries Josquin, Obrecht, Agricola, Isaac, and Ghiselin.

If music can be said to leave the imprint of its composer's personality—a debatable proposition, to be sure—Busnoys's gives the impression of an excessive, flamboyant character determined to experiment with his own way of doing things.[22] His works are rife with harmonic surprise, abrupt changes of tempo and texture, musical canons, extensive imitation, melodic sequences, and large-scale repetitions of motivic ideas and even of whole passages. He exceeded conventionally accepted limits of the gamut in cultivating wide-spanned melodic lines that prefigure those of Josquin and Obrecht.[23] And in extending the outer ranges of the upper and lower voices and enabling individual musical lines to operate unobstructed by interference with crossing parts,[24] Busnoys essentially reconfigured the existing boundaries of tonal space. Standing at the crossroads of an era that witnessed the ideological transformation of the composer from an able craftsman to an innately endowed creator, Busnoys emerges as a pivotal figure in a critical period of changing styles and one of the most powerful musical minds of the century.

Perhaps more than any other composer of the period, Busnoys seems almost obsessively preoccupied with transgressing accepted boundaries, resisting discursive containment, pushing the limits of musical expression, and flaunting accepted rules and practices when it suited his mode of musical expression. Even the admittedly fragmentary biographical evidence offers a tantalizing sketch of a

[22] Clearly, this somewhat psychologizing view of Busnoys cries out for further theoretical articulation with respect to poststructuralist debates on the author, particularly Roland Barthes, 'The Death of the Author,' in *Image–Music–Text*, trans. Stephen Heath (New York, 1977), 149–54, and Michel Foucault 'What Is An Author?' in *The Foucault Reader*, ed. Paul Rabinow (New York, 1984), 101–20, which I am disinclined to pursue in this particular forum. Suffice it to say that I do not seek naïvely to perpetuate the time-worn, positivist model of 'man-and-his-work' criticism so vociferously decried by Barthes: 'the *explanation* of a work is always sought in the man or woman who produced it, as if it were always in the end, through the more or less transparent allegory of the fiction, the voice of a single person, the *author* "confiding" in us' (p. 143). But I do believe, however, that their formulations, centred primarily on 19th-c. authors (Proust, Mallarmé, etc.), are of questionable relevance to composers, and especially to the late medieval 'composer'. Busnoys himself lived precisely during the time when the notion of a 'composer' as 'author' was barely nascent, and he was, moreover, deeply implicated in its formal articulation. In this respect, I am much more sympathetic to the far more subtly historicizing formulation of Foucault, who notes that the rise of the author coincides with the period in which ownership for texts came into being, which he dates to the late 18th and early 19th c. For music, however, questions of creative property and ownership were fermenting already in Busnoys's day, and were fully articulated in the 16th c. I pursue these questions further in my forthcoming book *Parents and Preceptors: Authority, Lineage, and the Conception of the Composer in the Late Middle Ages* (Oxford University Press).
[23] For a discussion of Busnoys as an innovator in the use of wide-spanned lines, hitherto regarded as one of the important style contributions of Josquin, see Higgins, 'Antoine Busnois', 55–9.
[24] Higgins, 'Antoine Busnois', 41–2, discussing Lynn M. Trowbridge, 'Style Change in the Fifteenth-Century Chanson: A Comparative Study of Compositional Detail', *Journal of Musicology*, 4 (1985), 146–70. Trowbridge suggests that Busnoys, 'more than any other composer studied achieved a texture in which the individual voices participate on an equal and independent footing. This arrangement, often attributed both to Ockeghem and Busnois, appears on the basis of the evidence gathered in the course of this study to be considerably more characteristic of Busnois than Ockeghem' (p. 162).

somewhat marginal, Villonesque character, headstrong and independent, 'living on the edge', defying ecclesiastical authority. This nascent if incomplete picture of Busnoys as a musical and social renegade may account in part for the irresistible attraction his life and music holds for us today, or at least helps to explain why some hundred scholars from six countries would choose to spend three days in collective isolation in a remote Midwestern enclave discussing it. Most of the twenty essays in this volume began life as papers presented at the 1992 Busnoys conference,[25] an event motivated not by sheer excess of commemorative fervour for the 500th anniversary of his death in 1492, but rather by the fortuitous coincidence of that occasion with an explosion of new historical interest in the composer and his music. Indeed, few musical personalities of the late Middle Ages have aroused an intensity of intellectual inquiry matching that currently surrounding Busnoys. The decade preceding the conference had witnessed the publication of the first complete critical edition of his Latin-texted works, more than a dozen articles and several lively exchanges in international journals, two doctoral dissertations, numerous conference papers, and several recordings.[26] Since then there have been additional articles, a monograph, new recordings, and a full-page story in the Sunday edition of the *New York Times* that spawned several weeks' worth of Internet threads.[27]

Such a remarkable turn of events could scarcely have been predicted, given how little attention Busnoys had received up until the mid-1980s. In that sense, the unexpected growth and dynamism of recent Busnoys studies does in itself represent a transgression of existing musicological boundaries, since the historical role carved out for the composer by traditional scholarship had been relatively modest. That Busnoys has never enjoyed canonical status within early music scholarship and the very reasons behind the belated and long-overdue attention to his music resonate somewhat uncannily with current postmodern concerns about the historical construction of scholarly canons: How is it that certain composers come to be privileged over others? How have historically constructed hierarchies of genre and their valorization informed assessments of musical significance? How have ideological blinkers, chronologically shifting aesthetic values, and tacit personal agendas resulted in the promulgation of the musics of certain cultural groups over those of others?

---

[25] Continuities and Transformations in Musical Culture, 1450–1500: Assessing the Legacy of Antoine Busnoys, held at the University of Notre Dame, 8–11 November 1992. Besides the present essay, the only one not presented at the conference itself is that of Honey Meconi (Ch. 19).

[26] For a summary of the most important developments in Busnoys scholarship antedating the conference see David Fallows's essay in this volume (Ch. 2).

[27] Paula Higgins, 'Love and Death in the Fifteenth-Century Motet: A Reading of Busnoys's *Anima mea liquefacta est/Stirps Jesse*', in Dolores Pesce (ed.), *Hearing the Motet* (New York, 1997), 142–68; Rob C. Wegman, ' "For Whom the Bell Tolls": Reading and Hearing Antoine Busnoys's *Anthoni usque limina*', ibid, 122–41; *Antoine Busnoys (d. 1492): In hydraulis and Other Works* (Pomerium; Alexander Blachly, director) (Dorian Recordings, 1993: DOR-90184); Richard Taruskin, 'The Trouble with Classics: They are only Human', *The New York Times*, Sunday, 14 Aug. 1994.

Much of the prior inattention to Busnoys has to do with the previous unavailability of his music: the complete edition of his Latin-texted music appeared only in 1990, and there is to this day no complete edition of his songs.[28] Moreover, and somewhat paradoxically, a long-standing historiographical tradition has cast Busnoys in the shadow of Ockeghem, a composer with whom he invariably shared equal billing in the eyes of his contemporaries. The historical construct of the 'Netherlands schools' as first promulgated by Raphael Georg Kiesewetter emerged in response to a patently nationalist cultural propaganda campaign: a prize competition launched by the Royal Netherlands Academy of Arts and Sciences for the best essay on the subject: What were the contributions of the Netherlanders to Music? Kiesewetter took the gold medal. Imbued with a kind of cultural chauvinism gone awry, his essay sought not only to establish the innate musical supremacy of composers from the Low Countries but also to prove that polyphony could not have flourished elsewhere.[29] It is thus probably no innocent accident of history that Ockeghem, with his patently Flemish surname, was proclaimed the head of the 'First Netherlandish School' at the expense of Busnoys, a French composer born within barely 100 kilometres from what is now modern-day Belgium. The role of bourgeois, Austrian-Catholic scholars in setting agendas that have laid the bedrock of early music scholarship would seem worthy of further investigation.[30] Tacit valorization of genres has also informed twentieth-century scholarly perceptions of Busnoys as a musical lightweight—a 'miniaturist'—known mainly for his courtly love songs, while Ockeghem, who left a more imposing and certainly more respectable body of masses, emerged as the more significant musical heavyweight.[31] Without wishing to endorse the

[28] See *Busnoys LTW*; Leeman L. Perkins is currently completing a critical edition of Busnoys's songs (originally begun by Catherine V. Brooks in the 1950s) for the Masters and Monuments of the Renaissance series, published by The Broude Trust.

[29] Raphael Georg Kiesewetter, 'Die Verdienste der Niederländer um die Tonkunst'. The silver medal in the competition was awarded to François-Joseph Fétis, 'Mémoire sur cette question: "Quels ont été les mérites des Néerlandais dans la musique, principalement aux 14ᵉ, 15ᵉ, et 16ᵉ siècles?" '. Both essays were published in *Verhandelingen over de Vraag: Welke Verdiensten hebben zich de Nederlanders vooral in de 14e, 15e en 16e Eeuw in het vak der Toonkunst verworven* (Amsterdam, 1829).

[30] For a discussion of the role of Kiesewetter and his nephew August Wilhelm Ambros in the promulgation of the 'myth of the Netherlands schools' and the centrality of Ockeghem to the historical constructions of their subjects see Higgins, 'Antoine Busnois', 32–3 and 216–26. Although Ockeghem was by far the linchpin in both scholars' efforts to demonstrate the musical supremacy of the 'Netherlanders', it is only fair to note that Kiesewetter published transcriptions of three Busnoys songs in an appendix to his 'Die Verdienste der Niederländer um die Tonkunst', in *Verhandelingen over de Vraag*. See also Higgins, 'Antoine Busnois', 218.

[31] 'It was in the field of secular music, however, that Busnois's talent was greatest, and in which his chief contribution was made' (Catherine V. Brooks, 'Antoine Busnois as a Composer of Chansons', 2 vols. (Ph.D. diss., New York University, 1951), i. 20); 'It is probably the small gem-like chansons that form Busnois's most significant contribution to music' (ead., 'Antoine Busnois, Chanson Composer', *JAMS* 6 (1953), 111–35 at 111); 'Busnois's mastery of small form and his refined treatment of detail appear to advantage in his secular music' (Gustave Reese, *Music in the Renaissance* (2nd rev. edn.; New York, 1959), 102); 'The sacred music of Busnois exhibits the same delicacy, refinement and great melodic gifts that mark his chansons. But his few motets and single Mass [*sic*] cannot compare in breadth of conception or depth of realization with Ockeghem's great achievement in this field' (Howard M. Brown, *Music in the Renaissance* (Englewood Cliffs, NJ, 1976), 88); 'Il n'est pas difficile de comprendre que ce qui classe Busnois au rang des

aesthetic hierarchies uncritically erected by earlier generations of scholars, it seems nevertheless important to point out that, in Busnoys's case, the survival pattern of sacred versus secular music is pure happenstance, and that what has come down to us—particularly in the realm of sacred music—is probably far less than what Busnoys actually wrote.[32] Moreover, it now appears that Busnoys, even more so than Ockeghem, had the most clearly discernible stylistic impact on the music of his younger contemporaries Josquin, Obrecht, and Isaac. With the wider diffusion of his music, Busnoys emerges ever more sharply as a pivotal figure in the histories of imitative counterpoint, melodic and harmonic sequence, and fifteenth-century tonality, and as the 'missing link' that helps bridge the stylistic chasm separating the musical styles of the Dufay and Josquin generations.[33]

Antoine Busnoys: Method, Meaning, and Context in Late Medieval Music brings together twenty original essays by some of the most distinguished and gifted scholars working in the field of early music today. All the articles have been revised, amplified, and in some cases transformed beyond recognition from their earlier incarnations as conference papers. While 'Antoine Busnoys', the catalyst for the original occasion, provides the title and thematic focus of the volume, the essays treat many of his contemporaries as well: Binchois, Dufay, Ockeghem, Obrecht, Tinctoris, Japart, Isaac, and others. The subtitle, 'Method, Meaning, and Context in Late Medieval Music', refers to the principal approaches exemplified in the essays rather than to discrete categories organizing the contents of the volume. Few of the essays, in fact, could adequately be described as exclusively methodological, critical, or contextual; some of them blend all three approaches; and all of them share the distinction of having responded to the problematic of the research situation itself, rather than to abstract paradigms or metanarratives arbitrarily imposed on the subject-matter. It is thus an essentially eclectic and pragmatist collection that resists neat, taxonomic labelling in terms of critical dispensations either 'new' or 'old'. Driven first and foremost by deep intellectual commitment to the study of late medieval musical culture, the contributors, like

petits maîtres de la musique religieuse, fait précisément de lui un grand maître de la musique profane' (Charles van den Borren, *Études sur le quinzième siècle musical* (Antwerp, 1941), 279). See also Higgins, 'Antoine Busnois', 25–34.

[32] Ibid. 30–3. As David Fallows has also noted, eight new masses had been attributed to Busnoys in the years immediately preceding the Busnoys conference (see Ch. 2). Moreover, felicitous references in random historical documents and theoretical works allude to the existence of at least five previously lost works, one of which, *Gaude caelestis Domina*, was recently rediscovered by Rob Wegman (Ch. 8).

[33] Higgins, 'Antoine Busnois', 45–54, summarizing the pioneering work of Edgar Sparks who was the first to draw attention to Busnoys's decisive and largely unrecognized contribution to the development of 15th-c. sacred styles. See *Cantus Firmus in Mass and Motet, 1420–1520* (Berkeley, 1963; repr. New York, 1975), esp. ch. 7, 212–18, and ch. 8. Earlier studies by Wolfgang Stephan, *Die burgundisch-niederländische Motette* (Heidelberger Studien zur Musikwissenschaft, 6; Kassel, 1937; repr. 1973) and van den Borren, *Études sur le quinzième siècle musical*, contained important discussions of Busnoys's motets. Both studies, however, concluded with the period of Ockeghem and Busnoys, and therefore did not explore the obvious stylistic ramifications of Busnoys's works for the next generation of composers.

Busnoys himself, have sought to experiment with their own way of doing things.[34] That such committed and passionate allegiance will inevitably change paradigms, transgress traditional disciplinary boundaries, and even lead to occasional excesses of interpretive zeal is obvious, and can be witnessed, if anywhere, in this volume itself. The reader will find a wealth of innovative methodologies for the study of late medieval music, novel interpretations of the music, theoretical treatises, and archival documents of the period, and virgin explorations into largely uncharted terrain impinging on the social, cultural, intellectual, devotional, and hermeneutic contexts of late medieval music. If any one all-encompassing theme does seem to emerge forcefully from virtually all the essays, it is that historical documents, theoretical treatises, and musical works can no longer be seen as isolated objects of specialized study but rather as colourful threads inextricably woven into the kaleidoscopic tapestry of late medieval culture. In the summaries that follow, I claim no role as ventriloquist for the authors (who may not necessarily agree with my formulations of their work), but seek rather to set the essays within a broader contextual framework to facilitate their reading and interpretation and to identify what I consider to be some of the key issues and shared resonances among them.

'You are trained and immersed in all musical delights', wrote Jean Molinet to Busnoys in a twenty-six-line letter of homage alternating the end-rhymes 'bus' and 'noys'.[35] As Busnoys's sometime pen-pal and one-time colleague at the

[34] In the past decade the field of musicology has undergone a dramatic paradigm shift that has provoked heated critical debates over the 'new musicology' and has singled out early music scholarship as the principal scapegoat in an increasingly vocal anti-positivist discourse. Inevitably, persistent assaults on early music fall squarely upon the shoulders of its practitioners and the curious silence from all but a few critical voices in its defence and the apparent lack of infiltration of the new trends into the discipline at large has perhaps unwittingly fostered the impression of a kind of collective indifference or complacency with the 'good old ways'. Viewed within the currently volatile political climate in the field, the publication of a hefty volume of essays paying homage to the creative legacy of a dead, white, European male composer and celebrating the élite musical culture of his day might even risk interpretation as a 'political act', and a rather retrogressive one at that: a last-ditch attempt to buttress a sagging field, a heroic effort to reassert the hegemony of a once-dominant but now moribund canonical tradition, and above all a flagrant violation of political correctness in seeming to advocate the enshrinement of yet another overlooked and undervalued male genius in the pantheon of musical greatness. The editor hopes that the present collection implicitly answers such charges, patiently and eloquently, with the only sensible answer that a constantly developing yet radically sceptical and questioning field can give: we are changing our paradigms from within and in response to a constantly shifting understanding of medieval musical culture itself, rather than out of a perceived historical necessity of methodological innovation for its own sake, or for musicology's sake.

For selected responses to the charges against early music with respect to the new trends see Margaret Bent, 'Fact and Value in Contemporary Scholarship', *Musical Times*, 127 (1986), 85–9; Lewis Lockwood, 'Communicating Musicology: A Personal View', *College Music Symposium*, 28 (1988), 1–9; Sandra Pinegar, 'The Seeds of Notation and Music Paleography', in Edmund Goehring (ed.), *Approaches to the Discipline: Current Musicology*, 53 (1993), 99–108; Paula Higgins, 'From the Ivory Tower to the Marketplace: Early Music, Musicology, and the Mass Media', ibid. 109–23 at 109–14; see also the exchanges between Pinegar and Higgins in *Current Musicology*, 55 (1993) and 56 (1994), 175–85; and Rob Wegman's numerous spirited postings on the amslist in September 1994.

[35] 'Je te rens honneur et tri*bus* | Sus tous aultres, car je cog*nois* | Que tu es instruis et im*bus* | En tous musicaulx esba*nois* . . .'. See the poetic exchange between Molinet and Busnoys in *Les Faictz et dictz de Jean Molinet*, ed. Noël Dupire, 3 vols. (Paris, 1936–9), ii. 795–801.

Burgundian court, Molinet undoubtedly spoke from a first-hand knowledge of Busnoys's songs, if the numerous allusions to them peppered throughout his poems is any indication. Taking up Molinet's epithet as the title of his essay, David Fallows conducts a magisterial survey and critical assessment of recent developments in Busnoys studies, and in the process adds several recommendations and major discoveries of his own.[36] 'Busnoys', he reminds us, 'was the most prolific song composer between Dufay and Claudin de Sermisy' and his song production warrants more serious critical attention. According to Fallows's tentative chronology of the songs, nearly two-thirds of Busnoys's songs must pre-date 1467, a revelation of rather startling proportions which will necessitate some serious rethinking of fifteenth-century style chronology. Similarly in need of greater study, according to Fallows, is the poetry manuscript Paris 9223, preserving a poem attributed to Busnoys as well as texts by a large number of poets associated with the court of Brittany, which he identifies as a hypothetical locus for an earlier and as yet undocumented phase of Busnoys's career in the 1450s.[37] And with his eagle eye for cryptograms, Fallows detects an acrostic formed by the initial letters of the first twelve songs in the Wolfenbüttel manuscript, thus identifying what is in all probability the first known owner of a major fifteenth-century songbook. The resulting name, 'Estiene Petit', corresponds to that of two officers in the French court—a father and son—and virtually clinches the case already constructed by others that Wolfenbüttel and its related manuscripts emanate from cultural circles surrounding the French royal court.[38]

The task of reconstructing the cultural, social, and devotional contexts for the production and diffusion of fifteenth-century musical works remains a central priority of early music scholarship. The first group of essays in the volume focus their attention on sacred music apparently written for performance within late medieval liturgical ceremony and ritual and explore methodologies for gaining deeper insights into its meaning and function. Howard Mayer Brown, comparing two versions of extant ordinances from the Burgundian court under Charles the Bold, illuminates the probable uses of and devotional contexts for Busnoys's music that survives in the court choirbook Brussels 5557, a manuscript containing what are thought to be Busnoys autographs. Documents like the Burgundian chapel ordinances, according to Brown, 'help us to understand better just what

---

[36] Fallows's article is a revised and expanded version of his Keynote Address that launched the Busnoys conference.

[37] Higgins, 'Parisian Nobles', 171–2 and 182–4 also treats Paris 9223 from the perspective of poets associated in the mid-1440s with the court of the dauphine of France, Margaret of Scotland, and raises the possibility of a redating of Busnoys's compositional activities to the 1450s (ibid. 190 and n. 133). A direct link of Margaret's court with that of Brittany, of course, comes by way of her sister Isabel, who, in the aftermath of Margaret's death in 1445, married Francis I, duke of Brittany.

[38] An extensive case amassing biographical, codicological, textual, and art historical evidence for the origins of the chansonniers Dijon, Laborde, Wolfenbüttel, Copenhagen, and Nivelle in French court circles in the Loire Valley in the 1460s is outlined in Higgins, 'Antoine Busnois', 234–96.

priests and singers did every day, what their responsibilities were in celebrating the Mass and Office, and what place music, whether chant or polyphony, had in the continuous celebration of the Christian faith'. Identifying those liturgical occasions which prescribed polyphony enables Brown to correlate many of the masses, motets, hymns, and antiphons of the Brussels 5557 repertory with the liturgical and paraliturgical services at which they may have been heard. More elusive to liturgical assignment are masses based on secular cantus firmi, like Heyns's *Missa Pour quelque paine*, which prompts Brown's concluding exhortation that music historians turn their attention to the more broadly hermeneutical question: why, given the vast body of plainsong available to them, did composers in the years around 1460 begin to base their masses on secular cantus firmi, particularly those derived from courtly love songs?

Of all the secular cantus firmi employed in polyphonic masses none captivated the musical imaginations of composers more than the *L'homme armé* tune. Despite the considerable attention devoted to the subject over the past fifty years, no one has yet succeeded in explaining the tune's extraordinary popularity and why more than thirty composers over the course of 150 years chose to base at least one and in some cases two masses on it. Flynn Warmington's perspicacious reading of Giovanni Rucellai's *Zibaldone quaresimale* of 1457 unearthed an intriguing reference to an ancient papal ritual—the 'Mass of the Armed Man'— that may bear on the origins of the tradition. Known for centuries to historians but entirely overlooked by musicologists, the Mass itself involved an elaborate ceremonial ritual during which powerful magnates received a papal sword and hat directly from the hands of the pope, or by proxy through an embassy dispatched to their own courts. Providing a hitherto unforeseen hypothetical context for the composition of these masses, Warmington isolates individual potentates, including the dukes of Burgundy and the kings of France, whose conferral ceremonies might well have prompted the commissioning of some of the earliest *L'homme armé* masses.

The long-standing music historiographical preoccupation with late medieval polyphony has tended to obscure the fact that plainsong remained a vibrant, living tradition throughout the late Middle Ages. Indeed, the centrality of plainsong in the daily lives of late medieval musicians whom we now regard exclusively as composers of polyphony can scarcely be overestimated. 'These men', as Jennifer Bloxam reminds us, 'sang and taught the plainsong dialect of the institutions they served; some supervised the preparation of new chant books, rendered judgements on analytic debates pertaining to plainsong, and even authored original texts and melodies for newly created feasts.'[39] The plainsong cantus firmi

---

[39] M. Jennifer Bloxam, 'Sacred Polyphony and Local Traditions of Liturgy and Plainsong: Reflections on Music by Jacob Obrecht', in Thomas Forrest Kelly (ed.), *Plainsong in the Age of Polyphony* (Cambridge Studies in Performance Practice, 2; Cambridge, 1992), 140–77 at 143.

adopted by composers of polyphonic masses like those in Brussels 5557 often reflected the local idioms of the regions and institutions in which peripatetic medieval musicians momentarily found themselves working. Bloxam's pioneering work in this fledgling field of early music scholarship has unearthed multiple layers of biographical, religious, and symbolic intertextuality embedded in composers' seemingly arbitrary choices of chant melodies.[40] In her essay here, she stresses the importance of these frequently significant divergences in plainchant practices and outlines a methodology for localizing, by means of contemporaneous service-books, the particular variants used by composers in their polyphonic compositions. Once linked to a specific liturgy, the cantus firmus adopted by a composer can not only yield unexpected insights into the initial performance context of a piece and sharper focus on matters of musical style and chronology, but can also raise more difficult hermeneutical questions: why did the composer select this particular cantus firmus? What did the quotation of the plainsong signify to the composer, the singers, and the listeners?

Similar questions of meaning and historical context inform the second group of essays, which encompass a more diverse group of topics relating to late medieval traditions of allegory, music pedagogy, mensural theory, and numerical exegesis. Michael Long subjects the *L'homme armé* question to more rigorous scrutiny by interrogating why the musical tradition of cantus-firmus masses seems to have arisen precisely in the years around 1460. With breathtaking interdisciplinary virtuosity, he weaves together disparate threads of mathematical, cosmological, literary, liturgical, mythological, and theological evidence suggesting that the earliest *L'homme armé* masses grew out of a direct response to the propaganda campaign launched by Pius II in support of the idea of a new crusade against the infidel Turks following the Fall of Constantinople in 1453. His argument hinges on Christian appropriations of pagan mythology through Virgil's vision of the lost Saturnian Golden Age and the allegorization of Pius II (Aeneas Sylvius Piccolomini) as Virgil's 'Aeneas', providing a motivation for the quotation of the 'Virgilian catchword' *Arma virumque cano* at the opening of the canon of the sixth Naples *L'homme armé* mass. In support of this hypothesis he underscores the 'readiness of medieval writers to appropriate non-Christian texts, characters, or topoi for allegorization and exegesis' and particularly 'the network of texts implicitly equating the literature and mythography of Imperial Rome with the fundamental precepts of the Roman Church and of her faithful warriors'.

A panorama of insights into several other of the more decisive social and cultural changes fermenting in the years around 1460 can be gleaned from sensitively contextual readings of archival documents. One momentous ideological shift during this period involved the increasing tendency to view the composer as

[40] M. Jennifer Bloxam, ' "In Praise of Spurious Saints": The *Missae Floruit Egregiis* by Pipelare and La Rue', *JAMS* 44 (1991), 163–220.

a creatively endowed individual. Paula Higgins sees the phenomenon as 'inextricably bound up with the evolving status of the *magister puerorum* from that of skilled pedagogue to creative mentor . . . a gradual shift in mentality that can be traced . . . in the patterns of recruitment and hiring of musical personnel in collegiate churches and cathedrals'. The focus of her essay centres on an unusual document of 1465 from Saint-Hilaire-le-Grand in Poitiers which recounts with rare precision the details of a heated debate among its canons over two candidates vying for the position of *magister puerorum*, Busnoys being one of them. What plainly emerges from between the lines of the rather remarkable discussion is that Busnoys, in probable complicity with the chapter's Dean, instigated a calculated (if not ruthless) and ultimately successful political move to usurp the position of the incumbent master. Contextualizing the incident with respect to roughly contemporaneous institutional hirings in nearby Bourges and elsewhere, she traces the emergence of the exceptionally competent master as a highly marketable commodity who, by the end of the century, seems invariably to have been a composer of complex mensural polyphony. The simultaneously evolving musical and theoretical discourse manifests a growing concern on the part of composers with acknowledging their masters, thereby implicitly legitimating their creative authority by situating themselves within a musical genealogy or lineage.

Busnoys as a composer benignly neglectful or (more likely) deliberately transgressive of received theoretical doctrine emerges forcefully in Rob Wegman's article, which scrutinizes Busnoys's 'single-minded adherence to notational practices that were edited out of his music almost everywhere else'. Tinctoris, the consummate *musicus*, consistently found fault with Busnoys's mensural usage and defended his own theoretical authority by underscoring that 'Busnoys *alone* disagrees . . .'. Seeking to explain Busnoys's persistence in perpetuating what many regarded as confusing mensural idiosyncrasies, Wegman develops the metaphor of 'mensural practice as language' and examines Busnoys's music as a means of understanding 'the way notational devices acquired meanings in history'. He observes that Busnoys's mensural usage hints at a personal allegiance to his own compositional training (possibly at the hands of Petrus de Domarto) and bears a curious resemblance to English practices of mid-century. Corroborating what we have already seen with respect to his music, his poetry, biographical documents, and contemporaneous assessments, Wegman suggests that even Busnoys's mensural profile can be read 'as an autobiographical text, tracing back its various strands to a range of historical intertexts'. Far from being of purely hermeneutical interest, this entirely original and unprecedented study of Busnoys's 'mensural intertextuality', as Wegman dubs it, leads him to identify the motet *Gaude caelestis Domina* in Cappella Sistina 15 with the purportedly 'lost' (but simply mistitled, through editorial error) motet *Animadvertere* attributed to Busnoys in Tinctoris's *Proportionale*.

The same 'single-minded persistence' typical of Busnoys's notational profile is also manifested, as we have seen earlier, by his interest in the hermeneutical and occult dimensions of late medieval thought, which seems to have exceeded by a long shot that of his contemporaries. This peculiar facet of his creative personality marks Busnoys as the virtually unrivalled *magister ludi* of late fifteenth-century music. Jaap van Benthem explores the possibility that an esoteric architectonic framework, obscured by faulty transmission in the manuscript sources, may have figured centrally in Busnoys's conception of *In hydraulis*, a piece that held undeniably personal meaning for him. In the light of Busnoys's penchant for cryptic and recondite canons, van Benthem demonstrates the probability that Busnoys originally wrote the ostinato tenor as a canonic entity (notated but once with instructions for resolving the mensuration of its successive statements) and proposes emendations necessary to effect a correct transcription of *In hydraulis* from its two relatively corrupt sources. From there he proceeds to explore a complex nexus of numerically significant textual and musical relationships that may represent an exegesis in 'sounding number' of Busnoys's identity and his relationship to Ockeghem.

Questions of authorship and attribution, particularly as they relate to edition-making, have long exercised the minds of musicologists. Some have objected to the seemingly disproportionate amount of time scholars of early music have devoted to these 'positivist' questions of establishing texts, rather than to their critical interpretation.[41] And yet it is difficult to devote serious critical thought to a body of music, like that of Busnoys, which has yet to become available in a standard 'text' that the complete critical edition represents. The methods of inquiry that characterize the third group of essays proceed from more broadly contextualized repertorial perspectives and focus attention on problems posed by conflicting attributions and anonymous works in late medieval music. In her survey of the vast repertory of fifteenth-century Magnificats, Mary Natvig draws attention to the anomalous and in some respects unique formal and stylistic features of Busnoys's single attributed Magnificat surviving in Brussels 5557 and in the light of these anomalies examines four anonymous Magnificats that scholars have linked with Busnoys. Several pressing questions come to the fore: How are we to develop sufficiently distinctive musical criteria for assessing questions of authorship? How much weight should be accorded to author attributions in the face of contradictory stylistic evidence? Having addressed these and other questions about the pieces under discussion, she concludes with some compelling thoughts about the possibility of a hitherto unexplored influence of Busnoys on the late works of Guillaume Dufay.

An overriding historiographical tendency for scholars to privilege works of

---

[41] Joseph Kerman, *Contemplating Music: Challenges to Musicology* (Cambridge, Mass., 1985), 48.

known authorship has consigned many outstanding anonymous works to historical oblivion. Andrea Lindmayr explores this time-honoured dilemma with
respect to the anonymous song-motet *Resjois toi terre de France/Rex pacificus*,
whose text links it to the coronation of Louis XI in July 1461. Previously attributed on the basis of circumstantial evidence to Ockeghem, the piece in actuality
bears a now fragmentary ascription to Busnoys in the Pixérécourt manuscript.
The question of Busnoys's authorship is of no minor import, providing as it
would a second securely datable piece with which to anchor a chronology of his
works (the only other being *In hydraulis*); it would also further corroborate his
interaction with musical circles of the French royal court. Ultimately, Lindmayr
sidesteps the question of authorship in favour of advocating greater attention to
the vast body of anonymous works of the period whose authorship can never be
known and without which we can never formulate a complete picture of the
music of the period.

Questions of authorship and authenticity assume more urgent practical concern for editors pressed to make hard-and-fast decisions about which works of a
composer to include or exclude from a definitive critical edition. Such decisions
are fraught with difficulties even in the relatively rare cases for which we have
more or less complete information about a composer's biography, firm datings of
the surviving manuscripts, and a number of securely datable pieces from which to
establish a chronology. As the editor of the complete edition of Busnoys's songs,
Leeman Perkins is forced to confront a woefully incomplete state of basic biographical and chronological information, large numbers of conflicting attributions, and the fragility even of those attributions that in the past scholars might
have considered relatively secure. Moreover, since Busnoys lived at a time when
author attributions were only beginning to become the norm, rather than the
exception, what does the editor of his music do about the large numbers of
anonymous works in those manuscripts emanating from cultural circles in which
he is known to have flourished and whose style suggests a connection with
Busnoys? The statistical predominance of combinative songs and virelais in
Busnoys's output leads Perkins to explore the possibility that a significant number of the anonymous songs in those genres transmitted in the central Busnoys
sources could be his, particularly those betraying what he has identified as a sufficiently idiosyncratic musical 'signature'. In conclusion, Perkins urges that musicologists unabashedly solicit the help of specialized computer technology to
assess questions of style as they impinge on conflicting attributions and anonymous works.

If such questions are already complex when only incomplete information
about a composer survives, they become all but insurmountable when nothing at
all is known about him—not even his first name. In these particularly murky cases
of composer identity, scholars have often turned to archival sources as a method

of last resort. In her essay here, Barbara Haggh tackles one of the thorniest bio-graphical problems of the fifteenth century: the identity of the composer 'Caron', several of whose works bear conflicting attributions to Busnoys. Combing a vast array of primary sources, she attempts to sort out the various personages by that name, and isolates musicians named Jean and Philippe as possible candidates for the composer. In the process she brings to light hitherto unknown information about Busnoys's curious beneficial career in Brussels churches—in one case the renunciation of a benefice after only four days of tenure.

Few topics impinging on the performance and study of early music have the capacity to cause scholarly tempers to flare more than interpreting the theorists on matters of *musica ficta*, compositional process, and mensurations and propor-tions. The three essays in the fourth section of the volume involve close readings of musical theorists towards a greater elucidation of the meanings of problematic and in some cases highly controversial passages dealing with these specific aspects of compositional procedure and performance practice in the music of Busnoys and his contemporaries. In the light of Tinctoris's apparent disapproval of allow-ing diminished fifths to stand without correction, Peter Urquhart undertakes a comprehensive study of the use of diminished fifths in Busnoys's song produc-tion, identifying some eighty-four places where a diminished fifth was found, and offering compelling reasons why in some thirty-one instances the troublesome interval would probably not have been altered. Busnoys, so it seems, emerges once again as the trangressor of higher theoretical authority. Urquhart's conclu-sions have far-reaching practical implications not only for the performance of the repertory, but especially for a reassessment of current editorial policies with regard to the introduction of accidentals.

Turning to the didactic treatises of Pietro Aaron, Richard Wexler attempts to tease out the intended meaning behind the controversial passage where Aaron asserts that the 'moderns' of his day 'considered all of the parts together' as they composed. He concludes that the passage refers to the need for compositional planning, not simultaneous conception of all the parts, and that the significant change in compositional method resulted from a growing tendency towards melodic assimilation of the individual parts, linked to the treatment of cantus firmi in paraphrase rather than in extended values, and the increasing prevalence of pervasive imitation as a compositional procedure in the late fifteenth and early sixteenth centuries.

Closely reading Tinctoris's treatises on mensuration and proportion, Alexander Blachly surveys a broad slice of contemporaneous music with the pur-pose of determining whether the proportions introduced in the linear progres-sion of a composition were the same as those introduced in simultaneous juxtaposition with the mensuration of other parts. Tinctoris, he observes, says nothing categorical about the stroke of diminution in his four statements on the subject, and from these Blachly extracts twelve axioms broadly applicable to the musical practice of the period and to modern-day performance of the repertory. With specific reference to Busnoys's individual mensural practice, Blachly, like Wegman earlier, notes that 'Busnoys's music occasionally breaks Tinctoris's rules'. As Blachly understands it, the crux of Tinctoris's message suggests 'that vertical and horizontal mensural relationships differed in kind' and that the context and the nature of the piece 'contribute to determining the degree of differentiation'. In other words, we must assess the significance of the difference 'on the merits of the piece in which it is found'.

The essays in the fifth and final section of the volume all relate to Busnoys's legacy and the reception of his works. Two particularly puzzling aspects of Busnoys reception are the predominance of his songs in manuscripts of Italian provenance, even though he has no known biographical connections with Italy, and his setting of two songs with Italian texts: *Con tutta gentileça* and *Fortuna desperata*. The papers by Picker, Meconi, and Rifkin all address aspects of the *Fortuna* problem, particularly as it impinges on the question of Busnoys's authorship. Martin Picker surveys Heinrich Isaac's involvement in the perpetuation and propagation of the *Fortuna desperata* tradition throughout Germany and identifies his six settings of the tune as an important secondary branch in the tradition's history which Ludwig Senfl and others clearly took as their point of departure. Picker himself considers the question of Busnoys's authorship unresolved, but concludes that its resolution probably has little bearing on the subsequent promulgation of the song in German spheres.

The essays by Honey Meconi and Joshua Rifkin should be read in tandem, representing as they do the scholarly analogue of two different 'art-song reworkings' of the same tune. Meconi takes on the *Fortuna* question from the hitherto unexplored angle of its Italian text. Through a study of its intertextual resonances with poetry lamenting the deaths of various Italian ladies of distinction, she links the text directly to the city of Florence and specifically to the circle of Lorenzo de' Medici and Angelo Poliziano. She then effectively contests the arguments against Busnoys's authorship and marshals substantial musical evidence from a wide variety of Busnoys's works to counter claims of *Fortuna*'s alleged contrapuntal flaws and stylistic deviations from Busnoys's normal practice. She raises the possibility of the song's authorship by lesser known Florentine musicians, including the 'Ser Felice' to whom a five-voice version of *Fortuna* bears ascription in Cappella Giulia XIII. 27. But in the virtual absence of other extant pieces by these native Florentines, 'opening the field to a new composer provides no more certainty than before . . . we may never be able to state definitively who wrote *Fortuna desperata*.' Thus consigned to the realm of the epistemological, the authorship question takes a back seat to the larger question that concludes her essay: 'If the original author were a nonentity or if later composers had no idea who wrote

Fortuna desperata, why rework this piece more than virtually any other fifteenth-century polyphonic model?'

Working with a virtually identical body of evidence, Joshua Rifkin arrives at conclusions diametrically opposed to those of Meconi.[42] Outlining the problems of Busnoys's presumed 'Italian period', Rifkin focuses on the two songs with Italian text. He ingeniously employs codicological evidence to demonstrate conclusively that *Con tutta gentileça* must be a contrafact and proceeds from there to undermine the reliability of the sole attribution of *Fortuna desperata* to Busnoys in the Segovia manuscript. In a virtuosic demonstration of positivist scholarship at its best, he exhaustively explores every conceivable codicological, repertorial, scribal, and musical piece of evidence remotely impinging on the question. On the weight of the evidence amassed, he categorically rules out Busnoys as the composer of *Fortuna desperata* and reassigns the work to the *piccolo maestro fiorentino*, Ser Felice.

Still, one feels compelled to ask whether the frequency with which Busnoys's music was emulated by and served as models for other composers (and whether or not he composed *Fortuna desperata* hardly contradicts the overwhelming evidence of his influence) may represent some tacit and otherwise undocumented evidence of the high regard in which he was held as a teacher, as an outstanding model to be emulated.[43] The advice of Hermann Finck and others that an aspiring student 'use an experienced teacher and devote himself totally to imitating him'[44] was already more or less formulated nearly a century earlier in Tinctoris's famous passage in his counterpoint treatise: 'just as Virgil took Homer as his model in his divine work, the Aeneid, so by Hercules, do I use these as models for my own small productions'.[45] That Busnoys served as master of the choirboys in at least two of the most renowned churches in western Christendom would undoubtedly have provided him with some of the finest raw musical talent around; yet the identities of his students will probably be for ever shrouded in anonymity. In the absence of known biographical links between composers, then, can one nevertheless find sufficiently compelling musical evidence to support the likelihood of such a pedagogical connection? Struck by the numerous similarities between the music of Busnoys and the little-known composer Jean Japart, Allan Atlas outlines a tentative methodology for exploring this intriguing

---

[42] Because Rifkin's essay arrived after editing of the volume was completed, it is published here virtually as received from the author.

[43] See in particular Stephan, *Die burgundisch-niederländische Motette*; Sparks, *Cantus Firmus*; van den Borren, *Études*; Higgins, 'Antoine Busnois', 21–5; ead., 'In hydraulis', 76–82; Richard Taruskin, 'Antoine Busnoys and the *L'Homme armé* Tradition', *JAMS* 39 (1986), 255–93, esp. 262–7; Richard Sherr, 'Illibata Dei virgo nutrix and Josquin's Roman Style', *JAMS* 41 (1988), 434–64 at 439–42 and 434; Thomas Brothers, 'Vestiges of the Isorhythmic Tradition in Mass and Motet, ca. 1450–1475', *JAMS* 44 (1991), 1–56 at 15–34, 38–49, and 56; Rob C. Wegman, 'Another Mass by Busnoys?', *ML* 71 (1990), 1–19; id., *Born for the Muses: The Life and Masses of Jacob Obrecht* (Oxford, 1994), 86–100, 213–17.

[44] Hermann Finck, *Musica Practica* (Wittenberg, 1556), beginning of Liber Quintus.

[45] Tinctoris, *The Art of Counterpoint*, trans. Albert Seay (MSD 5; [Rome], 1961), 15.

theoretical question. Identifying what he calls 'internal intersections' between the music of Busnoys and Japart—shared use of well-known tunes, combinative songs, and techniques of contrapuntal manipulation—as well as 'external intersections'—similar source transmission of the works of both composers—Atlas concludes on strength of the cumulative evidence that there may indeed have been a direct line of pedagogical influence from Busnoys to Japart.[46]

Jacob Obrecht, whose indebtedness to Busnoys is abundantly manifest in his direct imitation of Busnoys's *L'homme armé* mass, deployment of Busnoys's songs in his masses, and emulation of Busnoys's musical style, represents the unrivalled heir-apparent to Busnoys's musical legacy. Though the locus of personal contact between the two composers has long been thought to be Bruges, where both were working during the 1480s, Obrecht was already a mature composer by this time, as Rob Wegman showed in his second contribution to the conference proceedings.[47] Wegman sketches a scenario for a hitherto unforeseen context for their interaction during Obrecht's formative years: the late 1460s at the court of Burgundy where his father, Willem Obrecht, worked as a trumpeter. In the light of Obrecht's demonstrable musical indebtedness to Busnoys, Wegman concluded by reflecting on what Busnoy's death might have meant to the younger composer.

One wonders too what the prospect of his own imminent departure from life might have meant to Busnoys himself. As he soberly reflected on his life's transgressions and excesses on his deathbed in 1492, which of the two late medieval responses to his own mortality would have occupied his thoughts: 'to defy death, to prolong fame by deeds, to yearn for immortal glory'? Or would he have instead simply 'accepted death, fixed his hopes on eternal salvation', and found solace in the idea that his pre-established 'bonds of social and professional solidarity would ensure that [he] would always be remembered in the intercessions of the living'?[48] However grandiose his hopes for posthumous renown, even Busnoys could scarcely have conjured up a futuristic scenario five hundred years hence, where, in a strange New World discovered barely a month before he died, a group of scholars would convene in a peculiarly medieval spirit of community to commemorate the anniversary of his death, to perform his music, to discuss his

---

[46] Rob Wegman, noting the striking stylistic and mensural features shared by Petrus de Domarto's *Missa Spiritus almus* and Busnoys's *Anima mea liquefacta est* and *Missa O crux lignum triumphale*, has similarly suggested a pedagogical link between these two composers. See his 'Petrus de Domarto's *Missa Spiritus almus* and the Early History of the Four-Voice Mass in the Fifteenth Century', *EMH* 10 (1991), 235–303 at 240–4 and 261–71, and 'Mensural Intertextuality' (Ch. 8).

[47] 'Busnoys and Obrecht.' The material has since been published in full in Wegman, *Born for the Muses*, 86–100.

[48] See Rob C. Wegman, 'Singers and Composers in Flemish Urban Centres: A Social Context for Busnoys and Obecht', paper given at the Univeristy of Chicago, Musicology Colloquium Series, 3 March 1995.

life and works, and to engage in open dialogue about the directions for future studies of his work.

Taken together, the twenty essays in this volume powerfully reaffirm that early music scholarship is alive and well and continues to offer a virtually inexhaustible array of perspectives and approaches broadly applicable to the study of music of all periods. Challenging the stereotypes habitually coined for their work, the scholars whose essays appear here are working on retrieving historial evidence overlooked by earlier scholarship, on developing new methods for its evaluation, on bringing new critical insights and interpretations to time-honoured music-historical problems, and rethinking from more fully contextual historical and repertorial perspectives a century-long accumulation of received wisdom about late medieval music. These largely unprecedented discussions of the musical culture of Busnoys and his contemporaries lay the foundation of a new sub-discipline in music scholarship and open up vast, uncharted horizons for critical work yet to be done that will eventually reshape the discipline and study of early music for many years to come.

2

'Trained and immersed in all musical delights': Towards a New Picture of Busnoys

꙳ ❀ ❧

DAVID FALLOWS

I F Busnoys had died in 1482 rather than 1492, some things would have looked different. A conference ten years ago would have heard the first evidence that Busnoys had been in Tours in the early 1460s, though Paula Higgins in fact published this only in 1984; most delegates would have arrived with no certain information about the composer earlier than his appearance at the court of Burgundy soon before Philip the Good's death in 1467. A conference ten years ago would not have had to confront the eight mass cycles that have been attributed to Busnoys since then: the six *L'homme armé* cycles and the cycle *Quant ce viendra* attributed to him by Richard Taruskin as well as the cycle *L'ardant desir* attributed to him by Rob Wegman—all of them still controversial matters. It would not have been able to profit from Howard Mayer Brown's eloquent stylistic profile of the songs published in *A Florentine Chansonnier*, from the new biographical and social profile in Paula Higgins's thesis, from Richard Taruskin's edition of the sacred works, with its extensive commentary, from an enormous body of work on the manuscript sources, and so on. Nor would it have known two pieces only recently identified: the glorious motet *Gaude caelestis Domina*, which Rob Wegman located in Cappella Sistina 15 on the basis of the Tinctoris quote; and the ballade *Resjois toi terre de France*, for which Andrea Lindmayr noted traces of an ascription in Pixérécourt, traces that leave it virtually beyond doubt that it was ascribed there to Busnoys—though perhaps this would have been revealed at a Busnoys conference ten years ago, since it now turns out that Don Giller had independently reached the same conclusion in a seminar paper of 1980.[1]

This is a revised and expanded version of the Keynote Address delivered at the Busnoys Conference.

[1] As Giller informed me in a letter of 5 Oct. 1992. For the published items mentioned in this paragraph, see Paula Higgins, '*In hydraulis* Revisited: New Light on the Career of Antoine Busnois', *JAMS* 36 (1986), 36–86; Richard Taruskin, 'Antoine Busnoys and the *L'Homme armé* Tradition', *JAMS* 39 (1986), 255–93,

The main changes of the last ten years have been on two fronts. The first was to draw attention away from Busnoys's years at the Burgundian court, beginning to see the extraordinary richness of the central-French tradition, the importance of the entire Loire Valley circle both for Busnoys and for the history of music in the second half of the fifteenth century. If I had been invited to a Busnoys quincentenary conference in 1982 I would almost certainly have read a paper arguing that the 'central' chansonniers then thought to be Burgundian were from the Loire Valley area—as I did argue in an AMS chapter paper that year, reviving a paper originally presented in England five years earlier to mark fifty years of *Trois chansonniers* and *Der Kopenhagener Chansonnier* (both published in 1927). It now turns out that Paula Higgins was independently framing the same argument far more thoroughly and persuasively for her doctoral thesis; my paper was confined to the dustbin and that is now all old news.[2] But the fuller exploration of music in the Loire Valley area remains a major task for the next few years. The second main change has been to begin to appreciate the true quality and influence of Busnoys's music. Previously he seemed the quintessential Burgundian court composer; now he looks like the man who brought the newly cosmopolitan ideas of the French court to the Burgundian Netherlands, to a court that had earlier in the century been a major cultural centre but had recently seen little that was new. Previously Busnoys seemed a man whose brief and prolific career was almost immediately eclipsed by the brilliance of Obrecht and Josquin; now he begins to look like the main catalyst for the earlier works of both composers.[3] These are major changes in outlook; it is these that justify a conference marking the fifth centenary of his death. Ten years ago, it would have been much harder to raise the financial support for such an event.

It would also have been hard to raise the scholarly support. Certainly Busnoys had recently been given new prominence in 1979 with the edition of the Mellon Chansonnier, by Leeman Perkins and Howard Garey, the first publication of any substantial number of his works since *Trois chansonniers* of half a century earlier,

and ensuing correspondence; Rob C. Wegman, 'Another Mass by Busnoys?', *ML* 71 (1990), 1–19, and ensuing correspondence; Howard Mayer Brown (ed.), *A Florentine Chansonnier from the Time of Lorenzo the Magnificent* (Monuments of Renaissance Music, 7; Chicago, 1983); Paula Marie Higgins, 'Antoine Busnois and Musical Culture in Late Fifteenth-Century France and Burgundy' (Ph.D. diss., Princeton University, 1987); Richard Taruskin (ed.), *Busnoys LTW*, Commentary (New York, 1990); Rob C. Wegman, letter to *ML* 71 (1990), 633–5 at 635; Andrea Lindmayr, *Quellenstudien zu den Motetten von Johannes Ockeghem* (Neue Heidelberger Studien zur Musikwissenschaft, 16; Laaber, 1990), 69–73.

[2] Higgins, 'Antoine Busnois', ch. 5; the essence of her findings was already outlined in her introduction to the facsimile *Chansonnier Nivelle de La Chaussée* (Geneva, 1984). The case is also stated in Leeman L. Perkins, 'Modern Methods, Received Opinion and the Chansonnier', *ML* 69 (1988), 356–64. My own unpublished argument of 1977 was prompted primarily by a passing remark in Joshua Rifkin, 'Scribal Concordances in Some Renaissance Manuscripts in Florentine Libraries', *JAMS* 26 (1973), 305–28 at 391 n. 37.

[3] Again the gist of the matter is presented in Higgins, 'Antoine Busnois', though different aspects of his influence are outlined in Taruskin, 'Antoine Busnoys and the *L'Homme armé* Tradition', and in various articles by Rob C. Wegman.

and indeed the only such publication since *Trois chansonniers* in which a literary scholar has equal billing with a musicologist. Moreover, perhaps many of us here had our first major encounters with Busnoys through the marvellous 1970 record devoted to his songs, directed by Joshua Rifkin—aided, incidentally, by the spirited viol-playing of Richard Taruskin—and Bruno Turner's 1978 record of the mass *L'homme armé*.[4]

But within the last decade several scholars present here have moved Busnoys into the centre of the stage. They have brought out new dimensions of his character and musicianship. They have found hidden messages in his work. They have shown that we cannot understand Josquin and Obrecht, perhaps even Okeghem and Dufay, without further clarification of Busnoys's achievements, an insight pioneered by Edgar Sparks,[5] but in several ways still waiting there like a time-bomb. They have understood that one of the most fascinating features of his larger works is the way he explores the use of time, juxtaposing passages of intense activity with passages of almost total immobility, an exploration on which Josquin later built with such brilliance. They have helped musicians to realize how music that may once have seemed a little bland is not only driven by an unusually powerful musical mind but also crucial to the changes that shook the musical world in the years around 1480—changes that are still in the most urgent need of clarification.

On the other hand, it looks very much as though the body of surviving works would have been more or less the same if Busnoys had died ten years earlier: that is, most of his known music was probably written before 1482. Appendix A is a rough chronology of the songs—a fairly mindless listing, based on what seem to be the current views of source dates. Many people will have different views on some of these dates; moreover, the list gives very little attention to the obvious truth that any such date represents only a *terminus ante quem* and that many songs must be far earlier than the list suggests.

Even so, section 13 of the list shows that only nine songs make their first appearance later than the Pixérécourt songbook of about 1480; for five of these I have proposed an earlier date in any case, and two others look good cases for elimination as spuria. It would be very hard to argue that any song confidently by him is likely to be later than 1482.

Further than that, though, the list suggests that up to forty-two of his songs were composed before he appeared at the court of Burgundy, perhaps early in 1467. This case is harder to argue confidently, since much depends on the date of the Dijon songbook (I would put it around 1470, but some put it earlier, some

---

[4] *Antoine Busnois: Chansons*, The Nonesuch Consort, directed by Joshua Rifkin: Nonesuch H-71247; *Binchois motets and Busnois Mass L'homme armé*: Pro Cantione Antiqua, directed by Bruno Turner: Deutsche Grammophon Archiv Produktion 2533 404.

[5] Edgar H. Sparks, *Cantus Firmus in Mass and Motet, 1420–1520* (Berkeley and Los Angeles, 1963), ch. 8.

rather later), where it was copied, and how soon music composed at the court of Burgundy could reasonably have found its way into a central-French manuscript. Much may also depend on one's view of how much secular song it would have been appropriate to compose at the Burgundian court around the time of Philip the Good's last illness and his death in June 1467.

Moreover, some of this depends on my view that his virelais are from the earlier part of his career and that the virelai was a form not much cultivated at the court of Burgundy, hence the presentation in section 7 of the two virelais that first appear later than the Dijon chansonnier.[6]

Nevertheless, even Pixérécourt contains only twelve songs not found earlier. Given that manuscript's Florentine origin and its inclusion of several works up to forty years old at the time, it would be fairly easy to offer stylistic arguments that some of these pieces are also from well before 1470; and the alarming number of Pixérécourt ascriptions among section 15, the spuria, has already been used by others to question the authority of several more Busnoys ascriptions here and in Florence 229.[7]

In other words, a tendentious view of the chronology could almost make a case for saying that fewer than a dozen of his known songs are likely to date from his years at the court of Burgundy. Others may have a clearer view of whether such a case would be entirely fair or convincing. But even its possibility underlines a major change brought about by the source research of recent years. On balance, my suggestion that two-thirds of his known songs may be pre-1467 could well be a conservative estimate.

At the moment the chronology of his sacred music seems far less clear. Given the thin survival of the sources, a similar diagram would yield little sense, though far more may well date from his Burgundian years. In any case, much has been written about the sacred music over the past decade and very little about his songs. So these remarks today focus on the songs, because he is after all the most prolific French song composer between Dufay and Claudin de Sermisy (and the only challengers in any language would be Encina, Cara, and Tromboncino, all of whose works are far slighter). If I have a keynote to sound here, it is that it is time to give more attention to Busnoys the songwriter.

That is why Appendix A contains more information than is necessary for the simple chronological point it supports. The spread of the sources and of the ascriptions offers further useful clues. For example, most of the earliest songs appear in the Rohan poetry manuscript, and many of the next group are in early

---

[6] For a brief outline of the virelai form in these years, together with the reasons for preferring the term virelai to the more customary 'bergerette', see David Fallows, 'Bergerette', *Die Musik in Geschichte und Gegenwart: Zweite, neubearbeitete Ausgabe*, ed. Ludwig Finscher, i (Kassel and Stuttgart, 1994), cols. 1411–13.

[7] Gerald Montagna, 'Caron, Hayne, Compère: A Transmission Reassessment', *EMH* 7 (1987), 107–57 at 128.

sections of that most perplexing of all poetry sources, Paris 1719, a document that merits the most detailed exploration from a musical viewpoint.[8] As another example, the only early songs on the list that are not in the Dijon chansonnier apart from the ballade *Resjois toi* (sect. 1) are the two songs copied into Trent 89 apparently in the early 1460s (sect. 5).[9] Given also the very different pattern of their other sources, one must conclude either that there is an earlier and quite different stage of his career about which we still know nothing, or that the Trent 89 dating is wrong, or that Gerald Montagna was right to suspect their ascriptions in Pixérécourt and Florence 229 (he was judging purely from their style).[10] Similarly, the earliest songs all seem to appear in Nivelle, but again with the exception of *Resjois toi*. I have elsewhere stated my reasons for believing this was composed in about 1461, though, and further discussion would be more appropriate after hearing Andrea Lindmayr's latest thoughts on the matter.[11]

Obviously, though, this list draws attention to the matter of his earliest songs, more specifically to how early we can suspect that he started composing. If he had really composed two-thirds of his sixty-four songs by 1467, the chances are that his earliest works are from well before 1460.

That is where the poetry manuscript Paris 9223 becomes interesting—the one edited by Raynaud in 1889 as *Rondeaux et autres poésies*—more specifically its last section, in a different script and with an origin different from the rest, sharing, for example, nothing at all with the companion Paris 15771. In this last part of Paris 9223 there is a poem actually ascribed to Busnoys: it is in section 14 of

---

[8] The Rohan manuscript, Berlin 78 B 17, is edited in Martin Löpelmann, *Die Liederhandschrift des Cardinals de Rohan* (Gesellschaft für romanische Literatur, 44; Göttingen, 1923). For Paris 1719, see Françoise Féry-Hue, *Au grey d'amours . . . (Pièces inédites du manuscrit Paris, Bibl. nat., fr. 1719): étude et édition* (= Le moyen français, vols. 27–28; Montreal, 1991).

[9] Suparmi Elizabeth Saunders, *The Dating of the Trent Codices from their Watermarks, with a Study of the Local Liturgy of Trent in the Fifteenth Century* (diss., University of London, 1983; repr. New York, 1989), 206. On the other hand, she offers the same paper date for the anonymous *Missa Quant ce viendra*, also in Trent 89—that is, the Mass that Taruskin, 'Antoine Busnoys and the *L'Homme armé* Tradition', attributes to Busnoys; it is printed in *Busnoys LTW*, Music, 208. For the song *Quant ce viendra* in Trent 88 she offers (p. 198) watermark evidence for a date of about 1462. If we accept these watermark dates (and there is as yet no particularly cogent reason not to do so apart from one's natural hesitation in accepting a watermark date in a complicated manuscript without further supporting evidence), there could be a good case for putting the song *Quant ce viendra* well back into the 1450s.

[10] See above, n. 7.

[11] My remarks on *Resjois toi* are unfortunately rather scattered. I take the liberty of listing them here as witness of the way my own views evolved and may continue to evolve in the future: 'English Song Repertories of the Mid-Fifteenth Century', *Proceedings of the Royal Musical Association*, 103 (1976–7), 61–79 at 68 (initial identification of its occasion and suggestion that the composer is 'presumably Ockeghem'); 'Johannes Ockeghem: The Changing Image, the Songs and a New Source', *Early Music*, 12 (1984), 218–30 at 222 (statement that a better knowledge of Okeghem's work and hearing it on the recording of Okeghem's complete songs quite changed my mind and suggested it was a 'composer of lesser stature'); review of Martin Picker's *Johannes Ockeghem and Jacob Obrecht: A Guide to Research* in *ML* 70 (1989), 247–9 at 279 (eager endorsement of the work as being by Busnoys, based on the identification presented in the original typescript version of Lindmayr's thesis). Now that I know the work of Busnoys rather better, that too seems a little naïve, but I am not yet ready for my next glib observation on the work.

Appendix A since it has no music, the rondeau 'Lequel vous plairoit mieulx trouver'.[12]

In 1985 Barbara Inglis published what counts as the most recent literary study of that source. She gave very good reasons for believing that this last part of the manuscript was copied in 1458 at the court of Brittany. She impressively identified no fewer than eight of the fifteen named poets with men present at that court in that year, the single year of the reign of Duke Arthur III, famous earlier in his life for his military exploits as Arthur de Richemont.[13] Since it was not her main topic, Inglis mentioned this only briefly; but there are very full payment lists for the court in that year, and all eight poets were plainly present.

Within the new picture of Busnoys's early works, the possibility that he had written the poem by 1458 looks unavoidable. That same section of Paris 9223 also contains the poem 'En tous les lieux', here ascribed to Monseigneur Jacques, but found with a four-voice setting by Busnoys in Nivelle (sect. 2 of App. A). Again it was Barbara Inglis who very convincingly identified Monseigneur Jacques for the first time as Jacques de Luxembourg, brother-in-law of Duke Arthur III of Brittany, also known as Monseigneur de Saint-Pol and brother of the famous general Louis, Comte de Saint-Pol. Jacques is the main poet in this part of the manuscript, with his name above twenty-one of the sixty-four poems; his work is found in no other source apart from two musical settings, and Inglis makes a very good case for believing that this was his own personal collection.[14] If his poetry was not very widely distributed, it becomes very tempting to suggest that Busnoys was in fact present at the court of Brittany in the later 1450s, that is, before his first documented presence at Tours, in 1461. It may even be relevant that Saint-Pol is less than 20 miles from Béthune, where Busnoys seems to have grown up; so perhaps Jacques de Luxembourg or de Saint-Pol (whose wife, incidentally, came from nearby Roubaix) provides the link between the young composer and the court of Brittany.

Even more temptingly, there is another poem here by Jacques that survives in a musical setting: the rondeau 'Qu'elle n'y a je le mainctien', found in Dijon with

---

[12] *Rondeaux et autres poésies du XVe siècle*, ed. Gaston Raynaud (Paris, 1889), 153. Even though the poem has the rondeau form of most songs of that era, there must be some doubt as to whether it was intended for music. It has a kind of dialectic unsuitable for musical expression and rare in the surviving song repertory of the time. As Raynaud remarks (*Rondeaux*, p. xii), it is a kind of jeu-parti, posing a courtly question, elaborating it, and finally answering it.

[13] *Une nouvelle collection de poésies lyriques et courtoises du XVe siècle: Le manuscrit B.N. Nouv. Acq. Fr. 15771*, ed. Barbara L. S. Inglis (Bibliothèque du XVe siècle, 48; Geneva and Paris, 1985), app. A: 'Notice sur le manuscrit B.N. fr. 9223', 213–14.

[14] A brief outline of the life of Jacques de Luxembourg appears in Joseph Vaesen and Étienne Charavay (eds.), *Lettres de Louis XI roi de France*, 11 vols. (Paris, 1895), v. 364, where he is called 'Jacques de Saint-Pol ou, pour mieux dire, de Luxembourg, dernier frère du connétable [i.e. Louis], seigneur de Richebourg'; it reports that he had fought in the battles of Formigny (1450) and Gavre (1453), was a member of both the Order of the Golden Fleece and that of St Michel, and died on 20 Aug., 1487. On his elder brother Louis, see *Lettres de Louis XI*, ii. 227: he was born in 1418, appointed constable of France on 5 Oct. 1465, to the order of St Michel in 1469, and was executed for lèse-majesté at the age of 57 on 19 Dec. 1475.

anonymous music in a style not at all distant from that of Busnoys's early works. Moreover, in Dijon it immediately precedes two songs by Busnoys, only the second of which is ascribed to him there. The music is in Ex. 2.1. This is not the moment to explore it in detail, except to note that anyone familiar with Busnoys's early work will see several familiar details, among them the flawless treatment of dissonances that sets him apart from nearly all his contemporaries.

Ex. 2.1. Anon., *Qu'elle n'y a je le mainctien* (Dijon, fos. 106ᵛ–108ʳ)

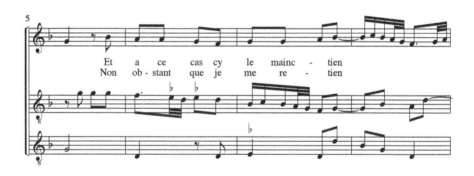

Ex. 2.1. *cont.*

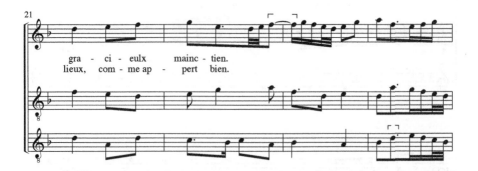

It is worth adding here that Inglis was working from the very full second documentary volume of Hyacinthe Morice's history of Brittany (1744).[15] Although

[15] Dom Pierre-Hyacinthe Morice, *Mémoires pour servir à l'histoire ecclésiastique et civile de Bretagne*, 3 vols.
(Paris, 1742–6); the entries quoted here are all from vol. ii (Paris, 1744). These volumes contain the
preparatory documentary work towards Dom Pierre-Hyacinthe Morice, completed by Dom Charles
Taillandier, *Histoire ecclésiastique et civile de Bretagne*, 2 vols. (Paris, 1750–6). I should add that I have made
no attempt to explore the original documents, which must surely yield further pertinent information.

Ex. 2.1. *cont.*

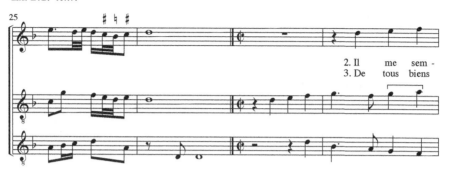

the particular court account she used (cols. 1722–7) contains hundreds of names, it frustratingly ends with a brief mention of '12 clercs of the chapel, nine trumpets and minstrels', none of them named. It is very hard to resist thinking that Busnoys may have been among them. Plainly these documents need to be rechecked. Incidentally, a search in Morice for anybody named Antoine, with the name Busnoys perhaps mistranscribed, was fruitless; but there is a certain Jean de la Haye, found in 1449 among the gentlemen of the Viscount de Rohan, being exempted military service (col. 1513), and in 1457 being appointed Capitaine au Baillage de Chastelaillon (col. 1710). There is nothing to say that he is the composer whose songs in Nivelle are in a style so like that of Busnoys; but at least the dates are more plausible than the 1443 generally associated with the composer Delahaye.[16] It is also worth adding that the brief comments Inglis offered about Paris 9223 were peripheral to her study, and the manuscript has not been considered thoroughly since Raynaud's edition of 1889. Like so many other poetic sources of the fifteenth century, it merits careful study as a chansonnier by a music historian; and this particular one points directly at the court of Brittany in the late 1450s as a substantial source of musical patronage, a matter that plainly invites the most urgent attention.

One point that emerges clearly from Appendix A is that there are several four-voice pieces among Busnoys's earliest known songs: *Resjois toi*, *En tous les lieux*, *Vous marchez*, and perhaps *On a grant mal/On est bien malade*. It is too easy to assume that a composer, any composer, will write four-voice songs later than three-voice ones. In the case of Busnoys and his secular work, that may well be the reverse of the true situation. In these apparently early works he shows himself a highly skilled composer in four voices.

Given that prevalence of four-voice music, the early history of the combinative chanson takes on a new interest. Another important recent event was the publication in 1989 of a substantial anthology of combinative chansons, edited by Maria Rika Maniates. Anyone glancing at that volume must have been struck by patterns of interrelationships between works, of which one concerns pieces by Okeghem and Busnoys. Between Okeghem's *Petite camusette* setting and Busnoys's *On est bien malade*, there are several similarities.[17] The most obvious is the way both run the borrowed melody in simple imitation through all three lower voices (rare within this repertory); another is how in both songs the upper voice shares in several details of that imitative network; yet another is the way both lay out their lower voices in a broad ABA pattern, that is, with the imitative network at the start returning in the second half. But there is more. The voice-ranges in the two pieces are almost identical, as are their lengths (forty-six breves for Okeghem, intriguingly forty-seven for Busnoys).

It is hard to put all this down to accident. Perhaps Busnoys was following the pattern set by Okeghem, just as his *Resjois toi* seems to follow the scheme of

---

[16] No dictionary entry quite gives the full and correct story on Delahaye, though it can be assembled from Higgins, *Chansonnier Nivelle de La Chaussée*, p. vi, and Higgins, 'Antoine Busnois', 280–1. A complete edition of his surviving music is in the press, edited by Jane Alden, to whom I am indebted for sharing information about the composer. [*Ed.*: Nevertheless, it seems pertinent to the argument that the Jean Delahaye of 1443 was evidently in the service of the Duke of Brittany. See Higgins, *Chansonnier Nivelle de La Chaussée*, p. vi.]

[17] Maria Rika Maniates (ed.), *The Combinative Chanson: An Anthology* (Recent Researches in the Music of the Renaissance, 77; Madison, 1989), nos. 20 and 29.

Okeghem's *Mort tu as navré*. It is equally possible that this reflects a kind of rivalry between the two composers; and there is just a chance that Okeghem was refining on a pattern set by Busnoys (though Okeghem's is surely the finer piece, more tautly constructed; and it survives in a large number of sources). But in any case both songs presumably date from the early 1460s when they were together in Tours: Okeghem's *Petite camusette* appears in both Nivelle and Wolfenbüttel, though *On est bien malade* is not found earlier than Dijon.

There is just one more combinative chanson that has a single melody shared between all three lower voices in this way, again by Busnoys, his *Vous marchez du bout du pied*, also first found in the Nivelle chansonnier.[18] This one stands just a little aside from the other two: its ranges are different; it is longer; and the top voice is rather less distinct from the three lower voices in its style. But technically it works in the same way; and it shares with Okeghem's *Petite camusette* that curious phenomenon of a single isolated note to open one of the lower voices (a detail found in several later pieces but not, I think, earlier). Plainly these three pieces belong together and add one further detail to the relationship between Busnoys and Okeghem—adding to the details already present in their two *L'homme armé* masses, in *In hydraulis*, in *Resjois toi*, in the documentation, and perhaps in *Ut heremita solus*. Nobody need be surprised if more emerges in the near future.

Another point about *On est bien malade* can be added here. In his edition of Florence 229, Howard Mayer Brown drew attention to the relation between this and another setting of the same materials.[19] Brown plausibly hinted that the new and bigger version could be the work of Isaac, an eager reworker of other people's music, though he would probably concede that the piece contains little trace of the compulsive contrapuntal ingenuity found in so many of Isaac's rewritings. In fact the keyboard intabulation in St Gallen 530 offers the missing link between the two versions.[20] With this, it becomes possible to suggest that Busnoys rewrote his own piece in two stages, perhaps even adapting it for an audience less interested in combinative chansons. Ex. 2.2 shows the opening of all three versions, with Dijon on the bottom. Again, one could spend a lot of enjoyable time exploring the differences, but for the moment it is enough to point out that the St Gallen version shares some details with Dijon and others with Florence 229.

So it looks as though this is another case of Busnoys rewriting, to add to the better-known cases of *Je ne puis vivre*, *Quant ce viendra*, and *Ung plus que tous*. It

---

[18] Ibid., no. 34. To the manuscripts named by Maniates should be added the Speciálník Codex, p. 255, and two much later sources in the hand once thought (wrongly) to be that of Lukas Wagenrieder: Munich 328–31, no. 122 (where it is headed simply 'Carmen in fa'), and Vienna 18810, no. 56, where it is (impossibly) ascribed to 'Henrichus ysaac'.

[19] Brown, *A Florentine Chansonnier*, Text vol., 65, 122–3, and 283; the two versions are both printed in the Music vol., nos. 183 and 183A.

[20] Fos. 67ᵛ–68ʳ (no. 75), with an ascription to 'Andreas Busnois'. It is now published in *St. Galler Orgelbuch: Die Orgeltabulatur des Fridolin Sicher (St. Gallen, Codex 530)*, ed. Hans Joachim Marx and Thomas Warburton (Schweizerische Musikdenkmäler, 8; Winterthur, 1992), 172.

Ex. 2.2. Busnoys, *On est bien malade*, mm. 1–13: (*a*) Florence 229, fos. 193ᵛ–194ʳ;
(*b*) St Gallen 530, fos. 67ᵛ–68ʳ; (*c*) Dijon, fos. 177ᵛ–178ʳ

begins to suggest a pattern which in its turn raises the name of another frequent
rewriter and adapter of his own materials among fifteenth-century songwriters,
Binchois.[21]

²¹ On Binchois and revision, see David Fallows, 'Embellishment and Urtext in the Fifteenth-Century
Song Repertories', *Basler Jahrbuch für historische Musikpraxis*, 14 (1990), 59–85 at 62–73. Further hints of

Ex. 2.2. *cont.*

This moves us on to slippery ground, but it is worth outlining. Okeghem declared his debt to Binchois much more openly, not just in *Mort tu as navré* but also in the mass on *De plus en plus*, though there is no documentation of direct

Binchois as a reviser of his own work can be seen in Dennis Slavin, 'Binchois' Songs, the Binchois Fragment, and the Two Layers of Escorial A' (Ph.D. diss., Princeton University, 1987), especially 43–72.

Ex. 2.2. *cont.*

personal contact between the two. For Busnoys the case is far trickier, and it is made more difficult by current uncertainty about which of the late pieces ascribed to Binchois are really by him. Perhaps it is easiest to begin with *Je ne vis onques la pareille*, ascribed to Dufay in Montecassino and to Binchois in the much more obviously trustworthy Nivelle: if there were no ascriptions at all, one would

Ex. 2.2. *cont.*

surely be inclined to guess that it was by Busnoys. The arguments against that were twofold: first that the piece was sung at the Feast of the Pheasant early in 1454, long before Busnoys was known to be active, though what I have just said about his earlier years tends to modify that objection; the second, which still seems to hold true, is that the Nivelle chansonnier seems to know the difference between Binchois and Busnoys. Strangely, one would reach the same view about *Tout a par moy*, ascribed to Walter Frye in Mellon and Laborde but to Binchois again in Nivelle, and also about *Comme femme desconfortee*, ascribed to Binchois only in Mellon. Perhaps the same could be said of the textless song in the Schedelsches Liederbuch, with a confusing ascription earlier read as being to Busnoys but now generally read as Binchois. All four plainly belong in the same stylistic world as the early songs of Busnoys. Moreover, Paula Higgins has pointed out that the decoration for several works of Busnoys in Nivelle and related manuscripts, the wild boar, also appears in the contratenor initial for the Nivelle copy of *Tout a par moy*.[22]

Now if these four pieces are all by Binchois, they are the only surviving works from the last decade of his life, so there is virtually no basis for evaluating the ascriptions from the viewpoint of style; all one can say is that the copyists of Nivelle and Mellon both knew that Binchois and Busnoys were two different people and presumably knew that they were men of entirely different generations. I think we must take their evidence on trust; in which case it looks as though Busnoys's early style grew out of Binchois's last style. His early songs are riddled with references to those pieces, most particularly to *Je ne vis onques la pareille*: Ex. 2.3 presents passages from Busnoys's *C'est bien maleur* in parallel with *Je ne vis onques*—and again it would be easy to devote a lengthy discussion to the similarities and differences between the two. Moreover, his *En soustenant vostre querelle* takes its opening text line from the last line of Binchois's *De plus en plus*, as Frederick Crane pointed out to me.

To broaden the picture a little, one could add that the opening music of *En soustenant* comes directly from a piece by Dufay, *Dieu gart la bonne sans reprise* (see Ex. 2.4), and that a very large number of Busnoys's early works include a cadence that matches the one at the end of Dufay's *Le serviteur* (Ex. 2.5 gives a few of them). But from the viewpoint of style it is those late works apparently by Binchois that seem to create the context for Busnoys's early songs. The Dufay references are more superficial and seem to betoken simply his fascination with earlier music, about which I have written elsewhere.[23]

---

[22] Paula Higgins, 'Parisian Nobles, a Scottish Princess, and the Woman's Voice in Late Medieval Song', *EMH* 10 (1991), 145–200 at 180–1. I should like to express my shame at reading there in n. 111 that I had informed Professor Higgins that I believed *Tout a par moy* to be 'in the style of neither Binchois nor Frye'; this is what I would now consider a thoroughly irresponsible and unconsidered remark. More to the point would be the bland impartiality of my comments in *Chansonnier de Jean de Montchenu*, ed. G. Thibault and D. Fallows (Publications de la Société Française de Musicologie, Première Série, 23; Paris, 1991), pp. cxii–xciv.

[23] David Fallows, 'Busnoys and the Early Fifteenth Century: A Note on "L'ardant desir" and "Faictes de moy"', *ML* 71 (1990), 20–4. Some conclusions offered there must now be modified in the light of Joshua Rifkin's paper for this conference (see Ch. 20); in particular, it can no longer be considered certain that *Faictes de moy* was originally composed for the much earlier text it now carries in Florence 229 and Pixérécourt, since Rifkin has shown that these are sources that elsewhere demonstrably added earlier and inappropriate texts to later music. Moreover, the rondeau has a four-line stanza, whereas Busnoys's music seems designed for a five-line stanza: both these sources add an extra line from the beginning of the third stanza; and one other source presents the music with a fragment of entirely unrelated text.

Ex. 2.3. Comparison of (*a*) Binchois(?), *Je ne vis oncques*, mm. 1–5 and 12–16 with (*b*) Busnoys, *C'est bien maleur*, mm. 1–5 and 15–19

Ex. 2.4. Comparison of (*a*) opening of Dufay, *Dieu gart la bonne* with (*b*) Busnoys, *En soustenant*

There might even be some room for wondering whether there wasn't a conscious decision involved when Anthoine de Busne chose the pen-name of Busnoys, just as Gilles de Bins was called Binchois; these pen-names are common enough, but the similarity of those two is intriguing. If so, that could even explain why Busnoys seems to have accepted a position in the household of Charles the Bold really rather suddenly, as we shall hear later from Paula Higgins. He may in a sense have liked to see himself as the true successor of Binchois.

With that in mind, it may be time to re-explore the dates and origins of the earliest songbooks on the list. Briefly, the latest information, mainly from Paula Higgins and Martella Gutiérrez-Denhoff and heavily supported by the art historians they consulted, is that all three—that is, Nivelle de la Chaussée, Wolfenbüttel, and the first layer of Laborde—date from the first half of the 1460s.[24] The way Appendix A works out might seem to suggest that Wolfenbüttel is the earliest of them all; but a fuller diagram of Wolfenbüttel, Appendix B, makes that seem unlikely, since there are several songs here found only among the additions to Nivelle and several found otherwise in the second

[24] Higgins, 'Antoine Busnois', 234–308; Martella Gutiérrez-Denhoff, *Der Wolfenbütteler Chansonnier* (Wolfenbütteler Forschungen, 29; Wiesbaden, 1985), ch. 4; further details on these manuscripts appear in Charles Edward Barret, Jr., 'A Critical Edition of the Dijon Chansonnier' (Ph.D. diss., George Peabody College, 1981), and Duff James Kennedy, 'Six chansonniers français' (Ph.D. diss., University of California at Santa Barbara, 1987).

Ex. 2.5. Final cadence of (*a*) Dufay, *Le serviteur* compared with cadences by Busnoys: (*b*) *C'est bien maleur*; (*c*) *Quant vous me ferez* (end); (*d*) *Ma plus qu'assez*; (*e*) *M'a vostre cueur*; (*f*) *In hydraulis*; (*g*) *Missa Quant ce viendra*; (*h*) *Gaude caelestis*; (*i*) *En tous les lieux*

Ex. 2.5. *cont.*

layer of Laborde (those below the line in App. B), among them Hayne's *De tous biens plaine*, which can hardly have been written before about 1465; it also contains a version of the anonymous *J'ay pris amours* with a low contratenor, apparently devised later than the one in Laborde.[25] That is, Wolfenbüttel could be the latest of these three early sources, even though it is also the one that contains the largest proportion of earlier classics. So it is of some interest in the study of how music by Binchois and others was received in the 1460s.

Higgins in particular has shown that the 'central' chansonniers have nothing to do with the Burgundian court area and has argued for their origins in French court circles in the Loire Valley; but their location has been no further specified than somewhere in the area between the Loire Valley cities and, rather south of the Loire, Bourges. This is mainly because the illuminators have been only approximately identified and none of the songbooks has been identified with a particular recipient—partly because in the case of Dijon and Wolfenbüttel the presumed dedication pages have been torn out.

In fact Wolfenbüttel contains a clear statement of its intended recipient. At my recent first personal encounter with the manuscript I was puzzled to notice that the labelling of the contratenor was confused in some of the early songs: the text scribe had written the initial letter 'C' as though he was not aware that the illuminator would later add a decorated 'C' at the beginning of the line. This was the case in nos. 2–5 but not thereafter. That obviously raised the question of why it had not happened for the first piece, Frye's *Ave regina celorum*, and it soon became clear from other palaeographical details that this had been added slightly later.[26]

[25] There are several songs from the years around 1450 that survive with two different and mutually incompatible contratenors, one in the same range as the tenor (following a pattern that goes back over a century) and the other in a range well below the tenor (reflecting the new preferences of the 1450s and after). In most cases the pattern of the sources clearly shows that the low contratenor is later. For *J'ay pris amours* the situation is not quite so clear, given that the equal-range contratenor appears, apart from Laborde, only in rather later sources—Paris 4379, fos. 27v–28r, and the intarsia (finished 1476) in Urbino, Palazzo ducale, Studiolo of Federico II da Montefeltro. But it seems reasonable to assume that the low contratenor is indeed later: there are enough cases of extremely close agreement between Wolfenbüttel and the first layer of Laborde for it to be clear that they were in general copied from the same exemplars; and it almost follows from this that the presence of the low contratenor in Wolfenbüttel makes its copying later than that of the first layer of Laborde—in other words, that the low contratenor was not yet available in that scribal workshop when the first layer of Laborde was copied. I spell out the case with all its uncertainties because this is in my view the crucial detail in their relative copying dates. The presence of Hayne van Ghizeghem's *De tous biens plaine* is another slightly slippery detail, since much depends on how young Hayne really was when he was described as a 'jeusne fils' in 1457 and on how old he would need to have been to have composed such an enormously influential piece. There is broad agreement, however, that it can hardly have been composed before 1465; and that happens to fit well with the pattern of the surviving sources, especially the pattern outlined here.

[26] It may be worth adding that Wolfenbüttel would be a particularly satisfying source for close analysis of all kinds. Thus the minimal trimming means that the marginal pricking is nearly all visible: evidently the pricker used a device that provided two parallel sets of five pricks: one set has a total breadth of about 9.5 mm. per system (this is the one actually used for ruling the staves in Wolfenbüttel); the other set, starting with the highest prick on the same level, was rather wider, with its fourth prick parallel to the fifth prick of the first set, and with a total depth of nearly 12 mm. That this ruling device is rather more elaborate than I, at least, had previously imagined makes it seem all the more probable that there is no accident in the number of central-French chansonniers with staves of either 9.5 or 12 mm.

That inevitably led to a closer look at the first twelve pieces originally copied into Wolfenbüttel and the realization that their initial letters form an acrostic, yielding the name Estiene Petit.

Curiously, that could explain why these twelve pieces contain more unica than the rest of the manuscript (there is otherwise only one unicum in its entire main layer). In the name Estiene Petit the letter E appears four times and T three times, both of them fairly rare as initial letters for songs of that era. It is hard to guess whether any of these songs was specially composed for the acrostic or whether the scribe simply drew on more obscure repertory to fill the gaps; but the question could perhaps be explored. (With hindsight, this acrostic should have been obvious, since two later songbooks have recently been identified from acrostics in the same way: the monophonic chansonnier de Bayeux for Charles de Bourbon, noticed by Jay Rahn, and Florence 121, with the name of Marietta [Pugi], noticed by Bonnie Blackburn.)[27]

There are two likely identifications for Estiene Petit, father and son, both of them closely linked to the French royal courts. The father was appointed royal *notaire et secretaire* on 2 October 1433 and died on 1 March 1465; presumably he was born in the first decade of the century. He was also *receveur general* for Languedoc from 1440 until his death, and he came to a certain prominence as the senior accountant assigned to explore the financial affairs of Jacques Cueur in the years 1450–3. He was raised to the nobility in 1452; and a royal charter of 1457 refers to him as 'nostre amé et feal conseiller maistre Estienne Petit'. The family home was in Montpellier, where he was mainly resident and where he was buried, though he evidently spent much time at the royal court and at Bourges, particularly in the later years of Charles VII's reign.[28]

But his son, Estiene Petit junior, seems to have a far stronger claim on the Wolfenbüttel songbook. He was born on 3 November 1449 (dying in 1523) and became *notaire et secretaire* to Louis XI on 1 August 1467 at the age of almost 18. In fact the position passed from Estiene senior to his eldest surviving son Jacques in 1463 or 1464; and he in his turn passed it on to the next son, Estiene junior in 1467. But in a letter exempting Estiene junior from the *tailles*, dated 4 November 1481, Louis XI refers to 'the services he has done me since the time of his youth, and which he still does every day in my presence'.[29] Wolfenbüttel could perhaps be a retirement

[27] Douglas Jay Rahn, 'Melodic and Textual Types in French Popular Songs, ca. 1500' (Ph.D. diss., Columbia University, 1978); Bonnie J. Blackburn, 'Two "Carnival Songs" Unmasked: A Commentary on MS Florence Magl. XIX. 121', *Musica disciplina*, 35 (1981), 121–78.

[28] The fullest documented account of his life is in André Lapeyre and Rémy Scheurer, *Les Notaires et secrétaires du roi sous les règnes de Louis IX, Charles VIII et Louis XII (1461–1515): Notices personelles et généalogies*, 2 vols. (Paris, 1978), i. 249. For the charter of 1457, see Gaston Du Fresne de Beaucourt, *Histoire de Charles VII*, 6 vols. (Paris, 1890), v. 429. Once again I must add that I have made no serious attempt to follow up the documents mentioned there and that any such search seems likely to prove useful.

[29] For an account of his life, see Lapeyre and Scheurer, *Notaires*, i. 249–52; for his elder brother Jacques, 252–3. For Louis XI's comment of 4 Nov. 1481, see *Lettres de Louis XI*, ix. 87–8.

present for the father; but it seems far more likely to have been a precious gift for the son, a rising courtier in the circle of Louis XI. Given the evidence already mentioned for thinking that Wolfenbüttel is later than either Nivelle or the first layer of Laborde, 1467 in fact looks an extremely attractive date—that is, the manuscript could have celebrated Estiene's receiving that royal position at the age of 18.

While so much else about these manuscripts remains uncertain, it may be premature to decide between the two. But in either case, the evidence connects the songbook with the royal court circle;[30] and that in its turn does the same for the three closely related manuscripts—Laborde, Dijon, and Copenhagen. That seems the important issue. Perhaps one of the main tasks for the next few years will be to reconsider the view that Louis XI was interested only in hunting and politics, discouraging culture of any kind—a view mainly derived from Commines.[31]

Another conclusion is rather more tentative. The first song in the Wolfenbüttel acrostic is by Busnoys, his *Est il mercy*. Its first four lines open with the words 'Est il', as a possible reference to Estiene; the second and fourth lines both contain within them all the letters of the name 'Estiene Petit'; and the first line contains all but the last T. There seems a possibility—as I said, tentative—that Busnoys composed *Est il mercy* specifically for Estiene Petit.

Be that as it may, there are some clearer conclusions to be drawn from these remarks about Busnoys: that his pre-Burgundy years show an astonishing profusion of songs, probably over two-thirds of what now survives; that he may well have been at the court of Brittany in the 1450s; that the songs of the early 1460s link up in various ways with those of Okeghem; and that he seems also to have owed much to the songs of Binchois, the man addressed in Okeghem's lament as 'pere de joyeuseté'—a slightly strange remark in the light of his known output. Perhaps, though, that is the sense of my title, 'Trained and immersed in all musical delights', which is an attempt to translate the words of Jean Molinet:[32]

> Car tu es instruis et imBUS
> En tous musicaulx esbaNOIS

Molinet's poetic exchange with Busnoys must date from a lot later, probably after 1475, when Molinet officially became Burgundian court chronicler.[33] The poem

---

[30] In the circumstances, it should be no surprise that the name 'Philippe St Symons', perhaps to be read on fo. 69ʳ of the manuscript, is that of the son of Louis St Symons, an écuyer of Charles VIII, as noted in Gutiérrez-Denhoff, *Der Wolfenbütteler Chansonnier*, 26–8; nor that she notes, pp. 24–6, that the binding fragments are of material related to royal court documents.

[31] A point already made in Higgins, 'Antoine Busnois', 300, drawing attention to the extended study by Alfred Gandilhon, 'Contribution à l'histoire de la vie privé et de la cour de Louis XI (1423–1481)', *Mémoires de la Société historique, littéraire, artistique, et scientifique du Cher*, 4th ser., 20 (1905), 335–97, and 21 (1906), 1–120.

[32] *Les Faictz et dictz de Jean Molinet*, ed. Noël Dupire, 3 vols. (Paris, 1936–9), ii. 795: 'Lettre à maistre Antoine Busnois', lines 3–4.

[33] Noël Dupire, *Jean Molinet: La vie—les œuvres* (Paris, 1932), 13–17; see also David Fallows, 'Jean Molinet and the Lost Burgundian Court Chansonniers of the 1470s' (forthcoming).

still remains to be explored and elucidated: most of it seems to be just obscene; to pull out the hard information there will take some skill, though it surely contains items of importance. That is just another of the many dimensions the study of Busnoys can take over the coming years as we continue to immerse ourselves in his musical delights.

Appendix A
Outline Chronology of Busnoys's Songs

The chronology is based almost entirely on earliest known sources as currently dated. In the listing of sources an asterisk (*) means that the source contains an ascription to Busnoys; sources after a semicolon (;) are text sources. Unless otherwise stated, everything is in ₵ mensuration and in three voices with the contratenor in a range below the tenor. Fuller details on all songs and their sources appear in the article by Leeman L. Perkins, below, Ch. 13.

1. c.1461
Resjois toi terre/Rex pacificus (ballade, 4vv; mens. O/₵)
   Pix* MC 871

2. *Nivelle (?early 1460s) but not in Wolf or Lab 1 or Mel; all also in Dij and most texts in Roh*
C'est bien malheur (rondeau; mens. O)
   Niv* Dij*; not in Roh
C'est vous en qui (virelai; mens. O, ₵; T=Ct)
   Niv* Dij*; Roh
En tous les lieux (virelai; 4vv; mens. O, ₵)
   Niv Dij*; Par1719 Par9223(Monsr Jaques) Roh
Laissez Dangier (virelai; mens. ₵)
   Niv* Dij BolQ16; Roh P7559
Ma damoiselle (rondeau; mens. O; T=Ct)
   Niv* Dij*; Roh
Quant vous me ferez (rondeau; mens. O)
   Niv Dij* Cop; Lo380 Roh Par1719 Par1722
Soudainement mon cuer (virelai; T=Ct)
   Niv* Dij Cop; Roh
Vous marchez/L'autrier/Vostre beauté (a 4)
   Niv* Dij Tr91 Spec Mun328 Vienna18810 (Henrichus ysaac); not in Roh

3. *Wolf (?mid-1460s); also in Niv, Dij, Mel, and Roh; all (but only these) also in Lab 1*

Est il mercy (rondeau; mens. O; extended Ct)
  Niv* Wolf Lab1 Dij Cord Mel*; Roh Jard
Le corps s'en va (rondeau)
  Niv* Wolf Lab1 Dij Mel*; Roh and 6 other text sources
Quant ce viendra (rondeau; mens. O)
  Niv Wolf Lab1* Tr88 EscB(hockengem) Dij* Tr89 Tr91 Mel Fl176; Roh

3a. *Wolf but not in Niv*

Ja que lui (virelai; mens. C, ₵) Hacqueville
  Wolf Lab1 Dij* Cop Mel Sev; not in Roh

4. *Remaining Jacqueline d'Hacqueville songs*

A vous sans autre (rondeau; mens. C; 3 equal voices)
  Dij* Mel; Jard
Ha que ville (rondeau; mens. C)
  Dij Cas* Sev* Fl229; Roh
Je ne puis vivre (virelai; mens. O, ₵)
  Dij*, revised in Mel; Jard

5. *Trent 89, apparently copied on paper of 1462–4 (Saunders)*

Chi dist on benedicite (rondeau)
  Tr89 Glog Pix* Fl229* Sev BolQ18
Mon seul et celé (rondeau)
  Tr89 Glog Pix* Fl176 Fl229 Par4379

6. *Dijon (?by 1470) but no earlier source*

A qui vens tu tes coquilles (rondeau)
  Dij Mel*
Au gré de mes ieulx (virelai; 2.p. a 2; mens. O, C2)
  Dij*
A une dame (virelai; mens. C) ?Haqueville
  Dij* Mel Fl176 BolQ16 Lab3* CG; Roh Par1719
Bel Acueil (rondeau; mens. O; 3 equal voices)
  Dij* Mel; Par1719
En soustenant (rondeau) [first line from *De plus en plus*]
  Dij Mel Cas* (FR2356 index); Roh Par1719
En voyant sa dame (rondeau; mens. C; 2 high voices over Ct)
  Dij* Lab2 BolQ16; Par1719 Par1722 *Chasse*
J'ay mains de biens (virelai)
  Dij Lab2 Cord Pix* Fl229* Sev Cape; Par1719
Je m'esbais de vous (rondeau; mens. O)
  Dij*; Roh

Joye me fuit (rondeau)
   Dij* Lab2 Tr91 Cas* Mel* Pix* Fl176; 4 text sources
Ma plus qu'assez (virelai; mens. O, ₵; 2 equal voices over Ct)
   Dij* Cop; Jard
M'a vostre cuer (virelai)
   Dij Lab2 Cop Cas* FR2794 BolQ16 Fl229 Sev; Par1719
Mon mignault musequin/Gracieuse plaisant (rondeau; *a 4*)
   Dij Fl229* Odh SG461*
On a grant mal/On est bien malade (rondeau; *a 4*)
   Dij*, revised in SG530(Andreas busnois), revised again in Fl229
Quelque povre homme [A] (rondeau; mens. O)
   Dij*; Par1719 *Fleur*
Vostre gracieuse accointance (rondeau; mens. O)
   Dij*

7. *Remaining virelais; apparently a form not favoured at the Burgundian court*

Ce n'est pas moy (virelai; mens. ₵, O2)
   Pix* BolQ16
Maintes femmes (virelai; *a 4*; mens. ⱺ, ₵)
   Sev CantiC*; cited Tinctoris in *Liber de arte contrapuncti* (1477)*

8. *In addition, I would add most of his other four-voice works to the pre-Burgundian period (further to the five already mentioned)*

Amours nous traite/Je m'en vois (rondeau; *a 4*)
   Pix* FR2794 Fl229*
Corps digne/Dieu quel mariage (rondeau; *a 4*)
   Fl229 Ber40021* CantiC*
Je ne demande aultre de gré (rondeau; *a 4*)
   CamR.2.71 Cas* Pix Fl229 Sev Odh* Seg* BolQ18 SpinacinoII
L'autrier la pieça/En l'ombre/Trop suis jonette (*a 4*)
   Sev*
L'autrier que passa (?rondeau; *a 4*)
   CantiB*
Une filleresse/Vostre amour/S'il y a (?rondeau; *a 4*)
   Fl229* CantiC

This excludes, as probably later: *Acordés moy, In mijnen sin, J'ay pris amours tout au rebours, Terrible dame*—thus giving a total of forty-two pieces (nearly two-thirds) that offer prima facie evidence (that is, before any stylistic considerations) of predating his Burgundian court years.

9. *Pieces in Mellon (c.1475) not already accounted for*

Au povre par necessité (rondeau)
   Mel Sev Glog Pix*

O Fortune trop tu es dure (rondeau)
    Mel Pix* Fl176* Sev (twice)
Pour entretenir (rondeau)
    Mel* Cas* Glog FR2794
Ung plus que tous (rondeau)
    Mel*, revised Pix Fl229 Sev; Jard Lille 402 Dres

10. *Pieces in Cas (c.1481) not already accounted for*

Acordés moy (rondeau; *a 4*)
    Cas* Pix Fl229 Odh (BolQ16 index)
Le monde est tel (?rondeau)
    Cas*; Par1719 Par1722
Pucelotte que Dieu vous gart (ballade)
    Cas* Pix Par16664
Seule a par moy (rondeau; mens. O2)
    Cas* Pix Fl229*

11. *Piece cited by Ramos (1482, though the book was reportedly written ten years earlier), as noted by Bonnie J. Blackburn*

J'ay pris amours tout au rebours (?rondeau; *a 4*)
    Odh* Seg(Johannes Martini)

12. *Pieces in Pixérécourt not already accounted for*

Advegne qu'advenir (rondeau)
    Pix* BolQ16
Bone chiere (?rondeau)
    Pix*
Con tutta gentileça (?rondeau)
    Pix Fl229*; much earlier source for text
Faictes de moy (rondeau)
    Pix Fl229* Sev Ver757; much earlier sources for text
Faulx mesdisans (?rondeau)
    Pix Fl229*
Ma tres souveraine (rondeau)
    Pix* BolQ16 Sev
Quant j'ay au cuer (rondeau)
    Pix*; Jard
Quelque povre homme [B: second and entirely different setting]
    Pix* Sev; Par1719 *Fleur*
Terrible dame (?rondeau; 4vv)
    Pix*
Ung grand povre homme (?rondeau)
    Pix* Fl229* Sev Linz529
(But remember, from above: *Ce n'est pas moy, Amours nous traite*.)

13. Remaining pieces not already accounted for

Fortuna desperata (strophic)
  Seg* Cape Sev and 25 more sources; Lo16439
In mijnen sin (4vv)
  FC 2439* *CantiC*
Je ne demande lialté (?rondeau)
  BolQ16 Fl229*
Sans avoir fait (?rondeau)
  BolQ16 Per431* Par676(Isach)
(But remember, from above: *Corps digne*, *L'autrier la pieça*, *L'autrier que passa*, *Maintes femmes*, *Une filleresse*.)

14. Appendix of poetic texts ascribed to Busnoys

'Cent mille fois le jour' (virelai)
  Roh Fabri*
'Lequel vous plairoit mieulx trouver' (rondeau)
  Par9223* (perhaps 1458)
'Reposons nous entre nous amoureux' (rondeau)
  Molinet sources* Namur Jard; music perhaps cited in Sev quodlibet

15. Appendix of conflicting ascriptions for songs unlikely to be by Busnoys and therefore ignored above

Amours amours (rondeau; *a 4*: Japart)
  Fl229 Odh(Japart) BolQ18(A busnois)
Amours fait moult/Il est de/Tant que nostre (rondeau; *a 4*: Japart)
  Cas(Jo Jappart) FR2794 Fl229(Jannes Japart) CG BolQ17(A busnois) Bas1-4(Pirson), etc.
    Both perhaps confused with *Amours nous traitte*.
Cent mille escus (rondeau: Caron)
  Wolf Dij Pix(?Busnoys) Fl229(Busnoys) Cas(Caron) CG(Caron), etc.
    Perhaps confused title with *Cent mille fois le jour*.
D'ung aultre amer (rondeau: Okeghem)
  Niv(O) Dij(O) Cas(O) FR2794(O) Par2245(O) BolQ17(O) Pix(Busnoys)
    Pix ascription is inexplicable.
Et qui la dira (?rondeau; *a 4*: Japart)
  Fl107bis(Japart) BolQ17(A busnoys)
J'ay bien choisi (Hayne)
  Cas(Hayne) Pix(Busnoys) Glog Fl229
Je ne fay plus (rondeau: Mureau)
  Fl176(G mueran) Fl229(Antonius busnoys) CG(Gil Murieu) Par2245(Mureau) BolQ17(A busnois) Seg(Loysette Compere)
Je suis venu vers mon amy (Hayne)
  Cas(Haine) Glog Pix(Busnoys) Fl229

Le serviteur hault guerdonné (rondeau: a 4, based on D and T of Dufay's song)
    Odh, but ascribed only in the first printing
Pour tant se mon volour s'est mis (rondeau: Caron)
    Sev Fl229(Caron) CG(Caron); cited perhaps by Aaron as Busnoys
Se brief je puis (rondeau: Caron)
    Cas Pix(Busnoys) Fl229(Caron) Sev

Appendix B
Inventory of Wolfenbüttel 287

All pieces are anonymous here: composers' names are taken from elsewhere. Concordant sources are listed only when they are likely to throw light on the possible date of this manuscript. Items in Nivelle and the first layer of the Laborde chansonnier (nos. 1–47 and 51–8, with often bizarrely close readings) are denoted by their serial numbers; numbers preceded by 'a' (as in 'a63' for no. 3) are later additions to the manuscript concerned.

The list shows: five of the seven unica come within the dedicatory acrostic ESTIENE PETIT (nos. 2–13); nos. 1–41 overlap heavily with the first layer of Laborde, which is not represented thereafter; the entire manuscript overlaps heavily with Nivelle, though the added pieces of Nivelle are to be found throughout Wolfenbüttel; and there is no case of even two pieces following one another in the same order as in either of the other two sources. This would seem to imply that all three sources drew on a common repertory, that Nivelle is comfortably the earliest of them, and that Wolfenbüttel was compiled shortly after the completion of the first layer of Laborde.

no.	title	composer	Niv	Lab1	others
1	*Ave regina celorum*	Frye		1	several pre-1460
2	*Est il mercy*	Busnoys	30	20	Dij, etc.
3	*Se mieulx ne vient*	Convert	a63	11	Dij, etc.
4	*Tout a par moy*	Frye	22	3	Ber 78.C.28, etc.
5	*Ja que ly ne*	Busnoys		41	Dij, etc.
6	*Et fusse je duc*	unique			
7	*N'aray je jamaiz*	Morton	a1	45	Dij, etc.
8	*Esse bien fait*	—		39	
9	*Pour refraindre*	unique			
10	*En m'esbatant (a 4)*	unique			
11	*Tant plus en ay*	unique			
12	*Jamaiz je sceray*	—		55	Dij only
13	*Tres noble et*	unique			
14	*De m'esjouir*	Basiron		13	FR 2794 only
15	*Nul ne l'a telle*	Basiron		5	Cop only
16	*Je ne requiers que*	—		29	Cop only
17	*Le joli tetin*	—		13b	Cop only
18	*Je le scay bien*	Basiron		7	

no.	title	composer	Niv	Lab1	others
19	*Mon cueur et moy*	Prioris		21	Cop FC2439
20	*Le serviteur*	Dufay		8a	Tr 90, etc.
21	*Malheureux cuer*	Dufay		18	Sched only
22	*Ma maistresse*	Okeghem		2	Tr 93, etc.
23	*Ma bouche rit*	Okeghem	41	23	Sched, etc.
24	*Comme femme*	Binchois		9	EscB, etc.
25	*Quant ce vendra*	Busnoys	4	19	Tr 88, etc.
26	*D'ung aultre aymer*	Okeghem	53	10	Dij, etc.
27	*O rosa bella*	Bedyngham			several pre-1460
28	*Par le regart*	Dufay		54	several pre-1460
29	*J'ay prins amours*	—	58	22	(Lab has high Ct)
30	*Je ne vis oncques*	Binchois	40	32	Tr 90, etc.
31	*Las ay je tort*	—			Fl 176 only
32	*Se la face ay palle*	Dufay		51	several pre-1460
33	*Mon seul plaisir*	Bedyngham		52	several pre-1460
34	*Chargé de dueil*	—	35	57	Dij, etc.
35	*Fors seullement*	Okeghem	3		Lab 2nd layer, etc.
36	*Le corps s'en va*	Busnoys	42	17	Dij, Mel
37	*S'il advient*	Michelet	a64	27	Dij, etc.
38	*Le souvenir*	Morton		43	Dij, etc.
39	*Ce qu'on fait*	—		13a	
40	*Helas que pourra*	Caron		4	(Lab diff. text); Dij, etc.
41	*Tant est mignonne*	—	a60	26	Dij, etc.
42	*O infame deloyaulté*	—			Dij only
43	*De tous biens plaine*	Hayne			Lab 2nd layer, etc.
44	*Ravi d'amours*	—			Dij, etc.
45	*Je ne seray plus*	Philipet			Sev, Fl 229
46	*La plus mignonne*	Dufay	51		
47	*Pour le mal*	—	6		
48	*Qu'ara d'amours*	—	unique		text: Roh
49	*Fortune laisse moy*	—			Cam R.2.71, Pav, Porto
50	*S'elle m'aymera*	Okeghem	43		Dij, etc.
51	*Au travail suis*	Barbingant	56		Dij, only
52	*Cent mille escuz*	Caron			Dij, etc.
53	*Jamais si bien*	—	48		Lab 2nd layer, Dij
ADDED PIECES					
a54	*Ma dame trop*	Charles			Tr 89, etc.
a55	*Belle de parler*	unique			
a56	*Entre Peronne*	Rubinus			Dij, etc.

PART I

MUSIC, CEREMONY, AND RITUAL
IN THE LATE MIDDLE AGES

3

Music and Ritual at Charles the Bold's Court: The Function of Liturgical Music by Busnoys and his Contemporaries

৯❦ ❦৪

HOWARD MAYER BROWN†

S HORTLY after Charles the Bold became duke of Burgundy, he had
drawn up a detailed set of regulations concerning the organization of his
household. These ordinances offer the most detailed information we have
about the people who worked for the court, and what duties they were required
to perform.[1] We learn from these ordinances of 1469 about the members of
Charles's kitchen staff, his heralds at arms, his secretaries, financial administra-
tors, gentleman pages, and so on. Five years later, in 1474, his secretary Olivier
de La Marche wrote another detailed description of Charles's household, this one
at the request of King Edward IV of England, who wished to model his own
court after that of the Burgundian duke. La Marche's *L'Estat de la maison du duc
Charles de Bourgoingne, dit le Hardy* reads less like a union contract than the earlier ordinances.[2] It gives us one man's impression of a late fifteenth-century court,
and thus serves as a foil to the 1469 regulations. La Marche evidently described
the court as he saw it, whereas the ordinances of 1469 described the court as it
ought to be.

---

† Howard Mayer Brown died on 20 Feb. 1993, some three months after the conference. He had submitted
the final version of his text six weeks earlier and we publish it here virtually unchanged.

[1] Oxford, Bodleian Library, MS Hatton 13. The passages from the court ordinances referring to music
are transcribed in David Fallows, 'Specific Information on the Ensembles for Composed Polyphony,
1400–1474', in Stanley Boorman (ed.), *Studies in the Performance of Late Mediaeval Music* (Cambridge,
1983), 109–59 at 145–59. For a summary of the organization of the Burgundian court, see Richard
Vaughan, *Valois Burgundy* (London, 1975), 95–122. On Charles, see, among other studies, id., *Charles the
Bold: The Last Valois Duke of Burgundy* (London, 1973).

[2] Published in Olivier de La Marche, *Mémoires*, ed. Henri Beaune and J. D'Arbaumont, 4 vols. (Paris
1883–8), iv. 1–94. For two later manuscript copies of La Marche's description, see *Charles le Téméraire:
Exposition organisée à l'occasion du cinquième centenaire de sa mort*, ed. P. Cockshaw *et al.* (Brussels, 1977),
129–30.

Among other things, the ordinances of 1469 give us a detailed view of the musical entourage of the Burgundian court. Under the rubric 'trompettes', for example, we learn that Charles had—or wanted to have—five 'trompettes de guerre', six 'trompettes de menestrelz', and three 'joueurs de instrumens bas'.[3] By 1474, La Marche reports that the duke had twelve 'trompettes de guerre' (whose duties he explains in some detail), six 'haulz menestrelz', and four 'joueurs de bas instrumens'.[4] Apparently Charles's musical establishment had grown in size during the first five years of his reign, and La Marche's report strongly implies what we might have assumed in any case from the earlier notice, that by 'trompette de menestrelz', the court reporter meant a wind band, doubtless consisting normally of shawms and sackbuts rather than trumpets. Charles's instrumentalists, in short, were organized in the way that became standard for courts throughout much of the fifteenth and sixteenth centuries, with a group of ceremonial trumpeters, a wind band, and a group of chamber musicians who must surely have played chiefly those soft instruments that had become the mainstay of courtly musical life by the second half of the fifteenth century: harp, lute, fiddle, and psaltery.[5] The court must also have had an organist, either among its chapel singers or among its chamber musicians, for the ordinances of 1469 also list a 'porteur d'orgues' among the permanent personnel of the duke's household.[6] La Marche in 1474, on the other hand, clarifies what was left unwritten in 1469, for he describes one or more organists among the chapel personnel.[7]

The greatest attention to music in the earlier description of Charles's court is given to the duke's chapel, which in 1469 was supposed to consist of twenty-five people: a first chaplain, twelve other chaplains, six *clercs*, five *sommeliers*, and one *fourrier*.[8] La Marche, on the other hand, describes a chapel of forty people, partly to be explained quite simply by an increase in the number of chaplain/singers during the intervening years and partly by the fact that La Marche included in his enumeration several clerics attached to the court in 1469 but not counted among the personnel of the chapel: a confessor and other chaplains, including the duke's own confessor and that of his *maistre d'ostel*, to which La Marche added a bishop, and three other 'Jacopins prestres et confesseurs', learned men who preached often. One of the manuscripts preserving La Marche's description, for example, reports that the chapel had fifteen chaplains, two 'demi-chapelains', four *clercs*, six *sommeliers*, and two *fourriers*.[9] In 1469 Mass was sometimes taken by an outside prelate, occasions when the singers could eat at the expense of the duke.[10] By

[3] Fallows, 'Specific Information', 146. [4] La Marche, *Mémoires*, iv. 70–1.
[5] See Howard Mayer Brown, 'Songs After Supper: How the Aristocracy Entertained Themselves in the Fifteenth Century', in Monika Fink, Rainer Gestrein, and Günter Mössmer (eds.), *Musica Privata: Die Rolle der Musik im privaten Leben. Festschrift zum 65. Geburtstag von Walter Salmen* (Innsbruck, 1991), 45.
[6] Fallows, 'Specific Information', 146. [7] La Marche, *Mémoires*, iv. 2.
[8] Fallows, 'Specific Information', 146–7. [9] La Marche, *Mémoires*, iv. 2.
[10] Fallows, 'Specific Information', 155.

1474, if La Marche can be taken literally, the duke had appointed a bishop as a regular member of his court. The discrepancies among the various accounts about how many people of each rank sang in the Burgundian chapel should caution us against claiming too precise an idea of the size of Charles's musical establishment, or even about its precise composition. We should take all the figures as approximate, and accept that for any given year, some differences between the table of organization and the real figures are bound to exist.

There was a hierarchical order among the members of the chapel, with the chaplains at the top of the pyramid. Their duties, which, as we shall see, mixed music with liturgy, are not specifically enumerated either in 1469 or by La Marche; nor, unfortunately, are the duties of the *clercs*, second in the chain of command, who must simply have been apprentice chaplains.[11] The court reporter of 1469 makes clear, on the other hand, that the *sommeliers'* chief duties were to serve at the altar, which included attending on the duke in his oratory, to guard the chapel, and to see that everything ran smoothly, although they did sing in the polyphonic choir on occasion.[12] At the bottom of the hierarchy the *fourrier* (or *fourriers*) served as verger, guarding the door at services, supplying whatever was needed for various special celebrations (for example, straw for the Christmas service, candles for Tenebrae, a white dove and other birds for Pentecost, and so on), acting as master of ceremonies in seating the courtiers at services, and overseeing all the arrangements for the physical comfort of the chapel both at home and while on tour with the duke.[13] Not all the members of the chapel were priests, although the regulations stipulate that those chaplains who were not should be paid as much as those who were, and that those priests who were *clercs* or *sommeliers* should be paid according to their rank in the chapel, rather than as priests. The regulations of 1469 indicate that promotions from *sommelier* to *clerc* or from *clerc* to *chapelain* were made on the basis of musical ability and good service.[14]

We should see Charles's musical establishment against the background of the past history of the ducal court. Jeanne Marix lists seventeen chaplains for most years between 1436 and 1450, and fourteen chaplains for the remainder of Philip the Good's reign. She lists two to six *clercs* during Philip's reign, and three or four *sommeliers* (although for some years there are more and for some years none at all). The first *fourrier* appears in her lists in 1464 and then again in 1468, although there must regularly have been such vergers employed by earlier dukes; Marix mentions *fourriers* in earlier ducal reigns in the body of her book.[15] Charles's

---

[11] On the duties of the first chaplain, see Fallows, 'Specific Information', 155–6.
[12] On the duties of the *sommeliers*, see ibid. 156–9.
[13] On the duties of the *fourrier* or *fourriers*, see ibid. 159.   [14] Ibid. 146.
[15] Jeanne Marix, *Histoire de la musique et des musiciens de la cour de Bourgogne sous le règne de Philippe le Bon (1420–1467)* (Strasbourg, 1939), 242–63, lists the members of Philip the Good's chapel from 1436 to 1477. For a summary of the regulations governing his chapel, and brief biographies of his chaplains, see 125–215.

chapel appears to have been organized very much like those of his predecessors, although he employed slightly fewer chaplains, but more *clercs* and *sommeliers*. Similarly, his instrumental ensembles were recognizably the same as those of Philip the Good, although their sizes differed slightly. Marix lists two to seven 'trompettes de guerre' and from three to ten other minstrels, whose precise duties—whether they were members of the wind band or the chamber musicians—cannot always be determined, even though some of them are more closely described as 'teneur des menestrelz' or 'trompette des menestrels' (presumably members of the wind band), or as 'harpeur', 'joueur de luth', 'joueur de vielle', 'petit menestrel', or 'menestrel de bas intruments' (all presumably among the chamber musicians), and the administrative head of the instrumental forces is often designed as 'roy des menestrels'.[16] The most radical difference between Charles's chapel and those of his predecessors was the apparent lack of boys in the chapel choir. Choirboys had been used by Charles's predecessors, and they were often called *clercs* in the payment records. Neither the 1469 ordinances nor La Marche's description of the court makes any mention of boys, however, and David Fallows has persuasively argued that none of the *clercs* serving in the Burgundian chapel in 1469 can have been a boy or even a youth.[17] In short, Charles's chapel seems not to have employed boys to sing either chant or polyphony.

A large proportion of the 1469 regulations is taken up with general problems of administration and the conduct of the chapel personnel that need not concern us here. The court reporter sets down rules concerning dress and behaviour and the means of resolving conflicts, and he outlines the normal agenda for the weekly meetings when specific duties are assigned each member of the chapel, and the previous week's performances are assessed. The regulations stipulate, among other things, that the first chaplain is allowed to give only two absences at any time, and makes provision for sick leave, professional expenses like clothing, and privileges, such as the number of horses each member of the chapel is provided (four for the first chaplain, two for each of the other chaplains, three horses for every two *clercs* and *sommeliers*, and a horse for the *fourrier*).[18] Nor need we be concerned with most of the details of the weekly liturgy, such as who officiated at Office Hours, who said the Epistle and the Gospels, or at what point in each service the various members of the chapel had to be present in the chapel.[19]

The only unambiguous reference to polyphony in the 1469 regulations occurs at the beginning of the description of the chapel, where it is stated that a high Mass 'à chant et deschant' was to be sung every day of the year, following the liturgical calendar and the usage of Paris.[20] La Marche confirms the practice, though he says only that the chapel members sang every day 'les heures du jour et

---

[16] The Burgundian minstrels from 1420 to 1474 are listed ibid. 264–75. One of the minstrels in Marix's list is described as 'ayde de l'eschansonnerie' (p. 266), and one as 'valet de chambre' (p. 273).

[17] Fallows, 'Specific Information', 112–14.

[18] Ibid. 148–55.   [19] Ibid. 148–9.   [20] Ibid. 147.

la grant messe solennel', without specifying polyphony.[21] Both documents make
the point that Charles came both to Mass and to Vespers every day (or at least on
those days when he was at court and holding audiences). Moreover, low Masses
were also said in the chapel from time to time. Among the duties of the *sommeliers*, for example, was the task of serving at low Masses, said by the duke's confessor or one of the other priests early in the morning, before the duke's arrival,
for the other members of the court.[22]

Three passages in the 1469 regulations take up the question of the size and
composition of the group of singers and priests needed to officiate at Masses and
Office Hours. The three passages are very difficult to construe, and they therefore
need explanation and interpretation.[23] All three are reproduced and translated in
Appendix A. From the first passage, it seems clear that the chapel functioned as
two flexible and constantly interchanging groups. Every month four priests from
among the chapel personnel were given the responsibility for saying Mass on
those days when there was no solemn feast (the regulations specify that even
those members of the chapel who were not priests had to take their turn performing this service). Since the four are described as those most easily spared
from polyphonic singing, the regulations imply that polyphonic music was not
normally sung at these ordinary Masses; but the 1469 regulations clearly state
that high Masses were to be given every day of the year, the four men on monthly
duty are described in the regulations as 'chapelains des haultes messes', and non-
priests were also required to do their monthly tours of duty.[24] All these circumstances strongly suggest that these 'ordinary' daily Masses were normally
celebrated in chant but without polyphony. Although the regulations do not
explicitly say so, they thus imply that polyphony was normally reserved for
solemn and double feasts (as we shall see, polyphony was also probably sung at
some combined Vespers and Compline services). At such solemn feasts, the first
chaplain was responsible for officiating at the altar, unless a visiting prelate from
outside the chapel personnel had come to say Mass. In either case, the celebrant
was assisted by the *sommeliers*.[25]

Altogether, there were nineteen chaplains and clercs (including the first chaplain) in the ducal chapel. If the four 'chapelains des haultes messes' were not
obliged to participate in singing polyphony during the month they were in service for ferial Masses, and the first chaplain officiated at the altar on solemn feast-
days, fourteen chaplains and *clercs* were left to sing polyphonically on such
occasions, precisely the number named in the regulations as needed for *chant du
livre*, almost certainly polyphonic singing.[26] David Fallows has already stressed
the important fact that the court reporter saw as an ideal distribution of voices

[21] La Marche, *Mémoires*, iv. 2.   [22] Fallows, 'Specific Information', 156–7.
[23] The three passages are taken from Fallows, 'Specific Information', 148, 149, and 154.
[24] Ibid. 147–9.   [25] Ibid. 155–6.   [26] Ibid. 149.

that six men should sing the top line, three each the tenor and contratenor lines, and two the *moien*, which I would interpret to mean the altus in four-part music.[27] The regulations, however, stipulate that the fourteen should be augmented by the four 'chapelains des haultes messes' and by the *sommeliers* if they were not otherwise engaged. On the one hand, then, polyphonic music was ideally sung by at least fourteen people although as many as twenty-three could take part (if all four weekly priests and all five *sommeliers* took part). On the other hand, although polyphonic singing should use *at least* three tenors and three contras, another section of the regulations makes clear that that was a slightly pious hope. The first chaplain had to ensure that there were at least two tenors and two contras at all times, suggesting that singers on the lower voices were in relatively short supply.[28]

The regulations of 1469 lead us strongly to conclude that polyphonic music at Mass was normally reserved for solemn feast-days, and doubles. And they show us vividly the sort of interrelationship between purely musical and liturgical duties expected of a member of the chapel. They were regularly expected to officiate at the altar (or at least to serve the celebrant) as well as to sing. Some members of the chapel were recognized as better at polyphonic singing, but all had to take part in the liturgical ceremonies, even those who were not priests. Even though their duties involved them in both spheres of activity, a premium was put on their musical ability, however, for they would be promoted from one rank to the next according to the quality of their voices as well as for their good service.

The 1469 regulations also clarify the liturgical occasions during the year when services were unusually elaborate. At those solemn feast-days listed in Appendix B, both first and second Vespers were to be said as well as high Mass and the little hours—all the morning Office Hours from Matins to None—services that were to be scheduled immediately following Matins.[29] A passing remark in the 1469 regulations makes clear that of all these solemn feasts, four were most important: Christmas, Easter, Pentecost, and All Saints.[30] Charles, moreover, stipulated that O antiphons, sung every morning during Advent, were to be reinstated, after having been dropped by his predecessors; that the chapel was required to sing obits and obsequies whenever a member of the ducal family died, or for whomever else the duke commanded them to commemorate; and that the chapel had also to sing at weddings, as the list of duties of the first chaplain explains.[31] There are few surprises in the list of solemn feasts, made up mostly of occasions celebrated solemnly everywhere in western Europe—and indeed still today—plus celebrations of the few saints most important to the ducal court. Not surprisingly, for example, many of the solemn feasts celebrate occasions in the life of the Virgin Mary. For our purposes, the list is most useful in that it offers detailed

---

[27] Fallows, 'Specific Information', 110–17.   [28] Ibid. 154.
[29] App. B is based on information given ibid. 147–8.
[30] Oxford, Bodleian Library, MS Hatton 13, fo. 34ᵛ.
[31] Fallows, 'Specific Information', 147, 148, and 155–6.

information about the occasions when polyphony would most likely have been included in the services, even if we cannot know how often it actually was.

In addition to the daily high Mass, the chapel at Charles the Bold's court also sang a combined Vespers and Compline service every day.[32] That information, too, should be of some interest to musicians, for those services offered the best opportunity to sing the many Marian motets that take up a large part of almost every surviving fifteenth-century manuscript of sacred music. Rather than singing the great Marian antiphons, for example, at a separate Compline service late at night, Charles's chapel sang them at the end of the day, immediately following Vespers. If Charles's singers were typical of those at other courts and collegiate churches in combining the two offices, then the 1469 regulations explain precisely the kind of occasion when a very important part of the surviving polyphonic repertory would normally have been performed.

If the 1469 regulations do not give us a detailed picture of the distribution between chant and polyphony at Charles's court, they at least offer a general idea of the times when polyphonic masses and motets could have been sung: at Masses and combined Vespers-Compline services most likely for more than twenty occasions during each year. We can only imagine that most of the services at Charles's court were dominated by chant, although we can begin to perceive the very special celebratory nature of those services when polyphony was deemed appropriate. Our view of the share polyphony had in enlivening sacred services could be made much more precise if we were able to compare the regulations of 1469 with all the music-books found at that time in Charles's chapel. We cannot of course make such a comparison, for very little of the music from the Burgundian ducal chapel in the fifteenth century has survived. In her dissertation on service-books from the Low Countries during the age of polyphony, Jennifer Bloxam has given us a very useful survey of the surviving chant manuscripts that can be associated with the Burgundian court.[33] But only one manuscript of polyphonic sacred music survives from Charles's chapel, Brussels 5557, to which can be added one other repertory of mass music, the cycle of six *L'homme armé* masses now in Naples, described in the manuscript as having been a part of the repertory of Charles's musicians.[34] The *L'homme armé* masses, however, may well have been intended for the singers at the Marian chapel of the Golden Fleece in Dijon, rather than for Charles's regular chaplains, and so we must rely on Brussels 5557 to give us our best view of the normal repertory of the ducal singers.

[32] Ibid. 147.
[33] Mary Jennifer Bloxam, 'A Survey of Late Medieval Service Books from the Low Countries: Implications for Sacred Polyphony, 1460–1520' (Ph.D. diss., Yale University, 1987), 67–88.
[34] Brussels 5557 is reproduced in facsimile as *Choirbook of the Burgundian Court Chapel: Brussel, Koninklijke Bibliotheek MS. 5557*, intro. by Rob C. Wegman (Peer, 1989). The six *L'homme armé* masses are published in a modern edition in Judith Cohen (ed.), *Six Anonymous L'Homme Armé Masses in Naples, Biblioteca Nazionale, MS VI E 40* (American Institute of Musicology, 1981). See also Cohen, *The Six Anonymous L'Homme armé Masses in Naples, Biblioteca Nazionale, MS VI E 40* (MSD 21; [Rome], 1968).

We cannot know precisely how Brussels 5557 fitted into the complete library of the chapel of Charles the Bold. The inventory of his library made shortly after his death in 1477 is not complete.[35] It lists only the books he had in Dijon but not in his other places of residence. The inventory reveals that Charles had retained the collection of service-books made for his predecessors, and that he owned at least two chansonniers (a volume of 'chançons notées' and another of 'chançons et choses faictes').[36] It does not, however, single out the books intended for his chapel (as at least one earlier inventory had done), it does not list Brussels 5557, and it does not make clear whether or not Charles had added other books of sacred polyphony to the ducal collections. On the other hand, we have some fairly precise idea of the size of the ducal library under the reigns of his predecessors. Craig Wright lists only five manuscripts of polyphonic music belonging to the Burgundian court under Philip the Bold and John the Fearless: two books of motets, two volumes of music by Machaut, and an anthology of motets, Credos, virelais, ballades, and other things said to have been sung in the chapel on great feast-days.[37] In short, the Burgundian chapel, like most other institutions of the time, possessed only a limited number of anthologies of polyphonic music. It is unlikely, therefore, that Charles had acquired in the ten years of his reign more than two or three volumes of polyphony intended for the use of his chapel. Brussels 5557 doubtless contains only a part of the music available to the chapel singers and not their complete repertory. Nevertheless, the manuscript almost certainly included a very substantial part of the music they sang, or at the very least a representative portion of the polyphony heard in the ducal chapel. In any case, Brussels 5557 is an unusually precious source, not only because of its relatively early date, but also because it is a rare example of a manuscript that gives the working repertory of a known institution.

Brussels 5557 can perhaps best be described as a 'starter manuscript', an anthology presented to Charles and his bride Margaret of York when they were married, in 1468.[38] It seems originally to have contained only five English masses, to which other masses and motets were added later in its history. Appendix C summarizes its contents, following the information given in Rob Wegman's facsimile edition, and identifies the liturgical orientation of the motets

[35] Excerpts from the 1477 inventory are published in Gabriel Peignot, *Catalogue d'une partie des livres composant la bibliothèque des ducs de Bourgogne au XVe siècle* (Dijon, 1841), 85–100.

[36] They are listed in Peignot, *Catalogue*, 95 and 97.

[37] Craig Wright, *Music at the Court of Burgundy, 1364–1419: A Documentary History* (Institute of Medieval Music Musicological Studies, 28; Henryville, Ottawa, and Binningen, 1979), 139–60.

[38] The introduction to *Choirbook* by Wegman offers the best summary of recent scholarship on the manuscript, and includes full references to earlier studies. On p. 5, Wegman cites his reasons for believing the manuscript to have been commissioned for the Burgundian court chapel at the time of the marriage of Margaret of York to Charles. On the provenance of the manuscript and the chronology of its contents, see especially Sylvia W. Kenney, 'Origins and Chronology of the Brussels Manuscript 5557 in the Bibliothèque Royale de Belgique', *Revue belge de musicologie*, 6 (1952), 75–100; and Wegman, 'New Data Concerning the Origins and Chronology of Brussels, Koninklijke Bibliotheek, Manuscript 5557', *TVNM* 36 (1986), 5–25.

and the cantus firmi of the masses. It would be good to be able to connect the contents of Brussels 5557 with what we know of the organization of liturgical services at the ducal chapel from the ordinances of 1469. Several obstacles, however, stand in the way of such an exercise. For one thing, we do not know how many other anthologies of polyphony the ducal singers normally used; and for another, the masses in Brussels 5557 do not obviously conform to the requirements for music described in the regulations, doubtless at least partly because it was a wedding gift. Nevertheless, we should make the effort to connect its repertory with what we know of the schedule of the chapel, for only in this way can we begin to understand how the artefacts of the past were actually used, and hence what significance they had in the society of their time.

In the first place, the manuscript offers a substantial and conceivably even sufficient number of compositions for use at the combined Vespers-Compline services we know to have been an important part of the services expected of ducal singers. Whenever else they might have been performed, all the Magnificats and motets in Brussels 5557 were most appropriate for the musically most elaborate office hour at the end of every feast day, the Magnificats, of course, as the canticle for Vespers, and the series of hymns, antiphons, and motets either for Vespers or for Compline. The manuscript includes music for the Christmas season at Vespers (Busnoys's *Noel noel* and his *Alleluia verbum caro*, based, as Bloxam has shown, on a chant that follows Paris usage);[39] music for the Easter season at Vespers (Busnoys's *Ad cenam agni* and his *Victimae paschali laudes*); and a number of Marian pieces most likely sung at Compline as well as at other Marian services (Busnoys's *Anima mea liquefacta est/Stirps Jesse*, the anonymous hymn *O quam glorifica luce*, and Busnoys's two settings of *Regina caeli*, both especially appropriate for the Easter season). Moreover, Brussels 5557 includes a Gregorian hymn for Passion Sunday, *Vexilla regis*; and a motet in honour of St Anthony Abbot, Busnoys's *Anthoni usque limina*, not a saint singled out for special veneration in the 1469 regulations, and included in the anthology possibly in deference to the duke's most distinguished composer, whose patron saint Anthony was.[40] In short, all these pieces fit easily into the liturgical framework outlined in the regulations; or rather, they can all easily be explained as decorative elements to the services themselves, conducted mainly in chant.

It is less easy to explain just how the masses in the manuscript fit into the liturgical year as outlined in the regulations. Which masses, for example, would the ducal chapel have sung for the four most important feasts of the liturgical year—Christmas, Easter, Pentecost, and All Souls' Day? Which masses were appropriate

[39] Bloxam, 'A Survey', 80–1; see also below, Ch. 4.
[40] On the place of each of the hymns, antiphons, and motets in the liturgy, see the Introduction to *Choirbook* by Wegman; Sylvia W. Kenney, *Walter Frye and the Contenance Angloise* (New Haven and London, 1964), 35–61; *Busnoys LTW*, Commentary, and the notes to editions of the complete works of the various composers.

and which were not for the other twenty-odd occasions when polyphony seems most likely to have been required? We have all operated under the only half-spoken assumption that the models on which masses were based determined the liturgical function of the resulting polyphonic cycle. We have assumed, for example, that a *Missa Ave regina caelorum* could only have been sung at Marian services, or that all (or at least some) of the masses based on the *L'homme armé* tune were originally intended for use in the Marian chapel of the Order of the Golden Fleece in Dijon.[41] We have not asked similar questions, however, about the masses for which there is no plausible liturgical connection—such as those based on songs and those for which no model can be posited—and we have not in any case tried to analyse the relatively few manuscripts that survive according to their usefulness for the musicians who first sang from them.

Brussels 5557 contains eleven polyphonic mass cycles and a fragment of a twelfth, plus an independent Kyrie by Dufay. Paradoxically, its original nucleus of five English masses fits easily into the view of services at the ducal court furnished by the regulations of 1469.[42] The manuscript opens with Walter Frye's *Missa Summe trinitati*, a mass appropriate for the reception of kings and queens and therefore an elegant tribute to the new duke and duchess; the mass could also serve for Trinity Sunday, one of the feast-days of the Burgundian liturgical calendar. Frye's *Missa Flos regalis* pays tribute to the duchess's home country, for it was almost certainly intended to honour St Etheldreda, the patron of Ely; and the third of his masses in the manuscript, his *Missa Nobilis et pulchra*, unfolds over a cantus firmus taken from a responsory for St Catherine of Alexandria, one of the few saints specially venerated at the Burgundian court, according to the 1469 regulations. The remaining two English masses, those by Plummer and Richard Cox, both have troped Kyries in the English manner, designating them, following Sarum usage, as masses appropriate for greater feasts. Nicholas Sandon suspects that Cox built his mass around a polyphonic model, and Plummer's mass, too, may also have been based on some model, either from chant or polyphony.[43] The models, however, have not as yet been identified, and therefore we have no choice but to suppose that both masses could have been sung at virtually any greater feast—they are all-purpose festival masses—until further information leads us to another conclusion.

In addition to the original nucleus of English music in Brussels 5557, six

---

[41] See William F. Prizer, 'Music and Ceremonial in the Low Countries: Philip the Fair and the Order of the Golden Fleece', *EMH* 5 (1985), 113–53; and also Ronald Woodley, 'Tinctoris's Italian Translation of the Golden Fleece Statutes: A Text and a (Possible) Context', *EMH* 8 (1988), 173–244. On the Mass of the Ceremony of the Armed Man and its possible connection with the series of *L'homme armé* masses written in the late fifteenth century, see also the essay by Flynn Warmington in the present volume, Ch. 5.

[42] On the five English masses and the liturgical propriety, see Wegman, *Choirbook*; Kenney, *Walter Frye*, 50–61; and Frye, *Collected Works*, ed. Kenney (CMM 19; [Rome], 1960).

[43] Nicholas Sandon, 'Cox', *New Grove*, v. 15. On the Kyrie tropes, see also Frank Ll. Harrison, *Music in Medieval Britain* (London, 1958), 72–3.

masses were either copied or bound into the manuscript at some later date.[44] Three of these additional masses were clearly intended for Marian services: Dufay's two late masses, the *Missa Ecce ancilla Domini* and the *Missa Ave regina caelorum*, and Johannes Regis's *Missa Ecce ancilla Domini*, built over a cantus firmus taken from an antiphon for second Vespers at the Feast of the Annunciation: *Ne timeas Maria*.[45] Two of the additional masses, on the other hand, may well have been intended to be sung whenever a polyphonic mass was required. It is, in any case, difficult to imagine that Ockeghem's *Missa Quinti toni* or the anonymous *Missa sine nomine* had any special liturgical propriety.[46] They, too, appear to be all-purpose festival masses like the two troped English masses, usable at any high Mass when polyphony would have been appropriate.

In sum, three of the five English masses appear to have had well-defined functions—to honour royalty (or the Holy Trinity) or to celebrate especially beloved saints—and three of the remaining masses celebrate the Virgin Mary, leaving four presumably all-purpose masses to be sung at the majority of sacred services during the year when polyphonic masses would have been expected at court. The one remaining complete mass cycle in Brussels 5557 is the only composition in the manuscript built over a secular song, the *Missa Pour quelque paine* by Cornelius Heyns, a composer associated with the city of Bruges during all of his known career.[47] Heyns's mass was probably copied into Brussels 5557 in the 1470s, fairly near the beginning of the history of song masses. Richard Taruskin points out in the commentary to his edition of Busnoys's Latin-texted music that the idea of basing a mass Ordinary cycle on a song seems to have been born in the second half of the fifteenth century, most probably in northern European courtly chapels.[48] The earliest examples include works by members of the Burgundian and the French royal chapels and other composers active in the north, works such as Bedingham's *Missa Dueil angoisseux*; Dufay's *Missa Se la face ay pale*; Ockeghem's *Missa Au travail suis* and *Missa Fors seulement*; Caron's *Missa Accueillie m'a la belle*; Frye's *Missa So ys emprentid*, and many others. The practice of basing masses on songs, however, only became widespread during the next generation, with works by Obrecht, Josquin, Martini, and their contemporaries.

[44] Nos. 7, 12, 18, 19, 20, and 23 in App. C.

[45] On Dufay's two masses, see Dufay, *Opera omnia*, ed. Heinrich Besseler, 6 vols. (CMM 1; [Rome], 1947–64), iii, pp. iv–v; and David Fallows, *Dufay* (London, 1982), 194–214. On Regis's mass, see Regis, *Opera omnia*, ed. Cornelis Lindenburg, 2 vols. (CMM 9; [Rome], 1956), i, pp. iv–v.

[46] Ockeghem's *Missa Quinti toni* seems not to be based on a cantus firmus; see Edgar H. Sparks, *Cantus Firmus in Mass and Motet 1420–1520* (Berkeley and Los Angeles, 1963), 174. For references in the musicological literature to this mass, see Martin Picker, *Johannes Ockeghem and Jacob Obrecht: A Guide to Research* (New York and London, 1988), 23–4.

[47] On Heyns's *Missa Pour quelque paine*, see Reinhard Strohm, *Music in Late Medieval Bruges* (Oxford, 1985), 131 and 196.

[48] See *Busnoys LTW*, Commentary, 95–100. The practice of basing a polyphonic setting of the Ordinary of the Mass on a secular model seems to go back to the 1450s. On this point, see, for example, Murray Steib, 'Imitation and Elaboration: The Use of Borrowed Material in Masses from the Late Fifteenth Century', 2 vols. (Ph.D. diss., University of Chicago, 1992), i. 8.

Musical scholars should begin to trace the history of these song masses and speculate about their purpose. It seems unlikely that we shall ever find much documentary evidence to shed light on the question of just why they were written, and Huizinga's theory that they simply reflect the interpenetration of sacred and secular elements in late fifteenth-century society no longer seems adequate as explanation.[49] Perhaps the vogue for song masses came about simply as another aspect of the playfulness of much late fifteenth- and sixteenth-century art, out of the joy in mixing disparate elements together. If so, such works are more apt to have been cultivated in courtly rather than religious circles. Religious institutions probably tolerated this sort of playfulness rather less well than secular courts. Craig Wright reports, for example, that the canons of Cambrai in 1517 asked that the *Missa Comment peult avoir joye* be deleted from the cathedral's mass books and not sung in the church again, possibly just because it was based on a secular song.[50] On the other hand, composers or their patrons may have wished to build or have built monumental musical structures quite simply on their favourite melodies. Such a theory would best explain the mass Nicholas Gombert apparently wrote for Emperor Charles V's coronation, the *Missa Sur tous regretz*, for it seems to me inconceivable that Gombert could have been making a negative political statement on such an official occasion.[51]

Since the chants on which many masses were based gloss the meaning and explain the liturgical propriety of particular cycles, we can also imagine that songs on which masses were based had some similar connection with the nature or the occasion of the polyphony, and we should therefore seek to find those meanings. Such an idea has been accepted, for example, with respect to the *L'homme armé* masses, and it may apply as well to other song masses.[52] It may be, for example, that song masses and especially those based on courtly songs that celebrate love were normally meant either to be dedicated to the Virgin Mary or to some other beloved saint, following the late medieval inclination to equate secular and sacred love, or else to have been intended originally for weddings, where a celebration of secular love would be most appropriate. The only rubric I have so far been able to find that may explain the liturgical destination of a song mass comes from a later Burgundian manuscript prepared by Margaret of Austria's scriptorium as a gift for Frederick the Wise of Saxony.[53] The opening two masses appear to pay homage

[49] Johan Huizinga, *The Waning of the Middle Ages* (New York, 1954), 156–7.

[50] Craig Wright, 'Performance Practices at the Cathedral of Cambrai 1475–1550', *Musical Quarterly*, 64 (1978), 299–300.

[51] On Gombert's mass for the coronation of Charles V, see Joseph Schmidt-Görg, *Nicolaus Gombert: Kapellmeister Kaiser Karls V., Leben und Werk* (Bonn, 1938), 180–3.

[52] See the literature cited above, n. 41.

[53] Jena, Universitätsbibliothek, MS 3. For the contents of the manuscript, see Karl Erich Roediger, *Die geistlichen Musikhandschriften der Universitäts-Bibliothek Jena*, 2 vols. (Jena, 1935), i. 4–7 and ii. 40–1. For a bibliography of studies of the manuscript, see *Census-Catalogue*, i. 288–9. On its origin as a gift for Frederick the Wise of Saxony, see Herbert Kellman, 'Josquin and the Courts of the Netherlands and France: The

to the recipient. It is one of the anthologies to include the Josquin *Missa Hercules dux Ferrariae*, but with the cantus firmus changed to 'Fridericus dux Saxsonie'. The manuscript opens with the *Missa Faisant regretz* attributed to Josquin, but here labelled *Missa Elizabeth*, in homage presumably both to Frederick's mother and to the patron saint of Thuringia, St Elizabeth of Hungary, but also, as Herbert Kellman has ingeniously proposed, most probably an allusion to the Visitation, the liturgical feast, in fact, for which the mass might well have been intended.[54] In any case, the anonymous rondeau *Pour quelque paine*, on which Cornelius Heyns's mass was based, could easily serve as a mass for Mary or some other saint.[55] The poet claims he will persevere in his love no matter what response he gets, an admirable attitude both for a Christian and a lover.

The question of the liturgical propriety of complete mass cycles and of the representative nature of anthologies of masses destined for particular institutions cannot, of course, be answered by recourse to Brussels 5557 alone. It would, for example, be instructive to look at the masses copied into manuscripts by members of the Habsburg-Netherlands scriptorium, manuscripts that preserve a later repertory from the same court. Most of the surviving Habsburg-Burgundian manuscripts, however, were presentation copies, made as gifts to other courts or to important individuals.[56] Only two anthologies containing only or mostly masses appear to have been prepared for actual use at sacred services in the Low Countries: Brussels 215–16, made for some chapel, probably in Brussels, dedicated to the Seven Sorrows of Mary, and containing two masses for the services for which the chapel was intended; and Brussels 6428, which probably records at least a part of the repertory of the Burgundian court chapel during the first decades of the sixteenth century.[57]

Evidence of the Sources', in *Josquin des Prez*, ed. Edward E. Lowinsky in collaboration with Bonnie J. Blackburn (London, 1976), 181–216 at 213.

[54] Kellman, 'Josquin', 198–200.

[55] The mass is published in a modern edition in Johannes Ockeghem, *Collected Works*, ii, ed. Dragan Plamenac (New York, 1947), 98–115. The anonymous song on which it is based is published ibid. 116.

[56] This information is taken from Kellman, 'Josquin', 209–16, who lists fourteen manuscripts containing only or mostly masses copied by the Habsburg-Burgundian scriptorium. Twelve of them were compiled as presentation copies for various rulers: Philip the Fair and Juana of Spain (Brussels, Bibliothèque Royale, MS 9126), John of Portugal and Catherine of Austria (Brussels, Bibliothèque Royale, MS 15075), Frederick of Saxony (Jena, Universitätsbibliothek, MSS 3, 7, and 21), Pope Leo X (Vatican, Biblioteca Apostolica Vaticana, MS Cappella Sistina 160), Manuel of Portugal and Marie of Spain (Vienna, Österreichische Nationalbibliothek, MS1783), MS 1783), and Maximilian I and Bianca Sforza (Vienna, Österreichische Nationalbibliothek, MS SM 15495); or for important private collectors: Pompejus Occo (Brussels, Bibliothèque Royale, MS IV. 922), Philippe Bouton (Vatican, Biblioteca Apostolica Vaticana MS Chigiana C VIII 234, the so-called Chigi Codex), and Raimund Fugger (Vienna, Österreichische Nationalbibliothek, MSS 4809 and 11778).

[57] The contents of Brussels 215–16 are listed in Charles van den Borren, 'Inventaire des manuscrits de musique polyphonique qui se trouvent en Belgique', *Acta musicologica*, 5 (1933), 66–71 at 69–70. See also *Census-Catalogue*, i. 91.

Brussels 6428 contains the following masses:[58]

Missa Conceptio tua (La Rue)
Missa Ista est speciosa (La Rue)
Missa Ave sanctissima (La Rue)
Missa de septem doloribus beatissime Marie virginis (La Rue)
Missa Virgo prudentissima ('De Assumptione beate Marie') (Isaac)
Missa Nos autem gloriari ('Missa de sancta cruce') (La Rue)
Missa Resurrexi ('Missa pascale') (La Rue)

The manuscript can be understood as a useful indicator of what a particular institution found most valuable to bind and preserve as a record of what they regularly sang during sacred services. It contains six masses by La Rue and one by Isaac: five Marian masses, a mass for the Holy Cross, and a mass for Easter. Regarding the contents of such manuscripts as significant portions of normal repertories helps us to understand better the relatively modest and yet highly important place polyphony had in the celebration of sacred services. The editor of the manuscript shaped its contents to reflect standard practices at a particular courtly chapel. The manuscript underscores the central importance the worship of the Virgin Mary had in the late fifteenth and sixteenth centuries, and in addition supplies masses for two important occasions during the liturgical year.

Documents like the two sets of regulations describing musical and liturgical practices at the court of Charles the Bold help us to understand better just what priests and singers did every day, what their responsibilities were in celebrating the Mass and Office, and what place music, whether chant or polyphony, had in the continuous celebration of the Christian faith. In order to offer a vivid picture of music in fifteenth- and sixteenth-century sacred ritual, however, we also need to compare such sets of regulations with the music that survives from particular institutions. Even though the pattern of survival of manuscripts is sketchy, we can assume that the manuscripts that do come down to us reflect at least a part of the core of the repertories regularly cultivated by court and cathedral chapels. In Charles the Bold's chapel, and probably in most other churches and cathedrals of the time, it was principally plainchant that embellished the sacred service, and allowed for heightened declamation of the sacred words. The chapel singers reserved polyphony for very special occasions, greater feast-days, and especially Marian services, including late afternoon Office Hours. Their repertory of polyphonic music probably did not extend beyond a dozen or so masses at any given time, plus a handful of motets and Magnificats for Vespers and Compline and possibly for other occasions as well. Charles the Bold's chapel may well have been typical for its time, but we need to continue our investigation of the conventions in use at a number of courts, emphasizing especially the liturgical propriety of the masses each choir cultivated, and continuing to ask when, where, and why composers based their mass cycles on secular songs, most of them extolling love.

[58] The contents of Brussels 6428 are listed in van den Borren, 'Inventaire', 70. See also *Census-Catalogue*, i. 93.

Appendix A
Passages from the 1469 Regulations at Charles the Bold's Court Concerning Singing

Item ou nombre de ceulx de la ditte chapelle a la discretion du premier chapelain, seront eslues quatre prestes propices pour officier a l'autel et desquelz on ce pourra le mieulz passer a la chanterie du livre, laquelle chanterie sera prealablement formé de tel nombres de haultes voix, teneurs et contres que cy apres est ordonné; lesquelz quatre prebstres seront députés et auront la charge des messes ordinaires es jours non solempnelz pour icelles messes; et ausi les evvangilles aux festes doubles et solempneles estre celebrées et dites par sepmaines sans ce que ceulx qui seront deputez a la dicte chanterie du livre, ne autres fors seulement les quatre dessusditz, se doient ocuper desdites messes ordinaires, et ce adfin qu'il n'y ait faulte de voix au livre; et le tour de quatre sepmaines fait par lesditz quatre prebstres, les autres prenans gaiges de chapelain, et chascun de eulx, aussi non prebstres, seront tenus par tour de faire desservier les messes de la chinquiesme sepmaine par ung des ditz quatre deputés aux messes en luy baillant ung escu d'or pour la dicte sepmaine.

(Item, from among the members of the said chapel, the first chaplain at his discretion will select four priests capable of officiating at the altar, and who can most easily be spared from polyphonic singing, which polyphonic singing will first and foremost be formed of such numbers of high voices, tenors and contras as are hereafter indicated. These four priests will be deputized and will have charge of ordinary masses on days without solemn feasts. And also the Gospels on double and solemn feasts will be said and celebrated each week without involving those who are deputized to sing polyphony; nor will anyone but the four above named need to occupy themselves with said ordinary masses, so that there will be no lack of polyphonic singers. And the assignment of four weeks having been finished by the four priests (the others having received chaplain's wages), each one of them [the other chaplains], even those who are not priests, will be obliged to take turns at serving mass during the fifth week in place of one of the said four deputized for masses, giving him a gold ecu for the week; Fallows, 'Specific Information', 148.)

Item pour le chant du livre y aura du moyns six haultes voix, troys teneurs, troys basses contres et deux moiens sans en ce comprendre les quatre chapelains des haultes messes ne les sommeliers lesquelz toutefoys s'ilz ne sont occupés a l'autel ou autrement raisonnablement seront tenus de servir avec les dessus ditz.

(Item, for the *chant du livre* there will be at least six high voices, three tenors, three *basse contres* and two *moiens*, without counting the four chaplains responsible for high masses or the *sommeliers*, who however, if they are not occupied at the altar or in some other reasonable manner, are obliged to serve with the above mentioned; Fallows, 'Specific Information', 149.)

Re: granting only two absences at a time: . . .
aussi il aura regard aux teneurs et contres tellement que le service soit tousjours fourny de deux teneurs et de deux contres.

(In addition, he [the first chaplain] will consider the tenors and contras so that the service will always have two tenors and two contras; Fallows, 'Specific Information', 154.)

Appendix B
Liturgical Occasions Celebrated with Special Solemnity at the Court of Charles the Bold[1]

La Nativité Nostre Seigneur
La Circumcision
L'Apparicion (= Epiphany)
La Purificacion Nostre Dame
L'Annunciacion
La Visitacion
L'Assumption
La Nativité et la Conception d'ycelle
Les festes de Pasques
L'Assention Nostre Seigneur
La veille et le jour de Penthecouste
La feste de la Trinité
Celle du Saint Sacrement
La Nativité saint Jhan Baptiste
La feste de saint Pierre en juing
La feste de Toussains
La Commemoracion des Trespassés
L[a] feste de sainte Katherine
[La feste] de saint Andrieu
[La feste] de saincte Barbe
Chascun jour de Karesme et de l'Avent
(plus funerals and weddings)

[1] From the ordinances of 1469; see Fallows, 'Specific Information', 147–8.

Appendix C
The Contents of Brussels 5557[1]

Original nucleus, copied in 1468 by Hand A

1. *Missa Summe trinitati a 3* (Frye)
   c.f.: responsory for Offices on Trinity Sunday (and also for the reception of kings and queens)

[1] After Wegman, *Choirbook of the Burgundian Court Chapel*, 6.

2. *Missa a 3* (Plummer)
   with Kyrie trope: *Omnipotens pater unigenite*

3. *Missa a 3* (Richard Cox)
   with Kyrie trope: *Deus creator omnium*

4. *Missa Flos regalis a 4* (Frye)
   c. f.: unknown but probably antiphon 'Flos regalis Etheldreda', for St Etheldreda, patron saint of Ely

5. *Missa Nobilis et pulchra a 3* (Frye)
   c. f.: responsory for St Catherine of Alexandria with Kyrie trope: *Deus creator omnium*

Copied after 1468 by Hand B

6. *Anthoni usque limina a 4* (Busnoys)
   for St Anthony Abbot

Copied c.1464–5 by Hand A'

7. *Missa Ecce ancilla domini a 4* (Dufay)
   Marian. c. f.: antiphon for the feast of the Annunciation, and also an antiphon (*Beata es Maria*) for the feast of the Visitation

Copied in the early 1470s by Hand D

8. *Magnificat secundi toni a 3* (anon.)

Copied after 1468 by Hands B and C

9. *Noel noel a 4* (Busnoys)
   for Christmas or Advent

10. *Magnificat sexti toni a 2–4* (Busnoys)

11. *Ad cenam agni* (probably *a 4*) (Busnoys)
    Easter hymn

Copied 1476–80 by Hand E

12. *Missa Quinti toni a 3* (Ockeghem)

Copied after 1476 by Hand B

13. *Anima mea liquefacta/Stirps Jesse a 3* (Busnoys)
    Marian (for Vespers service?)[2]

14. *Victimae paschali laudes a 4* (Busnoys)
    for Easter

15. *Regina caeli I a 4* (Busnoys)

---

[2] For the liturgical context of *Anima mea/Stirps Jesse* within the Parisian rite adopted by the Burgundian court see M. Jennifer Bloxam, below, Ch. 4.

16. *Regina caeli* II *a 4* (Busnoys)
    both Marian, sung during Easter season
17. *Alleluia verbum caro a 4* (Busnoys)
    for Christmas Vespers[3]

Copied in the early 1470s by Hand A'

18. *Missa a 3* (anon.)
19. *Missa Pour quelque paine a 4* (Cornelius Heyns)
    model: anon. rondeau *a 3*: *Pour quelque paine que j'endure*, publ. in Ockeghem, *Collected Works*, ii. 116

Copied in the early 1470s by Hand A"

20. *Missa Ave regina caelorum a 4* (Dufay)
    Marian. c. f.: Marian antiphon

Copied after 1468

21. fragment of *Missa*, possibly by Regis
22. *Vexilla regis* (monophonic hymn)
    for Passion Sunday

Copied probably in the late 1460s by Hand A"

23. *Missa Ecce ancilla/Ne timeas a 4* (Regis)
    Marian. c. f.: a series of antiphons mostly related to Mary

Copied after 1468

24. *O quam glorifica* (anon.)
    Marian hymn
25. *Kyrie* (Dufay)

---

[3] *Ed.:* M. Jennifer Bloxam has identified the plainsong upon which Busnoys's motet is based. See Ch. 4, Ex. 4.4.

4

On the Origins, Contexts, and Implications of Busnoys's Plainsong Cantus Firmi: Some Preliminary Remarks

ॐ ॐ

M. JENNIFER BLOXAM

HISTORIANS of medieval music and liturgy have amply demonstrated the astonishing richness of late medieval plainchant traditions. Far from being a fixed, immutable body of prescribed texts, tunes, and actions, the liturgy and ritual governing the daily life of composers manifested a staggering degree of regional variation. The veneration of local saints imparted a distinctive profile to the liturgical calendars of individual churches and towns, and the selection and ordering of readings and chants created a surprising malleability in the structure of universal feasts. Even the texts and melodies of universally known plainsongs often varied from place to place.[1]

Recent research has underscored the impact of local traditions of liturgy and chant upon a broad range of sacred polyphony, including twelfth-century organa,[2] fifteenth-century hymn settings,[3] and fifteenth- and sixteenth-century masses and motets based on one or more cantus firmi.[4] As these and other studies show, the plainsong used as a cantus firmus was a piece of music in its own

---

[1] A pioneering demonstration of the importance of regional variations in liturgy and chant in 15th-c. music is Manfred F. Bukofzer, '*Caput*: A Liturgico-Musical Study', in *Studies in Medieval and Renaissance Music* (New York, 1950), 230–56. By comparing the liturgy and chant for the Maundy Thursday service in a variety of French and English liturgies, Bukofzer was able to demonstrate the origin of the 'Caput' melisma in the Sarum rite.

[2] Craig Wright, *Music and Ceremony at Notre Dame of Paris, 500–1550* (Cambridge, 1989), 66–81.

[3] Tom R. Ward, 'The Polyphonic Office Hymn and the Liturgy of Fifteenth-Century Italy', *Musica disciplina*, 26 (1972), 161–88.

[4] Jacquelyn A. Mattfeld, 'Some Relationships between Texts and Cantus Firmi in the Liturgical Motets of Josquin des Pres', *JAMS* 14 (1961), 159–83; Jeremy Noble, 'The Function of Josquin's Motets', *TVNM* 35 (1985), 9–31; M. Jennifer Bloxam, 'In Praise of Spurious Saints: The *Missae Floruit egregiis* by Pipelare and La Rue', *JAMS* 44 (1991), 163–220; ead., 'Sacred Polyphony and Local Traditions of Liturgy and Plainsong: Reflections on Music by Jacob Obrecht', in Thomas Forrest Kelly (ed.), *Plainsong in the Age of Polyphony* (Cambridge Studies in Performance Practice, 2; Cambridge, 1992), 140–77.

right, with a particular, often locally defined function and context. Before their adoption as cantus firmi, these tunes possessed a life of their own; they existed at first in a dimension quite independent of the masses or motets that became, one might say, their hosts. The plainchants selected for quotation within a sacred polyphonic work were known to composers within the context of the liturgy and ritual that formed the framework of their daily experience, from their early training in the choir schools to their service as singers, chapelmasters, and composers in churches and secular courts throughout Western Europe.[5]

In the course of their frequently peripatetic careers, composers adapted to the idiosyncrasies of the local liturgies they encountered, and these peculiarities often found expression in their sacred compositions. Consequently, by ascertaining the connection of a particular cantus firmus with a specific liturgy, we often obtain unexpected new insights into music historical questions, such as a deeper understanding of the initial performance context of a piece (liturgical occasion, performing forces, architectural space, etc.), a more precise dating of a work (particularly when details of the composer's biography are known), and a sharper focus on matters of musical style and chronology. And in the process, more difficult questions of a hermeneutical nature often emerge: why did the composer select this particular cantus firmus? What did the quotation of this plainsong signify to the composer, the singers, the listeners?

The pioneering studies of cantus firmus in mass and motet relied primarily on the *Liber usualis* and other modern publications of chant and liturgy for the models and the liturgical context of the cantus firmi considered.[6] Although more recent studies and editions endeavour at least to cite the late medieval sources of chant available in facsimile,[7] scholars still often rely on plainsong collections of dubious relevance to the composer or repertory in question. For example,

---

[5] This generalization holds, of course, for a far broader temporal span than just the 15th c. Indeed, the needs of local liturgies have influenced sacred polyphonic composition from the formation of the earliest polyphonic repertories: the Winchester Troper (Cambridge, Corpus Christi College, MS 473), for example, includes polyphony for saints especially dear to the Old Minster at Winchester (see Andreas Holschneider, *Die Organa von Winchester: Studien zum ältesten Repertoire polyphoniker Musik* (Hildesheim, 1968).

[6] The central publications of modern plainsong are the *Liber usualis* (first issued by the Benedictines of Solesmes in 1896), the *Antiphonale Sacrosanctae Romanae Ecclesiae* (Rome, 1912), and the *Graduale Sacrosanctae Romanae Ecclesiae* (Rome, 1908), all of which reflect a modern distillation and universalization of the Roman Catholic liturgy and plainsong. Because of their accessibility, they have served a host of authors as the principal source of often erroneous information regarding the liturgical assignment and the melodic content of medieval chant. The central study devoted to the analysis of cantus-firmus technique in the 15th c., Edgar H. Sparks, *Cantus Firmus in Mass and Motet, 1420–1520* (Berkeley and Los Angeles, 1963), relied primarily on modern publications of chant, and many editions of medieval and Renaissance music have cited such sources, including such monuments as Guillaume Dufay, *Opera omnia*, ed. Heinrich Besseler, 6 vols. (Rome, 1951–66) and Josquin des Prez, *Werken*, ed. Albert Smijers (Amsterdam, 1921–).

[7] One exemplary effort to connect a repertory of sacred polyphony with the very liturgical tradition it was meant to adorn is the edition of the Old Hall manuscript (London, British Library, Add. MS 57950), whose critical apparatus relies exclusively upon late medieval sources of the Sarum rite for information about liturgical texts and cantus firmi. See *The Old Hall Manuscript*, 3 vols., ed. Margaret Bent and Andrew Hughes (CMM 46; [Rome], 1969–73). But such careful attention to the backdrop of liturgy, chant, and ritual behind the sacred polyphony of the late Middle Ages and Renaissance remains rare.

scholars treating Antoine Busnoys's small extant corpus of sacred music based on plainsong have relied on the *Liber usualis*, a thirteenth-century Sarum antiphonal, a sixteenth-century miscellany from 's-Hertogenbosch, a fourteenth-century troper from Dublin, a thirteenth-century breviary from Bayeux, and a thirteenth-century proser from Utrecht.[8] Of these, none but the Sarum source seems likely to have been been even tangentially associated with Busnoys's experience of liturgy and chant.[9] While the information gleaned from such a disparate array of sources is not necessarily incorrect, the materials and the methodology do exist to enable us to discern the outlines of a more complete picture of Busnoys's sacred music in relation to the traditions of liturgy and plainsong with which he was familiar. My purpose here, then, will be to outline and demonstrate some preliminary methodological steps towards a better understanding of the origins, contexts, and implications of Busnoys's plainsong cantus firmi.

Busnoys drew upon several different types of chant: antiphons, a responsory, hymns (all components of the Office), and sequences (usually part of the Mass celebration). Therefore, one must search for sources preserving both the texts and tunes of the Office as well as the Mass: breviaries, antiphoners, hymnals, and processionals for the Office chants, and missals, graduals, and sequencers for the Mass chants. Temporal and geographical details of the composer's biography will help circumscribe the particular liturgical usages for investigation. Busnoys, for example, is known to have served at least four ecclesiastical institutions in three different cities, each with its own distinct liturgical usage: the churches of St Martin and St Gatien in Tours, St Hilaire in Poitiers, and St Salvator in Bruges.[10] Additionally, one must consider the liturgical usage governing the musical chapel of the composer's most important secular employer, the Burgundian Duke Charles the Bold, his daughter Marie of Burgundy, and her consort Maximilian of Austria (whose musico-liturgical practices will be addressed shortly).

Locating the surviving manuscript and printed sources of liturgy and chant from these various institutions requires some detective work. One begins by scrutinizing a wide variety of catalogues of libraries, museums, and archives, as well

---

[8] See *Busnoys LTW*, Commentary, 46, 55, 60, 62, 87, 88, and Rob C. Wegman, 'Petrus de Domarto's *Missa Spiritus almus* and the Early History of the Four-Voice Mass in the Fifteenth Century', *EMH* 10 (1991), 243.

[9] Busnoys's service at the Court of Burgundy may well have exposed him to the Sarum rite. Duke Charles cultivated English liaisons, and his marriage to Margaret of York in 1468, as well as other state visits, would surely have exposed English chapels and their liturgical rite to continental listeners. On Charles the Bold's dealings with England, see Richard Vaughan, *Charles the Bold* (New York, 1974), esp. 41–83.

[10] Regarding Busnoys's association with the church of St Martin of Tours, see Paula Higgins, '*In hydraulis* Revisited: New Light on the Career of Antoine Busnois', *JAMS* 39 (1986), 36–86 at 69–76; Pamela F. Starr established his connection with the cathedral of St Gatien of Tours in 'Rome as the Centre of the Universe: Papal Grace and Music Patronage', *EMH* 11 (1992), 223–62 at 249–51. The composer's presence in Poitiers is discussed by Paula Higgins below, Ch. 7.

as specialized inventories of certain types of manuscript and printed sources.[11] However useful such secondary reference works may be, nothing can ultimately replace first-hand exploration of the various collections housed in churches, archives, and museums abroad, wherein one can still discover both manuscripts and prints not registered in the published catalogues.

Ideally, an inquiry into the liturgical and musical sources of a composer's chosen cantus firmi should comprise an investigation of all pertinent extant manuscripts and prints of liturgy and plainsong. One might hope to find liturgical books used during the same period by the very institution for which the composer worked, but the survival rate of such sources is poor indeed. Instead, one must frequently rely—and with great caution—on manuscripts and prints many decades removed from the composer and which are not necessarily from the particular church in which a composer worked, but rather from other institutions in the same city. Only by surveying all the surviving sources relevant to a particular usage can one verify the constancy of a chant's liturgical assignment and confirm its melodic and textual content within that usage.

A thorough-going study of the cantus firmi selected by Busnoys, then, would essentially involve four main steps: (i) locating the chants in question in as many textual and musical sources from each liturgical usage known to the composer as possible; (ii) determining the exact function of the plainsong within each of the sources that transmits it; (iii) recording the precise melodic and textual versions of the chant in each source; and (iv) comparing each version of the chant located against the cantus firmus as crafted by Busnoys. Among the most important questions to consider in undertaking this comparative musico-liturgical study are: was the chant used in all or only in certain of the locales in which Busnoys is known to have worked? Was its function within the framework of the service constant between usages, or did it vary? What might this function tell us about the context of polyphony based on this chant? Did the text and/or melody of the chant vary between locales, and if so, does the cantus firmus as employed by the composer bear a closer resemblance to one version over another? Are the intersections between the version of chant preserved in a cantus firmus and a local version of the tune persuasive enough to posit a direct link between the two? The answers to such questions are by no means clear-cut; each case must be weighed and interpreted on its own merits, taking into account the testimony of the sources while acknowledging the always incomplete nature of that testimony.

For however systematic and exhaustive our consideration of the sources relevant

---

[11] The sheer number of relevant catalogues prohibits listing them here, but a good start towards assembling a bibliography of pertinent manuscript sources of liturgy and chant can be made by consulting Victor Leroquais, *Les Bréviaires manuscrits des bibliothèques publiques de France*, 5 vols. (Paris, 1934), and id., *Les Sacramentaires et les missels manuscrits des bibliothèques publiques de France*, 3 vols. (Paris, 1924). For printed books, contact the RELICS project (*Renaissance Liturgical Imprints: A Census*), directed by Professors David Crawford and James Borders at the University of Michigan at Ann Arbor.

to the investigation of a certain cantus firmus, we can never be sure that we have taken into account all the local traditions of liturgy and chant that may have influenced a composer. In Busnoys's case, for example, the particular tradition within which the composer first learned as a choirboy is unknown, the extent of his familiarity with the liturgical traditions of institutions where he held prebends remains an open question, and there are still lacunae in his biography. And of course the survival of fifteenth-century sources from places where Busnoys is known to have been active is problematic indeed; there is, for example, no surviving antiphoner preserving the local usage of Bruges. Furthermore, liturgical sources from two locales in which Busnoys worked, Tours and Poitiers, still await investigation.

Inevitable gaps in our knowledge notwithstanding, the liturgy and plainsong tradition observed by the court of Burgundy offer a potentially fruitful avenue of investigation. Most of the sacred music by Busnoys survives, often as unica, in the manuscript Brussels 5557, a source compiled expressly for use by the chapel of Duke Charles the Bold and his bride Margaret of York.[12] Paula Higgins has shown that Busnoys entered the service of Charles between 1466 and 1467, and that he retained a connection with the court for almost twenty years.[13] There is every reason to believe, as Wolfgang Stephan first argued, that the pieces by Busnoys entered into Brussels 5557 were copied under his supervision, perhaps even by the composer himself.[14] Thus, the sacred compositions by Busnoys contained in Brussels 5557 were almost certainly sung during services conducted by the Burgundian court chapel.

To what liturgical usage did the court of Burgundy subscribe? Inventories of the collection of manuscripts from the Burgundian court during the time of Philip the Bold testify to its observance of the rite of Paris.[15] That this should be so is easily explained: the Valois Duke Philip the Bold received the duchy of Burgundy as a fief from his father King John II of France, and political expediency dictated that the rite of Paris should be transplanted to the Burgundian court, despite the fact that the Burgundian state soon established itself as a political entity largely independent of the Parisian court. Philip the Bold's Burgundian and Habsburg-Burgundian successors, from John the Fearless to Philip the Fair, inherited and continued to use the liturgical books amassed during Philip the Bold's rule. Manuscripts added to the collection during the fifteenth century attest to the continued celebration of the divine services at court according to the

[12] For the most recent research on Brussels 5557, see Rob C. Wegman, 'New Data Concerning the Origins and Chronology of Brussels, Koninklijke Bibliotheek, Manuscript 5557', *TVNM* 36 (1986), 5–19, and *Choirbook of the Burgundian Court Chapel: Brussel, Koninklijke Bibliotheek MS. 5557*, intro. by Rob C. Wegman (Peer, Belgium, 1989), 5–8.

[13] Paula Higgins, '*In hydraulis* Revisited', and below, Ch. 7.

[14] Wolfgang Stephan, *Die burgundisch-niederländische Motette zur Zeit Ockeghems* (Kassel, 1937), 89.

[15] See Craig Wright, *Music at the Court of Burgundy, 1364–1419: A Documentary History* (Institute of Medieval Music Musicological Studies, 28; Henryville, Ottawa, and Binningen, 1979), 140–2, and M. Jennifer Bloxam, 'A Survey of Late Medieval Service Books from the Low Countries: Implications for Sacred Polyphony, 1460–1520' (Ph.D. diss., Yale University, 1987), 67–75.

use of Paris; to this the famous breviary of Philip the Good (Brussels, Bibliothèque Royale, MSS 9511 and 9026), commissioned by the duke and copied in Paris according to the usage of the cathedral of Notre Dame, bears eloquent witness.[16] And the 1469 ordinance concerning the chapel under Charles the Bold (Oxford, Bodleian Library, MS Hatton 13) specifies the performance of the daily services 'following and keeping the usage of the church of Paris, as was customary during the time of the duke's predecessors'.[17]

Although the usage of Paris governed the celebration of the divine services at court, the manuscript Brussels 5557 preserving the polyphonic music that adorned these services does include works with no explicit connection with the rite of Paris. For example, the original layer of the source, apparently compiled for the wedding celebration of the English princess Margaret of York to Charles the Bold in 1468, transmits masses by English composers whose plainsong models derive from Sarum usage.[18] Busnoys, however, unlike the other known composers represented in Brussels 5557, sang and composed for the Burgundian chapel for many years, which raises the possibility that Parisian traditions of liturgy and plainsong directly influenced his sacred composition. Do any of his motets in Brussels 5557 betray the influence of Parisian usage, thereby suggesting their creation during the composer's tenure at the court? What can an exploration of the liturgy and plainsong of the Parisian rite tell us about the function of Busnoys's motets sung by the Burgundian court chapel? Four motets, selected for their inclusion of plainsongs with the most potential for localization, will serve as case studies: they are *Anima mea liquefacta est/Stirps Jesse*, *Ad cenam agni providi*, *Victimae paschali laudes*, and *Alleluia verbum caro factum est*.[19]

The three-voice Marian motet *Anima mea liquefacta est/Stirps Jesse* is generally regarded as Busnoys's earliest extant motet.[20] While the complete melody and text of the responsory *Stirps Jesse* unfold in the lowest voice, the upper voices deliver the text of the Marian antiphon *Anima mea*.[21] Both chants were univer-

---

[16] For a thorough study of this breviary, see Victor Leroquais, *Le Bréviaire de Philippe le Bon*, 2 vols. (Paris, 1929).

[17] 'et le tout en observant et gardant l'usage de l'eglise de Paris ainsi qu'il est acoustumé du temps des predicesseurs de monditseigneur'. See David Fallows, 'Specific Information on the Ensembles for Composed Polyphony, 1400–1474', in Stanley Boorman (ed.), *Studies in the Performance of Late Mediaeval Music* (Cambridge, 1983), 109–59 at 147. For a fuller discussion of this Burgundian court ordinance, see Howard Mayer Brown, above, Ch. 3.

[18] The *Missa Summe trinitati* and *Missa Nobilis et pulchra* by Walter Frye, for example, draw upon Sarum responsories for Trinity Sunday and for the feast of St Catherine of Alexandria, respectively; see Sylvia W. Kenney, *Walter Frye and the Contenance Angloise* (New Haven, 1964), 51. For further observations on the English masses and their cantus firmi, see Wegman, 'New Data', 10–11, and 18 n. 25.

[19] Omitted from discussion here are the *Magnificat* and the two settings of *Regina caeli*, all of which employ universally known plainsongs difficult to localize on the basis of either melodic variants or liturgical function; also not mentioned is *Noel noel*, whose plainsong model (if any) remains unknown.

[20] Sparks, *Cantus Firmus*, 223; *Busnoys LTW*, Commentary, 62.

[21] The superius occasionally paraphrases bits of the *Stirps Jesse* melody, and Brussels 5557 even provides the corresponding textual snippets from this chant in addition to the text of *Anima mea*; see Edgar H. Sparks, 'The Motets of Antoine Busnois', *JAMS* 6 (1953), 216–26 at 217 n. 10.

sally known, and served a variety of liturgical and paraliturgical functions within celebrations for the Blessed Virgin. Within the liturgy of Paris, however, a tantalizing detail proffers the possibility that Busnoys's inspiration for the wedding of these two chants may have derived, at least in part, from the Parisian rite. At first Vespers on the feast of the Assumption of the Virgin, according to the usage of Paris, the antiphon *Anima mea liquefacta est* stood as the fifth and final psalm antiphon, to be followed directly by the festal prolix responsory *Stirps Jesse*.[22]

The selection and ordering of the chants for the principal Marian feasts varied tremendously from place to place, and among the many local usages compared for this study, the contiguous placement of these two chants was unique to Paris.[23] Moreover, the rite of Paris was distinctive in the importance it accorded to prolix responsories at Vespers on important feasts, and the culmination of the antiphon series with *Anima mea liquefacta est*, crowned by the responsory *Stirps Jesse*, may have made a special impression on Busnoys.[24] But it would be premature to attribute too much importance to this coincidence of liturgical structure and musical invention; Busnoys's primary motivation for the combination of these two chants may well have had nothing at all to do with their liturgical context. Polytextuality has served since the thirteenth century as a way for composers to create a network of textual and musical associations within a piece, and the texts were chosen primarily for their content, and only secondarily for their liturgical associations. In the fifteenth century, polytextuality is relatively rare; this motet is Busnoys's only known use of the device within his sacred music, and the chants here chosen seldom appear in polyphonic settings. All this would suggest an extra-musical reason for the marriage of these two texts. As the purpose of this study is not to delve into the historical and biographical implications of the combination of these two texts, but rather to assess some of Busnoys's music in light of the usage of Paris, these extra-liturgical avenues of investigation must be left unresolved here.[25]

Within the services at the court of Burgundy, therefore, the textual and melodic materials of this motet might suggest performance in connection with Vespers on the feast of the Assumption. The florid style of *Anima mea liquefacta est*/*Stirps Jesse* and its polytextuality, however, separate the piece from the simpler

---

[22] These assignments are indicated, for example, in the early 14th-c. notated breviary of Parisian usage, Paris, Bibliothèque nationale, lat. 10482, fo. 486, as well as in printed breviaries of the late 15th and early 16th cc.

[23] These include the usages of Rome, Salisbury, Cambrai, Antwerp, Bruges, Utrecht, Thérouanne, Louvain, Brussels, Mons, and 's-Hertogenbosch.

[24] On the use of prolix responsories in the liturgy at Notre Dame of Paris, see Wright, *Music and Ceremony*, 105.

[25] For two different interpretations of the significance of this combination of texts, see Mary Natvig, 'The Latin-Texted Works of Antoine Busnois' (Ph.D. diss., University of Rochester, 1991), 279–301; and Paula Higgins, 'Love and Death in the Fifteenth-Century Motet: A Reading of Busnois's *Anima mea liquefacta est*/*Stirps Jesse*, in Dolores Pesce (ed.), *Hearing the Motet: Essays on the Motet of the Middle Ages and Renaissance* (New York, 1997), 142–68.

and obviously liturgical works among Busnoys's œuvre preserved in Brussels 5557.[26] While performance at Vespers cannot be ruled out, this motet may well have served a paraliturgical function, gracing one of the frequent Marian devotions of which medieval people were so fond.[27]

Although the melody of the responsory *Stirps Jesse* employed by Busnoys corresponds almost note for note to the version of this chant sung in the Parisian rite,[28] this version was widely known: the Sarum rite, for example, employed a melody that differed in only a few small details from that of Paris.[29] Melodic evidence thus allows the possibility that Busnoys turned to the usage of Paris for this cantus firmus, but cannot establish that the Parisian rite in fact furnished the version of the plainsong used by the composer.

Richard Taruskin has noted one small anomaly in the chant set by Busnoys: as shown in Ex. 4.1, the word 'virgam' beginning the second phrase (m. 35) lacks the initial descending minor third skip from *f* to *d* found in most plainsong versions of this chant (including Paris).[30] A comparison of the plainsong melody with Busnoys's cantus firmus, however, reveals that the composer simply chose to end the first phrase of his cantus firmus two notes prematurely in relation to the chant model, and to then commence the second phrase with the two notes concluding the first phrase of the chant model. The reason for this small licence in the phrasing would appear to be compositionally motivated: ending the first phrase of the cantus firmus two notes before that of the chant model permitted him to realize a neat cadential expansion from sixth to octave between the superius and tenor in mm. 29–30 that the cadence formula of the chant does not readily permit. If this explanation is correct, then the composer's deviation from the phrasing of the chant model would have no bearing on the provenance of that model. At this point, then, we can only state that the chant tradition of Paris may have furnished the model for the cantus firmus of *Anima mea liquefacta est/Stirps Jesse*.

Two of the sacred compositions by Busnoys transmitted in Brussels 5557 served to embellish the Eastertide celebration: the sequence *Victimae paschali laudes* and the hymn *Ad cenam agni providi*, for which only the bass and superius parts survive. Fortunately for the purposes of this study, Busnoys placed the cantus firmus of the hymn in the bass voice.

---

[26] For the liturgical contexts of Busnoys's works in Brussels 5557 see Brown, above, Ch. 3.

[27] The different functions served by works properly labelled motet, whose role is best described as paraliturgical, as opposed to explicitly liturgical settings such as hymns, psalms, and Magnificat antiphons, are explored by Anthony M. Cummings, 'Toward an Interpretation of the Sixteenth-Century Motet', *JAMS* 34 (1981), 43–59. Text type and musical style are key factors in drawing these functional distinctions. Although Cummings focuses on 16th-c. repertory, the pertinence of his findings to 15th-c. music is clear.

[28] Paris 10482, fo. 486ʳ.

[29] See the facsimile of the late 13th-c. antiphoner Cambridge University Library, MS Mm.11.9, ed. Walter Howard Frere as *Antiphonale Sarisburiense*, 6 vols. (London, 1901–24; repr. Farnborough, 1966), v. 519.

[30] *Busnoys LTW*, Commentary, 62.

Ex. 4.1. Busnoys, *Anima mea liquefacta est/Stirps Jesse*, mm. 23–45, and plainchant *Stirps Jesse* (Paris, B. n. lat. 10482, fo. 486ʳ; early 14th-c. notated breviary, usage of Paris)

Ex. 4.1. *cont.*

Like most hymns, *Ad cenam agni providi* was sung to any one of a number of different melodies, depending on the tradition of the particular locale. This diversity within the hymn repertory can help to circumscribe the locale of the liturgy for which a polyphonic hymn setting would have been appropriate: if a local usage associated a certain hymn text with melody X, and a polyphonic setting of that text quotes chant melody Y, then it is unlikely that the polyphony originated for that local liturgy.[31] The paschal text *Ad cenam agni providi* circulated in connection with no fewer than twelve different families of melody (with considerable variation possible within each family), and the tune family employed by Busnoys (Stäblein Melody 171) was by no means the most widely known.[32] It may therefore be significant that the Parisian version of the melody for this hymn concurs in virtually every detail with that of Busnoys's cantus firmus; indeed, it corresponds more closely than the exemplar for Stäblein Melody 171, Paris, Bibliothèque de l'Arsenal, MS 279, a thirteenth-century manuscript from Bayeux[33] (see Ex. 4.2).

Within the usage of Paris, *Ad cenam agni providi* served as the hymn at Vespers on Low Sunday, the Sunday after Easter.[34] The only polyphony within Brussels 5557 that would have been liturgically appropriate for performance on Easter Day is Busnoys's *Victimae paschali laudes*, a setting of the famous eleventh-century sequence melody by Wipo of Burgundy. Plainsong sequences usually decorated the Mass service, but *Victimae paschali laudes* had no place in any Mass according

---

[31] Ward, 'The Polyphonic Office Hymn'.

[32] Bruno Stäblein (ed.), *Hymnen (I): Die mittelalterlichen Hymnenmelodien des Abendlandes* (Monumenta monodica medii aevi, 1; Kassel, 1956), 113 *et passim*.

[33] Taruskin reproduces this version of the hymn tune in *Busnoys LTW*: Commentary, 60.

[34] See Wright, *Music and Ceremony*, 373–5, for the structure of the Parisian hymnal, extracted from Paris, Bibliothèque nationale, lat. 15181–2, a late 13th-c. manuscript.

Ex. 4.2. Busnoys, *Ad cenam agni providi*, bass, mm. 1–29, and plainchant *Ad cenam agni providi*: (*a*) Paris, B. n. lat. 10482, fo. 137ᵛ; (*b*) Paris, Arsenal 279, fo. 210ᵛ (13th-c. notated breviary, usage of Bayeux)

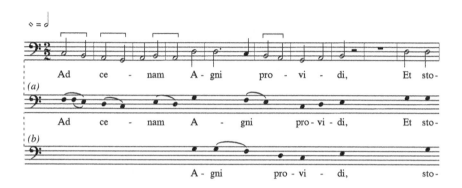

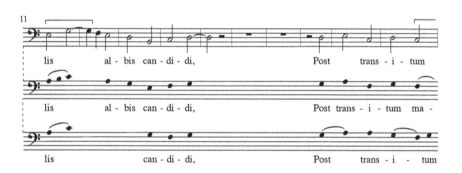

to the rite of Paris, in which the sequence sung at Easter Mass was *Fulgens praeclara*. Rather, the court of Burgundy, following Parisian usage, would have known *Victimae paschali laudes* as the substitute for the hymn at Matins and Vespers on Easter, as well as the hymn substitute at Vespers on the feast of St Mary Magdalene.[35] The select substitution of certain sequences for hymns on high feast-days was a distinctive (though not unique) feature of the Parisian rite, and the inclusion of Busnoys's *Victimae paschali laudes* within Brussels 5557 might suggest the work's performance by the Burgundian chapel choir in connection with the celebration of the Easter Office, not the Mass. Unclear, however, is the relevance of the liturgical role of the cantus firmus as a clue to the performance context of the polyphonic sequence. This is no simple, patently functional alternatim setting such as Dufay wrote; rather, Busnoys disregards the strophic structure of the chant in his setting and treats all verses in elaborate polyphony. Moreover, only the Matins Office on Easter in the Parisian rite called for this sequence in its entirety, while at Vespers the chant was to commence with the second strophe. Busnoys's setting would therefore appear to meet the particular requirements of the Matins celebration most exactly, but the Office of Matins generally did not merit elaborate polyphony. While it is possible that an opulent court's celebration of Matins on the most festive day of the liturgical year could have included such an ambitious work as *Victimae paschali laudes*, a paraliturgical role for this work appears more likely.[36]

A comparison of the melody for *Victimae paschali laudes* sung in the Parisian rite with the cantus firmus employed by Busnoys shows a close correspondence, but this melody varied only in small details from place to place, and Busnoys paraphrased the tune in such a way that the preservation of the small melodic discrepancies that do exist between local usages are difficult to detect within this cantus firmus. For example, in the first part of the fourth versicle (shown in Ex. 4.3), one phrase departs from the melody according to the usage of Paris, but the parallel segment in the second half of the versicle, while also differing from that of Paris, does not duplicate the first half of the versicle, as an exact quotation of the chant would. Suffice it to say that the usage of Paris cannot be ruled out as the source of Busnoys's cantus firmus for this motet, but neither can a persuasive case for this connection rest on the melodic comparison of the cantus firmus with the Parisian sequence.

Christmas is the other festal season for which Busnoys supplied polyphony that served the Burgundian court. Included in Brussels 5557 is the miniature Christmastide antiphon *Alleluia verbum caro factum est*, in a simple chordal style and hitherto believed to be without cantus firmus. Taruskin has characterized

---

[35] Wright, *Music and Ceremony*, 109.

[36] This suggestion concords with Cummings's findings regarding the elaborate sequence settings by Josquin and his followers; such compositions were clearly regarded as motets, distinct in function and style from small liturgical pieces used within the Office. See Cummings, 'Toward an Interpretation', 57.

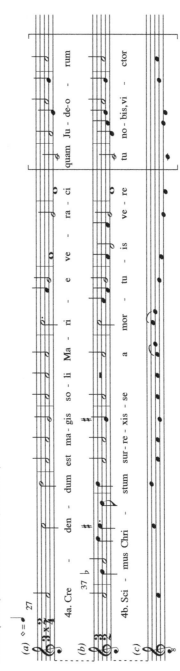

Ex. 4.3. Busnoys, *Victimae paschali laudes*, alto: (*a*) mm. 27–34, (*b*) mm. 36–44; compared with (*c*) plainchant *Victimae paschali laudes* (Paris, B. n. lat. 10482, fo. 176ᵛ)

Alleluia verbum caro factum est as a Magnificat antiphon for use at Christmas
Vespers, a reasonable suggestion, without a cantus firmus as a guide to liturgical
context.[37] An examination of the Christmas liturgy according to the usage of
Paris, however, reveals that this small motet is in fact based on a plainsong: the
superius presents a light paraphrase of the tune of the antiphon *Alleluia verbum
caro factum est*, which was sung with the canticle *Nunc dimittis* at Compline on
Christmas in the Parisian rite (see Ex. 4.4). While the liturgical placement of this
antiphon was not unique to Paris (it appears in the same context, for example, in
the Sarum rite),[38] it is the Parisian and not the Sarum version that corresponds
unequivocally to the plainsong melody Busnoys used.

The discovery of Busnoys's plainsong model not only enables us to ascertain
the original function of this composition within the liturgy of the Burgundian
court, it also helps to clarify the placement of text within the polyphony. A revised
texting of the superius according to the text placement of its plainsong model is
proposed in Ex. 4.4: the top line of text underlay duplicates that of the new
Busnoys edition,[39] while the bottom line shows the suggested revision. This
revised text underlay corresponds much more closely to the texting provided by
the scribe in Brussels 5557 (see Fig. 4.1), who, as noted earlier, may have been
the composer himself.[40] Discovery of the plainsong model for *Alleluia verbum*

Fig. 4.1. Brussels 5557, fo.89ᵛ

[37] *Busnoys LTW*, Commentary, 60.   [38] *Antiphonale Sarisburiense*, ii. 56.
[39] *Busnoys LTW*, Music, 129–31.
[40] Even the placement of text in the middle of a ligature (which, were the texting of the plainsong to be
followed strictly, would occur in m. 3) appears to be suggested by the text underlay in Brussels 5557. This
runs counter to 16th-c. theorists' prescriptions concerning text underlay for composers of Josquin's generation; see Edward E. Lowinsky, 'A Treatise on Text Underlay by a German Disciple of Francisco de Salinas',

Ex. 4.3. Busnoys, *Victimae paschali laudes*, alto: (*a*) mm. 27–34, (*b*) mm. 36–44; compared with (*c*) plainchant *Victimae paschali laudes* (Paris, B. n. lat. 10482, fo. 176ᵛ)

Alleluia verbum caro factum est as a Magnificat antiphon for use at Christmas Vespers, a reasonable suggestion, without a cantus firmus as a guide to liturgical context.[37] An examination of the Christmas liturgy according to the usage of Paris, however, reveals that this small motet is in fact based on a plainsong: the superius presents a light paraphrase of the tune of the antiphon *Alleluia verbum caro factum est*, which was sung with the canticle *Nunc dimittis* at Compline on Christmas in the Parisian rite (see Ex. 4.4). While the liturgical placement of this antiphon was not unique to Paris (it appears in the same context, for example, in the Sarum rite),[38] it is the Parisian and not the Sarum version that corresponds unequivocally to the plainsong melody Busnoys used.

The discovery of Busnoys's plainsong model not only enables us to ascertain the original function of this composition within the liturgy of the Burgundian court, it also helps to clarify the placement of text within the polyphony. A revised texting of the superius according to the text placement of its plainsong model is proposed in Ex. 4.4: the top line of text underlay duplicates that of the new Busnoys edition,[39] while the bottom line shows the suggested revision. This revised text underlay corresponds much more closely to the texting provided by the scribe in Brussels 5557 (see Fig. 4.1), who, as noted earlier, may have been the composer himself.[40] Discovery of the plainsong model for *Alleluia verbum*

Fig. 4.1. Brussels 5557, fo.89ᵛ

[37] *Busnoys LTW*, Commentary, 60.   [38] *Antiphonale Sarisburiense*, ii. 56.
[39] *Busnoys LTW*, Music, 129–31.
[40] Even the placement of text in the middle of a ligature (which, were the texting of the plainsong to be followed strictly, would occur in m. 3) appears to be suggested by the text underlay in Brussels 5557. This runs counter to 16th-c. theorists' prescriptions concerning text underlay for composers of Josquin's generation; see Edward E. Lowinsky, 'A Treatise on Text Underlay by a German Disciple of Francisco de Salinas',

Ex. 4.4. Busnoys, *Alleluia verbum caro factum est*, superius, compared with (*a*) plainchant *Alleluia verbum caro factum est* (Paris, B. n. lat. 10482, fo. 34ʳ)

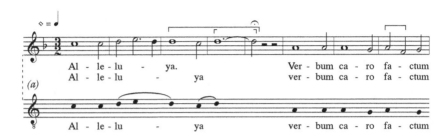

caro factum est thus suggests a certain authority for the text underlay of those works by Busnoys preserved in Brussels 5557, and supports the notion that composers translated even the details of their plainsong models' text underlay into their polyphonic settings.

Within the context of the liturgy and ritual observed by the Burgundian court chapel, the Vespers celebration on Assumption, Easter Sunday, and Low Sunday, and the Compline service on Christmas emerge as the most likely liturgical occasions for the rendition of four of Busnoys's cantus-firmus motets, though for two of these works a paraliturgical function appears more plausible. Moreover, in each case the possibility must be allowed that the plainsong tradition of Paris provided the composer with the models for his cantus firmi. But further investigation into the variety of usages known to Busnoys—particularly those of Tours and Poitiers—is necessary before even a tentative suggestion can be made as to the original destination or plainsong models of these four motets.

Although not included in the Burgundian court manuscript Brussels 5557, the *Missa O crux lignum* invites scrutiny regarding its possible association with that court. All recent literature about this mass mentions it in connection with the liturgy of Bruges, where Busnoys apparently spent his last years.[41] As Reinhard Strohm has observed, the people of Bruges venerated the Holy Cross with particular fervour, and, perhaps most suggestively, the particular strophe of the sequence *Laudes crucis attolamus* chosen by Busnoys as the basis for this mass stood by itself as the sequence for the feast of the Exaltation of the Cross in the liturgy of Bruges.[42] Recent research suggests, however, that the *Missa O crux lignum* was copied into its unique source, the papal choir manuscript Cappella Sistina 51, during Busnoys's period of service with Charles the Bold, possibly as long as a decade or more before the composer began his association with the church of St Salvator in Bruges.[43] Does the liturgy observed by the Court of Burgundy offer any clues to the original destination of this important work?

Within the rite of Paris, as in many French as well as other northern usages, well-established traditions favoured highlighting the internal verses of select sequences, identified in manuscripts by the rubric 'divisio'. One of the most popular *divisiones*, the strophe 'Ecce panis angelorum' from the Corpus Christi sequence *Lauda Sion salvatorem*, served a variety of special uses in churches from Lübeck to Langres, including Paris; this *divisio* also gave rise to several polyphonic settings.[44] Now *Lauda Sion salvatorem* employs the melody of *Laudes*

Festschrift Heinrich Besseler (Leipzig, 1961), 231–51, esp. 236; repr. in id., *Music in the Culture of the Renaissance and Other Essays*, ed. Bonnie J. Blackburn (Chicago and London, 1989), 868–83, esp. 873.

[41] Reinhard Strohm, *Music in Late Medieval Bruges* (rev. edn., Oxford, 1990), 142 and 253 n. 151; Wegman, 'Petrus de Domarto's *Missa Spiritus almus*', 263–4.

[42] Strohm, *Music in Late Medieval Bruges*, 145.

[43] On the dating of Cappella Sistina 51, see *Census-Catalogue*, iv. 51–2, where additional bibliography is provided.

[44] Bloxam, 'A Survey', 419–20.

crucis attolamus, and the verse 'Ecce panis angelorum' within the former corresponds melodically to the strophe 'O crux lignum' from the latter.[45] This coincidence may or may not be significant, but it appears likely that any usage
expressing a special fondness for 'Ecce panis angelorum', as did Paris, would also
acknowledge 'O crux lignum' in some fashion. And while the usage of Paris,
whose cathedral numbered among its prize relics a piece of the True Cross, did
not designate 'O crux lignum' for use alone on any feast-day, it did place special
emphasis on this verse during the performance of the complete sequence on the
feast of the Finding of the Cross. Missals according to the rite of Paris include
rubrics placed directly before the strophe 'O crux lignum' within the text of
Laudes crucis attolamus indicating the threefold acclamation of this verse.[46] This
repetition probably allowed for the execution of some ritual action, such as a
blessing (as was customary in connection with the 'Ecce panis angelorum' verse
at celebrations of the Holy Sacrament), or a congregational genuflection to the
reliquary. We cannot, therefore, on ground of its liturgical assignment rule out
the possibility that the *Missa O crux lignum* originated for use at the court of
Burgundy.

Melodic evidence, however, argues against the rite of Paris as the source of the
cantus firmus for this mass. As shown in Ex. 4.5, the tune of this verse differs dramatically from Busnoys's cantus firmus in the third phrase; not surprisingly, the
Parisian chant (Ex. 4.5*b*) here corresponds precisely to the melody created in the

Ex. 4.5. Busnoys, *Missa O crux lignum*, Kyrie II, opening of tenor, and plainchant:
(*a*) Bruges, Memling Museum, MS O.SJ210.I, fo. 220ᵛ (early 16th-c. gradual, usage of
Bruges(?)); (*b*) Baltimore, Walters Art Gallery, MS 302, fo. 239ʳ (early 15th-c. gradual,
usage of Paris)

[45] As was the case in the repertory of the hymn, the rhymed, metric text form of the late medieval
sequence lent itself to such wholesale recycling of existing melodies.
[46] This rubric appears, for example, in London, British Library, c. 29. l. 8, a missal for the usage of Paris
printed in Paris by Thielman Kerver in 1501.

twelfth century by the Parisian monk Adam of St Victor. Busnoys clearly modelled his cantus firmus on another version of the chant, and that version may well
have been that of Bruges. An early sixteenth-century gradual for the hospital of
St Mary Magdalene in Bruges, an institution under the jurisdiction of the collegiate church of St Donatian, transmits a version of the melody for 'O crux
lignum' that intersects exactly with the cantus firmus crafted by Busnoys (shown
in Ex. 4.5a). This gradual does not provide chants for the special feasts that identify the usage of Bruges; it is not certain, therefore, that the melodies preserved
in the book correspond to the indigenous chant tradition of the town.[47] At this
point we can simply observe that it appears unlikely that Busnoys composed the
Missa O crux lignum in response to the rite of Paris, and that Bruges remains a
possible destination for the piece. The next step for future research, for this piece
as for the other motets by Busnoys based on cantus firmi, requires delving into
the details of the musico-liturgical traditions that shaped the divine services at
Tours and Poitiers.

This preliminary inquiry into the origins, contexts, and implications of some of
Busnoys's plainsong cantus firmi demonstrates a variety of insights to be gleaned
even when the field of investigation is focused on only one particular liturgical
usage. Whether or not that local rite might have furnished a composer with his
plainsong model can be assessed, and the performance context of a mass or motet
evaluated in the context of that liturgical tradition. Recovery of the chant model
for an unidentified cantus firmus might clarify the function of and point to a
plausible origin for a particular polyphonic work. And reference to a composer's
possible plainchant sources might even spark reassessment of the text underlay
for a cantus firmus.

   Finally, the approach to fifteenth-century sacred polyphony here outlined and
exercised confirms that late medieval chant, in all its maddening richness and
diversity, furnished the scrim before which the ever-changing play of sacred
polyphony was acted out. To begin to appreciate the play in its entirety, we need
to keep that backdrop in constant view.

---

[47] A Hieronymite brother in Ghent copied the two volumes of this gradual (Bruges, Memling Museum,
MS O.SJ211.I and MS O.SJ210.I) for the hospital of St Mary Magdalene in Bruges in 1504 and 1506; see
Joseph Casier and Paul Bergmans, *L'Art ancien dans les Flandres (région de l'Escaut): Mémorial de l'exposition
retrospective organisée à Gand en 1913*, 2 vols. (Brussels, 1921), ii. 88–90. The gradual follows the usage of
the diocesan centre of Tournai.

5

The Ceremony of the Armed Man: The Sword, the Altar, and the *L'homme armé* Mass

୬ℜ ℜୢ

FLYNN WARMINGTON

WHILE the plague ravaged Florence in 1457, the prosperous merchant Giovanni Rucellai withdrew to a castle near Siena where, in enforced isolation, he began to set down a work imbued with the spirit of humanism, his *Zibaldone quaresimale*.[1] The title is witty: *zibaldone* was an odd Tuscan word for a minestrone or a large salad of mixed greens traditionally eaten in the penitential season of Lent, and its literary counterpart tosses together a great miscellany of food for serious thought. Here Rucellai, a member of the Florentine Academy, noted down quotations, ancient and modern, and memorabilia intended to assist his sons in the wise conduct of their lives.[2] A major church patron, Rucellai is remembered today mainly for donating the marble façade of the great Dominican church of Santa Maria Novella in Florence, a gift of which he was so immensely proud that, after the fashion of a Roman emperor, he had his name in Latin inlaid in majestic letters across the entire span of the building.[3] His religious concerns also appear in his *Zibaldone*, which we know from the excellent scholarly edition and commentaries edited by Alessandro Perosa.

Perosa, however, omitted a few passages he considered of minimal interest, such as 'some curious notices on the way of saying Mass'.[4] These he summarized

I am most grateful to Graeme Boone, Lewis Lockwood, Virginia Newes, Carla Zarilli, and Leeman Perkins for helping me to obtain rare materials for this paper, to Robert Levine for a translation, and to Paula Higgins for making it a possibility. The paper is dedicated to Hollace Schafer, who generously supplied a buoyancy critical to the author.

[1] See the edition and commentaries in Alessandro Perosa (ed.), *Giovanni Rucellai ed il suo Zibaldone. i: Il zibaldone quaresimale; ii: A Florentine Patrician and His Palace: Studies by Alessandro Perosa, Brenda Preyer, Piero Sanpaolesi, and Roberto Salvini*, intro. Nicolai Rubinstein (London, 1960–81). On the date, see i, pp. xii–xiii. On the meaning of the title, see Perosa, 'Lo Zibaldone di Giovanni Rucellai', in Perosa, *Giovanni Rucellai*, ii. 103–4.

[2] F. W. Kent, 'The Making of a Renaissance Patron', in Perosa, *Giovanni Rucellai*, ii. 15–16.

[3] See Perosa, *Giovanni Rucellai*, ii, pl. 33.   [4] Ibid. ii. 135 (quoted in translation).

in footnotes, and among them we find a laconic reference to a celebration of solemn Masses at the Abbey of Sant'Antimo, near Siena, during which an armed man stood 'beside the altar . . . with the bared sword in hand in defense of the Christian faith against whoever would contradict it'.[5] The existence of this curious ceremony naturally raises the question as to whether it might have any bearing, even obliquely, on the context surrounding the emergence of polyphonic masses based on the *L'homme armé* tune.[6] For what occasions were those masses written, and when were they performed? In this essay I shall investigate the armed Mass ceremonies Rucellai describes as possible contexts for *L'homme armé* masses. Although an improbable point of departure for this study, the Abbey of Sant'Antimo, situated about twenty miles south of Siena, stands next to the ancient *Via francigena*, the main pilgrimage road leading from Rome to Burgundy and France—the three locations associated with the origins of the *L'homme armé* tradition.[7]

The Mass of the Ceremony of the Armed Man at the Abbey of Sant 'Antimo

Fig. 5.1 shows the original manuscript of Rucellai's text. The portion that concerns us occupies a single folio (fo. 47^{r–v}) in the oldest layer of the manuscript, which is still owned by the Rucellai family.[8] The work of the main copyist evidently dates from 1457,[9] and an autograph insertion by Rucellai himself appears in the middle of the last column. A slightly abridged transcription and translation of the chapter are found in Appendix A. Rucellai begins with a historical introduction to the Abbey of Sant'Antimo explaining the authority the abbot has to use a special ceremony at Mass. He names Charlemagne as founder of the abbey and as the overlord who conferred full temporal powers on its abbot, including the power of the sword, the right literally 'to make blood', as Rucellai so neatly puts it. The abbey with its rich possessions is thus described as a fief of the Holy Roman Empire, with the abbot as both spiritual and temporal lord, whose duties include the defence of his territories.

---

[5] See Perosa, *Giovanni Rucellai*, 135 n. 6.

[6] On the *L'homme armé* tradition see Lewis Lockwood, '*L'homme armé*', in *New Grove*, x. 712–13; id., 'Aspects of the *L'Homme armé* Tradition', *Proceedings of the Royal Musical Association*, 100 (1973–4), 97–122; Richard Taruskin, 'Antoine Busnoys and the *L'Homme armé* Tradition', *JAMS* 39 (1986), 255–93, his correspondence with Rob Wegman in *JAMS* 42 (1989), 437–52, and *Busnoys LTW*, Commentary; Leeman L. Perkins, 'The *L'Homme Armé* Masses of Busnoys and Okeghem: A Comparison', *Journal of Musicology*, 3 (1984), 363–96; and Don Giller, 'The Naples L'Homme Armé Masses and Caron: A Study in Musical Relationships', *Current Musicology*, 32 (1981), 7–28.

[7] Richard Taruskin argues for a connection between some of the early *L'homme armé* masses and the Burgundian knightly Order of the Golden Fleece, which is certainly a strong possibility. See his article, 'Antoine Busnoys' and the correspondence cited above, n. 6. I do not argue against Taruskin's theories here, but seek to explore other possible contexts for some of the masses.

[8] Perosa, *Giovanni Rucellai*, ii, p. xiv.   [9] On the date, see ibid., ii. 135, and i, p. xii.

Though not entirely accurate, the historical information in Rucellai's account of Sant'Antimo reflects the traditional lore that was handed down even to this century. The originally Benedictine abbey does date back to Charlemagne's time, but no direct evidence indicates that he was the founder.[10] The earliest surviving document, a land grant from Louis the Pious, dates from December 813, a month before Charlemagne's death,[11] and the original ninth-century church still exists as the crypt. An imperial document probably dating from 952 conferred full temporalities upon the abbot.[12] The present monumental church was under construction in 1118, and at its peak the abbey held jurisdiction over thirty-eight churches.[13] By the end of the twelfth century, however, it had already fallen into decline, and after another hundred years it had degenerated into 'a state of temporal and spiritual collapse'. The lack of discipline among the Benedictines there led Pope Nicholas IV, in 1291, to turn the abbey and its possessions over to the Williamites.[14] They were a severe order of hermits founded a century earlier in a valley not far off that came to be known as 'Mala Valle' — 'Bad Valley' — a place of such fearsome desolation as to be virtually ideal for the mortification of the flesh.[15] But that site, prone to damaging floods, had also become infested with brigands.[16] By transferring the Williamites to Sant'Antimo, the pope sought to place the religious fervour of the hermits above the wealth and privilege of the abbey,[17] a union doomed from the start. Several documents of the fourteenth century attest to the strife-ridden cohabitation of Williamites and Benedictines.[18] By 1457, the time of Rucellai's writing, much of the abbey's fortune had been lost or squandered, and in 1462 it was to be secularized by Pius II. Until then, however, the abbot still claimed the prestigious imperial title of 'Count

[10] Charlemagne is first mentioned as founder of the abbey in a document of Emperor Henry III in 1051. See Antonio Canestrelli, *L'abbazia di S. Antimo: Monografia storico-artistica con documenti e illustrazioni* (Siena, 1910–12), 5 and 25 (Doc. II). On the legends about the foundation by Charlemagne, see pp. 3–4.

[11] Canestrelli (*Abbazia*, 4) gives the day as 29 Dec. The document is in the Archivio di Stato, Siena, prov. Riformagioni, parchment, under the date. Its text is printed in full as 'Documento I' in id., 'Ricerche storiche ed artistiche intorno all'Abbazia di S. Antimo', *Bullettino senese di storia patria*, 4 (1897), 72–4. Although one finds other dates for the foundation of the abbey in the literature, Kaspar Elm concurs with Canestrelli on the year and month of the land grant, but gives the day as 19 Dec. See his *Beiträge zur Geschichte des Wilhelmitenordens* (Münstersche Forschungen, 14; Cologne, 1962), 98.

[12] Canestrelli, *Abbazia*, 5 and n. 7. Also cited in Ferdinand Schevill, *Siena: The Story of a Mediaeval Commune* (New York, 1909), 41.

[13] Canestrelli, *Abbazia*, 11.

[14] Ibid. 15, and Doc. III, 25–6. In an earlier article, Canestrelli attributed the transfer of the abbey to a bull from Boniface VIII in 1298 ('Ricerche', 62).

[15] According to Alban Butler, St William, determined in 1155 to pursue a 'rigorous life', entered the 'frightful solitude' of 'a desolate valley for this purpose, the very sight of which was sufficient to strike the most resolute with horror'. His followers 'went barefoot, and their fasts were almost continual'. See *Lives of the Fathers, Martyrs and Other Principal Saints*, 5 vols. (London, [1928]), s.v. 'St. William of Maleval', i. 207–8.

[16] Canestrelli, *Abbazia*, 15.

[17] E[manuele] Repetti, *Dizionario geografico fisico storico della Toscana . . .*, 5 vols. (Florence, 1833–43), s.v. 'Abazia di S. Antimo', i. 3.

[18] Canestrelli, *Abbazia*, 15–16. Unless otherwise mentioned, the rest of this paragraph is based on this source. See App. A, n. 5 on the special claims of the Benedictines of this abbey.

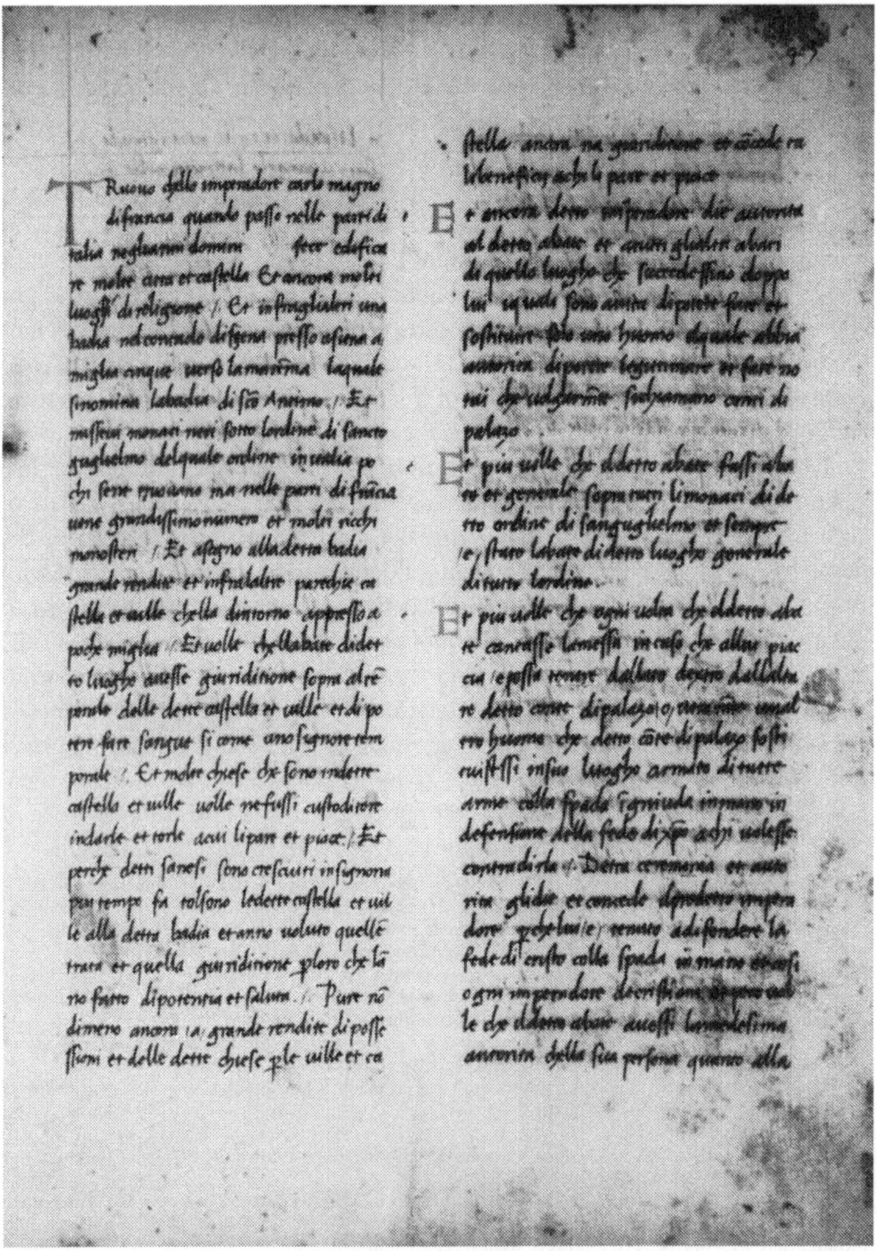

FIG. 5.1. Giovanni Rucellai, *Zibaldone quaresimale* (MS owned by Count Bernardo Rucellai), fo. 47ʳ⁻ᵛ. From a microfilm in the Warburg Institute, London

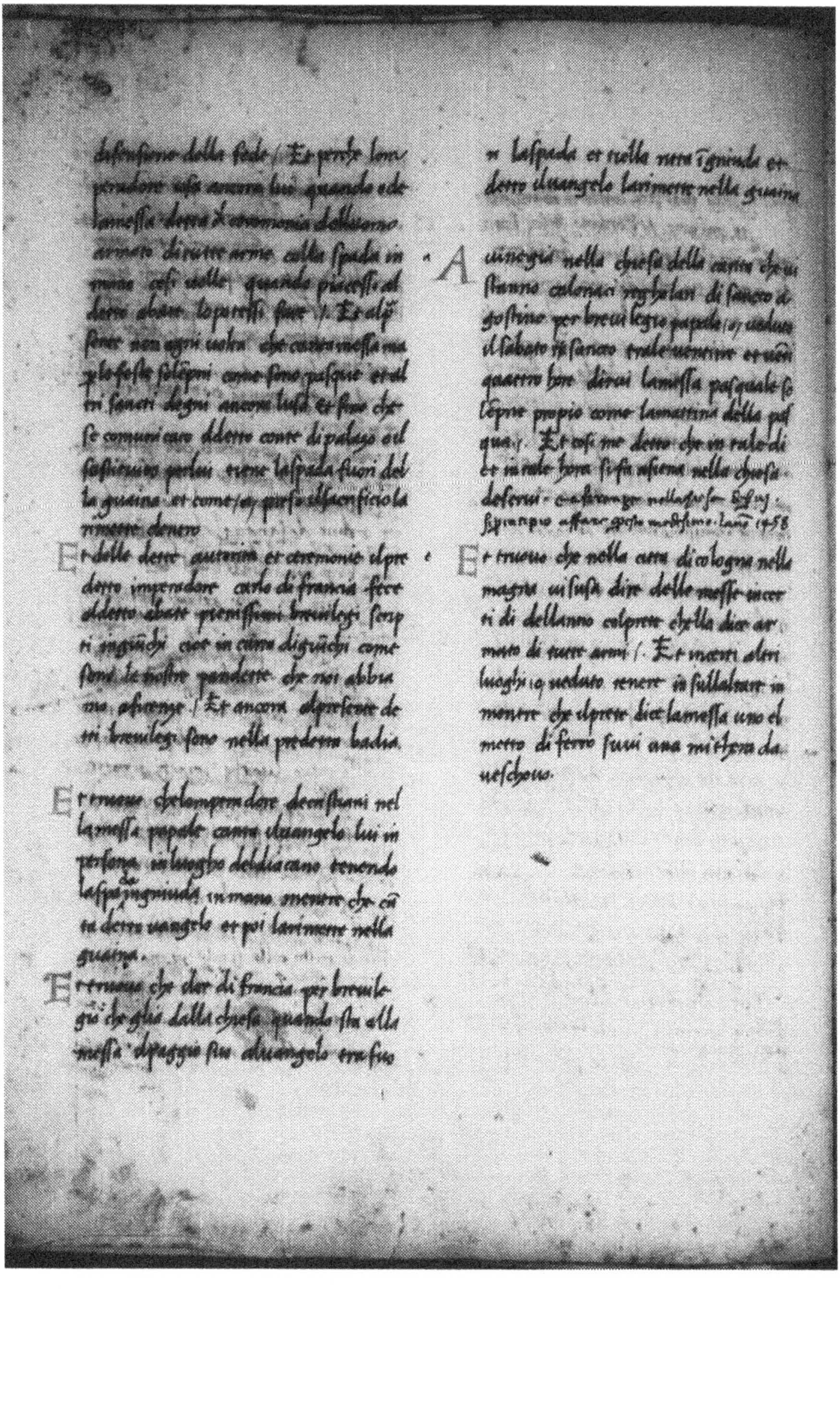
destrusione della fede / Et perche lom
peradore usa ancora lui quando e da
la messa detta d cerimonia dellaltorne
armato di tutte armi colla spada in
mano cosi stelle quando piacesse al
detto abate loparessi fare /. Et al
sono non ogni uolta che canta messa ma
p le feste solepni come sono pasque et al
tri santi degni ancora lusa et sono che
se comunicato ildetto conte di palagio et il
sustituto parlai tiene laspada fuori del
la guaina et come /e/ pursu il sacrificio la
rimette dentro

Et delle dette auctorita et ceremonie el pre
detto imperadore carlo di francia fece
aldetto abate pienissimi priuilegi scrip
ti insigniti cioe in citta diguachi come
sono le nostre pandette che noi abbia
mo afferma /. Et ancora el presente de
tti priuilegi sono nella predetta badia.

Et truouo che lomperadore de cristiani nel
la messa papale canta iluangelo lui in
persona in luogho deldiacono tenendo
laspada ignuda in mano mentre che cã
ta detto uangelo et poi larimette nella
guaina.

Et truouo che el re di francia per priuile
gio che glie dalla chiesa quando sta alla
messa el quale sta iluangelo tra fuo
ri laspada et tiella ritta ignuda et
detto iluangelo larimette nella guaina

A uinegia nella chiesa della carita che ui
stanno calonaci regholari di santo a
gostino per breui legge papale si costuma
il sabato santo tra le uentiere et uenti
quattro hore dirsi lamessa pasquale so
lepne propio come lamattina della pas
qua /. Et cosi me detto che in tal di
et in tal hora si fa a firenze nella chiesa
[illegible]
[illegible]

Et truouo che nella citta di cologna nelle
magiore uisusa dire delle messe certe
ri di dellanno elprete chella dice ar
mato di tutte armi /. Et in certi altri
luoghi io uedato tenere in sullaltare in
mentre che elprete dice lamessa uno el
metto di ferro suui una mitera da
ueschovo.

Palatine'[19] and accordingly used a seal permitted to imperial prince-bishops and prince-abbots: the sword crossed with the shepherd's crook,[20] a conjunction memorably condemned by Dante (see Fig. 5.2).[21] The imperial title and authority—temporal power claimed by an ecclesiastical leader—constitute the essential facts we need to know about Sant'Antimo.

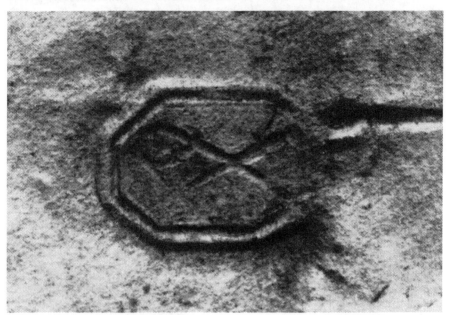

FIG. 5.2. Seal of Abbot of Sant'Antimo, with sword and crook, 1429. Siena, Archivio di Stato, Consistoro no. 1917, c. 2

[19] Under this title, the abbots exercised an almost sovereign power in their territory, where they made war, peace, and alliances (Repetti, *Dizionario*, i. 3, s.v. 'Abazia di S. Antimo'). Although the responsibility for military defence of the abbey had already been turned over to the city of Siena by the end of the 13th c., the title of 'Count Palatine' was retained until 1462, when it was transferred to the newly created bishop of Montalcino, who used it until the present century. See Canestrelli, *Abbazia*, 10 and 16.

[20] Significantly, the pastoral crook is on the heraldic dexter side, dominating the sword. The sword was used as an emblem of office by prince-bishops and prince-abbots until 1806. See the *Lexikon der christlichen Ikonographie*, 4 (Rome, 1972), s.v. 'Schwert'. A few other instances of the emblematic use of the sword by prelates give graphic confirmation of this practice. Jean de Cumenis, bishop and count of Le Puy en Velay, in 1307 used a seal (for his acts as count) that depicted him in episcopal habit and mitre holding the bared sword in his right hand and the episcopal cross in the left (Paul Delaroche, *Trésor de numismatique et de glyptique . . . xiii: Sceaux de communes, communautés, évêques, abbés et barrons* (Paris 1837), pl. 20, no. 7, and p. 37). See also the arms of the archbishop of Mainz (an imperial elector), which are marshalled on a sword, crozier, and pastoral staff in heraldic watermarks, in Charles-Moyse Briquet, *Les filigranes: Dictionnaire historique des marques des papiers de leur apparition vers 1282 jusqu'en 1600*, 4 vols. (2nd edn., Leipzig, 1923; repr. Amsterdam, 1968), i, nos. 2162 and 2164. See too nos. 1159 and 1160.

[21] For Dante's bitter remarks on the union of crook and sword, representing the Church's subjugation of temporal powers, see *Purgatorio* XVI. 106–14. Enlightening commentaries on this passage are found in James Bryce, *The Holy Roman Empire*, intro. by Hans Kohn (New York, 1961), 109, and in Dante Alighieri, *The Divine Comedy*, trans. with commentary by Charles S. Singleton, 3 vols. (Bollingen Series, 80; Princeton, 1973), ii. 365–70. Bryce refers to the jubilee year 1300, when Boniface VIII seated himself on the throne of Constantine and, with sword, crown, and sceptre, proclaimed himself emperor. Ferdinand Schevill made the connection between Sant'Antimo's temporal powers and the lines from Dante (*Siena*, 41).

After the historical introduction, Rucellai turns to the crucial paragraph of the text concerning the mass ceremony (see App. A, [4]):

And moreover he [Charlemagne] desired that every time the said abbot sang Mass, whenever he wished to he could have at the right side of the altar the said count of the palace, or another man that the said count of the palace would substitute in his place, armed with all arms with the drawn sword in his hand in defence of the faith of Christ against whoever would contradict it. This ceremony and authority was given and conceded to him by the aforesaid emperor because he is obliged to defend the faith of Christ with the sword in hand, and likewise every emperor of Christians, and therefore he wanted the said abbot to have the very same authority as himself with regard to the defence of the faith. And because the emperor himself, when he hears Mass, observes the aforesaid *ceremony of the armed man with all arms with the sword in hand* [italics mine], so he desired that when the abbot wished, he could do it. And at present, not every time that he sings Mass, but for solemn feasts like Easter and other worthy saints, he still does it. And until the said count of the palace or his substitute takes communion, he holds the sword unsheathed, and when he has partaken of the sacrifice, he puts it back in.

Rucellai clearly elucidates the ceremony and its meaning. The leading civil official appointed by the abbot stands in armour at the right side of the altar, the Epistle side. Opposite him would be the processional cross on the Gospel side, at the right hand of Christ on the Crucifix, a position of higher rank.

As Rucellai describes it, the ceremony was an imperial one that the abbot also had permission to use for Masses he celebrated himself in his own abbey—that is, for pontifical Masses, which have a more elaborate ritual than usual, with additional attendants. Though customarily required or expected for the major feasts of the year, such as Christmas, the main Marian feasts, and that of the abbey's titular saint, pontifical Masses could also be performed on other occasions that called for an extra degree of pomp. It is worth emphasizing that 'the Mass of the ceremony of the armed man' did *not* have any inherent topical connection, for instance, with soldier-saints. Only the importance of the feast and the desire of the abbot were criteria for its use.

The origins, or at least the age of the ceremony, are pertinent to our investigation because they surely impinge on the question of where else the Mass might have been performed. Rucellai states that Charlemagne used it and gave the authority to the abbot of Sant'Antimo, but this assertion cannot be taken as fact, since medieval institutions with historically nebulous origins often claimed Charlemagne, the hero of medieval romance, as their founder. A case in point is Rucellai's statement (found in Sienese chronicles as well) that Charlemagne gave Sant'Antimo to the Williamites: St William of Maleval, in whose honour that order was founded, lived more than three centuries after Charlemagne's death. There is also reason to think that the ceremony of the armed man was not as old as the abbey itself. First, it would not have been used at Sant'Antimo before the abbot received temporal powers, first documented in about 952. Secondly, it seems unlikely that Charlemagne used such a ceremony. The sword was not used in his imperial coronation, for instance;[22] it came to belong to the imperial insignia—bestowed by the pope—only in the later Middle Ages, when some of the Frankish and Saxon coronation rites were adapted for the emperor.[23] Rucellai gives another, less direct clue to the age of the ceremony (see App. A, [5]) when he states that the authority for it is given in privileges written on papyrus.

Papyrus? An inventory of important documents at Sant'Antimo, made in 1396, does mention three privileges evidently written on papyrus, 'tria privilegia de giunchis', but they no longer exist.[24] The material deteriorates when the climate is damp, and so we have lost most of the European documents in that medium. We do know, however, that papyrus documents could not date from after the early eleventh century, when even the most conservative institutions, like the Vatican chancery, had to give up using the venerable material when the necessary reeds from the Nile delta could no longer be obtained.[25] Rucellai's mention of a privilege written on papyrus, then, would lead us to believe that the ceremony of the armed man goes back at least to the eleventh century. This account poses some problems as well, however. The statement that the ceremony was instituted by Charlemagne—even in a broad reading—conflicts with the statement that the document is on papyrus: Charlemagne and his successors did not use papyrus.[26] The famous manuscript of the pandects of Justinian preserved

---

[22] For four accounts of Charlemagne's coronation, see Brian Pullan, *Sources for the History of Medieval Europe from the Mid-Eighth to the Mid-Thirteenth Century* (Oxford, 1971), 4–11.

[23] See Elisabeth Cornides, *Rose und Schwert im päpstlichen Zeremoniell von Anfängen bis zum Pontifikat Gregors XII* (Vienna, 1967), 34. Although she states that the first evidence of the bestowal of the sword in the imperial coronation rite is from the mid-12th c., she then refers to such a ceremony in the Ordo Cencius II, which she dates to the *first half* of the 12th c. Reinhard Elze gives the same date for the origin of this *ordo* in his edition of the Latin texts of the imperial coronation ceremonies, *Die Ordines für die Weihe und Krönung des Kaisers und Kaiserin* (Fontes Iuris Germanici Antiqui in Usum Scholarum ex Monumenta Germaniae Historicis Separatim Editi, 1, Ordines Coronationis Imperialis; Hannover, 1960), 35. According to Brian Pullan, however, the Ordo Cencius II (which he calls 'imperial coronation Ordo C') 'very likely' goes back another century and was first used in 1014 (*Sources*, 122 and 123–7 for an extract in English). In this source, the pope girds the emperor with the sword at the altar of St Maurice, in St Peter's, saying, 'Receive this sword, conferred on you with the blessing of God; and with this [by virtue of the Holy Spirit] may you succeed in resisting and expelling all the enemies of your own and of the Church of God and in guarding the realm entrusted to you and in protecting the fortresses of God with the aid of the invincible victor Our Lord Jesus Christ . . .' (Pullan, *Sources*, 126; the added clause is from Elze, *Ordines*, 43). For an earlier example of the sword in the coronation ceremonies of Frankish and Saxon kings, see the rite for the coronation of Otto of Saxony (the future Emperor Otto I) at Aachen in 936 (Pullan, *Sources*, 114–15). Cornides reviews the history of the sword in imperial coronations and the borrowings from German and Frankish rites (*Rose und Schwert*, 34–6) but she omits the texts of the two ceremonies quoted by Pullan.

[24] Canestrelli, *Abbazia*, 42. An early modern historian, Sigismondo Tizio, also claimed to have seen two documents from Charlemagne at Sant'Antimo. See ibid. 4.

[25] See H. Gerstinger, 'Papyrology', in *The New Catholic Encyclopedia*, x. 982, and Donald Jackson, *The Story of Writing* (New York, 1981), 68.

[26] See Edward Maunde Thompson, 'Papyrus', in the *Encyclopaedia Britannica*, 13th edn., xix. 745, who also states that papyrus was the exclusive material for papal deeds in the 10th c. There is at least one instance of a papal bull of 998 on papyrus that was 'jointly authorized' by Emperor Otto III, and thus could be seen as an imperial document. See George E. Holmes (ed.), *The Oxford Illustrated History of Medieval Europe* (Oxford, 1988), 140.

in Florence, moreover, is not written on papyrus, as Rucellai says, but on parchment.[27] Given the number of inaccuracies in Rucellai's information, we can draw from it only the most general conclusion: that at the time of his writing the ceremony was considered extremely old and authorized by imperial privilege.

The Emperor in the Papal Mass and Christmas Matins

The remainder of Rucellai's text deals with similar Mass ceremonies elsewhere. First, in paragraph six (App. A, [6]), he mentions the 'papal Mass' wherein the emperor serves as deacon and holds up the bared sword while he reads the Gospel.[28] To evaluate the authority of this statement, several elements must be separated: the emperor's acting as deacon in reading the Gospel, his baring of the sword, and the occasions suited to performing these rites. As part of the special reverence given to the Gospel as the Word of God, its reading was reserved for deacons or priests.[29] Many scholars report that the Holy Roman Emperor, alone among laymen, could be a Gospel reader.[30] Some authorities say that the medieval emperor read or sang the Gospel at Christmas Mass,[31] and the great

[27] This manuscript, in the Biblioteca Laurenziana, is the most important source of the pandects, or Digest, of Justinian law, and it probably dates from the second half of the 6th c. It was brought to Florence as part of the war booty after the conquest of Pisa in 1406. See H. F. Jolowicz, *Historical Introduction to the Study of Roman Law* (2d edn.; Cambridge, 1952), 500–1. The manuscript drew the attention of humanists in Florence, a group to which Rucellai belonged, and Angelo Poliziano transcribed the text late in the century. See Th. Mommsen, *Digesta Iustiniani Augusti*, 2 vols. (Berlin, 1870), i, p. xv, and ii, pl. 1–4, and Anna Lenzuni, et al., Biblioteca Medicea Laurenziana, Firenze (Le Grandi biblioteche d'Italia; Florence, 1986), pl. 6–7.

[28] A 'papal Mass' referred only to solemn high Masses (pontifical Masses) in which the pope was the celebrant. See *A Catholic Dictionary (The Catholic Encyclopedia Dictionary)*, ed. Donald Atwater (3rd edn.; New York, 1958), s.v. 'papal mass'. For the model ceremonial of a papal or solemn Mass, see Marc Dykmans, SJ, *L'Œuvre de Patrizi Piccolomini ou le cérémonial papale de la première renaissance*, 2 vols. (Studi e Testi, 293–4; Vatican City, 1980–2), ii. 176* ff.

[29] Joseph A. Jungmann, *The Mass of the Roman Rite: Its Origins and Development (Missarum Sollemnia)*, trans. Francis A. Brunner, 2 vols. (New York, 1955), i, pt. III, ch. 2, §6, p. 443.

[30] The explanation commonly given is that the emperor was made a cleric at his coronation. According to James Bryce, for example, the emperor 'is ordained a sub-deacon, assists the Pope in celebrating mass, partakes as a clerical person in the communion in both kinds, [and] is admitted a canon of St. Peter and St. John Lateran' as well as St Mary's in Aachen (*Holy Roman Empire*, 112 and 273). His sacred function 'was supposed to preserve' the title of *pontificatus maximus* of the ancient emperors (p. 273). Elisabeth Cornides, however, states that the emperor was not ordained, but only exercised certain ecclesiastical privileges, which came from the coronation rite and from the 'King's Canonry' the emperor or German king had in Germany and Rome, that of St Peter's going back to the end of the 12th c. (*Rose und Schwert*, 37). In addition to the three canonries just mentioned, there was another German king's canonry in Basle (*Rose und Schwert*, 38).

[31] J. Brückmann mentions the medieval emperor's Christmas Gospel reading at Mass as part of his 'special liturgical and canonical status': 'he was, at least before the Gregorian Reform [1076–1122], quite clearly not simply a layman but, by virtue of his position, stood equally above clerics and laymen. His name was read in the Canon of the Mass; he sang the Gospel in the sanctuary at Christmas . . .'. See J. Brückmann, 'The Holy Roman Empire', *New Catholic Encyclopedia*, vii. 93. Brückmann notes (p. 95) that after the Gregorian Reform the emperors were 'unable to maintain their liturgical sacred status'. Another authority, Joseph Jungmann, agrees that 'on Christmas night it became the privilege of the Roman Emperor to stand forth in full regalia to deliver the Gospel: *Exiit edictum a Caesare Augusto*' (*Mass*, 443). Archdale King concurs; see *Liturgies of the Past* (Milwaukee, 1959), 36. To document this practice, however, he has recourse to a single 18th-c. source, which in turn cites only three individual instances in which the emperors Charles IV, Sigismund, and Frederick III were observed to read the Gospel at Christmas. The last two of these cases, however, were actually readings of the seventh Matins lesson, as will be seen below.

nineteenth-century encyclopedist Gaetano Moroni notes that the emperor did this at Mass *in the papal chapel, holding up the bared sword*,[32] a statement that confirms Rucellai's but restricts the rite to a single feast-day.[33] Papal ceremonial books and a few passages in chronicles provide more exact information on the imperial ceremony in the fourteenth and fifteenth centuries.

The ritual practices of the popes are set down in the ordinals, or ceremonials, written by the masters of ceremonies.[34] The three earliest of these to prescribe such a rite, but for Christmas *Matins* rather than Mass, come from the papal court in the fourteenth century,[35] beginning with that by Jean de Sion at Avignon, *c*.1342–56,[36] followed by the collection of Bindo Fesulani, which has been dated 1377,[37] and ending with the more detailed work, dated between 1375 and 1400, of Pierre Ameil.[38] Ameil's ceremony, quoted in App. B, set the pattern for

[32] Gaetano Moroni (comp.), *Dizionario di erudizione storico-ecclesiastico da S. Pietro sino ai nostri giorni . . .*, 103 vols. in 53 (Venice, 1840–61), s.v. 'Evangelio', xxii. 231.

[33] Moroni also states that in his day, whenever the emperor appeared at Mass dressed in his imperial attire, he stood and raised his sceptre at the Gospel reading, holding the imperial globe in his other hand (ibid. 232). Perhaps this is a latter-day modification of the sword-bearing: both sword and sceptre are part of the imperial regalia. See Jonathan W. Zophy (ed.), *The Holy Roman Empire: A Dictionary Handbook* (Westport, Conn., 1980), s.v. 'Imperial Regalia'.

[34] For a critical list of manuscripts of papal ceremonials from the 13th through the early 16th c., see App. II in Marc Dykmans, SJ, 'Mabillon et les interpolations de son *Ordo romanus XIV* ', *Gregorianum*, 47 (1966), 338–42. For a review of papal ceremonial books from the 12th through the end of the 15th c., see Bernhard Schimmelpfennig, *Die Zeremonienbücher der römischen Kurie im Mittelalter* (Tübingen, 1973), 6–141.

[35] The complete series of six texts for this ceremony (plus a rewording of one text), from the 14th through the early 16th c., was published by Cornides in 1967, in *Rose und Schwert*, 136–42. Since then, the first five of the ceremonials containing these texts—all but the early 16th-c. text of Paride de' Grassi—have appeared in critical editions by Marc Dykmans and Bernhard Schimmelpfennig. These will be cited below. Because of the transmission pattern of the ceremony in papal sources, Cornides theorized that it originated in Avignon (p. 56).

[36] See Marc Dykmans, SJ, *Le Cérémonial papal de la fin du moyen âge à la Renaissance*, iii: *Les Textes avignonnais jusqu'à la fin du grand schisme d'occident* (Bibliothèque de l'Institut historique belge de Rome, 26; Brussels, 1983), 244, no. 267. Here it is not necessarily the emperor himself who performs the ceremony before the pope, but 'a certain one of the empire': 'In matutinis nativitatis Domini debet dicere quintam lectionem quidam de imperio, indutus pluviali, et super pluviali cinctus ense. Et cum legit ipsam lectionem, debet tenere ensem evaginatum in manu, et capellum de viebro, vel aliquod aliud solemne, folratum de variis, in capite. Et lecta lectione vadit ad osculum pedis domini nostri pape, amoto prius capello. Et facta huiusmodi reverentia dominus noster dat capellum predictum alicui de sibi circumstantibus.' A later source of de Sion's ceremonial, Dykmans's manuscript D, specifies for the reader of the fifth lesson: 'quidam de imperio: imperator vel rex si ibi intersit, aut alter nobilium ibidem presens' (Dykmans, *Cérémonial papal*, 244, no. 267). This manuscript seems to date from the period between 1370 and 1394 (ibid. 242 n. 158). For another edition of the passage, see Cornides, *Rose und Schwert*, 136–7, col. 1. Cornides also points out that the earliest armed readers were representatives of the emperor at the papal court (p. 64).

[37] The Bindo Fesulani collection was published by Bernhard Schimmelpfennig, *Zeremonienbücher*, 256, ch. 49, sect. 4. Here the reader of the fifth lesson, with bared sword in hand, is specified as 'the emperor, if he is present, or in his place another great nobleman, if he is in the chapel'. The sword and hat are described in greater detail: it is a 'noble sword with a golden belt', the cap is made of fur with pearls and precious stones, and both sword and cap are given by the pope to the emperor or nobleman after the ceremony. The text is excerpted by Cornides, *Rose und Schwert*, 137, under the title 'Vat. lat. 4726'.

[38] Marc Dykmans, SJ, *Cérémonial papal*, iv: *Le retour à Rome ou le cérémonial du patriarche Pierre Ameil* (Bibliothèque de l'Institut historique belge de Rome, 27; Brussels, 1985), 75–6, paras. 55–8. This is a critical edition of the text that has long been known as *Ordo Romanus XV*, as entitled in the publication of fifteen medieval Roman ordinals (the *Ordines Romani*) by Jean Mabillon and Michel Germain, *Musaeum italicum seu collectio scriptorum bibliotecis italicis . . .*, 2 vols. (1687–9; 2nd edn., 1724), ii. 452; reprinted by J.-P. Migne, *Patrologiae latinae tomus 78: Sanctus Gregorius Magnus* (Patrologiae cursus completus, Series latina,

the papal court after its return to Rome, in 1378, and presumably until after 1450.[39]

Ameil stipulates that the emperor, or a king, may take part in the papal service of Christmas Matins (immediately before midnight Mass). He is vested in a combination of ecclesiastical and military raiment. To the white pluvial (a priest's long cape) are added the sword, sword-belt, sheath, and pileus—a distinctive hat, sometimes called a ducal hat, used to lead troops in battle.[40] As in Rucellai's description, the emperor holds up the bared sword while he gives one of the readings, but here it is the fifth Matins lesson, a homily that could be read by a layman. There are additional elements here as well: the brandishing of the sword, the blessing by the pope, and the kissing of the pope's foot. The brandishing of the bared sword is an element traced back to a twelfth-century rite for the emperor's coronation in St Peter's and to the rites for dubbing knights.[41]

The later ceremonial books of Agostino Patrizi (written between 1486 and 1488) and Paride de' Grassi describe the rite in greater detail.[42] The precise mode

---

78; Paris, 1848), col. 1278 B–C. Cornides excerpts the sword ceremony from *Ordo Romanus XV* in *Rose und Schwert*, 138. The Ameil ceremony also appears, in varied wording, in marginal glosses added in the late 15th c. to the manuscript Rome, Biblioteca Apostolica Vaticana, MS Vat. lat. 5747, the main text of which is a ceremonial of Cardinal Jacobus Gaietani de Stephaneschi (d. 1341, according to Dykmans). A copy of this manuscript was used for Mabillon's edition of the Stephaneschi ceremonial, which thus conflated the main text with the glosses from Ameil: *Ordo Romanus XIV* (*Musaeum italicum*, ii. 325–6; reprinted in Migne (ed.), *Patrologiae latinae tomus 78*, col. 1182 C–D). This edition, long a standard reference, is now called 'pseudo-Stephaneschi'. See Marc Dykmans, SJ, 'Mabillon', 316–42, especially 317 n. 6, on the publication history of *Ordo Romanus XIV*, and 317 and 339 on the 1341 death date of Stephaneschi. For a critical edition of Stephaneschi's ceremonial, from which the Christmas Matins ceremony with the sword has been expunged, see Marc Dykmans, SJ, *Cérémonial papal, ii: De Rome en Avignon ou le cérémonial de Jacques Stephaneschi* (Bibliothèque de l'Institut historique belge de Rome, 25; Brussels, 1981). The version of the Ameil sword ceremony found in the marginal glosses in MS Vat. lat. 5747 also appears in Cornides, *Rose und Schwert*, 136–7, col. 2. Dykmans most recently gives the copying date for these glosses as *c*.1485 (*Cérémonial papal*, iv. 75 n. 18).

[39] A fourth papal ceremonial to contain the Christmas Matins rite (from the manuscript Rome, Biblioteca Apostolica Vaticana, MS 4727), was also published by Schimmelpfennig (*Zeremonienbücher*, 294, ch. 82, no. 5), and earlier by Cornides, *Rose und Schwert*, 137. Schimmelpfennig dates it to the time of the anti-pope Benedict XIII (*c*.1403–8) in Avignon; Dykmans associated it with Benedict's chamberlain François Conzié ('Mabillon', 341). One manuscript of the Ameil ceremonial, however, also transmits additions made by one of his successors, Pierre Assalbit, 'sacrist at least from 1417 to 1438', which suggests that Ameil's text remained in use in Rome (ibid. 341). In the time of Calixtus III (1455–8), another ceremonial is known to have been prepared by Antoine Rébiol, but it is lost (ibid.). A text of Rébiol's that describes the ceremony used at Christmas in 1454 is quoted in the early 16th-c. ceremonial of Paride de' Grassi, in a passage excerpted in Cornides, *Rose und Schwert*, 142.

[40] Some later ordinals use the word *galera* (helmet) instead of *pileus*, but the descriptive words used with it—'made of beaver with pearls'—suggest that the same kind of hat is being described. For example, the ceremonial of Agostino Patrizi, completed in 1488, refers to the 'ensem cum capello de bevaro cum perlis' (see Dykmans, *L'Œuvre*, ii. 285–6; on the date, see i. *27 ff.). In the version cited by Cornides (*Rose und Schwert*, 139), the phrase is *galera de bevaro cum perlis*.

[41] Cornides, *Rose und Schwert*, 35 and 59. According to Giuseppe Vale, sword-brandishing was mentioned as part of the 1366 ceremony of investiture for the patriarch of Aquileia, in the duomo of Cividale del Friuli, and it was also part of the coronation ceremony of the king of Hungary and the duke of Carinthia. See his article, 'La ceremonia della spada ad Aquileia e Cividale', *Rassegna gregoriana di liturgia*, 7 (1908), col. 43.

[42] For Patrizi's text, see Dykmans, *L'Œuvre*, ii. 285–9 (bk. 2, ch. 11, especially nos. 810–12 and 821–4; on the date, vol. i. 69*), also published with related texts (from a different source) in Cornides, *Rose und Schwert*, 139–40. For that of Paride de' Grassi, edited from Rome, Biblioteca Apostolica Vaticana, MS Vat. lat. 5634 *bis*, see Cornides, *Rose und Schwert*, 141–2.

of sword-brandishing, for example, corresponds with the description used for the coronation and dubbing: three vertical sword-strokes, down to touch the ground, after which the blade is drawn across the left sleeve to symbolize the wiping-off of the blood.[43] Nothing in the papal ceremonials, however, refers to the emperor's reading the Gospel at *Mass*, with or without the raised sword.

Apart from the papal ceremonials, a few chronicles describe the emperor's own Christmas rites. From the fourteenth century, something of Charles IV's practice in his own realm was described for the years 1347 (Basle), 1355 (Nuremberg), 1356 (Metz), and 1377 (Cambrai).[44] Since the pope was not present, these were clearly imperial rather than papal ceremonies. The first notice indicates that as King of the Romans (emperor-elect), Charles used an armed ritual when he visited Basle in 1347: on Christmas night in the cathedral, dressed as a deacon, he held up the bared sword while giving a reading. A contemporary chronicler states explicitly that he read the Gospel at midnight Mass, and this description was long accepted.[45] One recent authority, however, considers that the emperor more likely raised his sword for a Matins reading, as in the papal ceremony just considered, but with a shift from the fifth lesson to the seventh.[46] This lesson is a commentary on the Gospel of the midnight Mass (hence the confusion), and it begins by quoting the Gospel incipit: *Exiit edictum a Caesare Augusto, ut describeretur universus orbis*, 'An edict went out from Caesar Augustus, through all the world'. In addition to the religious privilege and honour of reading the words of the Gospel, the emperor's preference for this particular text has another obvious cause: it implies a parallel between himself, the new Caesar 'semper Augustus', and the Augustus whose peaceful reign was chosen by God for the coming of the Messiah. Revered in the Middle Ages as a prophet and the model for the Holy Roman emperors, Augustus could well be seen as the prototypical imperial armed man.[47]

---

[43] Cornides, *Rose und Schwert*, 59 and 140–1; Dykmans, *L'Œuvre*, ii. 288, no. 822.

[44] Cornides, *Rose und Schwert*, 38.

[45] The chronicle is quoted, with full bibliography, in Heinrich Modern, 'Geweihte Schwerter und Hüte in den k. h. Sammlungen des Allerhöchsten Kaiserhauses', *Jahrbuch der k. h. Sammlungen des A. H. Kaiserhauses*, 22 (1901), 133. Although the chronicler was previously identified as Mathias von Neuenburg, he has also been identified as Albert von Hohenberg. See Emil Werunsky, *Geschichte Kaiser Karls IV. und seiner Zeit*, 2 vols. in 3 (New York, 1961), ii, pt. 1, 102–3. The testimony that the ceremony in Basle was at the Mass is accepted by Modern and Werunsky, as well as King, *Liturgies*, 36. Trithemius, the German humanist (d. 1516), gives a similar account of the 1347 ceremony in Basle, which is also quoted by Modern, 'Geweihte Schwerter', 133 n. 3.

[46] Dykmans, *Cérémonial papal*, iii. 244 n. 164. According to Dykmans, Matins was confused with the Mass. Cornides simply refers to Charles IV's Christmas readings as either the Matins lesson or the Gospel in the Mass (*Rose und Schwert*, 38).

[47] On the imitation of ancient forms by the Holy Roman emperors, especially in connection with the emperor Augustus, see Bryce, *Holy Roman Empire*, 273–4. The title 'semper Augustus' or 'perpetuus Augustus' was 'the constant title of the Holy Roman emperor'; 'annalists usually number the place of each sovereign from Augustus downwards'; and the room in which the emperor-elect stayed in Rome in preparation for his coronation was called 'the room of Augustus'. Surpassing Augustus and all other models, the ultimate armed man was undoubtedly Christ, the 'invincible victor' (see n. 23 above and App. E).

We do have an unambiguous description of the emperor's Christmas ceremony thirty years later. Fig. 5.3 shows a miniature of Charles IV performing the
seventh lesson, sword in hand, at Christmas Matins 1377 in Cambrai, an occasion of importance amply treated in the chronicles of France.[48] On a state visit to
the king, Charles had planned to celebrate Christmas at Saint-Quentin, but his
escorts informed him that the king would not permit him to 'faire ses
magnificences et estaz imperiaulz', including the reading of the lesson (and by
implication the baring of the sword), on French soil.[49] Rather than give up the
imperial Christmas ceremony, he delayed his trip in order to celebrate it in
Cambrai, where the bishop held his territory as a fief of the Empire. This episode
demonstrates the importance the emperor attached to this ceremony, with its
dramatic display of the sacred authority for his military power. The practice evidently derives from the traditions of the German kings and emperors in exercising
their liturgical duties in churches in which they were titular canons.[50]

FIG. 5.3. Emperor Charles IV reading the seventh lesson
(from the Gospel) at Christmas Matins, Cambrai, 1377.
Paris, Bibliothèque nationale, MS f. fr. 2813, fo. 467ᵛ, col. 2
(14th c.)

[48] See R. Delachenal (ed.), *Chronique des règnes de Jean II et de Charles V*, 4 vols. (Les Grandes chroniques
de France; Paris, 1910–20), ii. 199; and iv, pl. 32, described on pp. 30–1.

[49] *Chronique des règnes de Jean II et de Charles V*, ii. 199. Marc Bloch states that this prohibition was
because 'they would not have allowed the Emperor to perform in public a religious office that could not be
carried out by the king of France'. See *The Royal Touch: Sacred Monarchy and Scrofula in England and France
(Les rois thaumaturges)*, trans. J. E. Anderson (London, 1973), 118.

[50] Cornides, *Rose und Schwert*, 39. See above, n. 30, for 'king's canonries'.

Later chroniclers on two occasions in the fifteenth century observed the emperor reading this seventh Matins lesson at Christmas, with the sword, in the presence of the pope (a departure from the fifth lesson specified in the early ceremonials). The emperor-elect Sigismund, King of the Romans and of Hungary, seems to have done so at the Council of Constance in 1414,[51] and in 1468, when Emperor Frederick III visited Rome on a pilgrimage to fulfil a penitential vow, he became the first emperor to perform the ceremony at the Vatican. Frederick insisted on reading only the beginning of the seventh Matins lesson—the Gospel text incipit without the homily—and he also made some other changes in the ritual.[52] His squire held the sword upright throughout the service and gave it to him just for the 'triple' brandishing before the pope. The emperor's dress was also somewhat modified.[53] Agostino Patrizi was later to use his observations of 1468 as the basis for his papal ceremonial of 1486–8, thus making the emperor's own practice official for Christmas Matins before the pope.[54] Rucellai's statement that the emperor held up the sword while he read the Gospel in the *papal Mass*, then, does not find confirmation from papal ceremonials or chronicles critically evaluated by earlier scholars, and so it would appear to be slightly inaccurate and to refer rather to Matins immediately before the first Christmas Mass; but if so, his was a common error made by early witnesses and repeated by modern liturgists.[55]

[51] *Chronique du religieux de Saint-Denys, contenant le règne de Charles VI, de 1380 à 1422*, ed. and trans. by L. Bellaguet (Collection de documents inédits sur l'histoire de France, series 1, Histoire politique, 5; Paris, 1844), 470: 'et pour complaire à l'empereur, il [anti-pope John XXIII] voulut que le jour de Noël, à l'office du matin, ce prince chantât, l'épée nue à la main, suivant l'usage, et en signe de sa dignité impériale, l'évangile *Exiit edictum a Caesare Augusto*'. A supposed eyewitness, Corrado Boiani, ambassador from Cividale, writes, however, that Sigismund read the *fifth* lesson, wearing a crown (Vale, 'Ceremonia', col. 28 n. 4). M. Creighton, Heinrich Modern, Joseph A. Jungmann, and Archdale King describe the reading (erroneously, it seems), as being in the [midnight] Mass on Christmas. They evidently follow early, but not contemporary chronicles. Vale (ibid., cols. 27–8) refers to Trithemius, and Modern cites Cochlaeus (d. 1552). Creighton adds that Sigismund acted as deacon and that the emblems of state (the sceptre, the drawn sword, and the 'golden apple of the Empire') were borne by the Margrave of Brandenburg, the Elector of Saxony, and the Count of Cilly, respectively. See M. Creighton, *A History of the Papacy from the Great Schism to the Sack of Rome* (London, 1919), i. 312; Modern, 'Geweihte Schwerter', 133 (with the date mistakenly given as 1415); Jungmann, *The Mass*, 443 n. 9 (based on secondary sources); and King, *Liturgies*, 36.
[52] Agostino Patrizi, the papal master of ceremonies, wrote about the service in his detailed description of the emperor's visit to Rome in 1468, *De adventu Friderici III*, reprinted from the first edition by Ludwig Biehl in *Das liturgische Gebet für Kaiser und Reich: Ein Beitrag zur Geschichte des Verhältnisses von Kirche und Staat* (Görres-Gesellschaft, 75; Paderborn, 1937), 155–7. (See also 100 ff. on Charles IV and Sigismund reading the Gospel lesson at Mass.) Heinrich Modern also published a detailed synopsis of the text ('Geweihte Schwerter', 134–5), and Cornides summarizes the changes Frederick III made in the ritual, in *Rose und Schwert*, 57. Patrizi reviewed some of this material in his ceremonial of 1486–8 (Dykmans, *L'Œuvre*, i. 147*–148* (synopsis), and ii, nos. 535–40 (text). Early editions of the full text are found in Lodovico Antonio Muratori (ed. and comp.), *Rerum italicarum scriptores . . .*, 23 (1733), cols. 203–16, especially 210–11*; Hieronymus Pez (ed.), *Scriptores rerum austriacarum*, 3 vols. (1721–45), ii. 615–16; and J. Mabillon, (ed.), *Musaeum italicum*, 2 vols. (1689), i, pt. 2, 255–72.
[53] The opening of his pluvial is in the centre, 'ad morem Sacerdotum' (rather than on the right side), with the stola in the form of a cross in front, as seen on the great imperial seal (Patrizi, *De adventu Friderici III*, in Biehl, *Das liturgische Gebet*, 156).
[54] Dykmans, *L'Œuvre*, i. 175*.
[55] It conforms with the description of the emperors Charles IV and Sigismund on their own territories in 1347 and 1377.

The King of France at the Gospel

In the seventh paragraph, Rucellai describes a ceremony at the court of France in which the king's page holds up a sword, again during a Gospel reading, but here we have no reason to doubt that it is the Gospel of the Mass. The Gospel, as the Word of God, has been accorded many ceremonies of special reverence over the course of the centuries, just as the book itself is often enclosed in particularly elaborate covers, sometimes studded with gems, or with silver or gold panels set with reliefs.[56] The immediate meaning of the French sword-baring ceremony parallels that associated with the emperor in his own territories: the king will defend the Church against the forces opposed to it.[57] The ceremony, however, is here reduced to a single element, the raising of the bared sword, and our text gives no hint of any connection with a particular feast. The presence of the sword-bearer, however, suggests that these were state occasions of some formality, and there are other pieces of information demonstrating that the French kings imitated the rituals of the emperor.[58] I have not been able to confirm their display of the sword during the Gospel, but an important sword, borne by a noble lord, was indeed used in French coronation rites and in royal entries, which culminated in Mass at a cathedral.[59]

A striking parallel to the French practice Rucellai describes can also be noted at the English court. Early in his reign, Henry VIII pressed Leo X to award him a title of honour like those of the kings of France and Spain,[60] 'Most Christian' and 'Catholic'.[61] At last, in 1521, Leo awarded Henry the title 'Defender of the Faith',

---

[56] See Jungmann, *Mass*, i. 442–55.

[57] In addition to the ancient papal title 'Most Christian' given to the kings of France, other titles also mirror those of the emperor and reflect the king's duty to protect the Church. See André Bossuat, 'The Maxim "The King is Emperor in his Kingdom": Its Use in the Fifteenth Century before the Parlement of Paris', in P. S. Lewis (ed.), *The Recovery of France in the Fifteenth Century*, trans. G. F. Martin (London, 1971), 185–95. Some examples are the titles 'protector of the Church of France' (1430) and *protecteur et deffenseur de l'église* (1493). See John A. F. Thompson, 'Popes and Princes, 1417–1517', in J. H. Shennan (ed.), *Politics and Polity in the Late Medieval Church* (Early Modern Europe Today; London, 1980), 52. For other examples, see M. G. A. Vale, *Charles VII* (Berkeley, 1974), 196–7.

[58] Cornides cites a treatise from the time of Louis XI in which it is stated that it is the duty of the Most Christian Kings of France to read the Gospel at Christmas in the presence of the pope (*Rose und Schwert*, 38–9). Here again there seems to be a confusion between the seventh Matins lesson and the Gospel at Christmas.

[59] See Vale, *Charles VII*, 197, 199, and 203. The sword *Joyeuse*, said to have been Charlemagne's, is often mentioned.

[60] On papal titles granted to Henry VIII, see J. J. Scarisbrick, *Henry VIII* (Berkeley, 1969), 33–4 and 115–17.

[61] From the time of Charles VII, it was admitted that the Church was the authority that conferred the ancient title *christianissimus* upon the French kings. On this and the general history of the title, see H. Leclercq, 'Roi très chrétien', in Fernand Cabrol and Henri Leclercq (eds.), *Dictionnaire d'archéologie chrétienne et de liturgie*, 15 vols. in 30 (Paris, 1907–53), xiv, pt. 2, cols. 2462–4. Further details are found in Moroni, *Dizionario*, s.v. 'Cristianissimo, e Cristianissima', xviii. 207–8. The title of honour *Cattolicus* was awarded to Ferdinand and Isabella by Innocent VIII, confirmed by Alexander VI in 1496, and made hereditary by Julius II. See Moroni, *Dizionario*, s.v. 'Cattolico'. Bryce sees these titles as imitations of imperial titles (*Holy Roman Empire*, 203).

another imperial and royal title,[62] and from then on Henry held up the bared sword when he heard the Gospel at Mass. He evidently discontinued the practice when he rejected the pope's authority in England, although the title became a permanent addition to the English royal dignities.[63] The religious knights of equestrian orders too drew out their swords at the reading of the Gospel 'to show that they were ready to shed blood for the faith of Christ'.[64]

Priests who Celebrate Mass in Armour

In his last paragraph, Rucellai cites two more related ceremonies (App. A, [9]). In Cologne, he writes, on some days of the year—that is, on certain feasts—the priest wears armour when he celebrates Mass. Rucellai usually refers to particular churches, and so his wording here seems to imply a general practice in more than one church of the city. Cologne was the largest and richest city in the Holy Roman Empire, and the archbishop was another imperial prince-bishop, ruler of sizeable territories. In the fifteenth century, however, his seat was in Bonn. While Cologne remained the administrative centre of the diocese, the city proper was independent of the Church, a free city directly subject to the emperor.[65] The cathedral provost, an archdeacon, wielded ecclesiastical power in the city.[66] Ceremonial practices could very well have been retained from an earlier time, when Cologne was the archbishop's seat, and there may have been regular occasions when the archbishop visited. We would expect the Mass ceremony Rucellai describes, with the priest in armour, to be held in the cathedral, and perhaps in other important churches as well, as imperial privileges.[67]

---

[62] According to Moroni, this title was given by the pope in 754 to Pepin, king of France, and to his sons. In its early history it was thus a papal title given to Frankish royalty, from which the French royal line descended. In 1014, the pope bestowed the titles of 'Advocate, Patron, and Defender of the Roman Church' upon the emperor Henry I at his coronation. See Moroni, *Dizionario*, s.v. 'Difensori della Chiesa Romana', xx. 37 and 39.

[63] King, *Liturgies*, 36–7. He notes that the Catholic King James II once more raised the bared sword at the Gospel during Mass as late as 1690. Ailbe J. Luddy recounts this event, which took place during the defeated king's exile in France at the abbey of La Trappe. Luddy states that this raising of the bared sword 'was the custom of the English Sovereigns since the time when Henry VIII received from the Pope the title *Defensor Fidei*'. See his book, *The Real De Rancé: Illustrious Penitent and Reformer of Notre Dame de la Trappe* (London, 1931), 252.

[64] Moroni, 'Evangelio', 231.

[65] *New Catholic Encyclopedia*, s.v. 'Cologne', iii. 1013. See also Zophy, *Holy Roman Empire*, s.v. 'Cologne'.

[66] *New Catholic Encyclopedia*, s.v. 'Cologne', iii. 1013–14.

[67] Philippe de Commynes mentions that the bishop of Liège, another imperial prince-bishop, was often attended by a canon (a priest) wearing full armour, and he attributes the custom to German prelates in general, although this particular bishop, Louis de Bourbon, was Franco-Burgundian. He writes of one of the horrifying events in the rebellion of 1468: 'The people were exceedingly happy at the capture of their bishop, the lord of Liège. They had caught several cathedral canons that day whom they hated, and they killed five or six of them straight off; among the rest was one of the bishop's close friends, called Master Robert, whom I had often seen attending him in full armor, for such is the custom of the prelates in Germany. They killed Master Robert in the bishop's presence and cut him up into several pieces, which they tossed at each other's heads with great laughter.' Quoted from *The Memoirs of Philippe de Commynes*, ed. Samuel Kinser, trans. Isabelle Cazeaux, 2 vols. (Columbia, SC, 1969), i. 171. A Master Robert accompanying the bishop that

This rite too has its parallels. We know from an anonymous chronicle that in 1340 the patriarch of Aquileia, Blessed Bertrand of Saint Geniès, celebrated 'the office of Christmas night' in armour as well as sacred vestments, assisted by a Benedictine abbot wearing a cuirass.[68] The service was performed in the country-side where the patriarch was assembling forces to besiege Gorizia, a town held by rebellious nobles, and a number of important personages, royalty from north of the Alps, and military men were present.[69] The patriarch, an imperial prince-bishop, clearly had privileges similar to those of Cologne and Sant'Antimo, including the right to wage war; but the chronicles do not tell us whether the celebrant's use of armour was a prescribed rite for the day or an exceptional event.[70]

For the normal ritual of Christmas Matins at 'the church of Aquileia', in use from an unknown date until the patriarchate was dissolved in 1751, we have the authority of an eighteenth-century witness: a canon, wearing a dalmatic and *bir-retto*, carrying a drawn sword, processes from the sacristy, reads the Gospel excerpt from the beginning of the seventh lesson, 'Exiit edictum . . .', and then brandishes the sword.[71] This rite seems to be closely modelled on the one associ-ated with the emperor that we have seen in chronicles and papal ordinals.[72] We might expect the ceremony to have ceased when the patriarchate ended and with it all possible pretence of temporal rule by the spiritual leader; but on the con-trary, hydra-like, the rite sprang up redoubled. Two new archbishoprics were formed, at Udine and Gorizia, and the metropolitan church in each of them per-formed the armed Matins ceremony until the mid-nineteenth century.[73]

Even today, a liturgical ceremony with a sword still takes place elsewhere in the former patriarchate of Aquileia. In Cividale del Friuli, in the duomo (the col-legiate church of S. Maria Assunta), the Mass of Epiphany is popularly known as the *Messa dello spadone*, the 'Mass of the Broadsword'.[74] Long an enormous

year is described by the papal legate as a venerable Carmelite doctor of theology. See Stanislas Bormans (ed.), *Mémoire du légat Onufrius sur les affaires de Liège (1468)* (Brussels, 1885), 32. Werner Paravicini identifies him as Robert de Morialmé, archdeacon of Liège, in *Guy de Brimeu: Der burgundische Staat und seine Führungsschicht unter Karl dem Kühnen* (Pariser historische Studien, 12; Bonn, 1975), 183.

[68] King, *Liturgies*, 36, who cites, in n. 2, the anonymous *Leoben. Chron. ad ann. 1340*, in Pez (ed.), *Scriptores*, i. 959. King gives the year as 1341 in his text, but this seems to be a misprint. See also Vale, 'Ceremonia', cols. 40–1. For a quotation from the patriarch's own memoir of this event, which supplies many details but does not mention the armour, see Pio Paschini, *Storia del Friuli*, rev. edn., 2 vols. (Udine, 1953–4), i. 91–2.

[69] Paschini, *Storia*, i. 91–2.

[70] The fact that the patriarch himself does not mention his armour in his narration of the siege and his celebration, 'in the fields', of 'the solemnities of the night of Christmas and the three Masses of the day', sug-gests that armed services were not unusual for him. See the excerpt ibid.

[71] See Vale, 'Ceremonia', cols. 28–9. He states that his source, Francesco Florio, must have witnessed the ceremony as canon of Aquileia before the patriarchate was dissolved, for he mentions it in his *Vita del beato Beltrando* (Venice, 1759), 89; but for his published description Florio refers to De Rubeis, *Dissertationes dua . . .* (Venice, 1754), 295.

[72] The basic link was noted by Vale, 'Ceremonia', cols. 27–9.   [73] Ibid., cols. 29–32.

[74] It is also called the *Messa della Spada*, the 'Mass of the Sword'. See Vale, 'Ceremonia', for a review of earlier literature on this ceremony and a detailed description of it. His own speculations about its origin seem improbable, however (cols. 44–6). Gino Fogolari calls the ceremony 'la messa dell'imperatore', which seems

tourist attraction,[75] this Mass is performed with the utmost majesty and solemnity before the entire chapter of canons, all the authorities, and many invited guests.[76] The deacon of the collegiate chapter[77] wears a traditional, plumed helmet[78] and carries the broadsword of the patriarch Marquard, inscribed with the date of his investiture in 1366.[79] In his left hand, pressed against his breast, the deacon holds a lectionary copied in 1433, which contains, in brief rubrics, the earliest known reference to the armed Mass at Cividale.[80]

The ceremony itself, as it was described in 1908 and later, begins with a procession in which the armed deacon is accompanied by two clerics; he brandishes the sword in three great, slow, downward strokes, facing the centre of the congregation and then the sides;[81] and he is then divested of the sword and helmet at the altar in order to perform the service. The deacon takes up the arms again in preparation for the Gospel reading. He repeats the brandishing, gives the arms to the two clerics,[82] sings the Gospel (according to a chant from the old rite of Aquileia), and then brandishes the sword a third time. He holds up the sword again while singing the announcement of Easter and the *Ite missa est* (which has an Aquileian trope), and in the recession he stops to brandish the sword a final time at the top of the steps of the sanctuary. The sword-brandishing is to be understood as a solemn military salute, the ancestor of modern salutes with rifles or cannon.[83]

---

to be a more formal name, although he cites no source for it; see *Cividale del Friuli* (Collezione di monografie illustrate, ser. 1, Italia artistica, 23; Bergamo, 1906), 64 and 76. Fogolari states that the ceremony recalls the military power of the patriarchs, who *resided* in Cividale, although their spiritual centre was in Aquileia (p. 64).

[75] Vale, 'Ceremonia', col. 32.

[76] Giuseppe Marioni and Carlo Mutinelli, *Guida storico-artistica di Cividale* (Udine, 1958), 571.

[77] The information summarized in this paragraph comes from Vale, 'Ceremonia', cols. 32–40, unless otherwise noted.

[78] In 1906 Gino Fogolari described the helmet as 'di cartone, moderno, e brutto', 'made of cardboard, modern, and ugly' (*Cividale*, 64; photograph on p. 76), and Vale describes it as modern ('Ceremonia', col. 35). Teresa Della Rovere, however, states that the helmet dates from the 1500s, in *La Messa dello Spadone e la rievocazione storica in costume a Cividale del Friuli* (thesis, Università di Bologna, Facoltà di Economia e Commercio, Scuola di Studi Turistici di Rimini, 1986/87), in *Milleservizi per l'immagine (Udine)*, 1 (1988), supplement to no. 2, p. [13]; photograph on p. [16].

[79] Vale, 'Ceremonia', col. 35. The sword is preserved in the Tesoro del Duomo. For a photograph of it, see Fogolari, *Cividale*, 76. A photograph of lesser quality appears in Marioni and Mutinelli, *Guida*, fig. 121, p. 324.

[80] Vale, 'Ceremonia', col. 34. There is some other evidence that the rite goes back at least to the 14th c. Vale (cols. 46–7) writes that in 1596, in the ecclesiastic province of Aquileia, all ceremonies that could not be proven to be older than two hundred years were abolished. The Mass of the Sword passed this test. The ceremony evidently is not included in the 14th-c. manuscript ceremonial of Cividale, *Ordo Civitatensis*, in the Museo Civico (Vale, 'Ceremonia', col. 44), which would suggest that the ceremony was instituted later on in that century. This manuscript is described in A. Zorzi, *Museo, archivio e biblioteca di Cividale del Friuli* (Cividale, 1899), 187, no. 16.

[81] Marioni and Mutinelli, *Guida*, 571.

[82] As described by Moroni, at an earlier period the deacon at Cividale sang the Gospel with the sword in hand and the helmet on his head (Moroni, 'Evangelio', 231).

[83] Marioni and Mutinelli (*Guida*, 571) refer to 'three great and slow downward strokes of salute'.

The Mass of the Broadsword has undoubtedly evolved somewhat over the centuries,[84] but the earliest sources do not give complete enough descriptions to permit any detailed conclusions about historical changes. The lectionary of 1433 has only the following rubric: 'Here follows the Gospel said at Mass on the day of Epiphany, having a drawn sword with which the helmeted deacon, escorting the priest and escorted by the subdeacon, proceeds to the altar.'[85] According to the extensive study by Giuseppe Vale, the next mention of the ceremony dates from 1668.[86] In the single example he quotes of an earlier scholarly description, from 1760, all the details that are included correspond with early twentieth-century use, but the sword-brandishing is not explicitly mentioned.[87]

Masses with Arms at the Altar

Finally, Rucellai (App. A, [9]) reports having seen an iron helmet with a bishop's mitre on it placed on the altar during Mass, in 'other places'. This is the only ceremony he claims to have seen personally, and in more than one location. The combination of bishop's mitre and helmet (the mitre taking precedence) clearly points to sovereign bishops. Gaetano Moroni confirms that bishops and abbots who had temporal sovereignty placed 'princely attributes' next to the altar for pontifical Masses,[88] and his most detailed example is Cahors, in southern France. There the bishop, in exercise of his temporal title of baron and count of the city, traditionally placed an array of arms and armour beside the altar for pontifical Masses: 'helmet, sword, burning fuse, gauntlets, or iron gloves, as well as boots and spurs'.[89] The temporal titles (and powers) associated with this rite are said to have been accorded the bishop to enable him to defend himself from the

---

[84] It was mentioned above that formerly the Gospel was read armed, with the sword held up by the deacon. Elsewhere in the former patriarchate of Aquileia, the ceremony underwent changes as recently as the last century of its use. After 1752, when Gorizia and Udine became the centres of new archbishoprics, they presumably adopted the same form of the service that had been used in Aquileia. According to the descriptions Giuseppe Vale was able to collect, however, there were differences a century later. In Gorizia, a *canon* read the seventh lesson wearing a *berretto* and holding up the bared sword, and afterwards he brandished the sword with *four* strokes in the air. In Udine, however, the deacon (also a canon) used the sword to make the sign of the cross over the people at that point. (See Vale, 'Ceremonia', cols. 29–32.) Guido Piovene states that the tracing of the sign of the cross with the sword was adopted in Cividale as well. See his *Viaggi in Italia* ([Verona], 1957), 53; his title and brief (second-hand) description of the rite also appear in *Grande dizionario della lingua italiana*, comp. by Salvatore Battaglia, 16 vols. (Turin, 1961–92), s.v. 'Messa; Messa dello Spadone'. In Marioni and Mutinelli, *Guida*, 571, however, sword-brandishing, rather than the sign of the cross, is specified.

[85] 'Sequens Evangelium dicitur ad missam in die sancto Epiphanie tenendo ensem evaginatum cum quo dyaconus galeatus sacerdotem concomitans et subdyacono concomitatus ad altare incedit.' Quoted in Vale, 'Ceremonia', col. 37.

[86] Vale lists earlier works on the Mass of the Sword in 'Ceremonia', col. 32 n. 4. The first is Basilio Zancarolo, *Antiquitates Forojuli* (Venice, 1668), 152 ff.

[87] 'Ceremonia', col. 33 n. 1.

[88] Moroni, *Dizionario*, s.v. 'Spada', lxviii. 9. For sovereign bishops and abbots, the sword, as the symbol of *jus gladii*, was generally among the princely attributes placed at the altar and used, as mentioned earlier, in heraldry on their seals and coats of arms (ibid.).

[89] Moroni, *Dizionario*, s.v. 'Cahors', vi. 225.

Albigensians,[90] heretical sects around Albi that were the objects of crusades begun in 1209.

Here at Cahors we have arrived at a liturgical Mass-ceremony with arms at the altar that was traditionally used in France, in at least in one cathedral. The 'princely attributes' next to the altar consist entirely of arms and armour, and the rite was like an inanimate version of the ceremony of the armed man at Sant'Antimo (though enlivened by the lit fuse), and used on the same occasions, pontifical Masses. The symbolic meaning is clearly the sanctified defence of the Church and her territories. According to Moroni, as noted above, sovereign bishops and abbots *generally* used such ceremonies. Sovereign bishoprics near Burgundy and under Burgundian control during the reign of Charles the Bold include Liège, Utrecht, and Cambrai, and others centred on Toul and Metz.[91]

Can we link any of these ceremonies with the *L'homme armé* tradition in France, Cambrai, and Burgundy? From what we have seen so far, there is only the practice at the French court of the king's page raising a bared sword at the Gospel, but this would appear to have been done regularly at Mass (at least when the king appeared in stately attire). While such a practice would provide a visible point of reference for any *L'homme armé* mass performed on state occasions, it does not provide us with any particular occasions to consider. Pontifical Masses at Cambrai, which the bishop celebrated on major feast-days or special days, are another matter; because Cambrai was a fief of the Empire, it seems very likely that some sort of military trappings adorned the altar on at least some of those occasions. A third possibility is that the duke of Burgundy, as Count of the Empire,[92] might have used a similar ceremony on important occasions in his imperial territories, in imitation of the emperor. The information gathered here about armour at the altar concerns ecclesiastical counts of the Empire, but what of their secular counterparts? The province of Dauphiné, for example, was also at least nominally under the Empire until 1457.[93] The key to this question probably lies in the coronation rites of the imperial counts, or the church ceremony performed upon their festive entry into the central town in the lands they ruled under the imperial title: did they receive or display a sword?

---

[90] Ibid. The fuse, or slow-match, was used to fire cannons, which were introduced into Europe early in the 14th c. (well after the Albigensian crusades). See John Keegan, *A History of Warfare* (New York, 1993), 320 and 328–30.

[91] See Commynes, *Memoirs*, p. xi.

[92] The duke of Burgundy held some of his territories as fiefs of France and others as fiefs of the Empire, in particular the County of Burgundy (Franche-Comté). See the map for 1477 in Commynes, *Memoirs*, p. xi.

[93] Bryce, *Holy Roman Empire*, 356.

Papal Gifts of the Blessed Sword and Hat

If we return briefly to the Vatican and pursue the subject of the sword at Christmas Matins, a new territory opens up for exploration. In the second half of the fourteenth century, in Avignon, the pope began to commission a special sword and cap to give away to the nobleman who performed the Christmas Matins ceremony.[94] These gifts represented works of art worth increasingly vast sums. The swords were of silver, worked in gold, the sheaths covered in velvet, often studded with precious stones. The ducal hat, in one typical fifteenth-century description, was of beaver edged in ermine, with the dove of the Holy Spirit sewn in pearls.[95] The Holy Spirit would thus be seen to protect the leader in battle and direct him in the right exercise of the sword, which symbolized Christ's temporal dominion and his victory over the Devil.[96] Sword and hat were blessed by the pope, usually on Christmas Eve, in a special ceremony that endowed them with sacred power.

Beginning with the pontificate of Martin V (1417–31), payment records for the manufacture of the gift sword survive for almost every year, although many of the recipients cannot be identified.[97] The available information suggests that another historical phase was beginning to unfold: rather than bestowing such gifts only on a nobleman present in the papal court on Christmas, the pope began more and more often to dispatch gifts of the newly blessed sword and cap to some distant sovereign or leader he wished to honour for political purposes, as a reward or encouragement to support his policies.[98] During the three papacies spanning the years 1417 to 1455, we know of eight such gifts to distant rulers. Under Martin V, the future Charles VII of France (ruling during his father's illness), probably received the blessed sword of 1419, and Louis III of Anjou, king of Naples, that of 1422. Both gifts confirmed the pope's support of the Angevin

[94] The first record of this gift dates from 1357 (Cornides, *Rose und Schwert*, 33). In 1365 Urban V bestowed a specially made, blessed sword and hat upon Duke Louis of Anjou, who read the fifth lesson at Christmas Matins (Modern, 'Geweihte Schwerter', 129). Cornides mentions that the name of one earlier recipient is known: Burchard von Magdeburg, the imperial ambassador to the papal court (*Rose und Schwert*, 64). Moroni traces the custom of these papal gifts to the legendary sword given in the 12th c. to Doge Ziani of Venice, which was unrelated to the Christmas ceremony (Moroni, *Dizionario*, s.v. 'Stocco e berrettone ducale', lxx. 44). Modern also mentions a precious sword given by Pope Paul I (d. 767) to Pepin ('Geweihte Schwerter', 143). Pepin was given the title of 'Protector of the Holy See'. See the *Dictionary of Catholic Biography*, compiled by John J. Delaney and James Edward Tobin [Garden City, NY, 1961], s.v. 'Pepin the Short'. On the history of these gifts, see also C. Burns, *Golden Rose and Blessed Sword: Papal Gifts to Scottish Monarchs* (Glasgow, 1970), 11–12.
[95] Moroni ('Stocco', 45) gives a description of the sword and cap given by Eugene IV to the Signoria of Florence in 1434. Two extant ducal hats (from 1567 and 1581), with the dove of the Holy Spirit in pearls, are reproduced in Modern, 'Geweihte Schwerter', pl. 22 and 23.
[96] The symbolism is made explicit from the time of Sixtus IV on, when his breve 'Solent Romani Pontifices' was used for the presentation. See App. E for the full text.
[97] Cornides, *Rose und Schwert*, 65.
[98] Ibid. Cornides reviews the extant material for the papacies of Martin V through Leo X (1417–1521) on 90–110.

claim to the throne of Naples, which was contested by Aragon.[99] In the pontificate of Eugene IV, the sword of 1443 was sent to the king of Poland, and that of 1446 (which still exists) to the king of Castile.[100] During the rather brief papacy of Nicholas V (1447–55), the practice accelerated. Four swords found their way to distant rulers, two of them conferred in response to the Turkish threat. The sword of Christmas 1449 went to the doge of Venice, and that of 1450 to Albrecht VI of Austria (the emperor's brother), both clearly chosen to promote a league against the Turks.[101] The gifts would generally be taken by an envoy to be presented ceremoniously in a great and solemn Mass. Here, in the presentation ceremonies for the papal swords, we find a striking possibility for a link with the *L'homme armé* tradition. The relevant questions concern the nature of the presentation ceremony, its dates and locations, and the identity of the recipients.

Notes in late fifteenth-century papal ceremonials clarify that the general formulas for presenting the sword away from the papal court were the same as those for the golden rose, a papal gift of greater antiquity. Only the breve and the prayer at the presentation had to be changed. Brief notes by Johannes Burckard preserve the instructions that were probably first used for the blessed sword in 1457, served again in 1461, and were adapted in 1491 for the golden rose.[102] They can be paraphrased as follows:[103]

A day's journey from the city or castle where the king resides, the apostolic nuncio will announce his arrival. The king must send nobles and others one or two miles to meet the nuncio in the name of the king and conduct him to his lodgings. Two of his dignitaries must go in front and bear the [sword and hat] uncovered, as is done [in the papal processions in Rome].[104]

---

[99] Cornides, *Rose und Schwert*, 91. The pope had traditional feudal rights over Naples, and the outcome of the rival claims of succession to the throne was a paramount political issue in preserving the authority of the papacy. Pope Martin V allied himself with Louis III of Anjou in 1420. See Thompson, *Popes and Princes*, 119–20. See also John Holland Smith, *The Great Schism, 1378* (New York, 1970), 226–7. Charles VII's backing of the House of Anjou was evidently rewarded by the papal gift.

[100] Cornides, *Rose und Schwert*, 93. The gift to the king of Castile is undoubtedly related to the campaign to oust the Moors from Spain.

[101] Ibid., 94. Nicholas sent the sword of 1454 to the 'king of Sicily'. The title undoubtedly refers to Alfonso V of Aragon, king of Naples, who ruled from 1442 to 1458. He came to terms with the papacy in order to secure the succession for his son (Thompson, *Popes and Princes*, 121). His representative in Rome, the count of S. Angelo, performed the Matins ceremony at Christmas that year and received the sword. The fourth sword under Nicholas V was sent to Luigi Bentivoglio of Bologna. See Cornides, *Rose und Schwert*, 94 and 142.

[102] See App. C, n. d.

[103] This paraphrase is based on the text used for the golden rose in 1491, published by Burns, *Golden Rose*, App. II, 38–9, from Vat. lat. 12343, fo. 148^r. According to Burns (p. 39), 'this page originally contained the instructions for the presentation of the blessed sword and hat to the duke of Burgundy in 1460, and these have been altered to suit the presentation of the golden rose to James IV'. In the paraphrase I have re-adapted the text, substituting the sword and hat for the golden rose and omitting the prayer of presentation.

[104] In the ceremonial of Agostino Patrizi, written in 1486–8, there is a detailed protocol for the procession with the sword and hat. See Dykmans, *L'Œuvre*, i. 183*–84*.

The papal breve is presented to the king, who must choose the day and place for the presentation ceremony. It must be on a Sunday or solemn feast-day in a church among the principal ones of the place, after the solemn Mass.

On the day of the presentation, the main altar will be prepared and the [sword and hat] placed upon it. The king and the nuncio come to hear the singing of the solemn Mass. When the Mass is over and the benediction has been given by the celebrant, the nuncio is vested in a suitable place and goes up to the altar and sits before it in a seat prepared for him, facing the congregation. The king goes to sit next to the altar in a prepared place, if he is not already there, where the nuncio reads the papal breve aloud to him. The king then kneels before the nuncio, and the nuncio goes to the altar, takes the [sword and hat], gives them to the king, and says the prayer on bestowing the gifts.

Then the king kisses the nuncio's hand and rises. The nuncio unvests and escorts the king to his palace, preceded and followed by the people in the customary order. The king moreover carries the [sword and hat] and when he has reached his palace, he places [them] on the altar of his chapel, or in another honourable place, where [they] will be kept reverently in honour of the Holy See.

A more detailed, but very similar prescription for the presentation of the blessed sword and hat *extra curiam* was drawn up for Julius II in 1507 by his master of ceremonies, Paride de' Grassi, based on earlier texts scattered in papal records.[105] It became the model thereafter.[106] For us the salient points of these prescriptions are that a special Mass was mandated for the sword presentation in a major church, in the presence of the papal commissioner, and that the king or lord chose the time and place. It was to be a major occasion joining church and state in a single Mass ceremony glorified by extraordinary gifts that were at once sacred and martial.

Recipients of the Blessed Papal Sword after 1453

The beginning of Appendix C lists the recipients who were sent the blessed sword and hat in the first years after the fall of Constantinople to the Turks (for the swords presented by the pope in person, see App. D). Three of them immediately catch the eye: Charles VII and Louis XI, kings of France, and Philip the Good, duke of Burgundy. We know from at least one letter that King Charles VII received the blessed sword and hat sometime between 1456 and 1458 (and in 1459 Pius II also awarded him the title 'Defender of the Faith').[107] The gifts to Philip the Good in 1461, and to Louis XI the following year, are securely documented.

---

[105] See Burns, *Golden Rose*, 18; for the text by Paride de' Grassi of the instructions for the sword presentation, see his App. IV, 40–2, published from Vatican City, Biblioteca Apostolica Vaticana, MS Vat. lat. 5634 *bis*, fos. 176ᵛ–178ʳ. The de' Grassi text for the presentation of the golden rose *extra curiam*, from fos. 226ᵛ–229ᵛ of the same manuscript, is published by Cornides, *Rose und Schwert*, 135–6.

[106] Burns, *Golden Rose*, 18. For a detailed description of the presentation of a blessed sword in Vienna in 1557, which captures the emotion of the event, see Modern, 'Geweihte Schwerter', 137–8.

[107] Moroni, *Dizionario*, s.v. 'Difensore della Chiesa, o della Fede', xx. 41.

Political considerations often motivated the papal gifts during this period, and Calixtus III and Pius II shared two pressing concerns: (i) to persuade the French to revoke the Pragmatic Sanction of 1438, which Pius called a 'pernicious poison', because it essentially freed the French Church from papal authority and gave many powers over it to the nobility; and (ii) to wage a crusade against the Turks.[108] The gifts from Calixtus to Charles VII were to no avail, but the political climate changed when Louis XI came to power in 1461, and an embassy from Pius II did succeed in obtaining the king's revocation of the Pragmatic Sanction.[109] Pius announced the news in December with tears of joy in his eyes, as he writes in his commentaries.[110] To a Sienese observer, it was 'the greatest news that could come to the Apostolic See. In one moment the Papacy has gained the Kingdom of France and has won the full obedience of all Christians. God be praised that during the reign of a Sienese pope Holy Church should be thus exalted.'[111]

The way was now clear to focus all energies on promoting the crusade. Pius immediately chose Louis to receive the blessed sword, and he composed a dedicatory poem that was inscribed on the scabbard, which was ornamented with gold and gems.[112] These lines, with their stirring call to arms against the Turks, vividly express the meaning of the pope's gift at this critical moment:

> EXERAT IN TVRCAS TVAS ME, LVDOVICE, FVRENTES
> DEXTERA; GRAIORVM SANGVINIS VLTOR ERO.
> CORRVET IMPERIVM MAVMETHIS ET INCLYTA RVRSVS
> GALLORVM VIRTVS TE PETET ASTRA DVCE.[113]

Let your [right] hand, Louis, draw me against the mad Turks. I shall be the avenger of the blood of the Greeks. The empire of Mahomet shall fall in ruins and the renewed valor of the French shall again soar to the stars under your leadership.[114]

As for the swords sent to the dukes of Burgundy, Philip the Good was clearly chosen to receive the one blessed at Christmas 1460 because of the combination of his great wealth and his willingness to launch a crusade. As it happens, Philip provided the only major support Pius was to have for his crusade, for a

---

[108] *Pii II: Commentarii rerum memorabilium que temporibus suis contigerunt*, ed. Adriano van Heck, 2 vols. (Studi e Testi, 312; Vatican City, 1984), i. 450. See also the abridged translation in Leona C. Gabel (ed. and intro.), *Memoirs of a Renaissance Pope: The Commentaries of Pius II, An Abridgment*, trans. Florence A. Gragg (London, 1960), 231. According to Pius, 'As a result of this law the prelates of France . . . were reduced to the most abject servitude and became practically slaves of the laity' (ibid. 211; see 209–11 for a full discussion). See also Cornides, *Rose und Schwert*, 65, 94–6; Thompson, *Popes and Princes*, 148–50; and Cecelia M. Ady, *Pius II (Aeneas Silvius Piccolomini): The Humanist Pope* (1913; repr. Ann Arbor, 1981), 207–14.

[109] According to Ady, Louis 'saw the alliance with the Papacy as a means of bringing the Gallican Church under his heel' (*Pius II*, 209). Louis soon reversed his position, however (ibid. 213).

[110] *Pii II: Commentarii*, i. 450. See also the abridged translation in Gabel, *Memoirs*, 231.

[111] Gregorio Lolli to Siena, 26 Dec., 1461, quoted by Ady, *Pius II*, 209.

[112] *Pii II: Commentarii*, i. 450.

[113] Ibid.

[114] Translated by Florence A. Gragg, in Gabel, *Memoirs*, 231.

Burgundian expedition did set out led by his bastard son Antoine. It had reached Marseilles when the pope died in 1464.[115]

A papal sword sent to Charles the Bold, duke of Burgundy from 1467 to 1477, would be especially intriguing for us because of his ties with two composers of early *L'homme armé* masses, Busnoys and Dufay, and his presumed ownership of the Naples manuscript containing six anonymous *L'homme armé* masses (or knowledge of the music).[116] The evidence in his case, however, requires evaluation. An undated inventory made by his *garde des joyaux* early in his brief reign lists two blessed papal swords.[117] The inventory cannot date from before 1469, since it has an entry for a goblet that was a New Year's gift from 'madame', who must be Margaret of York, Charles's wife from 1468.[118] At least the first part of the inventory, moreover, was completed before 12 February 1470 (modern style), for an added marginal note states that one of the items was given away on that date.[119] As there is no reason to suspect a protracted period for the drawing up of the inventory, it is probably safe to assume that the two papal swords had already been received by early 1470.

The inventory contains Charles's own valuables together with those inherited from his father, Philip the Good.[120] Philip's possessions are sometimes explicitly noted—especially if they bear his name, initials, or emblems—and we might expect to find here the blessed sword he received in 1461.[121] The wording of the inventory, however, implies that *both* papal swords were sent to 'MS'—that is, 'Mon Seigneur' the reigning duke, Charles; and they were sent, respectively, by 'nostre saint Père le pappe' and 'le saint Père', which would certainly suggest the current pope at the time of the inventory, Paul II (pope from 1464 to 1471).[122]

[115] See App. C, nn. *h* and *i*. See also Ady, *Pius II*, 127–8; Gabel, *Memoirs*, 125–8; and Richard Vaughan, *Philip the Good: The Apogee of Burgundy* (New York, 1970), 218, and 358 ff. for Philip and the crusade in general. Philip's decision not to lead the crusading party in person was, however, a bitter blow to the pope; see R. J. Mitchell, *The Laurels and the Tiara: Pope Pius II, 1458–1464* (London, 1962), 261.

[116] See Judith Cohen, *The Six Anonymous L'Homme Armé Masses in Naples, Biblioteca Nazionale, MS VI E 40* (MSD 21; [Rome], 1968), 62–71.

[117] The inventory, preserved in Lille in the Archives du Nord, exists in two versions, one better organized that the other. Both versions were published by Leon Emmanuel, SJ, Comte de Laborde, *Les Ducs de Bourgogne: Études sur les lettres, les arts et l'industrie pendant le XVᵉ siècle et plus particulièrement dans les Pays-Bas et le duché de Bourgogne*, 3 vols. (Paris, 1849–52), ii, nos. 2001 to 3988.

[118] Laborde, *Les Ducs*, ii. 41, item 312, and 156, item 3450. In the style of Brabant, the calendar year began on Easter. However, Margaret's gift 'au jour de l'an' would have been for 1 Jan. See Richard Vaughan, *Philip the Bold: The Formation of the Burgundian State* (Cambridge, Mass., 1962), 17.

[119] Ibid. ii. 28.

[120] Ibid. ii, p. iv.

[121] There is always a possibility, however, that Philip or Charles had already given away this blessed sword and hat, or kept it in another place. Eugène Müntz lists both the papal swords of Charles's inventory under the pontificate of Pius II (d. 1464), immediately after the entry for the sword sent in 1461 to Philip the Good but without explaining the implicit dates ('Les épées d'honneur distribuées par les papes pendant les XIVᵢᵉᵐᵉ, XVᵢᵉᵐᵉ, et XVIᵢᵉᵐᵉ siècles', *Revue de l'art chrétien*, 40 (1890), 285). This article was issued in three parts, of which the first covers the period up to 1405 (vol. 39 (1889), 408–11); the second, the period up to 1502 (vol. 40 (1890), 281–92); and a related note is in vol. 44 (1895), 491–2.

[122] The pair of swords is listed twice, in two parts of the first version of the inventory. (According to Laborde, this version contains the numbers from 2001 to 3351. He mentions that there are repetitions. See *Les Ducs*, ii, p. iv.) One listing appears under the heading 'Additions à l'inventoire', 'Déclaration des parties

We can question the accuracy of the *garde des joyaux* on these points,[123] however, and it would be unwise to give too strict a reading to the wording of the inventory.

The pope bestowed only one blessed sword each year, as a general rule.[124] As Appendix C shows, for the period from 1455 to 1470 (the year by which the inventory was probably finished), there are only four years for which the recipient of the Christmas sword is not already known: 1455, 1463, 1467, and 1469. On closer examination, none of these dates seems at all likely for a papal gift to Charles the Bold.

In conferring his first sword in 1455, Calixtus III would surely have broken all rules of diplomatic protocol by honouring Charles as a 22-year-old heir ahead of his powerful father, the emperor, and other sovereigns. Moreover, there is no known instance from the fifteenth century in which the pope sent a blessed sword to the heir to a duchy.[125]

From the papacy of Pius II, only the last sword, presumably blessed on Christmas Eve in 1463, has an unknown recipient. Pius's gifts are exceptionally well documented, in large part by the pope's own commentaries, and it is clear that his gift swords were all part of his efforts to launch a crusade. Philip the Good, chosen by Pius for the sword of 1460, joined the pope's league against the Turks in 1463.[126] The Burgundian embassy of that summer greatly raised the pope's crusading spirits,[127] and Philip remained his leading hope for support until the early spring of 1464, when the duke renounced his oath to lead crusaders in person.[128] Surely if a blessed sword had been sent to Burgundy again in early 1464, it would have gone to Philip rather than Charles. Although Charles cannot be ruled out absolutely as the recipient of the sword of 1463, then, he does not seem by any means a strong possibility.

à mettre encore en l'inventoire' (ibid., ii. 145): 'No. 3335. Item, une aultre espée benoite, que nostre saint Père le pappe a envoyée à MS, dont le pommeau et la gaine sont couvertes d'argent doré à pluseur ouvrages. No. 3336. Item, une aultre espée, aussi benoite, qui le saint Père a envoyée aussi à MS, le pommeau et le ghaine d'argent doré de pluseurs ouvrages.' This part of the inventory, devoted to valuable weapons, belongs to a section in the hand of a second scribe (ibid.142 n. 1), and the heading suggests that it is a preliminary list. The swords are also described, in nearly identical wording, near the end of the work of the main scribe, where the collection of arms is among the objects entitled 'Menues Baghes'. See ibid. 137.

[123] It seems likely that the *garde des joyaux*, as a matter of course, described each item before him according to what was visible on the object itself that would serve to identify it. There is also the possibility that some of the wording in this inventory was taken over from earlier lists. Papal swords, as we know from those that survive, usually had inscriptions with the pope's name, the year, and perhaps his arms. The recipient was not named, for he was usually chosen after the manufacture of the sword and scabbard, although those sent to Louis XI are a notable exception (for some of the early inscriptions, see Modern, 'Geweihte Schwerter', 140–2). Thus the *garde des joyaux* would not have known from the swords themselves whether the recipient was Charles or his father. Even though he would have known the name of the pope, he did not make it explicit.

[124] The blessed sword and hat given to Borso d'Este in 1471 are a special case.

[125] The sword of 1501 is the first exception to this rule, and the occasion—the marriage of the pope's daughter—is certainly unusual. Heirs to kingdoms were not *sent* blessed swords in the 15th c. either, the only exception being the blessed sword of 1419 sent to the future Charles VII of France, who was already ruling in his father's place, as mentioned above. The swords bestowed in Rome are a different matter, for they were sometimes given to representatives of monarchs. See App. 4.

[126] Moroni, 'Stocco', 46.   [127] Mitchell, *Laurels*, 256.   [128] Ibid. 261.

As for the swords blessed by Paul II in 1467 and 1469, it is unthinkable that Charles could have received one of them. At this time, the dominant political affair connecting Burgundy and the pope was the uprising in Liège (an episcopal principality) and its violent end. Soon after his accession in 1467, Charles pursued a brutal suppression of the rebellion in favour of his cousin Louis of Bourbon, who had been imposed by Burgundy as prince-bishop.[129] Although Charles proclaimed that his military action against Liège was to 'protect' the Church,[130] in the treaty he dictated on 28 November 1467 the Church's rights were 'totally disregarded'.[131] Paul II sent a legate early in 1468 with particular instructions 'to entreat, exhort, and admonish Charles, duke of Burgundy, to hold in check his offence of the Church . . .'.[132] In spite of the legate's attempt to negotiate an acceptable peace treaty, Charles's troops ultimately sacked and burned the city that year. Philippe de Commynes writes that most of the churches were plundered 'under the pretense of taking prisoners' and that 'for a long time afterwards, the pope issued severe censures against those who possessed anything which belonged to the churches . . .'.[133] Against this background, it is difficult to imagine that Paul II would send Charles any gift, and certainly not a blessed sword. It seems more likely that the two swords listed in his inventory were inherited from his father, in spite of the wording. One of them was presumably presented in 1461, and the other at an unknown date in Philip's long reign.

The Sword in the Papal Christmas Masses

The developing ceremonies at the Vatican connected with the blessed sword could also have provided an opportunity for the performance of a *L'homme armé* mass: at least by the late fifteenth century, the sword was a dramatic element on Christmas when the pope was present, not only at Matins and the first, night Mass that followed immediately afterwards, but also at the third, main Mass in the afternoon, which was celebrated as a solemn pontifical Mass in St Peter's. This was true even when the sword was not to be given to anyone present. Agostino Patrizi's ceremonial of 1486–8, the major source on this subject, can be paraphrased as follows:[134]

---

[129] The affair of Liège, 1468, is recounted in detail by Ornufrius de Santa Croce, the papal legate. See Bormans, *Mémoire*. For an authoritative modern appraisal, see Richard Vaughan, *Charles the Bold: The Last Valois Duke of Burgundy* (New York, 1974), 24 ff.

[130] Vaughan, *Charles the Bold*, 26.

[131] Ibid. 24.

[132] Bormans, *Mémoire*, 29–30.

[133] Commynes, *Memoirs*, i. 190. Commynes goes on to explain that Charles took pains to protect the interests of the Church and to carry out the pope's orders, but the large-scale devastation caused by the duke's troops and his usurpation of the Church's rights remain the salient aspects of the Liège affair.

[134] On the date, see Dykmans, *L'Œuvre*, i. 27*. For his summary of Patrizi's ceremonial for Christmas Matins, see ii. 174*–75*. For Patrizi's complete text, see bk. II, ch. xi, nos. 810–41, in ii. 285–93.

Before Matins on Christmas,[135] after the pope has blessed the sword (if he so desires), he goes in procession to the chapel preceded by the cross, and before the cross one of the clerics of the chamber carries the sword with the beaver hat with pearls.[136] The cleric places the sword and hat on the altar at the Epistle side.[137] Later in the service, if the nobleman who is to receive the sword is present and wishes to do so, he performs the ceremony of vesting in sacred vestments with the sword, going before the pope's throne, consigning the hat to his servant, begging the pope's blessing, brandishing the sword, putting the sword back in the sheath, going up to the pulpit, and reading the fifth lesson[138]—the seventh lesson for the emperor.[139] Modifications are made if the honoree is illiterate.[140] After this, the nobleman returns to the place where he was vested,[141] takes off the robe and sword, and is conducted back to his place. The sword is given to his servant, who holds it erect with the hat on the point, returns to his place, and sits holding the sword thus until the end of the service.[142] If the nobleman is not present, the cleric of the chamber nevertheless carries the sword and hat before the cross when the pope processes and recesses, at Matins [followed by the first Mass] and at the main [third] Mass.[143] The presentation ceremony for the sword and hat, with the reading of Sixtus IV's breve *Solent Romani Pontifices* [explaining the symbolism],[144] takes place after the Mass, either at the papal throne [in St Peter's] or else in the 'chamber of the parrot' [the *aula dei paramenti* in the papal palace], in the presence of the cardinals and other dignitaries. Finally, the recipient of the sword is escorted to his lodging in a formal procession accompanied by hosts of important figures in order of rank, with the sword and hat again borne by one of his men.[145]

Both the first and third Christmas Masses, then, became 'masses of the sword' when the pope was present, especially when the gift sword was presented in St Peter's.

Even in the absence of the pope the blessed sword was sometimes placed on the altar, or held next to it by a servant or armsman, for one or both of these services. A diary entry of Johannes Burckard, Patrizi's successor as master of ceremonies, states that in 1495 this took place 'according to custom' both at Christmas Matins and the main Mass: 'Sacrista tam in matutinis quam in missa majore (papa absente) poni fecit super altare ensem propter consuetudinem quem unus ex

---

[135] According to Marc Dykmans, Matins was celebrated at about three o'clock in the morning (ibid., ii. 174*).

[136] Ibid., ii. 285–6, no. 810. The sword is held upright with the hat on the point (174*).

[137] Ibid. 286, no. 812.   [138] Ibid. 288–9, nos. 821–3.

[139] Ibid. 293, no. 840.   [140] Ibid. 289, no. 825.

[141] This is specified as 'ad angulum retro banchum diaconorum cardinalium . . . vel alium locum convenientem' (ibid. 288, no. 821).

[142] Ibid. 289, no. 823.

[143] Ibid., no. 824. This third Mass was a 'papal' or solemn Mass in which the pope was celebrant. In the early Renaissance, only about five feasts during the year were celebrated as papal Masses, the others being Easter, sometimes Pentecost, Sts Peter and Paul, All Saints' Day, and rare special occasions (ibid. ii. 176*). The fact that in Patrizi's ceremonial the papal Mass at Christmas is designated as the model for other papal Masses suggests that a blessed sword might be used on those occasions, if one had been made and not already awarded. There are the examples of Epiphany in 1460, and Easter in 1471, listed in App. D.

[144] For the full text of the breve, see App. E.

[145] For the last two sentences, see Dykmans, *L'Œuvre*, ii. 183*; 316–18 (nos. 908–14).

familiaribus apportavit.'[146] In 1506, when Julius II was in Bologna, the blessed sword was at the altar of San Petronio during the main Christmas Mass, although the pope, who suffered from gout, was not present. He had blessed it after the second Mass at dawn, and a papal armsman carried it, in its sheath and borne horizontally rather than upright, and held it at the Epistle side of the altar.[147] Paride de' Grassi, the new master of ceremonies, criticized this practice and advised that the sword should not be used at Matins or the Mass when the pope was not present.[148] In 1510, however, Julius II gave express permission for the blessed sword to be used in the main Christmas Mass in his absence.[149]

The first and third Christmas Masses at the Vatican would seem to be occasions appropriate for a *L'homme armé* mass, in which the newly blessed symbols of the defence of Christianity and the victory of Good over Evil play a visible role in the drama of the sacred ritual. In the context of the Vatican, they assert the supremacy of the Church, headed by the pope, over temporal rulers.

Masses of the Armed Man and the *L'homme armé* Masses

All the Masses with armed men considered here would be suitable contexts for the performance of a *L'homme armé* mass: certain pontifical Masses performed by sovereign bishops and abbots, like the abbot of Sant'Antimo and the bishops of Cahors and presumably Cambrai; similar Masses in places like Cividale del Friuli, where special privileges were claimed for historical reasons; the emperor's Christmas Masses, following his armed Gospel reading at Matins; state occasions when the king of France's armsman draws his sword at the Gospel; papal Masses with the blessed sword at Christmas and sometimes other feasts; and especially the presentation ceremonies for the papal swords sent to France and Burgundy in 1457, 1461, and 1462. From what we know of somewhat later presentations, those outside the Vatican involved great, solemn, festive Masses celebrated in the presence of visiting ecclesiastical dignitaries and the local nobility in large numbers. They marked special occasions to honour a sovereign or great lord specifically in his capacity as a military leader with the duty to defend the Christian faith and the Catholic Church, particularly against the Turk. Individual gifts sometimes received artistic commemoration in paintings, poetry, sculpture,

---

[146] Johannes Burckard, *Diarium sive rerum urbanarum commentarii (1483–1506)*, ed. L. Thuasne, 3 vols. [Paris, 1883–5], ii. 345 (cited in Modern, 'Geweihte Schwerter', 135 n. 4). This edition has been superseded by Johannes Burckard, *Liber notarum ab anno 1483 ad 1506*, ed. E. Celani, 2 vols. (Rerum italicarum scriptores, 32, pts. 1–2; Città di Castello, 1910–42).

[147] The complete texts of Paride de' Grassi concerning the ceremonies with the blessed sword and hat in 1506 are found in Burns, *Golden Rose*, 26–7.

[148] Ibid. 25–6. See also in Modern, 'Geweihte Schwerter', 135–6, no. 4.

[149] This was reported and criticized by de' Grassi, who said that the pope had given permission 'per ignorantiam suam'. See Modern, 'Geweihte Schwerter', 135–6, no. 4.

anniversary rites—even in a coat of arms.[150] The legendary gift of a papal sword from Alexander III to Doge Sebastiano Ziani, for instance, furnished the subject for numerous historical paintings in Renaissance Venice, especially in the council chamber in the ducal palace,[151] and in Florence an annual Mass established by law commemorated the anniversary of the gift of a blessed sword to the Signoria in 1434.[152]

The connection between these various armed Masses and the *L'homme armé* masses remains in the realm of possibility alone. Both clearly stand at the conjunction of the spheres of church and state, where the ideal governing the relationship of the two great powers is given ritual expression in the Mass. We have seen that contemporary explanations of the armed Mass ceremonies have recourse to the same body of conceptual imagery. 'The emperor is obliged to defend the faith of Christ with the sword in hand', Rucellai wrote to explain the armed Mass at Sant'Antimo; 'May your hand remain firm against the enemies of the Holy See and of the name of Christ, and may your right hand be lifted up, intrepid warrior, as you remove them from the earth', Sixtus IV adjured the duke of Savoy in his breve for the presentation Mass of the blessed sword.[153] Likewise, in dedicating his gift of six *L'homme armé* masses to Beatrice of Aragon, queen of Hungary, the anonymous donor explained, 'Rex hostes fidei vincit—the king conquers the enemies of the Faith.'[154]

The context of the *l'homme armé* Mass remains a broad and various subject for further exploration.[155] For now, having reached France, Burgundy, Rome, and the Empire by a long and circuitous route from the abbey of Sant'Antimo, we shall end our journey.

---

[150] See Table 1, the notes to the sword of 1480, for Federico da Montefeltro, on the description of the award in *terza rima*, and the notes to the sword of 1488 for the commemorative use of the ducal hat in the coat of arms of the Trivulzi family. A late 16th-c. Roman marble relief of one of the ceremonies is reproduced in Modern, 'Geweihte Schwerter', fig. 1, and Burns, *Golden Rose*, pl. 16.

[151] See Modern, 'Geweihte Schwerter', 143–4. This gift reputedly took place in Venice in 1177 (Moroni, 'Stocco', 44). See also Gino Benzoni, *I dogi* (Milan, 1982), figs. 9 and 177.

[152] Moroni, 'Stocco', 45.   [153] See App. E.

[154] Naples VI E 40, fo. 64; Cohen, *Six Anonymous L'Homme Armé Masses*, 62–3.

[155] In Rome, for instance, the sense of threat to the Church and the military response to it in the late 15th c. found expression in interrelated kinds of symbolic display. Cardinals wore expensive swords, and even weddings could offer occasions for the pope to exhibit the power of the sword. In two nuptial Masses at the Vatican for which we have unusually detailed descriptions, those of Lucrezia Borgia in 1493 and 1498, the captain general of the Church and the captain of the papal guard, respectively, raised bare swords above the couples' heads (Ivan Coulas, *The Borgias*, trans. Gilda Roberts (New York, 1989), 62, 75–6, and 149).

Appendix A
Extracts Concerning the Mass Called the Ceremony of the Armed Man, from the *Zibaldone Quaresimale* of Giovanni Rucellai, fo. 47[r–v][1]

The Italian Text

[1] Truovo chello imperadore carlo magno di francia quando passo nelle parti ditalia negli anni domini ____ [*lacuna*] fece edificare molte citta et castella. Et ancora molti luoghi di religione. Et infra gli altri una badia nel contado di siena presso a siena a miglia cinque verso la maremma la quale si nomina la badia di sancto Antimo. Et missevi monaci neri sotto lordine di sancto guglielmo delquale ordine in italia pochi se ne truovano ma nelle parti di francia ve ne grandissimo numero et molti ricchi monosteri. Et asegno alla detta badia grande rendite et infra laltre parechie castella et ville chella dintorno appresso a poche miglia. Et volle chellabate di detto luogo avesse giuriditione sopra al temporale delle dette castella et ville et di potere fare sangue si come uno signore temporale. Et molte chiese che sono in dette castella et ville volle ne fussi custoditore in darle et torle a chi li pare et piace. Et perche detti sanesi sono cresciuti in signoria piu tempo fa tolsono le dette castella et ville alla detta badia et [h]anno voluto quellentrata et quella giuriditione per loro che l[h]anno fatto di potentia et saluta. Pure nondimeno ancora [h]a grande rendite di possessioni et delle dette chiese per le ville et castella ancora n[e h]a giuriditione et concede tali beneficii a chi li pare et piace.

[2] Et ancora detto imperadore die autorita al detto abate et a tutti gli altri abati di quello luoguo che succedessino doppo lui i quali sono a vita di potere fare et sostituire solo uno uomo il quale abbia autorita di potere legittimare et fare notai che volgarmente si chiamano conti di palazo.

[3] Et piu volle che il detto abate fussi abate et generale sopra tutti li monaci di detto ordine di sanguglielmo et sempre e stato labate di detto luogo generale di tutto lordine.

[4] Et piu volle che ogni volta che il detto abate cantasse la messa in caso che allui piaccia e[i] possa tenere dal lato dextro dellaltare detto conte di palazo o veramente un altro huomo che detto conte di palazo sostituissi in suo luoguo armato di tutte arme colla spada ingniuda in mano in defensione della fede di christo a chi volesse contradirla. Detta ceremonia et autorita gli die et concede il predetto imperadore perche lui e tenuto a difendere la fede di cristo colla spada in mano et cosi ogni imperadore di cristiani et pero volle che il detto abate avessi la medesima autorita chella sua persona quanto alla difensione della fede. Et perche lomperadore usa ancora lui quando ode la messa detta [d, *deleted*] ceremonia delluomo armato di tutte arme colla spada in mano cosi volle quando piacessi al detto abate lo potessi fare. Et al presente non ogni volta che canta messa ma per le feste solempni come sono pasque et altri sancti degni ancora lusa. Et fino che se comunicato il detto conte di palazo o il sostituito per lui tiene la spada fuori della guaina et come [h]a preso il sacrificio la rimette dentro.

---

[1] Transcribed from the microfilm of the original manuscript in the library of the Warburg Institute, London. I am grateful to the librarian Dr W. F. Ryan, for providing me with copies of these pages.

[5] Et delle dette autorita et ceremonie el predetto imperadore carlo di francia fece al detto abate pienissimi brevilegi scripti in giunchi cioe in carta di giunchi come sono le nostre pandette che noi abbiamo a firenze. Et ancora al presente detti brevilegi sono nella predetta badia.

[6] Et truovo che lomperadore de cristiani nella messa papale canta ilvangelo lui in persona in luogho del diacano tenendo la spada ingniuda in mano mentre che canta detto vangelo et poi la rimette nella guaina.

[7] Et truovo che il re di francia per brevilegio che gli [h]a dalla chiesa quando sta alla messa il paggio suo al vangelo tra fuori la spada et tie[ne]lla ritta ingniuda et detto il vangelo la rimette nella guaina.

[8] . . . .

[9] Et truovo che nella citta di cologna nella magna vi susa dire delle messe in certi di dellanno col prete chella dice armato di tutte armi. Et in certi luoghi [h]o veduto tenere in sullaltare in mentre che il prete dice la messa uno elmetto di ferro suvi una mithera da veschovo.

Translation

[1] I find that the Emperor Charles the Great of France, when he passed through Italy in the years of our Lord _____ [*lacuna*], founded many cities and castles. And also many places of religion. And among the others an abbey in the countryside near Siena, at a distance of five miles from Siena towards the Maremma,[2] which is called the Abbey of Sant'Antimo. And he put there black friars[3] under the order of St William,[4] of which order few are found in Italy but a great many in France, and many rich monasteries. And he assigned to the said abbey great revenues and among others many castles and country estates that are nearby at a distance of a few miles. And he wanted the abbot of the said place to have jurisdiction over the temporal matters of the said castles and country estates and to be able to shed blood like a temporal lord. And he wanted [the abbot] to be the guardian of many churches that are in the said castles and country estates, in giving them to and taking them from whomever he liked. And because the Sienese have grown in dominion, some time ago they took away from the said abbey the said castles and country estates, and they wanted that income and that jurisdiction for those who had made them powerful and strong. Nevertheless [the abbey] still has great revenues [from its] possessions, and of the said churches for the country estates and castles, it still has jurisdiction and grants benefices to whomever it likes.

[2] And also the said emperor gave authority to the said abbot and to all the other abbots of that place who should succeed after him, while they are alive, to be able to

---

[2] The abbey is actually more than twenty miles from Siena.

[3] The 'frati neri' here must be Benedictines. Sant'Antimo was among the earliest and most significant Benedictine monasteries in Italy, according to Elm, *Beiträge*, 98. The Williamites to whom the abbey was transferred were also Benedictines (Canestrelli, *Abbazia*, 15).

[4] As mentioned above, the Order of St William did not exist at the time of Charlemagne. It was begun after the death of William of Maleval in 1157 and given papal approval in 1202. See *Lexicon für Theologie und Kirche*, 11 vols. (Freiburg i. Br., 1957–67), s.v. 'Willhelm v. Malavalle'. Sant'Antimo was given to the Williamites in 1291 (Elm, *Beiträge*, 98).

designate and substitute only one man who would have the authority to be able to legitimate and work as notaries [chancellors], who are commonly called counts of the palace.

[3] And moreover he wanted the said abbot to be abbot and general over all the monks
of the said order of St William, and it has always been the abbot of that place who was general of the entire order.[5]

[4] And moreover he desired that every time the said abbot sang Mass, whenever he
wished to he could have at the right side of the altar the said count of the palace, or another
man that the said count of the palace would substitute in his place, armed with all arms
with the drawn sword in his hand in defence of the faith of Christ against whoever would
contradict it. This ceremony and authority was given and conceded to him by the aforesaid emperor because he is obliged to defend the faith of Christ with the sword in hand,
and likewise every emperor of Christians, and therefore he wanted the said abbot to have
the very same authority as himself with regard to the defence of the faith. And because the
emperor himself, when he hears Mass, observes the aforesaid ceremony of the armed man
with all arms with the sword in hand, so he desired that when the abbot wished, he could
do it. And at present, not every time that he sings Mass, but for solemn feasts like Easter
and other worthy saints, he still does it. And until the said count of the palace or his substitute takes communion, he holds the sword out of the sheath, and when he has partaken
of the sacrifice, he puts it back in.

[5] And of the said authority and ceremonies the aforesaid Emperor Charles of France
gave the said abbot the fullest privileges written in *giunchi* (reeds), that is, paper of reeds
[papyrus], as are our pandects that we have in Florence. And still at present the said privileges are in the aforesaid abbey.

[6] And I find that the emperor of Christians in the papal Mass sings the Gospel himself in person, in place of the deacon, holding the bared sword in hand while he sings the
said Gospel, and then he puts it back in the sheath.

[7] And I find that the king of France, by way of the privilege he has from the Church,
when he is at Mass, at the Gospel his page takes out the sword and holds it upright, bared,
and when the Gospel is over he returns it to the sheath.

[8] . . .

[9] And I find that in the city of Cologne in Germany,[6] Masses are said on certain days
of the year with the priest who says it armed with all arms. And in certain places I have seen
put on the altar while the priest says the Mass a helmet of iron with a bishop's mitre on it.

---

[5] Kaspar Elm writes that the abbots of Sant'Antimo came from the leading families of Tuscany and
claimed special privileges, immunities, and rights that were not consistent with membership in an order.
These included the use of the title of abbot and the claim to the office of perpetual vicar of the order. The
general prior of the order had lost authority over the abbots already in the 14th c. See Elm, *Beiträge*, 159
and 125 for the office of gereral prior, and Canestrelli, *Abbazia*, 15, for the abbey's claim of independence
from the [prior] general of the order in 1345.

[6] *Magna* is short for *Alemagna*. See the *Enciclopedia dantesca*, 6 vols. (Rome, 1971), s.v. 'magna'.

Appendix B
The Imperial or Royal Sword Ceremony during Christmas Matins from the Papal Ceremonial of Pierre Ameil, *c*.1375 –1400[1]

The Latin Text

Notandum etiam quod imperator vel rex, si sit in curia hac nocte, sacrista et clerici presentant sibi librum legendarum, in quo debet legere quintam lectionem. Et eum honeste instruunt de ceremoniis observandis in petendo benedictionem, in cingendo ensem cum vagina, et in extrahendo et ipsum vibrando, et de pluviali, pileo et aliis.

Item nobliliter paretur per camerarium et clericos camere ensis cum vagina, corrigia et pileo secundum nobilitatem principis.

Item dum cantatur quartum responsorium, si sit imperator vel rex, camerarius, sacrista et clerici capelle parant unum pulcrum pluviale album, et ante pulpitum sibi deponunt caputium et ipsum induunt ad modum clamidis illud pluviale, ita quod scissura sit ad manum eius dexteram. Et cingunt ei ensem, et ipsemet extrahit et facit vibrare. Et ponunt sibi super caput pileum, et ipse inclinat caput ad papam; et petit benedictionem, et legit lectionem, sibi predictis astantibus.

Qua lecta, ducunt eum sic indutum cum pileo super caput, ense extracto in manu, ad osculum pedis pape. Et quilibet revertitur ad locum suum.

Translation

It should also be noted that if the emperor or king is in the papal court this night, the sacrist and clerics present to him the lectionary from which he must read the fifth lesson. And they faithfully instruct him in the ceremony observed in entreating benediction, in girding on the sword with sheath, and drawing it and brandishing it, and about the pluvial, pileus, and other things.

Likewise the sword with sheath, belt, and pileus must be nobly prepared by the chamberlain and clerics of the chamber according to the nobility of the prince.

And while the fourth responsory is being sung, if the emperor or king is there, the chamberlain, sacrist, and clerics of the chapel prepare a pure white pluvial, and before the pulpit they remove his hood and put on him the said pluvial in the manner of a cloak, so that the opening is at his right hand. And they gird him with the sword, and he draws it himself and brandishes it. And they put the pileus on his head, and he bows his head to the pope; and entreats benediction, and reads the lesson, the aforementioned persons standing by him.

The lesson having been read, they conduct him so dressed with the pileus on his head and the drawn sword in his hand to kiss the pope's foot. And everyone returns to his place.

---

[1] Latin text from the critical edition edited by Marc Dykmans, SJ, *Le Cérémonial papal de la fin du moyen âge à la Renaissance*, iv: *Le Retour à Rome ou le cérémonial du patriarche Pierre Ameil* (Brussels, 1985), 75–6, paras. 55–8. See above, n. 38, on other publications of this text.

Appendix C
Papal Gifts of the Sword and Hat Blessed on Christmas and Sent to Distant Recipients, 1455–1503

* = sword survives

Date		Recipient	Remarks
Blessed	Sent		
Calixtus III, 1455–1458			
1455[a]	?		
1456[b]	1457?[c]	Charles VII	Probably to urge the king to revoke the Pragmatic Sanction and fight the Turks.[d]
1457*[e]	1458	Henry IV of Castile	Reward for victories over the Moors,[f] and call for renewed efforts against them.
Pius II, 1458–1464			
1458	7/1459[g]	Emperor Frederick III	All swords of Pius II were to induce the Christian princes to wage a crusade against the Turks.[h]

[a] Müntz reports on a document of the creation of the sword, in 'Les Épées II', 283–4.

[b] For the document on the manufacture of the sword, see ibid. 284.

[c] Dykmans gives the date of 1457, without citing a source for it, in *L'Œuvre de Patrizi*, i. 93*. Cornides states only that Charles VII was sent one of the two swords that were known to have been prepared in 1455 and 1456; it is mentioned in an envoy's letter and a later inventory (*Rose und Schwert*, 94). Müntz provides some details from the inventory (Amboise, 1499): the sword had the arms of Calixtus III, the scabbard was trimmed with gilded silver, the hat was of scarlet velvet seeded with pearls. See 'Les Épées II', 285.

[d] See Moroni, 'Stocco', 46, and Cornides, *Rose und Schwert*, 94, on Calixtus's crusading zeal. Moroni considers that the purpose for which Pius II, in 1459, gave Charles VII the title of Defender of the Faith was to press him to renounce the Pragmatic Sanction (and thereby accept the pope's authority). See Moroni, *Dizionario*, s.v. 'Difensore della Chiesa', xx. 41. It seems reasonable to suppose that the gift of the sword sent by Calixtus two or three years earlier had a similar purpose. The presentation formulas for Charles VII, the first to survive, were also used for Philip the Good, as noted down by Johannes Burckard in Vatican City, Biblioteca Apostolica Vaticana, MS Vat. lat. 12343, fo. 130ʳ⁻ᵛ. These formulas were retouched for the presentation of the golden rose to James IV, King of Scots, in 1491. See Dykmans, *L'Œuvre de Patrizi*, i. 93*. According to Burns, as mentioned above, Vat. lat. 12343, fo. 148ʳ, contains the instructions for the sword and hat given to Philip the Good, with alterations added for the golden rose of 1491 (*Golden Rose*, 39). For the altered text, see his App. II, 38–9. See above, pp. 110–111, for a paraphrase of the presentation text, based on Burns.

[e] According to Cornides, the sword sent to Henry was 'perhaps' that of 1457 (*Rose und Schwert*, 94). This is the date given by Moroni ('Stocco', 46). Müntz also gives the date of manufacture and blessing as 1457 and cites a Spanish chronicle, *Cronicon de Valladolid* (Madrid, 1848), that evidently states that the sword was sent in 1458. He also states that the blade still exists in the royal armoury in Madrid, and he describes the decoration and inscription; see 'Les Épées II', 284–5. Cornides mistakenly states that the scabbard still exists (*Rose und Schwert*, 94).

[f] Moroni writes that the gifts were a reward for some successes in battle against the Moors ('Stocco', 46), but Cornides states that they were rather an inducement (*Rose und Schwert*, 94).

[g] Cornides, *Rose und Schwert*, 95.

[h] Ibid. and Moroni, 'Stocco', 46. Moroni gives the proposed crusade as the purpose of the Congress of Mantua, which was under way when Pius sent the sword and hat to Frederick III. He explains that the emperor was held responsible, 'more than the other sovereigns, to protect the Church from the enemies of Christianity'. Cornides also states that there was probably a tradition of sending the first blessed sword of a pontificate to the emperor.

Date		Recipient	Remarks
Blessed	Sent		

[1459: see App. D]

1460	1/1461 embassy	Philip the Good, duke of Burgundy	Antonio de Noceto, ambassador.[i]
1461	1/1462 embassy	King Louis XI (r. 1461–83)	Antonio de Noceto and the Cardinal Bishop of Arras, Jean Jouffroy, ambassadors.[j]
1462*[k]	1463	Cristoforo Moro, doge of Venice	Indicates the importance of a Venetian fleet for a crusade.[l]
1463	?		

Paul II, 1464–1471

[1466: see App. D][m]			All swords of this papacy were given to promote the league against Islam.[n]
1467	?		
[1468: see App. D]			
1469	?		
1470	breve 4/1/1471	Matthias Corvinus, king of Hungary[p]	Sword to fight the Turks and the Bohemian heretics.[o]

[See also App. D for a second sword presented in 1471]

---

[i] Cornides, *Rose und Schwert*, 95–6. The January departure of the ambassadors is cited by Moroni ('Stocco', 46). On the presentation formulas, see n. *d* above on the sword for Charles VII. This sword was embellished with pearls and gems (Moroni, 'Stocco', 46).

[j] Cornides, *Rose und Schwert*, 95–6. Noceto also brought a letter from the pope to the king that is dated 13 Jan. 1462, which makes it clear that the ambassadors had not yet left Rome on that date. See Chr. Lucius, *Pius II. und Ludwig XI. von Frankreich, 1461–1462* (Heidelberger Abhandlungen, 41; Heidelberg, 1913), 48.

[k] Heinrich Modern argues that the doge received the sword that was blessed on Christmas Eve of 1462, and that inconsistencies in early practices of numbering the years have confused scholars, especially for the pontificate of Pius II ('Geweihte Schwerter', 141–2 and 161). He notes that the sword bears the year '1463', but that the new year at the Vatican began with Christmas Eve. (Cornides, following Müntz, erroneously gives 1463 as the year of the blessing of this sword and states that the recipient of the sword blessed in 1462 is unknown, in *Rose und Schwert*, 96.) Müntz mentions that there are documents of the manufacture of the papal sword in 1462 and that the price had gone up ('Les Épées II', 286). Mitchell reports that the blessed sword was sent to Venice early in 1463 (*Laurels*, 255). One side of the sword, which is preserved in the armoury in the ducal palace in Venice, is reproduced in Gino Benzoni, *I dogi* (Milan, 1982), 39, fig. 28, where part of the inscription on the blade can be seen. A drawing of the other side, with another inscription ('PIVS PAPA II ANNO V PONTIFICATVS'), appears in Müntz, 'Les Épées II', 286.

[l] Cornides, *Rose und Schwert*, 96. In 1463 Pius II announced his plan for a crusade that he would lead himself, together with the duke of Burgundy, and which the doge of Venice was also to join in person, along with a Venetian fleet. See John Julius Norwich, *A History of Venice* (New York, 1982), 344–5.

[m] Müntz quotes documents of the manufacture of two papal swords in 1466, but evidently no other such payment records survive from this papacy ('Les Épées II', 286). Cornides quotes an earlier article of Müntz in which the date of the two swords is given as 1467 (*Rose und Schwert*, 96 n. 9).

[n] See Cornides, *Rose und Schwert*, 96. [o] Ibid. 97.

[p] Moroni, 'Stocco', 47. He cites the papal breve *Suscipiat* of 4 Jan. 1471.

Date		Recipient	Remarks
Blessed	Sent		
?	?	Henry IV, king of Castile *q*	Related to the effort to expel the Moors from Spain. Probably the Christmas sword of 1467 or 1469.

Sixtus IV, 1471–1484

1474*r*	[1475]	Philibert I, duke of Savoy (r. 1474–82)	Sword sent with breve exhorting the duke to protect the church.*s*
[1477: see App. D]			
1480	soon after	Federico da Montefeltro, duke	Undoubtedly honoured for military actions on behalf of the pope.*t*
	25/12/1480	of Urbino	
1481	[1482]	Edward IV of England*u*	

[1482: see App. D]

Documented swords with unknown recipients: 1471, 1472, 1473, 1475, 1476, 1478, 1479.*v*

Innocent VIII, 1484–1492

?	?	Ferdinand II of Spain*w*	

[1484, 1486, 1488, 1491: see App. D]

Documented swords with unknown recipients: 1485, 1487, 1489.*x*

Alexander VI, 1492–1503

[1492: see App. D]

q Cornides, *Rose und Schwert*, 97 and n. 14. She quotes an article by Müntz of 1879 to the effect that this sword is still preserved in the royal armoury in Madrid; but Müntz states in a later article that this sword, although listed in an inventory of 1793, was lost after the revolution. See Müntz, 'Les Épées II', 286.

r Moroni, 'Stocco', 47; Müntz, 'Les Épées II', 287. Cornides, *Rose und Schwert*, 99, gives the year as 1477, which must be a misprint.

s Moroni, 'Stocco', 47. The breve *Solent Romani Pontifices*, 25 Dec. 1474, appears below in App. E. Part of it was later incorporated into the ritual for the presentation of the sword.

t The gifts were presented in Viterbo by the papal orator Pier Felici. See Giovanni Santi, *La vita e le geste di Federico di Montefeltro, Duca di Urbino: poema in terza rima*, ed. Luigi Michelini Tucci, 2 vols. (Studi e Testi, 305; Vatican City, 1985), ii. 621–2 (bk. 20, ch. 85, lns. 57–81). The main literature on the blessed sword and hat does not mention this award, but it is cited in Frederick M. Schweitzer and Harry E. Wedeck (eds.), *Dictionary of the Renaissance* (New York, 1967), s.v. 'Decoration of the Rose, the Hat, and the Sword'.

u Cornides, *Rose und Schwert*, 99. Moroni gives the date as 1477 ('Stocco', 47).

v Müntz reports on records of the manufacture of the swords for each year of this pontificate from 1471 to 1480, in 'Les Épées II', 286–7. It is worth noting that Louis XI would be an especially promising possibility for the Christmas sword of 1472, since he agreed to a major concordat with Sixtus IV in October of that year, essentially reiterating his promises of 1462. See Carlo Calisse, 'I concordati del secolo XV', in *Chiesa e stato: Studi storici e giuridici per il decennale della conciliazione tra la Santa Sede e l'Italia* (Studi storici, Pubblicazioni della Università del S. Cuore, ser. 2, 65; Milan, 1939), i. 137–41.

w Cornides, *Rose und Schwert*, 101; and Müntz, 'Les Épées II', 288, who reports that the sword still existed in 1793, according to an inventory of the royal armoury in Madrid. The gift was undoubtedly linked to the battles against the Moors, who were finally cast out of Spain in 1492.

x Müntz, 'Les Épées II', 287–8. Müntz states that two hats were made in 1489.

Date		Recipient	Remarks
Blessed	Sent		
1493	sent 6 Mar. 1494	Maximilian I, king of the Romans[y] (acting as emperor from 1493)	
[1494: see App. D]			
1495[z]	?	?	
1496	1497	Philip the Fair, archduke of Austria[aa]	
[1497: see App. D]			
1498	1499	King Louis XII of France[bb] (r. 1498–1516)	
1499[cc]	?	?	
1501	rec'd 6 Feb. 1502	Alfonso d'Este, heir to duchy of Ferrara	After his marriage to the pope's daughter, Lucrezia Borgia.[dd]

[y] Cornides, *Rose und Schwert*, 103. Müntz is evidently incorrect on the recipient of the sword made in 1493, whom he identifies as the future Ferdinand II of Aragon. He gives the date on which a blessed sword was sent to Maximilian I, however, as 6 Mar. 1494. See 'Les Épées II', 291.

[z] Müntz quotes Burckard on the pope's blessing of the sword on Christmas, but no recipient is named. See ibid. 291.

[aa] Cornides, *Rose und Schwert*, 103.

[bb] Ibid. Perhaps this might be the sword described in an inventory of the armoury at Arras in 1499 as having 'the scabbard white, the hilt trimmed with wood [?], on the pommel an Our Lady on one side and a St Martin on the other, called the pope's sword, who sent it to King Louis'. See Müntz, 'Les Épées II', 286. Müntz associates this inventory item with the papal sword sent to Louis XI in 1462, but the description does not match the one given in Pius II's commentaries, and in 1499 'Roy Loys' would presumably be Louis XII.

[cc] Müntz quotes Burckard's *Diarium* on the use of the sword and hat at St Peter's in 1499, at the altar at Mass on Christmas, but there was no immediate recipient. See ibid. 292.

[dd] The French ambassador to the Vatican delivered the gifts, with a papal bull, to Ferrara at the time of Lucrezia Borgia's festive entry. See Cornides, *Rose und Schwert*, 103–4. The solemn presentation took place in the cathedral there on 6 Feb. 1502. See Müntz, 'Les Épées II', 292.

Appendix D
Gifts in the Pope's Presence of the Blessed Sword and Hat, 1455–1503, in Rome (unless otherwise mentioned)

* = sword survives

Date of		Recipient	Remarks
Christmas blessing	Presentation		

Calixtus III, 1455–1458

—

Pius II, 1458–1464

| 1459 | 1/1460[a] (Mantua) | Margrave Albrecht of Brandenburg | Purpose: to urge the crusade against the Turks.[b] |

Paul II, 1464–1471

1466	1466	Scanderbeg, Albanian hero[c]	Scanderbeg was in Rome at Christmas to seek aid against the Turks.[d]
1468	1468	Emperor Frederick III	The emperor was in Rome for Christmas to fulfil a pilgrimage vow.[e]
?	Easter, 1471[f]	Borso d'Este, created duke of Ferrara	Elevation of Ferrara to a duchy; Borso joined league against Turks.[g]

Sixtus IV, 1471–1484

| 1477 | 1477 | Alfonso, duke of Calabria[h] | Heir to the kingdom of Naples (r. 1494–5). |
| 1482 | 1482 | Alfonso, duke of Calabria[i] | |

[a] Presented in the Mass of Epiphany. Moroni, 'Stocco', 46. This was during the Congress of Mantua.

[b] Cornides, *Rose und Schwert*, 95. Pius wanted him to lead the armies of the crusaders against the Turks. See Ady, *Pius II*, 175–6.

[c] R. J. Mitchell calls Scanderbeg (George Castriotes) 'a splendid picaresque leader of almost superhuman strength and courage' (*Laurels*, 259). See also J. B. Bury, 'The Ottoman Conquest', in A. W. Ward, G. W. Prothero, and Stanley Leathes (eds.), *The Cambridge Modern History*, i: *The Renaissance* (Cambridge, 1907), 66.

[d] Cornides, *Rose und Schwert*, 97.

[e] Ibid. 96–7.

[f] Ibid. 96. It is not clear when this sword and ducal hat were manufactured and blessed, since another sword had been sent to Matthias Corvinus in January.

[g] Ibid. Borso received papal gifts of a sword, ducal hat, spurs, and, the next day, the golden rose. Cornides specifically explains only the gift of the golden rose in connection with the league for the crusade, but the raising of Borso's position and all the attendant gifts are probably also to be seen in that light.

[h] The wording in Moroni, 'Stocco', 47, implies that Alfonso received the sword in person.

[i] Cornides, *Rose und Schwert*, 99.

Date of		Recipient	Remarks
Christmas blessing	Presentation		

Innocent VIII, 1484–1492

1484	1484	Francesco of Aragon, ambassador	Gift (for his declaration of obedience) of the king of Naples, his father, to the pope[j]
1486*	1486	Enea López de Mendoza, count of Tendilla, ambassador	Honoured for having declared the obedience of the king and queen of Castile and Aragon.[k]
1488	1488	Giovanni Giacomo Trivulzio, general of the ecclesiastical army	Honoured as a defender of the church for putting down the rebellious tyrant of Osimo.[l]
1491*	1491	Count Wilhelm of Hesse[m]	Recipient was returning from a pilgrimage to Jerusalem.[n]

Alexander VI, 1492–1503

1492	1492	Federico of Aragon, son of Ferrante[o]	Federico became king of Naples in 1496.
1494	1494	Ferdinand, duke of Calabria[p]	Now heir of the kingdom of Naples (r. 1495–6).
1497*	1497	Duke Boleslaw of Pomerania	The duke was returning from a pilgrimage to the Holy Land.[q]

---

[j] Ibid. 101. Moroni, 'Stocco', 47.

[k] Cornides, *Rose und Schwert*, 101.

[l] Moroni, 'Stocco', 47. From that time on, the ducal hat ornamented the Trivulzi coat of arms.

[m] Cornides, *Rose und Schwert*, 101. Müntz, 'Les Épées II', 288–90, including a drawing of the sword and scabbard, which are preserved in Kassel. Both sides of the blade bear the inscription 'ECCE * GLADIVM * AD * DEFENSIONEM * CHRISTIANEM (*sic*) * VERE * FIDEI'; there are also the pope's name, coat of arms, and *impresa*, the year of his papacy, and engraved and gilded images of St Peter and St Paul. Moroni erroneously places this sword and the ceremonies connected with it in 1492, in 'Stocco', 47.

[n] Cornides, *Rose und Schwert*, 101.

[o] Ibid. 103. Burckard describes the presentation in St Peter's after the main Mass (*Diarium*, ii. 26; quoted in Müntz, 'Les Épées II', 290–1).

[p] Cornides, *Rose und Schwert*, 103. She corrects the date of 1493 given by Müntz [and Moroni].

[q] Ibid. 102. For a drawing of this sword, together with the excerpt from Burckard's diary describing the presentation, see Müntz, 'Les Épées II', 290–1.

Appendix E
Text for the Presentation of the Blessed Sword and Hat, Instituted by Sixtus IV[1]

Solent Romani Pontifices in praeclara Natalis Domini celebritate christianissimo clarissimoque alicui principi ornatum ensem dare aut destinare, quae res profecto non caret mysterio. Unigenitus namque dei filius ut humanam naturam suo reconciliaret auctori, eam assumere dignatus est, ut inventor mortis diabolus per ipsam, quae vicerat, vinceretur, quae quidem victoria per ensem congrue designatur. Fuerunt insuper infideles Ariani, qui non veriti sunt Dei filium puram creaturam affirmare; cum tamen hodierni Evangelii scriptura testatur Deum omnia fecisse per Verbum. Largitur igitur praesenti die Maximus Pontifex emsem Dei infinitam potentiam signitatem in Christo Deo vero, Patrique aequali, et vero homini residentem, per quem facta sunt omnia iuxta Davidicum illud: Tui sunt caeli et tua est terra et plenitudinem eius tu fundasti, aquilonem et mare tu creasti. Sedes deinque Dei, Apostolica videlicet Sedes, a Christo suum sumpsit stabilimentum, exstititque praeparata Dei iusto iudicio, praemio atque iustitia, quibus salvator noster Jesus Deus et homo profligavit sedis ipsius adversarios, haereticos videlicet et tyrannos iuxta id quoque profeticum: Iustitia et iudicium praeparatio sedis suae. Figurat denique pontificalis his gladius potestatem summam temporalem a Christo Pontifici eius in terra vicario collatam iuxta illud: Data est mihi omnis potentia in coelo et in terra. Et alibi: Dominabitur a mari usque mare, et a flumine usque ad terminos orbis terrarum. Quam et declarat cappa illa serica, quam Pontifices gestare solent in nocte Nativitatis Domini. Nos ergo volentes, ut aequum est, approbatas sanctorum patruum consuetudines observare, statuimus te principem catholicam Sanctaeque Sedis a Deo utrumque gladium habentis filium devotissimum hoc nostro praeclaro munere insignire necnon hoc pileo in signum muniminis et defensionis adversus inimicos fidei et Sanctae Romanae Ecclesiae protegere. Firmetur igitur manus tua contra hostes Sanctae Sedis ac Christi nominis et exaltetur dextera tua, eos veluti ipsius assiduus intrepidusque propugnator de terra delendo et armetur caput tuum Spiritus Sancti per columbam perleam figurati protectione adversus eos, in quos Dei iustitia atque dignetur idem Dei filius qui cum Patre et Spiritu Sancto. Amen.

Translation

Roman pontiffs are accustomed, at the most splendid celebration of the Birth of the Lord, to give or to grant to some most Christian, most illustrious prince, a handsome sword; this is a custom certainly not without mystery. So that the only begotten Son of God might reconcile the human nature which he deigned to put on with his [divine] authority, so that the devil, the inventor of death, might be defeated by that which he had defeated, this victory is fittingly symbolized by a sword. Moreover, the faithless Arians were not afraid of arguing that the Son of God was a pure creature [i.e. was made entirely of created matter],

---

[1] Latin text quoted from Cornides, *Rose und Schwert*, 139, based on the ceremonial of Agostino Patrizi. (The critical edition of Patrizi's ceremonial in Dykmans, *L'Œuvre*, gives only the incipit of the breve *Solent Romani Pontifices*.) Moroni gives the date of 25 Dec. 1474 for the original breve ('Stocco', 47).

although the Gospel testifies that God made everything through the Word. Therefore the pope in these days grants the sword as a sign of the infinite power of God in Christ the Lord, who is co-equal with God, and truly became a man, by whom all those things were done, as David says: 'The heavens and the earth are yours, and you have established its plenty, and you have created the wind and the sea.' The seat of God, that is, the Apostolic See, takes its firmness from Christ, and has been prepared by the just judgement of God, with reward and justice, with which our saviour Jesus the Lord and man has struck down the enemies of the seat, that is, heretics and tyrants, about which it is prophesied: 'Justice and judgement are the preparation for his seat.' The pontifical sword symbolizes the highest temporal power conferred by Christ upon the pope, his vicar on earth, according to this [passage]: 'All power is granted to me in heaven and on earth.' And elsewhere [it is written]: 'His power will be from sea to sea, and from the river to the ends of the earth.' The silk cope [a full-length, semi-circular cape] which popes customarily wear on the Eve of the Birth of the Lord declares this. Therefore, wishing to observe the customs approved by the Holy Fathers, as is correct, we appoint you, holy prince, as another sword of the Holy See, which has, we declare by this fine gift, a most devout son in you, and also by this hat we declare that you are a fortification and bulwark to protect the holy Roman Church against the enemies of the Faith. Therefore, may your hand remain firm against the enemies of the Holy See and of the name of Christ, and may your right hand be lifted up, intrepid warrior, as you remove them from the earth, and may your head be protected against them by the Holy Spirit, symbolized by the pearly dove, in those things deemed worthy by the Son of God, together with the Father and the Holy Spirit. Amen.[2]

---

[2] Translation by Professor Robert Levine, Boston University.

PART II

INTERTEXTUAL, CONTEXTUAL, AND HERMENEUTIC APPROCHES TO LATE MEDIEVAL MUSICAL CULTURE

6

Arma virumque cano:
Echoes of a Golden Age

✿✿ ✿✿

MICHAEL LONG

THE Fall of Constantinople in 1453 marked a turning-point in European history the ramifications of which resonated far beyond the geographical limits of Byzantium. What appeared to be a stunning blow to the Church as a fundamental entity in fact ushered in several decades of increased prestige for the Roman papacy, and introduced a unifying theme into political discourse that affected both the polemical and actual interactions not only between the popes and secular princes, but among the secular powers of Europe. Neither the theme of a new crusade against the Turks, nor its implementation as a series of piecemeal preliminary expeditions,[1] was inherently new. What changed after 1453 was the status and number of papal exhortations on their behalf, as the church's financial demands on temporal authorities gained increased legitimacy, and the level of enthusiasm for the crusade (at least in terms of public posturing) grew in proportion to Turkish advances towards the heart of Roman Christendom. Crusade propaganda of the thirteenth and fourteenth centuries had established the principal themes that continued to be recycled as justifications for the Holy War in written and oratorical polemics, but now they were increasingly garbed in epic dress. As one historian puts it, the events of 1453 'sharpened the instinct for tragic drama in contemporary writers'.[2] The mythic proportions of Constantinople as a conceptual locus within the Christian tradition suggested literary analogies drawn from the canon of epic literature. Above all, the state of Christendom in the second half of the fifteenth century suggested parallels with those literary topoi connected with cataclysmic falls and quests for

---

[1] Concerning the organization of *passagia particularia*, in preparation for the grand *passagium generale* to the Holy Land itself, see Norman Housley, *The Avignon Papacy and the Crusades, 1305–1378* (Oxford, 1986), 3.

[2] Robert Schwoebel, *The Shadow of the Crescent: The Renaissance Image of the Turk (1453–1517)* (New York, 1967), 10.

restoration. In this paper I shall attempt to outline the relevance of these traditions to the *L'homme armé* phenomenon, and specifically to the masses of Busnoys and the anonymous creator or creators of the masses of the Naples VI E 40. If Busnoys is ultimately relegated to a peripheral role, I cite by way of model and apologia Paula Higgins's brilliant essay on the Hacqueville songs, in which the composer plays the part of a satellite orbiting a weightier centre of historical gravity.[3]

Let me first review the current evidence for associating polyphonic *L'homme armé* compositions with the crusading sentiment of the late fifteenth century,[4] and offer some conjectures regarding the song itself.

I

The polytextual rondeau transmitted anonymously in the Mellon manuscript and ascribed to 'Borton' in the Casanatense chansonnier, *Il sera pour vous conbatu/L'ome armé*, superimposes upon the *L'homme armé* song a cantus text in which the Burgundian musician Simonet le Breton is advised that the *doubté Turcq*, the feared Turk, will be fought for him (the implication being that Simon himself would not have to engage in hand-to-hand combat with a Turk). David Fallows's suggestion[5] that the song was composed in the spring of 1464 is especially compelling in light of historical circumstances, for at that point Burgundy's participation in the ill-fated crusade against the Turks to be led by Pope Pius II was still expected. The crusaders were scheduled to convene in Ancona in July of that year, and while ultimately the Burgundians did not show up, one can imagine that the preceding spring was a time of considerable anxiety for the less militarily inclined members of the duke's court.

In the dedicatory epistle to Beatrice of Aragon, queen of Hungary, that precedes the six masses of Naples VI E 40 in which tropes of Ordinary texts function simultaneously as tropes on the text of the *L'homme armé* chanson, the donor lauds the queen and her husband for their preoccupation with 'the enemies of the Faith'.[6] In the phrase *Rex hostes fidei vincit* (the king conquers the enemies of the faith) the letter refers specifically to King Matthias Corvinus' much-heralded victory over the Turks at Jajce in December of 1463, wherein he personally led his army against the *infidi Christiani*, as he termed the Turkish occupation forces in his own report of his 'victory for Christendom' dispatched to Pius II in January

---

[3] Paula Higgins, 'Parisian Nobles, A Scottish Princess, and the Woman's Voice in Late Medieval Song', *EMH* 10 (1991), 145–200.

[4] Brief discussions of *L'homme armé* and the 'Turkish connection' are included in Geoffrey Chew, 'The Early Cyclic Mass as an Expression of Royal and Papal Supremacy', *ML* 53 (1972), 267, and Ruth Hannas, 'Concerning Deletions in the Polyphonic Mass Credo', *JAMS* 5 (1952), 168–9.

[5] 'Simon le Breton', *New Grove*, xvii. 323.

[6] See Judith Cohen, *The Six Anonymous L'homme armé Masses in Naples, Biblioteca Nazionale, MS VI E 40* ([Rome], 1968), 62–3.

1464.[7] These instances are quite explicit, but they do not constitute in themselves a complete argument to support the ascription of all *L'homme armé* compositions to the crusade phenomenon. However, I would maintain that certain features of the text and musical structure of the song itself suggest a specific response to the crusading climate after the Fall of Constantinople, and thus represent an individual compositional act on the part of Busnoys or an as-yet-undetermined contemporary, rather than manifestations of some urban or popular tradition.

One of the most unusual aspects of the *L'homme armé* song is the reiteration of the word 'man', heard five times in the first statement of the opening section, and repeated at the end with a slight orthographical variation.[8]

> *Lo(m)me lo(m)me lo(m)me arme*
> *lo(m)me arme lo(m)me arme doibt on doubter*
> *doibt on doubter*
> *On a fait par tout crier*
> *que ch(asc)un se viengne armer*
> *du(n) haubrego(n) de fer*
> *Lo(m)me lo(m)me lo(m)me arme*
> *Lo(m)me arme*
> *Lo(m)me arme doibt on doubter*[9]

Since textual repetitions of such brief syntactic units do not form part of the conventional arsenal of musico-poetical strategies until the sixteenth century, this particular textual event demands a particular 'reading'. The phrase *L'homme armé* will admit two interpretations, that of the faithful knight and that of the enemy.[10] In its first invocation in the song, I think 'the man, the man, the man', whom one must fear, is meant to evoke the sheer numbers of Turkish invading forces which threatened Christian strongholds throughout the fifteenth century. Unlike the tactically inferior Christian troops, one hundred of which, according to contemporary reports, made more noise than ten thousand Turks, the infidels approached the battlefield from two or three miles away mounted in a massive continuous line that advanced methodically and rhythmically to the sound of a drum.[11] The superior numbers of Turks vs. Christians formed a pessimistic leitmotiv in crusade rhetoric of the later Middle Ages. As Pius II wrote in his autobiographical *Commentaries*: 'We longed to declare war against the Turks and to put forth every effort in defense of religion, but when we measure our strength

---

[7] Karl Nehring, *Matthias Corvinus, Kaiser Friedrich III. und das Reich: Zum hunyadisch-habsburgischen Gegensatz im Donauraum* (Munich, 1975), 23–4.

[8] The precise orthography of the final two statements (with upper case *L*s) may be related to a symbolic subtext. See below, pp. 151–2.

[9] The text is taken from the tenor of Mass VI in the Naples manuscript, fo. 58ᵛ.

[10] Geoffrey Chew, 'The Early Cyclic Mass', 267, suggested that 'the "Homme armé" of the song was an allegory of the Turk among other things'.

[11] Schwoebel, *The Shadow of the Crescent*, 104.

against that of the enemy, it is clear that the Church of Rome cannot defeat the Turks with its own resources . . . We are far inferior to the Turks unless Christian kings should unite their forces.'[12] The lack of parity between Christian and infidel troops is encapsulated in the Kyrie trope of Naples Mass V, in which the Christians, defended by the breastplate and helmet of God, are compared to David battling Goliath.[13]

Musically, the *L'homme armé* tune is a study in reiterations, the most striking perhaps being the thrice-repeated *d'* that precedes the cadential *g* at the end of the first section of the song. If both pitches are heard as a single unit, the dropping fifth might, as has often been suggested, represent the sound of a trumpet call; but surely the trumpet is to be associated with the opening of the second section of the song, based on a dropping fourth figure, and appropriately attached to the words *on a fait partout crier ‖ que chascun se viengne armer*, since the primary military purpose of the trumpet was the call to arms.[14] That function is described in the most widely read treatise on the art of war at the time, the *De re militari* of Vegetius, second only to Boethius in numbers of medieval vernacular translations.[15] Vegetius distinguishes between the horn, *cornicina*, which is to be used to signal the banner-carriers to move forth, and the trumpet, *tubicina*, which should be heard 'when the knights are called to battle'.[16] Naples Mass IV, based on the song phrase *on a fait partout crier*, includes several references to the *tuba* (trumpet) in its Kyrie trope. What, then, of the triple repercussion on *d'* at *doibt on doubter*? One possibility is suggested by the report of Bertrandon de La Broquière, a councillor of Philip the Good of Burgundy, who undertook an intelligence mission to Turkey in the 1430s at Philip's behest. In his account of Turkish battle strategy, La Broquière describes the method by which the Turks had so often defeated Christian forces. The Turks typically dispersed in order to draw their enemy out of formation, and then quickly would regroup in order to present a united front. An order to regroup was first signalled by the commander: three raps on the kettledrum. The other soldiers responded with the same signal.[17] For the Turkish soldier, the drum was one of the indispensable trappings of battle, and La Broquière himself carried one during his Turkish sojourn (and probably brought it back with him to the Burgundian court).[18] For a Christian soldier, the three-beat signal was certainly to be feared, as were the ricocheting

---

[12] See *Memoirs of a Renaissance Pope: The Commentaries of Pius II*, trans. Florence A. Gragg (New York, 1959), 237.

[13] *[Kyrie] O Deus excelse lorica casside tali protege Christicolas famulosque tuos velud olim David Goliam vicit et Israel hostem, eleyson* (fos. 44ʳ–45ʳ).

[14] Tinctoris, *Liber de arte contrapuncti*, iii. 6 illustrates the 'sound of bells and trumpets' with similar figures. See Johannes Tinctoris, *Opera theoretica*, ed. Albert Seay, 2 vols. (n.p., 1975), ii. 152–3.

[15] Geoffrey Lester, *The Earliest English Translation of Vegetius' De Re Militari* (Heidelberg, 1988), 15.

[16] Ibid. 97.

[17] Schwoebel, *The Shadow of the Crescent*, 104.

[18] Ibid. 101.

replies from throughout the field, a moment perhaps crystallized in such imitative passages as shown in Ex. 6.1, from Busnoys's *Missa L'homme armé*.

Ex. 6.1. Busnoys, *Missa L'homme armé*, Tu solus, mm. 4–7

The second half of the song, beginning *On a fait partout crier ‖ Que chascun se viengne armer*, might depict a sort of general call to arms that would have been heard in any number of situations, courtly, urban, or military. But whether royal, ducal, papal, or imperial, the polyphonic *L'homme armé* repertory existed in a courtly environment, and we may expect its text to have shared some strand of style, content, or referentiality with other contemporaneous poetry. I would point to the phrase *partout crier* and the subsequent *chascun* as constituting a particularly accurate depiction of the universal response to Constantinople heard, quite literally, everywhere in Christendom, and more specifically in one genre of courtly poetry, the political lament. Throughout Europe, the Fall of Constantinople inspired an outpouring of such works, as did later events like the Turkish seizure of Negropont in 1470. Similar in style, but arising out of the continuing Turkish crisis in general rather than specific Turkish victories, were scores of shorter orations and broadsides. All these poems, vernacular and Latin, shared certain features in common: portrayal of the Turks as monstrous enemies of Christendom and the sacraments, and textual calls, indeed cries, to arms (which were obviously intended for histrionic performance *alta voce*). These were directed at specific ears, that is, each potential defender of the faith is identified and petitioned. The voice issuing those cries is usually that of the anthropomorphized Church, or Constantinople. They are written in vocative style, with multiple strophes often beginning 'I cry' (*grido* or *chiamo* in Italian poems) 'O, Pope'

'O, King of France' 'O, Duke of Burgundy' 'O, King of Hungary'. Each name is followed by a plea, 'call your people to arms to defend me'. In the lament of Mother Church performed at the Feast of the Pheasant in 1454, the supplication begins with an invocation, 'O toy, o toy, noble duc de Bourgoingne', followed by an address to 'vous autres princes'. In an Italian *lamento* of 1453, Constantinople cries out strophe by strophe to the pope, the emperor, the king of Hungary, the king of Aragon, the king of France, the king of England, the duke of Burgundy, the duke of Milan, the Venetian doge, Florence, Pisa, Genoa, Siena, the French Dauphin, and strophesful of Italian princes to take up arms and 'fare a[i] Turchi dispietata guerra'.[19] Thus, I would take the second part of the *L'homme armé* text ('on a fait partout crier . . .') not as a naturalistic portrayal of a fifteenth-century urban soundscape, but as a comment upon the courtly rhetoric of vocative supplications exhibited in the contemporary Christian lamentations.[20] While this is not the place for a full exploration of these lament texts, a further link between the *L'homme armé* tradition and the lament genre is evidenced by several texts on the fall of Negropont in 1470,[21] which similarly describe that city's calls to Christians (for instance, 'when the renegades were seen, everyone cried '*siate armati!*', and 'immediately there appeared *ciascheuno cristiano* to the defence'). The Negropont laments open with invocations, ordinarily to God as Creator.

> O summo et ineffabile creatore
> De tute quante le cose create,
> Tu sey summa possanza e summo amore,
> Tu, summa sapientiae veritade,
> Che per levarci del antiquo errore
> Rendisti a' mortali humanitade
> E sostenisti morte acerba e dura
> Per dar salute a la humana natura.
>
>   .   .   .   .
>
> Signore, che fecesti el' umana natura,
> Factor, che fecesti el cielo e la terra,
> Signor, che fecesti lo omo a toa figura,
> Factor, che fecesti quello ce fa guerra,
> O creatore, che creasti omne cosa creata,
> Illumina la mente mia immaculata.

---

[19] For the Feast of the Pheasant see e.g. Schwoebel, ibid. 87–9. The Italian *lamenti* are collected in Antonio Medin and Ludovico Frati, *Lamenti storici dei secoli XIV, XV, e XVI* (Bologna, 1969). The citation is from *Lamento di Constantinopoli di frate Bernardino Cingolano*, 179. For German examples, see Schwoebel, *The Shadow of the Crescent*, 166–7.

[20] For the alternative interpretation, see Reinhard Strohm, *Music in Late Medieval Bruges* (rev. edn., Oxford, 1990), 130: 'The poet records the soundscape, the hectic activity of a town in a state of alarm, spinning his song round the vital three-note signal.'

[21] *Lamenti storici*, 254, 261.

The texts may be compared with the troped *Kyrie plasmator hominis mondique creator*; *Kyrie virtutis auctor virique creator*; *Kyrie summe Pater*; *Kyrie altitonans genitor Deus orbis conditor alme*; *Kyrie O Deus excelse*; *Kyrie alme Pater summeque Deus celi quoque rector* of the Naples collection.[22] The stylistic and substantive resemblance of these vernacular invocations with the Kyrie tropes found in the Naples masses is undeniable. Here again, the texts of laments and those of the *L'homme armé* masses are stylistically linked. The structure of the Negropont laments, with their prefatory invocations to the Lord, followed by gut-wrenching descriptions of the brutal attacks of the Turks and ultimate loss of the city, provides a frame in which to view the *entire structure* comprised of the six Naples masses as a coherent polemical composition. While the texts of the *Lamentations*, like that of *L'homme armé*, were intended to serve as inspiring exhortations to arms, their tone was in no way optimistic. They were infused with melodrama and pathos, representing the wails of a church in defeat. If the Naples masses are considered within this contemporary literary context, the significance of the canon for the sixth and final mass is clarified:

> Arma virumque cano vincorque per arma virumque
> Alterni gradimur hic ubi signo tacet.
> Sub lychanos hypaton oritur sic undique pergit
> Visceribus propriis conditur ille meis.

The canon, which explains the structure of the canonic *L'homme armé* tenor in that mass, begins 'Arms and a man I sing, and I am vanquished by arms and a man'. If the *L'homme armé* masses represent polemical exhortations to arms, they must proceed, as do contemporaneous literary polemics, from a posture of defeat and need. As I suggested earlier, there exists a fundamental ambiguity in the *L'homme armé* text, revolving around the identity of the armed man (as Turk or as Christian) within the context of the chanson. As a propagandistic slogan, the opening of *L'homme armé* must refer to the armed Turkish warrior (the *doubté Turcq* of Simonet le Breton), who commanded, more on the basis of his reputation than his weaponry, irrational fear among Christians. At the Congress of Mantua, convened by Pope Pius in 1459 to organize Christian forces for a crusade, the Burgundian representatives explained that 'a crusade against the Turks demanded very great strength, since, having been victorious for so many years, they inspired terror in Christians by their mere fame and prestige'.[23] Moreover, the Christian position in all crusade literature was one of defence: we have been defeated and now must take up arms to fight back and restore what was once ours. The donning of the defensive *haubregon* by a Christian would hardly inspire

---

[22] The Naples tropes are presented in convenient format in Barbara Helen Haggh, Communication to the Editor, *JAMS* 40 (1987), 139–43.

[23] *Commentaries*, 127.

fear in a Turkish soldier. The *haubregon*, as explained in vernacular translations of Vegetius, is necessary garb for footmen facing the shots of archers, who constituted, in fact, the initial offensive line of the Turkish army. Any fear on the part of the Turks would have to proceed not from confrontation with the weapons of the crusaders, but rather from the power of God, who, according to the Kyrie trope of Naples Mass III, inspires fear. By taking up the cross, by becoming a *crucesignatus*, the crusader was granted the protection of God and certain legal and spiritual rights by the Church.[24] These constituted the Christian's armour, and transformed him into a metaphorical *homme armé*.[25] Thus, the function of *L'homme armé* as avatar of the Christian knight exists in an ideal context outside that of the song's text, for it is only after the song, or the mass based upon it, has successfully served as an instrument of recruitment that the Christian becomes an armed man. The distinction is especially important for the final canon of the Naples masses, which opens with an allusion to Aeneas: *Arma virumque cano*, the first phrase of Virgil's *Aeneid*. As I hope to demonstrate, the text of the canon shares the same polar ambiguity as does the emblematic armed man. It allows for negative and positive readings, as does the opening of the *Aeneid* itself, for Virgil's epic is a tale of battles, and the arms of which Virgil sings are not just those of his hero.

The final canon of the Naples collection forges a link between the medieval battle of Christians and Turks and the world of classical epic poetry, and *Arma virumque cano* may serve us now, as it did in the Middle Ages, as a touchstone that unveils a network of images and emblems, visual and textual, bearing on the central literary theme of fifteenth-century crusade polemics, the theme of fall and restoration.

II

In a poem entitled *The Excursion*, William Wordsworth describes an encounter with an ancient hermit, identified only as 'the Wanderer', who dwells in a lonely woodland cottage. During a lengthy narrative the Wanderer recalls that

> I sang Saturnian rule
> Returned—a progeny of golden years
> Permitted to descend and bless mankind.[26]

Wordsworth's lines are modelled upon the Cumaean prophecy of Virgil's fourth Eclogue:

---

[24] The acceptance of the papal sword by a temporal ruler as described by Flynn Warmington, above, Ch. 5, may have had similar implications.

[25] On the legal ramifications of crusader status, see Housley, *The Avignon Papacy*, esp. 152 ff.

[26] *The Excursion*, bk. 3, ll. 756–8; cited in Frank Kermode, *The Classic* (New York, 1975; repr. Cambridge, 1983), 88.

> The great succession of centuries is born afresh
> Now too returns the Virgin; Saturn's rule returns
> A new begetting now descends from heaven's height
> O chaste Lucina, look with blessing on the boy
> Whose birth will end the iron race at last and raise
> A golden [one] through the world: now your Apollo rules.[27]

Wordworth's Wanderer is a conduit for the voice of Virgil, the singer of pastoral songs in the bucolic *Eclogues*, and of arms and war in the epic *Aeneid*. His song of the restoration of the golden rule of Saturn's kingdom through a new progeny descended from heaven is a late echo in an unbroken chain that constituted a post-Virgilian literary and artistic tradition associated with the Virgilian image of the Golden Age.

For the Church, the messianic implications as well as the prophecy of the Virgin in the fourth Eclogue contributed above all else to Virgil's elevation to unofficial status as a pagan saint, and it provided Christian commentators with unambiguous evidence for the equation of Christ's dominion on earth and the foundation of the Roman Church with the Saturnian *aurea saecula*, which was described in three well-known monuments of classical literature, Ovid's *Metamorphoses*, the fourth *Eclogue*, and the *Aeneid*.[28] Virgil and Ovid represent elaborations upon the basic theme of the Ages first set forth by Hesiod, in the less familiar *Works and Days*. Each tells of a time of earthly peace, security, and abundance, under the universal rule of Saturn (or Kronos, as he is named by Hesiod), whose throne was usurped by Jupiter. Saturn's fall at the hands of Jupiter marked the end of the Golden Age, and the beginning of the inferior age of silver.[29] In contrast to Hesiod, Virgil presents the myth in a prophetic context, and thus 'reverse[s] the downward movement of the four ages, and look[s] upward . . . to a time of cyclic regeneration.[30] In the *Aeneid*, it is Aeneas who is responsible for the restoration of Saturn's kingdom by his victory in the war in Latium, thus fulfilling a prophecy in Book Six of the poem concerning the grand and peaceful destiny of Rome. And according to post-Virgilian tradition, it was Aeneas's own son, Ascanius, from whom the line of Roman Caesars, the *gens Julia*, is descended. The link between the Saturnian Golden Age and Roman Italy was made explicit in the ancient name of the region, Saturnia.[31]

---

[27] Virgil, *Ecloga IV*, ll. 5–10: 'magnus ab integro saeclorum nascitur ordo. ‖ iam redit et virgo, redeunt Saturnia regna, ‖ iam nova progenies caelo demittitur alto. ‖ tu modo nascenti puero, quo ferrea primum ‖ desinet ac toto surget gens aurea mundo, ‖ casta faue Lucina: tuus iam regnat Apollo'. Trans. by Guy Lee (Middlesex, 1984), 56.

[28] The earliest poetic reference to the legend of the Golden Age appears in Hesiod's *Works and Days*: see M. L. West, *Hesiod. Theogony. Works and Days* (Oxford and New York, 1988), pp. xiv, 40.

[29] See Ovid, *Metamorphoses*, i. 85 ff.; Virgil, *Aeneid*, viii. 314–36.

[30] Harry Levin, *The Myth of the Golden Age in the Renaissance* (Bloomington and London, 1969), 17.

[31] The historical links between Rome and Saturnia are discussed in Marianne Wifstrand Scheibe, 'The Saturn of the *Aeneid*—Tradition or Innovation?', *Vergilius*, 32 (1986), 43–60.

In the Renaissance, the Romans were still viewed as part of this lineage. Pope Pius II referred to the Romans as 'successors of Trojan Aeneas'.[32] Virgil's epic tale of the re-establishment of peace and security in Latium represented a vision of restored Roman greatness he shared with his patron, the Emperor Augustus, and for Virgil, Augustus was the agent of Saturn's rule. He was, in a sense, the direct descendant of Saturn, since Saturn's daughter Venus was the mother and protector of Aeneas, whose line yielded the scions of Imperial Rome. Christian theologians had equated the time of the Augustan Peace, *pax augusta*, with that of the Advent for centuries. The notion appears in Eusebius, in Dante, even in Milton.[33] Thus, the new Golden Age of Rome coexisted with the new Golden Age of Christ's Kingdom, and the foundation of the Church. The 'universal peace', as Milton calls it, was a necessary pre-condition for the restoration of God's kingdom on earth in the Christian era; as in late medieval polemics, peace among all European rulers was deemed a prerequisite for the new crusade.[34] Needless to say, since the Golden peace was a Roman one, the Roman papacy took on the imperial lustre of Augustus as an emblem for the Golden Age.[35]

And, needless to say, the Golden Age metaphor was enthusiastically applied by fifteenth- and sixteenth-century poets and orators to virtually every patron in Europe. Since the fit between the Golden Age mythos and any individual leader hinged, following the model of the *Aeneid*, upon his ancestry and prowess in battle, this created some problems, as for instance in the case of Cosimo de' Medici, a 'banker and city boss'. Machiavelli objected to contemporaneous oratorical characterizations of Cosimo's rule as a Golden Age, since this equated him with God, pope, and emperor, an equation that did not suit, in Machiavelli's words, 'un uomo disarmato'.[36] Medieval moralists applied a process of syllogistic reasoning to the Trojan genealogy: Saturn begets Venus (not the embodiment of concupiscence, but rather, according to Bernardus Silvestris, the representation of *musica mundana*);[37] Venus begets Aeneas who begets Ascanius who begets the *gens Julia* and Augustus; Augustus implies the advent of Christ and Augustus implies Rome as a political institution; therefore, any figure in the genealogy might symbolize the institutionalized Roman Church or the papacy.

[32] *Commentaries*, 351. That Pius counted himself among them is made clear in his remark that he loved 'Rome as our own country . . . For we too are originally Roman. The house of Piccolomini, to which we belong, moved to Siena from this city, as the names Enea and Silvio so frequent in our family show' (p. 179).

[33] Kermode, *The Classic*, 50.

[34] Pius II called for a mandatory five-year truce among Christian rulers in preparation for the crusade against the Turks. See e.g. *Commentaries*, 258–9.

[35] For examples of the Golden Age and Saturnian themes in 15th- and 16th-c. political contexts, see Cecil H. Clough, 'Chivalry and Magnificence in the Golden Age of the Italian Renaissance', in Sydney Anglo (ed.), *Chivalry in the Renaissance* (Woodbridge, 1990), 25–48; also Ottavia Niccoli, *Prophecy and People in Renaissance Italy*, trans. Lydia G. Cochrane (Princeton, 1990), 54, 116, 186, 188; E. H. Gombrich, 'Renaissance and Golden Age', in *Norm and Form: Studies in the Art of the Renaissance*, i (London, 1966), 29–34.

[36] i.e. a 'man without arms'; see Gombrich, 'Renaissance and Golden Age', 33.

[37] Concerning this aspect of the 'moralized' Venus, see below, n. 49.

It was this syllogistic process of replacement that allowed the figure of Aeneas to serve as an allegorical stand-in for the Church and pope in medieval Christian literature, notably the *Ovide moralisé*. In that extremely influential fourteenth-century work, it is explained that Aeneas's foe in the battle for Latium, the fierce warrior Turnus, represents the Antichrist and his followers, who create grief and tribulation for the *champions de Sainte Yglise*, represented by Aeneas.[38] The battle between Aeneas and Turnus offered a natural prototype for the war between the Church and its foes, especially since Virgil depicts Turnus as insane with rage and blood-lust, attributes of the fifteenth-century stereotypical Turk. This suggests a motivation for the incorporation of the Virgilian catch-phrase *Arma virumque cano* into a mass likewise associated with the battle between the Turks (Antichrist or Turnus) and the Church (Aeneas). In light of Pius II's role as figurehead for the new crusade movement in the late 1450s and early 1460s, one might conjecture that the canon of the sixth Naples mass is, in fact, intended as a homage to the pope, whose Christian name was Aeneas Silvius Piccolomini. Pius's writings are full of explicit references to his Trojan lineage, which he supports with the evidence of his Roman names Aeneas and Silvius.[39] An unabashed humanist, he is reported to have taken the name Pius from Virgil's description of his hero as *pius Aeneas*.[40] Moreover, in a hymn by Agapetus, Bishop of Ancona, composed for a special Mass in 1462, Pius is lauded as the one who 'alone with unfailing courage dared to . . . raise the call to arms against the Turks',[41] and in Book Seven of the *Aeneid*, as Turnus's war (i.e. the attack of the infidels) on the Trojans begins, the alarm is first raised by Tyrrhus's daughter Silvia (the feminine form of the name Silvius). If a nod to Aeneas Silvius is implied in the Virgilian canon, it would suggest a date for the original composition of the Naples masses prior to Pius's death on his way to the crusade in 1464, although the notion of posthumous recognition of his leadership in the crusade efforts is not out of the question.

But, as I have indicated, the canon for Naples Mass VI also displays a darker side, for subsequent to the Virgilian reference, it continues 'and I am vanquished by arms and a man', concluding 'he is hidden in my own vitals (*viscera*)', describing the canonic double tenor. As I suggested earlier, I hear another voice behind the canon in addition to that of Virgil the prophet of the Christian peace. It is the voice of the captive Church, in whose vitals, particularly Constantinople and the Holy Land, the infidels had positioned themselves. In classical and post-classical Latin, the term *viscera* was often employed in this conceptual, geographical sense, especially in connection with places of origin. And, as Pius wrote of Islam in 1459, 'although the Bishops of Rome have tried in many ways to combat this plague, nevertheless it has continued to gain strength gradually to this day and

---

[38] C. de Boer, '*Ovide moralisé: Poème du commencement du quatorzième siècle publié d'après tous les manuscrits connus* (Amsterdam, 1938), v. 100–4.

[39] See above, n. 32.   [40] *Commentaries*, 88.   [41] Ibid. 248.

has penetrated to our very vitals'.[42] The language of the canon leads me back to a peculiarly French interpretation of the Golden Age as a literary topos. While some fifteenth-century French readers—at least those 'most competent in Latinity', as Tinctoris describes Busnoys—may have known the Saturn myth and the ensuing Trojan genealogy through classical sources or through the numerous medieval Christianized commentaries on the *Metamorphoses*, *Eclogues*, and *Aeneid*, more would have been familiar with the story as it is told (in abbreviated form, but on three separate occasions) in the vernacular *Roman de la Rose*. In classical versions of the tale, the Fall of Saturn's Kingdom is effected when Jupiter exiles Saturn, who flees to Latium. In the *Roman*, the end of the Golden Age is considerably more ignominious: 'Justice . . . reigned formerly at the time when Saturn held power—Saturn, whose testicles Jupiter, his hard and bitter son, cut off as though they were sausages and threw into the sea.'[43]

Despite its lurid quality, or perhaps because of it, the Saturn myth, which plays a relatively minor part in the *Roman* narrative, was a favourite choice for illumination. Fig. 6.1 reproduces a miniature from a late fifteenth-century

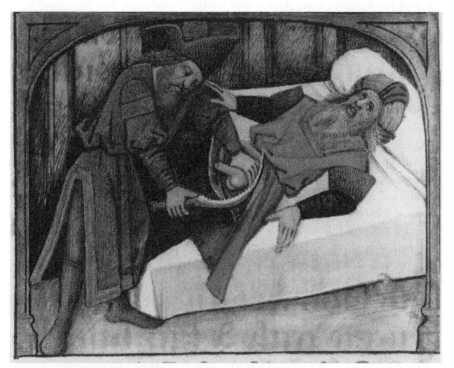

FIG. 6.1. The Castration of Saturn. Oxford, Bodleian Library, Douce 194, fo.76ᵛ

---

[42] See above, 92.
[43] Charles Dahlberg (trans.), *The Romance of the Rose* (Hanover, NH and London, 1983), 113.

manuscript of the *Roman*.[44] Here, the artist has depicted Saturn in the garb of a middle Eastern ruler, while he is castrated or eviscerated (and the term *viscera* was also used in the Middle Ages to describe male and female reproductive organs) by Jupiter, the son generated by Saturn's own *viscera*. Jupiter, the armed man in the picture, performs the ghastly deed with a sort of curved scythe, suggesting the Turkish scimitar. He wears a form of conical headgear with protective neckflaps that recalls the following description of Turkish soldiers related by the Burgundian La Broquière: 'They wore pointed head pieces, half a foot in height, to which were secured four pieces of metal on the front, back and two sides, designed to ward off sword-blows. Over these helmets they usually wore another head piece made of iron wire.'[45] La Broquière was also struck by the length of the coats of chain-mail and silk worn by the Turks, which fell to the calf of the legs. It would have taken no great leap of imagination for a fifteenth-century illuminator to envision the perpetrator of such a repulsive crime in what he or she took to be Turkish military garb, since Europe was inundated with spoken and written propaganda in which inflated tales of Turkish war atrocities were transmitted in painstaking and gruesome detail. From a Christian perspective, then, the miniature depicts the degradation of the Church (as personified by Saturn, Lord of the Golden Age),[46] but particularly (in light of Saturn's Eastern garb) the loss of its eastern dominions, Constantinople and the Holy Land, to the Saracen blade.[47] In another illumination of the same scene from the manuscript Valencia 387,[48] the artist illustrates the remainder of the *Roman* text which continues 'cut off . . . and threw into the sea, *thus giving birth to Venus*' (emphasis added). The miniature is laid out in linear fashion, concluding with the image of Venus, mother of Aeneas, rising from Saturn's genitals which are floating in the sea. In this portrayal, once again, the patrimony of Saturn to Aeneas via his mother Venus is secured, despite Jupiter's abrupt termination of the first Golden Age, and once again, the opportunity for restoration is born anew.[49]

---

[44] The miniature is included in Maureen Quilligan, *The Allegory of Female Authority: Christine de Pizan's Cité des dames* (Ithaca and London, 1991), 41.

[45] Schwoebel, *The Shadow of the Crescent*, 103.

[46] Saturn's turban resembles the nimbus cross associated in Christian iconography with the concept of God the Father. I am grateful to Flynn Warmington for calling this aspect of the miniature to my attention.

[47] The readiness of medieval redactors of the *Roman* to interpret its mythical and classical figures of good and evil in terms of the struggle with the Saracens is witnessed in the representation of Nero in some sources wherein he is identified with persecution of the Faith, and even as the progenitor of the Saracen lineage. See Sylvia Huot, *The Romance of the Rose and its Medieval Readers: Interpretation, Reception, Manuscript Transmission* (Cambridge, 1993), 184–5.

[48] For a facsimile, see John V. Fleming, *The Roman de la Rose: A Study in Allegory and Iconography* (Princeton, 1969), fig. 33.

[49] According to Bernardus Sylvestris's spiritual commentary on the *Aeneid*, Venus the mother of Aeneas is to be considered as distinct from Venus the mother of Cupid. The latter represents *voluptas carnis*, while the former represents *musica mundana*. See G. Riedel (ed.), *Commentarium super sex libros Eneidos Virgilii* (Greifswald, 1924), 10.

III

Providing corroborating evidence for the existence of a tradition of polyphonic responses to the menace of Islam is a polytextual motet of the late fourteenth century that explicitly conjoins the Golden Age metaphor with the call for a new papal crusade. The motetus text, *O terra sancta*, falls within the tradition of crusade laments discussed earlier.

> O terra sancta, suplica
> summo pastori gentium
> tuum adi Gregorium
> et fletus tales explica:
> 5   Nunc, sancte pater, aspicis,
> ecce conculcor misera,
> Christus hic lavit scelera
> Et fedor ab Arabicis.
> Junge leones liliis
> 10   et rosas cum serpentibus;
> indulge penitentibus.
> Pacem det pater filiis.
> Crucem in classe Syria,
> Agar cognoscat aquilas,
> 15   Farfar delphini pinulas
> et arma mittat Stiria.[50]

It pleads to Pope Gregory XI for assistance on behalf of the Holy Land, the place where Christ lived and worked, and which has been polluted and struck down by the Saracens (*ab Arabicis*). The heraldic images of lines 9 and 10 refer to an alliance between England, France, Milan, and the pope which will enable the launching of a crusade, proposed by Gregory in 1375, from the Farfarus, a tributary of the Tiber, supported by arms from the mining district of Styria. The triplum begins 'By the teachings of Pythagoras' (*Pictagore per dogmata*), and depicts the ordered workings of the cosmos, the *musica mundana*.

> Pictagore per dogmata
> fit virgo septenarius,
> librat dies et climata,
> quorum effectus varius,
> 5   et illa magna sidera:
> Sic Iupiter primarius,
> alter Mavortis opera
> gessit, exinde tertius
> nova dans mundo federa,

---

[50] The text and historical background of *Pictagore per dogmata / O terra sancta / Rosa vernans caritatis* are presented in Ursula Günther, *The Motets of the Manuscripts Chantilly, Musée Condé, 564 (olim 1047) and Modena, Biblioteca estense, α M. 5,24 (olim lat. 568)* (n.p., 1965), pp. xl–xlii.

10 surgit ut Phebi radius
post dulcis ut Citerea,
quam sequitur Cilenius,
Cinthia reddit trophea.
Mirari Neptunum cogit
15 sorte sumpta cum Enea,
hic almus, qui modo surgit,
iam consummato spatio
capiat, quicumque legit—
ut facta dicta ratio—
20 ubi caput fuit orbis.
Sedem firmabit Latio,
mentis ponet finem morbis,
nam tertia fert secula
auri, quae nectunt vincula.

According to the text, the virgin number 7 (*septenarius*), which accounts for the organization of the universe in a variety of ways, came about through the teachings of Pythagoras.[51] Its role in the cosmos was to balance the days, the *climata* (i.e. the latitudinal regions of the inhabited earth),[52] and the planets (*magna sidera*), six of which are named, and Saturn, always associated with the number 7, simply implied. Lines 14–24 equate Gregory's return of the papacy from Avignon to Rome with Aeneas's voyage to Latium. Gregory's return will set the stage for the new crusade and usher in the Third Golden Age (the *tertia secula auri* of the final lines), Aeneas's victory, as explained earlier, having laid the foundation for the second.

My attention was originally drawn to this work in connection with *L'homme armé* not by its text, however, but by its musical structure. The first statement of the unidentified tenor melody of the motet, which comprises the entire texted portion (the second *color*, in rhythmic diminution, is untexted) consists of four *taleae*, each comprised of thirty-one *tempora* in *tempus imperfectum*, major prolation:

Opening duo (mm. 1–4)

first *color*:
talea 1: mm. 5–35
talea 2: mm. 36–66
talea 3: mm. 67–97
talea 4: mm. 98–128
= 4 × 31 *tempora* in $\mathbb{C}$

Not only is such a large prime number unusual within the context of fourteenth-century *talea* structures, but this particular number stands as the 'egregious

[51] Ibid. xli.
[52] See G. J. Toomer, *Ptolemy's Almagest* (London, 1984), 19.

anomaly' in the midst of the Pythagorean framework of Busnoys's *Missa L'homme armé* proposed by Richard Taruskin.[53] Professor Taruskin's calculation of the number of *tempora* in the *Et incarnatus* of Busnoys's mass (and in several sections of other masses on the same tenor, including some in the Naples collection) has generated considerable controversy, much of it revolving around the question of whether or not to count final longs in cantus-firmus mass sections. Until a fifteenth-century analytical primer is uncovered, I fear we shall have to agree to disagree, and I, for one, agree with Taruskin, at least on the issue of final longs in non-isorhythmic Renaissance polyphony. To continue, here we are faced with a work in which statements of thirty-one *tempora* (coincidentally in the same mensuration linked by Pietro Aaron to the *L'homme armé* tenor) function as the primary structural units unambiguously (for *taleae* within isorhythmic structures do not entail *ultra mensuram* longs) in a motet inspired by late medieval crusade sentiment, and one in which the planetary actions of the universe described in the triplum are said to be generated by the teachings of Pythagoras, the organizing force in Taruskin's reading of Busnoys's mass. Based on William Prizer's research on the chivalric Order of the Golden Fleece, Taruskin suggested that within the *L'homme armé* complex of works, the number thirty-one was originally intended mathematically to embody the Order, whose membership through most of the fifteenth century comprised 31 noblemen in addition to its leader, the duke of Burgundy, and that *L'homme armé* masses like Busnoys's may have been intended to function liturgically as Masses for St Andrew, patron saint of the Order.[54] Andrew's role as patron, however, extended well beyond the *Toison d'or* to the crusade in general, as indicated by the grand ceremony, infused with crusade polemic, conducted by Pius II in Rome in 1462 to celebrate the arrival in the city of the apostle's head, which was to serve as a protective talisman for the crusade,[55] suggesting that the Burgundo-centric view of the tradition may require some revision.[56]

In June 1456, Pope Calixtus III had commanded that on the first Sunday of each month, processions were to be made in every diocese in order to pray that the Turkish invasion might be averted and furthermore that the *Missa contra paganos* (Mass against the infidel) was to be celebrated on those same days. Moreover, every priest, without exception, was to include in every Mass he said the prayer 'Almighty, everlasting God, to whom all power belongs, and in whose

[53] Richard Taruskin, 'Antoine Busnoys and the *L'Homme armé* Tradition', *JAMS* 39 (1986), 255–93. Taruskin writes (p. 271): 'There remains, of course, to account for the egregious anomaly that intrudes in the middle of [the mass's] proportional structure: the prime number 31, which is the number of tempora in the Et incarnatus section of the Credo. The anomaly occurs almost precisely in the middle, since, if we do not count the unwritten repetition of the Osanna, there are the equivalent of 202 perfect breves before it and 204 after it. Thirty-one, it so happens, is the number of measures (semibreves) in the cantus firmus tune . . . But there is obviously more to it than that.'

[54] Ibid. 272.   [55] *Commentaries*, 241–69.

[56] Flynn Warmington (Ch. 5) has proposed a link between the *L'homme armé* masses and the ceremonial bestowal of a papal sword. Since one such ceremony took place at the court of Philip the Good, the ascription of at least one mass to the Burgundian court is entirely within the realm of possibility.

hand are the rights of all nations, protect Thy Christian people and crush by thy
power the pagans who trust in their fierceness.'[57] Shortly thereafter, Calixtus sent
a brief to the Duke of Brittany, in which he specifically commended the Duke for
complying with the papal directive in his dominions, and informing him that the
prayers and Masses against the Turks were also being carried out in Italy,
Germany, Hungary, Spain, and, he believed, in the French kingdom.[58] In light
of David Fallows's suggestion that Busnoys may have been associated with the
court of Brittany in the late 1450s (see above, Ch. 2), it is tempting to speculate
that the composer's presence in an environment wherein anti-Turkish sentiment
was being officially and effectively promulgated could have provided motivation
for his interest in (or creation of) the *L'homme armé* song and mass or masses.
Calixtus' bull of 1456 addressed to all patriarchs, archbishops, bishops, and
abbots of Christendom in any case provides a universal context for the introduction of a specifically anti-Turkish bias into the liturgy on a regular basis, and
would thus accommodate the sudden magnitude of the *L'homme armé* phenomenon, as well as the generally accepted date for its inception about 1460. As for
the number 31, again, we might look to a less specific, less Burgundo-centric
explanation, one that would embrace both Busnoys and the anonymous author
of *Pictagore per dogmata*.

Since the Pythagorean balance referred to in the triplum extends the Golden
Age metaphor to a cosmological sphere, one in which all is balanced in the universe (the harmony of *musica mundana*), a potential model for the motet's mathematical structure might be sought in contemporary astronomical theory. The
'Table of straight lines in the circle, or chords', the very first table in Ptolemy's
massive treatise, the *Almagest*, begins as follows:[59]

Arcs	Chords		
½	0	(31)	25
1	1	2	50
1½	1	34	15
2	2	5	40
2½	2	37	4
3	3	39	52
.	.	.	.
(30)	(31)	3	30

[57] Schwoebel, *The Shadow of the Crescent*, 45. Also Ludwig Pastor, *Storia dei papi*, rev. Italian edn., ed. Angelo Mercati, i (Rome, 1942), 713.
[58] See Pastor, ibid., 713–14 n. 1, for a transcription of the text from the *Registra Brevium* of the Vatican archives (vol. 7, fo. 48ᵛ). There is some confusion about the intended recipient of the letter. Pastor's transcription of the salutation reads: 'duci Burgundie (Britanie)'. The document itself reads 'duci *Burgundie Britanic*'. It is impossible to judge whether either the underlined 'Burgundy' or 'Brittany' represents an error or a correction. I am extremely grateful to Pamela Starr for providing me with a photocopy of the document from the Vatican archives.
[59] The table of chords is taken from Toomer, *Ptolemy's Almagest*, 57.

Michael Long

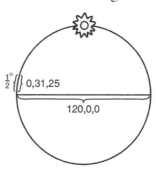

Fig. 6.2. The first (0, 31, 25) and greatest (120, 0, 0) chords of the ecliptic

Those aspects bearing upon my argument are illustrated geometrically in Fig. 6.2. Ptolemy's diagram is of very great significance, for without it most of the other diagrams could not be calculated. Forming the basis for all Ptolemaic measurement of planetary and stellar motion, the table, whose calculation Ptolemy supports with geometric proofs, assigns numerical values to astronomical distances. The first column represents distance in degrees along the 360° circle of the ecliptic, the path along which in the Ptolemaic system the planets, including the sun, and the fixed stars appeared to move. The second measures the size of that distance in terms of hypothetical units, 120 of which Ptolemy takes to represent the diameter of the ecliptic circle.[60] These units are divided on the Babylonian sexagesimal system into 60 *partes minutae primae*, each comprising 60 *partes minutae secundae*. The first measurable distance of planetary motion is 31 *partes minutae primae* and 25 *partes minutae secundae*. Again, these are mathematical values with no inherent physical referential meaning. Subsequent calculations are made by adding 31 to the second number in each row and 25 to the third. If either calculation yields a number of 60 or greater, 60 is subtracted from that sum, and 1 unit is added to the column to its left—as occurs in our decimal, or base ten, system when the sum of a column reaches ten or greater. Ptolemy was using the Babylonian sexagesimal, base sixty, system. So, for instance, in row 2, 31 + 31 = 62; 60 is subtracted, leaving 2 in the 31 column, while 1 is added to the column on the left, which started at zero. When a sum of 60 or more is reached, the addend 31 is increased to 32 for one step, and then the basal number 31 is reinstated. At 30 degrees of arc, i.e. one twelfth of the 360° ecliptic, the first figure in column 2 of the table reaches 31. If we take as our starting-point the entry of the sun into the sign of Aries (i.e. the beginning of the zodiacal year), the positions {0, 31, 25} and {31, 3, 30}—the first appearances of the number in each of the two columns of measurement—mark the boundaries of the sign which, owing to its temporal association with the vernal

[60] The choice of the number 120 was necessary to accommodate the sexagesimal ('base 60') system of fractions inherited from Babylonian mathematics. See e.g. Carl B. Boyer, *A History of Mathematics*, rev. Uta C. Merzbach (New York, 1991), 167.

equinox (which determines the position of Easter), is symbolically linked with the resurrection of Christ after the crucifixion (again, an image of restoration following degradation).[61] Most simply put, 31 is the first numeral of the *Almagest*, whose tables and proofs transmitted to the Latin world via Greek and Arabic exemplars in the late twelfth century provided the impetus for the new astronomy of the later Middle Ages.[62]

Thus, the number 31 bears an essential scientific relationship to the Pythagoras motet: it is the generating number of all positions in the cosmos, which constitute the *musica mundana*, and the root of all astronomical calculations involving the stars and planets, whose order and behaviour (the subject-matter of the triplum voice) was first described *per dogmata Pictagore*. But apart from the topical connections between the motet and *L'homme armé*, why incorporate the number into the masses, and in the case of Busnoys's possibly seminal work, at the point in the mass where the liturgical text most clearly approaches the meaning of the cantus firmus incipit, i.e. *Et incarnatus*, in which Christ is described as having been made man (*et homo factus est*)? A reading of our Ptolemaic table based not on the zodiacal, but rather the liturgical year (beginning with Christmas) would circumscribe the Nativity, rather than the Resurrection, by the two 31s.[63] But there is more to it than that, I would suggest. Given the unaspirated 'h' at the beginning of the French word for man, the three-word incipit, 'the armed man', actually consists of two, rather than three, sounding and visual letter groups: *Lo(m)me* and *arme*. Indeed, this perception survives today: Lewis Lockwood's 'L'homme armé' article in the *New Grove Dictionary* is found not in the *H*, but in the *L* volume, a rare instance of an encyclopaedia entry beginning with the definite article.[64] The precise acrostical representation of that phrase—which appears in most straightforward form in its last two repetitions in the third section of the Naples redaction of the song (staff three in Fig. 6.3 below), following the 'call to arms' of the second section—would be upper case *L*, lower case *a*.

Returning to the Ptolemaic table of chords in its original notation we read from left to right in the first row: one-half degree of arc represented by a Greek fraction; zero (a circle); and 31, represented in Greek mathematical notation as lambda–alpha:[65]

$$L' \quad 0 \quad \lambda\alpha$$

---

[61] The iconic link between Aries (the ram) and the sacrificial lamb of God (*agnus dei*) received considerable attention in medieval zodiologia. See e.g. Wolfgang Hübner, *Zodiacus Christianus: Jüdisch-christliche Adaptationen des Tierkreises von der Antike bis zur Gegenwart* (Königstein/Ts., 1983), 86.

[62] See David C. Lindberg, 'The Transmission of Greek and Arabic Learning to the West', in David C. Lindberg (ed.), *Science in the Middle Ages* (Chicago and London, 1978), 39–40, and Toomer, *Ptolemy's Almagest*, 3.

[63] There is, in fact, some evidence that the sign of Aries itself, despite its calendrical association with the paschal season, and its metaphorical association with the sacrificial aspect of the crucifixion, could be viewed as an icon for the incarnation. Arnaldus de Villanova (1235–1312) in *De sigillis* associates Aries with the scriptural text of John 1: 14: 'And the Word was made flesh.' Hübner, *Zodiacus Christianus*, 133.

[64] *New Grove*, x. 712.   [65] O. Neugebauer, *The Exact Sciences in Antiquity* (New York, 1962), 10.

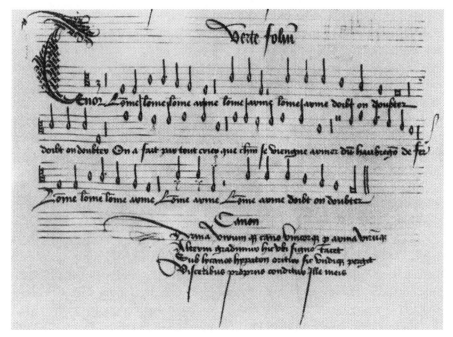

Fig. 6.3. The orthography of *L'homme armé* (Naples VI E 40)

As lambda is twice the height of alpha (in minuscule), the number stands as a precise acrostic for the phrase *Lo(m)me arme*, as it was written and heard. If Busnoys, whose fondness for alphabet puzzles has recently been demonstrated by Paula Higgins's exploration of anagrams and acrostics in the secular songs,[66] resolved to create a mathematical 'incarnation' of the phrase *L'homme arme* in the *Et incarnatus* (as a numerical embodiment of the archetypal new crusader or Christian Aeneas or heir to Saturn's universe), the number 31 would have been an obvious choice. Whether or not he was acquainted with astronomical theory, Busnoys would probably have been familiar with the basic principles of *gematria*, a well-known system of numerical exegesis which used the same Greek letter notation, and which Brian Trowell has applied with some success to the motets of John Dunstable.[67] *Gematria*, like acrostics and anagrams, was most closely associated, however, with cabbalistic writings, and these provided another possible source of significant numbers for medieval and Renaissance composers. The systems of *gematria*, *notarikon* (or acrostics), and *themurah* (or letter substitutions and anagrams), in all of which numbers and letters were interchangeable, was introduced by the school of Eleazar

    [66] Higgins, 'Parisian Nobles', esp. 175–9.
    [67] Brian Trowell, 'Proportion in the Music of Dunstable', *Proceedings of the Royal Musical Association*, 105 (1978–9), 100–41.

of Worms in the early thirteenth century.[68] *Gematria*, especially, was a favourite 'parlour game' in European Jewish communities, particularly in Rome.[69] By the end of the fifteenth century, Christian exegetes were beginning to realize the theological potential of cabbalistic mathematics.[70] Latin treatises based on the Hebrew *Zohar* and *Sefer Yetzirah*, the principal documents of medieval cabbalistic speculation, were commissioned by popes and princes (including Ferrante of Naples, the emperor Maximilian, and Pope Leo X). In cabbalistic thought, ten *sephiroth* (spheres or emanations), representing the path from God to man, corresponded to ten names for the divinity (a concept already encountered in St Jerome, who refers to *decem nomina mystica* (ten mystical names) recorded in the ancient sacred books).[71] The fourth *sephirah*, *chesed*, is 'the first sephirah of the formative world . . . in [which] forces first cohere into forms'.[72] The name of God in the fourth *sephirah* is *El* or *Al*, either of which is spelt lamed aleph (*l, a*, since Hebrew is read from right to left), and the number of God is 31, since, as in the Greek system, *l* (lamed) is equivalent to 30 and *a* (aleph) is equivalent to 1. 31, according to the Christianized cabbala, could also be derived from the ineffable Tetragrammaton, the four-letter representation JHVH (Jehovah or Jahweh). Its numerical value was 26, and if to it were added 'one for the unity of God and four, for the number of letters, the sum, thirty-one, is the numerical equivalent of EL'.[73] Christians were also quick to point out that the addition of the letter *s* in the centre of IHVH yielded IHSVH, or Jesu.[74] (See Fig. 6.4.)

El (God in fourth sephirah) = אל = 31

IHVH (Tetragrammaton)   = 26 + 1 (unity of God) + 4 (4 letters of IHVH)

+ S   = IHSVH

FIG. 6.4. Cabbalistic names and numbers

    There is no reason to rule out the possibility that Busnoys and other composers of the period might have been familiar with the basic precepts of the Christianized cabbala. In fact, cabbalistic interpretations of numerical structures in medieval and Renaissance music may be considerably less far-fetched than those based on Greek systems. Busnoys's 31-*tempus Et incarnatus*, which, as

    [68] Joseph Leon Blau, *The Christian Interpretation of the Cabala in the Renaissance* (Port Washington, NY, 1965), 7.   [69] Ibid. 8.
    [70] Ruth Tatlow, *Bach and the Riddle of the Number Alphabet* (Cambridge, 1991), 41–2, points to the medieval Christian knowledge of cabbalistic numerology but suggests that the late 15th c. marks the beginning of its decline. Her perspective, however, is from that of Protestant Germany, rather than Italy.
    [71] Adolph Franck, *The Kabbalah or the Religious Philosophy of the Hebrews*, revised, enlarged, and trans. by Dr I. Sossnitz (New York, 1926), 100.
    [72] Gareth Knight, *A Practical Guide to Qabalistic Symbolism* (USA: Helios Book Service, 1983), 113–14.
    [73] Blau, *The Christian Interpretation* (Port Washington, NY, 1965), 58.   [74] Ibid. 48.

Taruskin points out, lies at the centre of the masses,[75] as the cabbalistic Jesu is revealed in the centre of the omnipotent Jehovah, could be read not only as a mathematical gloss upon the phrase *L'omme armé*, via *notarikon*, but as a cabbalistic gloss upon the concept of the incarnation; the moment when, according to the doctrine of the fourth *sephirah*, 'forces first cohere into forms'.

The readiness of medieval writers to appropriate non-Christian texts, characters, or topoi for allegorization and exegesis was nowhere more evident than in the network of texts implicitly equating the literature and mythography of Imperial Rome with the fundamental precepts of the Roman Church and of her faithful warriors. Virgil's effective 'canonization' was based above all on the prophetic evidence of the Fourth Eclogue's invocation of a new Golden Age associated with the birth of a male child—a prophecy outranking those of the Old Testament in some minds.[76] With this conceptual foundation laid, all 'Virgilian' texts, including Ovid's redaction of the mythic time-line of the ages, and of the battles of Aeneas, could be mined for their instructive or polemical potential by Christian authors. Pythagorean, Platonic, Arabic, and Hebrew exegetes were no less welcome sources for material or methodology in a literary tradition that was primarily geared towards completeness and academic subtlety, despite its theologizing surface.

A fourteenth- or fifteenth-century composer faced with the task of creating a musical polemic *contra paganos* in a time of global insecurity would logically have looked to the imperfectly understood models of the distant past, filtered through the distorting lens of medieval moralization, for talismanic images of peace, stability, and supernatural power. In this paper I have endeavoured to suggest some ways in which those images might have affected the construction of the *L'homme armé* repertory. I have presented many conjectures, and few if any solutions to the riddles still posed by the concrete remains of the *L'homme armé* phenomenon. Busnoys's role in the tradition, and the cultural significance of its component elements, should continue to occupy us for some time, as befits the artefacts of a cultural process that encompassed the theological, geographical, and political essences of Christian Europe in the fifteenth century.

---

[75] Taruskin, 'Antoine Busnoys', 271.   [76] Kermode, *The Classic*, 39 n.

7

Musical Politics in Late Medieval Poitiers:
A Tale of Two Choirmasters

֍ ֍

PAULA HIGGINS

ATE medieval composers typically acquired their earliest musical training as choirboys in the *maîtrise* (choir school) of a collegiate church or
cathedral, yet remarkably few details about their musical education have
survived. Only for a handful of men can we identify the church in which they
served as choirboys and pinpoint masters who in all probability supervised their
musical studies and nurtured their nascent talents. Nor will further exploration of
neglected ecclesiastical archives necessarily clarify matters much further, since
choirboys tend to surface in the documents identified only by endearing diminut-
ives of their Christian names, thereby masking in perpetual anonymity many
would-be allusions to famous composers as children. As historian David Herlihy
so aptly put it, 'of all social groups which formed the societies of the past, children, seldom seen and rarely heard in the documents, remain for historians the
most elusive, the most obscure'.[1] However futile then may be the task of identifying the childhood mentors of those men we now consider the renowned composers of the late Middle Ages and Renaissance, it is clear that their young charges

Archival research in Poitiers undertaken for this article was made possible by a National Endowment for the
Humanities Summer Stipend in 1989 and an American Council of Learned Societies Fellowship for Recent
Recipients of the Ph.D. in 1989–90. Spoken versions of this article were read at the Conference on Medieval
and Renaissance Music, Royal Holloway and Bedford New College, 8 July 1990 and at the State University
of New York at Buffalo, 4 Oct. 1991.

[1] David Herlihy, 'Medieval Children', in *The Walter Prescott Webb Memorial Lectures: Essays on Medieval
Civilization* (Austin, 1978), 109–42. More recently, historian John Boswell has made a similar point: 'In the
case of the human family, what is missing is the "flesh and blood" in its most literal sense: children. The fos-
sil remains of ancient and medieval populations are almost entirely of adults; children left impressions too
fragile to survive, or no imprints at all'. See his fascinating study *The Kindness of Strangers: The Abandonment
of Children in Western Europe from Late Antiquity to the Renaissance* (New York, 1990), 5. The classic study
of children in the *ancien régime* is that of Philippe Ariès, *L'Enfant et la vie familiale sous l'ancien régime* (Paris,
1960), published in English as *Centuries of Childhood: A Social History of Family Life*, trans. Robert Baldick
(New York, 1962).

invariably followed in their footsteps to serve a stint or two as master of the choir-boys, often, but not always, as younger men.[2]

Despite the demonstrable importance of the *magister puerorum* in the choir schools of late medieval Europe, we know very little about the musical, ped-agogical, or philosophical criteria underlying individual appointments. While ecclesiastical scribes delight in recounting in often lurid detail the sexual pecca-dillos, moral transgressions, and derelictions of duty that led to the firing of vari-ous *magistri*, they rarely spell out the particulars concerning their hiring. In the context of the prevailing silence generally surrounding the subject, a document drawn from the chapter acts of the collegiate church of Saint-Hilaire-le-Grand in Poitiers emerges as somewhat remarkable, since it recounts with rare precision the details of a heated debate among its canons over two candidates vying for the position of master of the choirboys.[3] An ideological frame frozen in time, the document captures late medieval ecclesiastical bureaucrats in the process of decision-making, and the explicit opinions of the canons recorded in the docu-ment highlight their conflicting views about the place of music in their hierarchy of educational priorities as well as their attitudes towards musical competence. Beyond its intrinsic social historical value, the document incidentally furnishes hitherto unknown information about the career and reputation of Antoine Busnoys, one of the two contenders for the post.[4] This essay will offer some thoughts on the content and interpretation of the document and proceed from there to contextualize it as an artefact that mirrors the changing status of the *mag-ister puerorum* during the second half of the fifteenth century and his increasing valorization over time as a creative artist and mentor.[5]

However rich or unusual the information a document may offer, it poses

---

[2] A by no means complete list of 15th-c. composers from France and the Low Countries known to have held the office of *magister puerorum* at some point in their careers includes: Johannes Césaris, Nicholas Grenon, Richard de Loqueville, Jean Pullois, Jean Dusart, Cornelius Heyns, Jean Boubert, Rasse de Lavenne, Petrus de Domarto, Jean Cousin, Johannes Regis, Johannes Tinctoris, Guillaume Faugues, Antoine Busnoys, Philippe Basiron, Jean Hémart, Gilles Mureau, Éloy d'Amerval, Jacques Barbireau, Jacob Obrecht, Antoine Brumel, Jérome de Clibano, and Jean Mouton.

[3] Poitiers, Archives départementales de la Vienne (hereafter PADV), G 525, fos. 1–3, Actes capitulaires de Saint-Hilaire-le-Grand, 1465–9, *c.*14 Sept. 1465. See the Appendix for a transcription of the document. The volume is paginated both with folio numbers and with page numbers; all following citations of this vol-ume will refer to page numbers unless otherwise indicated.

[4] An article by historian Robert Favreau, 'Orgues et psallettes à Poitiers à la fin du moyen âge', *Bulletin de la Société des Antiquaires de l'Ouest* (series 4), 12 (1973), 47–64, mentions Busnoys in a footnote (p. 57 n. 80) among the masters of the choirboys at Saint-Hilaire-le-Grand. The article came to my attention after I had completed my dissertation ('Antoine Busnois and Musical Culture in Late Fifteenth-Century France and Burgundy' (Ph.D. diss., Princeton University, 1987)) and while independently pursuing research on the church of Saint-Hilaire-le-Grand in Poitiers, which was closely tied to the church of Saint-Martin of Tours, where Busnoys worked in 1465 (Paula Higgins, '*In hydraulis* Revisited: New Light on the Career of Antoine Busnois', *JAMS* 39 [1986], 36–86). Curiously, however, Favreau does not cite the document in question, which I discovered during a research trip to Poitiers in 1989.

[5] The document and its context will be treated in greater depth and scope in my book *Parents and Preceptors: Authority, Lineage, and the Conception of the Composer in Early Modern Europe* (Oxford, forthcoming).

inevitable problems of interpretation.[6] Even though the scribe has recorded the testimony of each participant in indirect discourse, presumably providing a reasonably accurate transcript of what was actually said, we shall never know how much editorial control he (or anyone else) might have exercised over the final product. In this respect, it shares much in common with the written minutes of a meeting of a late twentieth-century music department search committee, which often obscure subtle nuances of facial expression, emotional intensity, and colourful language, and whose retelling depends largely upon the political agenda and interpretative slant of the faculty secretary.

In September of 1465 one Johannes Le Begue, the incumbent master of the choirboys at Saint-Hilaire, had barely held office for two months when his position was threatened by another candidate who had evidently offered his services to the church. At the opening of an exceptional meeting called to discuss the matter, the Dean of Saint-Hilaire, Jean d'Amboise, identified the individual as one Antonius Busnoys and described him as follows (see App., [1]):

currently master of the choirboys at the church of Saint-Martin in Tours, who wishes very much to come and serve in the church of Saint-Hilaire-le-Grand, and who is highly competent and extremely expert in music, in the manner of instructing the boys in music, and in the other qualities essential to a good master of the choirboys with good morals.

The Dean then placed in motion a recommendation that Le Begue be deposed and removed from the office of master of the choirboys and that Busnoys be appointed and entrusted with their education, administration, and governance. At this point, the Dean polled each of the canons in attendance, and the scribe dutifully summarized and recorded their opinions and recommendations (App., [2]). The succentor, Geoffroy Rousseau, the highest ranking musical authority present, was of the opinion that, because of the skill, erudition, and productivity of Busnoys, who is said to be a very eminent man, that if he wishes to come, he should be invested with the choirboys' education and Le Begue deposed; but since Le Begue had assumed the position at the request of the chapter, he should continue to receive its emoluments until he could provide himself with another means of living (App., [3]). Canon Johannes Comitis proceeded from there to remind the canons that the chapter had spent a lot of money

---

[6] In its present state, this volume of chapter acts opens with four fragmentary pages barely one-fifth their original size. The entry from which the document under discussion derives appears on the first totally intact folio in the volume. Because the same folio is badly torn and worn at the top, the very first lines of the account have been obliterated, including its date. The entry immediately following it is dated 21 Sept. 1465 and a partial date on one of the preceding fragmentary folios reads 'Saturday, 24 [blank]'. Since Saturday the 24th happened to fall in the month of August, the document can be dated with virtual certainty sometime during the four weeks between 24 Aug. and 21 Sept. 1465, and in all likelihood to the previous Saturday, 14 Sept. 1465. In addition to the top of the page, the right-hand margin has lost between five to ten mm. of its original size, thereby truncating a number of words occurring at line-endings. Fortunately, the use of ultraviolet light permitted the retrieval of at least the beginnings of words, which in the case of Latin was enough to ensure their virtually accurate reconstruction.

looking for a master, and since they could not find one, had hired Le Begue, who governed and instructed the choirboys well, who intended to remain there, and who had made provisions for doing so; Busnoys is unknown to them and perhaps will stay only if the chapter provides his expenses, and the chapter will find no provisions for the choirboys if [he should then leave after] Le Begue is removed. Moreover, lest the canons of Saint-Martin of Tours be displeased with the canons of Saint-Hilaire, it should not appear to them that Busnoys is being taken away from their church. Le Begue should remain and no other received (App., [4]). Canon Jacques Boislesve, chancellor of the University of Poitiers, agreed with the succentor that Busnoys be installed and Le Begue dismissed (App., [5]), evidently refraining from further comment on the matter. The seemingly equivocal Canon Johannes Chaslarii felt that Le Begue should be retained, since he had just taken office two months earlier, but that if he were to be dismissed, the chapter ought to provide him with a means of making a living until it fulfilled its commitment to him (App., [6]). Canon Petrus de Albania alias Vassali, undoubtedly among the more politically shrewd members of the chapter, agreed that Busnoys should be hired, if he would come, seeing that he is a very dignified and eminent man (*multum solemnis et notabilis vir*); but since the chapter had appointed Le Begue master, since he has taught and governed the choirboys well, and since he has lived decently and honestly, perhaps he should remain and hold the position simultaneously with Busnoys, if possible; otherwise the chapter should ensure that he have a means of making a living (App., [7]).

At this point, the intensity of the discussion apparently heated up dramatically as canon René Du Bellay launched a vitriolic attack on the incumbent: Le Begue is inadequate to instruct and govern the choirboys, and has been insulting and offensive to many lords and choristers of the chapter; and because Busnoys is extremely qualified in music and poetry and would best instruct the boys, especially in music and in morals, Busnoys should be hired and Le Begue fired and ordered to vacate the choirboys' house as soon as possible (App., [8]). Du Bellay's caustic indictment of Le Begue and his enthusiastic endorsement of Busnoys evidently fell on deaf ears. Canon Julian Autier thought Le Begue should stay, invoking the opinion of Canon Comitis (who had opposed Busnoys, worried about how long he would stay, and feared the possibility of strained relations with the canons of Saint-Martin of Tours); to this Autier added that if Le Begue had indeed been insulting to members of the chapter, as Du Bellay had claimed, a hearing should take place, Le Begue should be able to tell his side of the story, and he should be removed, depending on the seriousness of the case (App., [9]). Canons Petrus de Brolio, Johannes Cardinalis, and Ynguerrand de Bouhayn (App., [10–12]) all agreed that Le Begue governed and instructed the boys well and should therefore not be removed. Having heard the opinions of each canon, the Dean concluded the assembly by announcing that Le Begue would be deposed and dismissed as master of the choirboys and that Busnoys would be hired as master of the choirboys in his place (App., [13]).

Clearly this ecclesiastical chapter was no citadel of democracy. No fewer than six canons preferred to retain Le Begue, and a seventh, though favouring Busnoys, felt that he and Le Begue should hold the position jointly if possible. After repeated allusions to Busnoys's eminence and exceptional competence in music, no one claimed that Le Begue was 'also a very eminent man', or 'also expert in music', much less in poetry; nor, apparently, did anyone defend Le Begue against the explicit charge of incompetence. Busnoys had only four real advocates: Amboise (the Dean), Rousseau (the succentor), Boislesve, and Du Bellay; of these, only Canons Rousseau and Du Bellay specifically underscored Busnoys's exceptional musical and literary expertise; and of all the canons, only Du Bellay invoked superlatives with regard to Busnoys's musical competence. Most of the canons seem unfazed by the allusions to Busnoys's eminence and particularly oblivious to the notion of finding the *most* qualified candidate who could *best* teach the choirboys. Even though Le Begue had been a candidate of last resort, as one of the canons plainly admitted, they were preoccupied with the ethical issues surrounding their commitment to him and perhaps even more so with the perceived risks, legal or otherwise, involved in hiring an illustrious stranger versus the security of retaining an inadequate, if less glamorous, colleague.[7]

How then does one explain the decision to hire Busnoys? For one thing, he clearly had the support of the Dean, Jean d'Amboise, a descendant of an ancient Angevin family that produced no fewer than five bishops. Jean d'Amboise resided at the French royal court as a counsellor and adviser to King Louis XI. His attendance at the meeting was itself somewhat exceptional, since the chapter acts contain complaints about his regular absence from the church in the service of the king.[8] Hence, d'Amboise's main base of operations must have been the royal city of Tours in the Loire valley, where Busnoys had by then worked for at least five years. Although judiciously refraining from active participation in the discussion, the Dean undoubtedly played a pivotal role in instigating, encouraging, and subsequently ensuring the success of Busnoys's candidacy. And while we know nothing about the extent of his own musical interests, his brother Louis d'Amboise, bishop of Albi in 1474, financed the construction of the important organs at Albi cathedral.[9] Like Dean Jean d'Amboise, Canon René Du Bellay, Busnoys's most

---

[7] Typical of the highly litigious climate of late medieval religious institutions, the chapter acts of Saint-Hilaire are replete with accounts of lengthy legal proceedings of all kinds, often initiated for the seemingly pettiest of reasons.

[8] PADV G 525, 132 (Saturday, 13 Sept. 1466). In 1467 d'Amboise requested from the chapter a dispensation of residence because he was continuously in the service of the king. See Robert Favreau, *La Ville de Poitiers à la fin du moyen âge: Une capitale régionale*, 2 vols. (Poitiers, 1977–8), ii. 426. For further information on d'Amboise see *Gallia Christiana*, 16 vols. (Paris, 1715–1865), ii. 1374 and iv. 631–2.

[9] On Louis d'Amboise, bishop of Albi, see *Gallia Christiana*, ii. 116 and Chan. Louis de Lacger, *Louis d'Amboise, évêque d'Albi, 1474–1503* (Albi, 1950).

articulate and best-informed advocate, had powerful ecclesiastical and political connections in the figure of his brother, Jean Du Bellay, bishop of Poitiers from 1462 to 1478.[10] Du Bellay too hailed from a noble Angevin family of ancient lineage whose descendants would include the sixteenth-century poet Joachim Du Bellay, interesting in light of his specific allusion to Busnoys as 'sufficientissimus in musica et poetria'.[11] And Canon Jacques Boislesve, though notably laconic in his endorsement of Busnoys, may have wielded political clout as rector of the University of Poitiers.

What was Busnoys's attraction to this select group of influential canons at Poitiers, and why did the others manifest indifference to him? Knowledge of the tacit ideological agendas concealed between the lines of the generally polite rhetoric would help answer the question, as would greater insight into the educational backgrounds of the canons themselves. Busnoys's advocates clearly favoured him because he was a distinguished and important man who would add considerable lustre to their church. And the basis for his eminence must have rested on his reputation as a composer, as the oblique allusions to his 'competence, knowledge, and productivity' seem to suggest.[12] Indeed, the evidence that Busnoys already in 1465 was considered a very famous man calls for serious rethinking of previous assumptions about the chronology of his career and his musical output. But the very notion of an individual attaining widespread renown for his work as a composer of music was barely nascent in 1465. Many of the canons, steeped in the legacy of a medieval philosophical tradition that viewed ostentatious display of one's talents with disdain and equated a composer with a shoemaker,[13] may have found the implications of such an idea troubling

[10] On the Du Bellay family see Favreau, *La Ville de Poitiers*, ii. 459.

[11] Canon Du Bellay's specific allusion to Busnoys's expertise 'in poetria' confirms beyond any doubt that Busnoys enjoyed a literary reputation as well. In the context of his remark, the version of this paper delivered at the Busnoys conference in 1992 included a lengthy discussion of Busnoys's *L'homme armé* mass and the anonymous Naples *L'homme armé* masses and drew attention to their possible indebtedness to literary procedures structuring Dante's *Divine Comedy*. The issues treated in the paper have assumed greater significance in the mean time, and I shall reserve discussion of them for my forthcoming book.

[12] If the chapter did indeed covet Busnoys for his skills as a composer, nothing in the canons' discussion or in subsequent documents alludes to any music he might have composed. Since we now know that Busnoys held two consecutive positions as master of the choirboys immediately preceding his arrival at the court of Burgundy, it is conceivable that some of the pieces by Busnoys added across the openings between fascicles in the Burgundian court choirbook Brussels 5557 may have been written either for Saint-Hilaire of Poitiers or Saint-Martin of Tours. One likely candidate is the motet *Victimae paschali laudes*, unique among Busnoys's Latin-texted works for its unusually high ranges. The notion that Busnoys would write a piece of such contrapuntal sophistication and rhythmic complexity with choirboys in mind would challenge received notions of their capacity to perform late 15th-c. sacred polyphony. But since so many late medieval composers held positions as masters of the boys, one must ask why they would have freely assumed, and indeed, actively sought such work unless the position provided an outlet and ample opportunity for them to exercise their creative skills.

[13] The medieval process of composition as a collaborative endeavour, such as one might find in a shoemaker's workshop, is the well-known formulation of 13th-c. Parisian theorist Johannes de Grocheo: 'In composing the aforesaid parts the artist must receive the text or subject matter from another person, the theologian must apply to it the appropriate form, whereupon the musician must apply to it in the appropriate form. Thus do the various crafts [*artes mechanicae*] support one another, as becomes evident in the shoemaker's or the tanner's workshop'. Quoted in Edward E. Lowinsky, 'Musical Genius: Evolution and Origins of a Concept', in id., *Music in the*

at best and at worst incongruous with the spirit of religious community.[14] Le Begue was a good artisan who exercised his craft competently and that seemed to satisfy the majority of the canons.

One surprising silence in the document concerns the absence of reference to the now infamous incident in which Busnoys, while a chaplain at the cathedral of Tours some five years earlier, had allegedly organized a gang assault on a priest, beating him on five separate occasions to the point of bloodshed (*usque ad sanguinis effusionem*), for which he and his cohorts incurred sentences of excommunication.[15] It does seem paradoxical that a man allegedly responsible for such a violent crime should be considered a paradigm of the 'good morals' necessary for the education of young choirboys, especially since upstanding moral character is the single most frequently mentioned qualification in the statutes of nearly every *maîtrise* in western Christendom. The master of the boys was in every respect a surrogate parent, largely responsible for the physical and spiritual exigencies of young male children and adolescents; he shared their house and had to take every precaution to prevent their exposure to malevolent influence of any kind. If the canons supporting Le Begue had needed powerful ammunition against hiring Busnoys, one would think that this ignominious incident from his past would have provided it—and yet no one seems to have mentioned it.

But however incongruous the idea of violence among clerics may appear to our modern sensibilities, the frequency of allusions in the chapter acts of Saint-Hilaire to physical assault 'to the point of bloodshed' suggests that it was a phenomenon so common as to be considered banal.[16] Indeed, Busnoys's incident must have seemed relatively tame in the context of far more grizzly beatings 'to the point of great bloodshed' involving 'the mutilation and mortification of flesh and limbs'.[17] Indeed, one has to wonder how seriously Busnoys and his companions

Culture of the Renaissance and Other Essays, ed. Bonnie J. Blackburn (Chicago and London, 1989), 50. See Lowinsky's eloquent discussion of the theological framework underlying medieval thought, espoused by St Augustine and St Thomas Aquinas, which 'ruled out the possibility of a concept of human creativity' on the grounds that 'solus Deus creat' (ibid. 49–50).

[14] The Rule of St Benedict for example, in discussing individuals authorized to read or sing, prescribes that 'If there are artisans in the monastery, they are to practice their craft in all humility, but only with the abbot's permission. If one of them becomes puffed up by his skillfulness in his craft, and feels that he is conferring something on the monastery, he is to be removed from practicing his craft and not allowed to resume it unless, after manifesting humility, he is so ordered by the abbot'. *The Rule of St. Benedict in Latin and English with Notes*, ed. T. Fry (Collegeville, Minn., 1980), 265.

[15] Pamela Starr, 'Rome as the Centre of the Universe: Papal Grace and Musical Patronage', *EMH* 11 (1992), 223–62 at 249–56 and 260 (Doc. 5).

[16] See for example PADV G 525, 156, 278, 281, 282, 283, 288, 297, 327, 427 (the last involving Petrus de Albania, one of the canons). The phrase 'to the point of bloodshed' itself is so vague as to encompass almost any kind of injury, regardless of degree, including a benign nosebleed provoked in a street brawl.

[17] For example the case involving two canons, one of whom 'maliciose iniuste et indebite absque causa racionabili manus suas in eumdem actorem ineicerat ipsum graviter percutiendo et ledando per plures sui corporis partes *usque ad magnam sanguinis effusionem sueque carnis et membrorum mutilacionem ac mortificacionem* . . .' PADV, G 527, fo. 146ʳ (8 Jan. 1481/2). The language involved in descriptions of such criminal litigation is highly precise because the tax penalties exacted by the Sacra Penitentiaria for absolution varied considerably, depending on the specific nature of the crime. See Emil Göller, *Die päpstliche Pönitentiarie von ihrem Ursprung bis zu ihrer Umgestaltung unter Pius V.*, 2 vols. (Rome, 1911).

intended to harm a man who, after five separate gang beatings, was still alive to talk about it. That the target of Busnoys's assault happened to have been a priest increased its gravity with respect to canon law, as did its repetition on four more occasions. But in the prevailing social context of clerical violence in late medieval France, and particularly since no homicide was involved, I suspect that the incident was unlikely to have attracted exceptional interest from the canons, even had they known about it. And Busnoys was, after all, pardoned by Pope Pius II, Aeneas Silvius Piccolomini.[18] Thus, whatever difficulties Busnoys might have had in Tours, they would seem to have been insufficiently grievous to have jeopardized his position in Poitiers.

Nevertheless, arriving at Saint-Hilaire as a privileged outsider, on the recommendation, if not the instigation, of a dean whose relations with the chapter seem to have been strained at best, cannot have created an ideally hospitable environment for Busnoys. Two weeks after the chapter's initial deliberation, Le Begue appeared before the canons to protest his deposition as master and to present them with a supplication that they provide him with a means of living to enable him to remain in the church's service.[19] No fewer than seven canons had explicitly expressed concern about Le Begue's financial welfare in the general meeting, but the Dean had apparently ignored the issue. An amended resolution, asking that Le Begue be provided with sufficient resources to enable him to remain at Saint-Hilaire,[20] evidently met with the approval of Le Begue and his allies, since Busnoys did come to Saint-Hilaire as master of the choirboys and Le Begue took his place among the supernumerary vicar-choristers.

News of Busnoys's appointment must have spread quickly, for within weeks of his arrival a flood of new musical talent descended upon Saint-Hilaire. The chapter accepted a new chorister named Étienne Aubry, 'expertus in musica', who lodged in Busnoys's house.[21] Shortly thereafter, the chapter admitted a 'poor tenor' into its ranks.[22] In the ensuing months, the chapter formally received many new choir clerks described as being 'expertus in musica' and whose admission was contingent upon satisfactory demonstration to the succentor of their competence in 'musica et letteratura'.[23] This may hint not only at the possibility that the chapter was beefing up its vocal forces as a result of Busnoys's arrival, but

[18] Starr, 'Rome as the Centre of the Universe', 260. Busnoys's petition for absolution was approved and signed by Cardinal Filippo Calandrini, Cardinal Penitentiary under Pope Pius II. The matter of Busnoys's excommunication as a result of this incident has yet to be fully explored. In my forthcoming book I examine Busnoys's crime in the context of medieval canon law, the penalties, both spiritual and material, exacted by a sentence of excommunication, and their implications for Busnoys's career. For an excellent overview of excommunication in the late Middle Ages, though focused mainly on England up to the early 15th c., see Elizabeth Vodola, *Excommunication in the Middle Ages* (Berkeley, 1986).

[19] [Saturday, 28 Sept. 1465], PADV, G 525, 14.   [20] Ibid.

[21] [Tuesday, 22 Oct. 1465]. 'Receptus est de choro et pannis presentis ecclesie Stephanus Aubry qui moratur cum magistro clericulorum presentis ecclesie et est expertus in musica.' PADV, G 525, 18.

[22] [Tuesday, 26 Nov. 1465]. 'Allocata est misia quinque solidorum datorum et traditorum per dominum succentorem cuidam pauperi tenori qui venit ad presentem ecclesiam.' PADV, G 525, 23.

[23] PADV G 525, 59 [1 Apr. 1466], 61 [ibid.], 72 [29 Apr. 1466] and [6 May 1466].

also that the presence of the 'distinguished and eminent' Busnoys himself was attracting unprecedented numbers of singers of polyphony to the church.

Four months after Busnoys's hiring, the residual political tensions over the matter had failed to subside. In January 1466, in response to a chapter decision to grant Busnoys ten *setiers* of wheat, Canon de Bouhayn, one of Busnoys's original opponents, accompanied by a canon absent from the meeting, approached the receiver to protest Busnoys's receipt of any more than four *setiers*[24] and appeared before the Dean and Canon Du Bellay later in the day to explain the reasons for his opposition. Similarly, in March 1466 the succentor and Canon Du Bellay, who had opposed Le Begue, together with a third canon missing from the general assembly, formally protested that 'supernumerary vicars', specifically naming Le Begue among them, were being given the same financial privileges as the regular vicars.[25]

Barely ten months passed before Busnoys disappeared from the records and Le Begue had his job back. On 19 July 1466 the chapter formally reinvested Le Begue with the governance of the *maîtrise*, with the provision that he and any future master would have to feed and maintain six boys and would not be able to hold a vicariate or benefit from its emoluments.[26] A document of 26 July 1466, one week later, describes Busnoys as 'master of the choirboys during the year just past', and charges the succentor and Canon Comitis with the final reckoning of his accounts.[27] The acts remain vexingly silent about the reasons for Busnoys's departure, but the explicitness of the conditions imposed on Le Begue's re-appointment, as well as the incidents previously mentioned, suggest that there may have been controversy within the chapter over responsibilities and financial arrangements during Busnoys's tenure as master. In any case, Busnoys's disappearance before his accounts were settled suggests that his departure was somewhat precipitous. Six months later, in early January 1467, the canons were still trying to find the best way of resolving their debt to 'Antoine Busnoys, former

[24] [25 Jan. 1465/6]. 'Item data fuerunt per capitulum decem sextaria siliginis magistro Anthonio Anthonio [*sic*] Busnoys magistro clericulorum presentis ecclesie verumptamen in mediate post capitulum ad me Johannem Mayeti scribam capituli etc accesscrunt prefati domini Johannes Reginaldi et Ynguerandus de Bouhayn qui dixerunt se non consentire quod ipse Busnoys habeat decem sextaria siliginis sed solum consenterunt quod habeat quatuor sextaria etc. et dictus de Bouhayn se opposuit ne dentur ultra quatuor sextaria.' PADV, G 525, 36.

[25] PADV G 525, 58 [Saturday, 29 Mar. 1466].

[26] [Saturday, 19 July 1466]. 'Magister Johannes Lebegue constitutus et deputatus est per capitulum magister clericulorum presentis ecclesie proviso tamen quod acetero ipse et quicumque alii magistri ipsorum clericulorum pro tempore futuro habebunt nutrire et intertenere seu manutenere sex pueros nec etiam ipse Lebegue nec alius quiviscumque magister etc habebit et percipiet vicariam seu lucrum vicarie presentis ecclesie. Et prefatus dominus succentor se opposuit ne fiat inquestam (?) etc.' PADV, G 525, 117.

[27] [Saturday, 26 July 1466]. 'Commissi fuerunt per capitulum prefati domini succentor et Comitis ad videndum et faciendum compotum magistri Anthonii Busnoys qui fuit magister clericulorum anno ultimo preterito cum Domino Johanne Brassay receptore et si dictus receptor aliquid debeat eidem Busnois quod residuum debiti tradatur in solutum furnerio, carnifici, alutario, et aliis quibus ipse Busnois tenetur ut dicitur et ut apparet per cedulas secundum quod melius per ipsos dominos succentorem et Comitis videbitur fiendum.' PADV, G 525, 118.

master of the choirboys'.[28] By then, Busnoys was well on his way to the Burgundian court, where he first turns up in records of early March 1467 as a singer in the service of the count of Charolais.[29] Meanwhile Le Begue, fulfilling the predictions of Canon Comitis (App., [3]), spent the next thirty years in the service of the church, with the exception of a four-year stint from 1476 to 1480 as *magister puerorum* at the cathedral of Chartres, where he had been a choirboy.[30] He figures prominently in the documents of Saint-Hilaire and gives the impression of being a highly industrious, self-motivated, and ambitious man, constantly seeking to improve his situation. He eventually received his bachelor's degree in canon law from the University of Poitiers, and became a priest.

The irregular circumstances surrounding Busnoys's appointment at Saint-Hilaire may well have generated petty power struggles, or exacerbated existing ones, within the chapter's hierarchy, thus precipitating his departure. Normally, a chapter initiated a search for a new master immediately upon a previous master's resignation or dismissal, writing to neighbouring chapters for recommendations. Sometimes they solicited a known master in another church, but hired someone else if he could not come or failed to respond in time;[31] sometimes a chapter persisted in trying to lure one particular candidate, settling with a series of interim masters until they could get their top choice.[32] Nor was it unheard of for masters in search of work or a change of scenery to send unsolicited offers of services to churches in desirable cities.[33] But the rather precipitous dismissal of an adequate incumbent master barely two months into his job in favour of a more eminent and exceptionally qualified outsider is unique among the cases with which I am familiar.

Coincidentally, a closely analogous situation took place at the nearby Sainte-Chapelle of Bourges, which I have written about elsewhere,[34] but will summarize here since it also involved the deposition of an incumbent master. The young

[28] [Saturday, 3 Jan. 1466/7]. 'Commissi et depputati fuerunt per capitulum prefati domini succentor et Comitis ad videndum et faciendum compotum Magistri Anthonii Busnoys nuper magistri clericulorum presentis ecclesie cum domino Johanne Brassay dicte ecclesie receptore.' PADV, G 525, 156.

[29] Higgins, '*In hydraulis* Revisited', 46.

[30] Evidence that he was a choirboy at Chartres survives in his testament, dated 10 Nov. 1494, PADV, G 515. On Le Begue at Chartres see André Pirro, 'L'Enseignement de la musique aux universités françaises', *Acta musicologica*, 2 (1930), 45. During Le Begue's absence from Saint-Hilaire he was replaced by the poet-composer Éloy d'Amerval, on whose activities I shall report fully elsewhere.

[31] For example, in 1458–9, the canons of the Sainte-Chapelle of Bourges dispatched a messenger to Poitiers to tell the newly appointed master of the choirboys not to come to Bourges because they had already found another master in the mean time (BADC, 8G1638, fo. 135).

[32] As did the canons of Notre-Dame of Cambrai in their quest to hire Johannes Regis. See David Fallows, 'The Life of Johannes Regis, ca. 1425 to 1496', *Revue belge de musicologie*, 43 (1989), 143–72 at 146.

[33] Some thirty years later Antoine Brumel did precisely the same thing at the cathedral of Notre-Dame in Paris, but in Brumel's case the canons of Notre-Dame approached him only after a series of failures with several other masters. See Craig Wright, 'Antoine Brumel and Patronage at Paris', in Iain Fenlon (ed.), *Music in Medieval and Early Modern Europe* (Cambridge, 1981), 37–60.

[34] Paula Higgins, 'Tracing the Careers of Late Medieval Composers: The Case of Philippe Basiron of Bourges', *Acta musicologica*, 61 (1990), 1–28 at 7–8.

composer Philippe Basiron, having served as musical adjunct to four different masters of the choirboys in as many years, finally approached the chapter to remind them of their promise to name him head of the *maîtrise*. He claimed that, in anticipation of this, he had turned down lucrative offers of employment from many important princes and prelates, including the bishop of Angers, Jean Balue, and Jean Cœur, the archbishop of Bourges. The incumbent master, Jean Laloyer, having heard talk of his imminent dismissal, confronted the canons with rumours that they were planning to get rid of him. Assuring Laloyer that they had absolutely no intention of firing him, the canons then proceeded one week later to do precisely that, and replaced him with Philippe Basiron.[35]

Internal politics undoubtedly fuelled the Bourges controversy as well, since it seems unlikely that ethical reasons alone prompted the Sainte-Chapelle's almost instantaneous granting of Basiron's request. Unlike Busnoys at Poitiers, however, Basiron was no stranger to the Sainte-Chapelle of Bourges, having spent nearly a decade in its service since he entered as a choirboy in 1458. Yet the cases are similar in involving attempts to replace what some people thought to be perfectly adequate masters with others having considerably more impressive credentials as well as political clout.

Such examples signal the rapidly changing position of the *magister puerorum* that took place throughout the second half of the fifteenth century. Choir schools had sprouted up all over France and the Low Countries since the mid-fourteenth century, possibly in response to endowments and foundations specifically requesting polyphonic music; and this in turn triggered an unprecedented and ever-growing concern with musical training and education.[36] One tangible by-product of this phenomenal growth industry was the emergence of the exceptionally competent master of the choirboys as a highly marketable commodity. Whereas earlier in the century a master's primary responsibilities seem to have been restricted to instructing the boys in plainchant and in the improvisation of vocal counterpoint, by the end of the century he seems almost invariably to have been a composer of complex mensural polyphony. Choir schools had to compete with an intensifying interest on the part of secular princes and influential prelates who sought to employ the best singers and composers in their personal entourages. The cases of Busnoys and Le Begue at Poitiers and of Basiron and Laloyer at Bourges epitomize the kinds of changes occurring in choir schools all

---

[35] Coincidentally, Laloyer had come to Bourges in 1466 directly from the choir school at Sainte-Radegonde in Poitiers, where he had served as master during the same year that Busnoys was at nearby Saint-Hilaire. Even more coincidentally, Laloyer had previously served as master at Tours cathedral in the early 1460s, while Busnoys had been master at Saint-Martin. Given this trail of coincidences, one cannot help but wonder if Laloyer, who must have known Busnoys personally, might have reported details of the Busnoys–Le Begue episode at Poitiers to his new colleagues at Bourges, thereby inspiring Basiron's audacious political manœuvre and unwittingly plotting his own demise.

[36] The only comprehensive study of choir schools during this period remains the unpublished dissertation of Otto F. Becker, 'The Maîtrise in Northern France and Burgundy during the Fifteenth Century' (Ph.D. diss., George Peabody College for Teachers, 1967).

over France and the Low Countries, and the polarized reactions of the canons
mirror the ambivalent attitudes and stubborn resistance that in all likelihood
accompanied them. By the late fifteenth century even students were getting the
idea that certain masters were 'better' than others, like the one at a *maîtrise* near
Grenoble who petitioned his own chapter to be transferred to the *maîtrise* of
Saint-André to study with the composer Jean Mouton.[37] In 1508, when the
canons of the cathedral of Saint-Étienne of Bourges were seeking to hire a new
master of the choirboys, they targeted a certain 'dominus Josquin' as the object
of their search. The chapter wrote letters to him, consulted an influential relative
of one of the canons about how best to induce him to come, and subsequently
dispatched a messenger from Bourges 'to Picardy' in order to search for him.
Apparently, 'dominus Josquin' never took up the canons' offer, but their persistence in attempting to find him suggests that the man in question was Josquin des
Prez.[38] Their determination to hire as their master a man who was by then the
most renowned composer of the day further corroborates my thesis that the position of *magister puerorum* was assuming unprecedented importance.

   With regard to the individual masters themselves, to what extent did a desire
to exploit the highly favourable market conditions motivate their frequent per-
ambulations? Did the mere prospect of improved material situations alone compel these men to leave the service of one church in favour of another, or did
certain *maîtrises*, such as those in cities with major universities, provide entice-
ments of a more subliminal kind, such as an intellectual climate more conducive
to the fullest expression of their exceptional creative gifts, or the promise of
skilled singers better capable of executing their works? To what extent, if at all,
did a quest for further artistic development, or greater opportunities for creative
expression, motivate these men? What, for example, ultimately compelled composers like Busnoys, Brumel, Mouton, and Obrecht, all of whom encountered
petty political problems or resistance of one sort or another in the routine performance of their duties, to abandon *maîtrises* for ever in favour of service at the
court of a secular prince?[39]

---

[37] Louis Royer, *Les Musiciens et la musique à l'ancienne collégiale Saint-André de Grenoble du XVᵉ au XVIIIᵉ
siècle* (Paris, 1938; repr. Geneva, 1972), 258–60.

[38] The documents in question, kindly brought to my attention by Jean-Yves Ribault, director of the
Archives départementales du Cher in Bourges, are discussed and published in my article 'Musical "Parents"
and Their "Progeny": The Discourse of Creative Patriarchy in Early Modern Europe', in Jessie Ann Owens
and Anthony M. Cummings (eds.), *Music in Renaissance Cities and Courts: Studies in Honor of Lewis
Lockwood* (Warren, Mich., 1997), 169–86 at 174 and 186.

[39] Busnoys, after Saint-Martin of Tours and Saint-Hilaire in Poitiers, settled in at the Burgundian court
of Charles the Bold; see Higgins, '*In hydraulis* Revisited'. Brumel, following short stints as master of the
choirboys at Geneva, Laon, and Paris, found employment at the court of Ercole d'Este in Ferrara; see
Wright, 'Antoine Brumel'. Mouton, after heading choir schools in Amiens, Nesle, and Grenoble, entered
the chapel of Anne of Brittany; see Royer, *Les Musiciens et la musique*. Obrecht, after an exceptionally active
career as choirmaster in Bergen-op-Zoom, Cambrai, Bruges, and Antwerp, ended his days at the court of
Ferrara; see Rob C. Wegman, *Born for the Muses: The Life and Masses of Jacob Obrecht* (Oxford, 1994),
346–54.

These questions seem particularly germane with regard to Busnoys's position in Poitiers. Why would a musician like Busnoys choose to leave Saint-Martin of Tours, then the most important church in western Christendom, only to serve in an identical capacity at its equally renowned sister institution seventy miles to the south, particularly when the extremely close ties of confraternity between the two churches theoretically precluded them from raiding each others' personnel?[40] Since the move would appear to have been a lateral one for Busnoys, it seems useful to question what particular attraction the city of Poitiers might have held for him.

The most obvious lure might have been that city's renowned university, established in 1432. Numerous allusions by fifteenth- and sixteenth-century theorists make it patently clear that the extent of Busnoys's learning and erudition vastly exceeded that of the average fifteenth-century musician. These in turn have prompted speculation that he held university degrees of some sort, although his alma mater has as yet never come to light. Busnoys may well have come to Poitiers with ambitions of pursuing university studies or perhaps continuing a degree already begun elsewhere, while supervising the most important musical *maîtrise* in the city. At least two other fifteenth-century composers seem to have followed precisely such a career trajectory: Johannes Tinctoris, *magister puerorum* at the cathedral of Sainte-Croix in Orléans while attending the university in that city, and the aforementioned Philippe Basiron, who taught the choirboys at the Sainte-Chapelle of Bourges while pursuing studies in canon law at the University of Bourges.[41] Busnoys may conceivably have matriculated at Poitiers, but it seems unlikely that he would have made substantial progress towards a degree during the ten months he remained in the city.

Nevertheless, in his capacity as *magister puerorum* at Saint-Hilaire Busnoys would have routinely interacted with university students and faculty. Of all the churches in Poitiers, Saint-Hilaire had the closest ties with the University. Besides counting the chancellor of the University among its ranks, the chapter of Saint-Hilaire also boasted a number of other canons who served as university regents. A number of the singers received into the choir Busnoys directed were students in the arts faculties, or already recipients of arts degrees. One of the earliest residential colleges of the University of Poitiers, the Collège de La Sereyne, was founded in 1463 with a bequest from the estate of a former Saint-Hilaire *cantor*, the dignitary charged with overseeing the administration of the

---

[40] The two churches, linked historically by an ancient bond dating back to the actual friendship between saints Martin and Hilary, continued to maintain extremely close ties of confraternity in the 15th c. Canon Comitis's remarks (App., [3]) seem explicitly to address his concern over the political ramifications for Saint-Hilaire of attempting to hire one of Saint-Martin's clerics.

[41] On Basiron's status as a university student while serving as master of the choirboys in Bourges see Higgins, 'Tracing the Careers', 11. On Tinctoris's activity in Orléans see Ronald Woodley, 'Iohannes Tinctoris: A Review of the Documentary Biographical Evidence', *JAMS* 34 (1981), 217–48. The documents concerning his matriculation at the University of Orléans are published in Hilde de Ridder-Symoens, Detlef Illmer, and Cornelia M. Ridderikhoff, *Les Livres des procurateurs de la nation germanique de l'ancienne université d'Orléans (1444–1602)*, 2 vols. (Leiden, 1971–8), i. 29–30 and ii. 69–70.

church's musical establishment. The College supported sixteen students—eight in arts, four in theology, and four in canon law. Eight of the positions gave first priority to choirboys exiting Saint-Hilaire's *maîtrise*.[42] While well-endowed *maîtrises*, such as those of Notre-Dame of Paris, the Sainte-Chapelles of Paris and of Bourges, and Notre-Dame of Chartres, routinely subsidized one or two university scholarships for gifted boys leaving the *maîtrise*, the intensity of interaction between Saint-Hilaire's *maîtrise* and the university at Poitiers seems extraordinary among comparable collegiate or cathedral choir schools in fifteenth-century France. Moreover, the *magister puerorum* and the choir school of Saint-Hilaire-le-Grand held a virtual monopoly on providing music for solemn university celebrations, judging from numerous documents alluding to musical performances by the master, choirboys, and other choristers.[43]

Curiously, while we have ample evidence of fifteenth-century *magistri puerorum* who held university degrees, usually the *maître-ès-arts*, those for whom music has survived—the ones we refer to today as 'composers'—are generally not among them. Of the fifteenth-century composers who served as masters of the choirboys, only two are known for certain to have had university training, and one of these is known primarily as a theorist—Tinctoris, whose twelve treatises represent the sum total of our knowledge of musical practice for the period.[44] While numerous pragmatic considerations, such as eligibility for plum ecclesiastical benefices, might have motivated a musician whose primary interests lay in the realm of musical composition to pursue a university degree, it seems clear nevertheless that the *maîtrise*, and not the university, served as the principal site of competition in the creative realm of musical endeavour.[45]

Indeed, the marked change in attitude towards the composer by the end of the fifteenth century seems inextricably bound up with the evolving status of the master of the choirboys from that of skilled pedagogue to creative mentor.[46] This gradual shift in mentality can be traced not only in the strategies of patronage employed at secular courts as the fifteenth century progressed, but especially in

---

[42] Robert Favreau, 'Aspects de l'Université de Poitiers au xvᵉ siècle', *Bulletin de la Société des Antiquaires de l'Ouest* (4th series), 5 (1959–60), 47.
[43] Ibid. 47.
[44] See above, n. 41. Dufay of course held a university degree, but so far as we know he never served as a master of the choirboys.
[45] Guillaume de Van already made this point some fifty years ago in 'La Pédagogie musicale à la fin du moyen âge', *Musica disciplina*, 2 (1948), 75–97 at 78.
[46] In his article 'Musical Genius' Lowinsky pinpointed the years around 1500, when composers were abandoning compositional procedures based on pre-existing melodies in favour of freely composed polyphony, as a period which gave rise to a growing awareness of the composer as a peculiarly gifted individual and creative artist, whose musical gifts were matched by an extraordinary and temperamental personality. In this subtle mixture of talent and temperament Lowinsky saw the ferment of the modern notion of musical genius. Lowinsky, however, overlooked a strongly competing strand of thought which is quite alien to the 19th-c. concept of genius: the indispensability of a master to the development and nurturing of one's creative talents. I have pursued this idea further in 'Musical "Parents" and Their "Progeny"'; see n. 38 above.

the patterns of recruitment and hiring of choirmasters and other musical personnel in collegiate churches and cathedrals, as we have seen. Accompanying this
changing role of the *magister puerorum* are growing manifestations of interest in
the establishment of his musical lineage as well as his musical progeny. By this
I mean of course not his biological ancestors or descendants, but rather the
teachers through whom he developed (or figuratively 'inherited') his musical
talent, and the disciples he in turn spawned as his creative offspring. Evidence of
this developing preoccupation with a composer's musical lineage can be discerned in the pages of theoretical treatises, in elegies on the deaths of famous
composers, in documentary records, and in the dedicatory prefaces to collections
of music and didactic works. Couched in rhetoric that frequently conflated the
actual music master/teacher/mentor with a metaphorical creative 'father', this
preoccupation with establishing the creative pedigree of composers developed,
over the span of some 150 years, into a veritable 'discourse of creative patriarchy'[47] of which Busnoys's acknowledgement of himself as Ockeghem's 'offspring' in the text of the motet *In hydraulis* may be one of the first examples.[48]
Significantly, a few years earlier Ockeghem had used the word 'père de joyeuseté'
to describe Binchois;[49] and some years later Jean Molinet and Guillaume Cretin
would call upon Josquin, Brumel, Compère, and their contemporaries to lament
the deceased Johannes Ockeghem as their 'maître et bon père'.[50] When Josquin
himself died in 1521, allusions to him as both a father and teacher proliferated as
rapidly as did the claims of younger composers purporting to have studied with
him. And a legion of sixteenth-century composers after Josquin, including
Gaffurius, Sermisy, Willaert, Gombert, Rore, Le Jeune, Byrd, Mauduit, and
numerous others, were all hailed by contemporaries as both important 'teachers'
and 'fathers'.

However real or figurative these allusions may prove to be, the trend around
1500 and beyond to acknowledge one's musical genealogy by claiming to have
studied under a particular 'maître' accompanied the relatively recent tendency for
masters of the boys to be accomplished composers. While most writers on music
before 1480 rarely mention teachers at all, neither their own nor those of
others,[51] sixteenth-century writers seem compelled to mention not only their

---

[47] See Higgins, 'Musical "Parents" and Their "Progeny" '.

[48] 'practiculum tuae propaginis arma cernens quondam per atria burgundiae ducis in patria per me busnoys illustris comitis de chaurolois indignum musicum . . .'.

[49] *Mort, tu as navré de ton dart*, edited in Johannes Ockeghem, *Collected Works*, iii, ed. Richard Wexler
with Dragan Plamanac (Boston, 1992), 77–8.

[50] Jean Molinet, *Nymphes des bois*, lament on the death of Johannes Ockeghem (1497): 'Acoutrez vous
d'abits de deuil | Josquin, Brumel, Pierchon, Compère | Et plorez grosses larmes d'œil | Perdu avez votre bon
père'; Guillaume Cretin, *Déploration sur le trépas de J. Ockeghem* (1497): 'Agricola, Verbonnet, Prioris |
Josquin Desprez, Gaspar, Brumel, Compère | Ne parlez plus de joyeux chantz ne ris | Mais composez un *Ne
recorderis* | Pour lamenter nostre maistre et bon père . . .'.

[51] An exception is Johannes Gallicus (Legrense) (d. 1474), who mentions his teacher Vittorino da Feltre.
See Johannes Gallicus, *Ritus canendi*, ed. Albert Seay, 2 vols. (Colorado Springs, 1981), i. 2.

own masters, but the real or putative teachers of many of the renowned composers of the day.[52] For example, despite numerous opportunities for self-revelation in his twelve surviving treatises, Tinctoris, tellingly, never mentions his own teacher; and only in his last work, generally thought to date from *c*.1481–3, during his years in Naples, did he refer to having once 'taught the choirboys at Chartres'.[53] Even though his documented activities as a choirmaster in Loire Valley churches dated back to the early 1460s, Tinctoris never mentions this in any of his earlier writings. In fact, one can discern a a subtle but striking shift in Tinctoris's conceptual language between the *Proportionale*, possibly written in the 1460s, when he described Ockeghem, Busnoys, and Regis, as having 'followed after' ('successerunt') Dunstable, Binchois, and Dufay,[54] and his much later *Liber de arte contrapuncti*, completed in 1477, where a rewriting of essentially the same passage described Ockeghem, Busnoys, and the other composers as 'having taken pride in having had the recently deceased Dunstable, Binchois, and Dufay as their teachers in the divine art of music',[55] thus symbolically joining the two generations of composers in a creative lineage as teachers and students, where no expressed connection between the two groups had existed in his previous discourse on the subject. Just one year earlier, Tinctoris had dedicated his treatise on mode to Ockeghem and Busnoys, as 'the most famous and most celebrated teachers of the art of music', the first known historical acknowledgement of these two figures as 'teachers'.[56] By the middle of the sixteenth century, the German theorist Hermann Finck formally articulated the idea that Tinctoris and others had understood for nearly a century:

And if it is important in the other disciplines who your first teacher and mentor is, certainly in this art it is of greatest significance that he who by nature burns with a love of music use an experienced teacher and devote himself totally to imitating him.[57]

No contemporary witness from the late fifteenth century has thus far come for-

---

[52] Just a few of the many mentor/student relationships proclaimed in the pages of contemporaneous treatises include: de Monte and Ramos; Ramos and Spataro; Glareanus and Cochlaeus; Gaffurius and Bonadies; Erasmus and Obrecht; Isaac and Senfl; Mouton and Willaert, Josquin and Mouton, and Ockeghem and Josquin.

[53] *De inventione et usu musicae*; see Karl Weinmann, *Johannes Tinctoris und sein unbekannter Traktat 'De inventione et usu musicae'*, ed. Wilhelm Fischer (Tutzing, 1961), 34.

[54] See Johannes Tinctoris, *Opera theoretica*, ed. Albert Seay, 2 vols. ([Rome], 1975), iia. 10.

[55] '. . . Johannes Okeghem, Johannes Regis, Anthonius Busnois, Firminus Caron, Guillermus Faugues, qui novissimis temporibus vita functos Johannem Dunstaple, Egidium Binchois, Guillermum Dufay *se prae-ceptores habuisse in hac arte divina gloriantur*' (italics mine). See ibid., ii. 12.

[56] 'Praestantissimis ac celeberrimis artis musicae professoribus Domino Johanni Okeghem, christianis-simi regis Francorum prothocapellano ac Magistro Antonio Busnois, illustrissimi Burgundorum ducis cantori . . .'; *Liber de natura et proprietate tonorum*; ibid., i. 65.

[57] *Practica musica* (Wittenburg, 1556), beginning of Liber Quintus. Quoted in Lowinsky, 'Musical Genius,' 54.

ward proclaiming himself as a pupil of Antoine Busnoys. And yet Busnoys was without question the master of his day most imitated by a younger generation of composers including Josquin, Obrecht, Isaac, Agricola, Ghiselin, and possibly Japart. In Busnoys's case, imitation may indeed have been the highest form of flattery; and it was in any case the only kind he could have expected at the time.

Appendix
Chapter Deliberation re: Busnoys v. Le Begue
Poitiers, Archives départementales de la Vienne, G525, fos. 1–3
Actes capitulaires de Saint-Hilaire-le-Grand, 1465–9
(*c.* 14 September 1465)

. . . [1] et moribus Magistri Johanni Lebegue magistri puerorum presentis [ecclesie][et] Busnoys qui nunc est magister clericulorum ecclesie beatissimi Martini Turonensis, multum affectat et desiderat deservire presenti ecclesie, esse multum sufficientem et maxime expertum in musica, in modo instruendi et docendi pueros in musica et ceteris requisitis ad bonum magistrum clericorum bonisque moribus. [2] Positoque in deliberacione capitulari per ipsum dominum decanum[1] de depp[onendo] et destituendo dictum Lebegue a regimine et gubernamento dictorum clericulorum presentis ecclesie et de constituendo et ordinando dictum Busnoys magistrum clericulorum regimen et administrationem eorundem sibi commictendo etc. Votisque [omnium] et singulorum dominorum capitulantibus singulariter et successive inquisitis, [3] primo [dominus] succentor[2] fuit oppinionis actenctis et consideratis sufficiencia, scientia [et] industria dicti Busnoys, qui ut dicitur est multum notabilis vir, quod si volet venire et accipere onus, regimen et administracionem dictorum clericulorum, constituatur in officio magistri ipsorum clericulorum et dictus Lebegue depp[onatur] et destituatur a regimine administracione et officio magistri clericulorum. Ve[rum] quia dictus Lebegue in primo suo adventu venit et accessit ad ecclesiam ad requestam capituli, fuit opinionis dictus dominus succentor quod [dictus] Lebegue largiatur de bonis capituli donec sibi providerit de modo viv[endi]. [4] Comitis[3] fuit opinionis quod cum alias capitulum fecerit plures misias habendo magistrum clericulorum in presenti ecclesia et quia non potuit reperire dictus Lebegue qui venit et constitutus fuit in dicto officio ad requestam capituli et dictos clericulos bene rexit et instru[xit], hic intendat residere et morari et fecerit suas provisiones notus quia etc. Dictus Busnoys est ignotus et forsan [*illegible*] et volet [*sic*] remanere in presenti ecclesia nisi capitulum faciat pro ipso [suas] [p. 2] expensas cum nullas provisiones reperiet [*top of page torn*] [pu]eris si dictus Lebegue destituatur Ne etc. domini ecclesie beatissimi Martini Turonensis sint male contenti a dominis presentis capituli ne eis videatur quod dictus Busnoys a sua ecclesia substrahatur. Dictus Lebegue continuetur in dicto officio magistri et non recipiatur alius. [5] Boilesve[4] fuit oppinionis prefati domini succentoris videlicet

---

[1] Johannes de Ambozia (Jean d'Amboise) (d. 28 May 1498), *in utroque jure licenciatus*, dean of Saint-Hilaire-le-Grand from Sept. 1462 until 1470; counsellor and adviser to Louis XI; bishop of Maillezais, 1470–81; bishop of Langres, 1481–97; governor of the estates of Burgundy under Louis XI, Charles VIII, and Louis XII. See *Gallia Christiana*, ii (Paris, 1720), col. 1374; iv, cols. 631–2.

[2] Gauffridus Rousselli (Geoffroy Rousseau) (d. 13 Nov. 1476), *in juribus canonico et civili licenciatus*, prebended canon of Saint-Hilaire-le-Grand by Nov. 1445 and succentor from at least 7 July 1461 until his death in 1476.

[3] Johannes Comitis, *in utroque jure licenciatus*, prebended canon of Saint-Hilaire-le-Grand.

[4] Jacobus Boilesve (Jacques Boislesve) (d. 1482), *in juribus canonico et civili ac aliis graduatus licenciatus*, rector of the University of Poitiers in 1466, and a prebended canon of Saint-Hilaire-le-Grand and Notre-Dame-la-Grande in Poitiers.

quod dictus Lebegue destituatur a dicto officio et Busnoys constituatur in eodem. [6] Chaslarii[5] fuit oppinionis quod dictus Lebegue, qui incepit annum in festo sancti Johannis Baptiste ultimo preterito, continuetur et non destituatur verumptamen si destituatur a dicto officio quod provideatur eidem per capitulum de modo vivendi donec et quousque sua debita eidem soluta fuerint. [7] De Albania[6] fuit oppinionis quod dictus Lebegue destituatur a dicto officio et regimine puerorum et quod constituatur in eodem officio Busnoys, si veniat, actento quod est multum sollemnis et notabilis vir, verumptamen quia dictus Lebegue a tempore quo fuit constitutus in officio magistri clericulorum presentis ecclesie dictos clericulos bene rexit et instruxit in scientia et moribus ac decenter et honeste vixit quod maneat et habeat expensas cum dicto Busnoys si possit fieri. Alias quod per capitulum provideatur eidem de modo vivendi et fiant ei tanta bona quod debeat contentari. [8] Dubellay[7] fuit opinionis actento quod dictus Lebegue est insufficiens ad dictos clericulos instruendum et regendum quia etc. est iniuriosus et iniuriatus fuit pluribus dominis presentis capituli et aliis choristis ecclesie et quia dictus Busnoys est sufficientissimus in musica et poetria et optime instruit pueros maxime in musica et moribus quod eidem Busnoys tradatur regimen et administracio dictorum clericulorum et deponatur et destituatur dictus Lebegue et precipiatur eidem ex parte capituli de vacuando domum dictorum clericulorum quam citius. [9] Anterii[8] fuit oppinionis quod dictus Lebegue continuetur et non destituatur causis et r[ationibus] [pre]tactis per dictum Comitis et ulterius dixit quod dictus Lebegue sup[er?] iniuriis pretactis citetur et audiatur et si ita reperiatur fiat iusticia et privatur [*sic*] secundum casus exigenciam et quod non debet destitui [nisi] eo audito. [10] De Brolio[9] fuit oppinionis quod dictus Lebegue qui est cognitus et bene regit et instruit clericulos tam in sciencia quam moribus quod continuetur in officio magistri dictorum clericulorum. [11] Cardinalis[10] fuit oppinionis quod dictus Lebegue non destituatur nec deponatur sed continuetur in dicto officio magistri puerorum cum dictos clericulos bene regat et instruat. [12] De Bouhayn[11] fuit oppinionis dicti de Brolio videlicet quod dictus Lebegue continuetur in dicto officio regimine et administracione dic-

---

[5] Johannes Chaslarii (d. 1482), *in juribus canonico et civili licentiatus*, prebended canon of Saint-Hilaire-le-Grand.

[6] Petrus de Albania, alias Vassalli (d. 8 July 1504), *in juribus canonico et civili licenciatus et in artibus magister*, prebended canon of Saint-Hilaire-le-Grand from at least 15 Jan. 1448 until 27 June 1476. Elected *cantor* 22 June 1482.

[7] Renatus Du Bellay (René Du Bellay), *in juribus canonico et civili licenciatus et in artibus magister*, prebended canon of Saint-Hilaire-le-Grand; resigned his benefice on 19 Apr. 1466; abbot of Notre-Dame-la-Grande in Poitiers; prebended canon of the cathedral of Saint-Pierre of Poitiers; brother of Jean Du Bellay, bishop of Poitiers from 1462 to 1474.

[8] Julianus Anterii (Julian Autier), *in legibus et decretis licentiatus et in artibus magister*, prebended canon of Saint-Hilaire-le-Grand.

[9] Petrus de Brolio (d. 29 Nov. 1476), *in juribus canonico et civili licentiatus*, prebended canon of Saint-Hilaire; already over 60 years old and ill on 2 Jan. 1467/8.

[10] Johannes Cardinalis (d. 1467), *in juribus canonico et civili licentiatus*, prebended canon of Saint-Hilaire-le-Grand; resigned his benefice on 23 June 1466 by permutation with Nicolaus Potruyelli, rector of the parochial church of Saint-Pierre de Montreuil-Bellay (PADV G 525, p. 101). His death is mentioned in the minutes of the chapter meeting of 15 Jan. 1467 (PADV G 525, p. 161).

[11] Ynguerandus de Bouhayn (d. 5 Nov. 1494), *in juribus canonico et civili licentiatus, scholasticus* of Saint-Hilaire-le-Grand from 10 July 1471 until his death in 1494. Probably the most politically influential of Le Begue's supporters, Canon de Bouhayn happened to be the nephew of Robert Poitevin, counsellor and physician to kings Charles VII and Louis XI (and hence another habitué of the French royal court at Tours), and Treasurer of Saint-Hilaire-le-Grand from 24 Apr. 1448 until July 1474.

torum clericulorum et quod non destituatur nec deponatur. [13] Quibus oppinionibus
auditis dictus dominus decanus presidens conclusit quod depponatur et destituatur dictus
Lebegue a regimine et administracione dictorum clericulorum, ipsum deposuit et desti-
tuit, et quod dictus Busnoys constituatur magister clericulorum et eidem tradatur onus
regimen et administracio dictorum clericulorum.

8

Mensural Intertextuality in the Sacred Music of Antoine Busnoys

⛧ ⛧

ROB C. WEGMAN

ONE can say many things about Johannes Tinctoris, but not that he was afraid to hold unpopular views on music theory.[1] His treatises show an unwavering adherence to 'truth' and 'reason', even in cases where no other compositions than his own (which modesty forbade him to mention)[2] exemplified those criteria. Faced with almost universal contrary practice on several of his teachings (including in the works of Antoine Busnoys), Tinctoris was fighting a losing battle, it seems, yet battling on nevertheless.

This is a position that must have required some intellectual courage, yet we should probably not overestimate that aspect. For in a sense Tinctoris belonged to two worlds. As a university teacher,[3] his primary allegiance was to the seven liberal arts (including music) as an internally consistent body of scientific knowledge. Here his criteria of 'truth' and 'reason' were backed by centuries of scholastic thought, and ultimately by the authority of 'the Philosopher', Aristotle.

The writing of this article was made possible through a British Academy Postdoctoral Fellowship. My original contribution to the conference (entitled 'Antoine Busnoys and the Late Fifteenth-Century Motet') was completely rewritten in the light of comments made to me by Paula Higgins. The present essay, which in many ways represents a sequel to my earlier article on Petrus de Domarto (cited below), is dedicated to Paula in acknowledgement of her pioneering work on Antoine Busnoys and her contribution to musicology at large, of which the memorable conference at Notre Dame was an outstanding example.

[1] References in this contribution are to Johannes Tinctoris, *Opera theoretica*, ed. Albert Seay (CSM 22; American Institute of Musicology, 1975–8), quoted here with corrections after the manuscripts (kindly supplied by Dr Bonnie Blackburn) and changed punctuation. Abbreviations are as follows: lower-case roman numerals refer to books, arabic numerals to chapters, and to sentences as numbered in Seay's edition; individual treatises are abbreviated as follows: *Liber de natura et proprietate tonorum* (*T*); *Proportionale musices* (*P*); *Liber de arte contrapuncti* (*C*); *Diffinitorium* (*D*); *Tractatus alterationum* (*A*); *Expositio manus* (*M*); *Liber imperfectionum notarum* (*I*); *Super punctis musicalibus* (*SPM*).

[2] Except when his works had been criticized by others, as in the case of the *Missa Nos amis* (*A* Prologus 3–6). For this work, see Reinhard Strohm, 'Die Missa super "Nos amis" von Johannes Tinctoris', *Musikforschung* 32 (1979), 34–51, and id., 'Meßzyklen über deutsche Lieder in den Trienter Codices', in *Liedstudien: Festschrift für Wolfgang Osthoff zum 60. Geburtstag* (Tutzing, 1989), 77–106.

[3] On the probability that Tinctoris taught law (and possibly music) at the university of Naples, see Rob C. Wegman, *Born for the Muses: The Life and Masses of Jacob Obrecht* (Oxford, 1994), 75.

Within this world it would have required much more courage to propose or defend violations of that consistency than to censure them.[4] Such violations had almost become the order of the day in the other world to which Tinctoris belonged, that of everyday musical practice. With that world the theorist had a far more uneasy relationship. Occasionally, when he criticizes the 'errors' of contemporary composers, one can almost sense him being embarrassed at what scholars in the other liberal arts might think (e.g. the 'arithmetici' in *P* iii. 2. 16–17).

It would seem, then, that Tinctoris felt at home in one world much more than in the other, and that this could perhaps explain his somewhat isolated position in the latter. Yet it is doubtful that he would have agreed with this view. For one thing, Tinctoris was a professional musician himself, with a distinguished career as a singer, teacher, choirmaster, and composer. For another, and more importantly, for him there could only be *one* art of music—not divided, but at most perhaps including practitioners who did not fully understand the art, and who were consequently in need of fuller instruction (*P* Prologus 13–19). Why dignify the incompetent with a world of their own? No musician could escape the teachings of the liberal arts, particularly mathematics (*T* 1. 6; *P* Prologus 15), even in such basic matters as pitch relationships (*Speculum musices*; see *M* 8. 20), the counting of rhythmic values (*I* 3. 53), proportional relationships (*P* i. 1. 3), and indeed any conception of number and multiplicity (*P* iii. 7). This being so, such teachings had best be worked out and applied consistently, lest musicians follow them in one case and contradict them in another (as he complained, for instance, in *P* iii. 5. 9–10).

It is this vision of a unified and intellectually respectable art of music that gave Tinctoris the courage to attack the most prominent composers of his day. In 1476 he dedicated a treatise to Antoine Busnoys and Johannes Ockeghem, two composers whom he had severely criticized four years earlier, in the *Proportionale musices* (*P*). In the preface to his new treatise, the *Liber de natura et proprietate tonorumi* (*T*), he firmly if somewhat undiplomatically stood by his criticisms, repeating that 'you have used the signs of proportion wrongly without any regard for censures or corrections' (Prologus 5).

Debates over proportions could make tempers rise even then. One northern musician, who apparently claimed expertise and authority in the art of music, had been so outraged by the criticisms in the *Proportionale* that he had threatened to make Tinctoris eat the treatise if ever he returned to his native land. Yet the theorist remained unimpressed even by threats of violence. Metaphorically, he

---

[4] It is probable, for instance, that Bartolomé Ramos de Pareja failed to obtain a public lectureship at the University of Bologna because of the unorthodox teachings in his treatise *Musica practica* (1482). See Bonnie J. Blackburn, Edward E. Lowinsky, and Clement A. Miller (eds.), *A Correspondence of Renaissance Musicians* (Oxford 1991), 463–5 and 1009–11.

replied, the treatise should indeed be digested, and in fact its contents had been gestated in him before he wrote it (*T* Prologus 13–16, confirming that much of *P* may have been worked out well before its completion date). Nevertheless, Tinctoris noted with glee that he had since then returned many times to the North, without suffering any harm.[5]

Tinctoris versus Busnoys

We are of course most fortunate in having contemporary criticisms of Busnoys's mensural habits, and indeed one can recognize most of these habits in his surviving works. Yet what do they tell us about the composer? For Tinctoris the answer would have been clear: Busnoys, although pre-eminent in Latinity (*P* iii. 3. 9), was not above committing errors that suggest a less than thorough grasp of mensural theory. Yet is not self-evident that we should necessarily see things Tinctoris's way. After all, it is Busnoys who was the more gifted, prolific, and successful composer. And to him, minor deviations from theoretical dogma might well have been a matter of relative indifference, representing either trifling variations in musical orthography, or perhaps the unavoidable consequence of artistic innovation. By contrast, Tinctoris, in seizing on such deviations, might conceivably be regarded as a hair-splitting pedant, a prototypical 'theorist' out of touch with practical reality. And when it comes to mensural usage, one might argue that Busnoys, in committing the alleged errors, gave them a certain authority based on practical currency. After all, what is theory more than the codification of practice? And even if we do not wish to 'take sides', might we not simply conclude that Tinctoris and Busnoys had different viewpoints on mensural theory, and that it is not our task to evaluate them in terms of right and wrong?

There are several historical assumptions involved in these questions—none of them necessarily inappropriate. One can defend Busnoys (if he needs our defence) by assuming that mensural notation can be likened somewhat to

---

[5] 'When the *Proportionale* became widely available, some persons, and one in particular, who is unworthy to be named not only here but in any other honourable and liberal work of instruction, as being devoid of all good arts, adjudged that I deserved rightly to be branded with the mark of abuse. In addition, this one man, who is the most ridiculous of all singers [*cantores*, not *musici*], was not afraid to threaten me with the forcible eating of that little book if ever I should return to my native land, on the ground that, as has been stated above, I had attempted to blame your misuse of signs of proportion. O words most worthy of a wise man! O menaces most seemly in a brave man! To be sure, what he predicted so wisely and what he threatened so bravely has happened to me honourably; I have repeatedly returned to my native land since this, time after time. For although my body is far removed from it, my mind, constantly remembering my family and friends, is only a short distance away or not at all. Have I not eaten the book too? Indeed I have, as the Spirit said to Ezekiel: "Thy belly shall eat, and thy bowels shall be filled with this book." [Ezek. 3: 3; Ezekiel continues: "And I did eat it, and it was sweet as honey in my mouth."] I am not ashamed to declare that it came true of me. For what is to eat a book but to consider what it contains with great care, and for one's bowels to be filled with it, but, having considered it, to remember it with an indelible memory? Both before and after I had published this *Proportionale* I had most diligently devoted myself to considering its content.' (*T* Prologus 6–18).

language, and by invoking linguistic concepts such as 'usage' and 'currency' (rather than 'truth' and 'reason'). This is a dynamic image, and it can do historical justice to the fact that mensural habits did indeed change over time,[6] that theory tended to accommodate such changes in the long run, and that several of Busnoys's 'errors' did eventually receive theoretical validation. In this view, Tinctoris's criteria of 'truth' and 'reason' would not have been timeless and objectively decidable, but subject to historical change—as the subsequent course of music theory only confirms. Mensural 'correctness' would be defined basically by historical precedent, and thus we could perhaps value Busnoys's role positively by assuming that he set several influential precedents.[7]

Yet this is not how Tinctoris would have viewed it, and we need to do justice to his position as well. He would not have denied that the mensural system comprises such a wide variety of available mensurations, proportions, and ways of notating their countless permutations, that it was quite possible for a composer to develop a personal 'usage', if only by consistently preferring some devices over others. (He did recommend, of course, that each composition cover as much of the available 'variety' as possible; see *C* iii. 8.) Nor would he have denied that such preferences could change over time.

Yet over and above such legitimate wanderings within the system he maintained the received view, in which the system itself was a science that proceeded from axioms, like mathematics or geometry (cf. *P* i. 1. 3). That is to say, the entire framework of musical knowledge was deduced in Aristotelian fashion from a number of given axioms (*elementa, principia, generales regulae*), such as note, value, hexachord, the rule of like before like, and so on. It was a closed system, in the sense that it was defined by what was logically possible, in the same way that mathematics allows valid theorems but rules out invalid ones. To move beyond its boundaries and still insist on theoretical validity was to lapse into logical contradiction. To use a modern analogy, it was like saying that, following the compass, one can move further north than the North Pole. In Tinctoris's view this would not be expanding or developing the system but corrupting it, and any invocation of historical precedent would be a matter of the blind leading the blind, wandering away from 'the clarity of truth' (*P* iii. 2. 20).

Tinctoris did not lay exclusive claim to 'truth' and 'reason'. Every composer who notated his music mensurally indicated, by the very act of doing so, his acceptance of established principles, thereby affirming the common ground from which the theorist could identify the few logical contradictions, rightly calling

---

[6] For a detailed study of the changing mensural habits of one 15th-c. composer, see Charles Hamm, *A Chronology of the Works of Guillaume Dufay Based on a Study of Mensural Practice* (Princeton, NJ, 1964).

[7] As Pietro Aaron, for instance, did in 1523, when he commented on Busnoys's use of *prolatio maior* augmentation: 'Since he was a great man and an excellent musician, this is not to be considered an error on his part, and the same thing is not to be condemned in Ockeghem and other ancients, and in Obrecht and Josquin, who followed the footsteps of their predecessors.' Quoted after Richard Taruskin, 'Antoine Busnoys and the *L'Homme armé* Tradition', *JAMS* 39 (1986), 255–93 at 290.

them errors. (It would have been pointless for him to proceed from the same basis in discussing details of tablature, score, or stroke notation, which represented different notational worlds altogether.) In this sense 'truth', as invoked by Tinctoris, was indeed objectively decidable.

Yet the historical truth is that mensural practice did change very much like a language, and frequently moved beyond its theoretically defined boundaries. In the fifteenth-century repertory one can find numerous notational conventions that had no logical relationship with any of the basic axioms, and often patently contradicted them.[8] Tinctoris reacted to such conventions in a way that could almost be described as intellectual overkill. Invariably he seized upon errors in compositions (rather than on viewpoints maintained in other treatises),[9] and proceeded to rebut them as if they were propositions defended in an academic disputation. As a rhetorical strategy this does indeed make the issue of 'truth' seem vitally important—much more so, one feels, than it would have been in the everyday lives of most musicians. But it also has the side-effect of elevating relatively trivial habits, even forms of shorthand (as with proportions, *P* iii. 2. 16–21), to theoretically grounded positions. The narrowly scholastic terms on which Tinctoris conducted these debates makes one feel that a split between two worlds was almost inevitable.

Returning to Busnoys, for instance, it is hard to say whether Tinctoris's criticisms point to anything as weighty as an actual difference of opinion. To be sure, when it comes to right and wrong, at least in medieval scientific terms, Tinctoris is invariably right. Yet whereas this evidently mattered a great deal to him, one cannot be sure how much it really mattered to Busnoys. That, in a way, is the central question of this essay: how seriously did Busnoys take his mensural usage, given that it was so idiosyncratic, and became subject to such heated dispute in the 1470s? One reason why this question is difficult to answer is that any simple juxtaposition between Busnoys and Tinctoris will inevitably stereotype either, and make us neglect a crucial complicating factor: the extensive common ground they in fact shared.

It might be tempting, for instance, to regard Busnoys as the prototypical creative genius, as an artist who could validate notational 'errors' simply by dint of writing them, or even transcend theoretical issues altogether by sheer force of musicianship. Yet this would involve a negative image of theory that is anachronistic as well as inappropriate. Whatever may have caused Busnoys to depart from the system as codified by Tinctoris, it cannot have been the irresistible force of artistic innovation, if only because the theorist emphasized in almost every case

---

[8] For a rich anthology of such conventions, with many musical examples from the contemporary repertory, see J. A. Bank, *Tactus, Tempo and Notation in Mensural Music from the 13th to the 17th Century* (Amsterdam, 1972).

[9] Except perhaps obliquely, for instance, when he observed that a minim under duple proportion is sometimes wrongly called semiminim 'as some unlearned babble' (*P* i. 4. 8).

that correct alternatives were available within the system. The alternatives may occasionally look a little contrived (as they tend to do in Tinctoris's own masses and motets),[10] but then Busnoys was hardly a man to shy away from mensural contrivance. Nor would the juxtaposition do much justice to Tinctoris and his teachings. The terms on which he discussed mensural theory may not have been popular, but within those terms he managed to convey a vision of mensural theory that commands respect for its intellectual profundity and integrity.[11] The modern tendency to sympathize with great composers more than with theorists should not lead us to overlook a very obvious (if even today perhaps unpopular) historical fact: that mensural theory, as codified by Tinctoris, is arguably among the great intellectual achievements of the late Middle Ages.[12] We might well be doing Busnoys's musicianship an injustice by setting it up in a perceived opposition with this.

Another juxtaposition might be the medieval one between *musicus* and *cantor*, crucially divided by the 'magna differentia' in literacy, learning, and thorough training in the liberal arts (*D* s.v. Cantor, Musicus). This, as we have seen, is the only internal division Tinctoris was prepared to acknowledge within the art of music. Since no one could be *musicus* without a degree in the liberal arts, there was (if nothing else) a social dimension to his refusal to dignify unlearned *cantores* with a world of their own. Their compositions might be widely distributed throughout the Christian world (more widely, in many cases, than his own), yet no amount of international success ought to validate errors committed demonstrably in ignorance. This was true of music no less than of, say, humanist Latin. Commenting on the widespread use of *prolatio maior* augmentation, Tinctoris hinted at this very parallel (*P* iii. 3. 7–8):

Indeed I am not surprised that Regis, Caron, Boubert, Faugues, Courbet, and many others have imitated Domarto in this error (as I have seen in their works), for I have been told that they are totally unlearned (*minime litterati*). And who can attain the truth not only of this but of any liberal science without learning?

Yet it is at precisely this point that the theorist acknowledged the common ground between himself and Busnoys, emphasizing the importance for men of their intellectual rank not to stoop to the level of the unlearned (9–10):

But that Ockeghem and Busnoys, men known to be sound Latinists, should stoop to their level in their masses *De plus en plus* and *L'homme armé* has aroused no small astonishment in our breast. What is more remarkable than that the sighted should enter upon the trackless (wastes) of blindness . . .

---

[10] e.g. *P* iii. 3. 10 and 5. 11–12.

[11] I have elaborated this point in two recent articles, and hope to expand it in others. See Rob C. Wegman, 'What is *Acceleratio mensurae?*', *ML* 73 (1992), 515–24, and 'Sense and Sensibility in Late-Medieval Music: Reflections on Aesthetics and Authenticity', *Early Music*, 23 (1995), 299–312.

[12] See also Rob C. Wegman, 'Petrus de Domarto's *Missa Spiritus almus* and the Early History of the Four-Voice Mass in the Fifteenth Century', *EMH* 10 (1990), 235–303 at 267–70.

Tinctoris judged Busnoys by a different standard, and this is a standard to which the composer himself aspired. By 1473 he had obtained the degree of master of arts (it is not known at which university),[13] and this means he had acquired all the knowledge and skills of disputation to answer Tinctoris's points, had he wanted to. And although he might not have relished public debate as much as his critic, there can be little doubt that matters of mensural theory did not leave him indifferent. Tinctoris may strike us occasionally as a cut-and-dried pedant, yet ironically, Busnoys was second only to him in ostentatiously foregrounding musical learning in his sacred works. And Tinctoris's style may overstate the intellectual dimension to the notational matters at issue, yet the composer applied the disputed practices self-consciously, in several cases uniquely, and seems to have persisted in them well after the dissemination of *Proportionale musices* (see below). If he was not making a theoretical point, what was he trying to communicate?

The Case Against Busnoys: Notational 'Errors'

If direct juxtapositions with Tinctoris yield no easy answers, examination of Busnoys's music and mensural profile only complicates the matter further. I shall focus in the first instance on notational details in his motets, as transmitted in the manuscript Brussels, Koninklijke Bibliotheek 5557. The reasons are twofold. First, the Brussels choirbook was copied and used at the Burgundian court throughout the period of Busnoys's employment,[14] and almost certainly contains direct transcripts from his autographs, if not copies in his own hand.[15] One of the Brussels scribes, as has often been pointed out, took an exclusive interest in copying Busnoys settings, did so with unusual care, and assumed the authority to make subsequent revisions or emendations in the music he had written down. Although one piece, the Magnificat, was not copied by him, it was he who supplied the attribution, and it must have been he, too, who emended a passage in the 'Deposuit potentes'. The scribes's notes look somewhat like stylized candle flames, with slightly curved top and bottom corners, and it is notes exactly like these that were

[13] Paula Higgins, '*In hydraulis* Revisited: New Light on the Career of Antoine Busnois', *JAMS* 39 (1986), 36–86 at 51 n. 67.

[14] Most of the Busnoys settings in this manuscript are found in the eighth gathering, whose paper dates 1476–80 (Rob C. Wegman, 'New Data Concerning the Origins and Chronology of Brussels, Koninklijke Bibliotheek, Manuscript 5557', *TVNM* 36 (1986), 5–25). Independent evidence that the choirbook was being used as late as 1479 is supplied by the French verse scribbled on the otherwise empty fo. 2ʳ (*Choirbook of the Burgundian Court Chapel: Brussels, Koninklijke Bibliotheek MS 5557*, with an introduction by Rob C. Wegman (Peer, 1989), 7 and fo. 2ʳ): 'Dis au Roy des Fauceurs qui n'use | Du treu d'un bonnier de Blangy | Il trouvera sans point de ruse | Quant la ses frans archiers perdy.' The 'Roy des Fauceurs' must be Louis XI, whose so-called 'faucheurs' pillaged the Hainaut countryside in 1477–8. The verse must have been written after the summer of 1479, since it refers to the battle of Blangy between Maximilian of Austria and Louis XI (7 Aug. 1479), which was lost by the latter's troops due to the lack of courage of his *francs archers* (M. Kervyn de Lettenhove, *Histoire de Flandre* (Bruges, 1874), iv. 172–5). Busnoys was in Maximilian's retinue at the time of the battle (Higgins, '*In hydraulis* Revisited', 64).

[15] Cf. Wolfgang Stephan, *Die burgundisch-niederländische Motette zur Zeit Ockeghems* (Heidelberger Studien zur Musikwissenschaft, 6; Kassel, 1937), 89, and Flynn Warmington's unpublished paper ' "A Very

written in the emendation, evidently over an erasure.[16] It would appear from this that the scribe's interest in works by Busnoys did not stop with his own copies: he intervened in another copy, attributing and possibly emending it. The second reason is that the Busnoys settings in Brussels are fully consistent notationally, even where they are in error, at least by Tinctoris's standards. This suggests a distinct mensural profile—which scribes elsewhere generally transmitted much less consistently, and sometimes even obliterated altogether (see below).

Ex. 8.1 gives a sample of usages that to my knowledge are unique to the sacred music of Busnoys. All these usages contradict not just the rules of mensural theory (particularly those of imperfection, coloration, and division) but, more seriously, the fundamental logic that holds the system together. The usages are identified by number, and would have been regarded as illogical for the following respective reasons:

1. The breve is to be counted with the preceding longa (imperfection *a parte post*), if only because it is followed by a group of notes that together make up a perfect longa. The dot of 'division' consequently separates what cannot be counted together in the first place. (For the principle that a dot of division can only separate what would otherwise be counted together, see *I* 3. 39 and *SPM* 2. 2.)

2. The coloured maxima is equivalent to two imperfect longas; the subsequent rest (or note) can only be counted together with the maxima, to form one ternary unit, and consequently the dot of 'division' cannot divide it from what follows.

3. The maxima in O2 is equivalent to two perfect longas. (This follows from the fact that coloured maximas elsewhere in this voice-part are equivalent to two imperfect longas; see above, under 2.) Since its value is binary, the maxima cannot be imperfected by a longa—even though both of its perfect longas can be imperfected by breves, of course. Hence the longa rest cannot imperfect it, even with the (redundant) dot of division. The intended rhythm should have been obtained by coloration.

4. Since imperfection *a parte post* takes precedence over imperfection *a parte ante*, the breve rest is to be counted together with the preceding maxima rather than the following longa, and consequently cannot be divided from the latter through the insertion of a dot.

5. The semibreve rest is followed by a ternary unit (three perfect breves), and consequently cannot be divided from that unit.

6. Dot of 'division' between notes that cannot be counted together in the first place.

7. Redundant coloration.

Fine Troup of Bastards"? Provenance, Date, and Busnois's Role in Brussels 5557', read at the national meeting of the American Musicological Society, Philadelphia, 1984.

[16] Brussels 5557, fo. 72r, about two-thirds into the second stave of the tenor. The emendation is clearly visible in the facsimile edition (*Choirbook of the Burgundian Court Chapel*).

Ex. 8.1. Mensural usages unique to Busnoys's Latin-texted music: (*a*) *Alleluia verbum caro factum est*; (*b*) *Regina caeli* I; (*c*) *Noel noel*; (*d*) *Victimae paschali laudes*

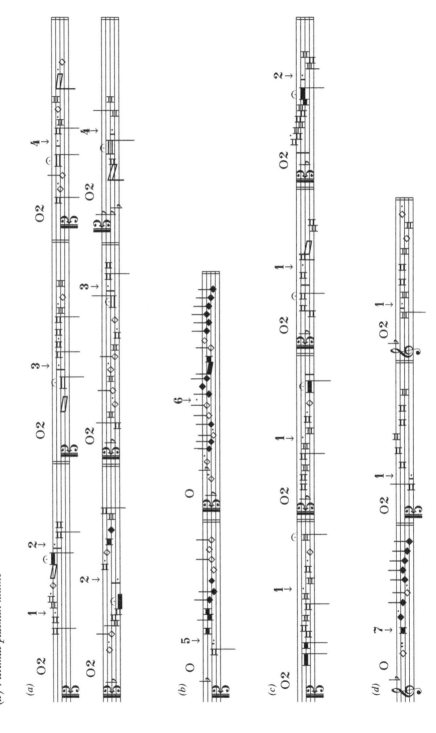

All these errors are quite basic: Busnoys demands imperfection of notes that cannot be imperfected, uses a dot of division in passages where there is nothing to divide, and uses coloration to effect a rhythm which is already there. In his defence one might perhaps suggest that he was conscious of potential misreadings on the part of his colleagues. Yet is seems improbable that the correct alternatives would have posed any problems that could not have been resolved at the first rehearsal. The Burgundian singers were thoroughly trained professionals, who were expected to cope with complex proportional signs such as Ɔ in *Anima mea* (fo. 83ᵛ) and 𝕯 in *Victimae paschali laudes* (fos. 85ᵛ–86ʳ). Nor is it likely that the over-notation might bespeak the involvement of inexperienced choirboys in an original performance context, prior to Busnoys's appointment at the Burgundian court (for instance, during this choirmastership at Poitiers, 1465–6), for the 'errors' are found in bass and tenor parts just as much as in the discantus.

Tinctoris did not censure Busnoys for these practices at the points where he might have done so (*SPM* 15. 2–3; *I* 2. 20). Yet he did criticize him in the *Proportionale musices* for a very similar type of over-notation: it is the redundant '3' under passages in *sesquialtera* coloration (*P* iii. 4. 11–12; my italics):[17]

Indeed, from all these three articles [concerning the indication of proportions], Busnoys *alone* dissents, for again and again he indicates his hemiolas, even though designated by the filling-in of notes, by placing underneath of the figure 3, as can be observed in this motet of his:

In this it is considered *by all* as superfluous, since the filling-in of notes suffices; inadequate, since even if it needed a sign in figures one figure would not be enough; and irregular, since what must be put at the beginning he puts underneath.

Emphasizing (twice) that the practice was unique to Busnoys, Tinctoris raised three objections: first, that coloration by itself already signifies 3/2 proportion, so that no figure is needed in addition ('superfluous'); second, that the proportional sign is incomplete, and should really consist of two figures ('inadequate'); and third, that the figure is placed *beneath* the passage rather than before it ('irregular'). From Tinctoris's point of view it is indeed difficult to see what alternative reading Busnoys was trying to prevent, for even without the '3' it is impossible to execute the coloured passage in any other way than he in fact spelt it out. *With* the '3', on the other hand, singers might well have been confused into thinking that *sesquialtera* should be applied twice over, leading to the cumulative propor-

---

[17] 'Ab his vero tribus pariter articulis Busnois unicus dissidet qui suas emyolias per impletionem notarum designatas suppositione istius cyphrae 3 iterum et iterum signat, ut patet in isto moteto suo animadvertere. [Example.] In quo superfluus, quia pro signo sufficit notarum impletio, diminutus, quia licet signo cyphrali indigeret unica cyphra non satisfaceret, et inordinatus, quia quod praeponendum est supponit, cunctis esse perhibetur.'

tion 9/4 (under which the passage would have taken up two-thirds of a perfect *tempus*, rather than a full *tempus*).

It may be this very possibility of confusion that motivated scribes elsewhere in Europe to omit the '3', or even renotate such passages altogether. Where we have more than one source for a sacred setting by Busnoys, the survival of a '3' in one manuscript almost invariably corresponds to omissions and renotations in its concordances.[18] This is true also of the unnamed motet from which Tinctoris cites his musical example. This work can be identified as the anonymous *Gaude caelestis Domina*, surviving uniquely in Cappella Sistina 15 (where it immediately follows Busnoys's securely attributed *Anima mea*).[19] Although the music for the contratenor and bass in bars 71–2 is clearly identical to that cited in the *Proportionale* (see the edition below, App.), neither of the figures '3' has been copied; moreover, the rhythm has been partly renotated.

The independent renotation of Busnoys's 'error' in different lines of transmission for several of his works places the Busnoys–Tinctoris issue in a different perspective. It is true that one might attribute the renotations to the influence of Tinctoris—or in his wake perhaps that of Gaffurius.[20] Yet this cannot explain why even the 'errors' listed in Ex. 8.1 (which Tinctoris had not criticized specifically in Busnoys) were renotated as well: in the only case where we have a concordance (Cappella Sistina 42, for *Regina caeli* I), the redundant dots of division turn out not to have been copied.[21] And so it would seem that Tinctoris, rather than being merely petty and fault-finding (and in an isolated position for these very reasons), voiced a more general sense of puzzlement at Busnoys's notational habits. 'Busnoys *alone* dissents . . . considered *by all* as superfluous': what could explain the composer's single-minded persistence in these and other confusing habits?

Historical Backgrounds

It is important to note that Busnoys's figures '3' always appear in passages where coloration is used in a very specific rhythmic pattern. Basically that pattern can be

---

[18] The Busnoys '3' is otherwise documented in *Victimae paschali laudes* (Brussels 5557, fo. 85ʳ⁻ᵛ), *Regina caeli* I (ibid., fo. 86ᵛ), *Magnificat octavi toni* ('Esurientes'), and *Missa L'homme armé* (Sanctus, bar 30 and Osanna, bar 27). Source variants exist for each of these passages except the one in *Victimae paschali laudes*, which is transmitted uniquely in Brussels 5557.

[19] Fos. 242ᵛ–245ʳ (edition below, App.). See Rob C. Wegman, Communication to the Editor, *ML* 71 (1990), 633–5 at 635. At the time I still assumed (on the basis of Albert Seay's edition of Tinctoris's theoretical works) that the motet cited in *P* was entitled *Animadvertere*. I am grateful to Leofranc Holford-Strevens for pointing out to me that the word 'animadvertere' was part of Tinctoris's Latin, and that he mentions no title at all. There is thus no longer any obstacle to accepting *Gaude caelestis Domina* as a work by Busnoys. For brief discussions of the motet, see Stephan, *Die burgundisch-niederländische Motette*, 18–20, and below.

[20] Franchinus Gaffurius, *Practica musicae*, trans. Clement A. Miller (MSD 20; American Institute of Musicology, 1968), 178.

[21] I am grateful to Bonnie Blackburn for verifying this for me in her microfilm of Cappella Sistina 42.

seen as a succession of two hemiolas on different levels, the first consisting of three against two semibreves, and the second of three against two minims.[22] One might assume that Busnoys, in using the figures '3', wished to clarify the distinction between these two levels. Yet it should once again be stressed that this clarification would not help the rhythmic interpretation in any way. Once one recognizes this highly distinctive pattern (it virtually leaps out from the surrounding white notation), it can be executed almost routinely, even at a first rehearsal. Rather than communicating the 'proper' reading, it seems, Busnoys must have felt that this was the right way to notate the pattern—the way, one is tempted to suggest, he had been brought up to do.

This brings us back to a possibility mentioned earlier: that of justification by precedent. In English music of the mid-fifteenth century we often find coloured rhythmic patterns of the very same type as described here, particularly in the cadential formula that has become known as the 'English Figure'.[23] Charles Hamm has documented the use of the redundant '3' in two English settings from the 1430s or 1440s, and, as it happens, in precisely this cadential formula.[24] Although the 'English Figure'—as the name suggests—is exceedingly rare in the Continental repertory, we do find it occasionally in Busnoys's music.[25]

Against this historical background we are forced to consider an entirely different possibility: that Busnoys was perhaps reared in an older mensural tradition to which he remained faithful, and which he was at pains to acknowledge, throughout his career. Perhaps we could compare this to the way Giovanni Spataro, to the end of his life, remained loyal to the somewhat eccentric precepts of his teacher Ramos de Pareja.[26] For Spataro this seems to have been a personal as much as a theoretical issue: when forced to defend 'mio preceptore', in 1529, he did not hesitate to call Tinctoris 'a fool [who] thought he knew a lot more than

[22] As illustrated in Rob C. Wegman, 'Another Mass by Busnoys?', *ML* 71 (1990), 1–19 at 4 n. 15.

[23] See Hamm, *A Chronology*, 52–4 and 92–4; Robert J. Snow, 'The Manuscript Strahov D. G. IV. 47' (Ph. D. diss., University of Illinois, Urbana, 1968), 92.

[24] *A Chronology*, 52–3. Hamm argues that neither the '3' nor the coloration is redundant: 'the former operates at the minim level, giving three minims in the time of two; the latter is semibreve coloration, putting three [semibreves] in place of two' (ibid. 52). This cannot be correct, however: the coloration fills one tempus in Φ, and should, if Hamm's interpretation were correct, contain four and a half semibreves in place of three, the proportion being 3 : 2. If the notated '3' represents an additional *sesquialtera* proportion on the minim level, as Hamm suggests, each of the four and a half semibreves should contain three minims, thus giving a total of thirteen and a half minims. However, in transcription it turns out that the intended number of minims was nine, and hence that *sesquialtera* was to be applied only once. The '3' is quite definitely redundant.

[25] For instance, in the *Missa L'homme armé*, Qui tollis, *tempora* 26–7, in the edition by Laurence Feininger (Monumenta Polyphoniae Liturgicae Sanctae Ecclesiae Romanae, I/i/2; Rome, 1948), where one can observe that the cadential formula was fully coloured in the English manner. This is the reading of Cappella Sistina 14 (partly renotated in its descendant, Cappella Sistina 63, but identical in Verona 759, which is extremely close to Cappella Sistina 14), and may well have been supplied originally with the figure '3' underneath. The formula has been fully renotated in Barcelona 454, and has been changed melodically, in different ways, in Chigi and SM 26—illustrating some of the vicissitudes that Busnoys's notational habits underwent in transmission.

[26] Blackburn, Lowinsky, and Miller (eds.), *A Correspondence of Renaissance Musicians*, 52–3, 55, and 1009–11.

he did'.[27] Yet even in the 1470s, as we have seen, there were singers who were prepared to make the theorist eat his words.

Busnoys's single-minded adherence to notational practices that were edited out of his music almost everywhere else, and were patently erroneous by the standards of Tinctoris, does seem to have such an element of loyalty to it.[28] Although I have not been able to discover precedents for the 'erroneous' practices listed in Ex. 8.1 (a more contemporary example will be discussed below), any composer of the previous generation who employed them consistently in exactly this way must have been close enough to Busnoys to have shaped his mensural outlook.

At the same time the hypothesis of a single formative influence, an influential teacher, does not satisfy. For Busnoys's mensural profile really is a complex of many diverse historical strands—one of which, as we have seen, can be traced back ultimately to English sacred music of the mid-fifteenth century. To unravel and trace back the other strands is a task that could not possibly be accomplished in a short contribution such as this. Even in the small *œuvre* that has survived we find a range of highly unusual mensuration signs, most of them 'erroneous', according to Tinctoris: Ɔ, Ɔ̸, ₵, C3, ₵3, Ɔ̸, O with perfect minor *modus*.[29] Several of these signs can be found in earlier repertory, and may go back to the years of Busnoys's training; others, however, could easily have been initiated by him.

One way forward might be to identify, however tentatively, different strata in the composer's mensural profile: primary and secondary. It is clear in several cases that Busnoys introduced mensural complexities almost for the occasion, creating intertextual meanings similar to those of canonic procedures and melodic quotations.[30] For instance, the sign C3 in the Tu solus of *Missa L'homme armé* is evidently an allusion to the pre-mass origins of the *L'homme armé* tune. Not only does the sign appear in the anonymous combinative song *Il sera pour vous/L'homme armé*, but it was in fact widely employed in other such songs in the 1440s and early 1450s, and the *L'homme armé* tune itself (notated in C3 in Naples VI E 40) is a typical *chanson rustique* of the 'chanson à refrain' form, such as found its way into numerous combinative songs.[31] Similarly, the curious juxtaposition

[27] Ibid. 406 and 411.

[28] I have made a similar assumption about Jacob Obrecht, who seems to have followed Busnoys in combining coloration with the figure '3' (*Born for the Muses*, 100 n. 13).

[29] See the survey in Wegman, 'Petrus de Domarto's *Missa Spiritus almus*, 263.

[30] On intertextuality in the music of Busnoys and his contemporaries see the seminal comments in Paula Marie Higgins, 'Antoine Busnois and Musical Culture in Late Fifteenth-Century France and Burgundy', (Ph.D. diss., Princeton University, 1987), 144–60.

[31] Maria Rika Maniates (ed.), *The Combinative Chanson: An Anthology* (Recent Researches in the Music of the Renaissance, 77; Madison, 1989); Rob C. Wegman, review of this edition, in *ML* 72 (1991), 510–13; Wegman, 'Petrus de Domarto's *Missa Spiritus almus*', 256 n. 45 and 258 n. 52. Further on the *chanson rustique* background of *L'homme armé*, see Reinhard Strohm, *The rise of European Music, 1380–1500* (Cambridge, 1993), 465–6; for another combinative song that quotes *L'homme armé*, see P iii. 4. 7. By all the criteria elaborated in my review of Maniates's edition, *Il sera pour vous/L'homme armé* is a typical combinative song of the 1440s or early 1450s (Group A). The original three-part version is anonymous; the later

of 𝄵 and 𝄴, in the Confiteor of the same mass, was surely inspired by the
'Genitum non factum' of Dufay's *Missa L'homme armé*, where the very same signatures appear in the very same relationship, albeit without strokes.[32] In the
L'homme armé mass, then, these mensural allusions seem to be part of a richer
intertextual tissue which also includes, for instance, an inversion canon in the bass
of the Agnus Dei—apparently a combined allusion to Dufay's retrograde canon
and Ockeghem's transposition to the bass in the respective Agnus Deis of their
settings.[33] Within Busnoys's total sacred *œuvre* all three signs, C3 (with perfect
prolation), 𝄵, and 𝄴, are unique to the *L'homme armé* mass, and although they
may be revealing of the composer's sense of tradition in the *L'homme armé* history, they are clearly secondary in terms of his mensural backgrounds.

Primary must be those mensural habits that are used consistently throughout
Busnoys's sacred *œuvre*. This includes the various practices listed in Ex. 8.1, the
redundant figure '3' (with its peculiar rhythmic pattern), but also, of course, the
signature O2.[34] Despite the criticisms of Tinctoris (*P* iii. 5. 8–10), Busnoys
employed this sign in a wide range of liturgical genres, involving nearly the whole
gamut of compositional styles and techniques: the two masses, a devotional tenor
motet (*Anthoni usque limina*), a sequence (*Victimae paschali laudes*), a Canticle
(Magnificat), and a short festive acclamation (*Noel noel*). An additional reason for
assuming that the composer's fondness for O2 may go back to the years of his training is that most of the 'errors' in Ex. 8.1 occur in this mensuration, and operate precisely on its distinguishing mensural level of perfect minor *modus*. O2 being
Busnoys's virtual trademark, it begins to seem increasingly doubtful that he would
have considered any of the practices listed in Ex. 8.1 as erroneous. For him they
must simply have represented the right way to do it (even if no one else did),
justified by a precedent somewhere in his past, which we have not as yet discovered.

---

four-part arrangement is attributed to 'Borton', who has been thought to be either Robert Morton or
Antoine Busnoys, and was recently identified tentatively with Pieter Bordon (Wegman, *Born for the Muses*,
71–2). For earlier discussions on the interpretation and significance of C3, see Richard Taruskin, 'Antoine
Busnoys and the *L'Homme armé* Tradition', 286–9, and Rob C. Wegman and Richard Taruskin,
Communications, *JAMS* 42 (1989), 437–43 and 443–52. The sign was condemned by Tinctoris in
Domarto (*P* iii. 5. 13–19; see also the discussion in Wegman, 'Petrus de Domarto's *Missa Spiritus almus*',
255–6).

[32] Wegman, Communication *JAMS* 42, 441–3. Richard Taruskin has argued that these two passages,
which involve two exceedingly rare signatures in identical superimpositions in two northern French
L'homme armé masses from the 1460s, were totally independently and differently conceived (ibid. 451–2).
Reversed signs of imperfect *tempus* (whether with major or minor prolation) were condemned by Tinctoris
as being 'so frivolous, so erroneous, and so far from all appearance of reason' that he chose not to dignify
them with musical examples from the works of 'those whom I fear to name [who] do not blush to use them'
(*P* iii. 2. 31–2). Busnoys was among these composers: see Wegman, 'Petrus de Domarto's *Missa Spiritus
almus*', 263, table 4, nos. 4, 17, and 18.

[33] Again the subject of considerable debate; see Taruskin, 'Antoine Busnoys and the *L'Homme armé*
Tradition', 263; David Fallows and Richard Taruskin, Communications, *JAMS* 40 (1987), 146–8 and
148–53 (at 152–3); D. Fallows, *Dufay* (rev. edn., London, 1987), 310–11.

[34] Taruskin first drew attention to Busnoys's special use of this sign; 'Antoine Busnoys and the *L'Homme
armé* Tradition', at 284–5.

One figure looms larger than any other composer in what we know of Busnoys's mensural and compositional backgrounds: Petrus de Domarto. Elsewhere I have drawn attention to a range of uniquely close parallels between the latter's famous *Missa Spiritus almus* and Busnoys's *Missa O crux lignum*. Yet I held back from speculating on possible personal encounters,[35] emphasizing instead the outlines of a more general picture: that of the fermenting musical climate in the Low Countries in the years around 1450.[36] However, my initial assumption, that Busnoys belatedly underwent the influence of that climate at some point after the mid-1460s, and became attracted to its distinguishing mensural and compositional practices mainly for their intrinsic interest,[37] now appears to me over-cautious. This is not just because of the apparent element of loyalty to which I referred above—although that element is placed in even sharper relief by the fact that Busnoys's mensural/compositional profile bears little trace of any influence on the part of Ockeghem (despite the five years he spent in the vicinity of that composer, at Tours in 1460–5), or indeed that of any other Northern musician active in the 1460s.[38] Crucial is also Paula Higgins's observation that Busnoys must have been an accomplished poet and composer by the mid-to-late 1450s, pushing back the years of his training to the early part of that decade at the latest.[39] Since all of Busnoys's prebends were situated in the south-western Low Countries, and his name moreover appears to be of Artois origin,[40] there is a strong circumstantial case for assuming that he originated from this area, and spent his formative years there.

The speculation that Busnoys might have been a pupil of Domarto in the early 1450s is exactly that: a speculation—albeit an attractive one. On musical grounds there is much to be said for it, yet in the absence of firm documentary evidence[41] we shall gain more from detailing the general musical picture of the southern Netherlands in the early 1450s, a picture in which both men can now be situated with some confidence. As for Petrus de Domarto, there is a highly suggestive piece

---

[35] 'Petrus de Domarto's *Missa Spiritus almus*', 262–72. [36] Ibid. 300–2.
[37] Ibid. 264–72. [38] Ibid. 264.

[39] See particularly Paula Higgins, 'Parisian Nobles, a Scottish Princess, and the Woman's Voice in Late Medieval Song', *EMH* 10 (1991), 145–200 at 188–90. The text of a rondeau 'Lequel vous plairoit mieulx trouver' is attributed to Busnoys in the mid-1450s poetry collection Paris 9223; see Higgins, 'Antoine Busnois and Musical Culture', 276–85. David Fallows, in his contribution elsewhere in this volume (above, pp. 26–30), suggests on the basis of this and other evidence pertaining to Paris 9223 that Busnoys might have been associated with the court of Brittany in the 1450s. In the light of comments made to me privately by Paula Higgins, I accept that Busnoys may have been much older than I previously thought (*Born for the Muses*, 64 n. 39, and 311). Pamela Starr suggests a birthdate between 1436 and 1439 ('Rome as the Centre of the Universe: Papal Grace and Musical Patronage', *EMH* 11 (1992), 223–62 at 251). It should be noted, however, that singers could be professionally active already in their late teenage years (as in the case of Pieter Bordon; see Wegman, *Born for the Muses*, 70–1), and that there is no problem in assuming exceptional precocity in Busnoys.

[40] Wegman, *Born for the Muses*, 65 n. 42; Higgins, '*In hydraulis* Revisited', 71 n. 109.

[41] The only written evidence that might suggest a teacher–pupil relationship is provided by Tinctoris: of the six passages in which he singles out Domarto for criticism, four mention Busnoys as well, either in one breath (*C* ii. 29. 3), or as having imitated or followed the older master (*I* 3. 56; *P* iii. 3. 7–9 and 5. 9).

to be added to the puzzle: Alejandro Planchart has recently discovered a new document mentioning this shadowy figure, and with characteristic generosity he has allowed me to publish it here. On 20 October 1451 the chapter of Cambrai Cathedral decided that their canon Guillaume Turpin should go to Tournai in connection with the vacancy of master of the choirboys. His specific task was to persuade a Paulus Iuvenis to accept the office, or alternatively to negotiate with Petrus de Domarto, 'who is also said to be a good musician':[42]

Vadat dominus Guillermus Turpin apud Tornacum . . . ad loquendum de uno magistro puerorum, et specialiter si possit faciat quod dominus Paulus Iuvenis acceptet officium, quia famatur bonus musicus et honestus, alioquin loquatur cum Petro de Domarto, qui etiam famatus est bonus musicus.

It emerges from this document that Domarto, two years after his brief employment at Antwerp,[43] was active in Tournai. He is mentioned neither as priest nor as master of arts (as was also the case at Antwerp), yet his reputation nevertheless made him a good second choice for a teaching post at a major musical establishment. What makes the document particularly interesting, of course, is the fact that Dufay was at this time a resident canon of Cambrai cathedral, and actively involved in the affairs of the chapter: surely the 'famatus est' must reflect his considered testimony.[44] Since the care and training of the Cambrai choirboys was at stake, Domarto could hardly have been considered for this responsible position unless he was a teacher of proven ability.[45] And as such we find him, then, in the very area where Busnoys's years of training may be plausibly located—the counties of Flanders, Artois, and Hainaut—in the very years during which his musicianship must have been formed.

It is also in this area, incidentally, that we begin to find a plausible historical background for the rhythmic pattern in which Busnoys combined coloration with '3' in the English manner. Scarcely 20 km. west of Tournai was Lille, at whose church of St Peter the master of the choirboys in 1450–1 and 1460–1 was a Simon de Vromont. Reinhard Strohm has persuasively identified this man with

[42] Cambrai, Bibliothèque municipale, MS 1059, fo. 1ᵛ. I am most grateful to Professor Planchart for sharing his discovery with me; he informs me that Iuvenis (probably De Jonghe or Le Jeune in the vernacular) was hired for the position five days later, on 25 Oct. 1452 (ibid., fo. 2ᵛ).

[43] Wegman, 'Petrus de Domarto's *Missa Spiritus almus*', 235–7.

[44] Craig Wright, 'Dufay at Cambrai: Discoveries and Revisions', *JAMS* 28 (1975), 175–229 at 188–9. Interestingly, Dufay and Domarto are the first known composers to have used the sign O2 for perfect minor *modus*, probably in the 1440s. See Wegman, 'Petrus de Domarto's *Missa Spiritus almus*', 258 n. 52, and Anna Maria Busse Berger, *Mensuration and Proportion Signs: Origins and Evolution* (Oxford, 1993), 22–3.

[45] The *Missa Spiritus almus* could well have existed by this time, adding to his reputation (Wegman, 'Petrus de Domarto's *Missa Spiritus almus*', 276–94). The duties of the master of the choirboys were defined in a chapter decision of 22 Sept. 1458, and included the teaching of liturgy, plainchant, proper behaviour, and Latin conversation, as well as supervision of the boys' playing, and responsibility for their sustenance and their language. See André Pirro, 'Obrecht à Cambrai', *TVNM* 12 (1927), 78–80 at 78–9, and also, more recently, Alejandro Enrique Planchart, 'The Early Career of Guillaume Du Fay', *JAMS* 46 (1993), 341–68 at 350–1.

the 'Simon of Lille' whose *Missa O admirabile commercium*, composed probably in the 1450s, survives in Trent 88.[46] Writing in a style that is clearly indebted to the anonymous English *Missa Caput*, Simon repeatedly uses the 'English Figure' in cadences, and the surviving notation is almost invariably in full coloration— albeit without figures '3'.[47]

This context is all the more plausible since freshly imported English music (particularly the anonymous *Missa Caput*) demonstrably had a major impact on composers working in the south-western Low Countries in the years around 1450. There is the famous case of Ockeghem's 'remake' of the *Caput* mass, for instance. His setting not only parallels Domarto's *Missa Spiritus almus* in style and compositional approach,[48] but it is among the exceedingly rare Continental works which (like Simon's *Missa O admirabile commercium*) employ the 'English Figure' in coloration.[49] More importantly—and this is where the web of musical interrelationships is pulled irresistibly tight—Ockeghem employs the almost exclusively English practice of telescoped text setting in the Credo.[50] This practice is exceptional for Continental mass music, but significantly, the only other known cycles to have telescoped Credo texts happen to be by composers who, like Ockeghem, were active at Antwerp in the 1440s: Petrus de Domarto in his three-part *Missa Quinti toni irregularis* (a cycle strikingly reminiscent of Leonel Power's mass settings),[51] and Jean Pulloys in his untitled three-part mass (a work so English in style and approach as to have had its ascription to Pulloys called into question).[52]

We should probably be careful not to overemphasize the Antwerp angle in the total picture,[53] if only because many musical centres in this region are still seriously understudied: Ghent, Courtrai, Thérouanne, Douai, Lille, Tournai, Arras, even Cambrai. What we can say, almost categorically, is that singers

[46] Fos. 304ᵛ–311ʳ; no published edition. See Wegman, 'Petrus de Domarto's *Missa Spiritus almus*', 301–2. Strohm made the suggestion in a paper read at the February meeting of the Royal Musical Association, London, 4 Feb. 1989.

[47] References are to *tempora*: Patrem, top voice, 35 and 79 (both in full coloration); Et incarnatus, 135–6 (partially renotated); Benedictus–Osanna, 88–9 and 107–8 (both in full coloration).

[48] Wegman, 'Petrus de Domarto's *Missa Spiritus almus*', 269–70 and 289–94.

[49] Credo, bar 34; see Johannes Ockeghem, *Collected Works*, ed. Dragan Plamenac (American Musicological Society, 1959–93), ii. 37–58. Other English-derived features which this mass shares with the settings by Domarto and Simon of Lille are simultaneous rests in duos (Gloria, bar 10, Credo, bar 11, Sanctus, bar 110; cf. Wegman, 'Petrus de Domarto's *Missa Spiritus almus*', 286–7, and *Missa O admirabile commercium*, Agnus Dei II, *tempus* 15), and extensive duos involving a scaffold tenor (Pleni and Agnus Dei II; cf. Wegman, ibid. 283, and *Missa O admirabile commercium*, Agnus Dei II).

[50] Credo, bars 144–208. The most extensive discussion of telescoping in English mass music is in Gareth R. K. Curtis, 'The English Masses of Brussels, Bibliothèque royale, MS. 5557' (Ph.D. diss., University of Manchester, 1979), i. 181–213. The single surviving copy for Simon's *Missa O admirabile commercium* supplies no text for the lower parts of the Credo beyond brief incipits, and consequently it cannot be ascertained whether the text in this movement might have been telescoped as well.

[51] Credo, bars 31–44; see David M. Kidger, 'The Music and Biography of Petrus de Domarto' (M.A. thesis, University of California at Santa Barbara, 1990), 197–8 and 349.

[52] Gareth R. K. Curtis, 'Jean Pullois and the Cyclic Mass—Or a Case of Mistaken Identity?', *ML* 62 (1981), 41–59 at 51–2.

[53] See also my cautionary remarks in 'Petrus de Domarto's *Missa Spiritus almus*', 293–4.

migrated freely within this area, and that their employment was rarely permanent enough for us to localize musical trends in the way that, for instance, art historians can postulate workshops and local 'schools'. If this was true of Domarto, as we have seen (Antwerp 1449, Tournai 1451), then clearly it would be pointless to speculate that Busnoys might have been trained by him directly for any length of time, in any particular place. Perhaps it is enough for us to be reasonably sure that he was trained somewhere in this region, as a young and impressionable aspiring musician, and that the sheer intensity of musical traffic made influence of some kind unavoidable. That in itself may be more than we could reasonably have hoped for: it means that Busnoys spent his formative years in one of the most exciting phases of fifteenth-century music history—singing, copying, and studying recent English music along with the latest Continental responses by Ockeghem, Domarto, Dufay, and Pulloys.

Tinctoris came from broadly this region as well, and he was of roughly the same age as Busnoys. Yet whatever musical influences he had undergone during his adolescence, in the end Tinctoris was to develop an adherence to the more narrowly scientific principles of 'reason' and 'truth', probably during his university years.[54] That makes him something of a special case (paralleled only, perhaps, by that of Dufay),[55] and we can now see that his first public attempts to reassert the traditions of Vitry and de Muris, in the early 1470s, came too late, and represented too 'learned' a voice, to make a significant impact on the ingrained habits of his contemporaries, even of the internationally famous Busnoys—himself by now a man of learning.

Yet in many ways Busnoys was a special case, too. As we have observed, there is something uniquely persistent and single-minded about the way he perpetuated mensural and compositional practices that many scribes elsewhere preferred to renotate, resolve, or remove. If his musicianship was formed in the years and the region that saw the creation of Domarto's *Missa Spiritus almus* and Ockeghem's *Missa Caput*, then this musical climate seems to have had a far more lasting impact on him than on anyone else—including Ockeghem, whose later masses and motets were to move in a different direction entirely. And even if we speculate that Busnoys, after returning to the North in late 1466, might have consciously reidentified with native traditions abandoned during his years with Ockeghem in France, that single-mindedness would only appear more striking, for it made him, in effect, the tradition's chief representative. In the end one is led

---

[54] In the years around 1460; see Ronald Woodley, 'Iohannes Tinctoris: A Review of the Documentary Biographical Evidence', *JAMS* 34 (1981), 217–48 at 226–9 and 242 (from which it appears that Tinctoris had obtained the degree of master of arts by 1462).

[55] I have emphasized in '*Miserere supplicanti Dufay*: The Creation and Transmission of Guillaume Dufay's *Missa Ave regina celorum*', *Journal of Musicology*, 13 (1995), 18–54 at 29 n. 22, that Dufay, in his later years, increasingly came to repent the mensural sins of his youth, aspiring to a notational 'correctness' that in many ways parallels the attitude of Tinctoris. It may be significant that Tinctoris came to work or study with Dufay for four months in 1460 (Planchart, 'The Early Career of Guillaume Du Fay', 367 n. 100).

to assume a profoundly formative, personal influence, well before his first documented appearance at Tours in 1460.

With that assumption we move beyond the question of justification by precedent, indeed beyond that of theoretical validation altogether. If we abandon the terms on which Tinctoris discussed musical theory, and return to the metaphor of mensural practice as language, we find that it is helpful in Busnoys's case for yet another reason: that it can do justice to the way notational devices acquired *meanings* in history: connotations, resonances, and overtones, to which no one was more sensitive, it seems, than Busnoys. Tinctoris's axiomatized musical system was closed, self-referential, and self-validating, but when we encounter signs like O2, C3 or ₵ (with implicit augmentation), or a practice like the redundant '3', we know—whether they are 'correct' or not—that each had a history of its own, that each can be associated with specific composers, works, and geographical areas, and that meaning and significance were read into them even then. In this sense one can read Busnoys's complex mensural profile almost as an autobiographical text, tracing back its various strands to a range of historical intertexts.

Excursus: *L'homme armé* Revisited

I have briefly illustrated such 'mensural intertextuality' in the case of the *Missa L'homme armé* (see above), but should now like to trace back its threads a little further, as a tentative essay in reading the 'text' of Busnoys's mensural profile. Busnoys's involvement in the *L'homme armé* history remains, like that history itself, a subject of some controversy. After the various recent debates I have become less and less persuaded, however, that there must be a single explanation to account for the genesis and development of the whole tradition, and that different hypotheses must therefore necessarily be incompatible. Perhaps the *L'homme armé* theme combined and attracted historical meanings in the same way as any other musical or literary text (or indeed notational device), and perhaps its polyphonic history eroded and engendered many such meanings—making the question of origins seem less relevant than that of enduring relevance in changing historical surroundings.

For instance, it is far from obvious that the *L'homme armé* tradition was consciously initiated as a tradition. After all, how could the composer of the first mass have suspected that others might follow his example, and have selected the *L'homme armé* tune in this awareness? There are many examples of mid-to-late fifteenth-century masses based on *chansons rustiques*, of which the anonymous *Missa Se tu te marie* in Trent 88 (composed probably in the 1450s) provides perhaps the most informative parallel.[56] The tenor melody of this cycle also appears in combinative chansons (like the *L'homme armé* tune), yet it is likely that both the mass and these chansons represent independent borrowings from the wide-spread tradition of the French monophonic song. *Se tu te marie*, like *L'homme armé* and many other popular melodies, must have been universally known in the cities of central and northern France. Against this background there is no objection to assuming that the first few *L'homme armé* masses might have been composed independently, having no closer historical connection to *Il sera pour vous/L'homme armé* than *Missa Se tu te marie* has to, say, *Robinet/Se tu te marie/Hélas, pourquoy*.[57] Indeed there are several such mass 'families' on common cantus firmi in the 1450s and 1460s (for instance, on *O rosa bella, Nos amis, Le serviteur*, and later *O Venus bant*), and as groups these show little more internal coherence than any randomly chosen group of masses from this period, never mind the strikingly dissimilar early *L'homme armé* masses by Ockeghem, Regis, and Caron. Nor do we necessarily need to read a deep intrinsic significance in the original choice of *L'homme armé* as a mass tenor. To extend the comparison: *Se tu te marie* might at most have been the somewhat inappropriate choice for an engagement or wedding mass ('If you get married, you'll regret it: And when? And when? Before the year is out!'),[58] but plainly there is little in its text and prior history to account for its elevation to a mass tenor.

The upshot of these considerations might be to remove the historical and explanatory weight from *Il sera pour vous/L'homme armé*, from the earliest *L'homme armé* masses, and perhaps even from the original meaning and context of the tune, and to locate the actual *creation* of the mass tradition at a later point.[59] Seen in this light, Busnoys's *L'homme armé* mass need not have been the first such cycle to have established the tradition. I have elsewhere expressed my agreement with Paula Higgins and Reinhard Strohm that the setting probably dates from the late 1460s,[60] yet see no necessary conflict with Taruskin's persuasive argument that its creation represents a decisive moment in the early *L'homme armé* history.[61] Perhaps one could view it as the point where a composer wrote so singular

---

[56] Fos. 77ᵛ–84ʳ, no published edition; cantus firmus identified by Reinhard Strohm, *Music in Late Medieval Bruges* (Oxford, 1985), 141. See Howard M. Brown, *Music in the French Secular Theater, 1400–1550* (Cambridge, Mass., 1963), nos. 154 and 273; further compositions listed in Maria Rika Maniates, 'Combinative Chansons in the Escorial Chansonnier', *Musica disciplina*, 29 (1975), 61–123 at 96–7.

[57] Edition in Maniates, *The Combinative Chanson*, 24–5.   [58] Ibid., p. xxvii.

[59] See also the pertinent comments by Richard Taruskin ('Antoine Busnoys and the *L'homme armé* Tradition', 288): 'The question of who wrote the first *Missa L'Homme armé* is distinguishable from the ultimately more interesting question of how the tradition got started. In the analogous and familiar case of the English *In nomine* fantasia, for example, the prototype, to be sure, was a Mass section by Taverner, but the origins of the tradition of emulation should probably be associated with the Elizabethan composer Christopher Tye, who wrote no fewer than twenty-one instrumental settings on its cantus firmus.'

[60] Paula Higgins, review of Strohm, *Music in Late Medieval Bruges*, in *JAMS* 42 (1989), 150–61 at 155 n. 15; Strohm, *The Rise of European Music*, 467–8; Wegman, *Born for the Muses*, 97 n. 10.

[61] 'Antoine Busnoys and the *L'Homme armé* tradition', 292–3; 'even if his *Missa L'Homme armé* should eventually turn out to be the second [or third, or fourth] to have been composed, Antoine Busnoys still stands as *fons et origo* of the great tradition'.

and significant a work that it invited imitation and playful allusion, thus trans-forming an ordinary mass family into a genuine tradition.

The meaning of the 'l'homme armé' theme itself need not have been singular and fixed, and it seems important to keep an open mind about the range of pos-sible meanings it could accumulate in history. It is entirely possible, as Richard Taruskin has suggested,[62] that Charles the Bold became identified with 'the armed man'—at least as soon as he could back up his political ambitions with mil-itary force, after 1465—yet in the crucial years around 1460 he was decidedly out of favour at the Burgundian court, and well removed from the corridors of polit-ical power.[63] The textual phrase 'l'homme armé' could become associated with many things: there was a 'maison l'homme armé' in de rue des Chanoines at Cambrai,[64] and a 'rue de l'homme armé' in Paris.[65] The song itself was to become associated with the Turkish threat, of course,[66] but one needs to read the texts of only a few *chansons rustiques* to realize that their concern with matters political, sexual, and religious is decidedly tongue-in-cheek, if not downright coarse.[67] Just as in the case of *Se tu te marie*, it must seem open to question whether the song's text and prior history must necessarily account for its elevation to a mass tenor in the 1450s, or indeed that we could conclude anything about its original meaning and significance on the basis of its subsequent polyphonic history.

On the other hand, it only illustrates the strength of 'mensural intertextuality' that a major obstacle to this interpretation should be Busnoys's employment of the sign C3 in the *L'homme armé* mass. As a conscious allusion to the pre-mass origins of the *L'homme armé* tune (see above), it seems to contradict my sugges-tion that the mass tradition might have transcended its monophonic background altogether. There is an additional reason why this seems significant. During his years in the Loire Valley (1460–5) Busnoys became actively involved in writing combinative songs, incorporating numerous *chansons rustiques* in 'chanson à refrain' form, just like *L'homme armé*. Yet none of his settings from these years looks remotely like *Il sera pour vous/L'homme armé*. Under his hands, and those of Ockeghem, the combinative chanson developed into a narrow formal type, char-acterized by the mensuration ₵ (rather than C, O, or C3), scoring in four parts

---

[62] 'Antoine Busnoys and the *L'Homme armé* Tradition', 273–83.

[63] Richard Vaughan, *Philip the Good: The Apogee of Burgundy* (London, 1970), 338–46. One should take this circumstance into account when considering Taruskin's speculation that Charles the Bold might have commissioned the first *L'homme armé* mass on behalf of the Order of the Golden Fleece, in 1461 (Communication *JAMS* 1987, 149).

[64] Wright, 'Dufay at Cambrai', 211.

[65] Isabelle Cazeaux, *French Music in the Fifteenth and Sixteenth Centuries* (New York, 1975), 147: 'One of the oldest streets of Paris, which was demolished about 1880 and whose original houses were said to date from the reign of Louis VII in the twelfth century, was the *rue de l'Homme armé* . . . Historians have specu-lated that the *rue de l'Homme armé* may have derived its name from the sign of an inn with the image of a man in armor—which is said to have existed as early as 1432.'

[66] See the text of *Il sera pour vous/L'homme armé*, as edited and translated in *The Mellon Chansonnier*, ed. Leeman L. Perkins and Howard Garey (New Haven, 1979), i. 330–5.

[67] Cf. the editions and lively translations in Maniates, *The Combinative Chanson*, pp. xviii–lvi.

with low contratenor (rather than three), and systematic use of canon and imitation.[68] Quick triple metres, if used at all, were now invariably notated in ₵3 with
perfect *tempus*, rather than in C3 with major prolation. Busnoys's awareness
(expressed in his Tu solus) that the *L'homme armé* melody would once have been
notated in C3 seems like an allusion to an earlier practice, a practice which both
he and Ockeghem had superseded in the years around 1460. C3 was a sign that
the tune could not cast off, it seems, at least not in 'ut iacet' notation, even though
it did in the settings of nearly all his contemporaries.[69] Yet by the late 1460s it
was an exceedingly rare and (according to Tinctoris) erroneous sign. We cannot
attribute Busnoys's use of it to a belated interest in historical backgrounds alone:
somehow the composer must have been personally acquainted with those backgrounds, possibly before his years in Tours.

Of course this is implicitly to open the door for Richard Taruskin's speculation
that Busnoys composed *Il sera pour vous/L'homme armé*,[70] perhaps now as early as
the late 1440s or 1450s. But that is only one of many possibilities. For the
moment it will be safer to note that the chanson evidently originated as an occasional piece. It is full of insider jokes, alludes to circumstances taken as understood (involving the Burgundian singer Symon le Breton), and borrows a
popular tune that should have been familiar enough for the quotation to be perceived as genuinely witty. A one-off piece of this kind could not plausibly bear the
explanatory weight even for the first few *L'homme armé* masses, let alone the subsequent tradition. A widely known popular tune, on the other hand, could easily
account for an early mass family as well as any number of combinative chansons—as the case of *Se tu te marie* illustrates. Busnoys may or may not have
known the setting during the years of his early training, but more significant, it
seems, is his acquaintance with the kinds of contexts in which such pieces originated. This would be the simpler explanation for his later use of C3, involving
fewer auxiliary hypotheses on the historical importance of *Il sera pour
vous/L'homme armé*.

What we know about these contexts musically is that they involved numerous
melodies in quick triple metre that were memorable enough not to require written transmission, yet were interpreted in C3 (with major prolation) as soon as
they were committed to paper. What we know about them historically is a great

---

[68] Wegman, review of Maniates, *The Combinative Chanson*, 512–13. I am somewhat hesitant to conclude
with David Fallows that the use of imitation in *Il sera pour vous/L'homme armé* parallels the much more systematic and extensive application of this device in combinative songs of the 1460s and 1470s—if only
because several phrases of the *L'homme armé* melody would have invited imitation in any context (as is true
also of *O rosa bella* and *Se la face ay pale*). See David Fallows, 'Robert Morton's Songs: A Study of Styles in
the Mid-Fifteenth Century' (Ph.D. diss., University of California at Berkeley, 1978), 214.

[69] A notable (and perhaps significant) exception can be found in the third of the six *L'homme armé* masses
in Naples VI E 40 (cf. Taruskin, 'Antoine Busnoys and the *L'Homme armé* Tradition', 287–9). Although I
would give my eye-teeth for six new masses by Busnoys, I remain highly sceptical that the Naples set is by
him.

[70] 'Antoine Busnoys and the *L'Homme armé* Tradition', 289–92.

deal less specific: most writers have agreed on a bourgeois social milieu, and a civic context involving theatrical performances and communal festivities of various kinds.[71] By some coincidence, it is in a context of exactly this kind that the phrase 'l'homme armé' happens to make yet another appearance—and, intriguingly, in direct association with the Turkish threat. Several years ago I came across a tantalizing (though sadly undocumented) reference to a 'jeu de l'homme armé', in a nineteenth-century study of street life in medieval Paris:[72]

> Le jeu de la quintaine ou *de l'homme armé*, dans lequel on combattait un mannequin habillé *en More* et placé sur un pivot, de telle sorte que les coups portés ailleurs que dans le tronc ou dans le visage faisaient tourner la machine, qui sanglait un rude coup d'estramaçon au maladroit . . . (my italics)

Attempts to follow up this promising lead in the extensive literature on the quintain have been disappointing. The practice of fighting Turk's heads (or manikins dressed as Turks) in civic games and jousts seems to have been universal in the cities of fifteenth- and sixteenth-century Europe,[73] but according to seventeenth-century tradition, at least, the custom of calling this *la course à l'homme armé* seems to have been specifically Italian.[74] What appears from the few leads we have, however, is that whenever or wherever the phrase 'l'homme armé' was associated with the quintain (a game which normally required no more than a barrel or a shield), it referred specifically to a Turk.

We are relatively well informed about chivalric (and mock-chivalric) games and jousts in the cities of northern France and the Low Countries: these were municipal activities, organized and financed along lines similar to mystery plays, involving public ceremonies of various kinds, the participation of trumpeters, minstrels, and heralds, and leaving no small impact on the population at large.[75] This is the kind of civic context in which *chansons rustiques*, and the *L'homme armé* melody in particular, must have thrived. Civic jousting festivities did not exclude

---

[71] Cf. Howard M. Brown, 'The *Chanson rustique*: Popular Elements in the 15th- and 16th-Century Chanson', *JAMS* 12 (1959), 16–26 at 18; *Music in the French Secular Theater, passim*.

[72] V. Fournel, *Les Rues du vieux Paris: Gallerie populaire et pittoresque* (Paris, 1897), 190.

[73] Certainly in France, Germany, and Italy, but also, for instance, in England; see J. R. V. Barker, *The Tournament in England, 1100–1400* (Suffolk, 1986), 150: 'The fifteenth century treatise, *Knyghthode and Bataile*, which is a verse paraphrase of the classical *De Re Militari* by Vegetius, says that young men should first be taught to fight by means of the quintain which the versifier urged him to imagine to be a Turk for "though he be slayn, noon harm is".'

[74] L. Clare, *La Quintaine, la course de bague et le jeu des têtes: Étude historique et ethno-linguistique d'une famille de jeux équestres* (Paris, 1983), 174 and 243, citing a French jousting treatise from 1669: 'Les italiens la nomment [i.e. the quintain] la Course à l'Homme Armé & le Sarrasin, parce qu'ils transfigurent ce Faquin en Turc, en More, ou en Sarrasin pour rendre ces Courses plus mysterieuses.'

[75] See particularly J. Vale, *Edward III and Chivalry* (Suffolk, 1982), ch. 2 ('Civic *festes* and Society in the Low Countries and Northern France'), 25–41, especially 28: 'Evidently the whole town [Lille] enthusiastically emulated the jousters on whatever came to hand, for besides barrels, small trucks or barrows . . . and even tables are mentioned. The re-enactment of these [14th-c.] bans, suggesting that the jousting "craze" was an inevitable annual phenomenon . . . are indications of the way in which the youthful population continued the activities of the *feste* in the Lille streets.'

the participation of the higher nobility: Charles the Bold, for instance, attended the jousts at Bruges in 1457, and his court accounts mention payments on this occasion to Ghent trumpeters and a Tournai singer.[76] Yet, returning to the young Busnoys, in whichever south Netherlands town he spent the years of his musical training, he could not possibly have escaped its annual jousting *festes*, nor perhaps active involvement as a musician.[77]

One might perhaps view quintains with Turkish manikins in psychoanalytic terms, as games meant to master collective anxiety and guilt—in this case over the Turkish victories in the East, and their occupation of the Holy Land. This could explain why the *L'homme armé* song—unusually for *chansons rustiques*—strikes a note of *fear*, and calls for collective armament: everybody would have known that 'the armed man' was in reality a mere puppet in the market square, dangerous only to the extent that it could revolve if mis-hit, and strike back at its attacker. The sense of fear could be comically exaggerated, in other words, precisely because there was a controlled outlet in the game itself, channelling public emotion in expressions of aggression, vindication, and laughter:[78]

The man, the man, the armed man is to be feared. All around it has been cried that everyone must arm himself, with an iron hauberk. The man, the man, the armed man is to be feared.

This interpretation may not exhaust all the contemporary meanings of the phrase 'l'homme armé',[79] yet it does pull together all the main threads pursued so far: the *L'homme armé* melody, the sign C3, the *chanson rustique* and its civic contexts, the quintain, the Turk, the sense of humour, and Busnoys's early years in the southern Low Countries. It might even yield a plausible face-value reading of *Il sera pour vous/L'homme armé*, if one accepts that this piece might have been written for a festive civic tournament in which Symon le Breton was somehow prominently involved:[80]

He will be fought for you, the dreaded Turk, Master Symon—there's no doubt about it—and struck down with an axe-spur. We hold his pride to have been beaten. If he falls into your hands, the felon, he will be fought for you, the redoubted Turk, Master Symon. In a

[76] Wegman, *Born for the Muses*, 35; Vale makes a similar point about Philip the Good (Valenciennes 1435, and Lille 1463 and 1464): *Edward III and Chivalry*, 30 and 115 n. 66.

[77] Among the towns which had prominent jousting *festes* were: Ghent, Bruges, Douai, Lille, Tournai, Valenciennes, Saint-Quentin, Saint-Omer, Arras, Ypres, Doullens, Sluis, Aardenburg, as well as many cities further south, in France (Vale, *Edward III and Chivalry*, 26).

[78] Trans. after Perkins and Garey, *The Mellon Chansonnier*, i. 334.

[79] In particular, no contradiction is implied with Flynn Warmington's important findings on ceremonies of 'the armed man' (above, Ch. 5): it would only be a tribute to medieval creativity and ingenuity if the *L'homme armé* tradition linked together a range of themes originating in different historical contexts—none of which should necessarily have been decisive on its own.

[80] Trans. Perkins and Garey, *The Mellon Chansonnier*, 332. The tenor and contratenor of the song repeatedly cry 'à l'assault! à l'assault!' For a different interpretation of this notoriously elusive text, see Fallows, 'Robert Morton's Songs', 210–13.

short time you will have beaten him, to God's pleasure. Then they will say 'Long live ol' Symon the Breton, because he has fallen on the Turk!' . . .

Whatever the strengths or weaknesses of this interpretation, it needs to be stressed that the mass tradition was to carry the *L'homme armé* theme to an entirely different intellectual and musical plane. The enduring relevance of the theme must have depended crucially on the typical medieval ability to transform even the slightest textual material by elaborating its verbal, musical, religious, and political resonances in totally unexpected directions.[81] One could think of no better parallel than the image of the Golden Fleece which, although of Greek mythological origin, became incorporated into ever more densely woven complexes of biblical imagery, in conscious literary and propagandistic efforts.[82] As with all traditions, we should probably expect less explanatory force from the unpromising origins of the *L'homme armé* history, and more from the astonishing flexibility and fertility with which composers transcended these in musical contexts resonant with new significance. In Busnoys's *L'homme armé* mass those origins still left a residue of meaning in the sign C3, suggesting the composer's personal acquaintance with an earlier history. Yet the very quality and complexity of his work only serve to highlight the comparative triviality of those origins, and remain, in the end, a tribute to his own extraordinary musical achievement.

Consequences for Attributive Research

Busnoys's use of the figure '3' has indirectly enabled us to identify the anonymous motet *Gaude caelestis Domina* as a work by him. This illustrates yet another aspect of the image of mensural practice as language: if the peculiar mensural 'language' of a composer is sufficiently idiomatic, we should be able to recognize it easily in works transmitted anonymously.

In some cases the suspicion that we may be dealing with a work by Busnoys in a reasonably authentic reading can be all but irresistible. A good example is the motet *Incomprehensibilia firme/Praeter rerum ordinem*, which survives anonymously in Verona 755.[83] The three sections of this piece have the successive mensurations of O, O2, and O3 (all in perfect minor *modus*), a layout identical to that of the Gloria of Busnoys's *Missa O crux lignum triumphale*. Yet it is in the small notational detail that one really feels on familiar territory. For instance, in the third section there are four occurrences of the English coloured pattern with

---

[81] For a particularly impressive example, see the verbal canons and tropes in the anonymous set of six *L'homme armé* masses in Naples VI E 40, as edited and translated by Barbara Haggh and Steven Moore Whiting (Haggh, Communication, *JAMS* 40 (1987), 139–43).

[82] Johan Huizinga, *The Waning of the Middle Ages* (London, 1955), 84–6.

[83] Fos. 101ᵛ–104ʳ; no published edition. I have speculated on the possibility of Busnoys's authorship in 'Another Mass by Busnoys?', 4 n. 15.

figures '3' written underneath.[84] Moreover, of the notational practices listed in
Ex. 8.1 above, the one itemized as (1) makes a frequent occurrence, and (2) also
appears once (see Ex. 8.2). This makes *Incomprehensibilia* the only known work
not attributed to Busnoys in which these curious practices are applied. The notation, in short, looks exactly as one would have expected in a 'lost' Busnoys motet.

Musically, too, there are close parallels with the motets of Busnoys. Each of the
three parts opens with a tenorless section in which one voice states the cantus
firmus in long note-values, before it is repeated in the 'proper' tenor statement in
the next section.[85] As a structural device this recalls *Victimae paschali laudes* (both
of whose parts open with literal pre-emptive statements of cantus firmus), and
also *Anima mea/Stirps Jesse* (whose two 'sections' similarly open with pre-emptive

Ex. 8.2. Mensural usages in Anon., *Incomprehensibilia/Praeter rerum ordinem* (Verona
755, fos. 101ᵛ–104ʳ)

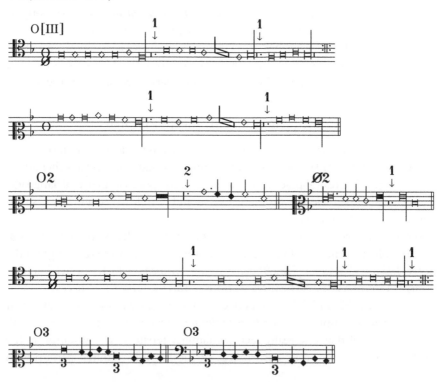

---

[84] In the section starting 'Impetra quod eius pater', top voice and bass, *tempora* 16–17 (stated twice in
succession, the two parts moving in parallel tenths, and the second '3' being omitted in all four patterns).
The coloured rhythmic pattern is also found in the second part (in the section starting 'In virgine mater', top
voice, *modi* 14–15 = *tempora* 41–2 and 44–5), but not with the figure '3'.
[85] Contratenor in the first part, top voice in the second, and bass in the third.

statements, albeit in different rhythmic elaborations).[86] What the pre-imitations in *Incomprehensibilia* share with those in the latter motet is that the text of the cantus firmus is written in the stave as an alternative to the motet text.[87] These are extremely rare (and at the very least Netherlandish) practices: they were to be applied extensively in the later masses and motets by Jacob Obrecht.[88]

Yet however irresistible Busnoys's authorship may seem, I am no longer persuaded of the benefits of attempting to drive it home. Here another case needs to be mentioned, that of the anonymous *Missa L'ardant desir*. When I first transcribed this remarkable work, in 1987, almost every feature seemed to suggest Busnoys's authorship: extensive use of O2, the absence of a tempo shift in this mensuration, mensural transformation, a range of other schematic manipulation procedures (including two which directly paralleled Busnoys's *Missa L'homme armé*), Greek-flavoured verbal canons, contrived Latin-Greek voice-names, motivic devices known to be typical of Busnoys, and transmission next to a mass securely ascribed to Busnoys. In my article 'Another Mass by Busnoys?' I tried to make the case, yet in hindsight, and particularly after two published exchanges with Richard Taruskin,[89] I feel that in staking everything on the problem of authorship, my approach ultimately became historically reductive. The *Missa L'ardant desir* is an extremely significant work, and vital to our understanding of Busnoys, and at the end of the day it deserves more sensitive historical treatment than one in terms of authorship alone.[90] The latter issue is not only fundamentally undecidable, but any extended discussion of it will implicitly affirm the questionable values underlying modern notions of canon and authorship, and in effect legitimate the historical distortion caused by those notions—in collected editions, encyclopaedias, recordings, and music histories.

Moving away from the issue of authorship, the question of historical significance proves to be refreshingly uncontroversial. For we can state without exaggeration that both *Incomprehensibilia* and *Missa L'ardant desir* belong firmly to the world of Busnoys's sacred music, and add significantly to its rich tissue of historical meanings and resonances. They do so in different ways, however. While *Incomprehensibilia* is clearly an intimate cognate of the Brussels 5557 motets, and crucial to our understanding of them, I am now inclined to suggest a much earlier dating for *Missa L'ardant desir*, possibly even in the years around

---

[86] See Stephan, *Die burgundisch-niederländische Motette*, 78–80; Edgar H. Sparks, *Cantus Firmus in Mass and Motet, 1420–1520* (Berkeley and Los Angeles, 1963), 212–15; Wegman, 'Petrus de Domarto's *Missa Spiritus almus*', 241–4.

[87] Verona 755, fos. 102ʳ, 102ᵛ, and 104ʳ; cf. Brussels 5557, fo. 83ᵛ.

[88] Wegman, *Born for the Muses*, 22, 88, 95, 101, 110–12, 116, 119–24, 126–7, 166–7, 175–8, 184–7, 202, 205, 208–11, 259, 288.

[89] Correspondence, *ML* 71 (1990), 631–5, and 72 (1991), 347–50.

[90] I have subsequently attempted to give it such treatment, in 'Petrus de Domarto's *Missa Spiritus almus*', 266–71.

1460.[91] Its style remains something of a mystery, totally unlike the two securely ascribed Busnoys masses, as Richard Taruskin has observed, and in some ways faintly reminiscent of Domarto's *Missa Spiritus almus* (with which it shares the D Dorian mode). Yet whereas the latter cycle is an exceedingly powerful work, and totally deserving of its remarkably successful career, it is difficult to find anything in *Missa L'ardant desir* to become genuinely excited about, either in its general stylistic profile or in any particular passage. Might we suspect in this mass the work of Busnoys's teacher, and a key, perhaps, to his later sense of loyalty—even if he never took his canonic complexities quite as far as did the *L'ardant desir* Master? If so, it may only strengthen the picture if I note the presence of no fewer than five cadential 'English Figures' in this work.[92] None of these is in coloration (let alone with the figure '3' underneath), yet I have demonstrated elsewhere that the tenors in the unique source of this mass are highly corrupt versions of canon resolutions, a circumstance which rules out proximity to the autograph in any case.[93]

It might seem, by now, as if the 'English Figure' was far more widespread in Continental music than the name suggests. Yet its frequency there is indeed significantly lower than in English music, and becomes all but negligible after the 1450s. It is precisely because my focus here is on the historical backgrounds of Busnoys's English-inspired habit that I have drawn attention to the exceptions that prove the rule—all of which must originate from the southern Netherlands, and find a context here (at least in the years around 1450) in other adoptions of English devices.

Moving still within the narrow circle of Busnoys's backgrounds, then, it reinforces rather than dilutes the picture if we note that the 'English Figure' (in coloration, this time) appears twice in the anonymous *Missa Quant ce viendra*, copied in Trent 89 in the mid to late 1460s.[94] Richard Taruskin has persuasively argued that this is a work by Busnoys, noting, amongst other things, that it is the earliest known cycle based on a chanson by him, and that the entire song is in fact incorporated as a contrafactum in the Et in Spiritum.[95] The notational picture is

---

[91] My previous dating, in the early 1470s, was based mainly on the prominent use of certain motivic devices ('Another Mass by Busnoys?', 12–18), yet is obviously weakened by the circumstance that very similar devices can be found in Dufay's *Missa Ecce ancilla Domini*, which must predate 1463 (see Sparks, *Cantus Firmus*, 230–1).

[92] Domine Deus, contratenor, *modus* 30 = *tempora* 89–90; Et incarnatus, top voice, *tempora* 59–60 (see 'Another Mass by Busnoys?', 14, Ex. 3, bar 20); Et resurrexit, top voice, *modus* 4 = *tempora* 11–12; Confiteor, top voice, *tempus* 48; Agnus Dei I, top voice, *tempus* 37.

[93] See 'Another Mass by Busnoys?', 7–12, and Correspondence (*ML* 1990), 635 n. For this reason, I am inclined not to read too much significance into the presence of a redundant dot of 'division' (identical to that itemized as (6) in Ex. 8.1) in the Sanctus, top voice, between *tempora* 33 and 34.

[94] Edited and tentatively attributed to Busnoys in *Busnoys LTW*, Music, 208–58 and Commentary, 94–100. The English Figures are in the Crucifixus, bars 18–19, and Et resurrexit, bar 9.

[95] A specifically Flemish context for this rare procedure can be found in the anonymous *Missa Nos amis* in Lucca 238, possibly a work by the Bruges composer Adrien Basin, who wrote the model. See Strohm, *Music in Late Medieval Bruges*, 128 and 238–49.

not otherwise suggestive of Busnoys, and the style is quite unlike that of *Missa L'ardant desir* as well as that of the two securely ascribed masses.[96]

Yet there is much to suggest that this is a very early mass, possibly even from the 1450s. Apart from the English cadential formula we find several simultaneous rests in duos—an English-inspired feature to which I have drawn attention also in Ockeghem's *Missa Caput*, Domarto's *Missa Spiritus almus*, and Simon's *Missa O admirabile commercium*,[97] but which is exceedingly rare in any Continental mass from the 1460s or after. In the long stretches of four-part writing, the bass tends to follow the rhythmic movement of the tenor, enhancing the sonorous relief to the more active top voices whenever the cantus firmus is augmented, and causing, in effect, a textural 'layering' that was quite common in the 1450s.[98] Imitation, even of the most incidental kind, is rigorously avoided in these stretches (the only exception being the contrafactum), but crops up as soon as the texture is reduced to two parts. The general sense is that of a relatively undifferentiated stream of four-part counterpoint, moving in distinct stretches sharply demarcated from the connecting duos. There is little or nothing to suggest awareness of the new stylistic trends of the 1460s:[99] *Missa Quant ce viendra* could easily be the first competent mass setting by Busnoys, recognizably 'personal' only in its choice of model, a chanson handled much more independently and confidently than the mass.[100]

Returning finally to *Gaude caelestis Domina*, this is, if anything, a worthy addition to the Busnoys canon: clean-textured, sonorous, and written with a superbly controlled sense of drive (see below, App.). These qualities are not accidental: just as in Busnoys's two masses, the tenor moves in long note-values (though it is not handled schematically), around which the other voices keep regrouping, almost imperceptibly, in parallel third and tenth relationships. The latter way of writing could be exaggerated to tedious extremes, of course: it was to become notorious particularly in the compositions of Gaffurius. Yet Busnoys continuously shifts the parallel relationships, and not infrequently disguises them by subtly differentiating the parts rhythmically, thus creating a sense of linearity that seems unaccountably euphonious. Meanwhile, in the midst of all this activity, the tenor moves imperturbably in its own time, organizing the shifting sonorities around its long-held notes, and firmly maintaining the general sense of long-term continuity. It is the tenor's contribution—transparently audible at all times—that accounts for the seemingly effortless sense of drive in this motet. This is a key feature of Busnoys's sacred musical style: rather than demanding the continuous investment of each singer's energy (as often seems the case in Ockeghem's more

[96] See my comments on the style of *Missa L'homme armé* and related works by Busnoys, as well as Obrecht's emulation in *Missa Petrus apostolus*; *Born for the Muses*, 88–97.
[97] See above, n. 49.   [98] See Wegman, 'Petrus de Domarto's *Missa Spiritus almus*', 282–8.
[99] Ibid. 277–82, and Sparks, *Cantus Firmus*, 219–41.
[100] Strohm, *The Rise of European Music*, 457–9.

densely written works), he creates and *ensemble* in which the voice-parts are constantly helped along by each other, and by the tenor more than most. But for the tenor, however (a genuine *fundamentum relationis* in Tinctoris's sense; *D* s.v. Tenor), each part is given enough melodic and rhythmic detail to relish individually. This is singer's music, if nothing else, seemingly as easy to write as it is to listen to. Yet nothing would require more hard work than to strike Busnoys's balance of sonority, linearity, rhythmic differentiation, drive, and long-term control: there can be no pastiche of vintage Busnoys.

Against the sheer luxuriance of Busnoys's part-writing, Tinctoris's objection to the notation of bars 71–2 (grateful though we must be to him for 'rescuing' *Gaude caelestis Domina*), seems to confirm all the stereotypes of the hair-splitting pedant. In the face of such artistic accomplishment, did the theorist really have nothing better to do than complain about the figures '3'—which he could easily have erased from his copy if they so annoyed him? Yet the truth, as I have attempted to show in this contribution, is that if we stereotype either Tinctoris or Busnoys, it is we who will be the poorer for it. As major fifteenth-century minds they should both be dear to us, and they deserve to have the common ground between them acknowledged. And thus it is only fair that I should end this essay with the observation that their common ground encompassed much more than mensural learning alone. For it is Tinctoris who, without any hint of envy, ranked his compeer Busnoys among the leaders of those whose works 'are so perfumed with sweetness that in my opinion, at least, they are to be considered most worthy not only for men and demigods, but even for the immortal gods themselves.'[101]

---

[101] *C* Prologus 17–18; see also Wegman, 'Sense and Sensibility in Late-Medieval Music'.

Appendix
Antoine Busnoys, *Gaude caelestis Domina*
(Cappella Sistina 15, fos. 242ᵛ–245ʳ)

an-ge - li ob-se - qui - o   Gau - de quod tu -
an-ge - li ob-se - qui - o   Gau - de quod
                                 Gau - de
                                 Gau - de   quod   tu -

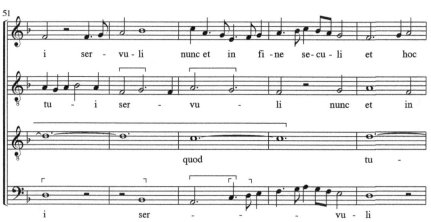

i   ser - vu - li   nunc et in fi - ne se-cu - li et hoc
tu - i   ser - vu - li   nunc et in
         quod   tu -
i   ser -   -   -   vu - li

in   i - ctu o - cu-li   ut fru - un -   tur
fi - ne   se -   cu - li
    - i   fru -
se -   cu - li et hoc in   i - ctu   o - cu - li

210

Rob C. Wegman

9

Text, Tone, and Symbol:
Regarding Busnoys's Conception of
In hydraulis and its Presumed Relationship to
Ockeghem's *Ut heremita solus*

❦❧

JAAP VAN BENTHEM

IN the early eighteenth century, Rembrandt's most famous painting, *De Nachtwacht* (The Night Watch), was moved from the Kloveniersdoelen, the building for which it was originally intended, and installed in the Town Hall of Amsterdam (today the Royal Palace on De Dam). As a result the painting had to be altered to suit its new physical surroundings: strips were cut off, foreshortening the painting's left side in particular. Fortunately, we still possess a seventeenth-century copy of *De Nachtwacht*, from which we learn that Rembrandt's original conception of space, particularly in the balance between foreground and background, was far more convincing then than it appears today. But what is left still faithfully portrays a group of seventeenth-century Amsterdammers—members of the city's militia—who served in the company of Captain Frans Banning Cocq.[1]

Far more damage has been done to Busnoys's motet *In hydraulis*, his musical testimony to his apprenticeship in Tours with Johannes Ockeghem.[2] Within

I wish to express my thanks for stimulating advice during the process of shaping the final version of this text to Dr Bonnie Blackburn, Prof. Paula Higgins, Dr Leofranc Holford-Strevens, Dr Keith Falconer, and Drs Wilma Roest.

[1] The painting's original size was approximately 440 × 500 cm. In 1715 the left side of the painting was cropped by approximately 60 cm. and smaller strips were cut off from the other sides. Today the painting's size is 363 × 437 cm. There are two 17th-c. copies of *De Nachtwacht*: a painted copy attributed to Gerrit Lundens (1622–after 1683), and a drawing in a family album of 1650 from the family Banning Cocq (or Cock). Both are on display in the Rijksmuseum, Amsterdam. The universally known name of the painting was only introduced in the early 19th c.

[2] For sources and modern editions of *In hydraulis* see App. A, which includes my hypothetical reconstruction of the motet's original form. For a detailed survey of the early career of Antoine Busnoys, and particularly on the notion of a pedagogical link between Busnoys and Ockeghem, see Paula Higgins, '*In hydraulis* Revisited: New Light on the Career of Antoine Busnois', *JAMS* 39 (1986), 36–86.

approximately ten years after its composition, copies of the motet found their way into two anthologies compiled in Central Europe: Munich 3154 and Trent 91 respectively (see App. A). Both sources have the same text incipits, but only the former offers the complete text, written in prose at the bottom of fo. 48 (28) (see Fig. 9.1).[3] Since no other sources for the composition are known, we have to accept as definitive the loss of the composer's intentions. Any attempt to reconstruct Busnoys's setting of the poem—which is the purpose of this essay—will therefore remain hypothetical.

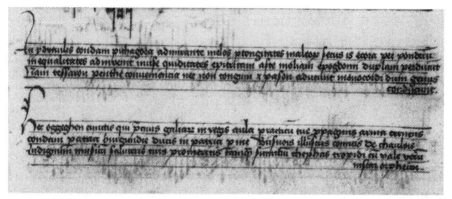

FIG. 9.1. Text of *In hydraulis* (Munich 3154)

Apart from the usual scribal corruptions and misunderstandings of the language, the orthography of the Latin text of *In hydraulis* in Munich 3154 betrays another aspect of the motet's early transmission: the copyist might have known the text at least partially by heart. Consequently, while notating the lines from memory, he used a French-orientated spelling: 'ydraulis' for 'hydraulis', 'condam' for 'quondam' (l. 1), 'emioliam' for 'hemioliam' (l. 6), and 'tongum' for 'phtongum' (l. 9). Equally possible, however, is that the scribe had the text dictated to him. The transmission of this text at the bottom of the page in two three-line paragraphs, corresponding to the complete texts of the *prima* and *secunda pars* respectively, is strange. The run-on nature of the text in the manuscript suggests that the scribe was not copying from an exemplar that reflected the original Latin poetry. In any case, Munich 3154 transmits an obvious mistake with regard to the poem's rhyme scheme in the second stanza; instead of the intended rhyme structure '-iam, -ducunt, -iam, -ducunt, -ducunt', the word 'nam' in the second

---

[3] According to Thomas Noblitt, 'Die Datierung der Handschrift Mus. Ms. 3154 der Staatsbibliothek München', *Musikforschung*, 22 (1974), 48–50, the watermark evidence suggests that Busnoys's motet was copied into that manuscript between 1471 and 1474; Suparmi Elizabeth Saunders, *The Dating of the Trent Codices from their Watermarks* (New York and London, 1989), 104–5, gives the period 1470–3 for the copying of the setting in Trent 91. This dating is confirmed in Peter Wright, 'Paper Evidence and the Dating of Trent 91', *ML* 76 (1995), 504. Apart from minor corruptions of the music in each source (see App. A), the two readings suggest a common ancestor.

line is considered to rhyme with 'hemioliam' at the end of the first line:

MS	*Reconstruction*
epitritam aste moliam	Epitritum ast hemioliam
epogdomi duplam perducu*n*t Nam	Epogdoum duplam perducunt nam
tessaron penthe conveniencia	Tessaron penthe convenientiam

While copying the motet, the scribe seems to have overlooked this irregularity in the text, and by starting the third line in each text paragraph with a majuscule — obviously intended as an adornment to the layout — it happened to be the word 'nam' that opens the third line of the first paragraph. That coincidence has led previous editors astray in their attempts to reconstruct the second stanza. Indeed, the scribe's copying of the second paragraph, where he adorned the word 'indignum' with a majuscule, notwithstanding its place in the middle of a poetic line, might confirm my suspicions. An alternative reading for the third stanza of the text was recently proposed by Dr David Howlett. His 'Galliarum in regis latria' (l. 12) convincingly restores the rhyme scheme of the third stanza, as does his 'practiculum' (l. 13) for the numbers of syllables. My reconstruction of the text reads as follows:[4]

TEXT IN MUNICH 3154	PROPOSED RECONSTRUCTION	
In ydraulis condam pithagora	In hydraulis quondam Pythagora	
admirante melos ptongitates	Admirante melos phtongitates	
maleor*um* secus is ecora	Malleorum secus is equora	
per ponderu*m* inequalitates	Per ponderum inequalitates	
adinvenit muse quiditates	Adinvenit muse quidditates	5

cont./

---

[4] For earlier attempts by Susan Hellauer, Ernest Sanders, and Leeman Perkins to reconstruct the original reading of the poem, see Leeman L. Perkins, 'The *L'Homme armé* Masses of Busnoys and Okeghem: A Comparison', *Journal of Musicology*, 3 (1984), 363–96. During the preparation of this paper Peter Urquhart graciously sent me a reading of the poem as included in his recording of the setting in *Motets by Busnoys, Josquin and Gombert*, Capella Alamire, Peter Urquhart, director, Titanic Records Ti 202 (1991). John Milsom provided me with a transcription of the setting by a collective of colleagues from Oxford, among which David Howlett, editor of the *Dictionary of Medieval Latin from British Sources*, contributed much to the understanding of the text. Their transcription appears in the liner notes to *The Brightest Heaven of Invention: Flemish Polyphony of the High Renaissance*, New London Chamber Choir, James Wood, director, Amon Ra Records CD SAR 56 (1992). While struggling myself with the poem's transmission I very much enjoyed the stimulating and critical support of Dr Leofranc Holford-Strevens, who has allowed me to quote from his letter to me, dated 23 Mar. 1992:

Although as you rightly observe the capital *N* of *Nam* need not be meant to mark a new line of verse, if in fact a new verse does start here, the manuscript text of line 8 would yield an alexandrine, *nam tessaron penthe* || *conuenienciam*, a perfectly good line in itself, but not acceptable as a casual variant among decasyllables. Hence the conjecture *nam tessaron penthe concordiam* [see Perkins, 'The *L'Homme armé* Masses', 364], the transmitted *conuenienciam* being due to synonym-substitution; the objection is that the less obvious word is substituted for the technical term, something likelier in poets than in scribes.

TEXT IN MUNICH 3154	PROPOSED RECONSTRUCTION	
epitritam aste moliam	Epitritum ast hemioliam	
epogdomi duplam perduncu*n*t Nam	Epogdoum duplam nam perducunt	
tessaron penthe conveniencia	Tessaron penthe convenientiam	
nec non tongum & pason aducunt	Nec non phtongum et pason adducunt	
monocordi dum genus conducunt.	Monochordi dum genus conducunt	10
Hec oggeghen cunctis qui pr*e*cnus	Hec Ockeghem cunctis qui precinis	
galiar*um* in regis aula	Galliarum in regis latria	
practicu*m* tue pr*o*paginis	Practiculum tue propaginis	
arma cernens condam p*er* atria	Arma cernens quondam per atria	
burgundie ducis in patria	Burgundie ducis in patria	15
p*er* me Busnois illustris comitis	Per me Busnoys illustris comitis	
de chaulois Indignum musicu*m*	De Chaurolois indignum musicum	
saluteris tuis pro meritis	Saluteris tuis pro meritis	
tamqu*am* summu*m* chephas tropidi cu*m*	Tamquam summum Cephas tropidicum	
vale veru*m* instar orpheicu*m*.	Vale verum instar Orpheicum	20

Long ago, when Pythagoras was wondering at the melodies of water organs and at the sounds [made] by hammers against surfaces, he discovered through the inequalities of the weights [of the hammers] the essentials of music: [5]

[The proportions of] *epitrite* as well as *hemiolia*, *epogdoum* [and] *dupla*; for they lead not only to the harmony of the *diatessaron* and *diapente*, but also to that of the *phthongos* and *diapason*, while they connect the species of the monochord.   [10]

You Ockeghem—who are chief singer before all [*premier chapelain*] in the service of the king of the French—strengthen the youthful/immature practice of your race when, at

> You transpose *nam*, with implicit punctuation after *duplam*, to give *epogdoum duplam, nam perducunt*, supposing that Busnoys pronounced *penthe* like the French word *pente* and ignored the extra unstressed syllable at the caesura. This gives very good sense, and avoids the difficulties inherent in previous explanations; but there are two obstacles to be overcome: (i) A Frenchman reading Latin or Greek did not treat a final *e* like a French *e féminin*, but as the full vowel now written *é*; before a pause, as at the caesura or the end of a line, it will be stressed. This is clear from puns and rhymes. (ii) Even in French, the extra syllable at the caesura was more frequent in the Old French epic, e.g. in the *Chanson de Roland*: 'Mult larges teres ‖ de vus avrai cunquises', than in lyric, which preferred either to elide *e féminin* (as a classical French poet was bound to do) before a vowel or to place the weak syllable in the *fourth* position: thus in two consecutive verses of Villon's *Epitaphe*:
>
> > Par justice ‖ Toutefois vous savez
> > Que tous hommes ‖ n'ont pas bon sens rassis.
>
> Hence, whereas French *pente* could stand in lyric verse as third and fourth syllable of the line (x x *pente* ‖ x x x x x X)—the so-called *césure lyrique*—but as the fourth syllable only, at least in general, when followed by a vowel (x x x *pen* ‖ *t(e)* x x x x x X), not by a consonant (x x x *pente* ‖ x x x x x X), which the metricians call the *césure épique*. . . . Even if Busnoys could have pronounced *penthe* as *pente* instead of *penté*, therefore, he was unlikely to place it as you suggest.
>
> Hence, if you are to justify your interpretation it must be by finding parallels, in a Latin poem written by a fifteenth-century French-speaker in syllabic metre, for the double anomaly of a final *e* treated as weak and placed hypermetrically at the caesura.
>
> Notwithstanding this distinguished analysis, I have decided to avoid any more drastic emendation for this line, and to accept its inherent message: 'tessaron penthe convenientiam'. See also my commentary to Appendix C: *In hydraulis*: Letter-Values and Golden Sections.

some time, you examine [the results of] these aspects in the halls of the Duke of Burgundy, in your fatherland.   [15]

Through me, Busnoys, unworthy musician of the illustrious Count of Charolais, may you be greeted—so to speak—as 'Cephas', as the first among the composers. Farewell, true image of Orpheus!   [20]

In writing *In hydraulis*, did Busnoys intend to present himself as a learned scholar qualified to pass on the basics of his profession? There was certainly no need for concern about the near future of 'this unworthy musician of the illustrious Count of [Charolais] (*illustris comitis de chaurolois indignum musicum*)', as he calls himself, nor his 'immature practice (*practiculum*)'. His newly established relationship with Charles the Bold must have been a challenge to the quick-tempered, adventurous Busnoys, who did not feel at all embarrassed about inviting the 'premier chapelain' of the king of France, whenever it suited him, to examine the results of his instruction—as presented now by his former apprentice—in the halls of the Duke of Burgundy, in his very homeland. Would that not have sounded rather provocative to a faithful servant of the French court?

Apart from a few small differences in pitch between the readings in the two manuscripts, the sources differ in the introduction of a key signature, B♭, in some of the voices of Trent 91: *prima pars*, contratenor altus; *secunda pars*, superius and bassus (see Fig. 9.2). However, strict application of these signatures would generate false harmonies and problematic hexachord combinations. Only a careful weighing of the notation in each source against the music can help us to neutralize these obstacles in modern transcriptions and performances.

The superius at measure 32 (see transcription, App. 1) offers the first *b′*, a note that can be sung as a B♭, even though the sources do not specify one until measures 38 and 41, where the note *b♭′* is singled out as *fa super la* in relation to the natural hexachord. Up to that moment *a* has been the lowest note in the superius, but in the line that starts at measure 51 it falls to *f* (see mm. 55 and 82), making the low *g* a *re* in the soft hexachord. Consequently, a low B♭ is appropriate in the continuation of that voice.

The contratenor altus has accidentals at measures 20, 49, and 75, of which two (mm. 20 and 75) again specify *fa super la*. In fact, that particular note occurs time and again in the melodic lines of the altus, and might well have prompted a copyist to add the B♭ signature to this part. More specifically, I presume that the copyist of Trent 91 worked from a source in which the fourth note of measure 3 was specified as *fa super la* by means of an accidental, a flat at the beginning of the first staff (see Fig. 9.2, in which I have marked the flats with arrows). After the copyist had completed the altus, he then must have supplied the remaining staves of that voice with a flat signature (see especially the fourth staff, where the flat is crowded in above the note), but by error included the first staff (and perhaps the

FIG. 9.2. Signatures in *In hydraulis* as transmitted in Trent 91

second?) of the bassus, where, of course, it appears to be an E♭. This obtrusive *e*♭ provokes the flat in measure 13 that time and again mars modern performances of the setting, since a B♭ signature is presupposed. Fortunately, the source from which Trent 91 was copied included a sign that immediately neutralized the E♭ signature: this is the flat before the *f* in the altus and bassus at measure 12, which explains the following note unquestionably as *e la mi*. Consequently, the flat before the note *e'* in the altus, measure 13, must be a corruption provoked by the erroneous B♭ signature in that voice.

A comparable situation is offered by the sources at the opening of the *secunda pars*. Munich 3154 specifies the second note in the superius and bassus as *fa super la* by means of a single accidental at the opening of the line, whereas Trent has an upper and lower flat signature in both voices. Many of the flats I have put over the note B in my transcription indicate either *fa super la* or a B♭ *fa* imposed by a *fa super la* in one of the other voices. But very often I have not specified B♭ because it is unnecessary.

Still another aspect of the transmission is worth exploring. Both sources of the motet give the tenor in *integer valor*, but the number of breve rests preceding the first and fourth statements of the cantus firmus are incorrect in both sources:

Fig. 9.3. Tenor of *In hydraulis* as transmitted in Trent 91

Jaap van Benthem

Ex. 9.1. Hypothetical reconstruction of tenor of Busnoys, *In hydraulis*

respectively four and two too few. Moreover, Trent has eight breve rests too many before the third statement of the cantus firmus (see Fig. 9.3). Fortunately, the sources offer *signa congruentiae* for the entrances of the cantus firmus. But there is more to ponder at. All four statements have the same melodic and rhythmic structure, but three are regulated by mensuration signs while the last is written out in *color*. Equally curious, the *tempus imperfectum* sign is introduced only before the second cantus firmus statement and not at the beginning of the preceding group of rests, as for the first and third statements in both sources. In my opinion, these bewildering aspects of the setting's transmitted reading all result from the clumsy transcription of a tenor part originally notated with time signatures as well as note-values and rests which deviated from those in the surrounding voices. In both *partes* of *In hydraulis* the proportion in time between the two statements of the cantus firmus is 3 : 2. This led me to consider the possibility of an alternative notation that would present the various statements of the cantus firmus *and* the preceding groups of rests by means of mensuration signs only (see Ex. 9.1). Notation of this kind might elucidate the origin and corruption of the transmitted tenor *ad longum* in Munich and Trent as well as its relationship with comparable tenors in Busnoys's masses.

The main obstacle to reconstructing such a notation is the impossibility of establishing a reasonable mensural relationship between the 68 imperfect breve rests preceding the third cantus-firmus statement (at m. 153) and the following group of 46 breve rests. Only 69 breve rests would produce a 3 : 2 proportion with the transmitted breve rests in the *secunda pars* of the motet. But neither the reading nor the transmission of the setting suggests any reworking that might have resulted in the elimination of one bar of music in the voices surrounding the tenor. However, we might hypothesize that the original form of the setting included an extra breve rest: in other words, a general pause. It is easy to imagine that such a breve rest could be lost in transmission, particularly when it no longer had a function in presenting a text. If so, is there any place in the layout of the setting between measures 85 and 153 where a general pause would make sense musically, and would it be possible to justify such a breve rest as a consequence of the poetic structure? My answer to both questions is envisaged in my transcription of *In hydraulis* (see App. A), which includes a general pause of a breve's length between measures 109 and 110, the only possible place in the setting between measures 85 and 153.[5] It incorporates an alternative notation for the

---

[5] In performance the sequence of mm. 109 and 110 gives a rather breathless impression. As an alternative to my proposed extra breve rest (which eliminates that impression) and my reasoning on this point one might conjecture that it was the corrupt number of 68 breve rests in the *tenor ad longum* that prompted a slight reworking at m. 109. In the original reading there might have been a longa in the superius and a breve followed by a breve rest in the altus. My extra breve rest has been incorporated in two recent recordings of *In hydraulis* by Pomerium, Alexander Blachly, director (Dorian-90184) and The Clerks' Group, Edward Wickham, director (ASV-CDGAU143).

tenor which allows a presentation of the various cantus-firmus statements and their preceding groups of rests by means of a far more sophisticated system of related mensuration signs. What we are missing is some sort of verbal canon to tell us how to derive the second and fourth cantus-firmus statements from our hypothetical reconstruction of the tenor's original notation. Such a canon might have been written in Latin (or even in a mixture of Latin and Greek[6]) with an instruction to interpret the note-values of the cantus-firmus statements, perhaps elucidating the origin of the coloration in the fourth cantus-firmus statement.

A consequence of my hypothetical reading of the tenor is that in the *secunda pars* of the setting the final harmony of a fifth as transmitted in Trent 91 can be realized at the end of both cantus-firmus statements (see Ex. 9.1). When we accept that final harmony as authentic, my hypothetical notation of the tenor comprises $18 + 19 = 37$ notes. We shall encounter this number again.

Although Busnoys's motet embodies Pythagorean principles such as the consonances of the octave, fifth, and fourth, its purpose is rather to hail Ockeghem, the 'Cephas' and first among the 'apostles', who introduced a new musical language to a new generation. However, for Busnoys's original conception of *In hydraulis* the classical dictum *Nomen est omen* appears to be the underlying principle for the contents of the poem as well as the musical layout of the setting. On the basis of the Latin natural-order alphabet in which a = 1, b = 2, c = 3 . . . i/j = 9 . . . u/v = 20 . . . z = 24, the number equivalence of the letters of the name 'Johannes Ockeghem'—in the spelling of his presumably authentic signature (Fig. 9.4; see App. B)—forms the proportion of the Pythagorean major third, which is 81 : 64 (i.e. two whole steps, $9/8 \times 9/8$).[7]

J	O	H	A	N	N	E	S		O	C	K	E	G	H	E	M
9	14	8	1	13	13	5	18		14	3	10	5	7	8	5	12

81   64

In this respect Busnoys's artful combination of Pythagoras and Ockeghem makes of the latter an emblem of classical principles.[8]

---

[6] Concerning Busnoys's tendency to 'pseudo-Hellenic word play' (Taruskin), see the canon concerning the tenor in the Credo of his *Missa L'homme armé*, 'Ne sonites cachefaton sume lychanosipaton' (correctly 'Ne sonites cacemphaton | sume lichanos hypaton', as pointed out by Leonfranc Holford-Strevens; 'cacemphaton' (= ill-sounding), which Busnoys probably got from Quintilian 8. 3. 44 and 47, was probably confused with 'cacophony'), and in his motet *Anthoni usque limina* (see below, n. 8). For the canons in his chanson *Maintes femmes* see Helen Hewitt, 'The Two Puzzle Canons in Busnois's *Maintes femmes*', *JAMS* 10 (1957), 104–10.

[7] For a survey of number alphabets, as well as for relevant bibliographical references, see Ruth Tatlow, *Bach and the Riddle of the Number Alphabet* (Cambridge, 1991), 130–8 and 168–77.

[8] It is unlikely that this coincidence between the spelling of the name 'Johannes Ockeghem' and its numerical connotation would have remained unobserved by the composer of the motet *Anthoni usque limina*. In this work the layout of the St Anthony bell exposes the name 'Busnoys' by means of 108 periods of time in both parts of the setting. The numerical equivalent of the name 'Busnoys' according to the Latin natural-order alphabet is 108 (2 + 20 + 18 + 13 + 14 + 23 + 18). The *prima pars* consists of 54 perfect breves

FIG. 9.4. Ockeghem's signature in E. Giraudet, *Les Artistes tourangeaux*

The *secunda pars* of the motet starts with the lines: 'Hec Ockeghem cunctis qui precinis Galliarum in regis latria'. The following line brings the former student's plea for lasting artistic support: 'practiculum tue propaginis arma'. The intention of the line seems to be highlighted by its canonic *Meister und Schüler* setting, starting at measure 110, and so it seems appropriate to stress the foregoing lines by means of the full cadence at measure 109. The setting of these opening lines starts with three voices (see Ex. 9.2), of which both superius and altus have exactly the same melody, comprising 14 notes, up to the first rest. The bassus offers only the first half of this phrase and continues with a melodic and rhythmic allusion to the cantus-firmus motif, three notes D–C–D in ligature, consisting of 9 notes in all. The opening notes in each of the three voices could represent the initials of 'Johannes Ockeghem', since the numbers 9 (i.e. the number of notes in the opening of the bassus) and 14 (the number of notes in the openings of both the superius and altus) represent the letters *J* (9) and *O* (14) in the Latin natural-order alphabet. But why, may we ask, is the phrase with 14 notes given twice (i.e. in *both* the superius and altus) in Busnoys's setting?

Significantly, both sources offer exactly the same reading for this section, and the strict imitation that underlies the conception makes their transmissions trustworthy. So the layout of measures 85–109, with 81 notes (37 + 44), becomes immediately understandable as a symbolic counterpoint to the exposition of the name 'Ockeghem' in the text, for 81 is the letter-value of the name 'Johannes'. Moreover, even an allusion to the name 'Ockeghem' can be easily detected since the number of notes the superius and altus have in common is 64 (32 + 32). But that is not the only reason why the opening phrase of the *secunda pars* includes 14 notes in both the superius and the altus. The total number of notes involved in the numerical exposition of the initials *J* and *O* is 37 (14 × 2 + 9), with 44 notes remaining to complete the total number of 81 notes for this section

under O, against which the bell thrice presents a group of 9 breve rests followed by 9 breves for the bell-ringing. In the *secunda pars* the voices have 108 imperfect breves arranged in groups of three in O2 mensuration, against which the bell thrice presents a group of 18 breve rests followed by 18 breves for the bell-ringing. Since the performance of the bell in the *secunda pars* of the motet is indicated as 'ubi supra', the overall structure of the bell part must be understood in *modus minor perfectus cum tempore perfecto et prolatione perfecta*, hence 6 longas, or 18 breves, or 18 × 6 minims = *108* periods of time.

For a modern edition of the composition, see *Busnoys LTW*, Music, 138–48; Commentary, 64–9. For recent studies of this motet, see Rob Wegman, 'Busnoys' *Anthoni usque limina* and the Order of Saint-Antoine-en-Barbefosse in Hainaut', *Studi musicali*, 17 (1988), 15–31, and id., 'For Whom the Bell Tolls: Reading and Hearing Busnoys's *Anthoni usque limina*, in Dolores Pesce (ed.), *Hearing the Motet* (New York, 1997), 122–41.

Ex. 9.2. Busnoys, *In hydraulis*, opening of *secunda pars*, mm. 85–109

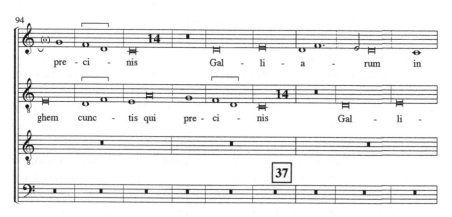

(i.e. mm. 85–109). The proportion of 44 : 37 nearly equals the traditional proportion of the Pythagorean minor third 32 : 27:

$$32 : 27 = 1184 : 999$$
$$44 : 37 = 1188 : 999$$

Is it really by accident that the musical layout of this opening section, so prominently exposing the numbers 81 and 64 in the setting of a text that names 'Ockeghem', seems to complete the reference to the Pythagorean major third with a reference to its proportional counterpart, the minor third, an interval which is, moreover, the first in the head-motif of the opening of the *secunda pars*?

I have already mentioned the pre-emptive allusion to the cantus firmus at the end of the nine-note bassus line. Unfortunately, the sources transmit no text for the cantus firmus. In contrast to the proposal in Taruskin's edition for solmizing the various statements of the cantus-firmus motif (i.e. *re–ut–re*, *la–sol–la*, *re–ut–re*), it seems more appropriate to me to mutate on the last note of the second statement (see also the transcription in App. A):

re	*ut*	*re*	/	*la*	*sol*	*la*	(= re)	/	*sol*	*fa*	*sol*		
22	39	22		12	43	12			43	7	43	=	243 or 3 × *81*
sol	*fa*	*sol*	/	*re*	*ut*	*re*	(= la)	/	*re*	*ut*	*re*		
43	7	43		22	39	22			22	39	22	=	259 or 7 × *37*

Note: The numbers below the syllables correspond to their numerical equivalent as calculated by means of the Latin natural-order alphabet.

The solmization syllables for the ascending line have a letter-value that forms a multiple of 81 (243 = 3 × *81*), and the syllables for the descending line form a multiple of 37 (259 = 7 × *37*). This compelled me to question the function of the isolated three-note cantus-firmus motif (bassus, mm. 89–92) within the group of 37 notes at the beginning of the setting's *secunda pars*. It was my hypothetical underlay of the poem's last line to the music that suggested the answer to me: the same three-note motif at measures 246–7 in the superius, and measures 249–51 in the bassus, perfectly fits the word 'vale'. Since 'vale' (farewell) is the emotional keystone of the text, its numerical equivalent being 37 (20 + 1 + 11 + 5), and since the original number of written notes for the tenor was presumably 18 + 19 = 37 (see Ex. 9.1), I feel justified in proposing that the word 'vale' be sung in the tenor. Further justification for my suggestion might be found in the text of the chant *O crux lignum triumphale*, on which Busnoys himself based a mass setting, in which the word 'vale' corresponds to the notes *d–c–d*, which Busnoys himself set in a rhythm identical with that of the tenor of *In hydraulis*.[9]

---

[9] The mass is edited in *Busnoys LTW*, Music, 49–93; Commentary, 46–52. My thanks to Paula Higgins for pointing this out.

TABLE 9.1. *Hypothetical number of notes surrounding the tenor in* In hydraulis

Part I,1 (mm. 1–54):
S   26 + 15   4 + 11 + 7 + 20 + 23 + 8 + 20 + 15 +
                         |
A   25 + 17 + 36   1 + 27 + 12 + 7 + 14 + 18 + 24 + 5 +
                         |
T   (6 × 3)
                         |
B   39 + 8   3 + 20 + 15 + 15 + 7 + 18 + 21 +

       166   315   = 481 or 13 × 37

Part I,2 (mm. 55–84):
S   8 + 30 1 + 21 + 25 + 5 + 5 + 27
                  |
A   1 + 1   13 + 26 + 10 + 3 + 6 + 3 + 19
                  |
T   (6 × 3)
                  |
B   5 + 30 18 + 27 + 3 + 6

       75   218   = 293 [296 or 8 × 37]

                                    21 × 37

Part II,1 (mm. 85–188):
S   14 + 26 + 7 + 11 + 36 + 25 + 23   1 + 26 + 31 + 23 +
                                            |
A   14 + 18 + 7 + 11 + 22 + 13 + 4 + 9 + 10 + 13 + 28   50 + 34 + 3 +
                                            |
T   (6 × 3 + 1)
                                    |
B   9 + 13 + [19] + 6   25 + 42 + 2 +

      37 44   257   237   = 575
      = 81   or *25 × 23*

Part II,2 (mm. 189–259):
S   1 + 8 + 7 + 29 + 5 + 8   1 + 23 + 15 + 5
                              |
A   1 + 8 + 7 + 22 + 5 + 10 1 + 6 + 39
                              |
T   (6 × 3 + 1)
                            |
B   6 + 33   16 + 11 + 7 + 2

           150   126   = 276 or *23 × 12*
                               +19
                               ===
                             145   *23 × 37*

Total number of notes 21 × 37 + 23 × 37 =   1628 or *44 × 37*
notes to be sung in the tenor   74

                                   1702 or *2 × 23 × 37*

By counting notes in the surrounding voices, we discover that the number of notes in the *prima pars* is apparently based on multiples of the number 37, and those in the *secunda pars* on multiples of the number 23 (see Table 9.1). These multiples are strictly bound by the layout of the tenor. In my presentation of these groups of multiples, the internal relationships among those in the *prima pars* appear to be based upon the Golden Section—*13* × 37 against *8* × 37 (that is, as successive terms in the Fibonacci series, 8 and 13 form a ratio of 1.625 : 1, which approximates the Golden Section, 1.618 : 1). (See also App. C.) This proportion confirms that we must reckon with the possibility of a slight corruption in the transmission of measures 55 to 84. In my estimation it is three notes short; in this connection, consider the transmission of the bassus at measure 59 against the superius at measure 60.

While acknowledging the hypothetical nature of my analysis, I find it significant none the less that the total number of notes in the superius, altus, and bassus (1628) equals 44 times 37, precisely the two numbers that appeared to be structurally important for the opening section of the *secunda pars* of *In hydraulis*. The total number of notes in the superius, altus, and bassus combined also divides into two equal parts between the groups of 37 and 44 notes:

$$I_1 \qquad I_2 \qquad II_1 \qquad\qquad II_2$$
$$481 + [296] + \mathit{37} + \mathit{44} + 494 + 276$$
$$\underbrace{} \quad \underbrace{\mathit{81} }$$
$$814 \qquad\qquad 575$$
$$\underbrace{}$$
$$814$$

Ex. 9.3. Josquin, ending of *Nymphes des bois*

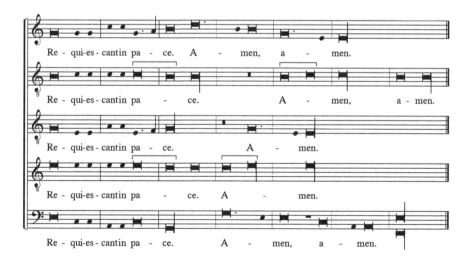

126 notes surround the last cantus-firmus statement which itself consists of 19 notes. In this final section of the motet exactly 145 notes hail the 'instar Orpheicum', 145 being the numerical equivalent of 'Johannes Ockeghem': *81 + 64*. Thirty years later the final line of *Nymphes des bois*, Molinet's lament for the same composer, would be set by Josquin des Prez with 64 notes (see Ex. 9.3).[10]

In my hypothetical notation of the tenor of *In hydraulis* (see Ex. 9.1), the first statement of the cantus firmus under *tempus perfectum cum prolatione maiori* (mm. 19–54) has a total duration of 12 breves, or 12 × 9 minims = 108 minims, 108, as we have shown (see n. 8), being the numerical equivalent of the name 'Busnoys'. The total duration of all four cantus-firmus statements is 300 minims:

Part I
6 × 9 minim rests	54	
12 × 9 minims of c.f. statement		*108*
3 × 6 minim rests	18	
12 × 6 minims of c.f. statement		72

Part II
23 × 6 minim rests	138	
12 × 6 minims of c.f. statement		72
23 × 4 minim rests	92	
12 × 4 minims of c.f. statement		48
		300

In the classical Greek Milesian number system the letter *tau* represents the number 300. In the unique transmission of Busnoys's motet *Anthoni usque limina* that letter crowns the St Anthony bell, the tau-cross being an iconographic attribute of that saint. In *In hydraulis* the four cantus-firmus statements—written out with 37 notes—amount to 74 tones (see Ex. 9.1); the numerical equivalent of the French name 'Antoine' is 74.

In the *secunda pars* of the motet, the cantus-firmus statements are preceded by 23 breve rests. That number may represent the sum of 9 + 14, the numerical equivalent of Ockeghem's initials. This leaves open the question as to how to accommodate my notation of last resort for the entrance of the tenor in the *prima pars* (see Ex. 9.1), for in performance the tenor repeats only half of my notated rests before beginning the second statement of the cantus-firmus, a procedure which results in a 2 : 1 proportion between these groups of rests. The obvious inconsistency can be explained by asking: who is singing 'vale' throughout the set-

---

[10] The pitch for this transcription, which is a fourth below all published transcriptions, has been suggested by the late Jean-Pierre Ouvrard (d. 13 Nov. 1992), formerly at the University of Tours, who shared his ideas about the setting's notation with me at the Josquin Symposium in Cologne, 11–15 July 1984.

ting? The answer has to be: it is the composer Antoine Busnoys, whose initials B and A, the second and first letters of the alphabet, figure at the opening of his chanson *Bel Accueil* (see the reproduction in the frontispiece of this volume).

This chanson offers an equally striking example of the numerological background to Busnoys's *œuvre*. In *Bel Accueil* the number of notes in the contra corresponds to the numerical equivalent of the name 'Jaqueline' (89), Busnoys's beloved lady; the numerical equivalent of 'Antoine Busnoys' equals the number of notes in the surrounding voices. And these two voices enter with groups of notes in a 2 : 1 proportion—18 and 9 notes respectively.[11]

Bel Accueil, le sergant d'amours (Mellon Chansonnnier, fos. 1ᵛ–2ʳ)

S	18 + 23	22 + 16 + 13	=	92
Ct	9 + 9 + 13 + 12	8 + 15 + 16 + 7	=	89
T	9 + 18 + 17	4 + 22 + 20	=	90
				182

J	A	Q	U	E	L	I	N	E		
9	1	16	20	5	11	9	13	5	=	89

A	N	T	O	I	N	E		B	U	S	N	O	Y	S		
1	13	19	14	9	13	5		2	20	18	13	14	23	18	=	182
		74								108						

It has been suggested on structural grounds that Ockeghem's motet *Ut heremita solus* 'might be regarded as a counterpart to Busnoys's *In hydraulis* . . ., assuming that the composition printed anonymously by Petrucci in 1504 is the one cited by Guillaume Crétin in his lament on Ockeghem's death'.[12] Several scholars have expressed the opinion that *Ut heremita solus* was composed as an emulatory response to Busnoys's motet.[13] Apart from a presumed melodic correspondence between the head-motif 'Ut heremita solus' and the phrase 'Hec Ockeghem' in Busnoys's motet (cf. Ex. 9.4 with Ex. 9.2), *Ut heremita solus* is a work of unusual complexity that makes use of a canonic device similar to that of Busnoys's chanson *Maintes femmes*. In the next part of this contribution I shall confine myself to some deductions from the unique transmission of *Ut heremita solus* in Petrucci's *Motetti C*. These are deductions which—together with my analysis of Busnoys's motet—might add to our assumptions concerning the relationships between

[11] On Jacqueline d'Haqueville and Antoine Busnoys, see Paula Higgins, 'Parisian Nobles, a Scottish Princess, and the Woman's Voice in Late Medieval Song', *EMH* 10 (1991), 145–200.

[12] Perkins, 'The *L'Homme armé* Masses', 369. For a modern edition of *Ut heremita solus*, see Johannes Ockeghem, *Collected Works*, iii, ed. Richard Wexler with Dragan Plamenac (Boston, 1992), 18–24.

[13] See Higgins, '*In hydraulis* Revisited', 78 n. 137.

Ex. 9.4. Ockeghem, *Ut heremita solus*: (*a*) mm. 1–12; (*b*) mm. 111–28

Busnoys's and Ockeghem's motets. They might equally have implications for our general understanding of the conception of such compositions.

Only the incipit of the text for Ockeghem's setting has been transmitted: 'Ut heremita solus'. Thanks to Andrea Lindmayr's inspired analysis of the tenor part, we now fully understand the function of its notation and know about the short poem artfully embedded in it (cf. Fig. 9.5 with Ex. 9.5):[14]

	syllables
O vere sol	4
Labes falaces solut	7
Ut remitere soles	7
Ergo lapsoque reo	7
Miserere	4

This poem apparently elucidates a central idea behind the composition:

> O veritable sun
> The deceitful stains have been cleansed (?)
> As thou art wont to forgive.
> Therefore have mercy on one who has fallen
> And is guilty.[15]

Apart from the customary *tenores ad longum*, Petrucci offers various instructions for the interpretation of the tenor part in its original notation. The first explains how to derive the complete tenor, and the second and third how to integrate that voice into both parts of the setting. In my view, the difference in structural quality between the second and third rhymed canons supports the authenticity of only one of them, the third:[16]

	syllables
Litteras caute notabis	8
pro qualibet tu pausabis	8
unam pausam temporis	7

[14] Andrea Lindmayr, 'Ein Rätseltenor Ockeghems: Des Rätsels Lösung', *Acta musicologica*, 60 (1988), 31–42. For a facsimile of the complete tenor part, see p. 34.

[15] I am grateful to Leofranc Holford-Strevens for the following translations, and his comments on *O vere sol*: '*Labe falaces solut*: *solut* is not a Latin word; the translation presupposes *solutae*, but if *-ae* (or *-e*) was accidentally omitted at the printer's between the two *ut* breves, that spoils the syllable count. Perhaps an abbreviation taken from commerce or law and properly meaning "paid" (Cappelli gives *solut* for *solutionis*, "of payment") has been pressed into service as a word. *Ut remitere soles*: *remittere* is good Latin for pardoning a fault, but also for waiving a debt, hence all the more suitable after *solut*. *Ergo lapsoque reo Miserere*: In medieval Latin *-que* is sometimes used as if it were *et*, joining a word to what follows instead of what precedes; that is what we have here. Both *falaces* and *remitere* ought to have had double consonants, *fallaces*, *remittere*, but I have encountered single spellings.'

[16] The wording of the second poem strongly suggests that it was derived from the third in order to fit Petrucci's *Resolutio* for the *prima pars* of the motet:
Pro qualibet littera duo tempora pausa
Sed vere prolationes
non petunt pausationes
Sed sunt signa generis

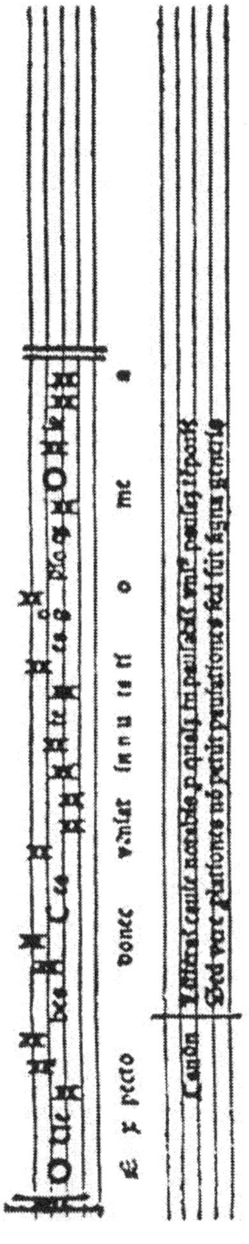

FIG. 9.5. *Motetti C* (Venice: O. Petrucci, 1504), tenor, fo. 13ʳ

EX. 9.5. Resolution of tenor of Ockeghem, *Ut heremita solus*

Sed vere prolationes	8
non petunt pausationes	8
sed sunt signa generis	7

You will carefully take note of the letters;
For each one you will rest one *tempus*.
But the prolations do not demand rests;
They are signs of the genus.

This third canon convincingly explains how to read the tenor in both parts of the setting. The only explicit indication missing is an instruction to perform *in duplo* the tenor in the setting's *prima pars*; accordingly, only the second of the two *tenores* given in Petrucci's *Motetti C* (i.e. the one on fo. 13ʳ; see Fig. 9.5) represents Ockeghem's original notation, whose rebus-like appearance is underlined by the added line *Expecto donec veniat inmutatio mea* ('I shall wait till my change comes'). The tenor part as derived from this notation consists of *64* breve notes and rests; up to the final breve its total length is 162 semibreves, a multiple of *81* (see Ex. 9.5). We have seen already that these two numbers represent the name 'Johannes Ockeghem' (81 + 64) in Busnoys's *In hydraulis*.

The reading of the short poem *O vere sol*, as transmitted in the original notation of the tenor, leaves no room for doubt about the spelling intended by the composer. The sum of its letter-values is 729, which is also a multiple of 81:

O vere sol	
14 47 43	104
Labes falaces solut	
37 45 82	164
Ut remitere soles	
39 89 66	194
Ergo lapsoque reo	
43 100 36	179
Miserere	
88	88

729 or 9 × *81*

We cannot be sure about the original number of notes intended for the setting, but Petrucci's version offers totals for both parts which are very near to multiples of *64* (part I: 1405 [1408 = 22 × *64*]; part II: 1023 [1024 = 16 × *64*]), and the total number of notes (2428) closely approaches 38 × *64* (= 2432). In relation to the poem *O vere sol* the number 38 is significant because of an incident described in the New Testament. In the Gospel of John, 5: 1–9 Christ visits a pool named Bethesda where he meets 'a certain man . . . who had an infirmity *thirty-and-eight* years . . . When Jesus saw him lying there, and knew that he already had been in that condition a long time, he said to him, 'Do you want to be made well?' The sick man answered him, 'Sir, I have no man to put me into the pool when the water is stirred up; but while I am coming, another steps down before me'. Jesus said to him, 'Rise, take up your bed and walk.'[17]

Only in the light of this episode does the short line of text added to the seventeen notes in the original notation of the tenor become fully comprehensible. The line is a quotation from the Book of Job: 'If a man dies, shall he live again? All the days of my hard service *I will wait, till my change comes*' (Job 14:14). Its inherent message seems to be underlined by the numerical equivalent of its wording in the Vulgate:

'Expecto donec veniat inmutatio mea'[18]

83   39   67   116   18 = 323

For only 324 will provide a multiple of *81*.

Such symbolic representation of human imperfection has its roots in early Christian number symbolism. According to St Augustine, 'the addition of one to any composite number unifies the whole, if a recognized limit is thereby reached. By the same token, the failure of a number to reach a recognized limit implies a defect or deficiency.'[19] As it is the number 1 which stands for God, the 'veritable sun, wont to forgive', it is only the complete tenor line that brings about the numbers *81* and *64*: *O vere sol, labes falaces solut!*[20]

If Ockeghem's *Ut heremita solus* is indeed a reaction to Busnoys's *In hydraulis*, with its frank disclosure of his name and rank, the fragment of text attached to the musical allusion at the very opening of the setting—'Ut heremita solus'—may provide us with a glimpse of the contrast in mentality between two artists who still enrich our lives as we assess their musical legacies.

---

[17] On the symbolic value of the number 38 see Vincent Foster Hopper, *Medieval Number Symbolism: Its Sources, Meaning, and Influence on Thought and Expression* (New York, 1938; repr. 1969), 82 and Heinz Meyer and Rudolf Suntrup, *Lexikon der mittelalterlichen Zahlenbedeutungen* (Munich, 1987), col. 709.

[18] Confirms the correctness of the spelling 'inmutatio'.

[19] See Hopper, *Medieval Number Symbolism*, 82, and Meyer and Suntrup, *Lexikon*, col. 7 for relevant quotations from early Christian authors.

[20] For a comparable analysis of a composition by Josquin des Prez, see Jaap van Benthem, 'Josquins Motette *Huc me sydereo*, oder Konstruktivismus als Ausdruck humanistisch geprägter Andacht?', in Herbert Schneider (ed.), *Die Motette: Beiträge zu ihrer Gattungsgeschichte* (Neue Studien zur Musikwissenschaft, 5; Mainz, 1992), 135–64.

Appendix A
Busnoys's *In hydraulis* and its Sources

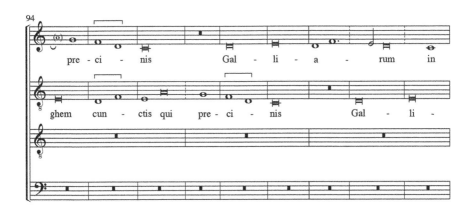

Sources

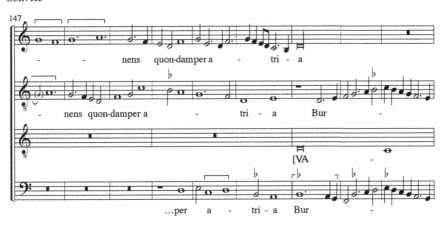

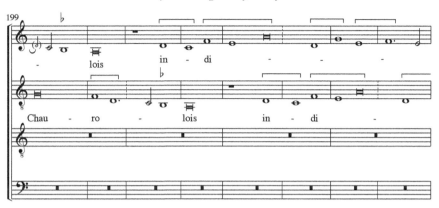

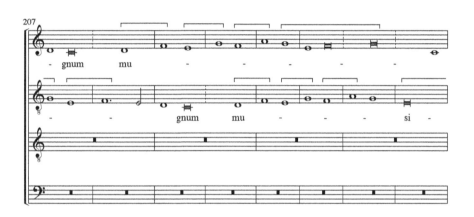

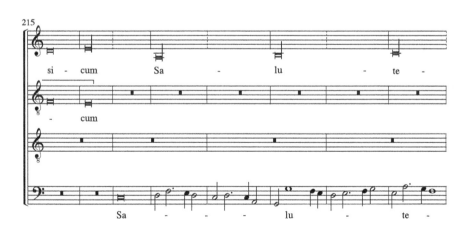

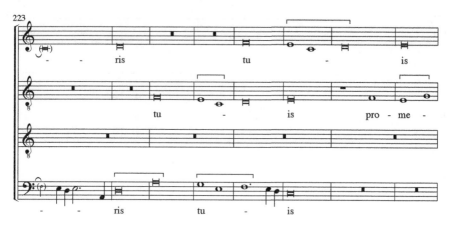

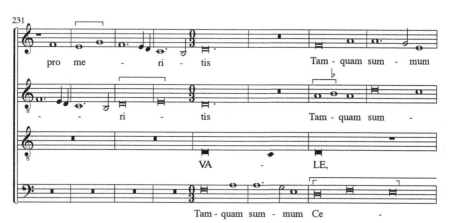

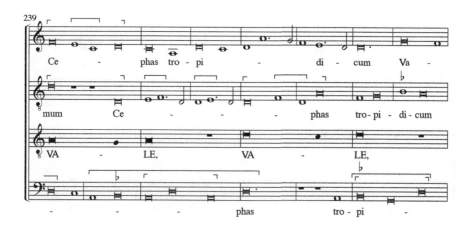

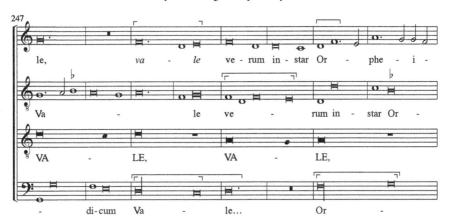

M	Munich, Bayerische Staatsbibliothek, Musiksammlung, Musica MS 3154, fos. 47v–49r (27v–29r), anon.
T	Trent, Museo Provinciale d'Arte, Castello del Buon Consiglio, MS 1378 (*olim* 91), fos. 35v–37r, busnoys

Musical Variants and Corruptions(*)

voice	measure	reading	source
B	10_3	*c*	T
T*	1–18	only 14 breve rests under O	M, T
B*	18_2	*c*	T
S*	38_1	no dot	M, T
S*	39_1	*d'*	T
B*	46_1	*e*	T
A*	49–50	not coloured	M, T
A*	50_2	semibreve	M
A	61_{1-2}	no ligature	M
voice	*measure*	*reading*	*source*

A*	63_2	c'	M
B*	67_1	g	M
B*	71_3	c	M
A*	79_{1-5}	semibreve d, coloured minim f, coloured semiminim e, dotted semibreve d	M
T*	85–152	8 breve rests too many under C2	T
S*	131_4	2 semibreves c' d'	T
A*	138_4	semibreve	T
B*	141_1	2 semiminims $f e$	M
		2 fusas $f e$	T
		see however, A 142	M, T
A	152	ligature	T
A	157_2–158	ligature	T
B	164–5	no ligature	T
T	186	Tenor *ad longum* has only d M, T	
S*	186_2	minim rest missing	M
S	186_2–187_1	2 semibreves $d' c'$	T
T*	189–234	only 44 breve rests under C/C2	M, T
A*	236	rest missing	T
A*	242_1–244	breve d, semibreve rest, 2 semibreves $f d$ in ligature, dotted breve a	T
T	257	only d	M

NB. The reading of the line 'genus dum conducunt' in mm. 79–84 instead of the transmitted reading of the poem in Munich 3154 ('dum genus conducunt') is editorial.

Modern Editions

Sechs Trienter Codices: Geistliche und weltliche Kompositionen des XV. Jhs., ed. Guido Adler and Oswald Koller (Denkmäler der Tonkunst in Österreich, 14/15; Vienna, 1900), 105–11.

Antoine Busnoys Collected Works, parts 2–3: The Latin-Texted Works, ed. Richard Taruskin (Masters and Monuments of the Renaissance, 5; New York, 1990), part 2 (Music), 151–65, part 3 (Commentary), 74–80.

Appendix B
The Fifteenth-Century Orthography of Ockeghem's Name

Since the publication of Leeman Perkins's article on musical patronage at the French royal court,[1] the spelling of the composer's surname with 'ck' has become suspect because — according to Perkins — in all official French documents the letter 'c' before the 'k' is missing. Pamela Starr has recently stated that in the spelling 'Okeghem', as it occurs in a collection of documents from the papal Curia relating to the acquisition of a benefice, 'we are virtually assured . . . of the correct spelling of Okeghem's surname'.[2] This is because 'An inaccuracy or a mistake in diction might have rendered the supplication suspect — or

[1] Leeman L. Perkins, 'Musical Patronage at the Royal Court of France under Charles VII and Louis XI (1422–83)', *JAMS* 37 (1984), 507–66.
[2] Pamela Starr, 'Rome as the Centre of the Universe: Papal Grace and Music Patronage', *EMH* 11 (1992), 223–62 at 231.

worse, invalid.'[3] These facts might indicate that there was an established French court-chancellery spelling of the composer's name.

However, this spelling is counterbalanced by the lifelong transmission of his music under various spellings of the name, including a 'c' before the 'k', from the early transmission of his setting of *O rosa bella* in manuscript Trent 90 up to the motet *Intemerata dei mater* and his polyphonic masses in the Chigi Codex. A presumed autograph signature by the composer is reproduced in Eugène Giraudet, *Les Artistes tourangeaux*: 'Peu de noms ont été aussi défigurés que celui de ce grand musicien et chanteur; ainsi, on l'a appelé tour à tour Ockenheim, Okekam, Okenghem, Obekhan, Obergan, Olkégen etc.; sa signature, que nous reproduisons ici, donne la véritable orthographe de son nom.'[4] Of about 360 artists and artisans mentioned, Giraudet's book reproduces thirty-three signatures and fourteen marks. Although he indicates the categories of the various documents or the collections from which most of these signatures were reproduced, some of them—among which Ockeghem's signature—are reproduced without further information. Since the document itself has never turned up, doubts about the reliability of the signature have been voiced. However, Ockeghem's presumed signature has a curious feature that underlines, at the very least, the reliability of Giraudet's reproductions: a superficial reading suggests the spelling 'Oekeghem', which, when taken together with Giraudet's commentary, pleads against any suggestion of a nineteenth-century attempt at forgery. It is just this particular ambiguity in the appearance of the signature which was tacitly eliminated in the unreliably traced reproduction of the signature in the catalogue of the Ockeghem exhibition in Dendermonde.[5] Already in the earliest document on Ockeghem (Antwerp, Kathedraalarchief, Register B), from 1443–4, the following versions of his name appear: Johannes okeghem (fo. 106^r), Jo okeghem (fo. 110^v), Jo de *oghe* (deleted) okeghem (fo. 109^r; the same version on fo. 109^v), Jo okegheem (fo. 106^v) and—in a second hand— Jo ockegheem (fo. 111^r).

Dozens of other spellings of his name in French court documents have been listed by Perkins: 'The variety of spellings given for this name is remarkable: Johannes (as well as Jehan) Oekghem, Okeghan, Hockeghen, Hocquergan, Hoiquergan, and perhaps others that have gone unrecognized in the troublesome script of the eighteenth century',[6] and by Michel Brenet: 'Johannes Okeghen, Johannes Hoquegan, Johannes Holreghan, Jehan Okeghan, Jean de Okenghem, Jehan de Ockeghem . . .'.[7] Moreover, recent research in the Archives municipales de Tours by Paula Higgins has brought to light a document which confirms that the spelling 'Ockeghem' was an acceptable orthography of his name in Tours at least in the early 1460s: 'A maistre Jehan de Ockeghem, tresorier en l'eglise monseigneur Saint-Martin de Tours' (Tours, Archives municipales, CC35, fo. 136^v;

[3] Pamela Starr, 'Rome as the Centre of the Universe: Papal Grace and Music Patronage', *EMH* 11 (1992), 223–62 at 231.

[4] Eugène Giraudet, *Les Artistes tourangeaux: Architectes, armuriers, brodeurs, émailleurs, graveurs, orfèvres, peintres, sculpteurs, tapissiers de haute lisse. Notes et documents inédits* (Mémoires de la Société Archéologique de Touraine, 33; Tours, 1885), 312–13.

[5] *Johannes Ockeghem en zijn Tijd* (Oudheidkundige Kring van het Land van Dendermonde, Buitengewone uitgaven, 24; Dendermonde, 1970), p. [3].

[6] 'Musical Patronage', 555 n. 7.

[7] Michel Brenet, 'Jean de Ockeghem, maître de chapelle des rois Charles VII et Louis XI', in *Musique et musiciens de la vieille France* (Paris, 1911), 23 n. 1.

31 Oct. 1461). The payment in question refers to income presented to Ockeghem annually on 31 October for the sale of wine on his barony of Chasteauneuf in Tours. I am grateful to Paula Higgins for sharing this document with me.

Appendix C
In hydraulis: Letter-Values and Golden Sections

Syllables:		Letter-values	Total
10	In hydraulis quondam Pythagora		
	22 111 80 105	318	
10	Admirante melos phtongitates		
	81 60 147	288	
10	Malleorum secus is equora		
	103 64 27 73	267	
10	Per ponderum inequalitates		
	37 100 146	283	
10 [50]	Adinvenit muse quidditates		
	93 55 124	272	1428
10	Epitritum ast hemioliam		
	125 38 81	244	
10	Epogdoum duplam nam perducunt		
	91 63 26 116	296	
11 [10?]	Tessaron penthe convenientiam		
	105 65 136	306	
10	Nec non phtongum et pason adducunt		
	21 40 108 24 61 84	338	
10 *51* [50?]	Monochordi dum genus conducunt		
	108 36 63 109	316	1500
10	Hec Ockeghem cunctis qui precinis		
	16 *64* 85 45 89	299	
10	Galliarum in regis latria		
	89 22 56 58	225	
10 (GS at 124)	Practiculum tue propaginis		
	130 44 118	292	(GS at 3639)
10	Arma cernens quondam per atria		
	31 74 80 37 47	269	
10 [50]	Burgundie ducis in patria		
	97 54 22 62	235	1320
10	Per me Busnoys illustris comitis		
	37 17 *108* 132 84	378	

Syllables:		*Letter-values*	*Total*
10	De Chaurolois indignum musicum		
	9 115 87 94	305	
10	Saluteris tuis pro meritis		
	118 66 46 89	319	
10	Tamquam summum Cephas tropidicum		
	81 94 50 122	347	
10	Vale verum instar Orpheicum		
[50]	*37 74 77 103*	291	1640
201 [200?]			5888

To this author's surprise, even the hypothetical reconstruction of Busnoys's text seems to underline the results of the analyses of the music and its transmission.

First, the letter-value of the complete poem is 5888 or 4 (*23 × 64*), and half of this number appears just before the name 'Ockeghem' (*64*) in line 11 of the poem: 1428 + 1500 + 16 = 2 (*23 × 64*). This division in two equal parts, violating the poem's formal structure, reminds us of the opening phrase of the setting's *secunda pars*, in which the motet's total number of notes 2 (*22 × 37*) in superius, altus, and bassus divides equally into groups of 22 × *37* notes (see Table 9.1). As for the construction of that opening phrase, the symbolic numbers *23* (*9 + 14*), *37*, *64*, and *81* appear to be as fundamental for the construction of the poem as they are for the music, since *37 × 81* (2997) is just inside the letter-value of the word 'Ockeghem' when added to 2 (*23 × 64*), which makes 2944. Secondly, the decasyllabic structure of *In hydraulis*, notwithstanding the problematic syllable structure of line 8 (see pp. 217–18, n. 4), results hypothetically in a total number of 200 syllables; the Golden Section of this number falls between 124 and 76, which marks 'tue propaginis' (123.6 : 76.4). The Golden Section of the letter-values for the complete poem falls between 3639 and 2249 (3638.784 : 2249.216), at the letter 'p' of 'propaginis'. These findings seem to suggest that Busnoys himself accepted the line 'tessaron penthe convenientiam' as decasyllabic.

PART III
ISSUES OF AUTHORSHIP, ATTRIBUTION, AND ANONYMITY IN ARCHIVAL AND MUSICAL SOURCES

10

The Magnificat Group of Antoine Busnoys: Aspects of Style and Attribution

⁂

MARY NATVIG

THE singing of the canticle of the Blessed Virgin Mary, the Magnificat (see the Appendix for text and translation), constituted the high point of the Vespers liturgy in medieval and Renaissance monasteries and collegiate churches. Beginning in the fifteenth century, large numbers of polyphonic Magnificats were copied into Continental manuscripts, particularly those from Italy.[1] The vast majority of these two- and three-voice elaborations were cast either as fauxbourdon or as *alternatim* settings of one of the eight Magnificat tones, with the odd-numbered verses sung in plainchant, and the even-numbered verses in polyphony.

Among extant fifteenth-century settings, the exquisitely crafted Magnificat of Antoine Busnoys is an unusual musical gem, beautiful in all its facets. Unlike the *alternatim* settings, which juxtapose polyphonic and monophonic verses, Busnoys's Magnificat is a thoroughly polyphonic setting with recurring musical sections. This feature alone does not distinguish it from contemporaneous settings, of course, since Dunstable, Dufay, Binchois, Agricola, and Weerbecke, among others, all set at least one Magnificat entirely in polyphony. Rather, the singularity of Busnoys's setting lies in its employment of a regular pattern of various formal delineators—number of voices, mensuration signs, and related musical materials—and his consistent and liberal use of imitation (exceedingly rare in fifteenth-century Magnificat settings). While a purely stylistic analysis of this work would offer many insights into Busnoys's compositional procedures, particularly with regard to imitative technique, my purpose in this study will be to examine four contemporaneous Magnificats that previous scholars have associated with Busnoys and which show certain formal and stylistic similarities to his

---

[1] See Edward R. Lerner, 'The Polyphonic Magnificat in 15th-Century Italy', *Musical Quarterly*, 50 (1964), 444–58 and Winfried Kirsch, 'Magnificat', *New Grove*, xi. 495–7.

own unusual work: (i) the anonymous San Pietro B 80/Milan 2269 Magnificat (hereafter San Pietro);[2] (ii) the anonymous Brussels 5557 Magnificat (hereafter Brussels);[3] 3) the anonymous Lucca Magnificat (hereafter Lucca);[4] and (iv) the *Magnificat tertii toni* attributed to Guillaume Dufay[5] (see Table 10.1).

The Busnoys Magnificat

Busnoys set the twelve verses of the Magnificat (the ten verses from Luke plus two verses of the lesser doxology) reflecting the formal pattern ABCD A′B′ED′ A′B′C′D′ (see Table 10.1). He divided the text into three four-verse segments, each of which presents successive verses in three, two, three, and four voices and in the mensurations O, C, Ф, and O2. No other fifteenth-century Magnificats, apart from the ones that form the basis of this study, show such a varied yet consistently recurrent formal pattern.[6] Most earlier settings consist of only one or two musical units (as in AA′A″. . . or AB A′B′, etc.), scoring for three voices (with some interspersed duos), and at most two mensurations, usually *tempus perfectum* and *tempus imperfectum* (O and C). Furthermore, few works use the diminution sign O2, which Richard Taruskin and Rob Wegman have shown to be a particular favourite of Busnoys's.[7] While younger composers such as Agricola and Weerbecke employ up to four voices, a variety of mensuration signs, and several repeating musical units, they do not utilize a regular patterning of the verses into small groups, nor do they display the sophisticated manner of musical repetition featured in Busnoys's work.

[2] San Pietro B 80, fos. 219ᵛ–224ʳ; Milan 2269, fos. 17ᵛ–20ʳ. For an edition see *Anonimi Magnificat*, ed. Fabio Fano (Archivum Musices Metropolitanum Mediolannese, 7; Milan, 1965). Richard Taruskin includes this work in the appendix of *Busnoys LTW*. The setting appears in two manuscripts containing a large number of Magnificats. Of the fourteen settings in San Pietro B 80, this is the only one not set in *alternatim*. Of the twenty-three Magnificats in Milan 2269, only two are non-*alternatim* settings, this one and the *Magnificat tertii toni* elsewhere attributed to Dufay and included in this study.

[3] Brussels 5557, fos. 62ᵛ–69ʳ. For a facsimile see *Choirbook of the Burgundian Court Chapel: Brussels Koninklijke Bibliotheek, Manuscript 5557*, ed. Rob C. Wegman (Peer, 1989). There is no modern edition of this work, which has been previously discussed in Charles van den Borren, *Études sur le XVᵉ siècle musical* (Antwerp, 1941); Taruskin, *Busnoys LTW*, Commentary; and Reinhard Strohm, *Music in Late Medieval Bruges* (Oxford, 1985), 136.

[4] Lucca 238, fos. 55ʳ–56ᵛ. There is no modern edition of this work, which is discussed in Strohm, *Music in Late Medieval Bruges*, 134–6.

[5] Montecassino 871, fos. 330ʳ–333ʳ (Dufay); San Pietro B 80, fos. 200ᵛ–203ʳ. (anon.); Milan 2269, fos. 8ᵛ–10ʳ (anon.); Trent 89, fos. 165ᵛ–166ʳ (anon.), and Cappella Sistina 15, fos. 95ᵛ–99ʳ (anon). Modern editions of the work can be found in *The Musical Manuscript Montecassino 871*, ed. Isabel Pope and Masakata Kanazawa (Oxford, 1978); *Anonimi Magnificat*, ed. Fano; and Guillaume Dufay, *Opera omnia*, ed. Heinrich Besseler, 6 vols. (CMM 1; Rome, 1951–64), v, no. 36.

[6] The Magnificat settings examined for this study include those by Dunstable, Dufay, Binchois, Feragut, Compère, Agricola, Weerbecke, Obrecht, the San Pietro B 80 anonymous settings, and the Milan 2269 anonymous settings. For further information on the 15th-c. Magnificat see Chris Maas, *Geschiedenis van het meerstemmig Magnificat tot omstreeks 1525* (Groningen, 1967). Unfortunately, this source became available to me only in the final stages of this project.

[7] For more on Busnoys's use of O2 see Richard Taruskin, 'Antoine Busnoys and the *L'Homme armé* Tradition', *JAMS* 39 (1986), 255–93, and Rob C. Wegman, 'Another Mass by Busnoys?', *ML* 71 (1990), 1–24. The isolated instances of this sign in Magnificats other than Busnoys's are found in two anonymous settings in Milan 2269 (nos. 2 and 4 in the Fano edition) and in Compère's *Magnificat primi toni*.

TABLE 10.1. *Comparison of Busnoys's Magnificat with four other settings: formal structure, number of voices, and mensurations*

verse	Busnoys			San Pietro B 80			Brussels 5557			Lucca			Dufay		
1	A	3	O	A	3	O	A	3	O	Xª	?	O	A	3	O
2	B	2	C	B	2	C	B	3	O	A	2	₵	B	2	O
3	C	3	₵	C	3	₵	C	2	C	B	4	₵	C	4	₵
4	D	4	O2	D	4	O2	A	3	O	C	3	C	D	2	₵
5	A'	3	O	B'	2	C	B	3	O	D	2	₵3	A'	3	O
6	B'	2	C	C'	3	₵	D	3	C	A	2	₵	B	2	O
7	E	3	C	E	2	O	A'	3	O	C	3	C	C	4	₵
8	D'	4	O2	D'	4	O2	B	3	O	B	4	₵	D	2	₵
9	A'	3	O	A'	3	O	D	3	C	D	2	₵3	A'	3	O
10	B'	2	C	B'	2	C	A'	3	O	C	3	C	B	2	O
11	C	3	₵	C'	3	₵	B	3	O	A	2	₵	C	4	₵
12	D'	4	O2	D'	4	O2	C	2	C	B	4	₵	D	2	₵

ª Only one voice survives.

In contrast to other Magnificats, in which minor variations between verses serve primarily to accommodate textual or mensural changes while preserving essentially the same music for related verses, Busnoys employs various compositional devices in order to create musically related but not identical verses. The first of these devices, which approximates a 'centonate' procedure, involves the recombination of modular units, wherein musical material from one verse appears essentially unchanged in another verse. For instance, the music for the second hemistich of the opening verse 'anima mea Dominum' (1*b*) returns as the music for the second half of verse 5, 'timentibus eum' (5*b*), and again (slightly modified) at 'Suscepit Israel' (9*a*) (see Ex. 10.1).

Busnoys fashions the B verses (2, 6, 10) and C verses (3 and 11) using a procedure different from the modular one described above. Here all the related verses begin with slightly modified material and resume the identical music only after the first four to eight bars.[8] In the duos (verses 2, 6, and 10) the beginnings of these identical sections are marked with a point of imitation, separating them slightly from their initial, non-identical phrases. In the C verses, however, since the opening material is so similar (for example, the beginning of verse 11 is really only a variation of the beginning of verse 3), the identical sections are not delineated at all, but flow smoothly from an internal cadence with no break in texture.

The four-voice verses (4, 8, and 12) display more complex relationships. Here the melodic material common to all three verses weaves in and out of newly composed material much as a single colour might twist through a densely textured cloth. The ground-plan of each verse is identical, however, with similar cadential patterns and short duos linking the first and second halves.

Busnoys's verse 7, set in fauxbourdon, serves as the focal point for the work, standing out because of its starkly homophonic texture, its clear presentation of the Magnificat tone (otherwise obscured beyond recognition in the other verses),[9] and its virtual absence of melodic material drawn from elsewhere in the work. In addition to its clear texture, the internal organization of verse 7 is also straightforward. A cadence ends the first half of the verse in measure 10, followed by a breve rest in all voices. The second half of the verse begins in measure 12 with the same rhythmic pattern that began the first half. Both halves of the verse become increasingly more complex, melodically and rhythmically, as they approach their cadences. The movement provides a solid and symmetrical centrepiece to the whole.

Verse 7 is not the only movement to reflect such a clear internal structure, since

---

[8] The only exception is the cadential material in verse 6 which differs slightly from its relatives, verses 2 and 10.

[9] Busnoys's Magnificat is based loosely on the sixth Magnificat tone. The tone, when audible, is in the cantus and proceeds at the same rhythmic pace as the other voices. Although it is most clearly presented in verse 7, even there it is embellished both rhythmically and melodically before the two major cadences. In most of the other verses the Magnificat tone is apparent only for the first few notes, if that.

Ex. 10.1. Busnoys, Magnificat: (*a*) verse 1, mm. 1–6; (*b*) verse 5, mm. 9–15; (*c*) verse 9, mm. 1–7

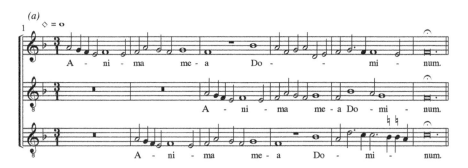

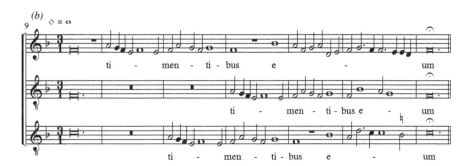

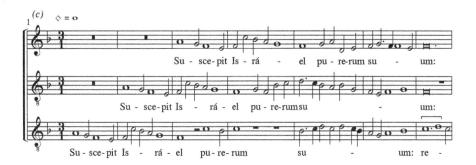

Busnoys usually divides each of the movements into two equal halves, one for each half of the written verse. Except for verses 3 and 11, which flow imperceptibly from one half of the verse to the next, all half verses are marked by a cadence (most often a complete stop) and a rest. Furthermore, all the verses (again except 3, 7, and 11) employ some type of textural demarcation at the half verse. As noted previously, verses 4, 8, and 12 separate the two halves with a short duo amidst a predominantly four-voice texture (the only instances where a three- or four-voice verse drops to two voices). The second halves of the remaining verses begin with a point of imitation.

Indeed, the consistent and liberal use of imitation represents the most striking aspect of Busnoys's Magnificat. With the exception of the homophonic verse 7, every movement begins with a point of imitation lasting approximately two breves. Five of the verses delineate the second half of the verse with another point of imitation, and the duos begin every phrase in such manner. (The duo movements also contain the longest imitations, up to five breves long, similar to the use of imitation in some contemporary mass duos.) While the frequent use of imitation in Busnoys's Magnificat is noteworthy, especially compared with the Magnificats of Dufay, Binchois, and the anonymous works in Milan 2269, its application is entirely regular, with little variety from one verse to the next. Most of the imitative entries are a breve (or its equivalent)[10] apart, except for the initial statements of verses 3 and 11, where the imitating voices follow after two breves. Most imitations occur at the octave (a few at the unison) and the tenor voice leads most often, with the cantus and contratenor occasionally taking the lead. In the four-voice verses and in one set of three-voice verses (3 and 11), only the cantus and tenor take part in the imitation; otherwise, all voices participate.

The melodic character of the Magnificat displays Busnoys's distinctive linear style, with its frequent leaps and sequences projecting a vigorous linear quality. The graceful stepwise motion at the beginning of the opening verse (Ex. 10.1*a*) gradually unfolds rhythmically into a more robust and energetic phrase ending. Rhythmic flow is achieved immediately here by means of semiminim motion on the second half of beat 1, as well as by the following syncopation that propels the line to the final cadence. Melodically, the second half of the statement (mm. 3–6) begins one step higher than the opening, on *bb′*, the highest note of the phrase. Instead of a smooth, stepwise descent, the line jumps down by third and fifth, filling in the leaps with stepwise motion in the opposite direction, thereby creating a brief but energetic sequence and expanding the range from a fourth to a sixth. Both these statements cadence on *f′*, but their respective approaches reveal Busnoys's flexibility in crafting a melodic line.

In verse 9 (Ex. 10.1*c*) Busnoys recasts the same melody through artful variation. The smooth, rolling opening has disappeared along with the semiminim motion, the ascent of a third in measure 2 has been replaced with the leap of a fifth from *f′* to *c″*, and the original two phrases are fused into one. The combination of downward leaps with short ascents (either steps or leaps themselves, as in Ex. 10.1*a*, m. 4) results in a kind of musical undulation that often produces a sequence. This, and the ascending leap that continues in the same direction, are hallmarks of Busnoys's vigorous style (see Ex. 10.2).

---

[10] In verses 4, 8, and 12 the imitative voice follows after three breves, but since the breve in O2 is equal to the former semibreve in O, the actual duration is that of the previous breve.

Ex. 10.2. Busnoys, Magnificat, verse 4, mm. 1–4

The duos often exhibit a type of varying contour contrasting the elegant and the robust (see Ex. 10.3). Here the middle statement of verse 2, 'spiritus meus', hovers gently around *c'*, with the only hint of what is to come foreshadowed in the upward expansions to *f'* and then to *g'*. The upper range, however, appears suddenly at the beginning of the next phrase, 'in Deo salutari meo'. This second line is fashioned with strength and energy, evidenced by its leaps and sequences. Note in particular the quick descending dip from *c''* to *e'* and back again at the beginning of 'salutari meo', and the cambiata figures, imitating each other in both voices, sequencing downward towards the cadence as the initial note of each figure traces the descent: *c''*, *a'*, *g'* to the cadence on *f'* (mm. 22 to end).

Ex. 10.3. Busnoys, Magnificat, verse 2, mm. 10–26

Ex. 10.3. *cont.*

Busnoys's melodies often climb swiftly up and down an octave in various ways. In measures 5–10 of verse 4 (Ex. 10.4), the contratenor falls gracefully from its highest note with two minims propelling the descent, both from the *f′* itself and from its temporary resting-point on *b♭*. The ascent, on the other hand, moves almost ploddingly back up the scale, after the initial leap of a third. The climb into

Ex. 10.4. Busnoys, Magnificat, verse 4, mm. 5–10, contratenor [1]

the higher register, however, does create a certain tension in preparation for the cadence. In general, the beginnings of Busnoys's melodic lines are often more graceful than the endings, which use more vigorous devices. In verse 3 (see Ex. 10.5) the juxtaposition of two expanding arches (the first to *d″*, the second to *e″*)

Ex. 10.5. Busnoys, Magnificat, verse 3, mm. 8–10, cantus

forms the basis for a long, slightly undulating melody, somewhat less dramatic than the extreme sweep seen above. Even here, however, Busnoys's stamp of vigour is applied to the second arch with its leap from *g′* to *c″*, which continues its upward path until it reaches the climax of the phrase.

This procedure, wherein one phrase or part of a phrase is expanded up a step in the next phrase, is typical of Busnoys. We have seen it already in the beginning of Ex. 10.3. It is at work again in verses 5 and 9, where the filled-in fourth at the end of the first statement forms the basis for the next phrase, and is expanded up to *c″* in the following one (see Ex. 10.6).

Ex. 10.6. Busnoys, Magnificat, verse 5, mm. 3–9, cantus

Et mi - se - ri - cor - di - a e - jus a pro - ge - ni-

e in pro - ge - ni - es:

One final observation on Busnoys's Magnificat concerns the musical units comprising verses 3 and 11, which stand apart from the other verses in matters of form and style. These are the only movements that do not delineate the half verse, and only two of the three voices join in imitation—with the entry after two breves instead of the usual one. Also in these verses the contratenor drops below the tenor, actually functioning as a contratenor bassus, while in the other verses *a 3*, the contratenor takes its usual place in the tenor range or slightly above. The final cadences of these verses, typical fifteenth-century cantus–tenor cadences with an octave leap in the contratenor, differ significantly from the more archaic sound-ing double-leading-note cadences found in verses 1, 5, 7, and 9. Furthermore, the melodic lines are somewhat quicker, more syncopated, and more playful than elsewhere in the work. Altogether, these verses are reminiscent of Busnoys's chansons, several of which employ a bass-functioning contratenor and limit the imitations to the upper two voices only.[11] Even the ends of the verses, with their parallel cadences, first to A, then to F, recall the first and second endings (although here sung consecutively) of Busnoys's bergerettes.

---

[11] e.g. *A qui vens tu tes coquilles* (*Mellon Chansonnier*, no. 10), *A une dame* (no. 5), and *Le corps s'en va*, second half (no. 21). See also Catherine Brooks, 'Antoine Busnois, Chanson Composer', *JAMS* 6 (1953), 111–35.

The 'Busnoys' Magnificat Group

The Anonymous San Pietro Magnificat

Charles Hamm considered this Magnificat 'a virtual twin to the Busnoys Magnificat' on the basis of its 'alternation of verses set for two, three and four voices, its canonic beginning, its use of the uncommon signature O2 and other details'.[12] Close comparison of the two works corroborates Hamm's conclusion. The overall structure of this anonymous work, including the precise alternation of the number of voices, mensurations, and musical units is indeed almost identical with Busnoys's setting (cf. Table 10.1). As in Busnoys's setting, verse 7 forms the centrepiece of the work, shares no repeated material with the other verses, and features an entirely homophonic texture. Unlike Busnoys's setting, though, the Magnificat tone is less clearly audible and the movement is explicitly marked as a 'duo' in both sources, rather than as 'fauxbourdon'; closer examination, however, reveals that a fauxbourdon voice could easily be accommodated.

Beyond the similarities in large-scale design, the composer of the San Pietro Magnificat used many of the same compositional techniques as Busnoys (and in almost the same movements) in constructing musically related verses. Furthermore, imitation figures as pervasively in this anonymous setting as in Busnoys's work, with somewhat less frequency, but more variety with regard to leading voice and temporal distance between entrances.

Melodic vigour, sequences, and wide-spanned arcs are all part of the linear writing in this anonymous setting, and the composer took pains just as carefully to mask the original tone as did Busnoys, with the only vestiges of it occurring, if at all, at the beginning of the verses. If Busnoys himself did not write this Magnificat, it can only represent the work of an extremely skilful imitator.

The Anonymous Brussels Magnificat

Several scholars have also considered the Brussels Magnificat a potential work of Busnoys since both are set entirely in polyphony, both paraphrase the plainsong, and both repeat musical sections to help produce unity.[13] And yet, the work seems a much less convincing example of Busnoys's style as manifested in his known Magnificat. First, the formal structure differs (see Table 10.1). While

---

[12] Charles Hamm, 'The Manuscript San Pietro B 80', *Revue belge de musicologie*, 14 (1960), 45. See the facsimile of the manuscript, *Vatican City, Biblioteca Apostolica Vaticana, MS San Pietro B 80*, ed. Christopher Reynolds (New York, 1986).

[13] Gustave Reese, *Music in the Renaissance* (rev. edn., New York, 1959), 108. Charles van den Borren tentatively attributed the work to Busnoys, saying: 'Certes, ce n'est pas le premier venu a composé ce magnificat d'allure si déliée; et, nous tenons à le redire, il ne serait nullement impossible que Busnois en soit l'auteur, encore que, ainsi qu'on va le voir par le second magnificat du codex 5557, qui lui appartient sans conteste, le maître ait une tendance à la complication dont il n'y a guère de trace dans l'œuvre que nous venons d'examiner'; *Études*, 216.

Busnoys and the anonymous composer of the San Pietro setting arranged the musical repetitions into three groups of four, the Brussels Magnificat (col. 3) organizes them into four groups of three, like Dufay's *Magnificat octavi toni*.[14] Scored mainly for three voices, the work employs only perfect and imperfect mensurations, aspects more typical of Magnificat settings of the first half of the fifteenth century. Only four of the verses have a definite break in all voices at the half verse, unlike both Busnoys's and the San Pietro settings, which consistently articulate the two hemistichs of the text.

In the Brussels Magnificat, verses 2, 5, 8, and 11 are virtually identical, exhibiting none of the clever melodic variations evident in the musically related verses of Busnoys's or the San Pietro Magnificat.[15] For example, verses 3 and 12 are identical, as are verses 6 and 9. An interesting relationship exists, however, between these two pairs of verses in that the first three measures of verses 3 and 12 are taken over by the cantus at the beginning of verses 6 and 9 (Ex. 10.7*a–b*). Busnoys's Magnificat exhibits a similar technique of sharing melodic material between two otherwise unrelated verses, occurring at the mid-point in verses 9 and 10 (and their related verses; see Ex. 10.8).

Ex. 10.7. Brussels Magnificat: (*a*) verse 3, mm. 1–5; (*b*) verse 9, mm. 1–4

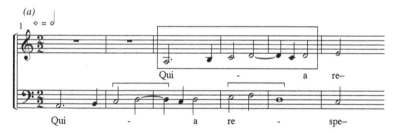

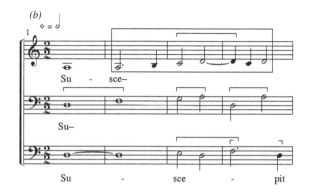

---

[14] Dufay, *Opera omnia*, v, no. 34. The formal structure is: ABC DBC DBC DBC.
[15] There is only a minute rhythmic change at the cadence in verse 2.

Ex. 10.8. Busnoys, Magnificat: (*a*) verse 9, mm. 9–10, cantus; (*b*) verse 10, mm. 15–16, cantus

re - cor - da - tus

A - bra - ham

The composer of the Brussels Magnificat also employed a somewhat modified version of Busnoys's modular method for verses 1, 4, 7, and 10. Unlike Busnoys, however, he used only the first six measures of verse 1, rather than the entire verse, and inserted them at the beginning of the related movements, rather than at the mid-point. He integrated verse 1 material smoothly into the new verses with no break in texture (unlike Busnoys's modular verses), and the division between old and new material does not mark the beginning of the half verse, as in the Busnoys and San Pietro settings.

Imitation also appears less consistently in the Brussels Magnificat than in either of the previously discussed works. Four verses employ brief initial imitations between two of the three voices and none makes use of it at the half verse. The duos, as always, have the most extensive imitations, one of which is nearly canonic. But even these duos differ from those of Busnoys and the San Pietro composer. In the first place, at the half verse, instead of imitation, a more homophonic style pervades. In addition, the Brussels duos are nearly three times as long as Busnoys's and cadences are further apart. Their melodic lines, though full of leaps, lack both the direction and the conciseness of the melodies in Busnoys's duets. Conspicuously absent from this work are sequences, cambiata figures, and drives to the cadence, the hallmarks of the melodic style of both Busnoys's and the San Pietro setting.

A number of other striking differences distinguish the Brussels setting from Busnoys's work. The extremely low cantus range spans a twelfth from *d* to *a'*. Since Busnoys's cantus lies a seventh above this, between *c'* and *e''*, it seems unlikely that these works were written for the same group of singers, although this factor alone does not preclude Busnoys's authorship (cf. the cantus of *Anima mea liquefacta est*). Moreover, none of the movements of the Brussels setting employs a contratenor bassus, as does Busnoys's. On the other hand, the sparing treatment of the Magnificat tone, including the use of only the first few notes at the opening of several verses, calls to mind both the Busnoys and the San Pietro setting. Despite a few common elements with Busnoys's securely attributed work, there is no sufficiently compelling reason to consider the Brussels Magnificat a work of Busnoys.

The Anonymous Lucca Magnificat

Reinhard Strohm described a Magnificat fragment from the Lucca Choirbook that shares certain characteristics with Busnoys's setting and noted that if the criteria for attributing to him the San Pietro and Brussels Magnificats were valid, then the Lucca Magnificat must also be regarded as Busnoys's.[16] As reconstructed by Strohm, the work consists of repeating polyphonic units governed by a changing number of voices (two, three, and four), four different mensuration signs (O, ₵, C, ₵3), and recurring musical units (see Table 10.1).[17] While the alternation of musical material in this work is not as regular as in Busnoys's Magnificat, this is not its most significant departure from Busnoys's setting. The two most conspicuous differences between the two works are: (i) the presentation of the Magnificat tone throughout Lucca in long notes in either the cantus or tenor voice,[18] and (ii) the virtual absence of imitation (although the work is not complete, there are at least two voices for most verses). Furthermore, like the Brussels setting, the Lucca fragment has a much lower cantus range than Busnoys's attributed Magnificat. Despite Strohm's assessment of its 'overall impression of . . . astounding variety, as well as great melodic and rhythmic energy',[19] the work does not compare favourably with Busnoys's Magnificat or the San Pietro setting in this regard. Though exhibiting Busnoys's typical vigour in its successive leaps and octave arcs, the overall melodic style of Lucca lacks the sequence-laden, cadence-directed lines so strongly characteristic of the settings by Busnoys and the San Pietro composer.

In summary, the three Magnificats examined here each bear in some way a resemblance to Busnoys's known setting. The San Pietro setting is very likely to be the work of Antoine Busnoys. The cases for the Brussels and Lucca Magnificats are less convincing. Although based on a repetitive multi-movement design, these works exhibit significant departures from Busnoys's known setting. Neither uses imitation as extensively as Busnoys's work, nor does either setting incorporate so many of the same formal techniques apparent in both Busnoys's and the San Pietro Magnificats. The more prolix linear writing lacks the rhythmic drive and motivic organization of Busnoys's energetic melodies. Furthermore, the undisguised appearance of the Magnificat tone in the Lucca fragment deviates from Busnoys's treatment of plainchant cantus firmi in general. Though one

---

[16] Strohm, *Music in Late Medieval Bruges*, 136.

[17] My thanks to Professor Strohm for making available to me his diplomatic transcription of the Lucca Magnificat.

[18] Strohm, *Music in Late Medieval Bruges*, 135.

[19] Ibid.

cannot entirely exclude the possibility that Busnoys composed these two works, a tentative attribution based on a stylistic comparison with Busnoys's known Magnificat would seem at best premature.

The Dufay Magnificat

The potential relationship of Busnoys's Magnificat to the setting attributed to Dufay in Montecassino 871,[20] thus far unexamined by previous scholars, warrants closer scrutiny. Commentators have noted the work's marked difference from Dufay's other Magnificat settings as well as its absence from the main source of Dufay Magnificats, Modena α. X.1.11 (ModB).[21] David Fallows considered the piece 'one of the few surviving works that might reasonably be ascribed to the last fifteen years of Dufay's life', because of its 'bolder use of open textures and a more relaxed mastery of supple line'. He does, however, note the unreliability of Montecassino 871's Dufay ascriptions.[22] In the light of the uncertainty about the attribution it may prove useful to re-examine the work given what we know about both Busnoys's Magnificat and the San Pietro setting, its 'twin'.

The formal structure of Dufay's piece closely matches that of both the Busnoys and the San Pietro settings: four musical units repeated three times (see Table 10.1, col. 5).[23] Although this Magnificat lacks the verse 7 centrepiece, verses 3, 7, and 11 (marked as C) share two important traits with Busnoys's verse 7. They are the only homophonic verses in an otherwise highly contrapuntal and imitative composition, and they present the Magnificat tone clearly, but without the long notes of the Lucca fragment. While the Magnificat tone in these verses is slightly more ornamented than in Busnoys's verse 7, the compositional procedure is similar: plainchant in the cantus, moving equally with the other voices, within a homophonic texture.

[20] See above, n. 5 for other sources of this work.

[21] 'Stylistically it is different from the other Magnificats by Dufay in that there is more frequent and extensive use of imitation (another Magnificat by him with imitational technique is the Magnificat in Tone VIII, which, however, also uses the old-fashioned technique of fauxbourdon). Our piece differs also in that it employs more complex rhythmic patterns in the melodies, contrasting notes of different value in wider variety; furthermore the cantus firmus is not consistently utilized and in fact often disregarded. The last feature is particularly important, since it was just for that reason that the two sources, Trent 89 and San Pietro B 80, could assign the setting for both Tones III and IV'; Pope and Kanazawa, *The Musical Manuscript Montecassino 871*, 603.   [22] David Fallows, *Dufay* (London, 1982), 150.

[23] A significant difference between the format of this setting and the other Magnificats we have examined is that the kindred verses in this setting are not only related, they are identical. Cappella Sistina 15 is the only source in which all the verses are written out separately. In Milan 2269 and Trent 89 the texts of the paired verses are grouped together and written under the same music. Montecassino 871 includes only the first five verses of the work and San Pietro B 80 contains only the odd-numbered verses (implying an alternatim performance). Both Trent 89 and Cappella Sistina 15 have an additional substitute setting for the seventh verse, which Pope and Kanazawa consider to be an 'anonymous appendix' to the piece, differing stylistically from the original Magnificat. It is obvious, then, that with the exception of verses 1, 5, and 9 mentioned above, none of the clever and subtle compositional techniques used for variety by Busnoys and the composer of the San Pietro B 80 Magnificat would be possible in this setting. Instead this composer (perhaps to save time?), has composed only four musical units for twelve verses of text.

Dufay's duos (verses 2, 6, and 10, marked as B in Table 10.1) are structurally similar to Busnoys's in their presentation of four points of imitation at the beginning of the phrases 'Et exultavit', 'spiritus meus', 'in Deo', and 'salutari meo'. In both settings the contratenor initiates all points of imitation, and the cantus always overlaps the beginning of the new imitation, except at the half verse, when both voices cadence together to create a break in texture. Moreover, the familiar modular procedure found in Busnoys's and the San Pietro setting, wherein verse 1 reappears in the second half of verses 5 and 9, also appears in Dufay's setting.

The work differs from Busnoys's setting, and indeed from most fifteenth-century settings, in that it is based on both the third and fourth Magnificat tones (however, only Trent 89 labels it as such). Therefore, the finals alternate between A and E and medial cadences occur on C, A, and D. None of the works discussed above manifests such a variety of cadential pitches, especially for the *finalis*. Although none of Busnoys's other Latin-texted works exhibits such regular alternation of cadential pitches, he does employ transposed and untransposed versions of the same chant in his two settings of *Regina caeli*, wherein alternating cadential pitches (as dictated by the plainchant versions) assume nearly equal importance until the very end of the piece, at which point Busnoys seems almost reluctantly to choose a final. In both this Magnificat, with its alternating finals on A and E, and in Busnoys's *Regina caeli* settings, the composer(s) appear to be manipulating the hierarchical expectations of the modal final. While these expectations are clearly not as strong as they were to become in tonal harmony, their presence in the modal language of the late fifteenth century is strong (at least to modern ears).

Vestiges of the mode 3 *repercussio* on C can be heard in several of the movements (verses 3, 5, 7, 9, and 11), resulting in a melodic style in these verses somewhat more declamatory than that of Busnoys's Magnificat. The composer created smoother, more gently flowing lines, without the sequential, cadential drives typical of Busnoys. Setting three verses to the same homophony (3, 7, and 10) instead of just one (verse 7) also differs from Busnoys's customary emphasis on a continuously contrapuntal texture. That is not to say that Busnoys never writes homophonically. One need only recall that his short motets *Noel, noel* and *Conditor alme siderum* resemble, at least in texture and rhythmic pace, the four-voice verses of this Magnificat.

Despite certain departures from Busnoys's usually typically vigorous melodic style, several melodic and harmonic aspects of the setting do recall Busnoys's Magnificat. For example, the duo used for verses 4, 8, and 12 (marked D in Table 10.1; and see Ex. 10.9) is imitative and illustrates several hallmarks of Busnoys's melodic style. Note the sequentially ascending thirds followed by the descending fifth in measure 14 (similar to the undulating line in Busnoys's verse 1) and the long string of parallel sixths (in mm. 16–17), a technique Busnoys used quite

Ex. 10.9. Dufay, *Magnificat tertii toni*, verse 4, mm. 13–22

regularly (as did Dufay occasionally) in his chansons and Latin-texted works alike.[24] In addition, the octave leap in the superius of verse 1 is typical of Busnoys, who often writes an octave leap in the top voice (usually returning by step) within the first twenty measures or so of either his motets or mass sections. Finally, this Magnificat, like Busnoys's work and the San Pietro setting, has a predominance of cadences without the usual suspension figure, which helps to create at least a moderate amount of flow from verse to verse. There are no double leading-note cadences in the work; in verses for more than two voices the final cadences have an octave leap in the middle voice and in medial cadences the lowest-sounding voice leaps down a fifth.

---

[24] The use of parallel intervals is not unique to Busnoys, of course. His penchant for them, however, is often cited as a component of his style. See e.g. Brooks, 'Antoine Busnois', 117 and Martin Picker, 'Busnois, Antoine', *New Grove*, iii. 504–8.

Apart from their formal structures, perhaps the most obvious stylistic connection between this work and the settings by Busnoys and the anonymous composer of the San Pietro Magnificat is its comparatively frequent use of imitation. Except for verse 1 and the four-voice verses (like San Pietro), all remaining verses begin with imitation, and several verses use it to delineate the half verse. As we have seen, the duos contain extensive imitations. Even in the three-voice verses 5 and 9 only two of the three voices imitate, two breves apart, as in verses 3 and 11 of Busnoys's authentic Magnificat, and verses 3, 6, and 11 of the San Pietro setting.

The last observation to be made regarding the Magnificat concerns the apparent structural 'weakness' implied by ending such a multi-verse work with a duo. Admittedly, Busnoys's known setting looks and sounds more coherent, with its central homophonic verse and its final verse in full texture. But there may be a method behind this Magnificat that subtly incorporates the drive to the cadence so common in late fifteenth-century music. The second duo in this work (comprising verses 4, 8, and 12), though diminutive in one respect, is actually the most complex, rhythmically intricate, and energetically charged of all the verses. The rhythmic pace begins slowly and somewhat regularly, quickly accelerating towards highly subdivided, syncopated lines that more than anything else remind us of the musical language of Busnoys.

How are we to assess this work with regard to its stylistic affinities with the work of Busnoys and its divergence from other Magnificat settings by Dufay? In many ways this Magnificat bears little resemblance to the three other Magnificats attributed with any certainty to Dufay. His *Magnificat sexti toni* is structurally similar (ABCD EBCD EBCD) but remains in three voices throughout, and lacks both the 'centonate' technique and imitation. His *Magnificat octavi toni* (ABC DBC DBC DBC) has somewhat more in common with this last setting since it uses short bits of imitation and some shared material between the A and D verses, with the A material found at the end of the D verses. Neither of these techniques, however, is as fully developed as in the Magnificat in question. Furthermore, Dufay's *Magnificat octavi toni* alternates between two and three voices and four of its verses are fauxbourdon settings. His *Magnificat quinti toni*, a three-voice *alternatim* setting, also uses what appears to be an early version of the 'centonate' method, but here, as in the *Magnificat octavi toni*, the shared material is not identical. Although the same polyphonic construct for verse 1 reappears in the cadence at the end of each of the following polyphonic verses, the melodic variation is significant and the formal structure of these verses is less well defined than in Busnoys's Magnificat.

The striking departures from Dufay's customary procedure in this Magnificat raise a number of thorny questions that cannot be satisfactorily answered at this time: does the *Magnificat tertii toni* represent the culmination of Dufay's experimentation with formal manipulation in Magnificat settings, and did it as such influence Busnoys's setting(s)? Conversely, did Busnoys's setting(s), with its reliance on imitation and formal clarity, stimulate the apparent innovations in Dufay's piece? Or, complicating the issue still further, is it conceivable that the attribution to Dufay in Montecassino 871 is incorrect, and that Busnoys or an imitator actually wrote the piece?

The musical influence of Dufay on Busnoys (or vice versa) has never been explored in detail except with regard to the *L'homme armé* debate, possibly because of the perceived generational difference between the composers, or because of Dufay's generally more transparent and more delicate style. If Dufay, like Busnoys, had a penchant for irregular, almost erratic, rhythms and melodies and intricate textures, perhaps it was tempered by his Italian sensibilities. Only in his later works, especially in the duos (for instance in *Missa Ecce ancilla domini*), do we see the rhythmic complexity and vigour typically associated with Busnoys. Here Dufay, like Busnoys, uses phrase-generated imitations, complex syncopa-tions, sequences, and rhythmic drives to the cadence. On the other hand, Busnoys himself did not consistently write in rhythmic 'high gear', so to speak, as his homophonic motets like *Noel noel*, *Ad cenam agni*, *Alleluia verbum caro factum est*, and his (probably) late work, the *Patrem de Village*, clearly remind us.

The question of influence between Dufay and Busnoys is less clear than schol-ars have assumed, mainly on the basis of Tinctoris's statement which names Ockeghem, Regis, Busnoys, Caron, and Faugues as having been 'taught' by Dunstable, Binchois, and Dufay.[25] And yet the careers of both composers over-lapped chronologically, raising the possibility of personal and musical interac-tions between them. Although questions of stylistic influence do not necessarily depend on biographical contact, one logical time-frame for Busnoys and Dufay to have met personally was during the autumn of 1468, after Busnoys's compos-itional style was clearly established, judging from his motet *In hydraulis*, written sometime before 1467. In September 1468, Busnoys, though not yet in the regu-lar employ of the Burgundian court, was called into the army to accompany Charles the Bold to Péronne.[26] On the way from Péronne to Liège, Charles the Bold and King Louis XI stopped in Cambrai, and Charles lodged only a few blocks from Dufay's house. The two composers might have had an exchange at that time, and, as Craig Wright speculated, perhaps even Ockeghem, chaplain to Louis XI, was along as well.[27] We also know that seven years later, shortly after Dufay's death, a new mass and a Magnificat by Busnoys were entered into the

---

[25] Johannes Tinctoris, *The Art of Counterpoint*, trans. Albert Seay (MSD 5; [Rome], 1961), 15.
[26] Paula Marie Higgins, 'Antoine Busnois and Musical Culture in Late Fifteenth-Century France and Burgundy' (Ph.D. diss., Princeton University, 1987), 74, and ead., '*In hydraulis* Revisited: New Light on the Career of Antoine Busnois', *JAMS* 39 (1986), 36–86 at 46.
[27] Craig Wright, 'Dufay at Cambrai: Discoveries and Revisions', *JAMS* 28 (1975), 208–9.

choirbooks of Cambrai Cathedral;[28] it does not seem too far-fetched to suggest that Dufay had known these works before his death.

While such speculation cannot bring us any closer to knowing for certain who wrote this Magnificat, it may help to explain why the work differs so significantly from Dufay's other Magnificat settings. In spite of the differences between this work and the known Magnificat(s?) of Busnoys there appear to be compelling reasons to group these two works together, and perhaps to re-examine the piece's existing attribution to Dufay. Although the striking stylistic differences between this work and Dufay's other Magnificats may well result from its later date of composition,[29] as Fallows proposed, it is formally more closely aligned with the Magnificat of Busnoys and the San Pietro Magnificat, both of them unusual works for their time.

What can we say, then, regarding the authorship of the 'Dufay' Magnificat? First, a somewhat tenuous attribution to Dufay has been weakened by evidence that it manifests musical traits possibly unique to Busnoys. While premature at this point, an attribution to Busnoys deserves serious consideration, especially as more information regarding the style and chronology of both composers continues to emerge. For instance, Edward R. Lerner proposed several years ago that late fifteenth-century Italian composers, although adopting the florid polyphony of the Northern composers in mass and motet, preferred a more declamatory style in their Magnificat settings.[30] If Busnoys wrote this work, one wonders whether geographical tastes or preferences might account for the more homophonic texture in this piece as compared with his known Magnificat. Several scholars have proposed an Italian sojourn for Busnoys, and although the evidence is circumstantial, at best, it could account for certain stylistic anomalies. On the other hand, if this piece is indeed the work of Dufay, then the nature of his relationship with Busnoys, whether personal or musical, clearly merits further exploration, because the similarity between these two Magnificats seems too close to be explained purely as coincidence.

For the time being, then, the authorship of the 'Dufay' Magnificat remains open and deserving of further study. While my own investigation suggests that it may be the work of Busnoys or an imitator, rather than Dufay, more conclusive evidence beyond precarious stylistic indications needs to surface. Until then, the question of authorship remains in the state of 'informed ambiguity' with which those of us who study fifteenth-century music have become all too familiar.

[28] Ibid.
[29] Of Dufay's later works, the chanson *Adieu m'amour* most closely resembles this Magnificat regarding its use and type of imitation. His motet from 1464, *Ave regina caelorum*, has some imitation consisting of either short snatches, or long canonic imitations, usually between only two voices.
[30] Lerner, 'The Polyphonic Magnificat', 44–5.

Appendix
Text and Translation of the Magnificat (Luke 1: 46–55)

1. [Magnificat] *Anima mea Dominum.
2. Et exultavit spiritus meus *in Deo salutari meo.
3. Quia respexit humilitatem ancillae suae: *ecce enim ex hoc beatam me dicent omnes generationes.
4. Quia fecit mihi magna qui potens est: *et sanctum nomen ejus.
5. Et misericordia ejus a progenie in progenies * timentibus eum.
6. Fecit potentiam in brachio suo: *dispersit superbos mente cordis sui.
7. Deposuit potentes de sede, *et exaltavit humiles.
8. Esurientes implevit bonis: *et divites dimisit inanes.
9. Suscepit Israel puerum suum, *recordatus misericordiae suae.
10. Sicut locutus est ad patres nostros, *Abraham et semini ejus in secula.
11. Gloria Patri, et Filio, *et Spiritui Sancto.
12. Sicut erat in principio, et nunc, et semper, *et in secula seculorum. Amen.

1. My soul doth magnify the Lord,
2. And My spirit hath rejoiced in God my Saviour.
3. For He hath regarded the low estate of his handmaiden; for behold from henceforth all generations shall call me blessed.
4. For He that is mighty hath done to me great things; and holy is His name.
5. And His mercy is on them that fear him from generation to generation.
6. He hath shown strength with His arm; He hath scattered the proud in the imagination of their hearts.
7. He hath put down the mighty from their seats, and exalted them of low degree.
8. He hath filled the hungry with good things and the rich He hath sent empty away.
9. He hath helped His servant Israel, in remembrance of His mercy;
10. As He spoke to our fathers, to Abraham and to his seed for ever.
11. Glory be to the Father and to the Son and to the Holy Spirit,
12. As it was in the beginning, now and ever shall be, world without end. Amen.

11

Resjois toi terre de France/Rex pacificus: An 'Ockeghem' Work Reattributed to Busnoys

Ꮥ❦ ❦Ꮣ

ANDREA LINDMAYR-BRANDL

THE image of Ockeghem as the great French court composer and of Busnoys as a lesser Burgundian master has dominated music historiography for generations. Despite their inexactitude, such classifications nevertheless serve to order our impressions, our experiences, and our knowledge. A similarly long-standing music historiographical bias towards works of known authorship has made it much more difficult to survey a repertory of anonymous compositions than a set of works classified as belonging to Josquin, Morton, Dufay, Busnoys, or Ockeghem. A single outstanding composition amidst the mass of anonymous works that still make up about half the late medieval repertory has little opportunity to draw attention to itself and consequently fades into music historical oblivion.

It is therefore hardly surprising that once an anonymous composition becomes potentially linked with a renowned composer our interest in it inevitably intensifies. Such is the case with the anonymously transmitted *Resjois toi terre de France/Rex pacificus*, which David Fallows signalled as a possible work of Ockeghem.[1] As its title makes clear, *Resjois toi* is an occasional composition referring to an explicitly political situation. The French and Latin texts of this song-motet stress 'l'honneur royal' and celebrate newly gained peace and freedom under the French king:[2]

The nucleus of this paper can be found in my thesis: Andrea Lindmayr, *Quellenstudien zu den Motetten von Johannes Ockeghem* (Neue Heidelberger Studien zur Musikwissenschaft, 16; Laaber, 1990), 69–72. I wish to thank the Musikwissenschaftliche Seminar of the University of Basle and Professor Wulf Arlt for providing a congenial working atmosphere and the possibility of using the excellent microfilm collection and library.

[1] David Fallows, 'Johannes Ockeghem: The Changing Image, the Songs and a New Source', *Early Music*, 12 (1984), 218–30 at 222.

[2] After Isabel Pope and Masakata Kanazawa, *The Musical Manuscript Montecassino 871* (Oxford, 1978), 626.

Superius:

Resjois toi terre de France!	Rejoice, o land of France!
Voici ton roy prest de venir.	Behold thy king, ready to come;
Aves espoir d'estre plus franche	Hope now to be free once again
En son tres joyeulx advenir.	With his joyful arrival!
C'est celuy qui fera unir	It is he who will cause to unite
Tout parcial;	Every part (of his land)
Car de son droit doibt obtenir	For as his right he should obtain
L'onneur royal.	The royal honour.

Contratenor altus:

I. Rex pacificus magnificatus est	The peace-making king is exalted;
II. Cuius vultum desiderat	The whole world desires to see his
[universa terra].	face.
III. Vivat rex in aeternum.	Long live the king to all eternity!

The historical events that inspired this musical setting would appear to fit very well into the last period of the Hundred Years War, when Charles VII recaptured, in quick succession, a number of French territories from English occupying armies. The conquest of the south-western province of Guyenne and the seaport of Bordeaux on 19 October 1453 marked the end of this dark period in French history.[3]

Some fifty years ago, André Pirro connected *Resjois toi* with the accession of Louis XI, who was crowned king in Rheims on 15 August 1461.[4] More recently, Leeman Perkins proposed a still later date,[5] suggesting that the motet might have been written for a triumphal visit of Louis XI to some newly regained territory in the mid 1460s or early 1470s. During that period, Louis successfully reunited his kingdom by fighting not only against the Burgundians, but also against one of several power-hungry dukes of his own realm, who repeatedly tried to secede from the crown.[6] Whatever the exact dating of *Resjois toi*, David Fallows had every reason to suppose that the piece was written by the only composer then known to have been working in the French royal chapel, Johannes Ockeghem.[7]

The transmission pattern of this exceptional composition reveals only two surviving sources: Montecassino 871 and Pixérécourt. The former, presumably a southern Italian source copied by a Benedictine monk and dating from 1480–1500, contains a mixed repertory of international and local, especially Spanish, music.[8]

---

[3] On the Hundred Years War see, among others, Jean Favier, *La Guerre de Cent Ans* (Paris, 1980).

[4] See André Pirro, 'Un manuscript musical du xvᵉ siècle à Montcassin', *Cassinensia*, 1 (1929), 205–8.

[5] See Pope and Kanazawa, *The Musical Manuscript*, 626 n. 29.

[6] See Paul Murray Kendall, *Louis XI* (London, 1971) and Ilja Mieck, *Die Entstehung des modernen Frankreich, 1450–1610: Strukturen, Institutionen, Entwicklungen* (Stuttgart, 1982).

[7] David Fallows, 'English Song Repertories of the Mid-Fifteenth Century', *Proceedings of the Royal Musical Association*, 103 (1976–7), 67–8; and id., 'Johannes Ockeghem', 222.

[8] Pope and Kanazawa, *The Musical Manuscript*.

Resjois toi appears in the seventh layer of the manuscript, together with a few other political or occasional works.[9] Pixérécourt,[10] also a source geographically removed from the actual political events recounted in the song-motet, was very probably written in Florence, since its decoration and musical readings are close to those of the well-known chansonnier Florence 229.[11] Allan Atlas, who considered Pixérécourt a 'pre-central' Florentine source and an important link between the Neapolitan and the 'central' Florentine tradition, dated the manuscript between 1480 and 1484.[12] Its two hundred parchment folios in a rather small format transmit 170 compositions, less than a quarter of them mentioning an author. The rest of the works are anonymous or, as one might suspect from the remnants of letters, have been consigned to anonymity at the hands of careless bookbinders who cropped the margins too closely.

Pixérécourt's scribe copied *Resjois toi* on to two consecutive openings (fos. 43ᵛ–45ʳ). At first glance it appears to be anonymous (see Fig. 11.1). Upon closer scrutiny, however, one discovers an open loop and a black spot to the left of it in the extreme upper margin (see Fig. 11.2). Initially the marking appears insignificant, or in any case too small to permit reconstruction of the name that originally occupied the now-trimmed margin. Theoretically, of course, the composer of *Resjois toi* could be any of the musicians we know from this time, not to mention those about whom we have no knowledge thus far. Nevertheless, it seemed plausible that the name might be the same as one of the composers mentioned elsewhere in the manuscript. This prompted me to copy the existing non-trimmed ascriptions, most of them easily readable, and compare them with the marks on the margin (cf. Figs. 11.2 and 11.3).

In the patchwork of names given in Fig. 11.3, Busnoys's exceeds the others by far, appearing some twenty-one times in a rather consistent calligraphy. Caron's name is given eight times, Ockeghem's three times—in three different spellings!—and Dufay, Cornago, Morton, and Ycart once each. All the names (like the manuscript as a whole) were obviously written by the same hand, an essential factor in permitting the next step of the reconstruction process. By copying the remnants of the ascription of *Resjois toi* onto a transparency and placing it over the different names, one can see that none of the *g*s in the 'Ockeghem' headings fits the open loop of the trimmed ascription of *Resjois toi*. For the same reason one can exclude the names 'Cornago', 'Morton', and 'Caron'. This leaves 'Ycart',

⁹ See Lindmayr, *Quellenstudien*, 67–8 and fig. 13.

¹⁰ The manuscript was described and edited (though not very carefully) by Edward Joseph Pease in 'An Edition of the Pixérécourt Manuscript: Paris, Bibliothèque nationale, fonds fr. 15123' (Ph.D. diss., University of Indiana, 1960).

¹¹ *A Florentine Chansonnier from the Time of Lorenzo the Magnificent: Florence, Biblioteca Nazionale Centrale MS Banco Rari 229*, ed. Howard Mayer Brown (Monuments of Renaissance Music, 7; Chicago and London, 1983), 14–15.

¹² Allan W. Atlas, *The Cappella Giulia Chansonnier (Rome, Biblioteca Apostolica Vaticana, C.G. XIII. 27)*, 2 vols. (Musicological Studies, 27; Brooklyn, 1975), i. 254–5.

FIG. 11.1. *Resjois toi terre de France* (Pixérécourt Chansonnier, fos.43ᵛ–44ʳ)

'Dufay', and finally 'Busnoys'. In this 'play with signs', as we may call it, only the letters of 'Busnoys' fit well, in fact almost perfectly.[13]

FIG. 11.2. Enlarged ascription of *Resjois toi*, from Pixérécourt Chansonnier

The implications of this potential ascription to Busnoys take on greater significance since David Fallows had hesitated to ascribe *Resjois toi* to Ockeghem in the first place:

I am bound to say that the musical evidence seems less than overwhelming: the song has none of the special gestures that make Ockeghem's work so individual . . . Hearing the work has emphatically not deepened my conviction that it is by Ockeghem.[14]

Though troubled by the stylistic evidence, Fallows had no compelling reason at the time to think of an alternative composer. It is now much easier to accept this work as a potential Busnoys composition since Paula Higgins has since brought to light documents that show that he was not only a Burgundian master but also, at an earlier stage of his career, a colleague of Ockeghem at Saint-Martin of Tours, a quintessentially French institution whose titular abbot was the king of France.[15] Thus Busnoys as well as Ockeghem might have been in a position to have received a commission for this occasional work.

Turning now to the music itself (see Ex. 11.1), one sees that the formal structure of *Resjois toi* is what modern scholars have called a 'song-motet': a secular piece with a sacred touch, so to speak. In this case we have the simultaneous combination of a ballade and a cantus-firmus setting, one of the newly created structures in the second half of the fifteenth century that were used for special occasions. The piece is written in four voices, with superius and a contratenor altus carrying full text, and two lower voices bearing only text incipits. The whole composition is divided into two *partes* by a change of mensuration from *tempus perfectum* to *tempus imperfectum*. Moreover, the last section of the *secunda pars* is written in coloration, producing a stretto-like feeling at the end of the composition.

The contratenor altus part, with its Latin text, is the most restricted. Lines 1 and 2 are based on the beginning of the plainsong *Rex pacificus*, the first antiphon at Vespers on Christmas Day (see Ex. 11.2).[16] Line 3 paraphrases another chant

---

[13] Using this rather primitive method one can also obtain clues about other trimmed ascriptions in Pix. For example, with regard to Busnoys's authorship of *Cent mille escus*, the remnants of the letters on fos. 10ᵛ-11ʳ do not fit his name as well as do those in *Resjois toi* because the loop goes in the wrong direction.

[14] Fallows, 'Johannes Ockeghem', 222. [*Ed.*: See also above, Ch. 2 n. 11.]

[15] Paula Higgins, '*In hydraulis* Revisited: New Light on the Career of Antoine Busnois', *JAMS* 39 (1986), 36–86 at 69–76.

[16] For a modern printed source of *Rex pacificus* see *LU* 364.

Fig. 11.3. Composite of ascriptions in Pixérécourt Chansonnier

Ex. 11.1. *Resjois toi terre de France/Rex pacificus*

(1) All sources: *e'*   (2) Pix: *a'*   (3) All sources: *c"*

Ex. 11.1. *cont.*

melody, which is apparently quoted in the first few measures and then partly repeated, a second higher and a second lower respectively. The sequence of notes is too short and insufficiently distinctive to permit conclusive identification of the melody of the plainsong model. Among the possible chant models, one melody for the *Pater noster* corresponds closely.[17] Its second half also resembles the end of the contratenor altus line and similarly ends on *d*. Another candidate, proposed by Jaap van Benthem, is the beginning of a *Benedicamus Domino*, whose cadential passage fits particularly well.[18] But the most promising model has been suggested by Don Giller: the hymn *Pater superni luminis*, sung during the office of 22 July, precisely the death date of Louis XI's father, Charles VII (see Ex. 11.3).[19] Taken as a symbol, this cantus firmus would confirm Pirro's dating, the coronation of the new king.

Whatever the actual plainsong model, the contratenor altus follows the liturgical melodies (marked in Ex. 11.1 with crosses) rather strictly throughout; only cadences are slightly florid and rhythmically sharpened. The *secunda pars* of *Resjois toi* opens in three-voice texture without the cantus firmus-bearing contratenor altus, which enters with text line 3 in measure 25 in steady breves, leading via a cadential phrase to *g*. The final departure from *g*, returning to *d*, is rather simply composed, using sequences and variations on a melodic pattern reminiscent of the opening measures of the superius in the *secunda pars*. Remarkable, too, are the pedal points on *d* closing each of the two *partes*.

In shaping the contratenor altus line the composer must have had in mind the dominating ballade structure demanded by the French text with its characteristic rhyme scheme abab bcbc and the musical form AAB, combined as follows:

formal scheme:	‖: A	:‖	B			coloration
mensuration:	O		C			
phrases:	1–7	8–17	18–24	25–30	31–5	36–42
text lines:	1/3	2/4	5	6	7	8
c.f. text:	1	2	—	3		

The opening section of A fortifies the plagal mode on G: the superius winds gently around *g′*, ascending to the fourth above, passing a cadence on *g′* and proceeding to *c″*. The first internal cadence, in measure 3, involves significant parallel fourths in the two upper voices. Together with the tenor they form a sequence of chords in first inversion, or fauxbourdon. Interspersed three-part sections structure the setting. The low-lying ranges of measures 8–9 have the same function as

---

[17] For a modern printed source of the *Pater noster* in question see *Graduale Triplex* (Paris and Tournai, 1979), 812 (Pater Noster A).

[18] For a modern printed source of the *Benedicamus Domino* in question see *LU* 125.

[19] A modern source for the hymn *Pater superni* can be found in *Antiphonale Monasticum pro diurnis horis* (Tournai, 1934), 975. The chant source as well as the attribution of *Resjois toi* to Busnoys was independently discussed in Don Giller, 'Busnois's Mass Compositions', App. A: 'A Motet-Chanson Newly Attributed to Busnois', unpublished seminar paper, Columbia University, October 1980.

Ex. 11.2. *Rex pacificus* (transposed)

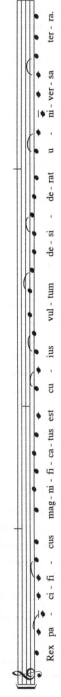

Ex. 11.3. *Resjois toi*: (*a*) beginning of *Rex pacificus*; (*b*) *Resjois toi*, contratenor altus, mm. 25–35, with plainchants *Pater noster, Benedicamus Domino*, and *Pater superni luminis*

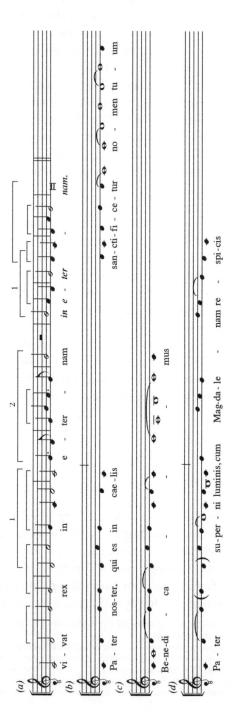

measures 29–30 in the *secunda pars*: they mark the formal mid-points of each *pars* and modulate from C to G. Both these three-voice sections show intricate rhythms and melodically fragmented parts, in the same style as the cadential passages in measures 13–17, and measures 22–3. The final measures of each half of the piece show the same characteristics: three animated voices, with the contratenor altus acting as a sonic filler. Particularly noteworthy is the smooth filling in by the superius of the fifth *g′–d″* in measures 15–16.

Both texted voices have very finely shaped 'top-voice' character, although the higher part can be heard more distinctly. The superius and the contratenor altus are partially set in counterpoint; the contratenor bassus has an extremely wide range and often crosses the contratenor altus and the tenor.

In the same layer as *Resjois toi* Montecassino 871 transmits two other famous song-motets that resemble it in structure and in compositional details: *O tres piteulx*, Dufay's lamentation on the fall of Constantinople to the Turks (datable 1455),[20] and *Mort tu as navré*, Ockeghem's lament on the death of Binchois (*c.*1460).[21] Both compositions have French and Latin texts, liturgical cantus firmi, four-voice texture, two-part structure with a change of mensuration from ternary to binary in the second section, and alternating three- and four-voice passages. *Mort tu as navré* is closer to *Resjois toi* in formal respects. It shows the same ballade pattern AAB, but has three verses. By contrast, *O tres piteulx* is through-composed with six internal sections in each *pars* and about a third again as long. Comparing the range of these three song-motets (see Ex. 11.4), one can recognize that *Resjois toi* is generally about a fourth higher than the other two. Significant for this comparison are the extremely wide ranges of the superius and contratenor bassus of *Resjois toi* (both spanning a twelfth) and the rather low range of the cantus firmus in *Mort tu as navré* (the cantus firmus of each is marked by arrows).

Ex. 11.4. Ranges of (*a*) *Resjois toi*, (*b*) *Mort tu as navré*, and (*c*) *O tres piteulx*

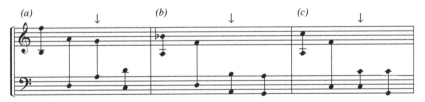

[20] Pope and Kanazawa, *The Musical Manuscript*, no. 102. See also Guillaume Dufay, *Opera omnia*, ed. Heinrich Besseler, 6 vols. (CMM 1; Rome, 1951–64), vi. 19–21.

[21] Ibid., no. 107. See also Johannes Ockeghem, *Collected Works*, iii, ed. Richard Wexler with Dragan Plamenac (Boston, 1992), 77–8. In giving the original four measures of rests in the upper voice at mm. 20 ff. and 30 ff. this new edition brings out more clearly the parallelism of the passages. Pope and Kanazawa turned three measures in ₵ into one large measure in 3/2 and thus condensed three original rests into one modern rest.

Three-voice passages structure all three settings. Ockeghem opened both *partes* of *Mort tu as navré* with a low-range section (the first with four measures, the second only with a single measure). To make the words 'pie Jesu domine' audible at the beginning of the final passage, he lets the upper voice rest again (see Ex. 11.5). Dufay opens the *secunda pars* of *O tres piteulx* with three voices and closes an inner section of the *prima pars* in the same way (mm. 19–21), with a separating and a modulating function (see Ex. 11.6).

Ex. 11.5. Three-voice sections in Ockeghem, *Mort tu as navré*: (*a*) mm. 1–5; (*b*) mm. 20–1; (*c*) mm. 30–2

Cadential passages with parallel fourths can also be found in both the Ockeghem and the Dufay compositions. The passage at measure 26 in *Mort tu as navré* is rhythmically fragmented (see Ex. 11.7*a*). *O tres piteulx* uses this special cadence four times, twice in each part (I: mm. 5–6, m. 25; II: mm. 5–6, m. 11) (see Ex. 11.7*b*).

Finally, if one takes the melodic shaping into consideration, it becomes clear that Ockeghem's typically long-breathed, flowing melodic lines without cadential drive seem incongruent with the much more structured melodies of *Resjois toi*. What the two pieces do have in common, however, is a striking descending melodic gesture at the very end of a line after the cadence proper, and a disconnected final cadential phrase (Ex. 11.8*a*; cf. superius of *Resjois toi* in mm. 12, 14, and 35 for the descending passage, and mm. 13 and 15 for the disconnected passage). Dufay's composition is more similar to *Resjois toi* in melodic respects. For example, the superius in the last section of the *prima pars* shows the same use of sequencing melodic and rhythmic patterns which result in a florid cadential passage as in *Resjois toi*, mm. 10 and following (see Ex. 11.8*b*).

The hypothetical ascription of *Resjois toi* to Busnoys obviously stands in need of confirmation by stylistic arguments; but in this respect there is little concrete evidence forthcoming. If this motet is really by Busnoys, it must be a relatively early composition in his repertory, written at a time when what we now consider to be typical characteristics of his style might not yet have developed. This may explain why typically 'Busnoysian' features like systematic use of imitation; intricate cross rhythms; syncopated rhythmic patterns and sequences; long arching,

Ex. 11.6. Three-voice sections in Dufay, *O tres piteulx*: (*a*) mm. 1–3 of *2.p.*;
(*b*) mm. 15–22

Ex. 11.7. Cadential passages with parallel fourths: (*a*) *Mort tu as navré*, mm. 26–7; (*b*) *O tres piteulx*, mm. 25–6

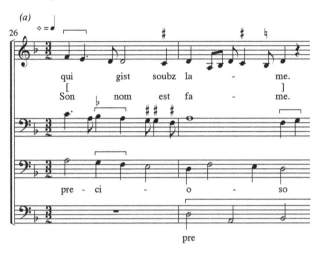

wide-spanned melodic lines; or syncopated, ascending scalar passages are missing, or can be traced only to a very small degree.[22]

Still, if there is any validity to my methodology of ascription (or reason to trust that the scribe of Pixérécourt put the real author's name on the top of the page) *Resjois toi terre de France/Rex pacificus* would represent a significant new composition that adds a number of new criteria with which to assess Busnoys's musical legacy: a hitherto unknown genre in his output (a song-motet); a datable

[22] For a summary of studies of Busnoys's musical style see Paula Marie Higgins, 'Antoine Busnois and Musical Culture in Late Fifteenth-Century France and Burgundy' (Ph.D. diss., Princeton University, 1987), 25–59.

Ex. 11.8. Shaping of melodic lines: (*a*) *Mort tu as navré*, mm. 14–19, superius;
(*b*) *O tres piteulx*, mm. 31–42, superius

composition for the chronology of his works (perhaps the occasion of Louis XI's
coronation, 15 August 1461, or a few years before or after) and thus far the earliest known work in his output; and further evidence of his close connections with
France and the French royal court.

And should none of this prove to be true? Then we have at least spent some
time on an anonymous composition worth being reconsidered and reanimated
for its own sake, even if only by a small group of scholars interested in the
musical life and culture of the fifteenth century.

12

Busnoys and 'Caron' in Documents from Brussels

&❧ ❧&

BARBARA HAGGH

A VISITOR to Brussels today can hardly imagine what the city must have been like when the court of Burgundy resided there. With the exception of the newly restored St Michael's Cathedral (formerly the collegiate church of St Gudula), only a few black and encrusted churches remain, traffic swirls around the Coudenberg where the palace once stood, and part of the church of St James, which was visited by the court on solemn occasions, now houses a bank.

Documents reveal more about daily life in the late medieval city than do surviving monuments, yet their evidence can be just as fragmentary and difficult to interpret. This is certainly true of two sets of fifteenth-century records that list three previously unknown benefices held by the composer Antoine Busnoys and concern the concierge Jean Caron, also a member of the Burgundian court chapel, and his son Philippe. The documents are intriguing because two songs (perhaps three) bear conflicting attributions to a composer named 'Caron' and to Antoine Busnoys: *Cent mille escus*,[1] *Se brief je puys ma dame*

I am grateful to the Catholic University of Leuven for the fellowship that enabled me to search archives in Brussels and Lille. Archives are abbreviated as follows: ASG = Archives Ste-Gudule; ASV, LA = Archivio Segreto Vaticano, Libri obligationum annatarum; ASV, RS = Archivio Segreto Vaticano, Registri suppliche; BAR = Brussels, Archives générales du Royaume; CC = Chambre des Comptes; ÉA = État et Audience; KB = Archives ecclésiastiques de Brabant/Kerkarchief van Brabant; F-Pan = Paris, Archives nationales. Abbreviations are resolved, i/j and u/v standardized, capitalization and punctuation added, and numerals modernized in the transcriptions. Editorial inserts concerning primary material are in brackets; other comments are in parentheses.

[1] *Cent mille escus* is ascribed to Busnoys and Caron. James Thomson, *An Introduction to Philippe (?) Caron* (Musicological Studies, 9; Brooklyn, 1964), 24, accepts Caron's authorship, pointing out that the scribe could have confused the chanson with Busnoys's *Cent mille fois*. Allan Atlas, *The Cappella Giulia Chansonnier (Rome, Biblioteca Apostolica Vaticana, C.G. XIII. 27)*, 2 vols. (Brooklyn, 1975), i. 97, thinks the Busnoys ascription refers only to the different bassus part found in Pixérécourt. His line of reasoning is developed further in 'Conflicting Attributions in Italian Sources of the Franco-Netherlandish Chanson, ca.1465–ca.1505: A Progress Report on a New Hypothesis', in Iain Fenlon (ed.), *Music in Medieval and Early Modern Europe: Patronage, Sources, and Texts* (Cambridge, 1981), 249–93; see 254–5 on the Caron

voir,[2] and *Pourtant se mon vouloir*.[3] Moreover, the works of these composers appear in many of the same manuscripts, evidence that they might have known each other personally.[4] A number of scholars have proposed a Philippe Caron as the composer 'Caron'.[5] However, the documents from Brussels demonstrate that Philippe did not belong to the Burgundian court chapel, even though he performed and taught music, and that he cannot have been the famous composer Firminus Caron lauded by Tinctoris.[6] Indeed, they do not record the physical presence in Brussels of Busnoys or Caron. Nevertheless, they provide new information about Busnoys's beneficial career and lay to rest unsubstantiated hypotheses about Caron.

ascriptions. Howard Mayer Brown, *A Florentine Chansonnier from the Time of Lorenzo the Magnificent: Florence, Biblioteca Nazionale Centrale, MS Banco Rari 229* (Monuments of Renaissance Music, 7; Chicago, 1983), i. 240–1, accepts Caron as the composer; see also Atlas, *Cappella Giulia*, discussion for no. 31. Judith Cohen finds a quotation of this same chanson, which she attributes to Busnoys, in the motto beginning of the *Crucifixus* of the second mass in Naples VI E 40, and uses this as evidence for Busnoys's authorship of the masses; see *The Six Anonymous L'Homme Armé Masses in Naples, Biblioteca Nazionale, MS VI E 40* (MSD 21; Rome, 1968), 68–70.

[2] *Se brief* also shares a conflicting attribution between Busnoys and Caron. Brown attributes it to Caron; see *A Florentine Chansonnier*, discussion for no. 74.

[3] The chanson *Pourtant se mon vouloir* is ascribed to Caron in Casanatense 2856 (see Thomson, *An Introduction*, 16). Pietro Aaron and Giovanni del Lago cite Busnoys as author of a chanson with the same title (see *A Correspondence of Renaissance Musicians*, ed. Bonnie J. Blackburn *et al.* (Oxford, 1991), letter 18, 350–1 n. 1). Howard Brown believed it was probably a different chanson (see Brown, *A Florentine Chansonnier*, discussion for no. 96); however, he was mistaken in saying that Aaron described the chanson as having a flat signature. Aaron said it was in the first mode ending on *d'*; the chanson ascribed to Caron fits that criterion as to the (rather unusual) high final of the tenor. However, since it descends to *a*, it would seem to be second rather than first mode; Aaron may have been looking only at the upper range, which reaches *b'*. The testimony of Aaron and del Lago (who may not be an independent witness) strengthen the case for it being the same chanson, but the question of attribution remains open.

[4] See *Census-Catalogue* for the sources containing works by each composer. Allan Atlas hypothesizes that conflicting ascriptions tend to involve composers who had known biographical connections. See his 'Conflicting Attributions'.

[5] On the tentative identification of Caron with the *petit vicaire* at Cambrai, Philippe, see James Thomson, 'The Works of Caron: A Study in Fifteenth-Century Style' (Ph.D. diss., New York University, 1959); id., *An Introduction*, esp. 1–6; Geneviève Thibault, 'Caron', *New Grove*, iii. 816–17; Christopher Reynolds, 'The Origins of San Pietro B 80 and the Development of a Roman Sacred Repertory', *EMH* 1 (1981), 257–304 at 286–7; id., 'Introduction' to facsimile, *Vatican City, Biblioteca Apostolica Vaticana, San Pietro B 80* (Renaissance Music in Facsimile, 23; New York and London, 1986), although Reynolds has retracted his claim (private communication); Adalbert Roth, *Studien zum frühen Repertoire der päpstlichen Kapelle unter dem Pontifikat Sixtus IV. (1471–1484)* (Capellae apostolicae sixtinaeque collectanea acta monumenta, 1; Vatican City, 1991), 286–94 *et passim*.

[6] Firminus Caron is named in the *Liber de arte contrapuncti* (11 Oct. 1477) with Johannes Okeghem, Johannes Regis, Anthonius Busnois, Guillermus Faugues, Johannes Dunstaple, Egidius Binchois, Guillermus Dufay, and Petrus de Domarto. See Johannes Tinctoris *Opera theoretica*, ed. Albert Seay (CSM 22; Rome, 1975–8), ii. 12, and again on ii. 156. He is called only Caron on ii. 143–4. He is listed in the *Complexus effectuum musices* (1472–5): 'Quis enim Johannem Dunstaple, Guillelmum Dufay, Egidium Binchois, Johannem Okeghem, Anthonium Busnois, Johannem Regis, Firminum Caron, Jacobum Carlerii, Robertum Morton, Jacobum Obrecht non novit?' (ibid. 176). Only Caron is named in the *Proportionale musices* (*c.*1473) (*Opera theoretica*, iia (Rome, 1978), 10, 49). On the composers cited in the *Proportionale*, see Paula Marie Higgins, 'Antoine Busnois and Musical Culture in Late Fifteenth-Century France and Burgundy' (Ph.D. diss., Princeton University, 1987), 250–1.

Busnoys

Until now, Busnoys was not known to have held benefices in any church in Brussels, even though he made occasional visits to the city with the Burgundian court chapel.[7] But two hastily scribbled entries buried among hundreds in the *acta capituli* of the collegiate church of St Gudula in Brussels show him trading local chaplaincies, as did his colleagues at the court.[8]

Such chaplaincies proliferated in the fifteenth century, and the *acta capituli* entries show how quickly they could pass from one chaplain to the next (see App. A, Docs. 1–3). On Tuesday, 10 November 1478, Walter Henrici, formerly a singer and *sommelier* of the oratory in the Burgundian chapel, gave up the chaplaincy of the Holy Spirit and Cross in the St Nicholas church in Brussels to exchange it with Busnoys, then a canon, probably in Andenne near Namur. The benefice had been obtained by Henrici only a day earlier, following the resignation of Nicholas vander Walter. Four days later, on 14 November, Busnoys resigned and exchanged the benefice in turn with Jehan Pintot *dit* Nicodemus, another Burgundian chaplain. Pintot resigned the benefice on 2 January 1479.[9]

Du Fay and Okeghem profited from rich prebends, but Busnoys seems not to have kept pace with them, as Paula Higgins has noted.[10] Thus it surprises us less that Busnoys, unlike many members of the court, did not have a benefice at St Gudula itself, the wealthiest and most influential church in Brussels.[11] Yet the church of St Nicholas, where Busnoys held the chaplaincy of the Holy Spirit and Cross, was not unimportant, despite being subordinate to St Gudula. Merchants'

[7] Busnoys's benefices are discussed in Higgins, 'Antoine Busnois', 114–24, and ead., '*In hydraulis* Revisited: New Light on the Career of Antoine Busnois', *JAMS* 39 (1986), 36–86 at 51–2. Busnoys was in Brussels with the chapel of Charles the Bold on 1 July 1474, with Mary of Burgundy's chapel on 7–8 June 1477, and with Maximilian's chapel on 7–8 and 23 Dec. 1479, in Oct., Nov., and Dec. of 1481, and in Jan. 1483 (ibid. 63–6).

[8] A chaplaincy was a benefice requiring the chaplain to celebrate assigned masses in a particular side chapel. Often a single chapel had several different chaplaincies. Chaplains were usually expected to participate in services held in the main choir as well as to celebrate their assigned chapel Masses. On chaplaincy foundations in Brussels, see Barbara Haggh, 'Music, Liturgy, and Ceremony in Brussels, 1350–1500' (Ph.D. diss., University of Illinois at Urbana–Champaign, 1988), 700–46, and cf. Jozef Van den Nieuwenhuizen, 'Het kapelaniewezen te Antwerpen tot 1477', *Bibliothèque de la Revue d'histoire ecclésiastique/Bronnen voor de religieuze geschiedenis van België, middeleeuwen en moderne tijden*, 47 (1968), 221–35, and id., 'Kapelaniewezen en kapelanen te Antwerpen van de oorsprong tot 1477' (Ph.D. diss., Katholieke Universiteit Leuven, 1963).

[9] The singer Nicolas van Oudenhagen received the chaplaincy (BAR ASG 910, fo. 115ᵛ). Walter Henrici (fl. 1445, d. 1494) had many benefices in the Low Countries and was responsible for introducing Guillaume Du Fay's plainchant for the office of the *Recollectio festorum beate Marie Virginis* to more than twenty churches. On Henrici, see M. Jennifer Bloxam, 'In Praise of Spurious Saints: The *Missae Floruit egregiis* by Pipelare and La Rue', *JAMS* 44 (1990), 163–220, esp. 172; Barbara Haggh, 'The Celebration of the "Recollectio Festorum Beatae Mariae Virginis", 1457–1987', *Studia Musicologica*, 30 (1988), 361–73, and *Trasmissione e recezione delle forme di cultura musicale: Bologna, 27 agosto–1 settembre 1987*, 3 vols., ed. A. Pompilio *et al.* (Turin, 1990), iii. 559–71; ead., 'Music, Liturgy, and Ceremony', 605–7; and Micheline Soenen, 'Un amateur de musique à Bruxelles à la fin du xvᵉ siècle: Gautier Henri, chanoine et écolâtre de Sainte-Gudule', in Hilda Coppejans *et al.* (eds.), *Album Carlos Wyffels* (Brussels, 1987), 423–36, esp. 427–9, for the most comprehensive list of his benefices. On *sommeliers* at the court, see below.

[10] Higgins, 'Antoine Busnois', 114–24.   [11] Cf. Haggh, 'Music, Liturgy, and Ceremony', 171–5.

guilds and their foundations made the church almost as wealthy as the collegiate church, and provided incomes for other well-known musicians: the papal singers Johannes Puyllois,[12] Jacobus Boni, and Johannes Raet, and, later, the composer Crispijne vander Stappen.[13] It maintained a choir of professional singers after 1472 and had several organs. Confraternities established foundations for the singing of polyphony.[14]

The documents from St Nicholas suggest that Busnoys's chaplaincy at the altar of the Holy Spirit and Cross was reserved for court chaplains or at least musicians, since Henrici and Nicodemus were both court chaplains and Nicolas van Oudenhagen was a singer at the church of St Gudula. Similarly, a number of non-resident papal singers held in succession the Marian chaplaincy in the same church.[15]

Busnoys kept the chaplaincy at the church of St Nicholas for only four days. Henrici, before him, and Nicodemus, after him, also resigned the chaplaincy after only a short time. The resignations may reflect circumstances at the church, because the many separate funds it supervised were reorganized in the 1470s. The church began to establish a *cotidiane* or choir of professional singers in accordance with the provisions of a papal bull of 1472.[16] This bull permitted the church to reassign incomes; thus the incomes from the chaplaincy may not have been secure. Whatever the situation at St Nicholas, the *acta* entries illustrate how often benefices could change hands, leading to two conclusions: that chapel foundations may have been neglected as a result of the frequent changes, and that we may never be able to document the number of benefices a fifteenth-century musician had at any given time.

The documents mention other benefices Busnoys held, some at churches not far from Brussels. He exchanged a canonicate, perhaps at Saint-Omer in Thérouanne, with Walter Henrici's chaplaincy at St Nicholas.[17] Later Busnoys exchanged the St Nicholas chaplaincy for another at an unnamed chapel in the park (*warande*) in Tervuren near Brussels, probably that located in the ducal

[12] Johannes Puyllois's illegitimate son, Cornelius, received legitimacy papers in Brussels in 1506 (BAR, CC 109). On Cornelius, see Pamela Starr, 'Music and Music Patronage at the Papal Court', 1447–1464 (Ph.D. diss., Yale University, 1987), 172.

[13] See Barbara Haggh, 'Crispijne and Albertijne: Two Tenors at the Church of St Niklaas, Brussels', *ML* 76 (1995), 325–44; Dutch translation in *Musica Antiqua*, 11 (1994), 14–21.

[14] Haggh, 'Music, Liturgy, and Ceremony', 51–4 and *passim*.

[15] Bernard Buillot, Busnoys's procurator when he obtained the St Nicholas chaplaincy, served in the chapel of Maximilian I as organ-carrier. Buillot had also acted as Busnoys's procurator in 1473 for a benefice at the chapel of St Silvester in the ducal castle in Mons. See Higgins, 'Antoine Busnois', 116–17, and ead., '*In hydraulis*', 52, on this benefice and on Buillot.

[16] On the bull of 1472, see Haggh, 'Crispijne and Albertijne'; on chaplaincies and discontinued foundations, see Jozef Van den Nieuwenhuizen, 'De koralen, de zangers, en de zangmeesters van de Antwerpse O.-L.-Vrouwekerk tijdens de 15e eeuw', in *Gouden jubileum gedenkboek van de viering van 50 jaar heropgericht knapenkoor van de Onze-Lieve-Vrouwekatedraal te Antwerpen* (Antwerp, 1978), 19–72, and above, n. 8.

[17] The word is difficult to decipher, but resembles 'Audomarensis' (Saint-Omer), and Busnoys is listed in the obligation of 5 Jan. 1477 (see Table 12.1) for a canonicate in the diocese of Thérouanne, in which Saint-Omer was located.

castle in the park where members of the court went hunting. Since Busnoys and Pintot *dit* Nicodemus, his successor in the Tervuren chaplaincy, both belonged to the court *chapelle*, this seems the most likely possibility, but others, such as the small Trinity chapel and chapels in the churches of St Nicholas and St John, all in Tervuren, also come into consideration.[18]

Busnoys probably sought benefices not only because there had been a change of ruler and administration following Charles the Bold's death on 5 January 1477, but also because of the prevalent economic insecurity. High inflation and political upheaval at many levels marked life in Brussels. In response to heavy taxes imposed by Mary and Maximilian at their accession, the guilds of Brussels seized the city hall, arrested all noble members of the city council, executed two council members, and banished others from the city.[19] Court service still ensured the best income for musicians and many stayed, but extra financial security would have been comforting during these years. Indeed, Busnoys was seeking other benefices actively at this time. His name appears in an obligation of 5 January 1477 for a canonicate in the diocese of Thérouanne, and in a collation list of 1480 for two benefices in Hainaut (Mons, Condé), and one in Zeeland (Tholen).[20]

The entries in the *acta capituli* of St Gudula reveal several previously unknown benefices held by Busnoys in a city where the court resided. Yet there is no evidence in the *acta* for Busnoys's presence in Brussels or at any of the establishments named in the documents. We still do not know where the composer stayed between 22 September 1477, when he visited Bruges with Mary of Burgundy's chapel, and 4 May 1479, when he returned to the same city with the chapel of Maximilian I.[21]

'Caron'

Archives in Brussels also name a Jean Caron, concierge, and his son, Philippe. The establishment of the identity of the Brussels Philippe is a matter of central importance for the history of fifteenth-century music, because no documentation

---

[18] In modern Dutch *warande* means park; in 15th-c. Brussels it referred to the woods of Tervuren in the north-eastern outskirts of the city where a castle (hunting lodge) of the court of Burgundy was located. On Tervuren and the ducal castle, see Geert Berings, *Tervuren in de middeleeuwen: Aspecten van de Brabantse geschiedenis* (Ghent and Tervuren, 1984). The church of St John (Haggh, 'Music, Liturgy, and Ceremony', 92) was subordinate to the church of St Géry in Brussels (Longnon, *Pouillés*, i. 341); the Trinity chapel and the church of St Nicholas in Tervuren were both subordinate to the Praemonstratensian abbey of Park near Louvain (ibid. 343).

[19] Haggh, 'Music, Liturgy, and Ceremony', 528–32.

[20] ASV, LA 25, fos. 95ᵛ–96ʳ; BAR, ÉA 1249a, fo. 2ʳ: fourth in line 'Aux prebendes de mons'; fo. 2ᵛ: first in line 'Aux prebendes de Conde'; fo. 3ʳ: third in line 'Aux prebendes de la tholne en zellande'. Both documents are discussed below.

[21] The two *escroes* are LADN B 3441, 119320, and B 3442, 119339 (Higgins, '*In hydraulis*', 63). Higgins found Busnoys's name in the wardrobe account for the funeral of Charles the Bold. Busnoys then passed into the service of Mary of Burgundy in 1477, but after her marriage to Maximilian I of Austria in August of that year, he was affiliated with Maximilian's household chapel, which was distinct from Mary's (ibid. 61–7, 85–8).

has been found for the composer Firminus Caron, praised by Tinctoris as one of the best of his time,[22] and because a Philippe Caron at the court has been put forth as this composer, most recently by Adalbert Roth.[23] The key document was cited by Fétis in his *Biographie universelle*: a charter of Charles the Bold appointing a certain Jean Caron as concierge of his *hôtel* on 12 August 1470. Unfortunately, Fétis did not assign a number to the charter.[24] Vander Straeten searched for it but could not find it.[25] The charters of Brabant have been catalogued since then, so I was able to locate the 'missing' letter of appointment (Doc. 4).[26]

The concierge named in the document and also described as 'nostre bien amé serviteur de nostre oratoire' must be the Jean Caron who was *sommelier* of the oratory of the court of Burgundy beginning in 1436, since no other individual with the same name held that position before 1470.[27] The *hôtel* must be the Coudenberg palace in Brussels, the principal residence of the courts of Philip the Good of Burgundy after 1450 and of Charles the Bold.[28] But since no other charters mention Jean Caron or a different concierge, we do not learn what duties he carried out in connection with that post or how long he held it. The importance of the charter lies in its documentation of a change in Jean Caron's duties, which raises the possibility that he was replaced as *sommelier* of the oratory when he became concierge.

This possibility is the source of Adalbert Roth's hypothesis regarding the identity and activities of Philippe Caron. A 'Carron' appears in a 1474 list of members of the Burgundian chapel published by Marix, and this evidence, together with a document Roth discovered in the Vatican archives, led him to propose that 'Carron' was a singer named Philippe Caron, rather than Jean Caron

---

[22] For Tinctoris's references to Firminus Caron, see above, n. 6. On the 1422 document naming Firminus Caron, see the discussion in Thomson, 'The Works of Caron', 13–14. Searches in the Archives départementales de la Somme and the Bibliothèque municipale in Amiens revealed no composer named Firminus Caron whose dates might correspond with Tinctoris's citation, but a number of Jean Carons were active at churches in the city between 1436 and 1480, although none can be confirmed as musicians or as relatives of the Burgundian court *sommelier*. It is striking that two early 16th-c. obituaries of Amiens Cathedral, Amiens, Bibliothèque municipale, G 2974–2975, list over 500 names, none of them Firminus or Jean Caron.

[23] See above, n. 5.

[24] François-Joseph Fétis, 'Caron (Firmin)', *Biographie universelle des musiciens et bibliographie générale de la musique* (2nd edn.; Paris, 1861), ii. 193–4.

[25] Edmond Vander Straeten, *Histoire de la musique aux Pays-Bas* (Brussels, 1867), i. 155.

[26] The content of the document is summarized in Alphonse Verkooren, *Chartes et cartulaires des duchés de Brabant et de Limbourg et des Pays d'Outre-Meuse, IIIᵉ partie: Chartes originales et cartulaires (1427–1789)*, iv: *1450–1469* (Archives générales du Royaume, Instruments de recherche à tirage limité, 47/4; Brussels, 1989). BAR, CC 134 was formerly cartulary 48 of the charters of Brabant.

[27] Jeanne Marix, *Histoire de la musique et des musiciens de la cour de Bourgogne sous le règne de Philippe le Bon (1420–1467)* (Strasburg, 1939; repr. Geneva, 1972), notes the arrival of Jean Caron as *sommelier* in 1436 and supposes that he remains at the court until 1474 (ibid. 261–2, list of 30 Aug. 1474). The duties of the *sommelier* of the oratory and last years of Jean Caron's career at the court are discussed below.

[28] On the court at the Coudenberg palace, see Haggh, 'Music, Liturgy, and Ceremony', 87 n. 317.

TABLE 12.1. *Names on obligation of 1477 and court escroes of 1476 and 1477*

obligation,[a] 5 Jan. 1477 ASV, LA 25, fos. 95ᵛ–96ʳ (names as in document; emphasis mine)	*escroe*, 7 Dec. 1476 LADN, B 3440 (names standardized)	*escroe*, 5 June 1477 LADN, B 3441 (names standardized)
Iohannis de Glimes	R. Olivier	C. Languebrouck
Iacobi Buckel	*M. Cocquel*	P. Canone
Nicolai Ruter	P. Canone	J. Pintot dit Nicodemus
Philippi Siron	J. Pintot dit Nicodemus	*M. Cocquel*
Dionisii Baudeti	*P. du Passaige*	*P. du Passaige*
Roberti Morton	W. Maes	R. Olivier
Claudii Petit	P. Desprez	P. Desprez
Thome France	C. Buerkel	W. Maes
Iohannis de Deckere	C. Petit	C. Buerkel
Paschasii Louis	A. Busnoys	A. Busnoys
Petri Basin	P. Basin	C. Petit
Iacobi Amoret	J. Amoury	P. Basin
Egidii Godeval	T. France	T. France
Iohannis Dupassage	G. Bousies	P. Louis
Innocentii de Creci	P. Du Wez	J. Sampain
Antonii de Busne	*J. Caron*	G. Bousies
Simonis de Hond	P. Louis	P. Beurse
Adriani Basin	J. Sampain	P. Du Wez
Iacobi de Casleto	P. Beurse	E. Blanc
Paschasii de Pratis	E. Blanc	
Petri Canonici		
Iohannis Bonart		
Roberti Oliverii		
Philippi Caron		
Egidii de Bonsies		
Eustacii Albi		
Philippi Cocquel		
Iohannis Pintot		
Petri Duwez		

[a] Transcribed in Roth, *Studien*, Anhang 1C, doc. 1, 542–3.

the *sommelier* of the oratory, and to argue that this Philippe was Tinctoris's composer, Firminus Caron.[29]

The Vatican document in question is an obligation of 5 January 1477, the date of Charles the Bold's death (see Table 12.1). The envoy and procurator for the duke of Burgundy, Henri de Berghes (later bishop of Cambrai), represents members of the Burgundian chapel as well as other favourites of Charles the Bold, and agrees to pay the annates on the benefices to which these individuals have been

[29] Roth, *Studien*, 290–3.

nominated.[30] The list of nominees includes Philippe Caron, canon of Cambrai, following Robert Olivier and preceding Egidius de Bousies and Tassin Le Blanc. Philippe's position in the list thus corresponds closely to the position of 'Carron' or 'Caron' in several published *escroes* of the court from the 1470s. Roth concluded that the Philippe Caron named in the obligation sang in the court chapel alongside Busnoys and Morton, two composers with whom Tinctoris's Firminus Caron—or Philippe Caron as Roth would have it—shares conflicting ascriptions.[31]

A collation list of the court of Burgundy from 1480 includes an entry proving that the Philippe Caron named in the obligation was the son of the Burgundian *sommelier* Jean Caron. 'Maistre Jehan parmentier, philippe filz de Jehan caron, Eustace le blanc, Jehan creuwin', and 'Pierre heddebault' are listed under 'Aux curés, chappelles, hospitaulx, personnages et cousteries de haynnau'.[32] Jean Caron, Philippe's father, can only be the first *sommelier* of the oratory of the ducal chapel. The collation list names many members of the chapel as well as some of their family members also employed at court, and names no other Jean Caron, nor do contemporary court documents. Moreover, Philippe was Jean Caron's legitimate son. Jean was not a priest, nor did his post as *sommelier* of the oratory require it,[33] and a supplication of 1460 confirms that he was married. In it, the duke of Burgundy requests permission for Jean Caron, *clericus coniugatus*, to keep the benefices he had acquired before his marriage and to obtain and permute new ones.[34] The document does not give the date of Caron's marriage, but presumably it took place just before 1460, since he needed the document to keep his benefices, a matter of utmost concern. If Jean Caron married just before 1460, then to be legitimate, Philippe would have been born in the 1460s. That accords with the hypothesis discussed below that Jean Caron's son and the Philippe Caron documented as an altarboy in Cambrai in the 1470s were the same individual.

[30] Annates, a one-time tax of one-half of the annual income of a benefice, had to be paid at a specified time after the incumbent had taken 'peaceful possession' of the benefice. Frequently, clergy-men pledged (and even paid) the annates in advance of taking possession of a benefice, in the hopes that this might help solidify their rights to the benefice (I thank Pamela Starr for this explanation).

[31] See above, nn. 1–3 on the Busnoys and Caron ascriptions. *C'est temps perdu* is attributed to Caron and Morton, but the Morton attribution in Perugia 431 cannot be correct. David Fallows points out that the scribe of this manuscript attributes four pieces to Morton that are unlikely to be his, but fails to add Morton's name to his most successful song, *Le souvenir* ('A Glimpse of the Lost Years: Spanish Polyphonic Song, 1450–1470', in Josephine Wright with Samuel A. Floyd, Jr. (eds.), *New Perspectives on Early Music: Essays in Honor of Eileen Southern* (Warren, Mich., 1992), 25–32, and id., 'Robert Morton's Songs' (Ph.D. diss., University of California at Berkeley, 1978), 325–481).

[32] BAR ÉA 1249a, fo. 2ᵛ. Parmentier, Le Blanc, and Heddebault were members of the chapel. The full list is transcribed and discussed in Higgins, 'Antoine Busnoys', 348–56, but she does not consider the entry naming 'philippe filz de Jehan caron' further.

[33] Cf. David Fallows, 'Specific Information on the Ensembles for Composed Polyphony, 1400–1474', in Stanley Boorman (ed.), *Studies in the Performance of Late Mediaeval Music* (Cambridge, 1983), 109–59 at 146, 156–9.

[34] ASV, RS 529, fo. 153ʳ. I thank Pamela Starr for this reference.

The 1480 collation list and the 1477 obligation both name persons not singing in the court chapel, however. The 1480 list describes many individuals explicitly as brothers, sons, and daughters of members of the court. Thus some individuals named in court records had families, and the family members could be supported with benefices as well.[35] Similarly, when the 1477 obligation is compared with two roughly contemporaneous *escroes*, a number of names do not match up. The names as they appear in this obligation carry weight, since, as Pamela Starr has noted, 'errors in fact, including incorrect orthography, might ultimately cause the papal provision to be invalid in law'.[36] This would have been an especially urgent concern here, since swearing that one was obliged to pay annates before the *Camera* was the last stage in the provision of benefices.[37] Roth noted Philippe Caron's name in the obligation and assumed that he was the 'Carron' in the *escroes*, but nowhere did he signal the presence of an *escroe* assigning the name Philippe to 'Carron', which would have proved his case. Moreover, other similar names in the two documents do not match up. The obligation names 'Philippe Cocquel', but the *escroes* list 'Matthias Cocquel'. Finally, 'Iohannes Dupassage' appears in the obligation, but only 'Philippe du Passaige' served in Charles the Bold's chapel.[38] I conclude that Philippe Cocquel and Iohannes Dupassage were sons or relatives of chapel members, like Philippe Caron, and not chapel members themselves. Therefore, the obligation does *not* constitute a list of chaplains *per se*, nor does it provide evidence that Philippe Caron ever sang in the Burgundian chapel, as Roth argues.

Above it was pointed out that the surname 'Carron' appears without a Christian name in a 1474 list of chapel singers published by Marix. It comes further down in the list than where Jean's name usually appears (the 1468 *escroes* do name 'Jean Caron' but not the 1470 list published by Marix). Roth concluded from this that 'Carron' was not 'Jean Caron'.[39] To test this hypothesis, which is based solely on published documents, I examined all known surviving *escroes* dating from 1471 to 1475 (see the results in App. B). A considerable lapse of time separates the Caron entries, none of which includes a first name. After being absent from the *escroes* of 8 March, 11 March, and 23 March 1471, Caron reappears on 30 March 1471, when the court spent the night at the gates of the city of Amiens.[40] He also visited Péronne and left the next day, just as the court departed for Abbeville. His name is absent from the surviving lists of 1472, from

[35] On the Burgundian dukes and benefices held by members of their court, see Adriaan Jongkees, *Staat en kerk in Holland en Zeeland onder de Bourgondische hertogen, 1425–1477* (Groningen, 1942).
[36] Pamela Starr, 'Rome as the Centre of the Universe: Papal Grace and Music Patronage', *EMH* 11 (1992), 223–62 at 231 n. 24.
[37] Starr, 'Music and Music Patronage', 61.
[38] The elder Jean du Passaige, father of the tenor Philippe, was dead by this time (see Haggh, 'Music, Liturgy, and Ceremony', 642). On Philippe, see ibid. and Karl Weinmann, *Johannes Tinctoris und sein unbekannter Traktat "De inventione et usu musicae"* (Tutzing, 1960; rev. repr. of 1917 edn.), 12.
[39] See Roth, *Studien*, 290. [40] See above, n. 22.

the summit at the abbey of St Maximin in Trier in 1473, reappears briefly in lists of July 1473, and more regularly in the last half of 1474, and periodically from April to December 1475. After Charles the Bold's death, Caron received retroactive payments for his work in 1474 and 1475.[41] But he was not with the chapel during the battle of Neuss in the first three months of 1475; other singers were also absent. The omission of Caron's first name may have been a scribal peculiarity. If Marix's lists reflect the documents accurately, accounts from 1453–5 that clearly concern Jean Caron also omit his first name.[42]

These intermittent notices and Caron's lower rank in the lists can be interpreted in two ways. Caron was probably appointed as concierge because he was older and had less stamina for travel. Yet we do not know how long his appointment as concierge lasted, nor do we know his duties or whether the duke gave him leave to travel occasionally. Given his seniority and the close relationship he must have had with Charles the Bold, whom he once protected from the wrath of his father,[43] it seems at least possible that the duke tailored his new appointment for him, allowed him to travel, but gave him fewer responsibilities, resulting in his lower rank in the lists.

Indeed, Charles the Bold's ordinance for his chapel dated 1 January 1469 (modern style) suggests that a *sommelier* could have been absent from time to time. The ordinance states that there will be five *sommeliers*, of which three will attend on the duke in his oratory and two will take turns serving at the altar. The former are the *sommeliers* of the oratory, the latter the *sommeliers* of the *chappelle*.[44] The oratory was the area enclosed in draperies where the duke and his close attendants, including the confessor and *sommeliers* of the oratory, sat during Mass, and can be seen in a famous miniature depicting Philip the Good at Mass.[45] The oratory was thus within the chapel of the palace, but when the court travelled, it was set up as a tent with a portable altar inside. Some of the liturgical regalia and books remained in the chapel of the palace while the court was away, and the *sommeliers* of the chapel must have guarded them.[46] Given that the ordinance specifies that two *sommeliers* take turns weekly and that the duties of the other three depended largely on the needs of the duke, a concierge given occasional leave could have served as *sommelier*.

---

[41] BAR CC 1796 is a list of retroactive payments made after Charles the Bold's death to members of his court. The payments are: 'A Caron pour l'annee [14]74 – 37 L. 14 S. 11 D.', and 'A lui pour l'annee [14]75 – 70 L. 3 S. 5 D.' I thank Paula Higgins for her transcription.

[42] Marix's lists are not from *escroes*, but are derived from sections of the accounts of the receiver general listing payments to members of the chapel. See *Histoire*, 252–3.

[43] Marix describes the incident in ibid. 197.

[44] See Fallows, 'Specific information', 146, 156–9.

[45] Brussels, Bibliothèque Royale, 9092, fo. 9ʳ, reproduced in Craig Wright, 'Burgundy', *New Grove*, iii. 465.

[46] On the movable oratory, see BAR CC 1924, fo. 37 and BAR CC 1925, fos. 504, 514, 542. I thank Paula Higgins for bringing these documents to my attention and for providing transcriptions. On the private oratory of the duke at meetings of the Order of the Golden Fleece, see Barbara Haggh, 'The Archives of the Order of the Golden Fleece and Music', *Journal of the Royal Musical Association*, 120 (1995), 1–43.

The positions of concierge and *sommelier* were thus not mutually exclusive. When the duke appointed Jean Caron concierge, Caron did not leave his duties as *sommelier* abruptly, nor did Walter Henrici appear *ex vacuo* to take his place. Walter Henrici is named in documents as *sommelier* in 1467 and 1468.[47] Then, an entry in the court accounts of 1469 calls Henrici 'par les nouvelles ordonnances clerc de l'oratoire'.[48] Evidently, Charles the Bold reconfirmed him in his post as *sommelier* when Charles reorganized the court chapel after the death of Philip the Good. Yet Henrici appears as first *sommelier* only from 1469 until 1473, except in two *escroes*, where he is second.[49] Since Jean Caron had been first *sommelier* before the 1469 ordinance, Henrici probably took Caron's place in 1469, as the result of the ordinance rather than of Caron's new appointment. Indeed, Caron continued to receive payments as *sommelier* throughout 1470, although the accounts record his new appointment. He served intermittently in 1469, however, even before he became concierge.[50] One reason for Caron to remain would have been to give Henrici instructions, since the latter had taken over tasks that Caron had accomplished for more than thirty years, all of which were crucial for the daily performance of the liturgy and, hence, for the salvation of the souls of the duke and his predecessors.[51]

An *escroe* of 7 December 1476 lists Jean Caron as *sommelier*, evidence that he never left those duties. 'Jean le Caron sommelier' is among the members of the chapel visiting Margaret of York on that day.[52] He appears for the last time in

---

[47] See LADN B 2064, fo. 44v (1467): '(Dons et recompensations) A Watelet Henry et Laurens Boucquery clercqs de la chappelle de mondit seigneur'; fo. 81v: '[after payment to Guillaume Dore] A Watelet aussi clerc de ladicte chapelle'; and LADN B 2068, fo. 67v (1468): '(Parties extraordinaires) A Watelet Henry clerc de l'oratoire de mondit seigneur . . . quie deue lui estoit pour semblable somme par lui donnee du commandement de mondit seigneur au baptisment de l'enfant de Pierre le Queux lequel il a nagaires lave sur les sains fons de baptesme ou nom dicellui seigneur'. I thank Paula Higgins for these references and for her transcription.

[48] BAR CC 1924, fo. 35 (1469): 'A Watelet Henry par les nouvelles ordonnances clerc de l'oratoire qui a servy ledit mois de mars 68 [1469 modern style] contenant 31 jours'.

[49] Walter Henrici was first *sommelier de l'oratoire* for eighty-three days in July–Sept. 1469 (BAR CC 1924, fos. 36v, 38v), from Oct. to Dec. 1469 (ibid., fos. 40r, 49v), and when he received back wages for fifty-nine days' service in Jan. and Feb. 1469 modern style (ibid., fos. 60v–61r). He received his wages and clothing allowance as first *sommelier de l'oratoire* for Jan. 1470 (BAR, CC 1925, fo. 49v) and for Feb. to Oct. 1470 (ibid., fo. 51v). On 8 Mar. 1471 Pierrequin du Wez was listed as first *sommelier* in the *escroes*, with Henrici second (LADN B 3435, 118619); on 8 June 1471 Henrici was listed first again (LADN B 3435, 118636), with Caron in fourth place; on 20 July 1472 Laurens Boucquery was first and Henrici second (LADN B 3436, 118738), but Henrici was first again on 12 Nov. 1472 (LADN B 3436, 118794), 18 Nov. 1472 (ibid., 118802), 2 Jan. 1473 (LADN B 3437, 118951), and in other lists of Jan. 1473. I thank Paula Higgins for providing transcriptions of these documents.

[50] Jean Caron was paid as *sommelier de l'oratoire* for thirty-one days in Jan. (1469) (BAR CC 1924, fo. 34v), but was absent from the lists of Apr.–June 1469 (fos. 35v–37v), July–Sept. 1469 (37v–39r) and Oct.–Dec. 1469 (39r–41v). He was present during this time none the less, because he was paid for 152 days' service later on, according to fo. 41r–v. Jean Caron *sommelier de l'oratoire* received his wages and clothing allowance for Jan. 1470 modern style (BAR CC 1925, fo. 54r) and for Feb.–Oct. 1470 (fo. 51v). I thank Paula Higgins for these references.

[51] Surely the court chapel was listed first in the *escroes* because the responsibility for the duke's soul rested on them.

[52] LADN B 3440, 119280 (cf. Higgins, '*In hydraulis*', 85): (7 Dec. 1476, after Pierre Duwez and before Pasquin Louis) 'Jehan le Caron sommelier – 6 S. 4 D. ob'.

court documents in the wardrobe account for Charles the Bold's funeral dated after 5 January 1477, again as *sommelier*.[53]

The scenario favoured by Roth makes a second, younger Caron the *sommelier*, who has a lower rank due to his youth and inexperience. In Roth's view, this is the Philippe of the 1477 obligation. Yet the name Philippe never appears in the *escroes*, not even in later years, and the obligation does not reflect a chapel list, as we already concluded.

Additional documents would tell us more about the concierge Jean Caron. But other biographical evidence about Philippe clinches the case, demonstrating that Philippe lived in Cambrai while 'Carron' travelled with the court. Roth's 1477 obligation lists Philippe Caron for a canonicate in Cambrai, and the 1480 collation list names 'Philippe filz Jehan caron' for benefices in Hainaut—the province in which Cambrai was situated. Indeed, Craig Wright documented a Philippe Caron in Cambrai. The Cambrai Philippe began his career as a choirboy at the Cathedral under Jean Hémart in 1471/2 (when 'Caron' was at the court, cf. App. B).[54] 'Philipo le caron' is the sixth altar boy listed under 'Magister Jo. hemart' on fo. 78[r] in Cambrai 28, a thirteenth-century psalter with later additions. He may also be the 'philippo' in the accounts of the *petits vicaires* of 1474/5 (again conflicting with the Caron in the *escroes*).[55] On 28 March 1480 Philippe Caron is listed as a cleric absent from Cambrai Cathedral and receives a chaplaincy in the parish church of Neuville, which he later exchanges by procurator for a chaplaincy in the collegiate church of St Géry in Cambrai.[56] Wright suggests that Caron may have been excused from his duties to study at the university, and one does find a Philippus Caron, albeit from the diocese of Tournai, matriculating at the University of Louvain on 14 June 1480.[57] In July 1483 Philippe Caron returns to the Cathedral and is inscribed as a *petit vicaire* at the lowest salary.[58] Soon afterwards, on 9 August 1484, the chapter gave him leave to go to Rome on a pilgrimage, and on 20 March 1486 they received him again as a *petit vicaire*.[59] Philippe Caron is named in 1486/7 for the last time; his name is miss-

[53] LADN B 3377, 113558, fo. [10ᵛ]: 'Aultres draps delivrez par ledict Henin . . . A Pierre du Wez – 7 aulnes . . . A Jehan le Caron . . . A Pasquier Louis'. I thank Paula Higgins for bringing this document to my attention and for her transcription.

[54] Craig Wright, 'Musiciens à la cathédrale de Cambrai 1475–1550', *Revue de musicologie*, 62 (1976), 204–28 at 216. Hémart was *maître des enfants* from 1469 until 1483.

[55] Thomson, 'The Works of Caron', 17–19; Jules Houdoy, *Histoire artistique de la cathédrale de Cambrai* (Lille, 1880), 83; see LADN 4 G 6791, fo. 4ʳ. The payment is for medicine for the altar boys Jo. Binchois and Philippe le Caron and was made on an unspecified date. The names are copied on a flyleaf (fo. 78ʳ) at the end of Cambrai, Bibliothèque municipale, MS 28.

[56] See Cambrai, Bibliothèque municipale, MS 1061, fos. 92ᵛ, 93ᵛ (transcribed in Wright, 'Musiciens', 216). This is most likely Neuville-sur-Escaut, but it could also be Neuville near Namur.

[57] Joseph Wils, *Matricule de l'université de Louvain*, ii: *1453–1485* (Brussels, 1946), 418. No Caron is listed in vol. i.

[58] See Cambrai 1061, fo. 164ʳ (transcribed in Wright, 'Musiciens', 216).

[59] Ibid., fo. 188ʳ (transcribed ibid. 216); 'philippus Charon' on fo. 248ᵛ (transcribed ibid.).

ing from the accounts of 1487/8 and from all later documents from the Cathedral.[60]

In 1489, when Busnoys may already have been in Bruges,[61] a Philippe Caron does turn up in Brussels at St Gudula, not long after the namesake disappears from Cambrai. Shortly after Philippe Caron's arrival in 1489, he bought a choir cap from another chaplain, Nicolas Mierlaer,[62] and served as procurator for the priest, Guilhermus Pesim (1489), and for the chaplain and priest, Guillelmus Prepositus (1490).[63] The accounts of the *villicus* of the church of St Gudula, the individual responsible for church property excluding prebends, demonstrate that Philippe Caron held the chaplaincies of Sts Michael, Lawrence, and George in that church intermittently, beginning in 1490,[64] and remained associated with the church as chaplain and later *zangmeester* until his death in 1509.[65] Since the Philippe Carons of Cambrai and Brussels both sang, the former disappears just

[60] 'Philipot' is last in the list of *petits vicaires* (LADN 4 G 6791, 1486/7, fo. 4ʳ); see Wright, 'Musiciens', 212, 215 ff., 232.

[61] Busnoys's whereabouts between 1483 and his presumed death in Bruges in 1492 are not known. See Higgins, '*In hydraulis*', 41, 52–3, 62.

[62] The biographical evidence for Philippe Caron at Brussels was first presented in Haggh, 'Music, Liturgy, and Ceremony', 567–8. On Mierlaer, see ibid., 632, and BAR, ASG 283, fo. 656ʳ (14 Oct. 1489): 'Rekeninge . . . executuren wijlen Claes Mierlaer, priester en capellaen der selver kerken van sinte Goelen . . . Item vercocht sijn choormutse her Philippus Caron ende gegeven in zwaren gelde om – 5 s.g.'

[63] A Jean Caron is listed as procurator in 1489, but a slightly later entry shows that this was in fact Philippe (emphasis mine). The confusion may have resulted from Philippe having only just arrived in Brussels: BAR, ASG 910, fo. 124ʳ: 'Eodem die [22 Jan. 1489 modern style] admissus est dominus Guilhelmus pesim presbiter In persona domini *Johannis caron* procuratoris sui ad capellaniam sanctorum Iohannis evangeliste et barbare dicte ecclesie [de capella] In vico katerine domini Johannis qui Iuravit et solvit Iuramenta consueta'; ibid., fo. 124ᵛ: (9 Oct. 1490) 'die sabbati nona octobris admissus est magister Guilhelmus prepositus clericus In persona domini *philippi caron* procuratoris sui constituti ut constat per Instrumentum exhibitum ad possessionem capellanie sancti Johannis baptiste situm In ecclesia de capella domino guillelmo collate ut constat Iuxta litteras domini Abbatis quas panes nos reservamus Iuravit et solvit Iuramenta consueta. [Left margin:] gratie Intuitu dicti domini Admissi' (emphasis mine).

[64] Philippe Caron served the first St Michael chaplaincy, with four weekly Masses, in 1490/1 (BAR, ASG 1391, fo. 176ʳ (1490/1; all accounts begin 24 Dec.); cf. Haggh, 'Music, Liturgy, and Ceremony', 717–18, on the chaplaincy), the third St Lawrence chaplaincy in 1495/6 (BAR, ASG 1391, fo. 288ᵛ (1495/6)), the fourth St Lawrence chaplaincy from 1498 to 1501 (ibid. 1392, fo. 8ʳ (1498/9): 'phillipus caron fit gratia'; fo. 33ʳ (1499/1500): 'Philippus caron [then in different ink:] Isti fit gratia totalis'; fo. 57ʳ (1500/1): 'Philippus caron Isti fit gratia totalis'; see Haggh, ibid. 713–14, on the St Lawrence chaplaincy, and the first St George chaplaincy from 1505 until his death. On this chaplaincy, see Haggh, ibid. 707–8. On Philippe as chaplain at the St George altar, see BAR, ASG 1392, fo. 186ʳ (1505/6), fo. 212ʳ (1506/7), fo. 238ʳ (1507/8), and fo. 264ʳ (1508/9). On fo. 283ʳ (1509/10), the chaplain holding this chaplaincy is Johannes Andree. Also see BAR, ASG 910, fos. 131ᵛ and 134ʳ, on Philippe Caron's admittance to the St George chaplaincy on 5 Dec. 1505 and on the admittance of his successor to the same chaplaincy on 26 Jan. 1510, respectively. Philippe Caron's career as chaplain corresponds well with the description of changing chaplaincy occupancy presented in the first part of this study.

[65] His musical duties included serving as *zangmeester* and teaching the *boni infantes* and *choraelen*, the choirboys of St Gudula. He is named in the accounts of the Fabric of St Gudula, BAR, ASG 9365 (Christmas 1493/4), and is documented as *zangmeester* in the accounts of the *bonifanten*, BAR, ASG 6398, fo. 361ᵛ (Christmas 1494/5): 'Alia exposita In premijs servitorum . . . Primo domino philippo Caron magistro cantus pro stipendio et salario Instructionis bonorum infancium – 2 L.g.' On the *bonifanten* and *choraelen* at St Gudula, see Lewis Baratz, 'St Gudula's Children: The Bonifanten and Choraelen of the Collegiate Church of Brussels during the Ancien Régime', in Barbara Haggh *et al.* (eds.), *Musicology and Archival Research: Proceedings of the Colloquium held at the Algemeen Rijksarchief, Brussels, 22–23 April 1993* (Archiefen Bibliotheekwezen in België, Extranummer 46; Brussels, 1994), 214–305. On the *zangmeesters* of St Gudula, see Haggh, 'Music, Liturgy, and Ceremony', 142–9. Philippe Caron's death in 1509 is documented in BAR, ASG 281, fo. 284ʳ (see App. A, Doc. 5).

before the latter appears, and the names are unique in the documentation, they may well have been the same individual.

Other evidence for the Philippe Carons of Brussels and Cambrai being the same son of Jean Caron is found in the life of the Brussels Philippe, which reflects his father's career and association with the Burgundian court, an association not documented for Philippe himself. Philippe owned a house on the Coudenberg, the area near the ducal palace populated mainly by the nobility,[66] and his neighbour was none other than the count of Nassau, probably Engelbert (d. 1504), a distinguished Burgundian soldier who fought in Charles the Bold's military campaigns in Switzerland and northern France, a diplomat and courtier of Maximilian and Mary of Burgundy who had been elected knight of the Order of the Golden Fleece in 1473 and also engaged to Anne of Brittany.[67] And in 1506 Philippe Caron read fifty 'vigils' for the soul of a member of Maximilian I's privy council, the canon and chaplain at St Gudula Marcus Steenberch, evidence that the two could have moved in the same circles.[68] In addition, Philippe Caron's executors' account shows that he was not buried in St Gudula as were most members of that church's clergy (see App. A, Doc. 5), but in Our Lady of the Sands, a church preferred by Charles the Bold, who had even asked for a street to be paved from his palace to it in 1470.[69] It seems extremely likely, then, that the Cambrai and Brussels Philippes were one individual, Jean Caron's son, probably

[66] BAR, ASG 9365 (Fabric accounts, 17 Oct. 1494), fo. 160ᵛ: 'Uuytgeven aen Erfrente dit Jair gecocht. Gecocht opten 17en dach octobris anno 94 tegen heer philipse le caron priestere opte 2/3 van eender hofstade metten huysen stallen en synen anderen toebehoirten opt coudenberch gelegen . . .'. There is no entry the next year; the accounts for 1496/7 do not survive. Next is ASG 9367 (Christmas 1497/8), fo. 2ʳ: 'heer philips caron priester van synen goeden opt coudenberch neven myns heeren van assouwen gelegen . . .'; the same property is also mentioned in ASG 9368 (Christmas 1499/1500), fo. 2ʳ, and ASG 9369 (Christmas 1501/2), fo. 2ʳ. The accounts following are missing, and there is no entry in ASG 9370 (Christmas 1531/2). No Caron or other Burgundian singers are listed in the surviving 15th-c. obituary from the priory of St James on the Coudenberg, BAR, KB 6906. On the wealthy neighbourhoods near the Coudenberg, see Guillaume Des Marez, *L'Origine et le développement de la ville de Bruxelles: Le Quartier Isabelle et Terarken* (Brussels, 1927), esp. chs. 4 and 5.

[67] On Engelbert of Nassau, see J. Arnoldi, *Geschichte der Oranien Nassauischen Länder und ihrer Regenten*, 5 vols. (Hadamar, 1799–1819), esp. iii, chs. 18–20 and 26; Emile de Borchgrave, 'Nassau, Engelbert, comte de', *Biographie nationale*, xv (Brussels, 1899), cols. 473–80; and C.-A. Serrure, *Notice sur Engelbert II, comte de Nassau* (Ghent, 1862), esp. p. 38.

[68] BAR, ASG 268, fo. 240ʳ (11 Jan. 1507 modern style). 'Reekeninghe der Executueren vanden Testamente wijlen des eerweerdighen heeren heeren ende meesteren Marcx steenberch In sijnre tyt Telkens Canonicx ende prochiaens Inder kercken van Sinte goedelen Inder stad van Bruessel'; fo. 265ʳ: 'Ander uutgeven en oncosten gedaen ten tyde vander afluicheit van mijn heere totten tyde toe vander dertichste'; fo. 266ʳ⁻ᵛ: 'Item betailt her philipse caron priester van vyftich vigilien voer den voirs. testaeteur te lesen van elcker een stuiver en desgelycx betailt heeren Janne steppe voer 42 werven onser liever vrouwen getijde te lesen'. Marcus Steenberch, major canon with the third prebend at St Gudula, had a doctorate in laws from Louvain and was a member of Maximilian's privy council (see Haggh, 'Music, Liturgy, and Ceremony', 665–6).

[69] See Haggh, 'Music, Liturgy, and Ceremony', 93. Unfortunately, none of the published inscriptions on graves or monuments in Our Lady of the Sands or other local churches names a Caron, and, with the exception of a few documents discussed in Haggh, ibid., no archives of musical interest from before 1600 survive from this church (I thank Father J. Windey, SJ, archivist responsible for the collection still in the church, for permitting me to study that archive). The documents from St Gudula do not list Caron for any chaplaincies at the church of Our Lady of the Sands.

a composer since he served as *zangmeester*, and certainly a musician,[70] but not a singer at the court of Burgundy.

Given that Roth's 1477 obligation lists individuals not belonging to the Burgundian chapel and that the Caron of the *escroes* cannot be Philippe Caron, we can only conclude that Roth's theory of a Philippe Caron who sang and composed as a Burgundian chaplain in the 1470s is entirely untenable. Moreover, Philippe Caron, the son of Jean, cannot be the famous composer. He was too young to have composed the works ascribed to Caron in manuscripts,[71] to have had a mass copied at Cambrai Cathedral in 1472,[72] and to have been regarded by Tinctoris as a leading composer in 1477.[73] Until the Tinctoris citation can be explained, his Firminus Caron will remain as enigmatic as the chaplaincy held by Busnoys at the church of St Nicholas in Brussels for only four days.

[70] Cf. Paula Higgins, 'Tracing the Careers of Late Medieval Composers: The Case of Philippe Basiron of Bourges', *Acta musicologica*, 62 (1990), 1–28, esp. 22.

[71] In the opinion of David Fallows, Caron's works must date from *c*.1465–80, given the dates presently assigned to the manuscript sources (private communication).

[72] Houdoy, *Histoire*, 200: 'Eidem [= Simon Mellet] pro duplici grossacione unius misse per Caron compilate et pro missa ex opere Johannis Fremiet – LX s'. It is possible that Caron only assembled mass movements and that some or all were by other composers.

[73] See above, n. 6.

Appendix A
Documents from Brussels on Busnoys and 'Caron'

Doc. 1. BAR, ASG 910 (acta capituli), fo. 115ᵛ

Die lune 9 Novembris [1478] capellaniam sanctorum spiritus et crucis ex simplici Resignatione domini Nicolai vander Walter ipsius possessoris vacantem contulimus domino Waltero Henrici scolastico et confratri canonico cum solemnibus solitis, similiter significat.

Doc. 2. BAR, ASG 910 (acta capituli), fo. 115ᵛ

Die martis 10 Novembris [1478] vacante predicta capellania sanctorum spiritus et crucis per Resignationem prenominati domini scolastici factam ex causa permutationis inite cum magistro Anthonio de busne Ad canonicatum et prebendam Audomarenses capellaniam ipsam contulimus predicto magistro Anthonio In persona bernardi buillot procuratoris dicti magistri Anthonii ad hoc constituti ut constat per notam procurationis retentam etc. Iuramenta hincinde ut moris est et nichil solverunt.

Doc. 3. BAR, ASG 910 (acta capituli), fo. 115ᵛ

Sabbato 14 Novembris [1478] capellaniam pretactam sanctorum spiritus et crucis vacantem per resignationem magistri Anthonii de busne ipsius novissimi possessoris factam ex causa permutationis Inite Inter eum et dominum Johannem Pintot capellanum capellanie de warandiis ad capellaniam suam huiusmodi contulimus dicto Jo. pintot et Iuramenta utrisque ut moris est nichil solverun. Quiquidem pintot constituit Fabri presentari(?) Ad Resignandum dictam capellaniam sanctorum spiritus et crucis In manibus capituli simpliciter promittens etc.

Doc. 4. BAR, CC 134, fo. 106ʳ

Commission de Jehan caron de conchierge et garde delostel de monseigneur sur coudenberghe a brouxelles

[left margin:] Hesdin, 12 August 1470

Collationne a loriginal qui est demoure devers ledit Jehan caron

[main text:] Charles Par la grace de dieu duc de bourgogne . . . Marquis du saint empire . . . A Tous ceulx qui ces presentes lettres verront salut Savoir faisons que pour consideracion des bons et agreables services que nostre bien ame serviteur de nostre oratoire Jehan Caron a faiz par cydevant a feu nostre treschere seigneur et pere que dieu absoille et a nous depuis son trespas tant oudit office de sommelier que autrement quil nous fait chacun Jour et esperons que encores faire nous doye ou temps advenir de bien en mieulx A Icellui Jehan Caron pour ces causes et autres ace nous mouvans Confians aplain de ses loyaulte preudomie et bonne diligence avons donne et ottroye donnons et ottroyons par ces presentes loffice de conchierge et garde de nostre hostel de coudenberghe en nostre ville de bruxelles a present vacant par le trespas de feu Jehan guillier derrenier possesseur dudit

office Lequel puis nagaires est alle de vie a trespas Comme entendu avons Pour icellui
office tenir excercer et desservir et faire bien et deuement tout ce quy y compette et appartient Aux gaiges droiz sallaires libertez franchises prouffiz et emolumens acoustumez et y
appartiennent Tant quil nous plaira Sur quoy Il sera tenu de faire le serment ace pertinent
es mains de noz amez et feaulx les gens de noz comptes a brouxelles que comectons ace Si
donnons en mandement ausdis gens de noz comptes que ledit serment fait Par ledit caron
comme dit est Ilz le mettent et Instituent ou facent mettre et Instituer de par nous en possession et saisine dudit office En lui baillant et delivrant ou faisant bailler et delivrer les clefz
et biens meubles estans et anous appartenant en nostre dit hostel Par bon et loyal
Inventoire le double duquel voulons estre mis et garde en ladit chambre de noz comptes a
bruxelles Et dudit office de conchierge ensemble des droiz libertez francises prouffiz et
emolumens dessusdis Ilz et tous autres noz officiers qui ce Regardera le facent souffrent et
laissent plainement et paisiblement Joir et user Cessans tous contrediz et empeschemens
Car ainsi nous plaist Il En tesmoing de ce nous avons fait mettre aces presentes nostre scel
de secret en absence du grant donne en nostre chastel de hesdin le 12 Jour daoust Lan de
Grace mil quatrecens Soixante dix Ainsi signee Par monseigneur le duc J. Gros Et sur le
doz dicelle est escript ce qui senssuit Le 15 Jour de septembre Lan mil cccc soixante et dix
fist Jehan Caron denomme en blanc de cestes Le serment pertinent de loffice de
Conchierge et garde de lostel de monseigneur sur le coudenberghe a bruxelles dont oudit
blanc alautre coste de ces presentes est faicte mencion En la chambre des comptes de mondit seigneur Illec et es mains de messires desdis comptes Moy present Ainsi signee N. le
prevost.

Doc. 5. BAR, ASG 281 (18 January 1509, modern style; excerpts)

fo. 282^r: Compotus executorum quondam domini et magistri Philippi Caron presbiteri
fo. 283^r: Rekeninghe en bewijs heeren Merttens vander Rijt, Claes Coels priesteren en
capellanen der kercke van sinte Goelen, Kaerls Caron en Wautelet Marii als executuren
wijlen zaliger gedachten heeren en meesters Philips Caron, doen hij leefde capellaen der
selver kercken, die sterf en afluich woordde den 18sten dach Januarij, Anno 1509 more
gallicano . . .
fo. 284^r: . . . Item den heeren Canonicke metten lichaem gaende tot opde Zavele daert
begraven Is elcken 2 stuivers anderen heeren priesteren en officieren vander kercken elcken
eenen stuiver. Ende Insgelijcx ter stoolen den Canonicken 2 solz en den anderen een stu-
ver tsamen – Rinsgulden 4 solz. . . . Premisse computaciones reddite fuerunt per antedictos executores coram venerabilibus viris dominis et magistris Judoco Cloet cantore,
Nicolao Mayoul, Judoco de Leenhere, Johanne Jacobi, Jacobo Vincentij et Nicolao van
Oudenhagen canonicis ecclesie collegiate beate Gudile Bruxellensis. In eorum loco capitulari capitulariter propter premissum congregatis die decimatercia mensis Martij, Anno
domini millesimo quingentesimo decimo more gallicano. Et fuerunt eedem computa-
tiones per antedictos dominos de capitulo passate et admisse. Necnon ipsi executores ab
onere huiusmodi executione eorum absoluti. Me Johanne Ets dictorum venerabilium
dominorum notario Jurato presente, quod signo meo manuali minuto attestor.

Appendix B
Summary of Burgundian Court *Escroes* Showing
Caron's Presence or Absence

1471

date	place	Caron named	source	
March				
8	Camp at Pont-de-Metz		LADN, B 3435:	118619
11	Camp near St-Acheul-lez-Amiens			118622
23	Camp near St-Acheul-lez-Amiens			118623
30	Amiens	Caron		118626
April				
5	Fosse Ferneuse [near Amiens]	Caron		118630
18	Péronne	Caron		118633
June				
8	Péronne	Caron		118636
13	Doullens	Caron [crossed out]		118638
18	LeCrotoy/Abbeville			118642
20	Abbeville			118645

1472

Caron is not mentioned on any of the thirty surviving lists dated from 20 July to 26 December 1472 (cf. Higgins, '*In hydraulis*', 55–6), LADN, B 3436, 118738–118825.

1473

date	place	Caron named	source	
January				
2	L'Ecluse/Arnemuiden		LADN, B 3437:	118951
6	Zierikzee			118953
14	Bruges			118954
15	Bruges			118956
23	Bruges/Ghent		PAN, K530[29]:	no. 31
31	Zierikzee/Biert		LADN, B 3437:	118959
February				
27	Antwerp			118960
July				
1	Camp near Nijmegen	Caron [crossed out]		118962
2	Camp near Nijmegen	Caron		118963
25	Château of Nijmegen			118972
26	Château of Nijmegen			118974
August				
1	Camp near the Abbey of Elten [county of Zuytphen]			118977
4	Camp at Baak-lez-Zuytphen			118979
22	Rolduc/Aachen			118987
31	Bastogne/Martelange			118988

date	place	Caron named	source	
September				
25	Château of Luxembourg			118999
26	Château of Luxembourg			119003
27	Luxembourg			119006
29	Luxembourg/Grevenmacher			119009
October				
2	St. Maximin's Abbey near Trier			119012
12	St. Maximin's Abbey near Trier			119016
13	St. Maximin's Abbey near Trier			119017
[illeg.]	St. Maximin's Abbey near Trier			119025
November				
24	St. Maximin's Abbey near Trier			119030
December				
4	Thionville			119034
10	Thionville			119039
13	Chambley/Château of Pierrepont			119040
26	Neuf-Brisach [Breisach]			119041
31	Neuf-Brisach/Ensisheim			119042

1474

date	place	Caron named	source	
January				
5	Ensisheim		LADN, B 3438:	119078
31	Dijon			119080
February				
23	Dole			119085
27	Dole		PAN, K530[29]:	no. 32
July				
1	Brussels		BAR, ÉA 9:	no. 257
13	Louvain/Saint-Trond	Carron		no. 242
20	Maestricht	Carron		no. 243
August				
6	gates of Neuss		Paris, Bibl. nat., fr. 8255:	no. 43
7	gates of Neuss	Carron	BAR, ÉA 9:	no. 244
14	gates of Neuss	Carron		no. 245
19	Neuss	Carron		no. 246
28	Neuss		Paris fr. 8255:	no. 44
29	Neuss	Carron	BAR, ÉA 9:	no. 247
30	Neuss	Carron	Paris fr. 8255:	no. 45
September				
10	Neuss			no. 48
14	Neuss	Carron	LADN, B 3438:	119091
15	Neuss	Carron		119092
21	Neuss	Carron		119094
26	Neuss	Carron		119096
October				
8	Neuss	Caron		119105
20	Neuss			119109
21	Neuss	Caron		119110

date	place	Caron named	source	
October				
24	Neuss	Caron		119111
November				
12	Neuss	Caron		119114
15	Neuss	Carron		119115
16	Neuss	Caron		119116
22	Neuss	Caron		119119
30	Neuss	Carron		119124
December				
18	Neuss	Carron		119130
21	Neuss	Carron		119131
23	Neuss	Carron		119132

1475

date	place	Caron named	source	
January				
5	Neuss	Caron [crossed out]	LADN, B 3439:	119180
15	Neuss			119183
20	Neuss			119185
22	Neuss			119188
February				
4	Neuss			119196
11	Neuss			119198
19	Neuss			119202
March				
1	Neuss		BAR, ÉA 9:	no. 250bis
3	Neuss		Paris, fr. 8255:	no. 28
4	Neuss			no. 29
7	Neuss			no. 31
9	Neuss		LADN, B 3439:	119203
10	Neuss		Paris, fr. 8255:	no. 32
11	Neuss			no. 33
12	Neuss			no. 34
13	Neuss			no. 35
14	Neuss			no. 36
15	Neuss			no. 37
16	Neuss			no. 38
31	Neuss			no. 49
April				
9	Neuss	Carron	BAR, ÉA 9:	no. 252
17	Neuss	Caron		no. 253
27	Neuss		Paris, fr. 8255:	no. 51
30	Neuss			no. 52
May				
8	Neuss			no. 54
12	Neuss			no. 55
14	Neuss	Carron	BAR, ÉA 9:	no. 255
25	Neuss		Paris, fr. 8255:	no. 56

date	place	Caron named	source	
June				
2	Neuss			no. 57
13	Neuss			no. 58
14	Neuss			no. 59
15	Neuss			no. 60
October				
6	Camp-lez-Bayon	Caron	LADN, B 3439:	119208
24	Siege of Nancy			119213
November				
3	Siege of Nancy	Caron		119222
December				
14	Nancy	Caron		119225
20	Nancy	Caron		119233
28	Nancy		Paris, fr. 8255:	no. 27
30	Nancy	Caron		119237
31	Nancy		Paris, fr. 3867:	fo. 2ᵛ

13

Conflicting Attributions and Anonymous Chansons in the 'Busnoys' Sources of the Fifteenth Century

வ๕ ஜ๑

LEEMAN L. PERKINS

IN attempting to bring at long last to fruition a complete edition of the chansons of Antoine Busnoys—a project begun decades ago by the late Catherine V. Brooks—it has been necessary to face anew the fundamental problems posed by such a task. Among the most vexing of these, perhaps, continues to be the establishment of a relatively reliable definition of the total repertory to have survived. Which of the pieces in the sources of the period were actually of Busnoys's composition, and therefore to be included in the edition? And should this question be construed to concern only those pieces ascribed to him, whether with or without conflicting attributions, as is usually the case? Or should there be serious consideration as well of those songs that were inscribed anonymously in the sources most central to the area and the period of his compositional activity?

No other composer of Busnoys's immediate generation is credited in the chanson sources of the fifteenth century with as many secular compositions as he. Among the masters of that age generally, in fact, only Binchois and Dufay have left a larger repertory of secular song. Fifty-nine pieces carry only his name (to the best of my knowledge), while another fourteen carry together with his that of at least one other person. However, in examining the ascriptions that link these pieces to Busnoys, one must be struck first of all by what slender a thread that connection is usually made (see App. A, where the chansons of Busnoys have been ordered according to the number of attributions for each). Forty-one of the fifty-nine songs that have been attributed only to him—more than two-thirds of the total number—carry his name in but a single source. Another fourteen have two surviving witnesses to his authorship; only four have as many as three, and none more than four.

Among these attributions some would appear to be more reliable than others. One generally assumes that the sources compiled closest to the time and place of a composer's primary activity have the best chance of correctly identifying those pieces that were actually his. On the strength of that assumption it is perhaps not too reckless to conclude that the ascriptions appearing in Nivelle and Dijon are those most likely to provide trustworthy evidence of Busnoys's authorship.

Nivelle is thought to be the earlier of the two, having originated between 1460 and 1465, most probably somewhere along the axis between Tours and Bourges.[1] Dijon is only about a decade later, for the most part, dating probably from the early 1470s, and its inclusion of a substantial number of compositions by musicians in the service of the ducal court of Burgundy would suggest that it was probably compiled in northern France, perhaps even close to the capital of the duchy where it is now found.[2]

Related to these two both geographically and temporally, and therefore also reasonably reliable in its attributions to Busnoys, presumably, is Laborde, which apparently dates from the late 1460s and originated in central France, most likely in one of the urban centres of the Loire Valley.[3] Unfortunately useless in this connection, because entirely wanting the names of the composers represented in them, are the other two related manuscript collections from roughly the same time and place: Copenhagen[4] and Wolfenbüttel.[5] In addition, although of Neapolitan provenance, Mellon would appear to be relatively dependable in its ascriptions because of the evident involvement in its compilation of the well-known theorist and composer Johannes Tinctoris, who in the early 1460s was at the University of Orléans and therefore not far from the French royal court.[6]

By contrast, ascriptions to Busnoys found only in secular sources of Italian, Spanish, or German origin ought perhaps to be regarded a bit more cautiously. To do so, however, is to face the slightly alarming circumstance that twenty-two of the forty-one songs carrying an attribution to Busnoys in a single source—

---

[1] See Paula Higgins, Introduction to the facsimile edition of the manuscript, *Chansonnier Nivelle de La Chaussée (Bibliothèque nationale, Paris, Rés. Vmc. ms. 57)* (Geneva, 1984), pp. iii, ix.

[2] See the Introduction by Dragan Plamenac to the facsimile edition of the collection, *Dijon, Bibliothèque publique, manuscrit 517* (Publications of Mediaeval Musical Manuscripts, 12; Brooklyn, NY, n.d.), 3.

[3] Concerning this codex, MS M2.1.L25 Case at the Library of Congress in Washington, DC, see the *Census-Catalogue*, iv. 125–6.

[4] Concerning this collection, MS Thott 291, 8° at the Royal Library in Copenhagen, see the edition by Knud Jeppesen, *Der Kopenhagener Chansonnier* (Copenhagen and Leipzig, 1927; repr. 1965), pp. xxv ff., who dated its compilation from the 1470s and placed it in northern France or Burgundy.

[5] Regarding this manuscript, MS Guelf. 287 extrav. of the Herzog August Bibliothek in Wolfenbüttel, see the study by Martella Gutiérrez-Denhoff, *Der Wolfenbütteler Chansonnier* (Wolfenbütteler Forschungen, 29; Wiesbaden, 1985), 22 and 48 ff., who dates the collection from the 1460s and places its illumination in the Loire Valley once again.

[6] Concerning this collection, MS 91 of the Beinecke Library for Rare Books and Manuscripts, Yale University, see the Introduction to *The Mellon Chansonnier*, ed. Leeman L. Perkins and Howard Garey (New Haven, 1979), i. 17–32; its compilation dates from the mid-1470s. Tinctoris's sojourn in Orléans has been documented by Ronald Woodley, 'Iohannes Tinctoris: A Review of the Documentary Biographical Evidence', *JAMS* 34 (1981), 217–48.

more than half—fall into this category.[7] One cannot of course conclude that because a manuscript is removed to a degree in time or place from the principal locus of a given composer's career that its ascriptions are necessarily in error. Nevertheless, the only source for nine of the composer identifications in question is the Pixérécourt chansonnier, which has proven to be generally less reliable in this regard than most collections of its kind.[8]

What is more, of the eighteen pieces with an attribution to Busnoys in two or more of the surviving sources, eight of them involve the Pixérécourt chansonnier and another Florentine source[9]—usually Florence 229, but also in one instance Florence 176[10]—raising the possibility that the two citations represent only one original witness for his authorship. Given the situation in the sources, then, it would be precious indeed if there were some other means available either to verify or to invalidate the meagre evidence that they offer.

The Conflicting Attributions

The group of fourteen pieces transmitted in the sources under Busnoys's name and that of at least one other composer represents a rather substantial repertory in its own right, one roughly a third the size of that linked only to Busnoys. Among these chansons there are only two for which a consensus appears to have emerged as to their rightful paternity. On the one hand is the widely disseminated *rondeau cinquain D'ung aultre amer*, which is credited to Okeghem in six of its fourteen musical sources and to Busnoys only in Pixérécourt, whose questionable authority in this respect has already been cited. No one appears ready in this instance to challenge seriously the statistically dominant ascription to Okeghem.[11]

On the other hand is the *rondeau layé Quant ce viendra*, which appears with Busnoys's name in two of the sources most central to his secular repertory, Dijon and Laborde, and with that of 'Hockenghem' only in the Italian source Escorial IV.a.24.[12] In this instance as well it appears to have been primarily the ascriptions

---

[7] In App. A, I: Works Attributed to Busnoys in a Single Source, these are nos. 1, 2, 6, 8–11, 14–16, 20, 23–6, 28, 30, 32–3, 36, and 38–40.

[8] Concerning this collection, MS 15123 of the fonds français at the Bibliothèque nationale in Paris, which was inscribed and decorated in Florence, probably in the 1480s, see the *Census-Catalogue*, iii. 23–4.

[9] In App. A, II: Works Attributed to Busnoys in Two Sources, these are nos. 1, 5, 6, 12, and 14; and in App. A, III: Works Attributed to Busnoys in Three or More Sources, these are nos. 2 and 4.

[10] Concerning the first of these, which was copied in Florence early in the 1490s, see the introductory study to the edition by Howard Mayer Brown, *A Florentine Chansonnier from the Time of Lorenzo the Magnificent* (Monuments of Renaissance Music, 7; Chicago, 1983), 1–51. Regarding the latter, which was inscribed in Florence in the late 1470s, see *Census-Catalogue*, i. 229–30.

[11] Paula Higgins omitted this chanson from her Catalogue of the Works of Antoine Busnois in 'Antoine Busnois and Musical Culture in Late Fifteenth-Century France and Burgundy' (Ph.D. diss., Princeton University, 1987), 313 ff.

[12] Concerning this collection, which may have been compiled in stages between 1450 and 1470 in Italy and brought to completion in Naples, see *Census-Catalogue*, i. 211–12; compare, however, the most recent review of its composition and contents by Denis Slavin, 'On the Origins of Escorial IV.a.24', *Studi musicali*, 19 (1990), 259–303.

in the manuscripts that have caused scholars to lean towards Busnoys as the more likely to have composed the piece.[13] It remains to be seen whether or not these conclusions will continue to stand in the face of a careful analysis of compositional style.

Evidence from the sources, when combined with some fairly well-established biographical detail, suggests a tentative resolution—one that is at least as secure as for the two songs just discussed—to yet another of the conflicts of attribution. The piece in question is *Vous marchez du bout du pié/Vostre beauté*, which is ascribed to Busnoys in Nivelle but to Isaac in Vienna 18810, a collection of primarily secular music that was probably copied in Augsburg or Munich between 1524 and 1533.[14] The latter witness, however, seems to me highly suspect. On the one hand, this late German source is far removed from Busnoys's time and sphere of activity. And on the other, the inclusion of *Vous marchez* under Busnoys's name in Nivelle, which could have been completed already in the early 1460s, would indicate that it was written when Isaac was still a child, possibly no more than 10 years of age, and was in any case as yet entirely unknown as a composer in the region of central France, where the songbook was copied.[15] And if, as it would seem, Busnoys is indeed the author of this lively little combinative chanson, that circumstance raises some interesting questions regarding his role in the development of what was then still a novel category within the genre, a point to which I shall return.

Every other instance of conflicting attributions involves manuscripts or prints compiled outside of the regions of France and Burgundy where Busnoys is known to have been in residence. In fact, the sources in which these multiple ascriptions are found are mostly of Italian provenance (see App. A, IV: Works with Conflicting Attributions). Not so the composers with whom Busnoys shares credit for the creation of these eleven pieces: most of them are Northerners. For some, such as Hayne van Ghizeghem, Gilles Mureau, and perhaps Caron—as, indeed, for Busnoys himself—there is no clear indication that they ever strayed in their travels south of the Alps.[16] For others, such as Johannes Japart, Johannes Martini, Loyset Compère, and Heinrich Isaac, an Italian sojourn, sometimes of considerable duration, is well documented.[17]

[13] Higgins, for example, has included this work in Busnoys's unchallenged canon ('Antoine Busnois and Musical Culture', 328) rather than among the Chansons with Conflicting Attributions (ibid. 331 ff.). See also the comments of Richard Taruskin, *Busnoys LTW*, Commentary, 95–100.

[14] Concerning the latter collection, see the *Census-Catalogue*, iv. 108–9.

[15] Concerning Isaac, see Martin Staehelin, 'Isaac, Heinrich', *New Grove*, ix. 329–32.

[16] Regarding Hayne, see Louise Litterick, 'Ghizeghem, Hayne van', *New Grove*, viii. 417–18; for Caron (Philippe or Firmin?), see Geneviève Thibault, ibid., iii. 816, who speculates on the evidence of the sources alone that he may have spent time on the peninsula, and Perkins, *The Mellon Chansonnier*, i. 9–10; but cf. the recent archival discoveries by Barbara Haggh, above, Ch. 12; on Mureau, see Gustave Reese, *Music in the Renaissance* (rev. edn., New York, 1959), 138.

[17] Concerning Japart, see Allan W. Atlas, 'Japart, Jean', *New Grove*, ix. 553; for Martini, see Lewis Lockwood, 'Martini, Johannes', ibid., xi. 726–7; on Compère, see Joshua Rifkin, 'Compère, Loyset', ibid., iv. 595–6; and regarding Isaac, see above, n. 15.

One might hastily conclude that an attribution in an Italian source to a composer known to have spent part of his career on the Italian peninsula is more likely to be accurate than one to a Northerner who apparently never ventured from his native regions. However, the fact that the conflicting ascriptions for these eleven compositions are in every case among sources of Italian provenance gives little support to that simple notion. Here, again, some means is badly needed beyond the codicological-biographical to determine which of the contradictory attributions is the more likely to be correct.

The Anonymous Compositions

In contrast to those chansons attributed both to Busnoys and at least one other composer—and posing a different and perhaps more intriguing problem—are those that flank pieces credited only to Busnoys but that have themselves no ascriptions at all in any of the sources in which they were inscribed. As has been noted, neither Copenhagen nor Wolfenbüttel names a composer for any of the songs entered upon their leaves. However, in Nivelle and Dijon, arguably the two most important sources for the chansons of Busnoys, a different situation obtains.

There pieces that can be credited to Busnoys, either directly by name or by a concordant source with an attribution, occur at times in small clusters and are separated from one another only by one or two anonymous songs. Assuming, as I believe we can, that the exemplars for larger collections such as these were smaller 'fascicles',[18] containing, for example, repertory from a given locality or, perhaps in some cases, by a single musician, it is tempting to speculate that some of the anonymous chansons nested (as it were) with others credited to Busnoys may also be his. This aspect of the constitution of the two sources in question is particularly suggestive with regard to compositions of two distinctive types: the combinative chansons and the virelais.[19]

In Nivelle the combinative chansons are few in number—there are only three—and they are scattered through the collection. The first, *D'une belle jeune fille/Coquille* (fos. xxxviii^v–xxxix^r) is without ascription and is sandwiched between rondeaux by Busnoys and Delahaye. (It was also included in the combinative fascicle of Dijon discussed below, a concordance that could prove to be especially worthy of note.) The second is Okeghem's well-known and widely disseminated *S'elle m'amera/Petite camusette* (fos. lv^v–lvi^r). And the third, *Tout au long/Il n'est Jacobin/Jennette des coqueles*, is signed with the name of Delahaye

---

[18] The concept, and this use of the term, we owe to Charles Hamm, 'Manuscript Structure in the Dufay Era', *Acta musicologica*, 34 (1962), 166–84.

[19] Meant, of course, is the one-stanza variety of the fixed form current during the 15th c., which is often referred to as a bergerette in the secondary literature.

(Jean?), a minor master known primarily through the small repertory of songs transmitted by this one source.[20]

In Dijon, by contrast, the repertory of combinative chansons is significantly larger, and their disposition in the manuscript is dramatically different. Apart from the anonymous *Souviegne vous/Ma bien amer*, which stands by itself at the end of the nineteenth gathering (fos. 146^v–147^r), all the pieces of this type were entered in the three consecutive quaterns coming immediately before the last gathering of the collection (22, 23, and 24, fos. 165–86).[21] All but one, *On a grant mal/On est bien malade*, which is signed Busnoys, are anonymous in this manuscript; however, three more have ascriptions in other sources, one to Okeghem—again his *S'elle m'amera/Petite camusette* (fos. 164^v–165^r)—and two more to Busnoys, *Mon mignault/Gracieuse plaisant* (fos. 181^v–182^r) and, assuming the solidity of the argument just made for its paternity, *Vous marchez/Votre beauté* (fos. 185^v–186^r).

Striking to me, and significant, I believe, is the fact that for the entire repertory found in those two manuscripts, only three composers are named in the sources: Okeghem and the little-known Delahaye with a single attribution apiece, and Busnoys with three. It is possible, of course, that none of the other pieces of this type is by any one of them. In view of the particular nature of the genre, however, and their—virtually anonymous—transmission in Dijon, I think it much more likely that at least some of the unsigned pieces are also by one of the composers linked to such pieces by ascription. And, clearly, on purely statistical grounds Busnoys is three times as apt as his two contemporaries to have unidentified combinative chansons among the compositions in the three contiguous fascicles given over to the genre in Dijon.

Interestingly, a similar situation exists with respect to the virelais in these two collections and in the other related manuscripts that are most important for the direct transmission of chansons by Busnoys. As may be seen from Appendix B, Virelais in the Sources Central for Busnoys, within the combined repertory of forty-nine virelais included in one or more of the six manuscripts consulted,[22] there are attributions to only ten composers, counting both Fresneau and Agricola for the single piece credited in separate sources to each of them. This is a significantly smaller group than that constituted by the masters who contributed to either Nivelle or Dijon generally but who have not been linked to a virelai by an ascription in any of the manuscripts in question. These include

---

[20] Regarding what little is known of a musician by this name who may have been the composer, see Higgins, *Chansonnier Nivelle de La Chaussée*, p. vi.

[21] Two motet-chansons, *Permanent vierge/Pulcra es/Sancta Dei* and *Mort tu as navré* (Okeghem's lament on the death of Binchois) were also included in this section of the manuscript.

[22] Basiron's *De mesjouir* was mistakenly identified as a virelai by Martella Gutiérrez-Denhoff in her inventory of *Der Wolfenbütteler Chansonnier*, 305, apparently merely because it occupies two full openings of the manuscript. As is evident from the form of both music and verse, however, not only in the Wolfenbüttel manuscript but also in the concordant sources, the piece is a *rondeau cinquain*.

Barbingant, Bedingham or Dunstable, Binchois, Boubert, Convert, Delahaye, Frye, Hayne, Michelet, Molinet, Morton, Pullois, Magister Symon (le Breton?), and Tinctoris, another fifteen composers.

Of those to whom at least one virelai has been ascribed somewhere, the greatest number by far have been credited to Busnoys, who is named for thirteen such pieces, as is shown in Appendix C, Inventory of Virelais in the Sources Central for Busnoys. Okeghem, who has the next greatest number, has been linked by attribution to only four. Fede—who was at one point a colleague of Okeghem in the French royal chapel[23]—is identified as the author of two virelais that were copied into Nivelle (but that were among the pieces subsequently erased rather thoroughly). All the others—Dufay, Basiron, Caron, Le Rouge, and (coming to the next generation of composers) Agricola, Compère, and Fresneau—have had their names signed in the sources to a single virelai apiece.

Statistically speaking, once again, the numbers suggest in this instance as well—and rather more dramatically—that Busnoys is much more likely than any of the others mentioned to be the author of one or more of the twenty-four compositions that remain anonymous in these sources. Okeghem, by comparison, although the next most probable, follows a distant second. In fact, if the proportion—thirteen to twelve—between Busnoys and the remainder of the musicians named in the segment of the virelai repertory having attributions were to hold for the pieces transmitted anonymously, Busnoys could be the composer of roughly half the latter as well. In any case, his numerical superiority in this part of the chanson repertory of the period may also help to explain why a fifteenth-century authority on the *seconde rhétorique* such as Pierre Fabri could mistakenly impute to Busnoys the invention of the genre.[24]

At this point, then, it is possible to ask which of the anonymous virelais in either of these two collections might possibly be by Busnoys. Let us consider once again the configuration of the sources. In Nivelle, for example, the sixth gathering contains only works that are either ascribed to Busnoys or are anonymous in all of the known sources. Included are three virelais, one that was inscribed under Busnoys's name in Dijon, *En tous les lieux*, and two others that have remained thus far without attribution.

The first of these, *Chargé de dueil*, is flanked on either side by a piece credited to Busnoys; preceding it is the *rondeau layé C'est bien malheur*, which carries his name in Nivelle itself; and following it the virelai just mentioned. Similarly, immediately following Busnoys's *En tous les lieux* and closing out the gathering is the anonymous virelai *Par Dieu, madame*. On the strength of the codicological

<hr>

[23] Regarding Fede, see David Fallows, 'Fede, Jean', *New Grove*, vi. 446, and Higgins, *Chansonnier Nivelle de La Chaussée*, pp. v–vi.

[24] See Fabri's *Le Grant et vrai art de pleine rhétorique* of 1521 as edited by A. Héron (Paris, 1889), ii. 71; this passage has been cited by Reese, *Music in the Renaissance*, 15 n. 69.

evidence alone, therefore, it appears at least conceivable that these two unattributed compositions could also be Busnoys's work.

No other gathering of Nivelle suggests in quite the same way that it may have
had as its exemplar a Busnoys 'fascicle', but there are several such gatherings in
Dijon. The tenth quatern, for example, opens with the virelai *A une dame*, and
closes with the rondeau *En voyant sa dame*, both of which are signed 'Busnoys' in
this manuscript. In between are four songs without ascription, one of which is
the virelai *La plus bruiant*, which is also found in Copenhagen. On similar
grounds, then, it, too, ought perhaps to be considered as possibly of Busnoys's
creation.

The twelfth gathering presents an analogous if significantly different situation:
it opens and closes with virelais, the first of which, *En tous les lieux*, once again carries Busnoys's name, while the last, *Je demeure seule*, has no attribution. In
between are pieces by both Molinet and Morton, indicating clearly that in this
sequence of pieces not all were by Busnoys; however, he is the only one of those
identified thus far known to have set polyphonically the virelai. Consequently, *Je
demeure seule* should perhaps be included as well among the anonymous pieces of
which Busnoys may have been the composer.

Bridging gatherings fourteen to fifteen of Dijon is another series of compositions, all of which are either attributed to Busnoys or of unknown authorship. It
opens with a virelai credited to Busnoys in Casanatense,[25] *M'a vostre cueur*, and
closes with another pair of virelais thought to be by Busnoys, *Laissez dangier*,
which is given to him in Nivelle, and *Au gré de mes ieux*, which carries his name
in Dijon itself. Sandwiched in between are two more that have been transmitted
anonymously: *Quant l'amoureuse* and *Qu'elle n'y a*, and both of them could therefore be viewed as possibly part of a group of songs copied from a 'Busnoys
fascicle'.

Similarly, from the end of the sixteenth quatern to the beginning of the eighteenth is another sequence of pieces that are either ascribed only to Busnoys in the
sources or transmitted anonymously. This one opens with the rondeau signed
there with his name, *Quant vous me ferez plus de bien*, and closes with *En soustenant
vostre querelle*, also a rondeau and another of the pieces assigned to Busnoys in
Casanatense. At the beginning of the sequence are two more pieces credited to
Busnoys in the sources, the rondeau *Le corps s'en va*, ascribed to him in both
Nivelle and Mellon, and the virelai *Soudainement mon cueur*. The second chanson
in this cluster of four is the anonymous virelai *S'il vous plaist*, which, to judge from
the surrounding pieces, may also be part of a Busnoys repertory. In addition, sep-

[25] The collection was almost certainly copied in Ferrara in the late 1480s; see the summary note in the
Census-Catalogue, iii. 112–14, and the bibliography listed there; cf. Lewis Lockwood, *Music in Renaissance
Ferrara, 1400–1505* (Cambridge, Mass., 1984), 225–7. Of particular note in this connection are the relatively close relations between Ferrara and the royal court of France, sketched by Lockwood elsewhere in this
same study.

arated from the same nest of four contiguous songs by a single unsigned rondeau, is the anonymous virelai *Par Dieu, ma dame*, identified earlier (p. 323 above) because of its placement in Nivelle as possibly a work by Busnoys.

Finally, beginning with the twentieth gathering, which seems to start afresh in a sense with a song-motet in honour of St Catherine, is another group of pieces transmitted either anonymously or—with one exception—only under Busnoys's name. That exception is the first of the attributed pieces, the rondeau *Cent mille escus*, which is credited to Busnoys in the Florentine manuscript, Florence 229, but to Caron in Casanatense. Following it immediately, however, is the virelai *J'ay mains de biens*, given to Busnoys by both the Florentine collections, Florence 229 and Pixérécourt,[26] and (with only one anonymous piece intervening) the rondeau *A qui vens tu tes coquilles*, ascribed to Busnoys in Mellon.

Separated from this nest of four pieces by just one anonymous rondeau and second in the series following the song-motet is the anonymous virelai *S'une fois me dictes ouy*. And at the end of the gathering, followed by a blank opening, is yet another, *Puis que je suis heritiere*. Working from the same assumption, therefore, that the fascicle exemplar for this series of pieces may have consisted entirely, or at least primarily, of chansons by Busnoys, these two could be added in turn to the list of those pieces to be considered as possibly from his pen.

There is perhaps one final anonymous virelai in Dijon to be included among the compositions for which there is codicological evidence for a link to Busnoys. It is *A ceste derraine venue*, which follows directly the virelai *Je ne puis vivre*, ascribed in the manuscript directly to Busnoys. Although Binchois is the only named composer for the following song, the *rondeau sixain Comme femme desconfortee* (the attribution being in Mellon), he is not one of the composers to whom a virelai has been attributed in the sources of the period. Moreover, of the six virelais inscribed in this section of the manuscript—that is the first nine quaterns (fos. 1–67)—four of the five that have attributions in relevant sources are credited to Busnoys and only one, *Presque transi*, to Okeghem.

Proceeding in the manner described, I have identified ten anonymous virelais among the twenty-four known to me as more likely than the others to be the work of Busnoys. This is less than half of the total number, which, as I observed earlier (p. 323), is not unreasonable in view of Busnoys's share of the pieces of this type that appear in the sources with a composer's name. The methods used establish little more than a list of possibilities, however, or at best of probabilities, but clearly no grounds for certainty of any kind. One could of course continue to interrogate in these or yet other ways the sources that are already known, and it may be that additional attributions to Busnoys will surface in secular sources still to be identified or discovered.

---

[26] See above, p. 319, however, for cautionary comments regarding attributions in the Florentine sources.

Ultimately, however, in my view, other means of confirmation will have to be found, not only in order to test the hypothetical possibilities suggested here but also, and more importantly, to assist in the other two areas in which similarly difficult problems have been identified: attributions based on but one or two sources, especially when in putatively peripheral sources, and conflicting ascriptions for a single composition. And, however slippery the ground may be, the best hope appears to me to be some sophisticated form of stylistic analysis.

Style Analysis for Authorship

As Lawrence Bernstein pointed out recently with particular clarity, one of the essential problems in attempting to utilize stylistic analysis to identify the composers of works whose authorship is for some reason in dispute, as well as those that have been anonymously transmitted, has been that analytical methods have been conceived for the most part to bring to light compositional traits that were consciously cultivated and that consequently became generally characteristic of a given style, genre, or composer.[27] The focus, in other words, has not usually been on what might be described as unconscious mannerisms or idiosyncratic stylistic features most likely to be unique to a particular context. Rather, definition was sought for those aspects of style that were either part of the common musical language or, at the very least, that could be perceived and imitated by other composers of the same period and general musical traditions.

This was, for example, the openly stated objective of Lynn M. Trowbridge in his stylistic study of the chansons of Binchois, Dufay, Okeghem, and Busnoys.[28] With the assistance of the computer he sought means to quantify such elements of melodic and harmonic facture as tendencies in intervallic movement (whether conjunct or disjunct), patterns of melodic direction, levels of rhythmic activity, preferences in the choice of consonance, and the use and incidence of dissonance. These data were then used in developing a method of analysis that he described as best adapted to 'collective processing and comparison of small repertories' in order to generate 'numerical profiles representative of the compositional practice of groups of chronologically related compositions and, through comparison of these profiles, to detect general stylistic trends'.[29]

Despite his declared intention to search for the general, he discovered in the process features that he regarded as more particularly characteristic of the chansons of Busnoys. These can be summarized as follows:

---

[27] See his 'Chansons Attributed to both Josquin des Prez and Pierre de la Rue: A Problem in Establishing Authenticity', in *Proceedings of the International Josquin Symposium: Utrecht 1986* (Utrecht, 1991), 125–52.

[28] 'Style Change in the Fifteenth-Century Chanson: A Comparative Study of Compositional Detail', *Journal of Musicology*, 4 (1985–6), 146–70.

[29] Ibid. 155.

1. Busnoys 'continued the tendencies of Dufay and Okeghem toward increased conjunct melodic motion' in the structural contrapuntal armature, meaning that there are fewer melodic thirds in the cantus, fewer fourths and fifths in the tenor. In the contratenor parts, by contrast, the number of fourths and fifths increased at the expense of smaller intervals, apparently reflecting 'an unusual disposition' for melodic movement in the lowest voice by fourth, fifth, and octave at the expense of movement by seconds, thirds, sixths, and sevenths.[30]

2. Busnoys also demonstrated a marked preference for using perfect consonances above the lowest sounding part—either the fifth or the octave (usually including the thirds into which the fifth could be divided) rather than the sixth—doing so almost two-thirds of the time.

3. More than other composers included in the survey—even more than Okeghem—Busnoys 'achieved a texture in which the individual voices participate [in the counterpoint] on an equal and independent footing'.[31]

4. Busnoys tended to keep the voice-parts separate, limiting the frequency with which they cross, by increasing the range encompassed overall while restricting the individual lines largely to the ambitus of a major tenth.[32]

5. Busnoys was more apt to cultivate what has been called the 'non-quartal' style of composition—'the avoidance of essential fourths between each pair of voices'.[33]

Although his analysis takes note of the recurrence of melodic intervals, it does not quantify what I have perceived to be the greater dynamism of Busnoys's melodic writing, that is the rapidity and energy with which he often traverses the tonal space of the gamut.[34] Trowbridge's observations are comparative in nature, in any case, and, as noted, are intended to reveal tendencies and preferences rather than features that could be used in any given composition to identify the author with some degree of certainty, whether it be the work of Busnoys or one of his contemporaries.

In a similar vein, Paula Higgins's perceptive observation, that 'the contrapuntal manipulation of musical motifs in retrograde and inversion is a hallmark of Busnoys's style',[35] concerns compositional procedures that would have been noticed by the more accomplished composers of his age, admired undoubtedly

---

[30] Ibid. 161.   [31] Ibid. 162.

[32] Trowbridge observes that, by contrast, the ranges used by Okeghem are, on the average, consistently wider than those adopted by the other composers. 'Thus, the melodic ranges of the Okeghem and Busnois repertories lie at opposite ends of the stylistic spectrum, the compositions of the former displaying the greatest diversity and widest compass and those of the latter exceptional consistency and moderation'. Ibid. 163.

[33] According to Trowbridge, the 'non-quartal' style is characteristic of both Okeghem and Busnoys, but is more marked in the chansons of Busnoys than in those of Okeghem; ibid. 164.

[34] See 'The *L'Homme armé* Masses of Busnoys and Okeghem: A Comparison', *Journal of Musicology*, 3 (1984), 368.

[35] Paula Higgins, 'Parisian Nobles, a Scottish Princess, and the Woman's Voice in Late Medieval Song', *EMH* 10 (1991), 145–200 at 149.

by all who did, and therefore probably emulated by the most skilful among them. So, too, with his adoption of 'curious' labels such as 'basitonans' for his voice-parts.[36] Once the pieces with which these terminological novelties were found began to circulate in written sources, they could be copied or imitated by other masters—or perhaps even by some of the scribes. Consequently, neither of these characteristic features—even if both were present in a particular composition—could be used as an absolute 'litmus test' for Busnoys's style.

As Bernstein concluded from his careful consideration of the problems involved in attempting to establish authorship for a work of doubtful parentage, 'The stylistic traits on the basis of which an anonymous work [can be] assigned an attribution must be idiosyncratic, as opposed to generic'. One must be able to show 'that they appear virtually nowhere else in music that is convincingly attributed to another composer'.[37]

It was stylistic criteria of this nature that Don Giller sought in attempting to isolate the compositional style of Caron for his study of the *L'homme armé* masses in the Naples manuscript.[38] And although questions may persist as to whether or not the traits to which he drew attention were sufficiently and distinctively personal to establish beyond reasonable doubt Caron's authorship,[39] the methodological concept underlying his work seems to me solid enough.

This method has been used with considerable success, it would seem, by Walter H. Kemp in his study of the song repertory of the earlier of the two songbooks at the Escorial (MS V.III.24).[40] A primary objective for him was to establish sound criteria for attributing as many as possible of the thirty-four unsigned pieces in the collection to one of the composers represented by its repertory, in particular Binchois, whose name can be linked with nineteen of its sixty-two pieces, largely on the basis of concordant sources.[41] To that end he isolated and illustrated the following elements of compositional style that he considers to be either uniquely, or, at least particularly, characteristic of Binchois's chansons:

1. a repetition of the final pitch of the contratenor in an iambic rhythm (semibreve, breve);

2. a pre-cadential melodic ornament in an anapaestic rhythm (two semiminims and a minim) where the second note is a dissonant neighbour to the first and last;

---

[36] Higgins, 'Parisian Nobles', 152.

[37] 'Chansons Attributed to both Josquin des Prez and Pierre de la Rue', 148.

[38] 'The Naples *L'Homme armé* Masses and Caron: A Study in Musical Relationships', *Current Musicology*, 32 (1981), 7–28.

[39] See e.g. Richard Taruskin, 'Antoine Busnoys and the *L'Homme armé* Tradition', *JAMS* 39 (1986), 255–93 at 279–80.

[40] *Burgundian Court Song in the Time of Binchois: The Anonymous Chansons of El Escorial, MS V.III.24* (Oxford, 1990), 1–64.

[41] See Kemp's Appendix, a catalogue of the contents of the codex, ibid. 120–4.

3. a rhythmic cliché in ternary metre often used to open a phrase, again in iambic rhythm (semibreve, breve) with the longer value often sub-divided by two or as a dotted figure;

4. the systematic use of imitative textures;

5. melodic progressions by thirds (thought to be typically English), together with melodic rhyme in structurally related phrases;

6. a dropping third in the cantus from the note of cadential closure.[42]

On the basis of these stylistic criteria, judged noteworthy because used consistently and simultaneously only by Binchois, Kemp thought it possible to propose his authorship for fourteen additional songs, to identify five more with a 'school of Binchois', and to assign three to a 'school of Dufay', leaving but a dozen of the thirty-four that are unsigned in the manuscript without a suggestion as to their composer.

Analysis of this kind is tedious, painstaking work and would clearly profit, as Trowbridge has seen, from the assistance made possible by computer technology.[43] In fact, specialized programs that can take advantage of the speed and flexibility of the most recently developed hardware may be the only hope of controlling and recalling the massive amounts of information needed to isolate those uniquely idiosyncratic compositional details capable of establishing convincingly the authorship of a composition whose parentage is in doubt.

One such set of protocols has been developed by David Cope. Although interested primarily in the possibilities for computer-assisted composition, his development of programming with LISP (list-processing) and his Experiments in Musical Intelligence (EMI) appear to offer the kinds of tools that I believe will be needed.[44] The first stages in the algorithm that he has developed for this purpose involve: (i) the encoding of works to be analysed; (ii) the matching of patterns within a given composition to create an 'image' of the work; and (iii) the superposition of two or more compositions to discover which patterns are peculiar to the melodic and rhythmic material of a specific piece and which are essentially inherent in the style of the composer and are thus 'work independent'.[45]

The latter may include a 'signature', defined by Cope as 'a set of contiguous intervals (exempt from key differences) found in more than one work by the same composer'.[46] In some instances, at least, such signatures may prove to be uniquely personal, perhaps even inimitable, and therefore a relatively reliable

---

[42] Ibid. 62 *et passim*. As a means of confirming the stylistic affinities pointing to Binchois as the composer, Kemp also considers the order in which the anonymous works are arranged in concordant sources, taking sequential proximity to be a significant indication in this connection.

[43] 'Style Change in the Fifteenth-Century Chanson', 146–7.

[44] See his most recent exposition of his work in computer-assisted composition, *Computers and Musical Style* (Oxford, 1991).

[45] Ibid. 152–3.

[46] Ibid. 46.

means of identifying the composer of works that have been transmitted in the sources anonymously or with conflicting attributions—provided, of course, that there are others by him that are securely ascribed. Obviously, any comparative analysis of the sort suggested here must have as its basis works attributable beyond reasonable doubt to the composer whose subconscious idiosyncrasies one is attempting to identify. With Busnoys, moreover—where, as we have seen, the evidence from the sources for his authorship is so slender—this principle will have to be observed with particular rigour.

Experience has taught us that getting a computer to help solve difficult problems is not usually quickly and easily done. Often, in order simply to formulate them in a manner that will lend itself to computer-assisted manipulation, they must be more clearly understood and articulated from the outset than might be the case were one to proceed more intuitively. Consequently, there are usually challenging new concepts to master, demanding new routines to learn, and a lot of patient effort is generally required to produce credible results. However, this may be one instance when, as the French would say, 'le jeu en vaut la chandelle'.[47]

Before proceeding to computer-assisted analysis, therefore, it is indispensable that one do all that can be done with conventional methods on the basis of the available evidence. The compositions ascribed to Busnoys that can most reasonably be taken as paradigms of his style are probably those included in one of the sources most central to the transmission of the Busnoys *œuvre*, either Nivelle or Dijon, and preferably, perhaps, the ten compositions that have been transmitted by both.[48]

Of particular significance in this connection will be, in addition, those compositions that can be linked biographically to the composer in some manner, most notably, of course, the four chansons that make textual reference to Jacqueline d'Hacqueville.[49] Also deserving of special consideration in this regard, it would seem, is the virelai *En tous les lieux*, not only because of its inclusion in both of the collections in question but also because of the ascription of its text to a certain Monsieur Jacques, who may have been one of the composer's connections with the ducal court of Brittany in the 1450s.[50]

---

[47] Professor Brad Garton, one of the most talented of the young composers working in the area known as 'computer music' (who is also a colleague in the Department of Music at Columbia University), has graciously agreed to assist me in setting up Cope's protocols for the analysis of chansons attributable to Busnoys.

[48] See my discussion of these works in 'Text and Music in the Chansons of Busnoys: The Editorial Dilemma', in *Atti del Convegno internazionale, L'Edizione critica tra testo musicale e testo letterario*, Cremona, 4–8 Ottobre 1992 (Lucca, 1995), 165–79.

[49] For a discussion of these pieces, including the French texts that have been ascribed on presumably (but unsubstantiated) biographical evidence, see my reflections on 'Antoine Busnois and the d'Hacqueville Connection', in Mary Beth Winn (ed.), *Musique naturelle et musique artificielle: In memoriam Gustav Reese = Le Moyen français*, 5 (1979), 49–64, but cf. Higgins, 'Parisian Nobles', 145–200.

[50] Regarding Busnoys's possible association with the court of Brittany, see David Fallows, above, Ch. 2.

Similarly, those anonymous works that should first be examined in order to determine whether or not they could be by Busnoys are undoubtedly those that seem to be the most likely candidates in the light of the evidence of the sources and general stylistic affinities with 'known' works of the composer. Although a comprehensive study along these lines is well beyond the scope of the present investigation, it may be instructive to test the methods that have been proposed here in order to discover, if possible, the kind of results they may be expected to produce.

As a limited sample, therefore, let us consider the three anonymous virelais that were included in both Nivelle and Dijon and that are 'nested' with chansons attributable to Busnoys in either one or the other or, for one of them, in both sources (see above, pp. 323–5). These are *Chargé de dueil*, *Par Dieu, madame*, and *S'il vous plaist* (nos. 2, 16, and 23 in the final series of App. C). Although rather different from one another in some fundamental ways, each of these compositions displays general characteristics also found in other chansons ascribed to Busnoys.

Chargé de dueil (see Ex. 13.1) is marked, first of all, by the point of imitation between cantus and tenor fashioned for the opening verse of the poem, and the same device was adopted again for the final line of the refrain (mm. 19–24). Although the imitative texture is not as well developed here as, for instance, in Busnoys's 'Jacqueline' virelai, *Je ne puis vivre ainsi*, where all three parts share some of the melodic material, it does present the same contrast between the contrapuntal writing of the refrain section and the essentially homophonic and declamatory texture with which the ouvert/clos section begins.

Less indicative of Busnoys's hand is the uniform mensuration for the two parts of the piece (¢); in the majority of instances he seems to have preferred a contrast—as between a ternary and a binary metre or an integral and a diminished one—but there are none the less several pieces bearing his name that follow the same pattern (see App. C, the list of virelais attributed to Busnoys, nos. 7, 9, 11, and 13).

With respect to the stylistic generalizations suggested by Trowbridge (see above), one does find a largely conjunct melodic ductus, even in the contratenor. The outer voices are confined to a total ambitus of an eleventh with the tenor spanning only an octave, and they are kept for the most part within their individual ranges, the only exceptions being the relatively brief crossing of tenor and contratenor at measures 3 and 9–10 and between cantus and tenor at measures 18 and 35–6. In addition, the consonance immediately above the lowest sounding part is most often perfect, the sixth being relatively rare and appearing usually in a conventional cadential formula, and a non-quartal harmonic style generally prevails.

By contrast, *Par Dieu, madame* (Ex. 13.2) makes almost no use of imitation; only one of the internal phrases in both the refrain and the ouvert/clos introduces

Ex. 13.1. Anon., *Chargé de deuil plus que mon fais* (Nivelle, fos. 42ᵛ–43ʳ)

teux sons tous mes fais, [Tant que pi -

teux sons tous mes fais.] Ha se mon en - ne - my
Je prans sur ma foy es -

mor - tel A - voit de mon mal la
- tre tel Que de luy me pran - droit

moi - tié,
pi - - - - - tié.

a verse with a brief point between cantus and tenor (mm. 17–20 and 38–40). The mensuration, conversely, does bring the juxtaposition of perfect and imperfect *tempus* that is most characteristic of Busnoys's virelais, and the latter appears under the (by then) somewhat archaic sign for an integral breve (C) that is to be seen with some frequency in chansons attributed to Busnoys in the earliest sources (see App. C).

Perhaps the most immediately arresting feature of this piece, however, is the use of an anacrusis, preceded by a breve and two semibreve rests in all the parts. This, too, is a device to be seen in other chansons attributed with some degree of reliability to our composer but to no other known to be represented in the two primary manuscript sources for his songs.[51]

In other respects this chanson is not unlike *Chargé de dueil*. The melodic ductus is largely conjunct in character. The ranges are restricted to a ninth in the cantus, an eleventh in the tenor, and a twelfth in the contratenor, and although there is some crossing of the lower two parts (e.g. mm. 6–8, 14–15, and 17–19 in the refrain) the cantus goes below the tenor only in measures 31–2. In addition, the contrapuntal style is basically non-quartal, with a preference for perfect consonances between the lowest sounding part and that immediately above.

None the less, the evidence to be garnered in this manner from general stylistic affinities between anonymous pieces, on the one hand, and those rather firmly established as by Busnoys, on the other, can be responsibly construed as little more than a general indication of his possible paternity. In the last analysis, it is no more conclusive than that to be drawn from a careful study of the sources themselves.

Turning, finally, to *S'il vous plaist* (Ex. 13.3), its general stylistic traits are again similar to those noted earlier as characteristic of works attributable to Busnoys. There is a modest reliance on imitation between cantus and tenor for the final two phrases of the refrain (with first the latter, then the former taking the lead) as well as the last line of the ouvert/clos, and the melismatic and contrapuntal character of the initial section yields at the beginning of the second, as in other instances, to a more syllabic declamation of the text and a more homophonic texture.

An integral imperfect *tempus* (O) at the beginning is followed in the second section by a shift to the diminished form of the same mensuration (Φ), and a short passage in a *sesquialtera* proportion introduced by the contratenor (mm. 11–13)

---

[51] See, for example, the rondeau *Quant vous me ferez plus de bien* (App. A, I, 34), and the virelai *Soudainement mon cueur* (App. A, I, 37), which latter piece is written, however, in diminished imperfect *tempus* (₵). The only other piece with an attribution in either Dijon or Nivelle to begin with silence in all parts is Delahaye's *Puis qu'aultrement ne puis avoir* (Nivelle, fos. xxix^v–xxx^r); otherwise four anonymous pieces in Nivelle (nos. 18, 19, 21, and 64 in Higgins's inventory) and two in Dijon, *Mon tout, mon souvenir* and *Puis que a chacun/L'autrier/Pardonnez moi* (fos. 135^v–136^r and 184^v–185^r respectively) start in a similar manner. However, only those pieces ascribed to Busnoys have first a full breve and then a semibreve (or two) rest preceding the first up-beat of the initial phrase.

Ex. 13.2. Anon., *Par Dieu, madame* (Nivelle, fos. 46ᵛ–48ʳ)

Ex. 13.2. *cont.*

mais   n'ay   riens   for - fait?   Pour - quoy mon fait
mon   veul   soit   par - fait?   Mais   im - par - fait

Ne doy-e es-tre beau - coup   meil - leur?
A   l'a-pe - tit de   grant   ri - - -

gueur,   [a   l'a - pe - tit   de grant   ri - gueur.]

provides a touch of the rhythmic complexity for which Busnoys shows such affection in his motets. The range is limited to an eleventh in each of the parts, and although the tenor and contratenor share essentially the same ambitus, having in common the ninth from *e* to *f'*, there is relatively little crossing between them (e.g. briefly in mm. 4, 6–8, 15, 18, 21–2 and 25–6 (= 27)). Finally, melodic motion of a predominantly conjunct character is combined again with a non-quartal harmonic style. As with the other two songs, then, there appears to be nothing here of a general stylistic nature to preclude Busnoys's authorship.

In the case of *S'il vous plaist*, however, there appears to be something more, a particular phrase that I have seen thus far among the composers of his generation only with Busnoys and that may be in the nature of a 'signature', the sort of

Ex. 13.3. Anon., *S'il vous plaist* (Nivelle, fos. 13ᵛ–15ʳ)

tié   vous   pren -   gne.

Car   que   je   sceus - se   vi - vre ain - si,
Ma - da - me,   sans   vous - tre   mer -   cy,

Veu   de   mon   mal   l'en - nuy   ter - ri -   ble,
Par   ma   foy,   il   est   im - pos - si -   -   -

ble.

idiosyncratic gesture or unconscious mannerism that a computer-assisted analysis may be able to discover. Early in the second phrase of the cantus, as its first descending figure (m. 6), is a melodic flourish in relatively rapid movement (here in semiminims) that drops stepwise through a third and then, after a step upward, through a fifth, encompassing in all a sixth, before turning back with a leap to the upper octave.[52] An identical configuration is found, for example, in the ouvert/clos of *Je ne puis vivre*.[53]

Interestingly, this particular melodic (and rhythmic) pattern is found only in what appears to be a revision of the latter song, the reading found in Mellon; the presumably earlier version of the piece found in Dijon moves instead primarily in semibreves and breves and is much more static melodically as well, rising from the *c'* at the bottom of the line (m. 29) no further than the fourth above before settling slowly back to cadence on the same *c'*, an octave lower than the concluding pitch of the same phrase in Mellon.

It is possible to wonder, of course, who was responsible for such a substantial reworking of the passage, and the answer is absolutely critical to the argument being made here. I am persuaded, however, that such a thorough-going recomposition of the passage can only have been an authorial revision. This is not the sort of alteration that scribes can be shown to have introduced on occasion—or that they would have been capable of making, for that matter—and another composer would have had no obvious motive for working changes of such a nature.

Whatever the case, the problems raised by the transmission of *Je ne puis vivre*, a 'Jacqueline' virelai, illustrate only too well the complexities and uncertainties with which we are faced, first of all in attempting to establish the authenticity of the Busnoys canon in the secular realm. Even more difficult, clearly, are the questions to be resolved in an endeavour to identify among the compositions transmitted anonymously in the sources those that may be from Busnoys's hand. In that enterprise every reliable method, whether deriving from the scholarly traditions of codicological study and stylistic analysis or from the application of new computer technologies, will surely be required to produce convincing results.

---

[52] As Barton Hudson has observed, this figure is not uncommon in the compositions of northern masters of the next generation, especially in the masses of Agricola and Obrecht, but he also points to its use in the chansons of Martini. See 'Two Ferrarese Masses by Jacob Obrecht', *Journal of Musicology*, 4 (1985–6), 276–302 at 280–1.

[53] For a transcription of this piece with commentary, see *The Mellon Chansonnier*, no. 12 (i. 64–7, and ii. 229–34).

Appendix A
Busnoys Chanson Attributions
(for sources see App. D)

I. Works Attributed to Busnoys in a Single Source

1. *Acordés moy ce que je pense*
2. *Advegne qu'advenir pourra*
3. *A qui vens tu tes coquilles*
4. *Au gré de mes ieulx*
5. *A vous sans autre*
6. *Au povre par necessité*
7. *Bel Acueil*
8. *Bone chiere*
9. *Ce n'est pas moy*
10. *Con tutta gentileça*
11. *En soustenant vostre querelle*
12. *En tous les lieux ou j'ay esté*
13. *En voyant sa dame au matin*
14. *Faites de moy tout [ce] qui vous plaira*
15. *Faulx mesdisans*
16. *Fortuna desperata*
17. *In myne zynn*
18. *Ja que lui ne si attende*
19. *Je m'esbais de vous*
20. *Je ne demande lialté*
21. *Je ne puis vivre ainsi tousjours*
22. *Laissez Dangier faire tous ces effors*
23. *L'autrier la pieça/Margot la hergiers*
24. *L'autrier que passa*
25. *Le monde est tel pour le present*
26. *Maintes femmes*
27. *Ma plus qu'assez et tant bruiante*
28. *Ma tres souveraine princesse*
29. *M'a vostre cueur mis en oubli*
30. *Mon seul et celé souvenir*
31. *On a grant mal par trop amer*
32. *Pucelotte, que Dieu nos quart*
33. *Quant j'ay au cueur*
34. *Quant vous me ferez plus de bien*
35. *Quelque povre homme que je soie*
36. *Quelque povre homme que je soie*
37. *Soudainement mon cueur a pris*
38. *Terrible dame*

39. *Une filleresse d'estouppes*
40. *Ung plus que tous est en mon souvenir*
41. *Vostre gracieuse acointance*

II. Works Attributed to Busnoys in Two Sources

1. *Amours nous traite honnestement*
2. *A une dame j'ay fait veu*
3. *C'est bien maleur qui me court seure*
4. *C'est vous en qui j'ay esperance*
5. *Chi dit on benedicite*
6. *Corps digne/Dieu quel mariage*
7. *Est il mercy de quoy l'on peust finer*
8. *J'ay mains de bien que s'il n'en estoit*
9. *Le corps s'en va et le cuer vous demeure*
10. *Ma demoiselle, ma maistresse*
11. *Mon mignault musequin/Gracieuse, plaisante muniere*
12. *O Fortune, trop tu es dure*
13. *Pour entretenir mes amours*
14. *Ung grand povre homme insanne*

III. Works Attributed to Busnoys in Three or More Sources

1. *Ha que ville et abominable*
2. *Je ne demande autre de gré*
3. *Joie me fuit et douleur me queurt seure*
4. *Seule a par moy en chambre bien paree*

IV. Works with Conflicting Attributions: Busnoys/?

1. *Amours, amours, amours* (Japart)
2. *Amours fait moult/Il est de bonne heure né/Tant que nostre argent* (Japart; Pirson)
3. *Cent mille escus quant je vouldroie* (Caron)
4. *D'ung aultre amer* (Okeghem)
5. *Et qui la dira* (Japart)
6. *J'ay bien choisi a mon vouloir* (Haine)
7. *J'ay pris amours tout au rebours* (Martini)
8. *Je ne fay plus, je ne dis ne escrips* (Mureau; Compère)
9. *Je suis venue vers mon amy* (Haine)
10. *Le serviteur* (à 4) (Anon.)
11. *Quant ce viendra* (Okeghem)
12. *S'amour vous fui* (Isaac)
13. *Se brief je puys ma dame voir* (Caron)
14. *Vous marchez du bout du pié/Vostre beauté* (Isaac)

Appendix B
Virelais in the Sources Central for Busnoys
A Summary Overview

Dijon: 27 of 160 compositions (16.8%)[1]
  Busnoys 12
  Okeghem 2
  Compère 1
  Anonymous 12

Nivelle: 14 of 66 compositions (21.2%)
  Busnoys 4
  Okeghem 2
  Fede 2
  Fresneau/Agricola 1
  Anonymous 5

Laborde: 17 of 106 compositions (16%)
  Busnoys 4
  Okeghem 3
  Basiron 1
  Dufay 1
  Anonymous 8

Copenhagen: 8 of 33 compositions (24.2%)
  Busnoys 4
  Basiron 1
  Anonymous 3

Wolfenbüttel: 9 of 56 compositions (16%)
  Busnoys 1
  Okeghem 2
  Basiron 1
  Dufay 1
  Anonymous 4

Mellon: 6 of 57 compositions (10.5%)
  Busnoys 3
  Okeghem 1
  Caron 1
  G. Le Rouge 1

---

[1] Totals include the compositions lost, both wholly and in part.

Appendix C
Inventory of Virelais in the Sources Central for Busnoys

Attributed to Busnoys[1]

1. *Au gré de mes ieulx* (O, C2)
2. *A une dame j'ay fait veu* (C, C)
3. *Ce n'est pas moy* (¢, O2)
4. *C'est vous en qui j'ay esperance* (O, ¢)
5. *En tous les lieux ou j'ay esté* (O, ¢)
6. *Ja que lui ne si attende* (C [Dij]; C, ¢)
7. *J'ay mains de bien que s'il n'en estoit* (¢, ¢)
8. *Je ne puis vivre ainsi tousjours* (O, ¢)
9. *Laissez Dangier faire tous ces effors* (C, C)
10. *Maintes femmes* (O, O2)
11. *Ma plus qu'assez et tant bruiante* (O, ¢)
12. *M'a vostre cueur mis en oubli* (¢, ¢)
13. *Soudainement mon cueur a pris* (¢, ¢)

Attributed to Okeghem[2]

1. *Ma bouche rit* (C, C)
2. *Ma maistresse* (O, ¢)
3. *Presque transi* (O)
4. *Tant fuz gentement resjouy* (C, ¢)

Attributed to Fede

1. *A la longue j'ay bien cognu*
   Niv, fos. xlix^v–li^r: Fede (largely erased) (O, ¢)
2. *Mon ceur et moy avons pensé*(?)
   Niv, fo. lxxii^v: Fede (cantus, refrain only) ([C or ¢?])

Attributed to Basiron

1. *Nul ne l'a telle*
   Cop, fos. 9^v–11^r (O, ¢)
   Lab, fos. 13^v–15^r: P. Baziron (O, C?)
   Wolf, fos. 15^v–17^r ([O], ¢)
   *Roh, fo. 184^v

Attributed to Dufay

1. *Malheureux cueur*
   Lab, fos. 26^v–28^r: Dufay (O, ¢)

---

[1] For sources see below, App. D.　　　[2] For sources see Johannes Ockeghem, *Collected Works*, iii.

Sched, fos. 101ᵛ–103ʳ
Wolf, fos. 25ᵛ–27ʳ ([O], ₵)
*Roh, fos. 128ᵛ–129ʳ

Attributed to Caron

1. *S'il est ainsi*
   Mel, fos. 46ᵛ–48ʳ: Caron (O, ₵)
   MC 871, fo. 148ʳ (p. 373), fo. 153ᵛ (p. 384)
   Pix, fos. 179ᵛ–181ʳ

Attributed to G. Le Rouge

1. *Se je fayz dueil*
   Mel, fos. 40ᵛ–42ʳ: G. le Rouge (₵)
   Sched, fos. 103ᵛ–105ʳ (refrain); fo. 24ᵛ (ouvert/clos)
   *Roh, fo. 74ʳ⁻ᵛ

Attributed to Fresneau/Agricola

1. *Ha qu'il m'enuye*
   Cop 1848, p. 46
   Fl 178, fos. 46ᵛ–47ʳ: Alexander
   Fl 229, fos. 128ᵛ–129ʳ (C2 and ₵ [tenor])
   Niv, fos. 79ᵛ–80ʳ (C)
   Par 1597, fo. 19ᵛ
   Par 2245, fo. 18ᵛ: Fresneau

Attributed to Compère

1. *Ne doibt on prendre*
   Bol Q18, fos. 87ᵛ–88ʳ
   Dij, fos. 189ᵛ–191ʳ: Loyset Compere (₵)[3]
   Fl 27, fos. 38ᵛ–39ʳ: Compere
   Zwi 78/3, no. 14
   Egenolff, no. 52
   Odh, fos. 50ᵛ–51ʳ: Compere

Anonymous in the Sources

1. *A ceste derraine venue*
   Dij, fos. 39ᵛ–41ʳ (C)
   *Jard, no. 293

2. *Chargé de dueil plus que mon fais*
   Dij, fos. 95ᵛ–97ʳ (₵, ₵)
   Fl 176, fos. 125ᵛ–127ʳ

---

[3] Later addition to the MS; 'Bourbon' written in left margin of the opening.

FR 2356, fos. 65^v–66^r (= 71^v–72^r)
Lab, fos. 70^v–71^r
Niv, fos. xlii^v–xliiii^r (₵, ₵)
Pix, fos. 61^v–62^r
Wolf, fos. 42^v–43^r (₵, ₵)
*Roh, fo. 126^v
*Jard, fo. lxxviii

3. *Dictes moi ce qu'il vous en semble*
Dij, fos. 135^v–137^r (O, ₵)

4. *Fortune, laisse moy la vie*
Cam R.2.71, fo. 2^r
Pav, fos. 19^v–21^r
Porto, fos. 62^v–64^r
Wolf, fos. 59^v–61^r (C)

5. *Greveuse m'est vostre acointance*
Lab, fos. 53^v–55^r (O, ₵)

6. *Je demeure seule, esbayee*
Dij, fos. 90^v–92^r (C, ₵)

7. *Je serviray selon qu'on me payera*
Lab, fos. 77^v–79^r (₵, O)

8. *La plus bruiant*
Cop, fos. 33^v–35^r
Dij, fos. 71^v–73^r ([O], ₵)

9. *Le joli tetin de ma dame*
Cop, fos. 21^v–23^r (₵)
Lab, fos. 21b^v–21d^r (i.e. only in table of contents)
Wolf, fos. 18^v–20^r (₵)

10. *Les desléaulx sont en la saison mis*
Lab, fos. 91^v–93^r (₵?)

11. *Ma plus amee de ce monde*
Niv, fos. ii^v–iv^r, (erased, quasi illegible) (C)

12. *Ne pour cela qu'esloigner me fauldra*
Lab, fos. 40^v–42^r (₵, ₵)

13. *N'est il secours que puisse avoir*
Lab, fos. 89^v–91^r (₵)

14. *O belle Dyane, la tresbelle*
Lab, fos. 59^v–61^r (C, ₵)

15. *Ostez la moi de mon oreille*
Cop, fos. 25^v–27^r (₵)
Dij, fos. 79^v–81^r (?, ₵)

16. *Par Dieu, madame, c'est a tort*
    Dij, fos. 125^v–127^r (O, C)
    Niv, fos. xlvi^v–xlviii^r (O, C)

17. *Puis que je suis heritiere*
    Dij, fos. 162^v–163^r (¢, ¢)

18. *Quant l'amoureuse et l'amoureux s'esbatent*
    Dij, fos. 107^v–108^r (¢)

19. *Qu'ara d'amours, belle*
    Wolf, fos. 57^v–59^r (O, ¢)
    *Roh, fo. 106^r

20. *Qu'elle n'y a, je le mainctien*
    Dij, fos. 109^v–111^r (C, ¢)

21. *Se je demeure despourveue*
    Niv, fos. vii^v–ix^r (fo. viii missing, with CT and ? on recto, cantus and tenor on verso)
    ([O], ¢)

22. *S'il ne vous plaist me faire allegement*
    Dij, fos. 169^v–170^r (¢, ¢)

23. *S'il vous plaist bien*
    Dij, fos. 119^v–121^r (C, ¢)
    Niv, fos. xiii^v–xv^r (C, ¢)

24. *S'une fois me dictes ouy*
    Dij, fos. 149^v–151^r (C, ¢)
    *Jard, no. 100

Appendix D
Catalogue of Chansons by Antoine Busnoys[1]

B = ballade; Comb = combinative chanson; Q = quodlibet; R4 = *rondeau quatrain*; R5 = *rondeau cinquain*; V = virelai

Acordés moy ce que je pense (a 4)   R4   (¢)
    Bol Q16 (index only)
    Cas, fos. 149^v–151^r: Busnoys
    Fl 229, fos. 160^v–161^r
    Pix, fos. 140^v–142^r
    Odh, fos. 35^v–36^r

---

[1] I should like to thank David Fallows for taking the time to check the following lists against his comprehensive unpublished catalogue of 15th-c. polyphonic songs and for providing me with better information in a number of instances. However, any remaining errors or imperfections are strictly my own responsibility.

Advegne qu'advenir pourra[2]   R5   (₵)
    Bol Q16, fos. 46ᵛ–47ʳ
    Pix, fos. 7ᵛ–8ʳ: Busnoys

Amours, amours, amours (a 4)   (R5)   (₵)
    Bol Q17, fos. 67ᵛ–68ʳ: A. Busnois
    Fl 229, fos. 172ᵛ–173ʳ: Japart
    Odh, fos. 25ᵛ–26ʳ: Japart
    *Chasse

Amours fait moult/Il est de bonne heure né/Tant que   Comb (4-part)   (₵)
    nostre argent (a 4)   arrangement)
    Bas F.X.1–4, no. 111: Pirson
    Bol Q17, fos. 63ᵛ–64ʳ: A Busnois
    Br IV.90, fos. 17ᵛ–18ʳ (discant of Tournai 94)
    Cas, fos. 160ᵛ–161ʳ: Jo. Jappart
    CG XIII.27, fos. 10ᵛ–11ʳ
    Fl 107bis, fos. 7ᵛ–8ʳ
    Fl 178, fos. 57ᵛ–58ʳ
    Fl 229, fos. 163ᵛ–164ʳ: Jannes Japart
    FR 2794, fos. 26ᵛ–27ʳ
    Tournai 94, fos. 18ᵛ–19ʳ (tenor of Br IV.90)
    Vat 11953, fo. 9ʳ⁻ᵛ (bassus partbook only)
    Reg C120, fos. 214ᵛ–215ʳ
    Odh, fos. 33ᵛ–34ʳ

Amours nous traite honnestement/Je m'en vois aux   Comb (4-part   (₵)
    vert boys (a 4)   arrangement)
    Fl 229, fos. 120ᵛ–121ʳ: Antonius Busnoys
    FR 2794, fos. 25ᵛ–26ʳ
    Pix, fos. 170ᵛ–171ʳ: Busnoys

A qui vens tu tes coquilles   R4   (₵)
    Dij, fos. 156ᵛ–157ʳ
    Mel, fos. 11ᵛ–12ʳ: Busnoys

Au gré de mes ieulx   V   (O, C2)
    Dij, fos. 113ᵛ–114ʳ: Busnoys

A une dame j'ay fait veu   V   (C, C)
    Bol Q16, fos. 29ᵛ–30ʳ
    CG XIII.27, fos. 88ᵛ–89ʳ
    Dij, fos. 67ᵛ–69ʳ: Busnoys
    Fl 176, fos. 6ᵛ–8 ʳ
    Lab, fos. 101ᵛ–102ʳ: Busnoys
    Mel, fos. 5ᵛ–6ᵛ

---

[2] Cited in the *Condamnacion du banquet*, c.1480.

*Par 1719, fos. 113ʳ
*Roh, fo. 115ʳ

Au povre par necessité   R5   (¢)
   Glog, no. 10 ('Regina regnancium')
   Mel, fos. 51ᵛ–52ʳ
   Pix, fos. 171ᵛ–172ʳ: Busnoys
   Sev, fos. 79ᵛ–80ʳ, no. 97

A vous sans autre   R4   (C)
   Dij, fos. 21ᵛ–22ʳ: Busnoys
   Mel, fos. 55ᵛ–56ʳ
   *Jard, lxviiiʳ

Bel Acueil   R4   (O)
   Dij, fos. 22ᵛ–23ʳ: Busnoys
   Mel, fos. 1ᵛ–2ʳ
   *Par 1719, fo. 91ᵛ

Bone chiere   (R4)   (¢)
   Pix, fos. 162ᵛ–163ʳ: Busnoys

Ce n'est pas moy   V   (¢, O2)
   Bol Q16, fos. 71ᵛ–72ʳ
   Pix, fos. 172ᵛ–173ʳ: Busnoys

Cent mille escus quant je vouldroie   R5   (¢)
   Bol Q16, fos. 147ᵛ–148ʳ
   Cas, fos. 26ᵛ–27ʳ: Caron
   CG XIII.27, fos. 34ᵛ–35ʳ: Caron
   Cord, fos. 29ᵛ–30ʳ
   Dij, fos. 152ᵛ–153ʳ
   Fl 178, fos. 61ᵛ–62ʳ
   Fl 229, fos. 71ᵛ–72ʳ: Busnoys
   Glog, no. 274
   Per 431, fos. 58ᵛ–59ʳ (different CT; cf. Pix)
   Pix, fos. 10ᵛ–11ʳ: Busnoys (different CT; cf. Per 431)
   Sev, fos. 45ᵛ–46ʳ, no. 55
   Ver 757, fos. 61ᵛ–62ʳ
   Wolf, 63ᵛ (cantus only)
   Canti C, fos. 122ᵛ–123ʳ (added 4th voice)
   +Spinacino ii, fos. 17ᵛ–18ʳ (intabulation for lute)
   *Lo 380, fo. 242ʳ
   *Roh, fo. 184ʳ

C'est bien maleur qui me court seure   R *layé*   (O)
   Dij, fos. 24ᵛ–25ʳ: Busnoys
   Niv, fos. xliᵛ–xlijʳ: Busnois

C'est vous en qui j'ay esperance	V	(O, ¢)

Dij, fos. 45ᵛ–47ʳ: Busnoys
Niv, fos. xxxiijᵛ–xxxvʳ: Busnois
*Roh, fo. 180ʳ

*Chi dit on benedicite*³	R5	(¢)

Bol Q18, fos. 36ᵛ (*a 4*, 'De tous bien plein')
Fl 229, fos. 55ᵛ–56ʳ: Antonius Busnoys
Glog, no. 14 ('Laudem demus parvulo')
Pix, fos. 86ᵛ–87ʳ: Busnoys
Sev, fos. 70ᵛ–71ʳ, no. 89
Tr 89, fos. 420ᵛ–421ʳ, no. 774 (no text)

Con tutta gentileça	Ballata	(¢)

Fl 229, fos. 52ᵛ–53ʳ: Antonius Busnoys
Pix, fos. 13ᵛ–14ʳ
*Lucca 184, fo. 18ᵛ (musical setting by Andrea Stefani)

Corps digne/Dieu quel mariage (*a 4*)	Comb?⁴	(¢)

Ber 40021, fo. 59ʳ: Businos
Fl 229, fos. 192ᵛ–193ʳ ('Bon me larim bom bom')
Canti C, fos. 105ᵛ–106ʳ: Busnoys

D'ung aultre amer	R5	(¢)

Bol Q17, fos. 40ᵛ–41ʳ: Okeghem
Cas, fos. 16ᵛ–17ʳ: Okeghem
CG XIII.27, fos. 105ᵛ–106ʳ
Cop, fos. 32ᵛ–33ʳ
Cop 1848, fo. 145ʳ
Dij, fos. 42ᵛ–43ʳ: Okeghem
Fl 178, fos. 62ᵛ–63ʳ
FR 2356, fos. 73ᵛ–74ʳ (= 79ᵛ–80ʳ)
FR 2794, fos. 19ᵛ–20ʳ: Okeghem
Lab, fos. 18ᵛ–19ʳ
Niv, fos. 66ᵛ–67ʳ: Okeghem
Par 2245, fos. 13ᵛ–14ʳ: Okeghem
Pix, fos. 189ᵛ–190ʳ: Busnoys
Sev, fos. 51ᵛ–52ʳ; 132ᵛ–133ʳ (*a 4*)
*Roh, fo. 118ʳ
*Jard, fo. lxxxiiiʳ

En soustenant vostre querelle	R5	(¢)

Cas, fos. 70ᵛ–71ʳ: Busnois
Dij, fos. 131ᵛ–132ʳ
FR 2356 (index only)

---

³ Cited by Molinet, *c.*1470.
⁴ According to Fallows, the tenor of this composition appears to be embedded in a Sanctus in the Speciálník Codex, pp. 12-15, and in a Benedictus in Perugia 431, fos. 4ᵛ–7ʳ(no. 5).

Mel, fos. 2ᵛ–3ʳ
*Par 1719, fo. 93ʳ⁻ᵛ
*Roh, fo. 161ʳ⁻ᵛ

En tous les lieux ou j'ay esté (a 4)   V   (O, ¢)
  Dij, fos. 83ᵛ–85ʳ: Busnoys
  Niv, fos. xliiijᵛ–xlviʳ
  *Par 1719, fo. 62ʳ⁻ᵛ
  *Par 9223, fo. 101ʳ: Monseigneur Jaques
  *Roh, fo. 181ᵛ

En voyant sa dame au matin   R4   (C)
  Bol Q16, fos. 123ᵛ–124ʳ
  Dij, fos. 74ᵛ–75ʳ: Busnoys
  Lab, fos. 83ᵛ–84ʳ
  *Par 1719, fo. 113ʳ
  *Par 1722, fo. 48ʳ
  *Chasse

Est il mercy de quoy l'on peust finer   R5   (O)
  Cord, fos. 36ᵛ–38ʳ
  Dij, fos. 59ᵛ–60ʳ
  Lab, fos. 29ᵛ–30ʳ
  Mel, fos. 8ᵛ–9ʳ: Busnoys
  Niv, fos. xxxvijᵛ–xxxviijʳ: Busnois
  Wolf, fos. 2ᵛ–3ʳ
  *Roh, fos. 100ᵛ–101ʳ
  *Jard, fo. lxviʳ

Et qui la dira (a 4)   4-part   (¢)
  Bol Q17, fos. 66ᵛ–67ʳ: A. Busnois   arrangement?
  Fl 107bis, fos. 5ᵛ–6ʳ: Japart

Faites de moy tout [ce] qui vous plaira   R5   (¢)
  Fl 229, fos. 238ᵛ–239ʳ: Antonius Busnoys
  Pix, fos. 132ᵛ–133ʳ
  Sev, fos. 97ᵛ–98ʳ ('Amours me tient en son domaine')
  Montserrat 823 (text only)
  Urb 1411, fos. 4ᵛ–5ʳ (text only)
  Ver 757, fos. 38ᵛ–39ʳ

Faulx mesdisans   ?(R5)   (¢)
  Fl 229, fos. 57ᵛ–59ʳ Busnoys
  Pix, fos. 190ᵛ–191ʳ

Fortuna desperata (a 3)⁵   3-part   (¢)
  Fl 121, fos. 25ᵛ–26ʳ   arrangement?
  Lo 35087, fos. 11ᵛ–12ʳ

⁵ There are various versions of this piece for four voices with different texts; see below, Chs. 19 and 20.

Per 431, fos. 83ᵛ–84ʳ
Seg, fo. clxxiiiiʳ: Anthonius Busnoys
Wolfenbüttel fragment⁶
*Lo 16439

Ha que ville et abominable   R4   (C)
   Cas, fo. 8ʳ ('Trinitas in unitate'): Busnoys
   Cas, fos. 8ᵛ–9ʳ ('sanse fuga'): Busnois
   Dij, fos. 18ᵛ–19ʳ ('Trinus in unitate')
   Fl 229, fos. 213ᵛ–214ʳ ('Trinitas in unitate')
   Sev, fos. 98ᵛ–99ʳ, no. 116 ('Que ville'): Busnois
   *Roh, fo. 183ʳ

In myne zynn (*a 4*)   B   (¢)
   FC 2439, fos. 29ᵛ–30ʳ: Bunoys
   Canti C, fos. 55ᵛ–56ʳ ('Le second jour d'avril')

Ja que lui ne si attende   V   (C, ¢)
   Cop, fos. 37ᵛ–39ʳ
   Dij, fos. 61ᵛ–62ʳ: Busnoys
   Lab, fos. 52ᵛ–54ʳ
   Mel, fos. 17ᵛ–18ʳ
   Sev, fos. 57ᵛ–58ʳ, no. 77
   Wolf, fos. 5ᵛ–7ʳ

*J'ay bien choisi a mon vouloir*⁷   ?   (¢)
   Cas, fos. 42ᵛ–43ʳ: Haine
   Fl 229, fos. 112ᵛ–113ʳ
   Glog, no. 258 ('Virgo pudicicie', *2.p.* of *O stella maris*)
   Pix, fos. 125ᵛ–126ʳ: Busnoys

J'ay mains de bien que s'il n'en estoit   V   (¢)
   Cape, fos. 117ᵛ–118ʳ ('O mira circa nos'; 'O felix
     culpa')
   Cord, fos. 26ᵛ–28ʳ
   Dij, fos. 153ᵛ–155ʳ
   Fl 229, fos. 56ᵛ–57ʳ (refrain only): Busnoys
   Lab, fos. 85ᵛ–87ʳ
   Pix, fos. 178ᵛ–179ʳ (refrain only): Busnoys
   Sev, fos. 90ᵛ–91ʳ
   *Par 1719, fos. 109ʳ

J'ay pris amours tout au rebours (*a 4*)   R4   (¢)
   Seg, fo. 110ᵛ: Johannes Martini
   Odh, fos. 44ᵛ–45ʳ: Busnoys⁸

---

⁶ See the exhibition catalogue, ed. by Martin Staehelin, *Musikalischer Lustgarten* (1985), 70–1.
⁷ Perhaps a *réponse* to *Je suis venue*.
⁸ Ascription to Busnoys also by Ramos, *Musica practica*, 1482.

Je m'esbais de vous   R5   (O)
    Dij, fos. 53ᵛ–54ʳ: Busnoys
    *Roh, fo. 114ʳ⁻ᵛ

*Je ne demande autre de gré*⁹   R4   (¢)
    Bol Q18, fos. 39ᵛ–40ʳ
    Cam R.2.71, fo. 1ʳ (tenor and contra of 2nd half)
    Cas, fos. 151ᵛ–152ʳ: Busnoys
    Fl 229, fos. 151ᵛ–152ʳ
    Lab, fo. 121ᵛ (Textual incipit only; no music)
    Pix, fos. 153ᵛ–155ʳ: Busnoys
    Seg, fos. 112ᵛ–113ʳ: Anthonius Busnoys
    Sev, fos. 105ᵛ–107ʳ, no. 133
    Odh, fos. 47ᵛ–48ʳ: Busnoys
    +Spinacino ii, fo. 9ʳ (intabulation for lute)

Je ne demande lialté (no text)   ?(R5)   (¢)
    Bol Q16, fos. 58ᵛ–60ʳ
    Fl 229, fos. 59ᵛ–61ʳ: A. Busnoys

Je ne fay plus, je ne dis ne escrips   R *layé*   (¢)
    Bol Q17, fos. 37ᵛ–38ʳ: A. Busnois
    CG XIII.27, fos. 12ᵛ–13ʳ: Gil Murieu
    Cop 1848, fo. 97ʳ
    Fl 121, fo. 26ᵛ
    Fl 176, fos. 73ᵛ–75ʳ: G. Mureau
    Fl 178, fos. 40ᵛ–41ʳ
    Fl 229, fos. 54ᵛ–55ʳ: Antonius Busnoys
    FR 2356, fos. 6ᵛ–7ʳ
    FR 2794, fos. 50ᵛ–51ʳ
    Par 2245, fos. 23ᵛ–24ʳ: Mureau
    Pix, fos. 177ᵛ–178ʳ
    Seg, fo. 181ᵛ: Loysette Compère
    Sev, fos. 25ᵛ–26ʳ, no. 17
    SG 462, p. 85
    Tur I.27, fo. 47ʳ ('Au joly moys de may')
    Wolffheim, fos. 90ᵛ–91ʳ (*a 4*; 4th part, later hand)
    Odh, fos. 10ᵛ–11ʳ (4th part; cf. Wolffheim)
    *Par 1719, fo. 39ʳ⁻ᵛ (mostly crossed out)
    +Ber 40026, fo. 51ʳ
    +Spinacino i, fo. 21ʳ
    +Thibault, fos. 16ᵛ and 54ʳ

Je ne puis vivre ainsi tousjours   V   (O, ¢)
    Dij, fos. 37ᵛ–39ʳ: Busnoys
    Mel, fos. 14ᵛ–16ʳ (revision)
    *Jard, lxxxivʳ

        ⁹ Cited by Molinet, *c.*1470, by Tinctoris, 1477, by Aaron, 1525, etc.

Je suis venue vers mon amy[10]   ?   (¢)
    Cas, fos. 43ᵛ–44ʳ: Haine
    Fl 229, fos. 28ᵛ–29ʳ
    Glog, no. 258 ('O stella maris')
    Pix, fos. 127ᵛ–128ʳ: Busnois

Joie me fuit et douleur me queurt seure   R5   (¢)
    Cas, fos. 13ᵛ–14ʳ: Busnoys
    Dij, fos. 29ᵛ–30ʳ: Busnoys
    Fl 176, fos. 13ᵛ–15ʳ
    Lab, fos. 100ᵛ–101ʳ
    Mel, fos. 36ᵛ–38ʳ: Busnoys
    Pix, fos. 163ᵛ–164ʳ: Busnoys
    Tr 91, fos. 258ᵛ–259ʳ ('Je me sans')
    *Par 1719, fos. 33ᵛ–34ʳ
    *Par 2798, fo. 71ᵛ (later addition)
    *Par 7559, fo. 64ʳ
    *Jard, fo. xcviijʳ

Laissez Dangier faire tous ses effors   V   (C)
    Bol Q16, fo. 103ʳ
    Dij, fos. 111ᵛ–113ʳ
    Niv, fos. xxvijᵛ–xxixʳ: Busnois
    *Par 7559, fo. 51ᵛ (R4 with same refrain stanza)
    *Roh, fo. 111ᵛ

L'autrier la pieça/Margot la bergiers/En l'ombre du   Q (4-part   (¢)
    buissonet/Trop suis jonette (a 4)   arrangement)
    Sev, fos. 103ᵛ–105ʳ, no. 132: Busnois

L'autrier que passa (a 4)   ? (no text)   (¢)
    Canti B, fos. 11ᵛ–12ʳ: Busnoys

Le corps s'en va et le cuer vous demeure   R5   (¢)
    Dij, fos. 123ᵛ–124ʳ
    Lab, fos. 25ᵛ–26ʳ
    Mel, fos. 26ᵛ–27ʳ: Busnoys
    Niv, fos. livᵛ–lvʳ: Busnois
    Wolf, fos. 45ᵛ–46ʳ
    *Dres
    *Lille 402, fo. 31ʳ
    *Ox Taylor, p. 23
    *Par 1719, fos. 3ʳ, 74ᵛ, 182ʳ
    *Roh, fo. 154ʳ⁻ᵛ
    Chasse
    Fleur, fo. iiiᵛ

---

[10] Cf. *J'ay bien choisi*, which may have been written as a *réponse* to this chanson.

Le monde est tel pour le present[11]   R4   (¢)
    Cas, fos. 41^v–42^r: Busnoys
    *Par 1719, fo. 118^r
    *Par 1722, fo. 47^v

Le serviteur (a 4)[12]   [R5]   (O)
    Odh (Bologna), fos. 37^v–38^r: Busnoys[13]
    *Par 1719, fo. 87^r
    *Roh, fo. 91^v
    *Jard, fo. 87^r

Ma demoiselle, ma maistresse   R5   (O)
    Dij, fos. 15^v–16^r: Busnoys
    Niv, fos. xl^v–xli^r: Busnois
    *Roh, fo. 156^r (first stanza only)

Maintes femmes (a 4)[14]   V   (O, ¢)
    Sev, fos. 107^v–109^r
    Canti C, fos. 117^v–118^r: Busnoys

Ma plus qu'assez et tant bruiante   V   (O, ¢)
    Cop, fos. 15^v–17^r
    Dij, fos. 31^v–33^r: Busnoys
    *Jard, fos. lxxiiij^v

Ma tres souveraine princesse   R4   (¢)
    Bol Q16, fos. 62^v–63^r
    Pix, fos. 131^v–132^r: Busnoys
    Sev, fos. 84^v–85^r, no. 102

M'a vostre cueur mis en oubli   V   (¢)
    Bol Q16, fos. 41^v–43^r ('Terribile fortuna')
    Cas, fos. 72^v–74^r ('Ma doulce ceur'): Busnois
    Cop, fos. 12^v–14^r
    Dij, fos. 101^v–103^r
    Fl 229, fos. 245^v–247^r
    FR 2794, fos. 36^v–38^r
    Lab, fos. 95^v–97^r
    Sev, fos. 55^v–56^r, no. 75
    *Par 1719, fo. 113^v

Mon mignault musequin/Gracieuse, plaisante muniere (a 4)   Comb   (¢)
    Dij, fos. 181^v–182^r
    Fl 229, fos. 194^v–195^r: Antonius Busnois

---

[11] Fallows has observed that the first stanza of this poem is also known in a setting by Crecquillon, published in RISM 1545[14].

[12] Based on the cantus and tenor of the chanson attributed to Dufay.

[13] According to Helen Hewitt, *Harmonice Musices Odhecaton*, 8, the attribution to Busnoys, included in the earliest known edition of the collection ('perhaps too hastily'), was eliminated from later printings.

[14] Cited by Tinctoris, *Liber de arte contrapuncti*, 1477.

SG 461, p. 65: Busnoys
Odh, fos. 19^v–20^r

Mon seul et celé souvenir   R5   ($\mathbb{C}$)
Fl 176, fos. 17^v–19^r
Fl 229, fos. 48^v–49^r
Glog, no. 7 ('Ave rosa rubicunda')
Par 4379, fo. 72^v
Pix, fos. 124^v–125^r: Busnoys
Tr 89, fo. 414^r

O Fortune, trop tu es dure   R5   ($\mathbb{C}$)
Fl 176, fos. 15^v–17^r: Busnois
Mel, fos. 48^v–49^r
Pix, fos. 126^v–127^r: Busnoys
Sev, fos. 31^v–32^r, no. 23
Sev, fos. 78^v–79^r, no. 96

On a grant mal par trop amer/On est bien malade pour amer   Comb (4-part   ($\mathbb{C}$)
  trop[15] (*a 4*)   arrangement)
Dij, fos. 180^v–181^r: Busnoys
+SG 530, no. 75: Andreas busnois
  (keyboard intabulation)

Pour entretenir mes amours   R5   ($\mathbb{C}$)
Cas, fos. 22^v–23^r: Busnoys
FR 2794, fos. 57^v–58^r
Glog, no. 271 (no text)
Mel, fos. 19^v–20^r: Busnoys
*Jard, fo. lxx^r

Pucelotte, que Dieu nos guart   B   ($\mathbb{C}$)
Cas, fos. 108^v–109^r: Busnoys
Par 16664, fos. 87^v–88^r
Pix, fos. 186^v–187^r

Quant ce viendra   R5 *layé*   (O)
Dij, fos. 7^v–8^r: Busnoys
EscB, fos. 121^v–122^r: Hockenghem
Fl 176, fos. 69^v–71^r
Lab, fos. 28^v–29^r: Busnoys
Mel, fos. 20^v–22^r (*a 4 si placet*)
Niv, fos. vj^v–vij^r (erased)
Tr 88, fo. 411^r ('Gaude mater')
Tr 91, fos. 70^v–71^r ('Gaude mater miserere')
Wolf, fos. 32^v–33^r
*Roh, fo. 157^r

---

[15] A related work, perhaps a revision of this one, is found in Florence 229, fos. 193^v–194^r; cf. Howard Mayer Brown, *A Florentine Chansonnier from the Time of Lorenzo the Magnificent* (Monuments of Renaissance Music, 7; Chicago, 1983), 283–4, nos. 183, 183A.

Quant j'ay au cueur [16]   R5   (¢)
    Pix, fos. 184ᵛ–185ʳ: Busnoys
    *Jard, fo. lxxxiijʳ

Quant vous me ferez plus de bien   R4   (O)
    Cop, fos. 30ᵛ–31ʳ
    Dij, fos. 118ᵛ–119ʳ: Busnoys
    Niv, fos. xviiiᵛ–xixʳ
    *Lo 380, fo. 247ʳ
    *Par 1719, fo. 92ᵛ
    *Par 1722, fo. 43ʳ
    *Roh, fo. 141ᵛ

Quelque povre homme que je soie   R5   (O)
    Dij, fos. 65ᵛ–66ʳ: Busnoys
    *Par 1719, fo. 86bisᵛ
    Fleur, sig. G1ᵛ

Quelque povre homme que je soie   R5   (¢)
    Pix, fos. 164ᵛ–165ʳ: Busnoys
    Sev, fos. 74ᵛ–75ʳ, no. 93
    *Par 1719, fo. 86bisᵛ
    Fleur, sig. G1ᵛ

S'amour vous fui   ?   (¢)
    Bol Q16, fos. lxxxxiiᵛ–lxxxxiijʳ ('Sans avoir')
    Par 676, fos. 78ᵛ–79ʳ ('Malagrota'): Isach
    Per 431, fos. 65ᵛ–66ʳ (55ᵛ–56ʳ): Busnois

Se brief je puys ma dame voir   R5   (¢)
    Cas, fos. 29ᵛ–30ʳ
    Fl 229, fos. 75ᵛ–76ʳ: Caron
    Par 4379, fos. 38ᵛ–39ʳ, no. 125
    Pix, fos. 128ᵛ–129ʳ: Busnoys

Seule a par moy en chambre bien paree (a 4)   R5   (O2)
    Cas, fos. 21ᵛ–23ʳ: Busnoys
    Fl 229, fos. 61ᵛ–62ʳ: A. Busnoys
    Pix, fos. 156ᵛ–157ʳ: Busnoys
    *Lille 402, no. 19
    *Ox Taylor, p. 136

Soudainement mon cueur a pris   V   (C, ¢)
    Cop, fos. 28ᵛ–30ʳ
    Dij, fos. 121ᵛ–123ʳ
    Niv, fos. xxxvᵛ–xxxvijʳ: Busnoys
    *Roh, fo. 72ᵛ

---

[16] Cf. the mass by Isaac based on this chanson.

Terrible dame (*a 4*)   ?(R5)   (₵)
  Pix, fos. 159ᵛ–160ʳ: Busnoys

Une filleresse d'estouppes/S'il y a compagnon/Vostre amour   4-part   (₵)
      (*a 4*)   arrangement?
  Fl 229, fos. 63ᵛ–64ʳ: Busnoys
  Canti C, fos. 91ᵛ–92ʳ (a fifth lower)

Ung grand povre homme insanne   ?(R5)   (₵)
  Fl 229, fos. 62ᵛ–63ʳ ('Seyense an mains'): A. Busnoys
  Linz 529, fo. 5ᵛ
  Pix, fos. 130ᵛ–131ʳ: Busnoys
  Sev, fos. 77ᵛ–78ʳ, no. 95 ('Un grand pons')

Ung plus que tous est en mon souvenir   R4/R5   (₵)
  Fl 229, fos. 51ᵛ–52ʳ (R5) (revision)
  Mel, fos. 9ᵛ–10ʳ (R4): Busnoys   (C)
  Pix, fos. 71ᵛ–72ʳ (R5) (revision)
  Sev, fos. 17ᵛ–18ʳ, no. 9 (R5) (revision)
  *Dres
  *Lille 402, no. 518
  *Jard, fo. lxviiiʳ ('L'ung plus que tous')

Vostre gracieuse acointance   R5   (O)
  Dij, fos. 63ᵛ–64ʳ: Busnoys

Vous marchez du bout du pié/Vostre beauté (*a 4*)   Comb (4-part   (₵)
  Dij, fos. 185ᵛ–186ʳ   arrangement?)
  Mun 328–31, no. 122
  Niv, fos. lviijᵛ–lvixʳ: Busnois
  Spec, p. 255 ('Magne olimpii')
  Tr 91, fos. 42ᵛ–43ʳ
  Vienna 18810, fos. 21ʳ: Isaac

PART IV

READING THE THEORISTS ON
COMPOSITIONAL PROCEDURES
AND CHANGING STYLES

14

False Concords in Busnoys

ᢒᢓ ᢒᢓ

PETER URQUHART

THE modern editorial practice of adding accidentals to fifteenth- and sixteenth-century music has been shaped in part by centuries of counterpoint instruction according to rules based on the pedagogy of J. J. Fux and the music of Palestrina. Editors commonly apply the harmonic rules of counterpoint quite strictly, and then proceed to correct all the perceived problems by means of editorial accidentals in the name of 'musica ficta', or more properly, performer's accidentals.[1] However, a number of recent empirical studies of the music have suggested that these supposed contrapuntal flaws may well be characteristic stylistic features.[2] Thus, an editorial method designed to correct these features tends to mask an essential aspect of the music.

The theoretical literature of the period does not furnish many explicit references to the contrapuntal features that editors often choose to emend.[3] Tinctoris, at the end of the second book of his counterpoint treatise, provides us with a few statements about false concords—imperfected fifths, octaves, and unisons—which, if we were to believe him, might curb our zeal to correct slight deviations from harmonic perfection. In previous studies, I have concentrated on evidence

[1] Margaret Bent began the shift among English-speaking musicologists away from equating the term 'musica ficta' with the accidentals that modern editors add on behalf of performers: 'Musica Recta and Musica Ficta', *Musica disciplina*, 26 (1972), 73–100. As I have suggested elsewhere, the difference is not trivial, especially in our understanding of the step B♭/B♮, and the flat sign in general. See my review of Karol Berger, *Musica ficta* (Cambridge, 1987) in *Historical Performance*, 2 (1989), 35–8.

[2] See especially Jeremy Noble, 'Clash and Consonance in the Sixteenth Century', *Musical Times*, 104 (1963), 555–7 and 631–2; James Haar, 'False Relations and Chromaticism in Sixteenth-Century Music', *JAMS* 30 (1977), 391–418; Jaap van Benthem, 'Fortuna in Focus', *TVNM* 30 (1980), 1–50; Thomas Noblitt, 'Chromatic Cross-relations and Editorial Musica Ficta in the Masses of Obrecht', *TVNM* 32 (1982), 30–44; Stanley Boorman, 'False Relations and the Cadence', in Richard Charteris (ed.), *Altro Polo: Essays on Italian Music in the Cinquecento* (Sydney, 1990), 221–64; Robert Toft, *Aural Images of Lost Traditions: Sharps and Flats in the Sixteenth Century* (Toronto, 1992); and Peter Urquhart, 'Cross-relations by Franco-Flemish Composers after Josquin', *TVNM* 43 (1993), 3–41.

[3] For a discussion of imperfect octaves and unisons in music by Josquin and Gombert by one late Renaissance theorist (Correa de Arauxo), see Willi Apel, 'Punto intenso contra remisso', in Thomas Noblitt (ed.), *Music East and West: Essays in Honor of Walter Kaufmann* (Festschrift Series, 3; New York, 1981), 175–82.

for the imperfect octave and unison; in this essay, Tinctoris's famous passage about diminished fifths in chansons by Busnoys and others will be my point of departure. In contrast to the case of imperfect octaves and unisons, there can be no doubt that harmonic diminished fifths and augmented fourths were meant to exist in this music. The question to consider is, under what circumstances did composers allow or intend these harmonic intervals to occur?

The modern pedagogy of counterpoint, which stems from Johann Joseph Fux's *Gradus ad Parnassum* of 1725, allows diminished fifths and augmented fourths in music of three or more voices as consonances, but only when the bass does not take part in the diminished or augmented interval. Thus, for the 'white-note' diatonic collection, the naturally occurring dissonant interval between B and F is handled as though consonant when it is supported by D (Ex. 14.1*a*). Modern writers of course refer to it as a diminished triad in first inversion, and stress that only the first-inversion form of the diminished triad is consonant.[4] In fifteenth- and sixteenth-century music, such diminished triads occur frequently in the approach to cadences. In the theory and practice of the time, two voices only were necessary in order to define a cadence by their approach to an octave or unison by step from the nearest possible imperfect consonance, either a major sixth or a minor third.[5] For example, a cadence on C (Ex. 14.1*b* and *c*) would be defined by the approach from B and D; if these pitches are carried by the cantus and tenor respectively, the third pitch in an upper contratenor would be F, thereby causing the diminished or augmented interval between the cantus and contratenor with which we are concerned. In fact, when the contratenor is in an upper voice, F is the *only* pitch available, outside of doubling a note that is already

Ex. 14.1. 'Consonant' augmented fourths and diminished fifths (contratenor set in blackened noteheads)

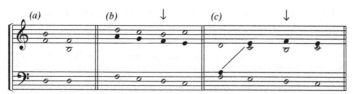

    [4] The counterpoint texts that discuss this matter include: Knud Jeppesen, *Counterpoint*, trans. Glen Haydon (Englewood Cliffs, 1939; repr. New York, 1992), 175–8; Arnold Schoenberg, *Preliminary Exercises in Counterpoint*, ed. Leonard Stein (London, 1963), 94–5; Felix Salzer and Carl Schachter, *Counterpoint in Composition* (New York, 1969), 27–8. All are indebted to the species counterpoint model provided by Fux. While Fux's discussion of diminished fifths in three voices is cursory at best, his examples of first-species counterpoint in three voices freely use the first-inversion diminished triad, but eschew the root-position chord, a usage emulated in all subsequent counterpoint texts: Johann Joseph Fux, *The Study of Counterpoint from Gradus ad Parnassum*, trans. and ed. Alfred Mann (New York, 1965), 76–85.

    [5] Cadence theory of the 15th c. is briefly outlined by Putnam Aldrich, 'An Approach to the Analysis of Renaissance Music', *Music Review*, 30 (1969), 7–9, and is placed in contrast to a triadic interpretation by Richard L. Crocker, 'Discant, Counterpoint, and Harmony', *JAMS* 15 (1962), 11–14, and Don M. Randel, 'Emerging Triadic Tonality in the Fifteenth Century', *Musical Quarterly*, 57 (1971), 75–9.

present, which may in turn present difficulties for voice-leading. It is this restriction that probably created the need to make an exception to the rules about consonant intervals in simple counterpoint in the first place. Unless the F is sung as F♯, resolving to G in a 'double leading-tone' configuration, the penultimate chord in these cadences will contain the problematic diminished or augmented interval, dissonances which eventually had to be accepted by theory.[6]

Of course, fifteenth-century cadences on C are not always preceded by chords over the pitch D. The contratenor could be the lowest voice, in which case it would probably choose the pitch G, thereby avoiding the dissonant interval, and resulting in a cadence that we now would identify as 'V–I' harmonic motion (Ex. 14.2*a*). Or, if the cantus/tenor duo were to approach the final pitch from a minor third (or compound thereof) with the tenor on B, an upper contratenor voice might intone either G or F. In the latter case the resultant diminished triad would be, to use modern terminology, in 'root position' (Ex. 14.2*b*). Modern contrapuntal pedagogy forbids the use of this chord, and it is not very common in Palestrina, although Jeppesen did find two examples.[7] Otherwise, the root-position configuration of the diminished fifth results from the same linear progressions that created the accepted form of the cadence in Ex14.1*c*, but with the cantus and tenor functions reversed.

Ex. 14.2. Other cadences on C

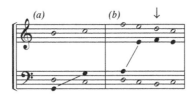

An approach to the cadence by means of root-position diminished fifths can be created for cadences on all the degrees of the diatonic scale with the exception of B, as shown in Ex. 14.3.[8] In most cases, the diminished fifth can 'resolve' inward to a third. The word 'resolve' is used here with some circumspection, because the interval, a false concord by definition, is not dissonant in quite the way that seconds, fourths, or sevenths are, nor does its resolution proceed in the same

---

[6] As long as the double leading-tone cadence inflection was common (F♯ to G coexisting with B♭ to C), the penultimate sonority in a cadence to C could be free of dissonance. But this practice probably fell away sometime in the latter half of the 15th-c., possibly with the increasing frequency of four-voice textures and the resulting dominance of the 'V–I' harmonic effect at cadences. The contrapuntal logic driving this development is discussed in a most elegant and concise fashion by Don Randel, 'Emerging Triadic Tonality', 73–86.

[7] Knud Jeppesen, *The Style of Palestrina and the Dissonance* (Oxford, 1946; repr. New York, 1970), 158.

[8] Most of the accidentals inserted into Ex. 14.3 are the appropriate inflections for each cadence; although only rarely signed in 15th- and 16th-c. music, cadential accidentals were probably added by performers on a routine basis.

manner.[9] Nevertheless, practice tended to follow this pattern of stepwise motion, so that by the time of Zarlino theoretical support for the stepwise resolution of diminished fifths was in order.[10] Only in the case of the cadence to E in Ex. 14.3 is there no opportunity for a diminished fifth to resolve into a third on the cadence pitch, because there is no diminished fifth available above the tenor; A♭ would have no place in a cadence on E.[11] On the other hand, a contratenor added below an E cadence will create a root-position diminished fifth, one for which the possibility of a stepwise resolution to a third is not available, unless the contratenor were to move up to C, thus undermining the effect of the cadence on E.

Ex. 14.3. Cadences using 'root-position' diminished fifths (contratenor set in blackened noteheads)

Given the variety of contexts for diminished fifths that are available, I find it quite striking that Tinctoris chose the particular examples that he did; all three of his examples of diminished fifths (Ex. 14.4) derive from contexts in which the diminished interval is in root position as in Ex. 14.3, not in first inversion as in Ex. 14.1. Furthermore, in all three cases, the contratenor is below the tenor, and the upper voice falls by a half step into the cadence pitch; these examples thus bear the closest resemblance to the E-cadence paradigm of Ex. 14.3, the one that is least susceptible to 'resolution' by step in both voices, except through upward motion in the contratenor that undermines the arrival at the cadence pitch. Following the title of his 33rd chapter from Book II of the counterpoint treatise, 'Discords which they call false concords must be completely avoided', Tinctoris writes:

Nevertheless, I have discovered the opposite most frequently among many, many composers, even the most famous, as with Faugues in his *Missa Le serviteur*, with Busnois in his chanson, *Je ne demande*, and with Caron in one chanson which is named, *Hellas*, just as is

---

[9] In describing Palestrina's practice, Jeppesen calls the diminished fifth 'a mild dissonance . . . which vibrates between consonance and dissonance; this interval is also used in other instances where, according to strict rules, only consonance was allowed . . .'; *The Style of Palestrina and the Dissonance*, 158.

[10] '[W]e may on occasion write the semidiapente [diminished fifth] in a single percussion. We may do so when it is immediately succeeded by the ditone [major third].' Gioseffo Zarlino, *The Art of Counterpoint*, trans. Guy A. Marco and Claude V. Palisca (New Haven, 1968), 67–8.

[11] Similarly, E♭ would have no place in a cadence on B. When the contratenor occurs below the tenor in a cadence on B, F might be chosen, following the example of cadences on E, but a linear diminished fifth would result.

Ex. 14.4. Tinctoris's examples of diminished fifths

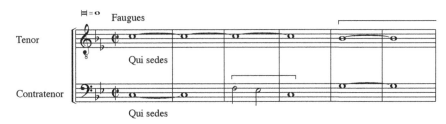

seen here: [*see Ex. 14.4*] And, indeed, when I see such evident errors committed by so many composers, I think that these men can be excused in absolutely no other way than by this statement of Horace, 'When the good Homer nods', that is, as Acro explains, when the good poet erred; hence, it is not to be wondered that a good musician also errs sometimes.[12]

The examples Tinctoris provides show only the two voices that create the diminished fifths at cadences in works by three of his fifteenth-century contemporaries. When all the voices are scored, the cantus/tenor cadential frameworks become clear, along with the supporting role of the contratenor.[13] The cadences by Faugues and Caron in particular are comparable to the E cadence of Ex. 14.3, but are transposed by two flats to the pitch D, and by one flat to A, respectively (Ex. 14.5).[14]

In all three of Tinctoris's examples, the root-position diminished fifths are strong, emphasized metrically and agogically. An editor might well be tempted to perfect these fifths by means of editorial accidentals, were it not for Tinctoris's statement about them. Karol Berger states that the 'fact that they were not meant to be so corrected, clearly implied by Tinctoris, means that they were found tolerable'. The point hiding behind Berger's word 'tolerable' is that Tinctoris found it necessary to comment on these intervals at all, meaning that Tinctoris, and therefore Berger, did not assume they would be corrected by performers on their own. 'Tolerable' also implies 'intended by the composer', and Berger looks for the purpose for that intention in the counterpoint: 'the conditions which make these intervals tolerable must lie in their context, in the way in which they are followed ('resolved') and preceded ('prepared')'.[15] However, as shown above, these examples have a very poor context in terms of preparation and resolution. The Caron passage in particular weakens our hope for preparation by step and resolution by motion inward to a third. While the Faugues passage certainly resolves, it is because the contratenor does not move to the cadence pitch. If it had moved to D, would the passage be judged any less 'tolerable', that is, would the singer

---

[12] Johannes Tinctoris, *The Art of Counterpoint*, trans. Albert Seay (Musicological Studies and Documents 5; [Rome], 1961), 130–1; the example is taken from Berger, *Musica ficta*, 96.

[13] The chanson by Caron has a *si placet* fourth voice in four sources. According to Albert Seay, it is likely that Tinctoris knew the work from a source close to Dijon, which carries the work in three voices only. See Johannes Tinctoris, *Opera theoretica*, ed. Albert Seay, 2 vols. ([Rome], 1975), ii. 143. Busnoys's *Je ne demande* may also have originated as a three-voice work. According to Bernhard Meier, the higher contratenor voice (the one quoted by Tinctoris!) was not original to the piece; Meier, 'Studien zur Messkomposition Jacob Obrechts' (Ph.D. diss., Freiburg im Bresgau, 1952), 19. Thomas Noblitt has translated and reprinted Meier's comments in a more accessible source: 'Problems of Transmission in Obrecht's *Missa Je ne demande*', *Musical Quarterly*, 63 (1977), 211–23 at 221.

[14] Complete editions of the pieces may be found as follows: Faugues, Qui tollis, from *Missa Le serviteur* in *Collected Works of Guillaume Faugues*, ed. George C. Schuetze, Jr. (2 vols.; Brooklyn, 1960), 16 ff.; Busnoys, *Je ne demande autre degré* in *A Florentine Chansonnier from the Time of Lorenzo the Magnificent*, ed. Howard Mayer Brown (Monuments of Renaissance Music, 7; Chicago, 1983), no. 147; Caron, *Hélas!*, in *Les Œuvres complètes de Philippe(?) Caron*, ed. James Thomson (Brooklyn, [1976]), ii. 175–8. The excerpt from the Caron work is found on p. 177, at the end of the second system.

[15] Berger, *Musica ficta*, 96–7.

Ex. 14.5. (*a*) Faugues, *Missa Le serviteur*, Qui sedes, mm. 77–82; (*b*) Caron, *Helas que poura devenir*, mm. 43–6

on the tenor line have been more likely to adjust his part because of what the contratenor was *about* to do? This does not seem likely.

Unlike Berger and most other commentators, I believe that if Tinctoris assumed that these particular diminished fifths would be performed unaltered by singers, he would probably assume the same of most diminished fifths, whether they were judged tolerable or not.[16] And there is at least some indication in the sources of the Busnoys example that this strong diminished fifth was not entirely tolerable at the time; in two sources of *Je ne demande* a corrective flat is added, not to the contratenor given by Tinctoris, but to the lowest voice (Ex. 14.6).[17] No

---

[16] Tinctoris's other famous example of a diminished fifth is found in the chapter on the sixth mode in his treatise on the modes; this example, which is used by many commentators today to justify modern editorial practices regarding harmonic diminished fifths, will be discussed fully at the end of this paper.

[17] Ex. 14.6 is adapted from Berger, *Musica ficta*, 98. A flat appears in the lowest voice on the low E in the Segovia and Casanatense MSS. No accidental appears at this point in Bologna Q18, Pixérécourt, Seville, or *Odhecaton*. Questions about the authenticity of the higher contratenor voice are mentioned in n. 13.

Ex. 14.6. Busnoys, *Je ne demande*, mm. 19–23

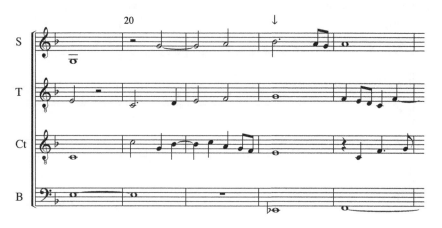

source provides a flat in the contratenor, and indeed the possibility of adding an Eb to this voice is contraindicated by the linear augmented fourth that would be created thereby. On the other hand, in the chanson *Fortuna desperata* (Ex. 14.7), such augmented linear fourths are explicitly indicated in the contratenor by means of accidentals that occur in certain sources, precisely in order to avoid the harmonic diminished fifths in that work.[18] These contradictory details are raised

Ex. 14.7. Busnoys, *Fortuna desperata*, mm. 33–6

[18] Ex. 14.7 is adapted from Jacobus Obrecht, *Opera omnia editio altera*, ed. A. Smijers (Amsterdam, 1954), i. 171. Two of the four sources that transmit the three-voice version of the work contain this contratenor flat at m. 35 (London 35087 and Florence 121); numerous four-voice versions also carry it. A similar, even more striking passage occurs in mm. 54–5 of the same chanson. It is also marked with a flat in London 35087. The two explicit linear tritones caused by these accidentals stand out as unusual features in *Fortuna desperata*, contrary to the stylistic background provided by Busnoys's other chansons. Questions about its authenticity have been raised: Julie E. Cumming, 'The Goddess Fortuna Revisited', *Current Musicology*, 30 (1980), 7–8; Barton Hudson, 'Two Ferrarese Masses by Jacob Obrecht', *Journal of Musicology*, 4 (1986), 290–6, and by Joshua Rifkin, below, Ch. 20. See also the articles in the present volume by Martin Picker (below, Ch. 17) and Honey Meconi (below, Ch. 19).

to indicate that there is evidence available to support any number of interpretations.

The problems involved in sorting out the meaning of Tinctoris's statements, the inferences we may draw from them, and the priorities that should be applied when dealing with examples, led me to a study of diminished fifths in Busnoys's three-voice chansons. The study was limited to the three-voice works because they are a larger and more homogeneous group than the four-voice chansons, in which questions regarding the addition of voices to pre-existent compositions are minimized. The goal was to find out when Busnoys wrote fifths that are potentially diminished, a preliminary step necessary before deciding when to correct these false concords with accidentals, and when not to. In all, 84 diminished fifths in the 47 three-voice chansons were collected.[19] For most of these 84 cases, we cannot know for certain whether or not performer's inflections might have been applied to correct the diminished interval. However, in some 31 cases corrective inflection seems unlikely, either because linear and contrapuntal restrictions appear to confirm the use of the diminished fifth (as in Ex. 14.8), or because the effort necessary for the singer to correct them would be out of proportion to the size of the flaw (as in Ex. 14. 9).[20] The 31 instances that were judged most likely to be diminished fifths are listed in Appendix A.

A few useful generalizations can be drawn from this collection of 84 diminished fifths. In 51 cases the diminished fifth resolves inward to a third, but in 33

Ex. 14.8. Busnoys, *Quelque povre homme* I (Dijon), opening

[19] App. A of Paula Marie Higgins, 'Antoine Busnois and Musical Culture in Late Fifteenth-Century France and Burgundy' (Ph.D. diss., Princeton University, 1987) provides an alphabetized list of Busnoys's works with source concordances and references to published editions. The forty-seven chansons referred to in my study are the three-voice works taken from category I of that list, beginning on p. 313. Chansons that were not available in published editions were transcribed by myself and my graduate students Scott Atwell, David Ballou, Ted Mann, Melinda McMahon, Tamara Rozek, Mary Smith, and Gordon Ward, whose contributions I would like to acknowledge here.

[20] Ex. 14.9, adapted from Brown, *A Florentine Chansonnier*, no. 57, also shows how rough the counterpoint may often be; the importance of the diminished fifth between the tenor and contratenor in m. 43 pales next to the dissonance between the cantus and the contratenor.

Ex. 14.9. Busnoys, *J'ay mains de biens*, mm. 41–4

it does not. Within the smaller group of 31 fifths that are unlikely to be altered, the proportion of those that resolve inward is higher, but there still remain six cases that do not resolve, including the one in Ex. 14.8. Diminished fifths in root position, that is, involving the lowest pitch of the texture, far exceed those in first inversion, and this is probably due to the one generalization that is most striking: in 74 out of the 84 cases, the diminished fifth involves a lower contratenor voice, just as in Tinctoris's examples. The remaining ten diminished fifths between the cantus and tenor show much more care and planning: they are most often in first inversion with the contratenor supporting the dissonance, and with only one exception they resolve inward by step, whereas the 74 diminished fifths involving the contratenor are far less orderly. This statement corroborates another common observation about the fifteenth-century chanson repertory: the contratenor appears to be the third voice composed. Cadences in Busnoys's chansons involving the contratenor as a structural voice occur less frequently than cadences between the cantus and tenor, and no chanson ends with a cadence between the contratenor and another voice. In most cases the contratenor can be stripped away without harming the contrapuntal framework of the piece, even though Busnoys normally places his contratenors as the lowest voice of the three.[21]

These observations about the contratenor highlight the most important differences between Busnoys's three-voice writing and that of modern counterpoint pedagogy. In counterpoint, and in the musical training of most modern editors, the bass determines the acceptability of the sonority; the bass cannot be involved in creating the dissonant interval, which therefore limits the use of diminished fifths and augmented fourths to first-inversion chords. In Busnoys's chansons,

---

[21] In only two chansons are these generalizations about the contratenor and the cantus/tenor framework clearly not true: the equal-voiced chansons *Bel Acueil* and *A vous sans autre*. As George Perle pointed out more than forty years ago, these two works, which appear on adjacent folios in the Dijon chansonnier, foreshadow the more homogeneous style of the next generation. See 'The Chansons of Antoine Busnois', *Music Review*, 11 (1950), 89–97 at 96.

this bass predominance plays no part, for there really was no such concept operating. Indeed the opposite is true. The contratenor is the source of most of the dissonant intervals, and because the contratenor is most often on the bottom of the texture, the bass is more often involved in diminished fifths than not. Using concepts related to modern counterpoint training—inversion, preparation, or resolution—in order to judge the acceptability of a particular dissonance or the need for corrective editorial accidentals in Busnoys is clearly misguided.

How then might we be able to judge which diminished fifths were considered acceptable during the fifteenth century, and which would be considered harsh, unnecessary, and subject to correction? The theory of the time will not help us here; Tinctoris does not appear to approve of harmonic diminished fifths at all, yet his statements simply help confirm their use by composers. What is needed is an empirical methodology to study the question, in which we look at the repertory itself for clues hidden in its patterns and in its internal consistency: are there particular circumstances in which composers actually *intended* diminished fifths? The search is beyond my scope here, but perhaps a look at one work in depth may serve to point out the kinds of questions that could be raised, and possibly answered, by an empirical approach. The piece I would like to consider is *C'est bien maleur*. Ex. 14.10 presents the entire piece, following the version found in the Dijon chansonnier.[22] (For a complete edition, with text, see App. B.)

C'est bien maleur contains four fifths that are potentially diminished, in measures 13, 14, 23, and 24; all four cases involve the contratenor voice and coincide with cadential motion in the upper voices to the pitch A. In each case the diminished fifth resolves inward to a third, except in the last instance, which presents a very unusual final cadence. One could argue that this cadence harmonically demands a B♮ in the tenor, which also suggests that B♮ is appropriate in measures 23 and 24 in the tenor and cantus. This solution operates well at the end, but it is less reasonable to demand B♮s in the tenor or cantus in measures 12–14, for reasons of counterpoint: the entire passage here is linked by imitation between the cantus and tenor, and by the simultaneity between the contratenor and tenor in measure 12. Given the B♭ in the contratenor voice, the diminished fifths in measures 12–14 seem to require acceptance. The primary question about the piece that remains is: should the chanson end with the odd diminished-fifth cadence of measure 25?

Initially, three contrasting answers seem possible. First, we could claim that final cadences cannot involve diminished fifths on the penultimate sonority, especially ones that do not resolve. The cadence looks like a modern V–I progression to A, and was probably meant to sound that way; therefore the tenor Bs must be

[22] Dijon, fos. 24ᵛ–25ʳ. The reading provided in the other source, the chansonnier Nivelle de La Chaussée, fos. xliᵛ–xliiʳ, differs only in slight details.

Ex. 14.10. Busnoys, *C'est bien maleur*

natural. A second position would begin with the claim that the contratenor is not as important as the cadencing cantus and tenor, and that this diminished fifth cadence is possible because that is exactly what it says in the sources; altering it to suit our harmonic preconceptions would obscure the composer's intentions. The third possibility is also the strangest: we could flat the E in the contratenor, and claim that the importance of attaining the harmonic perfect fifth in measure 24 overrides the fact that in so doing we create both a melodic tritone and a melodic diminished fifth in the contratenor. While I do not offer this third possibility seriously, there is a piece in a sixteenth-century English manuscript that ends with such a cadence (Ex. 14.11). Based on the pitch B, the work seems designed in order to prove that a composition in the chimerical 'Locrian' mode could be written.[23] The final cadential motion of F to B is the only direct diminished fifth or tritone leap in the entire work, and its authenticity, or resistance to correction, cannot be doubted, given what precedes it. It makes of the piece a demonstration, a *tour de force*, ending with an exclamation point; the final cadence sums up the entire purpose and point of such a work.

It may well have been Busnoys's intention to show that a diminished fifth could form even the penultimate sonority of a chanson, and that, like the work of Ex. 14.11, *C'est bien maleur* is some sort of demonstration of what is normally impossible. But before accepting this viewpoint, we should consider the other cadences on A and E in Busnoys's three-voice chansons to see whether such a cadence, either internal or final, ever occurs elsewhere. Out of a total of some 276 cadences in the three-voice works, there are only six cadences on E.[24] In none of these is a B employed in the contratenor beneath the penultimate F–D of the

[23] The work, 'Consort VII' by [William] Cornish, is no. 60 in John Stevens's edition, *Music at the Court of Henry VIII* (Musica Britannica, 18; London, 1973). Stevens claims that the work was also intended to operate with three flats, making it 'an English example of a so-called *catholicon*'. The idea has little to commend it, for the observation does not derive from the work itself, which is written in an entirely explicit notation; nothing about the work suggests a three-flat interpretation of the notation, except that it allows one to avoid the telling use of the diminished fifth leap at the end.

[24] To count these events, I have used a rather limited definition of cadence which requires that at least one of the voices of the two-voice framework comes to a halt, typically marked with a rest. I have also counted medial cadences where all voices come to a halt, but which frequently lack the two-voice framework.

Ex. 14.11. Cornish, Consort VII, beginning and ending

cadencing pair of voices, which would have resulted in the diminished fifth cadential pattern that we find at the end of *C'est bien maleur*. Most often the cadence on E is supported by contratenor motion from D to A, as in Ex. 14.12.

Ex. 14.12. Busnoys, *Quant j'ay au cueur*, mm. 15–16

Cadences on the pitch A, on the other hand, are much more plentiful. Many form the medial cadences of works in D-mode, and, like many medial cadences, have no cantus/tenor cadential framework at all (Ex. 14.13). Of those twenty-eight cadences on A that do contain the cantus/tenor framework, most are in a

Ex. 14.13. Busnoys, *Pour entretenir mes amours*, mm. 16–17

no-flat context, and tend to use E as a bass, such as the cadence in Ex. 14.14*a*.[25] Eight cadences on A occur in a one-flat context: of these eight, one occurs in a passage with no contratenor, three use the pitches G–D in the contra, in the manner of 'Phrygian' cadences on E (Ex. 14.14*b*), and four use E in the contra, much like *C'est bien maleur*. Of these four, only the one shown in Ex. 14.14*c*, from *Est il mercy*, bears much similarity to our final cadence in question. In the other three, the contratenor either briefly brushes against the pitch E, as in Ex. 14. 9, or, in

Ex. 14.14. Contratenor form in cadences on A: (*a*) in a B♮ context, *En soustenant*, mm. 29–30; (*b*) with 'Phrygian' contratenor, *Quand ce viendra*, mm. 21–2; (*c*) using E in B♭ context, *Est il mercy*, mm. 8–9

Among a total of **28** cadences on the pitch A:
> **17** are in a B♮ context (Ex. 14*a*)
>> **3** are in a context that is not clearly B♭ or B♮
>>> **8** are in a B♭ context, of which:
>>>> **3** use a 'Phrygian' contratenor (Ex. 14*b*)
>>>> **4** use the pitch E (Ex. 14*c*)
>>>> **1** has no contratenor

---

[25] Ex. 14.12 is adapted from A. Smijers (ed.), *Van Ockeghem tot Sweelinck*, 6 vols. (Amsterdam, 1951), vi. 185–6; Exs. 13, 14*a*, and 14*c* are from *The Mellon Chansonnier*, ed. Leeman L. Perkins and Howard W. Garey, 2 vols. (New Haven, 1979), i. nos. 15, 2, and 7, respectively. Ex. 14*b* is adapted from *Trois chansonniers français du XVe siècle*, ed. Eugénie Droz, Geneviève Thibault, and Yvonne Rokseth (Paris, 1927; repr. New York, 1978), no. 3.

the case of the cadence in *Fortuna desperata* mentioned before (Ex. 14.7), the E is flatted by an explicit accidental in some sources. In *Est il mercy* (Ex. 14.14c) the diminished-fifth sonority is metrically and agogically accented, and appears to be similar to that in *C'est bien maleur*. Nevertheless, the contratenor here does resolve inward to an F, after a brief rest. Only in *C'est bien maleur* does the contratenor leap out from the diminished fifth to the pitch A in a final cadence.

Finally, of the three cadences on A where the flat signature context is not absolutely clear (including the cadence in *C'est bien maleur* itself), two of them should in all probability use B♮ in the tenor. In the first, *Ma demoiselle, ma maistresse* (Ex. 14.15a), an accidental flat in one source (cantus, m. 25) is probably an error stemming from the presence of earlier flats in the middle of the work; in any case, its presence need not affect the choice of tenor inflection at the penultimate sonority.[26] In the second work, *C'est vous en qui j'ay esperance*, the B♭ signature in the tenor is probably mistaken, given the linear motion in the vicin-

Ex. 14.15. Two ambiguous cadences on A: (*a*) *Ma demoiselle*, mm. 24–6; (*b*) *C'est vous en qui j'ay esperance*, mm. 21–3

[26] Both works, *Ma demoiselle, ma maistresse* and *C'est vous en qui j'ay esperance*, are edited in *Trois chansonniers*, nos. 12 and 39. As printed in that edition, *Ma demoiselle* is provided with editorial flats over every B in measure 25.

ity of the cadence and in other passages (Ex. 14.15*b*). It is conceivable that the final cadence of *C'est bien maleur* is similarly clouded by inappropriate B♭ signatures, for otherwise it stands alone among all the A cadences in its form.

One other question might shed some light on the diminished-fifth cadence in *C'est bien maleur*: into what mode or tonal type would this chanson fit? George Perle pointed out in 1950 that *C'est bien maleur* is 'altogether exceptional in its modal implications'.[27] The opening of the piece gives the impression of a G one-flat tonal type, Busnoys's favourite mode. However, there is not a single cadence on G in the entire work, and a final cadence on a pitch one step above the final would be unprecedented in any mode. Is there another modal category which would better fit the pitch content and cadential profile of the piece?[28]

The three-voice chansons by Busnoys organize themselves readily into modal groupings (see Table 14.1). The great majority of pieces may be grouped under just two categories. The term 'Dorian' will suffice for works with D finals and those with G finals under a B♭ signature; there is also a single work with a two-flat signature in all three voices, ending on C. The second most numerous category can be dubbed 'Major'; it includes eight works with F finals, four works with C finals, and a single work ending on B♭. The F-mode works occur most often with one-flat signatures, although partial signatures are common, just as they are in the 'Dorian' works. Unique works that remain outside these two categories include the single G no-flat chanson, *Seule à par moy*, which, with its cadences on B♮, seemed so unusual to Catherine Brooks that she added enough editorial accidentals to transform it into a G-Dorian work.[29] None of Busnoys's chansons ends with an E cadence, which is striking, given Ockeghem's preference for this mode, a taste that was handed down to Josquin in the next generation.[30]

---

[27] Perle, 'The Chansons', 94.

[28] Modal studies have long been a standard, if not completely unambiguous tool for the study of 15th- and 16th-c. music. As of late, modal analysis has been under a kind of siege, as traditionally accepted terminologies and assumptions have been questioned, especially by Harold Powers in a series of influential articles. However, the main purpose to modal categories, or tonal types, is simply to group pieces together that have certain similarities of pitch content and procedure, which is all that will be attempted here. Since the authenticity of the flat signatures in our chanson is in question, consideration of Busnoys's typical choices of signature and final may be of help.

[29] Catherine Brooks, 'Antoine Busnois, Chanson Composer', *JAMS* 6 (1953), 111–35 at 129–30. Cadences on the pitch B♮ are very unusual in this repertoire, possibly because they are not easily created. Composers must take care to avoid certain linear motion in accompanying voices, or have those voices drop out, in order to accomplish the feat. The two B cadences in *Seule à par moy*, the only cadences on B♮ in the body of three-voice chansons, do appear to have been written with an awareness of these difficulties and should not be transformed into B♭ cadences by editors. See Peter Urquhart, 'Three Sample Problems of Editorial Accidentals in Chansons by Busnoys and Ockeghem', in Jessie Ann Owens and Anthony M. Cummings (eds.), *Music in Renaissance Cities and Courts: Studies in Honor of Lewis Lockwood* (Warren, Mich., 1997), 465–81.

[30] Not included in this summation is *C'est bien maleur*, the work under scrutiny, and *Pucellotte que dieu vous guart*, a piece that firmly resists modal categorization because of its canonic structure. Since the work contains no internal cadences at all, its absence from the statistics of Table 14.1 has no effect other than to make the total number of chansons surveyed amount to just forty-five.

TABLE 14.1. *Modes and cadence profiles of Busnoys's three-voice chansons*

'Dorian' chansons

14 D-mode works, with cadences on:	D	E	F	G	A	B	C
finals:	12	—	—	—	2	—	—
all cadences:	52	5	6	1	21	—	—
15 G(1♭)-mode works, with cadences on:	G	A	B♭	C	D	E	F
finals:	14	—	—	—	1	—	—
all cadences:	46	6	9	—	24	—	2
1 C(2♭)-mode work, with cadences on:	C	D	E♭	F	G	A	B♭
finals:	1	—	—	—	—	—	—
all cadences:	3	—	—	—	2	—	—

'Major' chansons

8 F-mode works, with cadences on:	F	G	A	B♭	C	D	E
finals:	8	—	—	—	—	—	—
all cadences:	28	3	3	—	10	1	—
4 C-mode works, with cadences on:	C	D	E	F	G	A	B
finals:	4	—	—	—	—	—	—
all cadences:	17	1	—	—	8	2	—
1 B♭-mode work, with cadences on:	B♭	C	D	E♭	F	G	A
finals:	1	—	—	—	—	—	—
all cadences:	3	—	—	—	3	—	—

Other chansons

G(no ♭)-mode: *Seule à par moy*, with cadences:	B	D	D̂	G	B	G	G	G
A(no ♭)-mode: *Ma demoiselle*, with cadences:	A	E	C	Ĉ	G	E	A	

Of Busnoys's four chansons ending with cadences on A, only *Ma demoiselle* would seem to earn the description of A-mode, with its prominent cadences on A, C, and E. Two other works, *En soustenant* and *Le monde est tel*, have beginnings that look strikingly like the D-mode works. Given their cadence profiles (Table 14.2), they are perhaps best thought of as D-mode works that end on the confinal, a not uncommon choice for a final cadence in other works of the period.[31]

The cadence profile of *C'est bien maleur* also resembles these D-mode works. With cadences only on D and A, a D-mode assignment fits well; what argues against it is the opening sonority on G and the one-flat signatures. A look at the beginning of the piece (Ex. 14.10) shows that a G-Dorian hearing of the opening is really due more to the contratenor than to the cantus/tenor pair. With just those two voices in mind, it is possible to think of this opening as that of a D-mode work, especially in the cantus voice. D is indicated by the first substantive cadence in measure 10; first cadences normally provide the definition of the

---

[31] Another Busnoys chanson that ends on its confinal is *Joye me fuit*, of the G (1♭) mode.

TABLE 14.2. *Four chansons ending on A*

Titles	Cadences
Ma demoiselle	A E C $\widehat{C}$ G E A assigned to A-mode
En soustenant vostre querelle	D A $\widehat{D}$F D A assigned to D-mode (no ♭)
Le monde est tel	D D $\widehat{A}$ D A assigned to D-mode (no ♭)
C'est bien maleur	D $\widehat{D}$ A

modal final.[32] The one-flat signatures appear to be the main obstruction to acceptance of a D-mode assignment, yet flat signatures are notorious for their mutability in this repertory. The two sources for *C'est bien maleur* both carry flat signatures in all voices, but the flat drops out from the cantus in measure 15 of the Dijon manuscript. Flat signatures are very common in D-mode works: about half of Busnoys's D-mode chansons have partial or intermittent signatures in at least one source. The sources of one piece in particular, *M'a vostre cueur*, transmit quite a variety of signatures (Table 14.3), ranging from no flats in any voice to one flat in all voices. Despite this confusion, there is little question of what mode or what inflections to use in *M'a vostre cueur*. The variety of flat signatures is probably the result of errors or creativity on the part of the scribes; however, it should warn us that the meaning of the flat signature is far less reliable or specific during this period than we today would like to assume.

TABLE 14.3. *Flat signature differences in two chansons*

M'a vostre cueur (beginning)								*Soudainement* (beginning)		
	Fl 229	Cas	Bol Q16	Lab	Fl 2794	Cop	Dij		Cop	Dij	Niv
C	—	—	—	—	—	♭	♭	C	♭	—	—
T	—	—	—	—	—	—	♭	T	—	—	♭
Ct	—	—	♭	♭	♭	♭	♭	Ct	—	—	♭

If we consider the possibility that the flat signatures of *C'est bien maleur* are in error, the evidence clearly points towards a final cadence that uses B♮. The editorial alteration necessary for the tenor would best be thought of as an emendation of that voice's flat signature in the vicinity of measure 15, while the inflections in the cantus in measure 24 (G♯ and F♯) would result from performer's accidentals. Concluding with such a cadence, the chanson would rejoin its neighbours in the repertory, not as an experiment in indeterminate modal form with an unlikely final

---

[32] In 38 out of 45 chansons surveyed, the first cadence occurs on the same pitch as the final of the mode.

cadence, but as a D-mode work with an independent and wayward contratenor. It would also correlate with our observation that securely diminished fifths found in Busnoys's chansons do in fact resolve inward most of the time, in accordance with the practice that was eventually described by Zarlino. But, and this is most important, the converse does not necessarily follow; I have not attempted to show that fifths that do not resolve are therefore not diminished. Indeed, this cannot be claimed, for there remain a small number of diminished fifths in Busnoys's other chansons that are as secure in their diminished quality as any diminished fifth that resolves inward.[33] We may not like such diminished fifths any more than did Tinctoris, but that does not mean that they are not there.

In his discussion of the examples of diminished fifths from Tinctoris's treatise on counterpoint (above, Ex. 14.4), Karol Berger asks that we consider 'the conditions under which such discords may be tolerated'.[34] One naturally wonders about those discords that are judged not tolerable. Berger presumes that such intervals were corrected by performers then, and should be corrected by editors today. Certainly the composer, or scribe, or anyone wielding a pen or eraser could have effected such corrections.[35] But Berger, and most editors of fifteenth-century music, assume that performers would also make these alterations, without written signs: 'In particular, flats correcting melodic tritones may be easily left unwritten, but also accidentals required for contrapuntal-cadential reasons need not always be expressly notated, and even those required to correct mi-against-fa discords may sometimes be left out.'[36] With regard to the last category, which includes our diminished-fifth discords, one must wonder how such correction was possible, given that a performer singing from only his own line could not tell whether a particular diminished fifth was acceptable or not, until after he had already sung the interval. Judging acceptability on the basis of correct resolution is possible for a score-reader, but not necessarily for a singer. For this practical reason, it must be questioned whether the inflections that were added by performers during the normal course of singing—which comprise sharp inflections of cadences, and flat inflections of lines that span augmented fourths—

---

[33] Ex. 14.8, from *Quelque povre homme I*, is one of these. [34] Berger, *Musica ficta*, 96.

[35] The second half of the chanson *Je ne puis vivre ainsi* may provide an example of where a scribe or composer made corrections because of his distaste for the diminished fifths in Busnoys's work. A comparison of the version of the second half found in Dijon with the version in Mellon reveals major reworking that coincides in two separate passages with the occurrence of strong diminished fifths in the Dijon version. The Dijon version was probably Busnoys's original. For this version see *An Anthology of Early Renaissance Music*, ed. Noah Greenberg and Paul Maynard (New York, 1975), 171, or Droz, *Trois chansonniers*, no. 33; for the Mellon version, see *The Mellon Chansonnier*, i. 67. For a comparison of the versions, see Urquhart, 'Three Sample Problems'; for a different interpretation, see Wulf Arlt, 'Vom Überlieferungsbefund zum Kompositionsprozeß: Beobachtungen an den zwei Fassungen von Busnois' "Je ne puis vivre ainsy"', in Gerhard Allroggen and Detlef Altenburg (eds.), *Festschrift Arno Forchert zum 60. Geburtstag* (Kassel, 1986), 27–40.

[36] Berger, *Musica ficta*, 165.

should include harmonic *mi-contra-fa* corrections. Tinctoris would have had no reason to write his chapters 33 and 34 about false concords if *mi-contra-fa* sonorities were corrected on the fly by performers, in the same way as they would inflect cadences or correct linear problems.

The distinction I am drawing here is crucial in the case of a quite famous diminished fifth corrected by Tinctoris in his treatise on the modes. The example, from the chapter on the sixth mode, is famous because it has been understood by many commentators to uphold the modern editorial tendency to give preference to harmonic over linear considerations when adding editorial accidentals. Karol Berger highlights the importance of the passage to the modern editor in the clearest manner, and thus is quoted below in full:

What did one do then when a correction of a melodic relation produced an unwanted vertical one, or the reverse? The question is of a considerable practical importance, but—like all the subtler questions of musical practice—it is generally not discussed by theorists. We are fortunate, however, to possess Johannes Tinctoris's discussion of this very problem:

It must not be overlooked, however, that in composed song, so that a fa against a mi may not happen in a perfect concord, occasionally it is necessary to use a tritone. Then, to signify where ♭ normally ought to be sung in order to avoid the tritone, but where mi must be sung, I believe that the sign of hard b, that is, square b, must be prefaced, as is proven here.[37]

Berger, along with other previous commentators, takes this passage as evidence that 'when one must choose between two non-harmonic relations, one melodic and the other vertical, one should correct the latter'.[38] However, the passage has precisely the opposite meaning if modern editorial accidentals are added to represent what singers would do or were expected to do during performance. The passage does suggest that Tinctoris had a preference for harmonic over linear adjustment in his counterpoint teaching, but what it really ought to signify for modern editors is that singers would sing diminished fifths freely unless expressly told not to. Although I have made this point elsewhere, I raise it here because of the wide misuse to which the passage has been put, and because it directly relates to our questions about diminished fifths in Busnoys.[39]

---

[37] Ibid. 118–19. See Johannes Tinctoris, *Concerning the Nature and Propriety of Tones*, trans. Albert Seay (Colorado Springs, Col., 1976), 13. The passage comes from Ch. 8.

[38] Other commentators include Perkins, *The Mellon Chansonnier*, ii. 133; Lewis Lockwood, 'Musica ficta', section 1(v), *New Grove*, xii. 806; Margaret Bent, 'Diatonic Ficta', *EMH* 4 (1984), 1–48 at 24–6.

[39] See my 'Cross-relations', 27–31.

Tinctoris is saying the following: if the sign of square b were not present, the eighth harmony in the passage would be sung as a diminished fifth for linear reasons, a *'fa* against a *mi'* in a vertical concord. Although such harmonic events do happen in music by 'many, many composers, even the most famous', such as Busnoys, Tinctoris the theorist is opposed to such forbidden intervals on principle. For that reason, he wishes to point out that it is sometimes necessary to use a linear tritone in one part in order to gain the desired harmonic interval with another. In this chapter on the sixth mode, the linear tritone Tinctoris means is that from F to B♮. He has spent the previous three paragraphs showing how this linear tritone in the fifth and sixth modes is normally avoided by singing through the soft hexachord ('per ♭ molle cantabitur'), and that the sign of ♭ does not even need to be present for this to happen ('Neque tunc ♭ mollis signum apponi est necessarium'). This comment, including the famous phrase that the use of the sign with certain melodic figures is 'asinine', is followed by a monophonic example that makes the meaning clear—the linear context provided by the melody is sufficient to cause the singer to use the soft hexachord (see Ex. 14.16). A singer

Ex. 14.16. Tinctoris's example to be sung through the soft hexachord

will sing 'per ♭ molle' any line that rises from F to B and then descends again, unless told not to by some sign. In order to contradict this tendency in the two-voice example, 'the sign of square b must be prefaced'. The verb chosen here is 'praeponere'; use of the verb 'ponere' (*positum, apponi, praeponetur*) throughout this chapter relates to the placement of signs, not to how the passage will be sung, which is indicated by the verb 'cantare' or 'canere' (*cantabitur, canetur, canendum*).[40] The separate use of the verbs ensures that the separate functions remain clear. If the person writing down symbols wishes the singer to sing a linear tritone in order to avoid a harmonic diminished fifth, he must *write* down the sign of ♮; otherwise the singer will sing 'per ♭ molle' and thus cause a diminished fifth, which in this case Tinctoris, the theorist, does not want.

The meaning of the passage is clear. The problem that remains is determining how to relate editorial accidentals to this meaning. I submit that modern editors who add accidentals to this repertory, and musicologists who write the 'rules of *musica ficta*', tend to forget on whose behalf they are acting. Are they adding performers' accidentals, or are they 'correcting' the composers' counterpoint? Performers' accidentals are added by editors in order to indicate the inflections that singers would normally have added on their own, as expected by Tinctoris

---

[40] Tinctoris, *Opera theoretica*; the chapter on *De formatione sexti toni* begins on p. 73.

and composers alike, neither of whom would bother to add these unnecessary signs. When editors add accidentals that could not reasonably be expected from singers, they are correcting the counterpoint, placing signs, such as the one in the example from the chapter on the sixth mode (p. 381), that they have determined *should* have been placed by scribes, but were not by error or for some reason— signs for which composers, not singers or theorists, were ultimately responsible.

Clearly, both kinds of editorial activity are necessary, but they are by no means the same, and must not be confused.[41] In the first place, performers' accidentals ought to be added by editors, including cadential inflections and *b molle* linear inflections that singers could normally have been expected to add while sightreading. Secondarily, and hopefully less often, editors must deal with corrections of the sources, adding accidentals that should normally have been present but were not.[42] If my analysis of the chanson *C'est bien maleur* is correct, then we were dealing with the second type of editorial accidental or signature alteration for the final cadence. Harmonic corrections more likely fall into the second group of alterations than the first, because singers were primarily responsible for and aware of their own line, and the symbols presented to them in their part. Editors should be very careful about their actions in the second category of editorial accidentals, or they may obliterate intentions the composer had. Despite Tinctoris's schoolmasterly prohibitions, composers clearly did not always wish to avoid *mi-contra-fa* in perfect concords, nor were performers automatically expected to correct them. Otherwise, Tinctoris would have had no reason to complain of false concords in music by Faugues, Busnoys, or Caron.

---

[41] It is perhaps time that two separate classes of signs be developed for editions in order to distinguish performers' accidentals from purely editorial, and therefore potentially meddlesome, additions.

[42] Sometimes one must *delete* accidentals present in sources. Many sources are clearly corrupt, and accidental and signature indications are among the first corruptions to occur for music of this period. Preliminary investigations of how the process of regularization of partial signatures operates in the transmission of Josquin's works can be found in my dissertation, 'Canon, Partial Signatures, and "Musica ficta" in Works by Josquin and his Contemporaries' (Ph.D. diss., Harvard University, 1988), especially for the *Missae De beata Virgine*, *Ad fugam*, and *Sine nomine*, the chansons *Plaine de dueil* and *Faulte d'argent*, and the motet *Inviolata, integra et casta es, Maria*.

Appendix A
Thirty-one Harmonic Fifths in Busnoys's Three-Part Chansons that are Probably Diminished

Chanson title	Measure*	Voices	Duration	Resolve?	Harmony	Remarks
C'est bien maleur	13	C/Ct	♩	yes	5/3	confirmed by counterpoint
	14	T/Ct	♩–♩	yes	5/3	confirmed by counterpoint
C'est vous en qui	9	T/Ct	♩–♩	no	5/3	confirmed by linear constraint on T
Chi dit on benedicite	36	T/Ct	♩–♩	yes	5/3	in Pix, d5 is ♩ in a dotted figure
Con tutta gentileça	28	C/Ct	♩–♩	yes	5/3	passing motion in both voices
En voyant sa dame au matin	17	C/Ct	♩	yes	5/3	confirmed by linear constraint on Ct
Est il mercy	3	T/Ct	♩–♩	yes	5/3	passing motion in T
	8	T/Ct	♩–♩	yes	5/3	Ex. 14.14c; linear constraints
Ja que lui ne si attende	11	C/Ct	♩–♩	yes	5/3	passing motion in C
	12	T/Ct	♩–♩	yes	5/3	passing motion in T
	15	C/T	♩–♩–♩	yes	6/3	passing motion in C and T
	16	C/T		no	6/3	sequence
J'ay mains de biens	43	T/Ct		yes	5/3	Ex. 14.9
Je m'esbaïs de vous	2	C/Ct	II	yes	6/3	cadential 6/3 that resolves
Je ne puis vivre ainsi	14	C/Ct	II	yes	5/3	cadential
	32	C/Ct	♩	yes	5/3	in Dij, not Mel; see mm. 44 and 46
	37	T/Ct	♩–♩	yes	5/3	in Dij, not Mel; see mm. 44 and 46
	44	T/Ct	♩	no	5/3	in Dij; linear constraint; see m. 48
	46	C/Ct	♩	no	5/3	in Dij; linear constraint; see m. 48
Joie me fuit	29	C/T	♩–♩–♩	yes	6/3	6/3 that resolves
Le corps s'en va	18	C/Ct	♩–♩	yes	5/3	cadential
	24	C/T	♩–♩	yes	5/3	passing motion in T

Chanson title	Measure*	Voices	Duration	Resolve?	Harmony	Remarks
Le monde est tel	40	T/Ct	◊	yes	5/3	cadential; compare mm. 38 and 42
	42	C/Ct	◊♩	yes	5/3	cadential; compare mm. 38 and 40
Ma tres souveraine princesse	5	C/Ct	♩◊	yes	5/3	slight; consider m. 6
Mon seul et celé souvenir	58	C/Ct	◊	no	5/3	confirmed by linear constraint on Ct
Quelque povre homme (I)	3	T/Ct	◊♩	no	5/3	confirmed by linear constraint on Ct
	26	T/Ct	◊	yes	5/3	confirmed by linear constraint on Ct
Ung grand povre homme	37	C/T	♩◊	yes	6/3	confirmed by linear constraint on T
	41	C/T		yes	n.a.	passing motion in C and T
	51	T/Ct	◊	yes	5/3	confirmed by linear constraint on T

* Regardless of their note-value reductions, most editions place bars every two or three semibreves of original notation, depending on the mensuration. Some chansons edited in the *The Mellon Chansonnier* differ; because of the 1:4 reduction used there, these chansons are barred by four-semibreve measures: *Ja que lui ne si attende, Joie me fuit,* and *Le corps s'en va.*

Appendix B

Busnoys, *C'est bien maleur* (Dijon 517, fos. 24ᵛ–25ʳ)

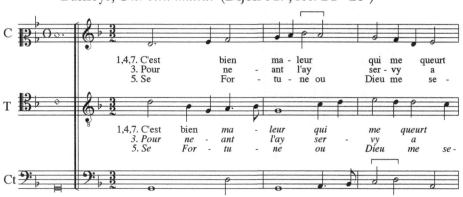

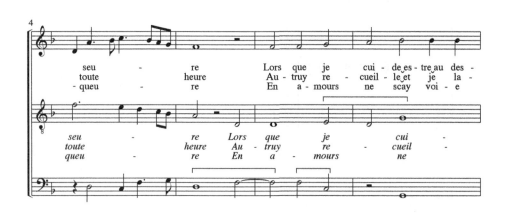

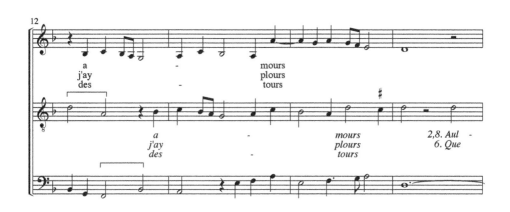

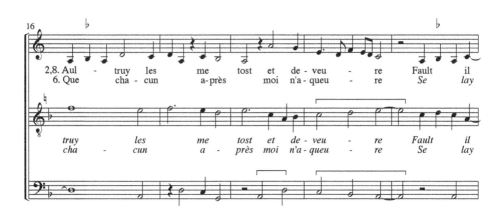

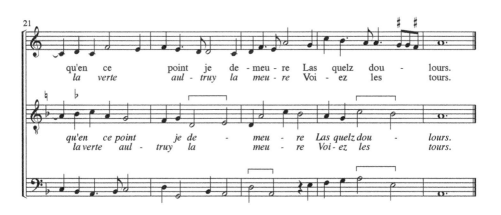

15

Simultaneous Conception and Compositional Process in the Late Fifteenth Century

❧✸✷❧

RICHARD WEXLER

B Y placing each voice in its own individual range, making the voices equal in terms of their overall character and rhythmic values, substituting a paraphrase cantus firmus that migrates throughout the texture for the old-fashioned long-note cantus firmus, and providing a point of imitation at the out-set of each phrase of counterpoint, composers of the late fifteenth century formulated what some have called the '*a cappella* ideal'.[1] It may well be that the migrating paraphrase cantus firmus provided a rationale for the employment of pervading imitation. Because segments of the cantus firmus could be borne in theory by any voice in any given phrase, composers may have thought it more 'artful' to obscure its destination by starting all voices alike at phrase beginnings.

A well-known passage in Pietro Aaron's *Thoscanello de la musica* of 1523 has provided what many have taken to be a significant hint concerning the origins of the style associated with the *a cappella* ideal—or at least it has seemed fairly cer-tain that this is the style about which he is writing.[2]

La imaginatione di molti compositori fù, che prima il canto si dovessi fabricare, da poi il tenore, et doppo esso tenore il con-trobasso. Et questo avenne perchè man-corno del ordine et cognitione di quello che	Many composers were of the opinion that the soprano should be composed first, then the tenor, and after the tenor the bass. This happened because they lacked the order and understanding of what was necessary

---

[1] Whether or not this expression has any legitimacy with respect to instrumental accompaniment or the lack of it, it has been used in connection with the stylistic traits listed here, which taken together represent one of the prevailing styles of composition in the sixteenth century. Cf. Paul Henry Lang, *Music in Western Civilization* (New York, 1941), 194 and 223 ff., and Donald Jay Grout, *A History of Western Music*, 3rd edn., with Claude V. Palisca (New York, 1980), 174.

[2] Pietro Aaron, *Thoscanello de la musica: A Facsimile of the Venice [1523] Edition* (Monuments of Music and Music Literature in Facsimile, 2nd series, 69; New York, 1969), ii, ch. 16 ('Come il compositore possi-dare principio al suo canto' ['How the composer might get a song started']). The passage is reproduced after the edition of 1529 in Bonnie J. Blackburn, 'On Compositional Process in the Fifteenth Century', *JAMS* 40 (1987), 210–84 at 215; her translation is used here.

si richiede nel far del controalto: et però facevano assai inconvenienti ne le loro compositioni: perchè bisognava per lo incommodo che vi ponessino unisoni, pause, salti ascendenti et discendenti, difficili al cantore overo pronontiante: in modo che detti canti restavano con poca soavità et harmonia: perchè facendo prima il canto over soprano, di poi il tenore, quando è fatto detto tenore, manca alcuna volta il luogo al controbasso: et fatto detto controbasso: assai note del contro alto non hanno luogo: per la qual cosa considerando solamente parte per parte, cioè quando si fà il tenore, se tu attendi solo ad accordare esso tenore, et così il simile del controbasso, conviene che ciascuna parte de gli luoghi concordanti patisca. Onde gli moderni in questo meglio hanno considerato; come è manifesto per le compositioni da essi a quatro a cinque a sei, et a più voci fatte: de le quali ciascuna tiene luogo commodo facile et grato: perchè considerano insieme tutte le parti et non secondo come di sopra è detto. Et se a te piace componere prima il canto, tenore o controbasso, tal modo et regola a te resti arbitraria: come da alcuni al presente si osserva: che molte fiate danno principio al controbasso, alcuna volta al tenore, et alcuna volta al contro alto. Mà perchè questo a te sarebbe nel principio mal agevole et incommodo, a parte per parte comincerai: non dimeno di poi che ne la pratica sarai alquanto esercitato, seguirai l'ordine et modo inanzi detto.

to compose the alto. Thus they had many awkward places in their compositions because they had to insert unisons, pauses, and ascending and descending leaps difficult for the singer or performer, so that those works had little sweetness and harmony. For in composing the soprano first and then the tenor, once the tenor was made there was sometimes no room for the bass, and once the bass was made, there was no place for many notes in the alto. Therefore, in considering only part by part, that is when the tenor is being composed, if you pay attention only to harmonizing this tenor [with the soprano], and the same with the bass, it is inevitable that each part will suffer where they come together. Therefore the modern composers had a better idea, which is apparent from their compositions in four, five, six, and more voices, in which each part has a comfortable, easy and agreeable place, because they take all the parts into consideration at once and not as described above. And if you prefer to compose the soprano, tenor, or bass first, you are free to follow that method and rule, as some at present do, who often begin with the bass, sometimes with the tenor, and sometimes with the alto. But because this will be awkward and uncomfortable for you at first, you will begin part by part; nevertheless, once you have gained some experience, you will follow the order and method described before.

It is not completely clear what Aaron meant in saying 'they take all the parts into consideration at once and not as described above [with regard to composing the voices one after another in a particular order]'. But it seems doubtful he intended to imply that a composer of his day who considered all the parts together was capable of what Mozart reputedly could do: the composition of a piece in minute detail, from start to finish, in his head, as though he were working it out on paper, while simultaneously engaged in a game of billiards.[3] This is a kind of 'simultaneous conception' perhaps no more than one person in the whole history of music was able to manage—assuming the legends concerning such prodigious feats on Mozart's part are true.

Be that as it may, Jessie Ann Owens has published a description by Luzzasco Luzzaschi written in 1606 of Cipriano de Rore's method of composing in which Luzzaschi says that Rore, using a *cartella*, 'used to write the compositions made first by him in his mind, as was always his custom'. The description is contained in an affidavit concerning the authenticity of a set of autograph partbooks once belonging to Rore (Milan, Biblioteca Ambrosiana, Ms. A.10.sup. [*olim* S. 691]).[4]

Io Luzzasco Luzzaschi Cittadino Ferrarese, faccio fede che questa Cartella fù del famosissimo, et Eccellentissimo Cipriano Rore Fiammengo Musico, et Maestro di Cappella del già Eccellentissimo Signor Duca Ercole d'Este secondo di Ferrara. Sopra la qual Cartella scriveva le compositioni fatte prima da lui a mente, come'era sempre suo costume. Io in quel tempo essendo suo discepolo lo vidi à scrivere sopra detta Cartella la Gloria d'una Messa che fece in Ferrara et altre sue compositioni fatte in diversi tempi. Et detta Cartella donò à me quando parti di qui, che fù l'Anno 1557 [recte 1559] insieme con l'annesso Miserere composto da lui in Fiandra quando era giovine, et scritto di sua mano, et hora ne facc'io presente all'Illustrissimo et Reverendissimo Signor Cardinale Borromeo mio Signore et patrone Colendissimo affermando quanto hò detto di sopra esser' la verità.

Io Luzzasco Luzzaschi hò scritto di mia propria mano la presente fede, in Ferrara alli 29 Settembre 1606.

I, Luzzasco Luzzaschi, Ferrarese citizen, swear that this *cartella* belonged to the most famous and most excellent Cipriano Rore, Flemish composer and *maestro di cappella* of the late most excellent Lord, Duke Ercole II d'Este of Ferrara, on which *cartella* he used to write the compositions made first by him in his mind, as was always his custom. I, being at that time his student, saw him write on the aforementioned *cartella* the Gloria of a Mass that he made in Ferrara and others of his compositions made at various times. And he gave the aforementioned *cartella* to me when he left here, which was in 1557 [recte 1559],[5] together with the attached *Miserere*, composed by him in Flanders when he was young, and written in his hand, and now I make this known to the most illustrious and most reverend Lord Cardinal Borromeo, my lord and most cherished patron, affirming that what I have said above is the truth.

I, Luzzasco Luzzaschi, wrote the present affidavit with my own hand, in Ferrara on September 29, 1606.

[3] See Erich Hertzmann, 'Mozart's Creative Process', in Paul Henry Lang (ed.), *The Creative World of Mozart* (New York, 1963), 18.

[4] Jessie Ann Owens, 'The Milan Partbooks: Evidence of Cipriano de Rore's Compositional Process', *JAMS* 37 (1984), 270–98 at 276 ff., from which the text and translation are taken. Luzzaschi's affidavit is bound into the set of partbooks as its first folio (ibid. 280). The *cartella* to which he refers is apparently lost.

[5] Rore is known to have left Ferrara in 1559, not 1557. Owens believes Luzzaschi's recollection of the departure date may have been faulty in 1606. See her n. 10.

As Owens indicates, a *cartella* was a kind of pasteboard with a specially pre-pared surface from which it was possible to erase whatever had been written.[6] She goes on to propose that Rore employed the *cartella* to write down at least some voices of a phrase that began with a point of imitation, for she does not believe he needed a full score. Then he copied the result into a set of partbooks, erased the *cartella*, and perhaps used it either to work out the remaining voices of the phrase or else to begin fashioning the next point of imitation.[7] If Owens is right, then what Luzzaschi meant by 'compositions made first by him in his mind' does not mean the same thing as some have supposed Aaron intended by 'they take all the parts into consideration at once'.[8] If it was Luzzaschi's intention to suggest that Rore could compose all the voices of an entire piece at the same time, then the composer should have had no need of the intervening *cartella*.

Aaron, in his *De institutione harmonica* of 1516, after explaining that the older composers generally wrote the cantus first, followed in order by the tenor, bass, and alto, seems to imply that four composers with whom he was acquainted, Josquin, Obrecht, Isaac, and Agricola, composed using a newer method.[9]

Nostri tamen temporis compositores facile deprehenduntur: hanc non servare veterum consuetudinem: ut partes, quas diximus: quattuor tali semper ordine concinnent: quod nos quoque crebro facimus: summos in arte viros imitati praecipuae vero Iosquinum. Obret. Isaac. et Agricolam: quibus cum mihi Florentiae familaritas: et consuetudo summa fuit.	It is easily apprehended, however, that the composers of our time do not follow the custom of older composers in putting these four parts together always in this order, which we ourselves often do, having imitated the most outstanding men in this art, especially Josquin, Obrecht, Isaac, and Agricola, with whom I had greatest friendship and familiarity in Florence.

It has been inferred from this comment that these four are among the modern composers who 'take all the parts into consideration at once' not named by Aaron

---

[6] For further information about the *cartella*, gleaned from letters written between Pietro Aaron, Giovanni del Lago, and Giovanni Spataro, see Bonnie J. Blackburn, Edward E. Lowinsky, and Clement A. Miller (eds.), *A Correspondence of Renaissance Musicians* (Oxford, 1991), 120–3.

[7] Owens, 'The Milan Partbooks', 292–3.

[8] See in particular Edward E. Lowinsky, 'The Concept of Musical Space in the Renaissance', *Papers of the American Musicological Society* for 1941 (1946), 57–84 at 68, and id., *Music in the Culture of the Renaissance and Other Essays*, ed. Bonnie J. Blackburn (Chicago and London, 1989), 6–18 at 11, where he writes: 'Of all the changes in the manner of composition since the emergence of polyphony, the change described by Aron seems to my mind the most vital and the most fateful one. How novel, how difficult it was to train the musical imagination to perceive a complex of four or more voices as one unit and to organize the different parts of a composition by looking at all of them simultaneously from one point, is not easy to realize today.' See also Lowinsky 'On the Use of Scores by Sixteenth-Century Musicians', *JAMS* 1 (1948), 17–23 at 21 (repr., 800).

[9] Pietro Aaron, *De institutione harmonica* (1516), iii, ch. 10; see *Libri tres de institutione harmonica: A Facsimile of the Bologna [1516] Edition* (Monuments of Music and Music Literature in Facsimile, 2nd series, 67; New York, 1976). Blackburn, from whom the translation is taken, considers the sense of this passage to be obscure and suggests that the scholar who translated Aaron's Italian into Latin omitted a key phrase. See her 'On Compositional Process in the Fifteenth Century', 213–14.

in the passage from *Thoscanello* quoted above,[10] and that may well be the case. Nevertheless, Aaron was not suggesting that four composers he knew personally could write detailed works in their minds in the manner imputed to Mozart, even if they were among the greatest of his time. He must have been talking about something rather more modest, which is probably not that they could write a whole mass or multipartite motet, nor perhaps even a single movement or *pars*, in four or five voices in their heads from start to finish. More likely, they would have been able to compose four or five voices more or less simultaneously for a single phrase, which, after all, was the basic structural unit of most masses and motets composed in Aaron's time.

Even though the vast majority of music from the period survives in choirbook or partbook format, it seems probable that composers created counterpoint in score. In fact, there is at least some reason to suppose that Josquin and Isaac used scores of one kind or another. Martin Ruhnke reads the German theorist Lampadius as saying, in his *Compendium musices* of 1537, 'By the time of Josquin and Isaac it was usual to write the parts together in score.'[11] But as Owens has pointed out, Lampadius's meaning is rather more difficult to interpret than that.[12]

Da tabulam compositoriam, quam veteres illi musici usurparunt?	[Student:] What of the tablets for composition that these old musicians used?
Tabulam qua usus Iosquinus et Isaac et reliqui eruditissimi, nemo verbis neque exemplis tradere potest. Eius ratio est, quod veteres illi, tabulis ligneis vel lapideis non contenti fuerunt, non quod ijs non usi fuerint, verum magis se ad Theoricam quam ad practicam applicarunt quare qui hanc artem ignorant nihil certi component, sed plane operam luserint.	[Lampadius:] No one is able to offer a description or examples of the tablet that Josquin, Isaac, and the other most learned composers used. The reason for this is that these old [composers] were not content with tablets of wood or stone; not that they did not use them, but they applied themselves more to theory than to practice, which is why those ignorant of this art compose nothing with certainty, but utterly waste their labours.

Lampadius may be saying that Josquin and Isaac employed scores of a type similar to the woodcut of a score (in the modern sense) he provides by way of

---

[10] Cf. Blackburn, ibid. 214–16.

[11] 'zur Zeit Josquins und Isaacs sei man jedoch dazu übergegangen, die Stimmen in einer Partitur zusammenzuschreiben'. Martin Ruhnke, 'Lampadius, Auctor', *Die Musik in Geschichte und Gegenwart*, ed. Friedrich Blume, 17 vols. (Kassel, 1949–86), viii. 150–1.

[12] 'The Milan Partbooks', 295. From Lampadius (of Lüneberg), *Compendium musices, tam figurati quam plani cantus ad formam Dialogi* (Berne, 1537). See further the discussions and translations in Lowinsky, 'On the Use of Scores', 18–19 (repr., 798–9); Siegfried Hermelink, 'Die Tabula compositoria', in *Festschrift Heinrich Besseler zum sechzigsten Geburtstag* (Leipzig, 1961), 221–2; and Owens, 'The Milan Partbooks', 295–6. The translation is after Lowinsky, Hermelink, and Owens.

illustration.[13] Or he may be saying only that they used *tabulae compositoriae*, which might or might not be the same thing.

Whatever he means, he does indicate that these composers used at least some writing materials while composing. A *tabula*, which is what the predecessor of Rore's *cartella* was called, consisted of a writing surface made from slate or wood.[14] It may be that few autographs or drafts of compositions have come down to us because composers worked out their counterpoint on slate with a chalk-like substance or on a wooden tablet coated with beeswax. Once a scribe had made a fair copy of the music on parchment or paper, the slate could be erased with a damp rag or the tablet smoothed with a hot iron. The poet Crétin, in his lament for Jean Braconnier, dit Lourdault, who died in 1512, enjoins Johannes Prioris to 'take your slate and, in your fashion, there compose a *Ne recorderis*'.[15] One should bear in mind that Prioris was a contemporary of Josquin and Isaac and that Crétin mentions his composing in this manner only a few years before the appearance of Aaron's *De institutione harmonica*.

A closer look at the passage from Aaron's *Thoscanello* suggests there may be good reason to doubt that he even intended what some have come to call 'simultaneous conception' at all.[16] He says 'perchè considerano insieme tutte le parti' ('because they *take all the parts into consideration* at once'), not that they *compose* all the voices, note for note, at the same time. In other words, he is advocating planning all the voices together in order that each might occupy its own range within the texture without unduly overlapping the others and thereby avoiding 'unisons, pauses, and ascending and descending leaps difficult for the singer or performer'.[17] This kind of planning could have resulted in a certain amount of composition of more than one voice at a time, but perhaps nothing on the scale hitherto imagined by some modern writers on this subject.[18]

---

[13] See Lowinsky, 'On the Use of Scores', 23 (repr., 799), a reproduction after Lampadius of five 'measures' in barred score from a work by Verdelot.

[14] See Guillaume de Van, 'La pédagogie musicale à la fin du moyen âge', *Musica disciplina*, 2 (1948), 75–97 at 94.

[15] 'Prenez l'ardoyse et de vostre faczon, composez cy ung *"ne recorderis"*.' Ibid., n. 44.

[16] In addition to the writings of Lowinsky mentioned above, see, for example, Manfred F. Bukofzer, 'The Music of the Old Hall Manuscript', in *Studies in Medieval and Renaissance Music* (New York, 1950), 46, who is in turn quoted by Edgar H. Sparks in *Cantus Firmus in Mass and Motet, 1420–1520* (Berkeley and Los Angeles, 1963), 18.

[17] Blackburn presents essentially the same interpretation of this passage ('On Compositional Process', 211 and 216–17) but seeks an explanation for its meaning in earlier and contemporaneous writings concerned with the terms 'harmony' and *res facta*.

[18] The interpretation of Aaron's remarks as referring to 'simultaneous conception' came to the attention of musicologists principally as a result of the two articles by Lowinsky cited previously, 'The Concept of Physical and Musical Space' (see above, n. 8), and 'On the Use of Scores'. Lowinsky acknowledged Dagobert Frey as the originator of this reading of Aaron, invoking the latter's *Gotik und Renaissance als Grundlagen der modernen Weltanschauung* (Augsburg, 1929), and he also found support for it in Gioseffo Zarlino's *Le istitutioni harmoniche* (Venice, 1558); see 'The Concept', 68 (repr., 11), where he quotes Zarlino's edition of 1573, iii. 63. Evidently, Lowinsky was quite taken with Frey's suggestion that the introduction of 'simultaneous conception' in music could be considered analogous to that of perspective in painting. There can be no question that the significance of perspective was very great to the artists of the 15th c., as abundant testimony makes clear. In relating the biography of Paolo Ucello (1397–1475), for

It may be that too much has been read into Aaron's remarks. Aaron himself does not seem to make a great deal of this new method. He does not give much reason for the change, except to say that what he recommends would provide a place for each part and avoid unisons, rests, and difficult leaps; and in fact he advises novices, for whom he was writing after all, to compose part by part anyway, presumably without trying to take into account in advance what the other voices will do. Therefore, rather than proclaiming a new way of composing and making this new method the momentous central subject of his treatise,[19] he mentions it only in passing in book ii, ch. 16. This might be because he was well aware that for years the composition of certain kinds of pieces, as has been pointed out by numerous commentators,[20] may well have involved a certain amount of the actual creation of more than one voice at a time—in particular, canons, *fauxbourdon* and *falsobordone* settings, and perhaps pieces with note-against-note texture, such as the lauda, the frottola, the villancico, the polyphonic Lied, and other similar types.

Nevertheless, we should perhaps resist assuming that the composition of all such pieces necessitated the creation of more than one part at a time. One can imagine easily that a composer could create a frottola, for example, by inventing the melody for the top voice first, then supplying it with an appropriate bassus that might imply certain 'harmonies' but not specific note choices, and finally adding the inner voices one at a time according to those implications. By suggesting that such notions as 'implied harmonies' could have existed, I realize that

example, Giorgio Vasari writes (as retold by Dmitri Merejkovski) that 'taken up with abstract mathematics, which he compared with art, and with brain-racking problems of perspective, contemned and abandoned of all, Ucello had fallen into penury and had almost gone out of his head; he passed whole days without food, whole nights without sleep; at times, lying in bed, with wide-open eyes staring into the darkness, he would waken his wife by exclaiming: "Oh, what a delectable thing is perspective!" He died, bemocked and not understood.' (See Dmitri Merejkovski, *The Romance of Leonardo da Vinci*, trans. Bernard Guilbert Guerney (New York, 1938), 380; see also Giorgio Vasari, *The Lives of the Painters, Sculptors, and Architects*, rev. edn., trans. William Gaunt [London, 1963], 239). Little in the way of testimony, however, not even from the inordinately talkative Heinrich Glarean, remains to suggest that any composer of that time was absorbed in and distracted by the problems of musical style and composition to such an extreme degree.

[19] In contrast, the author of a well-known early 14th-c. treatise uses his title to announce change with a grand flourish. See *Philippi de Vitriaco: Ars nova* [*c*.1320], ed. Gilbert Reaney *et al.* (CSM 8; [Rome], 1964). It is chiefly on this point that I differ with Blackburn, who begins her article 'On Compositional Process', 'Hardly any development in the history of music has been more vital and fateful than the change from "successive composition" to "simultaneous conception" ', and shortly afterwards quotes Lowinsky as proposing that 'this change in the method of writing music down coincides with a momentous change in the technique of composition—the change from the successive conception of the single voices to the simultaneous conception of the polyphonic complex' ('On the Use of Scores', 20; repr., 799). She goes on to present a divergent reading of the passage in which she points out that what Aaron describes as the newer practice 'could also result from successive composition' (216–17). It seems to me that the amount of planning of the voices together required for composing imitative polyphony in Aaron's time was not very much greater, for example, than what Perotinus needed to do in planning the composition of the voice-exchange passages in his three- and four-voice *organa*.

[20] See especially Blackburn, 'On Compositional Process', 211 (summarizing Lowinsky) and 219; and Edward E. Lowinsky, 'Canon Technique and Simultaneous Conception in Fifteenth-Century Music: A Comparison of North and South', in Robert L. Weaver (ed.), *Essays on the Music of J. S. Bach and Other Divers Subjects: A Tribute to Gerhard Herz* (Louisville, 1981), 181–222, esp. 198 n. 17 (repr., 891).

I am also suggesting that there might have been a concept of a 'chord' long before Rameau's day. But no matter what a frottolist singing a melody and accompanying himself on a lute may have called the resulting simultaneities, the fingers of his left hand were indeed gripping two or more strings at the same time, and his right hand was sounding several notes together.

With regard to music in the style associated with the *'a cappella* ideal' described here at the outset, Bonnie Blackburn has pointed out, 'It would be very difficult indeed to write a three-part piece in pervading imitation without constantly adjusting one voice to another. When composers began to write in this manner we can confidently say that they were not only considering all voices together, they were conceiving all voices in relation to each other'.[21] And the same thing is true of a four-voice piece, or for that matter anything with more than two voices.

But to what extent, using the stylistic traits mentioned at the beginning of the present essay—equality of voices, diversity of vocal ranges, a migrating cantus firmus, and a point of imitation at the outset of each phrase—would it have been necessary to conceive all the voices in relation to each other? In writing such a piece, one would first have to determine what the basic ranges of the voice-parts should be, perhaps based on the ranges of the singers for whom one was composing (who were in any event probably chosen in the first place to provide the desired contrasting ranges). Next, one might need to recast the cantus firmus in order for it to match the melodic type to be used in the non-cantus firmus voices (assuming no plan to paraphrase it in the course of composing). Then one could begin to compose the first phrase, conceiving the voices simultaneously, as though writing in canon—but only necessarily for the duration of the point of imitation. Once the phrase was begun with all voices presenting the initial portion of a segment of the cantus firmus in imitation, one then faced a decision concerning which voice should continue with the concluding portion of the segment. That voice could be taken to the end of the phrase first, with the remaining voices then being added in free counterpoint, perhaps even one at a time, until the phrase was completed.

Admittedly, the method just described sounds like a rather prosaic way of creating polyphony, but not every composer who wrote in this style had the transcendent abilities of a Josquin or an Isaac, to name only two composers of that time who probably had little need of following it doggedly. However, it is entirely in keeping with what Aaron recommended, that being the taking of 'all the parts into consideration at once'. The important thing to bear in mind is that the principal stylistic factor demanding the composition of more than one voice simultaneously is the consistent use of canonic points of imitation. A relatively significant change of style may have occurred in the last several decades of the

---

[21] Blackburn, 'On Compositional Process', 267.

fifteenth century, but the method of composing had to change only just enough to accommodate what was new in stylistic terms, which is to say not very much, since there had been abundant imitation in earlier music even if all voices did not participate in points of imitation at the outsets of phrases.

Therefore, it should not be necessary to impose a 'close reading' on Tinctoris in order to examine why, in his *Diffinitorium*,[22] the words 'Armonia', 'Melos', 'Melodia', and 'Eufonia' all share a single meaning and to determine how this has a bearing on 'simultaneous conception'.[23] I suspect it has none. I also suspect that whatever Tinctoris did mean by *res facta* and *cantare super librum*, trying to follow what he is saying about them in terms of 'simultaneous conception' and 'successive composition' will not shed much light on what Aaron was talking about many years afterwards.[24] By 1523 Aaron must have heard a great deal of music, unknown to Tinctoris in the 1470s, in which the voices occupied separate ranges, the voice parts were alike in character, the cantus firmus (if there was one) was paraphrased and perhaps migrated, and each phrase began with a point of imitation; in other words, music in which the relationship of one part to another required a certain amount of planning, a consideration of all the parts together, in ways not needed earlier. To find out when the approach to composition alluded to by Aaron gained currency, it is merely necessary to identify, in the surviving music, where imitation in combination with a migrating cantus firmus begins to assume the role of dictating as a matter of course a need for working out the parts together. This, however, is no easy matter.

If one looks in the music of Dufay and Ockeghem for the stylistic traits just enumerated, one finds such characteristics at various times in one work or another, and both composers must have engaged now and again in the kind of planning Aaron mentions in connection with other composers known to him personally. But for the most part the music of Dufay and Ockeghem contains a key stylistic ingredient, imitation, only in an incidental way. Except in several noteworthy and exceptional instances, such as Ockeghem's *Missa Prolationum*,[25] a phenomenal *tour de force* that transcends all workaday method, imitation is not employed by them as a structural principle and could have been worked into the

---

[22] Ibid. 211, and Johannes Tinctoris, *Dictionary of Musical Terms (Terminorum musicae diffinitorium)*, ed. and trans. Carl Parrish (London, 1963), 8, 40, and 30.

[23] Blackburn, 'On Compositional Process', 211 and 224 ff., esp. 226 and n. 24.

[24] See Margaret Bent, '*Resfacta* and *Cantare Super Librum*', *JAMS* 36 (1983), 371–91 at 387, where she writes: 'The "mutual obligation" of the parts in *resfacta* almost suggests that we might find here a statement about simultaneous conception, fifty years earlier than the first unequivocal testimony to this way of composing in Aaron's *Toscanello*; however, none of Tinctoris's examples of *resfacta* gives us a good justification for claiming that they have broken with the successive principles that so clearly apply to his "pure" counterpoint.' For a contrasting view, see Blackburn, 'On Compositional Process', 265–8.

[25] In his 'Canon Technique and Simultaneous Conception in Fifteenth-Century Music', Edward Lowinsky gave special prominence to the *Missa Prolationum* as an example of conceiving the voices simultaneously; see 187 and n. 23 (repr., 892). The mass is published in Johannes Ockeghem, *Collected Works*, ii: *Masses and Mass Sections IX–XVI*, ed. Dragan Plamenac (2nd corr. edn.; New York, 1966), no. 10.

counterpoint as the context permitted in the process of composing the voices successively.

Nevertheless, Dufay and Ockeghem, and with them Busnoys, as well as the composers Aaron named, Agricola, Isaac, Josquin, and Obrecht, laid the groundwork for the style later associated with the so-called *a cappella* ideal. Rather than perpetuating an expression, 'simultaneous conception', that tends to evoke visions of momentous transformations[26] having near mythic proportions, we should perhaps think about seeking a less fanciful way of describing the more natural, evolutionary continuity of musical style in the late fifteenth century.

[26] See above, n. 19.

16

Reading Tinctoris for Guidance on Tempo

୫୨ ୨୨

ALEXANDER BLACHLY

JOHANNES TINCTORIS, today probably the most highly esteemed theorist of the fifteenth century, never discusses the concept of tempo directly. He limits his statements on tempo to some brief observations concerning cut signatures and time-beating. But so great is his authority that modern misapprehensions concerning Tinctoris's passing observations on mensuration and tempo have led to a distorted view of fifteenth-century mensural relationships generally. When Carl Dahlhaus equated in a diagram the workings of the fifteenth-century beat with the sixteenth-century two-motion *tactus* described by Martin Agricola (1532),[1] Giovanni Lanfranco (1533),[2] and Sebald Heyden (1540),[3] he helped bolster the notion that Tinctoris's views on time-beating foreshadow the teachings of these sixteenth-century writers.[4] Yet Tinctoris's term for the beat is *mensura*, which he identifies with a single note.[5] Others in our time, including Fritz Feldmann, Eunice Schroeder, and Anna Maria Busse Berger, have each, from different vantage points, associated Tinctoris's statements on cut sig-

I should like to thank Alejandro E. Planchart, Leeman L. Perkins, Rob C. Wegman, Bonnie J. Blackburn, and Leofranc Holford-Strevens for reading this paper prior to publication and making helpful suggestions for its improvement. The last-named kindly provided corrections to the Latin/English excerpts from Renaissance treatises. Rob C. Wegman's 'What is "Acceleratio mensurae"?', *Music and Letters*, 73 (1992), 515–24, cites several of the Tinctoris passages discussed below, and, I am happy to say, comes to conclusions similar to those presented here.

[1] *Musica figuralis deudsch* (Wittenberg, 1532; facs. repr. Hildesheim, 1969).
[2] Giovanni Maria Lanfranco, *Scintille di musica* (Brescia, 1533; facs. repr. Bologna, 1970).
[3] *De arte canendi* (Nuremberg, 1540; facs. repr. Monuments of Music and Music Literature in Facsimile, 2nd series, 129; New York, 1969), trans. Clement A. Miller, *Sebald Heyden: De Arte Canendi, Translation and Transcription* (MSD 26, 1972). See Carl Dahlhaus, 'Die Mensurzeichen als Problem der Editionstechnik', in *Musikalische Edition im Wandel des historischen Bewußtseins* (Kassel, 1971), 174–88, esp. 178.
[4] This is ironic, because elsewhere Dahlhaus argued strenuously against the modern projection of 16th-c. theory onto 15th-c. repertory. See, most importantly, his 'Zur Theorie des Tactus im 16. Jahrhundert', *Archiv für Musikwissenschaft*, 17 (1960), 22–39.
[5] This point is discussed in detail in ch. 3 of my study, 'Mensuration and Tempo in 15th-Century Music: Cut Signatures in Theory and Practice' (Ph.D. diss., Columbia University, 1995).

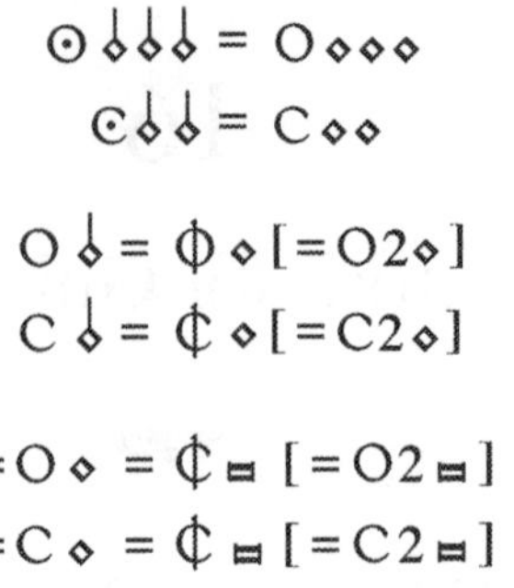

⊙ ♩♩♩ = O ◇◇◇

₵ ♩♩ = C ◇◇

O ♩ = ɸ ◇ [= O2◇]

C ♩ = ₵ ◇ [= C2◇]

⊙♩ = O ◇ = ₵ ▭ [= O2 ▭]

₵♩ = C ◇ = ₵ ▭ [= C2 ▭]

FIG. 16.1. Sixteenth-century 'proportional' relationships

natures with proportionally based systems,[6] systems best known today from their
advocacy by sixteenth-century theorists we may refer to as 'proportionalists'
(Andreas Ornithoparchus, Martin Agricola, and Sebald Heyden).[7] The present
study attempts to correct Feldmann's, Schroeder's, and Busse Berger's representations of Tinctoris's understanding of mensuration and tempo—proposing
instead an understanding of such flexibility that it alone can account for the myr-
iad contrasting uses of cut signatures in fifteenth-century music. The interpretation of Tinctoris proposed here relies on two of his treatises dating from the
1470s: the *Proportionale musices* (*c*.1473) and the *Liber de arte contrapuncti*
(1477).[8]

'Proportionalism' teaches that the relationships between the three 'grades' of
mensuration are always restricted to 2 : 1 proportions as one ascends from the
first level (⊙, ₵) to the second (O, C), and from the second to the the third (ɸ,
₵, O2, C2), regardless of the context in which the signs appear (see Fig. 16.1).

Even those who see Tinctoris as a precursor of this system, however, recognize

---

[6] Feldmann, in the Introduction to Johannes Tinctoris, *Opera omnia* (CMM 18; [Rome], 1960), states
on p. iii: 'The general character of melody in Tinctoris' period is best brought out by transcribing the semibreve as a half-note: ◇ = ♩ [1 : 2], while the frequent use of *tempus diminutum* demands diminished equival-
ents: ₵◇ = ♩ [1 : 4]. We can confirm that *tempus diminutum* signifies reduction by a half of the normal values,
owing to his remarks in chapter 2 of the *Proportionale, Liber tertium* . . . The accompanying example in the
Proportionale shows clearly enough that the notes of the *alla breve* Discantus are to be taken twice as quickly
as the normally notated Tenor.' For a discussion of the passage from the *Proportionale* referred to by
Feldmann, see below, Statement 2, where it is shown that, contrary to Feldmann's understanding, Tinctoris
allows a duple proportion between C and ₵ only with the greatest reluctance and only under special circumstances. Eunice Schroeder's views are found in 'The Stroke Comes Full Circle: ɸ and ₵ in Writings on
Music, ca.1450–1540', *Musica disciplina*, 36 (1982), 119–66. For Anna Maria Busse Berger's argument, see
'The Relationship of Perfect and Imperfect Time in Italian Theory of the Renaissance', *EMH* 5 (1985),
1–28, and 'The Myth of *diminutio per tertiam partem*', *Journal of Musicology*, 8 (1990), 398–426; it may also
be found in her book, *Mensuration and Proportion Signs: Origins and Evolution* (Oxford, 1993), esp. 129–39.

[7] For a full discussion of these theorists' views, see Blachly, 'Mensuration and Tempo', ch. 4. Neither
Ornithoparchus' nor Agricola's proportionalism represents a wholly consistent system.

[8] For a modern edition of Tinctoris's treatises, see Tinctoris, *Opera theoretica*, ed. Albert Seay (CSM 22;
Neuhausen-Stuttgart, 1975–8).

that he does not approve of the top equations in Fig. 16.1. In fact, Tinctoris not only condemns proportional relationships in which ☉ and ℭ are used as signs of proportion, he condemns the use of any mensuration sign whatever as an indicator of a proportional relationship.[9] Evidently unpersuaded by this message, which the theorist sends to the reader repeatedly in Book iii of the *Proportionale musices*, Feldmann contends that Tinctoris equates ₵ with duple proportion; Schroeder concurs in this reading and also asserts that Tinctoris equates ⏀ with *sesquialtera*. Feldmann hangs his entire argument on a misreading of the second of Tinctoris's excerpts discussed below. Schroeder seeks support for her interpretations in the writings of Anonymous 12, whose treatise was written by 1471,[10] and in numerous 'non-proportionalist' treatises dating from the early years of the sixteenth century.

Anonymous 12 and the later writers Schroeder cites do advocate the relationship shown in Fig. 16.2, but Tinctoris is purposely vague: he merely allows that by means of a stroke through the sign of *tempus* (i.e., ⏀) Ockeghem could have indicated an 'excited *sesquialtera*' in his chanson *L'autre d'antan*.[11]

$$ O \diamond \diamond = \varnothing \diamond \diamond \diamond $$

FIG. 16.2. Tinctoris's view of ⏀, according to Eunice Schroeder

Anna Maria Busse Berger contrasts Tinctoris's teaching, which she characterizes as one endorsing 'equal minim',[12] with that of Bartolomeo Ramos de Pareja and Giovanni Spataro, who, she declares, base their systems on the premiss of 'equal breve', a phenomenon she traces to the fourteenth century.[13] According to Busse Berger, the relationship for which Spataro, in particular, wished to account may be expressed formulaically as in Fig. 16.3.

---

[9] See *Proportionale musices*, iii. 2 (Opera theoretica, iia, 47–8). Tinctoris asserts that proportions may correctly be signalled only by means of two-numeral fractions. He berates Domarto and Cousin for using such signs as ℭ and C3 to indicate augmentation, *sesquialtera* at the semibreve level, and *sesquialtera* at the breve level; he criticizes 'some of the older composers' for writing out the name of a proportion instead of using a (two-numeral) sign; and he later lists three different uses for the signs of major *prolatio* (as indicators of *sesquialtera* and *subsesquitertia*, and as signs sharing minim equivalence with O, respectively). He approves only of the last of these.

[10] According to Jill M. Palmer (ed.), *Anonymus: Tractatus et Compendium cantus figurati* (CSM 35; Neuhausen-Stuttgart, 1990), the date 1471 appears in one of the two sources for the treatise: Regensburg, Proskesche Musikbibliothek, MS 98 Th. 4°.

[11] See below, Tinctoris Statement 1.

[12] See 'The Relationship of Perfect and Imperfect Time', 23 (= *Mensuration and Proportion Signs*, 79), where she claims that Tinctoris's views eventually prevailed: 'After about 1510 Tinctoris's reform succeeds, and minim equality takes over as the leading theory to such an extent that most theorists do not even bother to discuss it, but simply assume it.'

[13] See 'The Origin and Early History of Proportion Signs', *JAMS* 41 (1988), esp. 407–13 (= *Mensuration and Proportion Signs*, 57–66). The most accessible source for Spartaro's view on this matter is Letter no. 40 (Giovanni Spataro to Pietro Aaron) in Bonnie J. Blackburn, Edward E. Lowinsky, and Clement A. Miller (eds.), *A Correspondence of Renaissance Musicians* (Oxford, 1991), 473–5.

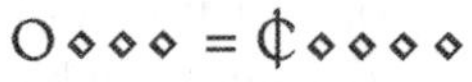

$$O \diamond \diamond \diamond = \mathbb{C} \diamond \diamond \diamond \diamond$$

FIG. 16.3. Ramos's and Spataro's view of $\mathbb{C}$ following O, according to Busse Berger

Alejandro Planchart has shown that 'equal breve' could also arise as a consequence of regarding the signs $\mathbb{C}$ and $\supset$ as interchangeable (for most of its history, beginning in the fourteenth century, the sign $\supset$ functioned solely as a sign of proportion, specifically as an indicator of *sesquitertia*, i.e., four values in the place of three).[14] According to this argument, $\mathbb{C}$ would derive its meaning from $\supset$ (see Fig. 16.4).

$$O \diamond \diamond \diamond = \supset \diamond \diamond \diamond \diamond = \ \mathbb{C} \diamond \diamond \diamond \diamond$$

FIG. 16.4. The evolution of the 4 : 3 relationship between O and $\mathbb{C}$, according to Planchart

Busse Berger, however, prefers to view the 4 : 3 relationship between O and $\mathbb{C}$ from the perspective of 'breve equivalence'; that is, she begins with the top line in Fig. 16.5 to arrive at the bottom one. So far as I have been able to ascertain, this approach originates with Ramos in the 1480s.

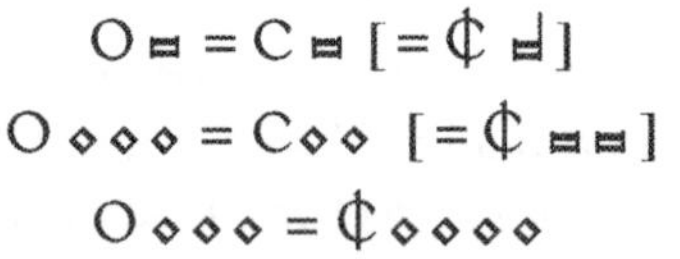

$$O \ \rlap{=}\sqcup = C \ \rlap{=}\sqcup \ [= \mathbb{C} \ \rlap{=}\sqcup]$$
$$O \diamond \diamond \diamond = C \diamond \diamond \ [= \mathbb{C} \ \rlap{=}\sqcup \ \rlap{=}\sqcup]$$
$$O \diamond \diamond \diamond = \mathbb{C} \diamond \diamond \diamond \diamond$$

FIG. 16.5. The evolution of Spataro's equation, according to Busse Berger

A 4 : 3 relationship between a passage in $\mathbb{C}$ following a passage in O in music of the fifteenth century has also been proposed in recent years by Margaret Bent.[15] The 4 : 3 relationship between O and $\mathbb{C}$ is attractive to modern inter-

---

[14] Alejandro E. Planchart, in 'The Relative Speed of *Tempora* in the Period of Dufay', *Royal Musical Association Research Chronicle*, 17 (1981), 33–51, notes that in Aosta, a Gloria by Johannes Brassart indicates a 4 : 3 proportion with the sign $\supset$, but in Bologna Q15, Trent 90, and Trent 93 the same notes are signed with $\mathbb{C}$.

[15] Introduction to *Fifteenth-Century Liturgical Music II: Four Anonymous Masses* (Early English Church Music, 22; London, 1979). Bent states that for English works from the period in question, 'vertically coincident conflicts of signature . . . invariably presuppose minim equivalence. In isorhythmic motets, too, numerical proportions are occasionally provided which confirm minim equivalence between one section and another. This relationship often fails to work well between major sections of Mass movements, suggesting that a different convention may have been in force. The duple-time sections have a markedly slower rate of harmonic movement, and use fewer short note-values. In all surviving English sources of this period the diminution signature $\mathbb{C}$ is rigorously avoided; yet Continental scribes show a strong tendency to convert the English C into $\mathbb{C}$. Taken literally, the one is too slow, the other too fast. A 3 : 4 relationship betwen triple and duple (i.e. perfect breve of O = imperfect long of C or $\mathbb{C}$) seems appropriate, and has been suggested editorially. Objective evidence to support this proportion is slight but not entirely lacking: it draws on late fourteenth-century English practices.'

preters because it allows sections in both O and ¢ to move in moderate tempos (as would seem appropriate in an age that extolled balance, moderation, and the 'mean' as aesthetic ideals),[16] whereas a 2 : 1 ratio between passages in these two mensurations forces both away from moderate tempos: O towards extreme slowness, ¢ towards extreme speed, as Richard Taruskin has noted in his recent edition of the Latin-texted works of Antoine Busnoys.[17]

From what might be termed a 'mathematical' point of view, however, it is difficult to reconcile the 2 : 1 ratio between cut and uncut signatures when both occur in a simultaneous context[18] with some other relationship, such as the proposed *sesquialtera* (for ¢ following O) or *sesquitertia* (for ¢ following O), when cut and uncut signatures occur in a successive context. To do so admits an inconsistency into the science of musical notation—namely, a double meaning for the stroke of diminution, with the (vertical or horizontal) context alone determining which meaning will obtain. From the time of Franco of Cologne,[19] the general trend in notational evolution had been to move away from contextual understandings, such as those dependent on the ligature patterns used in modal notation, towards concrete, absolute meanings for the elements of notation, independent of context.[20] It should not be stretching matters to assume that both Tinctoris and Ramos recognized the problematic nature of cut signatures in the musical practice of their time. At the very least, they must have realized that the use of cut signatures undermined the traditional French principle of a constant minim between all mensurations—a principle inherent in the writings of Philippe de Vitry and Johannes de Muris (see Fig. 16.6).

[16] The idealization of the mean is so pervasive in the culture of the 15th c. as to need little demonstration. A typical expression of the concept posited man as the centre of the universe, the mean between the very small and the very large. Marsilio Ficino, for example, referred to the individual as 'the center of nature, the middle point of all that is, the chain of the world, the face of all, and the knot and bond of the universe' (*Platonic Theology* [3, 2], as translated by J. L. Burroughs, in *Journal of the History of Ideas*, 5 (1944), 227–39; cited by Giancarlo Maiorino in *Adam, 'New Born and Perfect': The Renaissance Promise of Eternity* (Bloomington, Ind., 1987), 36). Similarly, the Florentine architect Francesco di Giorgio (1439–1501), seeing the physical proportions of the human body as expressions of a 'divine proportion', devised an 'anthropomorphically derived modular grid in which the proportions of the human body are used to determine a temple plan' (Henry Millon, 'The Architectural Theory of Francesco di Giorgio', in Creighton Gilbert (ed.), *Renaissance Art* (New York, 1970; repr. 1973), 135).

[17] Richard Taruskin, in *Busnoys LTW*, Commentary, 78 n. 11: 'To the admittedly slender documentary evidence for the sesquitertial proportion . . . one might legitimately add the oft-lamented dilemma faced by conductors of Renaissance church music, to wit, that if one adopts a duple proportion (semibreve under O equals breve under ¢), one either has to take the section in O too slowly or the section in ¢ too quickly for comfort or (apparent) sense. The sesquitertial interpretation of the mensural relationship seems to solve this problem.'

[18] Vertical 2 : 1 ratios are discussed below on pp. 414–15. An example of a piece that presupposes a 2 : 1 ratio between ¢ and O when they are vertically aligned is Isaac's *Tartara* (*Canti C*, fos. 136ᵛ–138ʳ). Though rare, the simultaneous use of O and ¢ does occur in the musical sources, as, for example, in Du Fay's *Missa Sancti Anthonii de Padua*, in the 'Amen' of the Credo, where the relationship between a semibreve of ¢ in the superius and a semibreve of O in the tenor and contratenor is 2 : 1. Both examples are given in Blachly, 'Mensuration and Tempo', Introduction.

[19] See Andrew Hughes, 'Franco of Cologne', *New Grove*, vi. 794–7.

[20] Although the mensural notation of the 13th–16th cc. retained some significant contextual features, such as the length of an imperfected note, which, in the case of an imperfected breve of ☉, could vary in length anywhere from eight to five minims, depending on what other notes were in its immediate vicinity.

$$\odot \, \flat = \mathbb{C} \, \flat = \mathrm{O} \, \flat = \mathrm{C} \, \flat$$

FIG. 16.6. Minim equivalence among French fourteenth-century mensurations (with fifteenth-century signs)

Possibly Ramos and Tinctoris were each trying to account for the same musical practice, but by way of different reasoning. Tinctoris, as already noted, does not actually present a direct argument. Most likely, he shied away from an explication of cut signatures because he could not formulate an explanation for them free from the contextual inconsistency noted above. Unlike Ramos, Tinctoris refused to make a break with French mensural theory, upon which so much else in his treatises depended. He therefore sidestepped the issue, referring briefly to cut signatures when the discussion required him to do so, using them in his own compositions and in his musical examples in the manner customary at the time, but never attempting to integrate an explanation of their various uses into the otherwise coherent and consistent musical universe his writings describe.

The variety of contexts in which cut signatures relate to uncut ones illustrates why one unchanging equation cannot account for all of them. Ex. 16.1 shows the beginning of a short mass movement signed with C in a source from Milan but with ¢ in a source that originated in Ferrara. How should we interpret this difference? According to the teachings of the sixteenth-century proportionalists (Ornithoparchus, Heyden, etc.), the Benedictus was sung twice as slowly in Milan as in Ferrara. Who today could believe this? The late fifteenth-century repertory contains many similar cases, including an entire mass by Guillaume Du Fay (his last one, *Ave regina caelorum*), which has all the passages in duple metre signed with C in two of the sources but with ¢ in the third.[21]

Even when all sources for a given piece agree on the mensuration sign, as in Ex. 16.2, Hayne van Ghizeghem's *De tous biens plaine*, the sign may not convey to today's interpreter an unambiguous meaning. Is the stroke in the sign ¢ merely a warning not to sing the piece too slowly? Does it indicate a beat on the breve, and if so does this imply a duple proportion to a piece in C, such as Antoine Busnoys's *Ha que ville*? (The Dijon Chansonnier preserves both chansons in the same hand; see Ex.16.3.)

In the most problematic relationships between signs, two or more contrasting mensurations occur in immediate juxtaposition within a single piece (that is, deliberately juxtaposed by the composer). Contrasting mensurations further divide into 'vertical' or 'horizontal' types. The best-known examples of 'vertical' usage in late fifteenth-century music are found in *L'homme armé* masses, where,

---

[21] In Brussels 5557 and Modena α.M.1.13 the mass is signed throughout with O and C, while in San Pietro B 80 it is signed with O and ¢. The notation itself is the same in the three manuscripts.

Ex. 16.1. Johannes Martini, *Missa Ma bouche rit*, beginning of Benedictus: (*a*) Milan 2268; (*b*) Modena 456

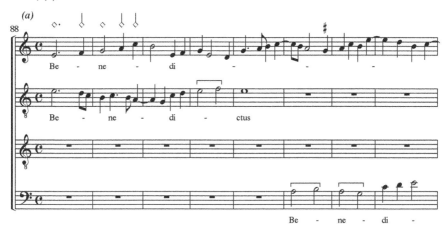

typically, a tenor voice in, say, ℭ, sounds simultaneously against other voices in O or ₵ (see Ex. 16.4, the opening of Ockeghem's *Missa L'homme armé*). In a modern score, one observes literally a vertical alignment of the signs. In 'horizontal' usage, a section governed by a new signature follows a previous section in a contrasting signature (see Ex. 16.5, Busnoys's Kyrie I and Christe from the *Missa O crux lignum triumphale*, where the Christe in ₵ follows the Kyrie I in O without any overlap of voices to define the relationship).

Both forms of the immediate juxtaposition of contrasting mensurations—the horizontal as well as the vertical—force us to face head-on the issue of precisely how the respective mensurations relate to one another. Vertical relationships

Ex. 16.2. Hayne van Ghizeghem, *De tous biens plaine*, opening

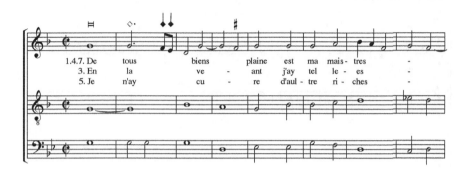

1.4.7. De tous biens plaine est ma mais- tres -
3. En la ve - ant j'ay tel le - es -
5. Je n'ay cu - re d'aul - tre ri - ches -

se, Chas -
se, Que
se, Si

rarely lead to questions on this matter, since the demands of counterpoint almost always clarify the intended relationships. In horizontal relationships, however, the issue of contrasting mensurations remains much in dispute, especially when the mensurations involved include an 'undiminished' and a 'diminished' signature (such as O followed by ₵).

It should be noted that Tinctoris himself shows no reluctance to use cut signatures in his own compositions or in the musical examples in his treatises. Moreover, he never criticizes a composer for a use or misuse of a cut signature as such. He only objects to the practice, common in his day, of allowing mensuration signs of all types to stand for various arithmetical proportions. According to Tinctoris, all real (arithmetical) proportions should be signed with two-numeral fractions, such as $\frac{2}{1}$, where the top numeral indicates how many notes governed by the proportion are to replace the number of notes of the same type specified by the bottom numeral. Tinctoris not only recommends these fractions in the *Proportionale*; he insists on them, and, indeed, criticizes at some length various instances in which his contemporaries depart from minim equivalence by some

Ex. 16.3. Busnoys, *Ha que ville*, opening

other means. He thus makes it clear that he disapproves of multiple meanings for single signs, i.e., of contextual dichotomies.

Despite Tinctoris's reluctance to formulate a theoretical explanation for cut signatures, his understanding of how they function in the actual musical practice of his day appears implicitly in four passages in his treatises. If viewed as expressions of an interlocking network of underlying principles— if each of the four statements is taken to be consistent with the other three—Tinctoris's statements imply

Ex. 16.4. Ockeghem, *Missa L'homme armé*: Kyrie I, Christe, and beginning of Kyrie II

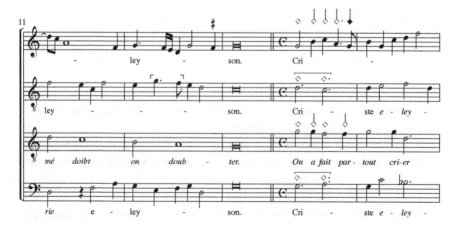

several additional unspoken axioms of practice. When examined in this way for their full potential, Tinctoris's four passages go a long way towards clarifying 'immediate' mensural relationships, both vertical and horizontal, in the music of Busnoys and other composers of the second half of the fifteenth century.

Ex. 16.5. Busnoys, *Missa O crux lignum*: Kyrie I and Christe

Ex. 16.5. *cont.*

1. *Proportionale musices*, i. 3: a discussion of proportions of equality (each note
in one voice relating to its respective counterpart in another voice in a 1 : 1 ratio),
with a criticism of Ockeghem for using a sign of proportion of inequality as an
initial signature in all voices.[22]

²² All translations are my own. The italicized passages in the English column represent the most pertinent aspect of Tinctoris's thinking on the matter at hand. Italic in the Latin reproduces original underlinings
found in Brussels, Bibliothèque royale, MS II 4147; a conflated edition of this source and six others is found
in Tinctoris, *Opera theoretica* ed. Seay, iia. Statement 1 is found on fos. 102ᵛ–103ʳ (Seay, iia, 14–15). This
passage has frequently been cited by recent writers, most of whom, however, tend to see it as Tinctoris's
endorsement of Φ as a sign of 'diminution by a third'. The discussion in the following pages attempts to correct this view.

cum in aliquo cantu nullum inequalitatis signum videmus eum per equales numeros compositum esse iudicamus ut hic patet

whenever we do not see a sign of inequality in a given composition, we judge it to be composed of equal numbers, as can be seen here:

Ex quo confunditur inexcusabilis error Okeghem qui suum carmen bucolicum lautre dantan ab omni parte numeris equalibus compositum nedum signo proportionis/sed illo qui a quibusdam triple ab aliis sesquialtere per se et male attribuitur signavit. Et hoc sic

In the light of this, Ockeghem's inexcusable error is refuted, for he signed his pastoral chanson *L'autre d'antan* — composed with equal numbers in every voice — not even with a sign of proportion, but with [a sign] that is assigned by itself, wrongly, to *tripla* by some and to *sesquialtera* by others, as appears here:

Eodem autem signo dufay suum *Qui cum patre* in *patrem de sancto anthonio* per duplam sesquiquartam proportionatum signare voluit quo fit ut si ille bene/iste male signavit. Diverse enim proportiones diversa signa requirunt. Sed sicut illum hic ita istum suo loco male signasse probabo. Dum vero carmen premissum scilicet *lautre dantan* aut aliud similiter signatum habent imperiti dicunt repente canamus Sesquialtera est. O puerilis ignorantia equalitatis proportionem inequalitatis asserere. Nec existimo compositorem/quamvis ita secundum

With this same sign, however, Du Fay chose to mark the 'Qui cum patre' of the *Patrem* of his [*Missa*] *Sancti Anthonii* [*de Padua*], which is a duple sesquiquarta proportion [i.e., 9 : 4]. Therefore, if the one has signed well, then the other has signed badly, for different proportions require different signs. But I will show that just like the former, here, so also the latter in his piece has signed badly. For when the unskilled get hold of the abovementioned chanson, *L'autre d'antan*, or some other [piece] signed similarly, they say at once,

aliquos signaverit/ ita dici voluisse/sed ut carmen suum concite instar sesquialtere cantaretur. Ad quod efficiendum virgula per medium circuli cuiusque partis traducta sufficiebat. Nam proprium est ei mensure accelerationem significare/sive tempus perfectum sive imperfectum sit/ut in infinitis etiam suis compositionibus apparet. Cuius in utroque forma talis est Ꝺ, ₵.

'Let us sing; this is a *sesquialtera*'. Oh, childish ignorance, to assert a proportion of equality to be one of inequality! *Yet I do not believe that the composer—even if he signed his chanson thus, following certain persons' [practice]—wanted it performed thus, but rather wished that it should be sung like an excited* sesquialtera, *for which the drawing of a line through the middle of a circle in each part would have been sufficient; for it is proper for it [this line] to signify an acceleration of the* mensura, *whether the* tempus *is perfect or imperfect, as is clear in a great many of his own compositions, where its appearance in either form* [tempus] *is thus:* Ꝺ, ₵.

2. *Proportionale musices*, iii. 2: a discussion of the simultaneous use of C against ₵ to create a duple proportion. Tinctoris only grudgingly acknowledges the legitimacy of this practice, terming it 'tolerable'. His distaste for allowing a mensuration sign to function in a proportional capacity is evident in his *caveat* that he does so here only to please de Domarto and Faugues, two composers who have adopted the practice.[23]

Alii vero pro signo duple signum temporis imperfecti minorisque prolationis cum tractulo traducto accelerationem mensure ut premissum est denotante quo cantus vulgariter ad medium dicitur tantummodo ponunt ut hic.

But others write, instead of the sign of duple proportion [i.e., C_1^2 in Tinctoris's system], a sign of imperfect *tempus* with minor *prolatio* with a stroke drawn through it denoting an acceleration of the beat (as has been said above), whereby the piece is called in the vernacular 'à demi'[24] ('by half'), as here.

---

[23] Brussels II 4147, fo. 112ʳ (Seay, iia, 45–6).
[24] I wish to thank Leofranc Holford-Strevens for this suggestion.

Quod ut *de domarto* et *faugues* in *missis spiritus almus* Et Vinus ita signantibus placeam tolerabile censeo propter quandam equipollentiam illius proportionis ac istius prolationis dum enim aliquid ad medium canitur 2 note sicut per proportionem duplam uni conmensurantur.

In order that I may please Domarto and Faugues, who have signed thus in their masses *Spiritus almus* and *Vinus, I will grant that this is tolerable—because of an approximate equivalence of the former proportion [i.e. duple] and the latter* prolatio *[i.e. cut with a stroke]; for when something is sung 'à demi' two notes are measured through duple proportion [in the place] of one.*

3. *Liber de arte contrapuncti*, ii. 29: a discussion of the length of a dissonance relative to the length of the beat (*mensura*) in a well-written composition, with a criticism of Domarto and Busnoys for allowing the dissonance to last the length of an entire beat.[25]

Quod multi nunquam supra integram partem dimidiam note secundum quam mensura cantus dirigitur immo supra minorem tantum assumunt. Capitulum 29.

How many never use [a discord] larger than an integral half part of that note according to which the *mensura* of a song is beaten, but rather only a smaller part. Chapter 29.

Multi tamen adeo exacte discordantias evitant ut nunquam supra dimidiam partem integram immo super terciam aut quartam aut minorem tantum cuiusvis note secundum quam mensura dirigitur discordantiam assumant. Et ut mea fert opinio tales potius imitandi sunt quam *Petrus de domarto et anthonius busnois* quorum ille in prima parte *et in terra* misse *Spiritus almus* iste vero in cantilena *Maintes femmes* non solum dimidiam partem note mensuram dirigentis hoc est semibrevis minoris prolationis in tempore perfecto/immo totam ipsam semibrevem discordem[26] effecerunt ut hic patet:

Many [composers], however, avoid dissonances to such an extent that they never allow a dissonance on a half, but rather only on a third or a fourth or a lesser part of the note according to which the mensura *is beaten. And in my opinion, they are more to be imitated than* Petrus de Domarto and Antonius Busnoys, *of whom the first, in the first part of the 'Et in terra' of his* Missa Spiritus almus, *the second in his chanson* Maintes femmes, *have produced dissonances not merely half the length of the note defining the* mensura, *namely, the semibreve of* tempus perfectum prolatio minor, *but [lasting] an entire such semibreve, as is evident here:*

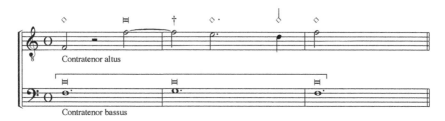

Contratenor altus

Contratenor bassus

[25] Brussels II 4147, fo. 95ʳ (Seay, ii. 139).
[26] This word is incorrectly given as 'discordam' in Brussels II 4147, fo. 95ʳ, but correctly as 'discordem' in Valencia, Biblioteca Universitaria, MS 835, fo. 136ᵛ.

Tenor

4. *Proportionale musices*, iii. 3. A discussion of how best Ockeghem and Busnoys might have indicated in their *L'homme armé* masses the 2 : 1 proportion between the voice in ℭ and the other voices in O. Tinctoris rules out the option of signing the voices in O with a diminishing sign of duple proportion (O_1^2). He recognizes that on the contrary it is the voice in ℭ which must be augmented in value, preferably by means of a verbal canon:[27]

Quid enim admirabilius est quam videntes avia cecitatis ingredi Sed quoniam in tali eorum componendi modo/si ita signaretur O_1^2 pro ut ars requirit difficultas pronunciationis immo tocius melodie destructio propter nimiam velocitatem oriretur. Melius tenori canon apponeretur scilicet Crescit in duplo vel equivalens sicut laudabiliter fecit *dufay* in missa *Se la face ay pale*.	For what is more remarkable than that the sighted should enter upon the trackless (wastes) of blindness? But since, in composing their works in the way they did, *had* O_1^2 *been signed, as art requires, a difficulty of performance, or rather the destruction of all melody would arise because of the excessive speed.* It would have been better to have appended a canon to the tenor, such as 'Let it grow twofold', or the equivalent, as Du Fay has laudably done in his mass *Se la face ay pale.*

Assuming that the four passages just cited belong to a coherent view of fifteenth-century practice, at least twelve axioms of practice follow from them:

1. The stroke through a sign of *tempus*, whether the sign be a complete circle or an incomplete one, causes an 'acceleration of the beat' that may vary by context. In one example it approximates an 'excited *sesquialtera*' and in another a duple proportion. However, both Φ and ₵, when used as initial or independent mensurations, lie outside the domain of true proportions.

2. The note receiving the beat may usually be determined by an examination of dissonance treatment, since in a well-written composition a dissonance will normally last not more than one-half the value of the note receiving the beat.

3. The beat is normally on the semibreve in pieces in O and also at least sometimes on the semibreve in Φ: Tinctoris shows it to be on the semibreve in Busnoys's *Maintes femmes*, which is signed Φ in his musical example.

---

[27] Brussels II 4147, fo. 113ᵛ (Seay, iia, 50).

4. That (i) the stroke of diminution could cause an 'acceleration of the beat' and that (ii) Tinctoris could consider re-signing a voice in O with a sign of duple proportion (though immediately rejecting the idea) shows that he understood there to be a certain degree of latitude in determining the tempo of a piece — that is, he understood tempo to be somewhat flexible.

5. The tempo of a piece in O, while flexible to a degree, cannot be doubled from its 'normal' interpretation, for this would result in 'the destruction of all melody because of the excessive speed'.

6. Therefore, pieces in Φ which show the same surface activity and level of dissonance as pieces in O cannot move in a 2 : 1 ratio to the latter: the 'acceleration of the beat' produced by the stroke through the sign of *tempus* must be less than a 2 : 1 doubling of tempo.

7. There is no inherent difference in the degree of acceleration to be inferred from a stroke through a O and a stroke through a C. Therefore, causing a passage in ₵ to move twice as fast as a passage in C, assuming that both passages have the same degree of surface activity and the same level of dissonance treatment, would also result in the 'destruction of all melody'.

8. Tinctoris acknowledges only one case where ₵ may equal a duple proportion (Statement 2), and in this one case the voice in ₵ shares the same beat as the voice beneath it, written in C. Consequently, for the voice in ₵ the beat is on the breve. This would suggest, as do Axioms 6 and 7, that when the beat remains on the semibreve in a cut signature, the acceleration caused by the stroke is *less* than a duple proportion.

9. The converse of this argument would be that a cut signature can only equal a duple proportion when the beat *is* on the breve.

10. To judge from the above, a passage in ₵ with a beat on the semibreve will not move twice as fast as a passage in O with a beat on the semibreve. The fact that both mensurations have a beat on the semibreve precludes a 2 : 1 ratio between them.

11. Since Tinctoris avoids stating that cut signatures produce specific proportions when they occur outside of simultaneous contexts, it would appear that the stroke through the sign of *tempus* may cause a variety of accelerations, depending on the perceived needs of the piece.

12. The 4 : 3 acceleration favoured by Busse Berger, Bent, and Planchart is one of the many possibilities implicit in Tinctoris's formulation.

Returning now to our Ex. 16.1 — Martini's Benedictus — Tinctoris's teaching indicates that the beat remains on the semibreve in both the version in C and the version in ₵. This in turn implies that the difference in tempo between Ex. 16.1*a* and Ex. 16.1*b* does not constitute a 2 : 1 proportion, but something less extreme. Of course, if the stroke originated with the composer himself, we would expect the stroke through the sign of *tempus* in Ex. 16.1*b* to represent only a minor adjustment, a slight acceleration. That the stroke in this case did originate with the composer seems entirely possible, given that in the early 1470s Martini was stationed in Milan (where Milan 2268 originated), and that he moved in the later 1470s to Ferrara (where Modena α.M.1.13 originated). To phrase this the other way around, the historical evidence suggests that the simplest explanation for the stroke through the sign of *tempus* in the Ferrarese source is to assume that a particular performer (either Martini or someone else), wishing for the Benedictus to move slightly faster, added the stroke as a sign of *più mosso*. To assume a 2 : 1 ratio between Exs. 16.1*a* and *b*, on the other hand, is to attribute to Martini a major miscalculation the first time around.

The four Tinctoris passages may be seen to support the idea that a simultaneous (i.e. vertical) relationship differs in kind from a successive (horizontal) one. Thus, C and ₵ in a vertical relationship function in a 2 : 1 ratio, as in the example in Tinctoris's Statement 2, whereas in a horizontal relationship the difference between them appears to be much less—as suggested by the two sources for Martini's Benedictus. We have noted already that a contextual differentiation such as this contradicts the notion of a 'mathematical' system. Moreover, just such a contextual differentiation for the meaning of mensuration signs was emphatically rejected in the sixteenth century by the proportionalists (Andreas Ornithoparchus, Martin Agricola, Sebald Heyden, and others)—at least with regard to signs of diminution.[28] In our own time an apparent equating of vertical and horizontal relationships has been championed either explicitly, in an article or preface, or implicitly, in an edition, by Dragan Plamenac, Fritz Feldmann, Ludwig Finscher, Heinrich Besseler, Armen Carapetyan, Edward Lerner, Leeman L. Perkins, William E. Melin, Richard Taruskin, and many others. What evidence might be sufficient to overpower both the modern-day desire for consistency in the mensural system and the sixteenth-century viewpoint of Ornithoparchus, Agricola, and Heyden—evidence that would show convincingly that in Busnoys's day vertical relationships functioned *differently* from horizontal ones? Short of an explicit statement to this effect from a contemporary theorist, the best evidence would be a musical work in which two contrasting signs, in passing from a vertical to a horizontal context, fail to maintain a proportional relationship.

Ockeghem's *Missa L'homme armé* happily meets the requirement (see Ex. 16.4). Moreover, this work can hardly be called an obscure piece. As one of the earliest examples in the long *L'homme armé* mass tradition, if not the earliest, it must have been familiar to all the leading composers of the time. In it, the rare, dual meaning of a single sign (₵ used in a single voice as a sign of augmentation in Kyrie I and II, but governing all voices together as a sign of perfect *prolatio* in

---

[28] See below, n. 31, for Ornithoparchus' and Agricola's inconsistency on this point with regard to ☉ and ₵ used as signs of augmentation.

the Christe), allows us to prove the fallacy of equating the vertical and horizontal uses of contrasting mensurations. Because of the apparent continuity of the tenor, which bears the sign C in Kyrie I, Christe, and Kyrie II, one might be tempted to regard it as an unvarying standard by which to gauge the other voices. To judge from his edition of the mass, Dragan Plamenac evidently took this view, for he transcribes the tenor in augmented values not only in Kyrie I and Kyrie II, but also in the Christe (along with the other three voices). Thus, the Plamenac edition presents a classic instance of equating the relationships between contrasting mensurations in both vertical and horizontal contexts.

However, the writings of numerous early sixteenth-century theorists imply another relationship between the Kyries and the Christe of Ockeghem's mass. Their treatises declare unanimously that C in all voices does *not* constitute augmentation but rather perfect *prolatio*. Johannes Cochlaeus, in 1504 and again in 1511, defines the two contexts for a sign of major *prolatio* in terms of the *tactus*:[29]

Johannes Cochlaeus, *Musica*:

De augmentatione.	Concerning Augmentation.
Augmentatio est alicuius cantilene in suis notulis plurificatio. ut ponendo minimam pro semibrevi: semibrevem pro brevi et huiusmodi. Et cognoscitur per circulum vel semicirculum cui inscriptus est punctus; plerumque penes unam dumtaxat cantilene partem positum. hec modo ☉ C et sic minima valet tactum. Si autem omnes cantilene partes punctum in circulo vel semicirculo contineant prolatio perfecta declaratur. in qua tres minime aut perfecta semibrevis tactu mensuratur. Verum intrinsecum augmentationis indicium est. paucitas notularum in una carminis parte dispositarum sine signo repetitionis. In augmentatione insuper pause non secus ac notule augentur.	Augmentation is a multiplication of a certain type of piece, regarding its notes, as in putting a minim for a semibreve, a semibreve for a breve, and so forth. And it is recognized by a circle or semicircle in which a dot is inscribed, generally placed in only one part of a piece, in this manner: ☉ C. And thus a minim equals a *tactus*. If, however, all parts of the piece contain a dot in a circle or semicircle, this indicates perfect *prolatio*, in which three minims or one perfect semibreve are measured by a *tactus*. An intrinsic sign of augmentation, on the other hand, is a scarcity of notes in one of the parts of a piece, without a sign of repetition. In augmentation, moreover, the rests are augmented in the same way as the notes.

Cochlaeus, *Tetrachordum musices*:

Quid est augmentatio? Est quantitatis notularum maioramentum. Fit enim in prolatione perfecta/quando minimauna/	What is augmentation? It is an increase in the quantity [i.e. duration] of the notes. It occurs in perfect *prolatio* when one minim

---

[29] *Musica*, sig. [G. iv^v]; *Tetrachordum musices*, sig. E iii^v. For an English translation of the latter, see *Johannes Cochlaeus: Tetrachordum musices, 1511*, trans. and ed. Clement A. Miller (MSD, 23, [Rome], 1970). For a discussion of Cochlaeus's *tactus*, see Blachly, 'Mensuration and Tempo', ch. 4.

/tactu integro mensuratur. semibrevis vero perfecta/tribus tactibus.

is measured by an entire *tactus*, and a perfect semibreve by three *tactus*.

Quod est signum eius extrinsecum. Circulus vel semicirculus/cui inscribitur punctus/circa unam duntaxat cantilene partem repertus hoc modo ☉ ₵.

What is its 'external' sign? A circle or semicircle in which a dot is inscribed, occurring in only one voice-part of a piece, as here: ☉, ₵.

Nam si in omnibus eius partibus reperiatur/non est augmentatio/sed perfecta simpliciter prolatio/in qua tres minime uno mensurantur tactu.

For if [such a sign] is found in all parts of a piece, this is not augmentation but simply perfect prolatio, in which three minims are measured by one tactus.

These are the first specific approbations in musical treatises of the concept of major or perfect *prolatio* used in a single voice to signify augmentation (although Tinctoris had commented unfavourably on the practice in the *Proportionale* as early as *c.*1473). Once Cochlaeus showed the way, many other theorists followed suit. Thus, Johannes Volckmar in 1513:[30]

Augmentatio est quantitas notularum maioramentum. Fit enim dumtaxat in prolatione maiori. Signumque eius extrinsecum est circulus vel semicirculus cui inscriptus est punctus, atque circa unam cantilene partem repertus minime tactu mensuratur. nam si in omnibus eius partibus reperiatur: non est augmentatio ut quidam dicunt sed perfecta simpliciter prolatio. in qua tres minime ad unum tactum proferuntur.

Augmentation is an increase in the quantity of the notes, and it occurs only in major *prolatio*. Its external sign is a circle or semicircle in which a dot is inscribed, found in only one voice-part of a piece; it is measured with a *tactus* of one minim. *For if it is found in all the voice-parts, this is not augmentation, as certain people say, but simply perfect prolatio, in which three minims are performed to one tactus.*

Bernard Bogentantz in 1515 rephrases Cochlaeus' definition, retaining, however, his term *prolatio perfecta*:[31]

Augmentatio . . . cognoscitur per circulum vel semicirculum cui inscriptus est punctus. plerumque penes unam duntaxat cantilene partem positum hoc modo. ☉ ₵ & sic minima valet tactum. Si autem omnes cantilene partes punctum in circulo vel semicirculo contineant prolatio perfecta declaratur. in qua tres minime aut perfecta semibreuis tactu mensuratur.

Augmentation is recognized by a circle or semicircle in which a dot has been inscribed; such a sign is most frequently placed to pertain only to one voice-part in a piece, like this: ☉, ₵ , such that a minim lasts one *tactus*. *If, however, all voices of a piece contain a dot in a circle or semicircle, this is called perfect prolatio, in which three minims or a perfect semibreve are measured by a tactus.*

---

[30] *Collectanea quedam musice discipline utilia quam necessaria* (Frankfurt an der Oder, 1513), sig. D iᵛ.
[31] *Collectanea utriusque cantus* (Cologne, 1515), sig. D iiᵛ.

Michael Koswick in 1516 makes the same distinction between augmentation and regular perfect *prolatio*:[32]

Tactus specialis est triplex: Augmentationis. Est enim augmentatio/ secundum consequentem descriptionem cantilene in suis notulis plurificatio. Fitque in prolatione perfecta cum una ♭ tactu mensuratur. Signa eius sunt ☉ ℭ cum circa unam partem cantilene ponuntur. Signum vero intrinsecum eius/est paucitas notarum/sine signo repetitionis/circa unam cantilene partem positarum	The special *tactus* is threefold: of augmentation, where there is an augmenting or increase in the notes of a piece according to the following description: it occurs in perfect *prolatio* when one minim is measured by a *tactus*. Its signs are ☉ ℭ when these are placed in one voice-part of a piece. Its intrinsic sign is a paucity of notes without a sign of repetition, within one voice-part of a piece
. . . . Similiter in his ☉ ℭ cum circa omnes voces ponuntur/non est augmentatio/sed perfecta simpliciter prolatia qua tres minime tactu mensurantur.	. . . . *Similarly when all voices are written in these* ☉ ℭ, *this is not augmentation but simply perfect* prolatio, *in which three minims are measured by one* tactus.

Even Ornithoparchus, the earliest proponent of what would become the 'proportionalist' point of view, subscribes to the augmentation/perfect *prolatio* distinction in his treatise of 1517:[33]

Augmentatio tria sunt signa, Primum est paucitas notarum, in una cantilene parte.	There are three signs of augmentation: the first is a paucity of notes in one of the voices of a song.
Secundum est canonis inscriptio, dicendo brevis sit maxima, Semibrevis longa, ac minima brevis. Vel crescit in duplo, triplo, hexagio numero etc.	The second is a canonic inscription, declaring, Let a breve be a maxima, a semibreve a long, and a minim a breve. Or Let it grow twofold, threefold, sixfold, etc.
Tertium est punctus in signo temporali, circa unam dumtaxat cantilene partem repertus. Unam dico, nam si apud omnes offenditur, non augmentationis: sed maioris prolationis: erit indicium.	The third is a dot in the sign of *tempus* found in only one voice-part of a song. *I say one, for if it appears in all, this will indicate not augmentation but major* prolatio.

Georg Rhaw, in his treatise *Enchiridion utriusque musicae practicae* (Leipzig, 1520), also mentions the difference between perfect *prolatio* written in only one voice-part of a piece (so as to cause augmentation) and perfect *prolatio* written in all voice-parts. In the latter case,[34]

---

[32] *Compendaria musice artis aeditio* (Leipzig, 1516), sig. L ii[r–v].

[33] *Musice active micrologus* (Leipzig, 1517), sig. [F iiii[r]]. It is interesting that neither Ornithoparchus nor Martin Agricola after him seems to realize that a dual standard with regard to ☉ and ℭ undermines the logic of the 'proportionalist' outlook. Sebald Heyden does appear to have been aware of this internal contradiction; he admits neither a dual interpretation for major *prolatio* nor any other contextual differentiation in meaning for mensuration signs.   [34] Sig. D ii[r].

... non est Augmentatio/sed perfecta simpliciter prolatio. ubi tres minimas/vel
unam semibrevem/integer tactus con-
tinebit.

... this is not augmentation, but simply
perfect *prolatio*, where a complete *tactus*
contains three minims or one semibreve.

On the question of augmentation, Martin Agricola in 1532 accepts the prevailing view of Cochlaeus, Koswick, Ornithoparchus, and Rhaw:[35]

Das eußerliche zeichen der Augmentation.

The external sign of augmentation.

Ist/wenn ein Punkt im gantzen odder
unvolkomen ringe beschlossen/bey einer
stym allein erfunden wird also ℂ ☉. und so
gilt eine volkomen Semibre. drey
gantze/und eine Minima ein gantzen
Tact/Wo aber ein solch zeichen bey allen
stymmen erscheint/so bedeuts nicht eine
grösserung/sondern die volkomen
Prolation/in welcher drey Mini. oder eine
volkomen Semibrevis auff den Proportien
Tact/wie oben im iiii. Cap. inn dem
Exempel von der volkomen Prolation
gemelt/gesungen wird.

Is when a dot inscribed in a whole or half
circle is found in only one voice-part, like
this, ℂ ☉, and then a perfect semibreve is
worth three whole *tactus*, and a minim one
whole *tactus*. *But if such a sign appears in all
voices, this does not signify augmentation, but
rather perfect* prolatio, *in which three minims
or one perfect semibreve is sung to the propor-
tionate* tactus, as pointed out above in the
4th chapter in the example concerning perfect *prolatio*.

Glareanus, writing as late as 1547, still acknowledges a dual interpretation of
☉ and ℂ, with its meaning dependent on context:[36]

De augmentatione diminutione ac semidi-
tate, Caput VIII.

Chapter 8. Concerning augmentation,
diminutio, and *semiditas*.

Consueverunt autem Musici ad unam duntaxat Cantilenae partem ponere, vel circulum, vel semicirculum cum puncto sic ☉ ℂ
ac tunc vocare augmentationem. Nam sic
minima valet semibrevi, semibrevis perfecta tribus semibrevibus. At si haec signa
omnibus cantilenae partibus apponantur,
prolatio perfecta est, quae nunc in raro usu
est.

Musicians have been accustomed to place,
in only one voice of a piece, either a circle
or a semicircle with a dot, thus: ☉, ℂ, and
then to call this augmentation. For thus a
minim is worth a semibreve, and a perfect
semibreve three [imperfect] semibreves.
*But if these signs are placed in all voices of a
piece, then this is perfect* prolatio, *which is
rarely in use now.*

To what specific music might all these theorists be referring? If they have in
mind augmentation versus perfect *prolatio* within a single work, there may be
only one candidate: Ockeghem's *Missa L'homme armé*.[37] Volckmar's observation

[35] *Musica figuralis deudsch* (Wittenberg, 1532), sig. [G vii^v].
[36] *Glareani Dodecachordon* (Basel, 1547), viii. 8, pp. 204 ff.
[37] It should be noted that this work was copied into the Chigi Codex in the early years of the 16th c.,
shortly before the appearance of the German treatises just discussed. See Herbert Kellman, 'Introduction' to
the facs. edn. of Vatican City, Biblioteca Apostolica Vaticana, MS Chigi C VIII 234 (Renaissance Music in

that 'this is not augmentation, *as certain people say*', may well reflect the confusion Ockeghem caused by using 𝄴 with opposed meanings in such close proximity. The candidacy of Ockeghem's *L'homme armé* mass receives considerable support from Pietro Aaron's specific reference to it in this very connection in his *Toscanello* of 1523 (where he refers not to the Christe but to a parallel passage in the Credo):[38]

Ma se tutte le parti del canto saranno per segno puntato segnate, si tenera altro ordine: perche a l'hora per una misura over battuta passera una semibreve perfetta overo tre minime, come da Ockechen è stato osservato in una parte de Patrem de la sua messa di lome armé.	But if all the voices of a song are signed by a sign with a dot, [i.e. ⊙ or 𝄴], this is deemed to be another category, for now one perfect semibreve or three minims occur in one *mensura* or beat, as Ockeghem observed in a part of the Patrem in his *Missa L'homme armé*, [i.e., the Et resurrexit].

Ironically, while Ockeghem's use of signs provides us with valuable evidence in clarifying the non-equivalence between vertical and horizontal relationships in fifteenth-century practice, it is likely that other composers in his own time found fault with it. Thus, the motivation behind Busnoys's use of C3 as a new sign of perfect *prolatio* in his own *L'homme armé* mass could well be his wish to avoid the very confusion suggested by Volckmar's comment. (As if to confirm the meaning of Busnoys's C3 , Josquin, in the Osanna of his *Missa L'homme armé super voces musicales*, instructs the tenor, governed by ⊙ 𝄴 ⊙, to 'rejoice' with the other voices, governed by C3: 'Gaudet cum gaudentibus'.)[39] Despite its decisiveness in clarifying mensural practice for the present study, there can be no denying that Ockeghem's mass has also given rise to confusion (not least in Plamenac's edition).

In support of Cochlaeus's reliability as a guide to usage in Ockeghem's time, we discover that with regard to the sign ₵ he proves a faithful student of Tinctoris. Like the author of the *Proportionale musices*, the author of the

---

Facsimile: Sources Central to the Music of the Late Fifteenth and Sixteenth Centuries, 22; New York, 1987), p. v, where the author states that 'all evidence points to the years 1498–1503 as the period within which the Chigi Codex was prepared'. Bertrand Vaqueras's *Missa L'homme armé* (a work which survives uniquely in Cappella Sistina 49) provides the only other case known to me where a passage that juxtaposes 𝄴 in the tenor against a contrasting mensuration (O2) in the other voices (Qui tollis) is followed directly by a passage with all voices in 𝄴 (Cum sancto spiritu). From a 20th-c. vantage point, however, Vaqueras's mass seems an unlikely candidate for the attention of the 16th-c. theorists, whereas they showed great interest in several of Ockeghem's works. Vaqueras's *Missa L'homme armé* has been edited by Laurence Feininger (Monumenta polyphoniae liturgicae, ser. 1, i (Rome, 1948)) and Richard Sherr, in Vaqueras, *Opera omnia* (CMM 78; Neuhausen-Stuttgart, 1979).

[38] *Toscanello della Musica* (Venice, 1523), i. 38.

[39] See Edward E. Lowinsky (ed.) in collaboration with Bonnie J. Blackburn, *Josquin des Prez: Proceedings of the International Josquin Festival-Conference* (London, 1976), 237, 708. It should be pointed out that the diagram on p. 708 of the *Proceedings* erroneously places the rubric 'Gaudet cum gaudentibus' next to Confiteor rather than Osanna. For the Confiteor, which notates all four voices in ₵, Petrucci has no rubric for any of the voices. Further confusing the issue is that for the repeat of the Osanna Petrucci erroneously prints 'Osanna ut jacet' in the tenor voice, rather than 'Osanna ut supra', as in the other three partbooks.

Tetrachordum musices understands a voice governed by ₵ to be in a 2 : 1 diminution only when it occurs simultaneously against a voice governed by an uncut sign. Cochlaeus terms the relationship between one voice in ₵ against another in C a *semiditas*:[40]

Quid est semiditas? Est alterius partis temporalis mensure imminutio. fit solum in tempore imperfecto/per hoc signum ₵ vel per hec signa O2, C2. Due namque semibreves sic unicum complent tactum/in una cantus parte/quando unica tactum perficit in altera parte signo non diminuto per virgulam scindentem/aut numerum appositum.

What is *semiditas*? It is the removal of a half the measure of time, and occurs only in imperfect *tempus*, under this sign ₵, or under these signs: O2, C2. *For thus two semibreves complete a single* tactus *in one voice-part of a piece, while one [semibreve] completes a* tactus *in another part under a sign that is not diminished by an intersecting line or by a number placed beside.*

Also of interest is Cochlaeus's definition of Ø, which he terms a sign of *diminutio*:[41]

Quid est diminutio? Est abstractio quantitatis ab ipsa mensura. Fit enim in tempore perfecto/per virgulam circulum integrum scindentem/hoc modo Ø.

What is *diminutio*? It is the removal of value from this *mensura*. It occurs in perfect *tempus* when a complete circle is divided by a line, as here: Ø.

In diminutione namque non notularum numerus minuitur (manet enim signum perfectum) sed tercia mensure pars adimitur. Velocior nanque sic est tactus quam si virgula circulum non intersecet/ quamvis utrobique idem sit notarum valor et ternaria perfectio.

In *diminutio* the number of notes is not lessened (for the sign remains perfect) but *a third part of the* mensura *is removed*. So the *tactus* is faster than if the line did not intersect the circle, although in both cases the value of the notes and their ternary perfection remain unchanged.

Cochlaeus's position on *diminutio*, in turn, appears to be taken directly from Melchior Schanppecher, in a treatise dating from 1501:[42]

Diminutio autem fit in tempore perfecto quando circulus dividitur per tractum ut hic Ø, ibi enim solummodo 3a pars notarum aufertur. Vult enim cantum in tali signo modicum velocius tangi debere quam in illo. O.

Diminutio occurs in perfect *tempus* when a circle is divided by a stroke, like this: Ø, *whereby only a third part of the notes is removed. It causes a song to be beaten a little faster than [a song] in this:* O.

---

[40] *Tetrachordum musices*, sig. E iiii^r. The term *semiditas* is found as early as 1471 in the treatise by Anonymous 12 (see Palmer (ed.), *Anonymus*, 64–5).

[41] *Tetrachordum musices*, sig. E iiii^r.

[42] *Musica figurativa* [= Nicolaus Wollick, *Opus aureum*], sig. [F vi^v]. Both writers may well have been aware of Anonymous 12, who claimed a reduction of the value of notes by a third for the sign Ø in his treatise of *c*.1471.

We should note with regard to Schanppecher's two definitions—'a third part of the notes is removed', and 'it causes a song to be beaten a little faster'—that the vagueness of the second prescription cancels out the apparent precision of the first, reducing Φ to an undetermined acceleration of the beat analogous to Tinctoris's.

Finally, Cochlaeus presents a *tactus* table which includes the figures shown in Fig. 16.7.[43]

O	12	6	6	1
C	8	4	2	1
Ø	12	6	3	1
₵	8	4	2	1
⊙	12	6	3	1
₵	8	4	2	1
	⊟	⊟	⊟	◇

Fig. 16.7. Cochlaeus's *tactus* table in abbreviated form

Since ₵ receives here the same number of *tactus* per note-value as C, it follows that the line intersecting the sign ₵—when ₵ occurs as an independent mensuration unmodified by the presence of C in another voice-part—cannot cause a shift of *tactus* to the breve. Had that been the case, Cochlaeus would have marked ₵ in his table with the numbers shown in Fig. 16.8.[44]

₵	4	2	1	1/2
	⊟	⊟	⊟	◇

Fig. 16.8. Values of notes in ₵ when the *tactus* falls on the breve

[43] Cochlaeus's table is reproduced in part and discussed in Dahlhaus, 'Zur Theorie', 32; it appears in the *Tetrachordum* on sig. E iii[v].

[44] This argument assumes that Cochlaeus would not allow two diametrically opposed methods of doubling of the tempo of the semibreve: one in which the *tactus* remained on the semibreve and moved twice as fast and another in which the *tactus* moved at the same speed but shifted to the breve. See above, Axiom 12.

But without a shift of the *tactus* to the breve, ₵ can only call for an acceleration of the beat, similar to that caused by Φ. This constitutes solid evidence for the fifteenth-century style of 'variable *tactus*'. Like Schanppecher's Φ, Cochlaeus' ₵ bears a close resemblance to the *acceleratio mensure* described in Tinctoris's Statement 1.

Problematic Mensural Usages in the Music of Busnoys

In two respects, Busnoys's music concords imperfectly with Tinctoris's prescriptions:

1. Busnoys's music occasionally breaks Tinctoris's rules. As we have seen, *Maintes femmes*, with a semibreve *mensura* in Φ, allows a dissonance to last the full length of the *mensura* (see Statement 3). From this it follows that dissonance treatment in Busnoys pieces does not always clearly indicate which note receives the *mensura*. Evidently, to achieve certainty on this issue requires reference to other works or passages by Busnoys that are free of the ambiguity. Thus, in the Christe of Ex. 16.5, the cadential figure in measure 25 leaves open the question of which note receives the *mensura*, but the minim dissonances in measures 35 and 55 make it clear that the *mensura* equals the semibreve. We must assume that performers in the Renaissance puzzled over and resolved this type of issue during rehearsal, as still happens today.

2. Busnoys uses not just Φ and ₵, but also O2 and C2 as independent mensurations that may follow sections in O or C. In Busnoys's works, however, there is no apparent difference between ₵ and C2 or O2, except that in O2 the long is perfect. Again, the level of dissonance determines other matters of interpretation. A beat on the semibreve in any of the diminishing signs just listed rules out a duple proportion to O or C in a horizontal context. Yet there may still be differences in tempo between, say, Φ and O2. In Busnoys's *Magnificat sexti toni*, for example, it can be seen that in passages in O2, where the dissonance lasts a semibreve and the beat must therefore be assigned to the breve, the prevailing note-values exceed by one level those in the verses in Φ. The combination of a beat on the breve and larger prevailing note-values may indicate a semibreve in O2 intended in this piece to be faster than the semibreve in Φ. In the *Missa O crux lignum triumphale*, however, where both O2 and Φ retain a beat on the semibreve,[45] the tempo of the one sign may be intended to equal that of the other.

---

[45] The sign Φ appears twice in this mass as an independent mensuration shared by all four voices simultaneously: in the Osanna and at the end of the final Agnus. Taruskin's edition incorrectly shows three of the voices at the end of the final Agnus to be in ₵, leading to the erroneous statement in the Commentary, p. 49, that at this point in the mass the sign Φ 'is vertically aligned with ₵ in the other parts, so that a semibreve

In conclusion, it would appear that we have misunderstood the intended meaning of cut signatures and other 'diminishing' signs in fifteenth-century music if we view all diminished/undiminished relationships as being identical. Tinctoris's four passages (and the twelve axioms of practice derived from them) suggest that vertical and horizontal mensural relationships differed in kind in the fifteenth century. Therefore, the intended tempo relationship between contrasting mensurations in a horizontal context cannot be restricted to the proportional relationship that would obtain if the same two mensurations were aligned vertically. It appears rather that the range of meanings for horizontal relationships extended from the *più mosso* we have suggested for the two sources of Martini's Benedictus (Exs. 16.1*a* and *b*) to a much greater divergence in tempo (see Exs. 16.2 and 3).[46] Thus, both the context (vertical or horizontal relationship) and the nature of the piece contribute to determining the degree of differentiation. In horizontal contexts, an undiminished signature has a suggestion of a slower tempo, a diminished signature the suggestion of a faster one; but neither is necessarily slower or faster in any specific proportion or degree. In such cases, we must understand the significance of the diminished signature on the merits of the piece in which it is found. That, I believe, is the kernel of Tinctoris's message.

in Φ equals a semibreve in ₵'. Curiously, both Taruskin and I agree that Φ ◇ = ₵ ◇. The difference is that he argues for O ◇ = ₵ ≡ (O ◇ : ₵ ◇ = 2 : 1), whereas, as argued here, I believe the evidence from Tinctoris indicates that the difference between O ◇ and ₵◇ is less than 2 : 1. Expressed formulaically, it might approximate O ◇◇◇ = ₵ ◇◇◇◇; but all that can actually be specified on the basis of Tinctoris's statements is that O ◇ > ₵ ◇ and ₵ ≡ > O ◇.

46 Why Busnoys would wish to notate *Ha que ville* in C and Hayne *De tous biens plaine* in ₵ is not easy to determine. Most likely, however, the difference is connected with tempo. On the basis of what has been proposed above, it would appear that the *mensura* of *Ha que ville* (beaten on the semibreve) was intended to be slightly faster than the *mensura* of *De tous biens plaine* (beaten on the breve).

PART V
BUSNOYS'S LEGACY

17

Henricus Isaac and *Fortuna desperata*

❧❧❧

MARTIN PICKER

AMONG the most frequently copied and widely disseminated compositions of the late fifteenth century is the Italian song *Fortuna desperata*. It
comes down to us as a three-part piece in five sources, and in some fourteen others with an added fourth part.[1] Eleven of those sources have a particular
altus added to the original superius, tenor, and bassus; three others have different altus voices.[2] Most of these sources, especially the earlier ones, are of Italian
provenance: these include Paris 4379, part I, probably written in Naples in the
1470s or 1480s (with the most common altus part added in another hand);
Perugia 431, copied mainly in Naples around 1485 and containing both three-
and four-part versions; Paris 676 (with the same added altus), written in Mantua
or Ferrara and dated 1502; and Florence 121, written in Florence *c*.1510 and
containing the three-part version.[3] Only one of the eighteen sources names a
composer; this is a Spanish manuscript of the late fifteenth or early sixteenth century now in the archive of the cathedral of Segovia, attributing the work to
'Anthonius Busnoys'.[4]

Fortuna desperata has given rise to one of the largest families of compositions
of the Renaissance. Its relatives and descendants consist of four masses and thirty-
five shorter works composed within seventy-five or eighty years from its first
appearance in Italian songbooks around 1475 to the publication of its last

---

[1] The original three-voice setting (see App., no. 1) has been widely published, most recently after Seg in
Jacob Obrecht, *Collected Works*, iv, ed. Barton Hudson (Utrecht, 1986), pp. xxx–xxxii. To the sources listed
there should be added Wolf 78, fo. 2ᵛ (anon.). The bassus alone is found in Basle F. X. 10, the single surviving partbook of an original set of four.

[2] The best-known four-voice version (App., no. 2(*a*)) is published after 1504[3] in *Werken van Josquin des
Prés, Missen*, iv, ed. Albert Smijers (Amsterdam, 1929), 106. Another version, with a different altus (see
App., no. 2(*d*)), is published ibid. 107, after Lon 31922.

[3] See *Census-Catalogue*, i. 226–7; iii. 14–15, 29–30, and 43–4; and iv. 372 for descriptions and further
references.

[4] Ibid. iii. 137–8.

descendant in the mid-1550s.[5] Some of these provide a full text, either the original or a *contrafactum*, but most have only the incipit *Fortuna desperata* or merely *Fortuna*. (See App. for a list of these thirty-five works.)

The attribution of the original *Fortuna* to Busnoys was accepted by Catherine Brooks, whose 1953 dissertation and subsequent article on Busnoys's chansons were the first significant studies of his work.[6] This attribution was challenged by Julie Cumming in her 1980 study of *Fortuna* pieces and by Barton Hudson in a 1986 article, but defended by Paula Higgins in her 1987 dissertation.[7] Although my purpose here is not to focus on the identity of the composer, it is nevertheless necessary to begin with a presentation of the evidence for and against Busnoys's authorship in order to clarify the family history of *Fortuna desperata* as a whole and Isaac's contribution to it in particular.

The argument for Busnoys's authorship rests on the credibility of the attribution in the Segovia manuscript, which contains a large number of works in French, Latin, Dutch, Italian, and Spanish by a wide range of composers, most of them named in the manuscript. Scholars have not been unanimous in their evaluation of the attributions, but in her 1978 dissertation on the manuscript Norma K. Baker concluded that it 'compares favorably with most contemporary sources' and that 'there is little reason to dispute out of hand the testimony of its attributions'.[8] Some of the attributions are demonstrably incorrect, but many others are confirmed by concordances. For example, Busnoys's *Je ne demande* for four voices, contained in the Segovia manuscript under his name, is confirmed as his work in Rome Casanatense 2856 and in Petrucci's *Odhecaton* (1501).

Evidence against Busnoys's responsibility for *Fortuna desperata*, according to Cumming and Hudson, includes its Italian text and predominantly Italian sources despite a lack of documentation for a stay by Busnoys in Italy, and its styl-

---

[5] Some of these works are discussed in Otto Gombosi, *Jacob Obrecht, eine stilkritische Studie* (Leipzig, 1925), 99–116. Three attempts at listing and comparing all such settings have been made in recent years: Alfred Loeffler, 'Fortuna desperata: A Contribution to the Study of Musical Symbolism in the Renaissance', *Student Musicologists at Minnesota*, 3 (1968–9), 1–30; Julie E. Cumming, 'The Goddess Fortuna Revisited', *Current Musicology*, 30 (1980), 7–23; and Honey Meconi, 'Art-Song Reworkings: An Overview', *Journal of the Royal Musical Association*, 119 (1994), 1–42 at 31–3. For a new, expanded list, see the Appendix to the present paper.

[6] Catherine V. Brooks, 'Antoine Busnois, Chanson Composer', *JAMS* 6 (1953), 111–35.

[7] Cumming, 'The Goddess Fortuna Revisited', 8; Barton Hudson, 'Two Ferrarese Masses by Jacob Obrecht', *Journal of Musicology*, 4 (1985–6), 276–302 at 294–6; Paula M. Higgins, 'Antoine Busnois and Musical Culture in Late Fifteenth-Century France and Burgundy' (Ph.D. diss., Princeton University, 1987), 22–5. Joshua Rifkin, in his paper 'Busnoys and Italy: The Evidence of Two Songs', read at this conference (see below, Ch. 20), also strongly questions Busnoys's authorship of *Fortuna desperata*. This paper directly preceded mine at the conference and was first made known to me at that time. I am grateful to Mr Rifkin for sending me a copy, but I have decided not to make substantial alterations to my own paper since there is no dispute about the facts of the situation. My own position is that Busnoys's authorship remains in doubt, but is not disproven. References to Rifkin's paper will be made in the present notes as appropriate.

[8] Norma K. Baker, 'An Unnumbered Manuscript of Polyphony in the Archives of the Cathedral of Segovia' (Ph.D. diss., University of Maryland, 1978), i. 62. Joshua Rifkin disputes the reliability of the Segovia manuscript, but I do not find it easy to dismiss it so lightly. As indicated here, I consider the question to remain open.

istic distance from most of his other works.[9] None of these arguments is conclusive, however, and until clear evidence is offered that Busnoys did not compose *Fortuna desperata* it is reasonable to consider him its probable author and therefore the most likely founder of this large musical family.

Why did *Fortuna desperata* so quickly spawn such an extensive progeny? Part of the answer may lie in the interest in *imitatio* that pervaded Renaissance intellectual life and literary activity in the fifteenth and sixteenth centuries, as pointed out by Howard Brown.[10] But the rather modest musical materials of the original *Fortuna desperata* are insufficient to explain the large number of compositions based on it. Many writers, from Edward Lowinsky to Alfred Loeffler and Julie Cumming,[11] believe that the underlying reason for its attraction to composers is its emblematic nature, joining simple but memorable melodic ideas to a text describing the fickleness and mutability of Fortune. The key to the symbolism that made the piece so compelling is found in the opening words: 'Fortuna desperata, iniqua e maledetta'.[12]

Borrowing has been limited mainly to the superius and tenor voices, which form a duo that is structurally self-sufficient and 'non-quartal', that is, involves no harmonic fourths requiring support by a bass (see Ex. 17.1).[13] This feature is characteristic of much but not all three-part music composed in the fifteenth century, including that of Busnoys. While the bassus undoubtedly enriches the texture and strengthens the harmony, the piece can be performed without it, and

---

[9] Another Italian song, *Con tutta gentileça*, attributed to Busnoys in the authoritative Florentine source Florence 229, dating from around 1492, has been seen as supporting the theory that Busnoys may have spent time in Italy and composed songs to Italian texts (see *A Florentine Chansonnier from the Time of Lorenzo the Magnificent*, ed. with an Introduction by Howard Mayer Brown (Monuments of Renaissance Music, 7; Chicago, 1983), Text, 130; Music, 106–7; also the contribution by Brown to the symposium 'Critical Years in European Musical History 1500–1530', in the *I.M.S. Report of the Tenth Congress, Ljubljana 1967* (Kassel, 1970), 90–1). However, Walter Rubsamen, 'From Frottola to Madrigal: The Changing Pattern of Secular Italian Vocal Music', in James Haar (ed.), *Chanson and Madrigal 1480–1530* (Cambridge, Mass., 1964), 52–3, notes that the piece 'may be based on a French model'. Joshua Rifkin, in 'Busnoys and Italy', demonstrates that *Con tutta gentileça* is in fact a contrafact, probably of a bergerette, and thus it does not support the theory of Busnoys's residence in Italy or his authorship of *Fortuna desperata*.

[10] The classic discussion of the musical aspects of Renaissance *imitatio* is Howard Mayer Brown, 'Emulation, Competition, and Homage: Imitation and Theories of Imitation in the Renaissance', *JAMS* 35 (1982), 1–48.

[11] Edward E. Lowinsky, 'The Goddess Fortuna in Music', *Musical Quarterly*, 29 (1943), 45–77; revised repr. in id., *Music in the Culture of the Renaissance and Other Essays*, ed. Bonnie J. Blackburn (Chicago and London, 1989), i. 221–39. The discussion of *Fortuna desperata*, occurring towards the end of the article, touches on the salient aspects of its symbolism, especially the transpositions of its melodies. For the articles by Loeffler and Cumming, see above, n. 5.

[12] The full text has been reconstructed by Fausto Torrefranca, *Il segreto del quattrocento* (Milan, 1939), 297. New information was discovered by Honey Meconi; see below, Ch. 19. The most important of Meconi's discoveries is a textual source that places the origins of the piece in Florence during the 1470s and differs in significant respects from the versions of the text preserved in musical sources. Meconi suggests that *Fortuna* concerns actual persons and events in Florence and that this may have led to its choice as a subject for *imitatio*. I am grateful to Professor Meconi for sending me a copy of her paper.

[13] See Charles Warren Fox, 'Non-Quartal Harmony in the Renaissance', *Musical Quarterly*, 31 (1945), 33–53. As Rifkin points out, the sources disagree on the first note in the superius in m. 13. Segovia and some other sources have *f'*, while still others have *c'*, each reading being found in both three- and four-part versions. This matter is discussed below (n. 34) in connection with Isaac's settings.

Ex. 17.1. *Fortuna desperata* (superius and tenor)

(1) Variant in Isaac, nos.19-21 (see Appendix):

no composer has chosen it alone as a cantus firmus. I shall review the family's history briefly before turning to the settings by Isaac and his followers that are the main subject of this paper.

The four known *Fortuna desperata* masses include two by acknowledged masters of the late fifteenth century: Obrecht, who uses the original tenor as a cantus firmus, and Josquin, who employs all three voices as individual cantus firmi and as a polyphonic unit, anticipating the development of the full-blown 'imitation' or 'parody' mass.[14] In addition there is a mass by Periquin in a manuscript at Tarazona (which I have not seen) and an anonymous mass copied by Giovanni Spataro at S. Petronio, Bologna, around 1525, quoting the original superius and tenor.[15]

Of the individual settings, besides the four that add altus parts to the original three voices (see App., Nos. 2(*a–d*)), there are three that incorporate two or more of the original voices (nos. 3–5). Two of these, one attributed to Josquin and another to a certain Felice, tentatively identified by Frank D'Accone as the Florentine singer Ser Felice di Giovanni Martini (d. 1478), substitute a new bassus of distinctly instrumental character for the original one (nos. 3 and 4); and Alexander Agricola adds three new voices to the original three (no. 5).[16]

All the remaining settings employ either the original superius or tenor as cantus firmus. Excluding the settings of Isaac and Senfl, which I shall discuss separately, there are five settings of the tenor at its original pitch or transposed down

[14] The Obrecht mass is published in Jacob Obrecht, *Werken: Missen*, ed. Johannes Wolf (Amsterdam, 1908), i. 85–135; *Opera omnia: Missae*, ed. Albert Smijers (Amsterdam, 1953), i. 113–69; and *Collected Works*, ed. Barton Hudson (Utrecht, 1986), iv. 49–91. The Josquin mass is published in Josquin des Prez, *Werken: Missen*, ed. Albert Smijers (Amsterdam, 1929), iv. Concerning their cantus-firmus usage, see Edgar H. Sparks, *Cantus Firmus in Mass and Motet, 1420–1520* (Berkeley, 1963), 248–9, 317–20; on the imitation mass, see J. Peter Burkholder, 'Johannes Martini and the Imitation Mass in the Late Fifteenth Century', *JAMS* 38 (1985), 470–523.

[15] The contents of the Tarazona MS are listed in Higinio Anglés, *La música en la corte de los reyes católicos*, i. *Polifonía religiosa* (Barcelona, 1941), 124. A catalogue of the S. Petronio manuscripts is given in Frank Tirro, *Renaissance Musical Sources in the Archive of San Petronio in Bologna* (Neuhausen-Stuttgart, 1986); the *Missa de Fortuna desperata*, in MS A. XXXVIII, is listed on p. 71. The thematic incipits of all five movements, given by Tirro on pp. 90, 111, 123, 135, and 147, show that the S and T of the original are quoted at the beginning of each movement; it is likely that the T is the principal cantus firmus.

[16] For no. 3, see *The Collected Works of Josquin des Prez*, 27. *Secular Works for Three Voices*, ed. Jaap van Benthem and Howard M. Brown (Utrecht, 1987), 66–7. In the *Critical Commentary* (1991), 77–8, Benthem and Brown describe the work as doubtful, citing musical problems, inconsistencies with the readings in Josquin's mass, and the unreliability of the Segovia MS, the unique source. Concerning another setting that may be by Josquin, see no. 34 below.

For no. 4, see Allan W. Atlas, *The Cappella Giulia Chansonnier* (Brooklyn, 1976), ii. 38–42; concerning Ser Felice, see Frank A. D'Accone, 'Some Neglected Composers in the Florentine Chapels, ca. 1475–1525', *Viator*, 1 (1970), 263–88 at 280–1. Felice's name in the documents cited by D'Accone suggests that he may have been a pupil of Johannes Martini, composer of another *Fortuna desperata* setting (see no. 12). Since Ser Felice died in 1478, the original *Fortuna desperata* had to have been composed before that date if he is the composer of the new bassus. (The source, Cappella Giulia XIII.27, has the original three voices and the most common added altus (no. 2(*a*)) plus Felice's bass, but the latter is not compatible with either the original bassus or the added altus. Therefore it is apparent that Felice intended his bassus to replace the original one and that his setting is *a 3*, not *a 5*, as it appears to be at first glance.)

For no. 5, see Alexander Agricola, *Opera omnia*, ed. Edward R. Lerner (Neuhausen-Stuttgart, 1961–), v. 68–70.

a fourth or octave, preserving its intervallic structure (nos. 6–10). One anonymous setting, marked 'a 3', survives only as a superius, but the *Fortuna* tenor fits with it until nearly the end (no. 6).[17] Another, an unicum of which three voices are given in Munich 328–31, may lack its original altus, like most other pieces in this section of the manuscript (no. 7).[18] In its present form it adds two voices entirely in breves to the original tenor. The four-part setting (no. 8) is unusual in that the tenor has been freely paraphrased, a rare procedure in these settings.[19] Two three-part settings survive only in organ arrangements under their intabulators' names, Othmar Nachtgall (also known as Luscinius) and Hans Buchner. In these the original tenor is transposed down an octave, explicitly to be played *pedaliter* (nos. 9, 10).[20] Both settings make use of a variant in measure 30 of the tenor that is also found in three settings by Isaac (see Ex. 17.1). These tenors may have been borrowed from Isaac, or it is even possible that the models for Nachtgall's and Buchner's arrangements are compositions by Isaac, a point to which I shall return later.

One extraordinary late setting, Matthias Greiter's *Passibus ambiguis* (published in 1553), borrows only the first six notes of the tenor, using this phrase as a transposing ostinato moving by ascending fourths from its original starting pitch of F to end on C♭ (no. 11).[21] Its Latin text makes the symbolism explicit: *Passibus ambiguis Fortuna volubilis errat* ('inconstant Fortune wanders with uncertain steps'). By Greiter's time the *Fortuna desperata* motto was widely recognized in Germany and its symbolism had become familiar.

Seven settings employ the superius as cantus firmus (nos. 12–18). One, an instrumental setting emphasizing a scalar motif in dotted rhythm intensively imitated in all but the borrowed voice, is probably by Johannes Martini, to whom it is attributed in Casanatense 2856, written in Ferrara around 1480 (no. 12). It is attributed in the Segovia manuscript to Isaac, but in this case the Ferrarese manuscript deserves credence, since Martini was a central figure in Ferrarese

[17] Donald G. Loach, 'Aegidius Tschudi's Songbook (St. Gall MS 463)' (Ph.D. diss., University of California at Berkeley, 1969), ii. 48–50.

[18] See Don Smithers, 'A Textual-Musical Inventory and Concordance of Munich University MS 328–331', *R. M. A. Research Chronicle*, 8 (1970), 36–7.

[19] See *Das Liederbuch des Johannes Heer von Glarus*, ed. A. Geering and H. Trümpy (Schweizerische Musikdenkmäler, 5; Basle, 1967), 14–17. As noted in the edition, the tenor is written in the tenor clef, as if were transposed to *mi*; the music requires that it be read in baritone clef a third lower, thus transposed down a fourth as well as paraphrased. There may be a symbolic purpose for the transposition and paraphrasing of the tenor, but this is not clear.

[20] Both are in Berlin 40026 (the Kleber tablature), attributed to M.O.N. (Magister Othmar Nachtgall) and H.B. (Hans Buchner) respectively; see *Die Orgeltabulatur des Leonhard Kleber*, ed. K. Berg-Kotterba (Das Erbe deutscher Musik, 92; Frankfurt, 1987), 64–7, 67–70. German organ settings often place the cantus firmus in the left hand or pedal, and this transposition probably does not have symbolic significance in these cases.

[21] See the study by Edward E. Lowinsky, 'Matthaeus Greiter's *Fortuna*', *Musical Quarterly*, 42 (1956), 500–19, and 43 (1957), 68–85; revised repr. in *Music in the Culture of the Renaissance*, i. 240–61. This includes a transcription of Greiter's piece.

musical life at the time.[22] The persistent motif is repeated some twenty times in the bass at various pitch levels (F, B♭, and C) to reflect Fortune's mutability. An anonymous setting in a Bolognese manuscript associated with Giovanni Spataro also features repetitive ostinati in three of its four voices (no. 13).[23] A setting by Johannes Pinarol in Petrucci's *Canti C*, which is criticized by Gombosi for its awkwardness,[24] places the original superius in the bass as yet another representation of mutability (no. 14). An anonymous Italian *zibaldone* (quodlibet), probably by a Netherlander living in Italy and one of many such pieces in Italian songbooks, quotes the entire superius of *Fortuna desperata* and fragments of popular Italian songs, such as *La Tortorella* and *Dammene un poco* (no. 15).[25] Finally, there is a richly textured six-part setting by Robertus Fabri that unfortunately lacks two of its voices in the fragmentary sources (no. 16).[26]

All the settings thus far discussed are by different composers or anonymi. We turn next to multiple settings by single composers: one group of six by Henricus Isaac (nos. 17–22), and another of seven, plus a possible eighth, by Isaac's pupil and disciple, Ludwig Senfl (nos. 23–30). Two of Isaac's settings use the *Fortuna* superius, while another four, and all Senfl's settings, are based on the tenor. In these we come to a decisive stage in the evolution of *Fortuna desperata* as an emblematic model for imitation. Given the rarity of attributions of the model piece to a composer, it is unlikely that Isaac or Senfl knew or greatly cared who its composer was. Their choice of it as a model was determined by its ready recognition and potential symbolism, well established in Italy from its earliest appearance. It is probably through Isaac, who spent many years in Florence and then worked in German territories, that *Fortuna desperata* was adopted as a model in Germany, particularly by Senfl. Greiter's familiarity with the tenor reflects the continuity of the German *Fortuna* tradition, of which he is possibly the last representative. Thus Isaac appears to be the main link between the Italian and German branches of the *Fortuna* family.

Isaac's two settings employing the superius of *Fortuna desperata* are combinative pieces uniting borrowed melodies from disparate sources. One, analogous to the Italian *zibaldone*, is his setting for four voices uniting the superius of *Fortuna desperata* with the German Lied *Bruder Conrat*, paraphrased in the three 'free' voices (no. 17).[27] (The first five notes of the *Fortuna* bassus are also quoted at the

[22] See Lewis Lockwood, *Music in Renaissance Ferrara, 1400–1505* (Cambridge, Mass., 1984), 167 *et passim*. For the music, see Johannes Martini, *Secular Pieces*, ed. Edward G. Evans, Jr. (Madison, 1975), 19–21. Lowinsky discusses its symbolic aspects in 'The Goddess Fortuna', 74–5 (repr., 238).
[23] Susan Forscher Weiss, 'The Manuscript Bologna, Civico Museo Bibliografico Musicale, Codex Q 18 (*olim 143*)' (Ph.D. diss., University of Maryland, 1985), 454–6.   [24] Gombosi, *Jacob Obrecht*, 101–2.
[25] See Obrecht, *Werken*, ed. Wolf, i. 138–40. Gombosi compares the version of the tune *Dammene un poco* in this piece with the versions in similar *zibaldoni* by Isaac and Japart, and considers its composer to have been a Netherlander resident in Italy (*Jacob Obrecht*, 103).
[26] Loach, 'Aegidius Tschudi's Songbook', 400–3.
[27] Heinrich Isaac, *Weltliche Werke*, ed. Johannes Wolf (Denkmäler der Tonkunst in Österreich, 28; Vienna, 1907), i. 74.

beginning.) Influences of both the Italian *zibaldone* and German *Tenorlied* are evident in this piece, as is the conceptual relationship between the two borrowed songs. (*Bruder Conrat* refers to a gravely ill monk, and *Fortuna*, as we have seen, to the injustice of Fortune.) As in the *zibaldone*, but unlike a typical *Tenorlied*, Isaac's work paraphrases *Bruder Conrat* rather than quoting it literally, breaking up and reassembling its fragments in imitation among various voices.[28]

More complicated, conceptually as well as musically, is Isaac's five-voice setting of the *Fortuna* superius combined with a Litany chant formula, *Sancte Petre/Ora pro nobis*, divided antiphonally between two tenors, a work found uniquely in the Segovia manuscript (no. 18).[29] Cumming views the incorporation of the Litany of the Saints in this composition as an invocation of divine aid against the vicissitudes of Fortune, while Maniates, in a survey of quodlibet types, finds the combination 'mocking and slightly blasphemous'.[30] Either interpretation may be correct, but it should be noted that there is a fifteenth-century tradition of combining the Litany of the Saints with popular melodies, suggesting that Isaac may have intended no special symbolism here but merely indulged in a playful uniting of opposites in accordance with the quodlibet tradition. One such Litany setting is Jean Japart's *Vray dieu d'amours* in Petrucci's *Canti C* (1504[3]), and another is an anonymous Dutch song of the fifteenth century celebrating the coming of spring, *Ich zei den claren dach*.[31] It is difficult to interpret any of these three pieces as emblematic, although it is likely that a late medieval tradition of mocking conventional piety underlies them all.

The implications of Isaac's setting are difficult to assess. Its presence in the Segovia manuscript suggests that it is an early work composed in Flanders before Isaac's emigration to Italy in 1484.[32] On the other hand, Isaac may not have encountered *Fortuna desperata* before arriving in Italy. Three possibilities offer themselves: Isaac may have known *Fortuna desperata* in Flanders, where Busnoys worked (the theory I prefer); it may have been written by Isaac in Italy and brought to Spain along with other Italian works; or, as Just suggests in his dissertation on Isaac's motets, it may not be by Isaac at all.[33] Its vigorously inter-

---

[28] See Gombosi's analysis of Isaac's 'deconstruction' of the Lied in his *Jacob Obrecht*, 104–5.

[29] Transcribed in Baker, 'An Unnumbered Manuscript', ii. 840–7.

[30] Cumming, 'The Goddess Fortuna Revisited', 17; Maria Rika Maniates, 'Quodlibet Revisum', *Acta musicologica*, 38 (1966), 174.

[31] I am grateful to David Fallows for drawing my attention to Japart's setting. The Dutch song is published in Nanie Bridgman, 'Paroles et musique dans le manuscrit Latin 16664 de la Bibliothèque nationale de Paris', in Ursula Günther and Ludwig Finscher (eds.), *Musik und Text in der Mehrstimmigkeit des 14. und 15. Jahrhunderts* (Kassel, 1984), 407–8. Concerning the Paris manuscript, see *Census-Catalogue*, iii. 27.

[32] This is one of the pieces dealt with in my paper 'Isaac in Flanders', in Albert Clement and Eric Jas (eds.), *From Ciconia to Sweelinck: Dona natalicium Willem Elders* (Amsterdam, 1994), 153–65 at 161–2.

[33] Martin Just, 'Studien zu Heinrich Isaacs Motetten' (Inaug.-diss., Eberhard-Karls-Universität, Tübingen, 1960), i. 167–8, doubts Isaac's authorship on the basis of a few structural and stylistic anomalies. I consider these as evidence more of immaturity than inauthenticity, and note that the division of a borrowed melody between two voices is found in a much more sophisticated form in a textless composition by Isaac in Florence 229 (*Weltliche Werke*, 121; also Brown, *A Florentine Chansonnier, Music*, 387–8).

active polyphony, however, strikes me as consistent with Isaac's style, and I see no reason to reject it as his work.[34]

Four settings of the *Fortuna* tenor are attributed to Isaac. One in three parts, found in two Italian sources, places the original tenor in the highest voice, transposed up a fifth and with a five-bar extension (no. 19).[35] The textless, active lower voices, with an unusual passage of hocket just before the end, exhibit Isaac's habitual leaning towards an instrumental idiom. The placement of the tenor in the position of superius may reflect a preference for its melody over that of the original superius. As Gombosi points out in his monograph on Obrecht, the tenor is the more graceful and convincing of the two voices.[36] In his setting, Isaac introduces a syncopated cadential elaboration in measure 30 that adds rhythmic and contrapuntal interest without violating the original, although this variant is found in none of the sources of the model (see Ex. 17.1).

Isaac also uses the variant of measure 30 in his two settings in *mi*, discussed below. It appears in other settings as well, including the organ transcriptions by Nachtgall and Buchner previously mentioned (nos. 9 and 10), and at least one other setting in *mi* (no. 33). It is possible that Isaac originated the variant in the course of composing his three-part song-setting of the *Fortuna* tenor, the simplest of the settings attributed to him, and continued to use it subsequently. The occurrence of the variant in the keyboard arrangements by Nachtgall and Buchner suggests that their models may have been otherwise lost settings by Isaac or by a composer close to him.

The most interesting of Isaac's three-part settings are the two pieces in which the tenor is transposed down a semitone, from *fa* to *mi* (nos. 20–1). This strikingly illustrates the mutability of Fortune by changing the tonality of the song from F Lydian to E Phrygian. These pieces emphasize their Phrygian character by sustaining the final E in the tenor to accommodate a coda. In these settings, generally identified by title as *Fortuna in mi*, the two free voices are more imitative and the texture better integrated than in his setting with the borrowed tenor in the highest voice, suggesting that they are later, more mature works. There is no reason to doubt Isaac's authorship, although Wolf relegates one of the settings to the category of doubtful works and includes the other only among keyboard arrangements.[37] These two compositions, which are among Isaac's best short

---

[34] Nevertheless, an indication that it may have arisen at a different time than *Fortuna/Bruder Conrat* is the variant reading of the first note in m. 13 of the superius. As Rifkin points out in 'Busnoys and Italy', the sources of the original *Fortuna* do not agree on this note. Some have *f'*, which makes better counterpoint with the bass but a weaker melodic line, while others have *c'*, which creates parallel fifths with the bass but a better melody. Isaac's *Fortuna/Bruder Conrat* has *c'* at this point, but *Fortuna/Sancte Petre* has *f'* (and cannot have *c'* because that would make fifths with its bass). The original reading was probably *f'* and Isaac would have encountered it early in his career. The *c'* may have been an 'improvement' by an unknown hand, which the mature Isaac would readily have accepted for its stronger melodic profile.

[35] Isaac, *Weltliche Werke*, 74.   [36] Gombosi, *Jacob Obrecht*, 100.

[37] No. 20 is attributed to 'Isac' in the Kotter tablature (Basle, Öffentliche Bibliothek der Universität, MS F.IX.22; *Weltliche Werke*, 144–5). No. 21 is attributed to 'H. Isaac' by hand in two copies of the print 1538[9],

pieces, are apparently designed to form a composite work in two *partes*: they are so presented in Zwickau 78/3, and are indeed complementary, a descending motif in the opening of the bass of no. 20 being inverted to become an ascending motive in the upper voice of no. 21.

Another setting by Isaac based on the *Fortuna* tenor is problematic, having the incipit 'Sanctus' in all four voices but no further text (no. 22). This piece appears in Bologna Q 17, a predominantly secular anthology. Staehelin, in his study of Isaac's masses, doubts that this 'Sanctus' has anything to do with a mass.[38] However, the free treatment of the cantus firmus, its mensuration in *tempus perfectum*, and its presentation in quasi-canon between superius and tenor suggest that this may well be part of a larger work in which the *Fortuna* tenor functions as a cantus firmus subject to rhythmic and contrapuntal manipulation, perhaps an otherwise unknown *Missa Fortuna desperata* by Isaac.

Isaac's multiple *Fortuna* settings gave impetus to further examples of *imitatio*, particularly in Germany. Seven or eight works by Isaac's pupil Ludwig Senfl appear to have as their goal the surpassing of Isaac's multiple settings. All settings by Senfl are of the *Fortuna* tenor joined to a second borrowed or artificially constructed voice. Except for one four-part setting entitled *Fortuna ad voces musicales* (no. 23), Senfl's settings are for five voices (nos. 24–9).[39] Three of these are dated 1533 in the source, which may be the year in which all were composed. None of these is a clone of any of Isaac's pieces, but they appear to have been inspired by his combinative settings, especially *Fortuna/Bruder Conrat* (no. 17), despite the fact that Isaac uses the *Fortuna* superius and Senfl the tenor in these works. Senfl incorporates the popular Lieder *Ich stuend an einem morgen* (no. 25) and *Es taget vor dem walde* (no. 28); the Latin liturgical chants *Helena desiderio plena* (no. 26), *Virgo prudentissima* (no. 27), and *Pange lingua* (no. 29); and a voice based on the hexachord (no. 23). The emblematic text *Nasci, pati, mori* (you are born, suffer, and die) is set to an ostinato-like motto that is persistently imitated in the 'free' voices, reinforcing the symbolism of the *Fortuna* tenor (no. 24). To the seven that come down to us under his name can be added another work, incorporating a verse of the hymn *Vexilla regis*, and which is anonymous in two sources but is surrounded in both by works of Senfl and is similar to the *Fortuna* pieces bearing his name (no. 30).[40]

---

as well as appearing anonymously in tablature (*Weltliche Werke*, 134, 143). Both works are anonymous in Zwickau 78/3, where they are labelled as *1a* and *2a pars*.

[38] Martin Staehelin, *Die Messen Heinrich Isaacs* (Berne, 1977), i. 47–8.

[39] The following settings are published in Ludwig Senfl, *Sämtliche Werke* (Wolfenbüttel, 1937–): no. 23 (iv. 20–3); no. 24 (vi. 60–2); no. 25 (iv. 12–13); no. 26 (vi. 62–5); no. 27 (vi. 66–8); no. 28 (iv. 18–20); and no. 29 (iv. 132–3). In Vienna 18810, nos. 24, 26, and 27 are dated Sept./Oct. 1533; these and no. 25 are presented there in succession, suggesting that they were composed as a tetralogy or part of an even larger cycle.

[40] See Martin Staehelin, 'Möglichkeiten und praktische Anwendung der Verfasserbestimmung an anonym überlieferten Kompositionen der Josquin-Zeit', *TVNM* 23 (1973), 86.

Senfl is single-minded in using the *Fortuna* tenor unmodified, but other composers employ the *Fortuna in mi* version. One such work is a four-part setting found in a keyboard arrangement by Hans Buchner (no. 31).[41] It is also found anonymously in two German sources of the 1520s that reflect the Munich and Vienna court repertories: Munich 328–31 (where it lacks the essential altus) and Regensburg C 120 (the so-called 'Pernner Codex').[42] The sources are close to Isaac, but that composer's distinctive variant is not found in this setting.

More surprising is a five-part Marian motet, *Ave mater, matris Dei/Fortuna desperata*, attributed to 'Jachet' (Jacquet of Mantua) in Bologna, Civico Museo Bibliografico Musicale, MS Q 19, written in northern Italy and dated 1518 (no. 32).[43] *Fortuna in mi*, with the variant in measure 30 that may be Isaac's modification, forms its tenor. Although this motet seems far removed in style from the German *Fortuna in mi* settings, it is worth remembering that Isaac spent much of his later life in his beloved Florence, dying there in 1517. It is therefore possible that one or more of his settings of *Fortuna* came to Jacquet's attention and that Jacquet borrowed this tenor from him.

Three other settings of *Fortuna in mi* appeared in the early sixteenth century. One by Wilhelm Breitengraser for four voices was printed by Ott in 1534 (no. 33). In the tradition of the *Tenorlied*, Breitengraser paraphrases the *Fortuna in mi* tenor in the two lower voices.[44] Another is an anonymous five-voice chanson, *Consideres mes incessantes plaintes/Fortuna desperata*, constructed on an isorhythmic tenor consisting of the first two phrases of the *Fortuna in mi* tenor stated twice, first in *integer valor* and then in diminution (no. 34). Found in Vienna 18746, a manuscript copied by Pierre Alamire at the Netherlands court around 1523, this subtle and expressive piece, clearly a complaint against misfortune although only the first line of text is present, exploits the symbolism of *Fortuna* to the full. It may have been composed for the regent Margaret of Austria, to whose taste in poetry and music its elegiac character conforms so closely. Since the entire tenor melody is not present, it is impossible to say if it owes anything directly to Isaac's settings, but almost certainly the composer was aware of *Fortuna in mi*. In a study devoted to the Vienna manuscript, Jaap van Benthem has attributed this chanson to Josquin, comparing it particularly to

---

[41] Hans Joachim Moser (ed.), *Frühmeister der deutschen Orgelkunst* (Leipzig, 1930), 62–3. This edition is marred by a misreading of the first note of the tenor as *c* instead of *e*.

[42] Concerning the Munich manuscript, see above, n. 18; also *Census-Catalogue*, ii. 245 and iv. 449. On the Regensburg manuscript, see ibid. iii. 102–3 and iv. 470.

[43] *Selections from Bologna, Civico Museo Bibliografico Musicale, MS Q19 ('Rusconi Codex')*, ed. Richard Sherr (Sixteenth-Century Motet, 7; New York, 1989), 28–34.

[44] I am grateful to Honey Meconi for sending me a copy of her transcription of this piece. There is no modern edition, but its musical incipits are published in *Das Tenorlied*, ed. N. Böker-Heil, H. Heckmann, and I. Kindermann (Kassel, 1979), i. 41. Professor Meconi is presently preparing an edition of all *Fortuna desperata* settings.

Nymphes des bois.[45] We might carry this speculation a step further and say that Josquin may have remembered his rivalry with Isaac for appointment at Ferrara, and consciously or unconsciously attempted to match Isaac in composing a *Fortuna in mi*. It must be added that this setting exhibits no resemblance either to Josquin's mass or to the three-part setting attributed to him.

Finally, in a five-voice motet *Anima mea/Amica mea–Fortuna desperata* attributed to 'Cabbiliau' in Susato's *Liber nonus ecclesiasticarum cantionum quinque vocum vulgo moteta vocant* (Antwerp, 1554) (no. 35), the first two phrases of the *Fortuna in mi* tenor are stated successively in *integer valor* and diminution, exactly as in no. 34, on which this work is evidently modelled. It is difficult to see a connection between 'Fortuna desperata' and the motet text (from the Song of Songs); indeed, the motet seems more a pedantic exercise in *imitatio* than a composition in its own right. Of the various musicians called 'Cabbiliau' (or 'Cabilliau'), one who can be readily placed at the Netherlands court, where the manuscript containing no. 34 originated, is a certain 'Joachim de Tollenaere dit Cabilliau', who in 1528 served as a choirboy under Margaret of Austria and Charles V.[46]

In summary, it can be said that an able composer, who may or may not have been Busnoys, created in *Fortuna desperata* a viable model for *imitatio*, and that both its words and music provided many composers with a memorable symbol of unpredictable Fortune. In the large family of *Fortuna* compositions, Isaac occupies a central position by his contribution of secular, sacred, and instrumental settings that stimulated others, notably his pupil Senfl, to further efforts at *imitatio*. One of the last in the family line is the most remarkable descendant of all, Greiter's far-reaching experiment in hexachord mutation. The founder of the *Fortuna* family may or may not have been Busnoys, but the composer who most effectively enlarged it and set a standard for the next generation was Henricus Isaac.

[45] Jaap van Benthem, 'Einige wiedererkannte Josquin-Chansons im Codex 18746 der Österreichischen Nationalbibliothek', *TVNM* 22 (1971), 18–39 at 32–6.

[46] See the entry under 'Cabilliau' in Robert Eitner, *Biographische-Bibliographisches Quellen-Lexikon der Musiker* (Leipzig, 1898–1904), ii. 162; also the documents cited by Edmond vander Straeten, *La Musique aux Pay-Bas avant le XIXe siècle* (Brussels, 1867–88), i. 116 and vii. 232. I am grateful to Dr Bonnie Blackburn for drawing my attention to this motet.

Appendix
Fortuna desperata: A List of Individual Settings of Voices Borrowed from the *Canzona* Attributed to Busnoys (Excluding Masses)

No.	Title	Voices	Composer	Sources	Comments
I. The original (for 3 voices) and settings with added or substitute A and/or B (3–6 voices)					
1	*Fortuna desperata*	3	A. Busnoys?	Seg + 4 anon.	
2(a)	*Fortuna desperata*	4		*Canti C* + 10, all anon.	+ A(*a*)
(b)	*Fortuna desperata*	4		Bol Q16, anon.	+ A(*b*)
(c)	*Fortuna disperata/[Poi che te hebi]*	4		Fl 27, anon.	+ A(*c*)
(d)	*Fortune esperee*	4		Lo 31922, anon.	+ A(*d*)
3	*Fortuna desperata*	3	Josquin?	Seg	ST + new B
4	*Fortuna desperata*	3	Felice	CG XIII.27	ST + new B
5	*Fortuna desperata*	6	Agricola	Aug 142a	STB + 3
II. Original T as cantus firmus (excluding Isaac and Senfl)					
6	*Fortuna desperata quae te dementia*	3?		SG 463, anon. (inc.)	T=T?
7	*Fortuna a*	3(4?)		Mun 328–31, anon. (inc.?)	T=T
8	*Fortuna desperata*	4		SG 462, anon.	T=T down a 4th, paraphrased
9	*Fortuna in fa*	3	O. Nachtgall	Ber 40026 (tablature)	B=T down an octave
10	*Fortuna in fa*	3	H. Buchner	Ber 40026 (tablature)	B=T down an octave
III. T motto as ostinato cantus firmus					
11	*Passibus ambiguis*	4	M. Greiter	Faber 1553	mutation study

No.	Title	Voices	Composer	Sources	Comments
IV. Original S as cantus firmus (excluding Isaac)					
12	*Fortuna desperata*	4	J. Martini?	Cas ('Ysaac' in Seg)	S=S
13	*Fortuna desperata*	4		Bol Q18, anon.	S=S
14	*Fortuna desperata*	4	J. Pinarol	Canti C + 1	B=S down an eleventh
15	*Fortuna (zibaldone)*	4		Fl 164–7, anon.	S=S
16	*Fortuna desperata quae te dementia*	6	R. Fabri	SG 463, 464 (inc.)	S=S
V. Settings by H. Isaac					
17	*Fortuna/Bruder Conrat*	4		Vienna 18810	S=S, T=Lied
18	*Fortuna/Sancte Petre*	5		Seg	S=S, T=litany
19	*Fortuna desperata*	3		CG XIII.27; Fl XIX.121, anon.	S=T up a fifth
20	*Fortuna in mi* (I)	3		Zwi 78/3, anon.; Bas F.IX.22 (tabl.)	T=T down a step
21	*Fortuna in mi* (II)	3		Zwi 78/3, anon.; 1538^9 + 2 tabl.	T=T down a step
22	*Sanctus*	4		Bol Q17	S/T=paraphrased
VI. Settings by or attributed to L. Senfl					
23	*Fortuna ad voces musicales*	4		1534^{17} + 3	T=T, S from hexachord
24	*Nasci pati mori/Fortuna*	5		Vienna 18810 (dated 21 Sept. 1533)	T=T

No.	Title	Voices	Composer	Source	Relationship
25	*Ich stuend an einem morgen/ Fortuna*	5		Vienna 18810; 1534[17]	T=T, A=Lied
26	*Helena desiderio/Fortuna*	5		Vienna 18810 (dated 28 Sept. 1533)	T=T, S²=antiphon
27	*Virgo prudentissima/Fortuna*	5		Vienna 18810 (dated 1 Oct. 1533)	T=T, S²=antiphon
28	*Es taget vor dem walde/ Fortuna*	5		1534[17]	T=T, S=Lied
29	*Herr durch dein Blut (Pange lingua)/Fortuna*	5		1534[17]	T=T, S=hymn
30	*O crux ave (Vexilla regis)/ Fortuna*	5	(Senfl?)	Reg C120; Vat 11953, both anon.[a]	T=T, S=hymn

VII. Fortuna in mi *(excluding Isaac)*

No.	Title	Voices	Composer	Source	Relationship
31	*Fortuna in mi*	4	H. Buchner	SG 530 (tabl.); Mun 328–31 (A lacking); Reg C120, both anon.	T=T down a step
32	*Ave mater matris dei/ Fortuna*	5	Jacquet	Bol Q19	T=T down a step
33	*Fortuna in mi*	4	W. Breitengraser	1534[17]	T/B=paraphrased T, down a step
34	*Consideres mes incessantes plaintes/Fortuna*	5	(Josquin?)	Vienna 18746, anon.[b]	T=phrases 1–2 of T, down a step
35.	*Anima mea/Amica mea– Fortuna desperata*	5	Cabbiliau	1554[9]	T=phrases 1–2 of T, down a step

[a] Attributed to Senfl by Staehelin, 'Möglichkeiten', 86.
[b] Attributed to Josquin by van Benthem, 'Einige wiedererkannte Josquin-Chansons', 32–6.

18

Busnoys and Japart: Teacher and Student?

෨෪ ෪෨

ALLAN W. ATLAS

O assert that one fifteenth- or early sixteenth-century composer studied composition (whatever that entailed) with another composer is tricky even when there is contemporary or near-contemporary testimony for such a relationship. How many scholars, for instance, whether on the basis of Zarlino's sober reference or Cosimo Bartoli's somewhat mythologizing statements, would accept unequivocally that Josquin studied with Ockeghem,[1] or that the seemingly self-serving Adrian Petit Coclico had been Josquin's student,[2] or, finally, that Ockeghem taught all the composers who are made to address him as 'nostre maistre et bon pere' in the famous passage from Guillaume Cretin's *Déploration*?[3] Among such would-be student–teacher relationships, those involving Senfl and Isaac or Willaert and Mouton seem at least plausible; they are, at any rate, two student–teacher relationships that have gained widespread acceptance.[4]

[1] Gioseffo Zarlino, *Istitutioni harmoniche*, 2nd edn. (Venice, 1573; facs. edn. Ridgewood, NJ, 1966), 329: '. . . Giovanne Occheghem, che fu maestro del detto Giosquino . . .' (and see below, n. 4). Cosimo Bartoli, *Ragionamenti accademici* (Venice, 1567), fo. 35ᵛ: '*et* che Iosquino discepulo di Ocghem. . .'; for Bartoli's text, see James Haar, 'Cosimo Bartoli on Music', *EMH* 8 (1988), 37–79 at 54; Jessie Ann Owens, 'Music Historiography and the Definition of "Renaissance" ', *Notes*, 47 (1990–1), 305–30 at 311; Alfred Einstein, *The Italian Madrigal* (Princeton, 1949), 21–2.

[2] Adrian Petit Coclico, *Compendium musices* (Nuremberg, 1552; facs. edn. Kassel, 1954); Coclico's most explicit claim to having studied with Josquin appears in the title of the treatise: *descriptum ab Adriano Petit Coclico discipulo Iosquini de Pres*; see also fo. B [iv]. For Coclico's text, see Owens, 'Music Historiography', 311, and Adrian Petit Coclico, *Musical Compendium*, trans. Albert Seay (Colorado Springs, Col., 1973), 8. For doubts about this and other of Coclico's autobiographical assertions, see Albert Dunning, 'Coclico, Adrianus Petit', *New Grove*, iv. 513–14.

[3] The composers include Agricola, Verbonnet (Ghiselin), Prioris, Josquin, Gaspar (van Weerbeke), Brumel, and Compère. Originally edited in Ernest Thoinan, *Déploration de Guillaume Cretin sur le trépas de Jean Okeghem* (Paris, 1864), 19 and 40, the passage appears conveniently in, among other places, Barton Hudson, 'Brumel, Antoine', *New Grove*, iii. 377, and Gustave Reese, *Music in the Renaissance* (rev. edn., New York, 1959), 137, both of whom, of course, take the claim with a grain of salt.

[4] On Senfl's having studied with Isaac, see, most recently, Martin Picker, *Henricus Isaac: A Guide to Research* (Garland Composer Resource Manuals, 35; New York, 1991), 15. On the general acceptance of Willaert's having studied with Mouton, see, among others, Reese, *Music in the Renaissance*, 280; Lewis Lockwood, 'Willaert, Adrian', *New Grove*, xx. 421, and 'Adrian Willaert and Cardinal Ippolito I d'Este: New Light on Willaert's Early Career in Italy, 1515–21', *EMH* 5 (1985), 85–112 at 86; Howard Mayer Brown,

If, then, we generally place little stock in such testimony, how do we establish a student–teacher relationship when even that kind of 'documentation' is lacking? Obviously, we speculate, though we should probably insist that three conditions be met: (i) the lives of the would-be student–teacher pair must intersect both geographically and chronologically, and that at a time when the presumed student would have been approximately the right age (mid to late teens?) to fill the student role; (ii) there should be a discernible generation gap between student and teacher, since our young composition student is more likely to have studied with an older composer than with a direct contemporary; and (iii) there should probably be some kind of recognizable trace of teacher-to-student compositional influence, whether in terms of shared general stylistic traits, specific compositional techniques, or even, perhaps, a predilection for one or another genre.

And having shown that precisely these conditions prevailed in connection with the presence of both the young Philippe Basiron and the older Guillaume Faugues at the Sainte-Chapelle of Bourges in the early 1460s, Paula Higgins has argued quite convincingly that Basiron studied with Faugues and that a less direct, possibly emulatory relationship might have obtained between Basiron and Ockeghem.[5] Likewise, Peter Wright has recently implied that there may have been a student–teacher relationship between the well-documented Johannes Brassart and the relatively obscure Johannes de Sarto, most likely when the careers of these two musician-singers overlapped at the Habsburg court during the 1430s.[6] Finally, David Fallows has recently referred to Johannes Regis as Guillaume Dufay's 'favoured pupil', pointing out that the young Regis served as Dufay's *clerc* at Cambrai during the 1440s.[7]

But what if one or more of the abovementioned conditions does not obtain? How far can we go in persuasively positing a student–teacher relationship if the life and career of one member of the hypothetical pair is so thinly documented that there are no known intersections with the career of the other, and if even the

'Mouton, Jean', *New Grove*, xii. 657; and Lawrence F. Bernstein, *La Couronne et fleur des chansons a troys* (Masters and Monuments of the Renaissance, 3; New York, 1984), ii. 20. Though the above references repeatedly cite Zarlino's *Dimostrationi harmoniche* (Venice, 1571; facs. edn. Ridgewood, NJ, 1966) as the source for the Willaert–Mouton relationship, there has been some confusion about the precise location of the testimony, and none of the references actually reproduces it. Zarlino's testimony about Willaert's having studied with Mouton appears on pp. 88–9 (the latter misnumbered as 77), where Zarlino has Willaert say: '. . . Et mi ricordo, che innanzi di noi quei buoni Antichi Giosquino, il suo Maestro Gio. Ocheghem: Gascogne, & il mio precettore Gio. Motone . . .'. I am grateful to Dr Vered Cohen, who communicated the precise location of the Zarlino testimony to me in a letter of 26 Oct. 1992.

[5] Paula Higgins, 'Tracing the Careers of Late Medieval Composers: The Case of Philippe Basiron of Bourges', *Acta musicologica*, 62 (1990), 1–28 at 12–15. Higgins (pp. 15 and 17) also points out that Basiron, in turn, may have taught both Karolus de Launay (active at Florence and Mantua in the 1480s and 1490s) and Johannes Soupison, who are probably the composers 'Colinet de Lannoy' and 'Souspison' represented in Casanatense 2856.

[6] Peter Wright, 'Johannes Brassart and Johannes de Sarto', *Plainsong and Medieval Music*, 1 (1992), 41–61 at 59–60.

[7] David Fallows, 'The Life of Johannes Regis, c. 1425 to 1496', *Revue belge de musicologie*, 43 (1989), 143–72 at 162.

TABLE 18.1. *Conflicting attributions involving Japart*

Piece	Attribution to Japart	Attribution to other composers
Amours, amours	Odh	Busnoys in Bol Q17
Amours fait molt/Tant que nostre argent/Il est de bonne heure né	Fl 229 and Cas	Busnoys in Bol Q17; 'Pirson' in Bas F.X.1–4
Et qui la dira	Fl 107bis	Busnoys in Bol Q17
J'ay bien nourri (= J'ay bien rise tant)	Fl 229	Josquin in Fl 178; 'Johannes Joye' in Seg
Je cuide	Cas	'Congiet' in Fl 229
T'meiskin was jonck (= De tusche in busche)	Fl 178	Isaac in Odh and Schlick, *Tabulaturen* (1512); Obrecht in Seg

generation to which he belonged can be surmised only approximately from the style of his music and the sources that transmit it? And given the complete absence of documented biographical interactions, how many and what kind of musical correspondences must there be to compensate?

I ask these questions because they are central to the hypothesis that I shall pursue: that the composer Jean Japart may have studied composition with Antoine Busnoys. In an earlier essay I had formulated some hypotheses about the likelihood of biographical connections between composers whose works seem consistently to bear conflicting attributions in the manuscript sources. A brief overview of Japart's output[8] reveals that thirty-three sources from the late 1470s to circa 1540 (including tablatures and one treatise) transmit seventy-eight redactions of twenty-three chansons that carry attributions to Japart in at least one source. Of these, six pieces have conflicting attributions in other manuscripts (see Table 18.1). Pieces with conflicting attributions are crucial to my central hypothesis, for not only is Busnoys the composer with whom Japart most frequently conflicts, but he is also the only composer with whom Japart conflicts more than once. Thus the possibility of some biographical relationship between the two composers would follow logically from my earlier hypothesis. And it was this

[8] See my article, 'Conflicting Attributions in Italian Sources of the Franco-Netherlandish Chanson, *c*.1465–*c*.1505: A Progress Report on a New Hypothesis', in Iain Fenlon (ed.), *Music in Medieval and Early Modern Europe: Patronage, Sources and Texts* (Cambridge, 1981), 249–93. The summary of Japart's output is based on the data compiled for a forthcoming edition of Japart's works for the series Masters and Monuments of the Renaissance, published by the Broude Trust. For a list of Japart's works, see Atlas, 'Japart, Jean', *New Grove*, ix. 553. In addition to the works listed there, the *Riemann Musiklexikon. Personenteil*, ed. Wilibald Gurlitt (Mainz, 1959), i. 870, incorrectly attributes to Japart the *Missa super Princesse et amorette* by Gaspar van Weerbeke. Likewise, Gerhard Croll, 'Weerbeke, Gaspar van', *New Grove*, xx. 291, assigns to him (with the comment 'probably by Japart') *Bon temps je ne te puis laissier* and *Que faict le cocu au bois* (both ascribed to 'Gaspart' in FC 2442, nos. 49 and 50), and, with somewhat less conviction (now the qualification 'possibly by Japart'), *Sans regretz veul entretenir* (attributed to 'Jaspar' in FC 2439, fos. 79ᵛ–80ʳ). In each case, however, the attribution is far more likely to refer to Weerbeke.

observation, together with some striking stylistic musical correspondences between their pieces, that led me to ask about the possibility of a Busnoys and Japart teacher and student relationship.

The problem centres around our scanty knowledge about Japart, whose precise whereabouts are known for no more than a span of approximately four and one-half years. The earliest known reference to Japart places him at the Milanese court of Galeazzo Maria Sforza in July 1476.[9] Japart was still at Milan in February 1477, though since his name now appears on a 'safe-conduct' pass of that year, it seems evident that he was about to leave.[10] And upon quitting Milan, Japart apparently headed directly for Ferrara, where he is recorded among the chapel singers of Ercole I d'Este from mid-1477 through January 1481.[11]

Beyond his Milanese and Ferrarese sojourns, Japart's life is open only to speculation. Though Osthoff has suggested that Japart might be identified with the 'Jaspare' who is recorded as chapelmaster of the Guild of Our Lady at Bergen op Zoom in 1507,[12] the identification remains both unconfirmed and chronologically irrelevant (as is, for that matter, at least in terms of our hypothetical Japart–Busnoys relationship, Japart's activity at Milan and Ferrara). Similarly unconfirmed and equally irrelevant are the statements by Fétis and Vander Straeten that Josquin welcomed Japart either to or back from Italy with a now-lost chanson that began: *Revenu d'oultremonts, Japart, je n'ai du sort que mince part*.[13]

These scanty biographical details about Japart bring the problem into focus: (i) the only years for which there is documentation about Japart are those that he spent at Milan and Ferrara from mid-1476 through early 1481, years during which Busnoys was a member (as Japart never was) of the Habsburg-Burgundian

[9] Edward E. Lowinsky, 'Ascanio Sforza's Life: A Key to Josquin's Biography and an Aid to the Chronology of his Works', in *Josquin des Prez: Proceedings of the International Josquin Festival Conference*, ed. Edward E. Lowinsky with the collaboration of Bonnie J. Blackburn (London, 1976), 31–75 at 41 n. 30 (repr. in id., *Music in the Culture of the Renaissance and Other Essays*, ed. Bonnie J. Blackburn (Chicago and London, 1989), 541–64 at 546 n. 30). Although the document fails to record the year, Lowinsky describes it as 'with great certainty belonging to the year 1476'.

[10] Ibid. 40–1. Neither of the Milanese documents is mentioned in Atlas, 'Japart'.

[11] See Lewis Lockwood, *Music in Renaissance Ferrara, 1400–1505* (Cambridge, Mass., 1984), 153, 176, 239, 272, 320–2; Atlas, 'Japart', 553.

[12] Helmuth Osthoff, *Josquin Desprez*, 2 vols. (Tutzing, 1965), ii. 339 n. 1, who gives the name as 'Jaspart'. It is recorded as 'Jaspare' in Rob C. Wegman, 'Music and Musicians at the Guild of Our Lady in Bergen op Zoom, c. 1470–1510', *EMH* 9 (1990), 175–249 at 245. As it happens, the orthography of Japart's name in the music sources—that is, the attributions that must unequivocally refer to Jean Japart the composer—may argue against Osthoff's suggestion; while the name is variously spelled 'Japart' (most often), 'Jappart', 'Japarth', 'Zapart', and even 'Haeppart', it is never spelled with the combination 'sp'. Nor can the 'Jaspare' at Bergen op Zoom be identified with Gaspar van Weerbeke, since the latter was at Rome in 1507; see Croll, 'Weerbeke', 290. On another problem involving Japart and Weerbeke, see above, n. 8.

[13] François-Joseph Fétis, *Biographie universelle des musiciens* (2nd edn.; Paris, 1869), iv. 428–9; Edmond Vander Straeten, *La Musique aux Pays-Bas avant le XIXᵉ siècle* (Brussels, 1867–88; repr. New York, 1969), vi. 104. Vander Straeten himself never saw the chanson, and simply cites Fétis as his authority. Finally, though Osthoff, *Josquin Desprez*, ii. 154, doubts that the piece ever existed, Lowinsky, 'Ascanio Sforza's Life', 41 n. 30 (repr., 546 n. 30), thinks it somewhat likely that it did exist.

chapels;[14] (ii) Japart's style and the pattern in which his works were disseminated (see below) make it virtually certain that he was a member of the Josquin generation, probably born during the decade 1440–50; so that (iii) any student–teacher contact between Japart and Busnoys would almost certainly have occurred by the mid to late 1460s, a period during which Busnoys was associated first with the collegiate church of Saint-Martin at Tours—where, among other things, he served as master of the choirboys (so that we know that he functioned as a teacher)—then for a few months with both the collegiate church of Saint-Hilaire-le-Grand in Poitiers and the court of Burgundy, and, finally, possibly with Paris,[15] but during which Japart's own whereabouts are completely unknown.

In all, there is no documentary biographical evidence that points to a career association between Japart and Busnoys, much less to a pedagogical relationship. And to posit such a connection we must turn to their music.

There are five distinct kinds of intersections between the works of Japart and those of Busnoys: (1) shared tunes; (2) predilection for combinative chansons; (3) use of 'serial' procedures; (4) conflicting attributions; and (5) paired transmission in the sources. These fall neatly into two categories: internal intersections, or those that appear in the music itself (intersections 1–3), and external intersections, or those associated with the dissemination of the works (intersections 4–5). In dealing with the internal or musical intersections, I have excluded certain pieces from consideration: (i) all works by either composer that involve conflicting attributions, (ii) the 'Gaspart/Jaspar' pieces assigned to Japart (incorrectly, I believe) by either Gerhard Croll or the *Riemann Lexikon*, and (iii) those works that have been assigned to Busnoys on stylistic and/or circumstantial grounds but for which there are no attributions in the sources.

Thus for the internal intersections, I have restricted my field of inquiry only to those works with uncontested attributions: seventeen by Japart, all of which are French chansons, and seventy-three by Busnoys, of which fifty-nine are secular and fourteen sacred.[16] Finally, my discussion of the intersections carries with it

[14] The most complete account of Busnoys's activity in these chapels is Paula Higgins, '*In hydraulis* Revisited: New Light on the Career of Antoine Busnois', *JAMS* 39 (1986), 36–86 at 61–9; and ead., 'Antoine Busnois and Musical Culture in Late Fifteenth-Century France and Burgundy' (Ph.D. diss., Princeton University, 1987), Ch. 2. In addition, see her forthcoming book about the composer.

[15] On the connections with Tours, Burgundy, and Paris, see Higgins, '*In hydraulis* Revisited', 39–76 and 'Antoine Busnois', chs. 3 and 4. On Busnoys as master of the choirboys at Tours and at Poitiers see Paula Higgins, above, Ch. 7.

[16] For a complete edition of Busnoys's sacred works, see *Busnoys LTW*. For the secular works, I have relied on Higgins, 'Antoine Busnois', 313–41. We might note that there are twelve chansons that involve Busnoys in conflicting attributions (see below, Table 18.5), including *Quant ce viendra* (also ascribed to Ockeghem), which, however, Higgins (p. 328) includes in her list of Busnoys's authentic works. Finally, I have not counted the setting of *Le serviteur* that is ascribed to Busnoys only in the first edition of *Odhecaton*.

For a list of works that have been assigned to Busnoys on stylistic or circumstantial grounds, see Higgins, 'Antoine Busnois', 339–40, to which should now be added—without counting works that are attributed to

two *caveats*: first, though I take up the internal intersections in roughly ascending order of significance, intersections 2 (use of combinative chansons) and 3 (use of 'serial' procedures) could just as well be reversed; and second, although the five intersections when considered together form an intriguing picture, no single intersection demonstrates anything by itself.

Internal Intersections

1. Shared Tunes

Busnoys, of course, not only set the *L'homme armé* melody with a mass that may have been the progenitor of that rich mass tradition, but perhaps even composed the famous tune itself.[17] Japart, too, utilized the *L'homme armé* tune, and did so, as we shall see, in a thoroughly Busnoysian way, combining it with another popular melody to form the double chanson *Il est de bonne heure né/L'homme armé*. Moreover, both Busnoys and Japart used the same G Dorian version of the tune, and, more specifically, with the note g' (instead of e') in the first phrase of the middle section.[18] On the other hand, since the extremely popular *L'homme armé* tradition includes at least five other secular settings from the late fifteenth century,[19] and since the combination of G Dorian with the version of the tune

Busnoys in articles included in this volume (see below)—the *Missa L'ardant desir* in Cappella Sistina 51, recently assigned to Busnoys by Rob Wegman (see below); the well-known chanson *Tout a par moy*, which, despite its conflicting ascriptions only to Binchois and Frye, has been suggested as being Busnoys's by David Fallows (see below); and possibly the chanson *Pour les biens*, which Higgins maintains has a 'connection' with Busnoys. In addition, see the articles in the present volume by Rob C. Wegman (Ch. 8), Mary Natvig (Ch. 10), Andrea Lindmayr (Ch. 11), and Leeman L. Perkins (Ch. 14), all of which would expand still further the corpus of Busnoys's works.

On the *Missa L'ardant desir*, see Rob C. Wegman, 'Another Mass by Busnoys?' *ML* 71 (1990), 1–19. Further on the question of Busnoys's authorship of this piece, see the exchange of views between Taruskin and Wegman in *ML* 72 (1991), 347–50. Taruskin (p. 349) describes the piece as being 'dogged, panting, redundantly cadential motivic work . . .', and then goes on to speculate about its composer: 'I cannot think it the work of any more major a master than . . . Basiron . . . a kind of poor man's Busnoys'. Wegman, however, has since altered his original position on the mass (see above, Ch. 8). Perhaps, if my arguments in the present essay are convincing, another nominee will come into view: Japart. On *Tout a par moy* and *Pour les biens*, see Paula Higgins, 'Parisian Nobles, a Scottish Princess, and the Woman's Voice in Late Medieval Song', *EMH* 10 (1991), 145–200 at 173, 179–80 and n. 111.

[17] For a discussion of both the priority of Busnoys's mass and his authorship of the tune—and thus of the double chanson *Il sera pour vous/L'homme armé* in Casanatense 2856 (four voices with ascription to 'Borton') and Mellon (three voices without attribution)—see *Busnoys LTW*, Commentary, 4–8, 35–7; and Richard Taruskin, 'Antoine Busnoys and the *L'Homme armé* Tradition', *JAMS* 39 (1986), 255–93; see also Leeman L. Perkins, 'The *L'Homme armé* Masses of Busnoys and Okeghem: A Comparison', *Journal of Musicology*, 3 (1984), 363–96 at 391. For questions about both of Taruskin's points, see the Communications of David Fallows and Reinhard Strohm in *JAMS* 40 (1987), 146–8 and 576–7, respectively.

[18] On the use of g' vs. e' as a means of delineating sub-traditions among the *L'homme armé* masses, see Lewis Lockwood, 'Aspects of the *L'Homme armé* Tradition', *Proceedings of the Royal Musical Association*, 100 (1973–4), 97–122 at 103; Perkins, 'The *L'Homme armé* Masses of Busnoys and Okeghem', 371; Taruskin, 'Antoine Busnoys and the *L'Homme armé* Tradition', 293 and n. 64.

[19] For a nearly complete list of masses and secular compositions based on *L'homme armé*, see Judith Cohen, *The Six Anonymous L'Homme armé Masses in Naples, Biblioteca Nazionale, MS VI E 40* (MSD 21; [Rome], 1968), 72–4; see also Walter Haas, *Studien zu den 'L'Homme armé'-Messen des 15. und 16. Jahrhunderts* (Kölner Beiträge zur Musikforschung, 136; Regensburg, 1984), 28–52.

having the note g' in the middle section also occurs in masses by Basiron, Vaqueras, Caron, and the Naples anonymi,[20] one cannot attribute excessive importance to the Japart–Busnoys *L'homme armé* intersection.[21]

2. Combinative Chansons

The Busnoys–Japart *L'homme armé* intersection assumes greater significance when one considers that, as both Taruskin and Picker have noted, Busnoys was particularly fond of the polytextual, combinative chanson in which a popular melody and its text were combined either with another popular tune or with a freshly composed setting in one of the *formes fixes*.[22] And as Table 18.2 makes clear, Japart also cultivated the technique.[23] Of Busnoys's fifty-nine securely attributed secular works (that is, works either without conflicting attributions or not ascribed to him conjecturally), six—or just over 10 per cent—are of the combinative chanson variety, while for Japart the percentage of such works is even higher: four unchallenged chansons out of seventeen, or about 23.5 per cent.[24] And just how high these percentages are becomes apparent when we compare them with the percentage of combinative chansons in the output of a number of other composers (Table 18.3).[25] Given that eleven of the nineteen polytextual

[20] Taruskin, 'Antoine Busnoys and the *L'Homme armé* Tradition', 293 n. 64.

[21] If the *J'ay pris amours* attributed to Busnoys in both *Odhecaton* and indirectly in Bartolomeo Ramos de Pareja's *Musica practica*, but to Martini in Segovia, is by Busnoys, this intersection would add two more pieces, since Japart set *J'ay pris amours* twice. That the conflicting attribution prevents the Busnoys/Martini piece from being considered is doubly unfortunate for the central hypothesis, since its verbal canon and use of inversion would also have placed it among the works in intersection 3 (see below). I am grateful to Bonnie Blackburn for calling my attention to Ramos's attribution of the canonic inscription in the piece to Busnoys; see now Blackburn, 'Obrecht's Missa *Je ne demande* and Busnoys's Chanson: An Essay in Reconstructing Lost Canons', *TVNM* 45 (1995), 18–32 at n. 25.

[22] Taruskin, 'Antoine Busnoys and the *L'Homme armé* Tradition', 290; Martin Picker, 'Busnois, Antoine', *New Grove*, iii. 507. Taruskin (p. 290) uses Busnoys's predilection for the genre as evidence that Busnoys—rather than Robert Morton—composed the three-voice version of *Il sera pour vous/L'homme armé* in Mellon (see above, n. 17). On the combinative chanson, see Maria Rika Maniates, 'Combinative Chansons in the Dijon Chansonnier', *JAMS* 23 (1970), 228–81; 'Combinative Chansons in the Escorial Chansonnier', *Musica disciplina*, 29 (1975), 61–126.

[23] The list of combinative chansons by Busnoys in Table 18.2 is based on Higgins, 'Antoine Busnois', 313–31, and does not include works with conflicting attributions.

[24] The percentage for one of the two composers would become even higher if the well-travelled *Amours fait molt tant/Tant que nostre argent/Il est de bonne heure né*—with ascriptions to Busnoys, Japart, and 'Pirson'—were included, since the ascription to 'Pirson' (= Pierre de la Rue?) in the peripheral Basle F. X. 1–4 must probably take second place to the Busnoys and Japart attributions in Bologna Q 17 and Florence 229, respectively (though see below). Finally, Busnoys's percentage would increase still further if, as is likely, he can be credited with the *Vous marchez du bout du pié/Vostre beauté* ascribed to him in Nivelle, but to Isaac in Vienna 18810. (Maniates, 'Combinative Chansons in the Dijon Chansonnier', 255, overlooked the concordance with the Isaac ascription.)

[25] The statistics for Table 18.3, which, for all the composers cited, excludes pieces with conflicting attributions, are drawn from the following: for Agricola: *Opera omnia*, ed. Edward R. Lerner (CMM 22; [Rome], 1970), v, pp. iv–xcviii; for Compère: Joshua Rifkin and Barton Hudson, 'Compère, Loyset', *New Grove*, iv. 598, and Ludwig Finscher, *Loyset Compère (c. 1450–1518): Life and Works* (MSD 12; [Rome], 1964), 47–54; for Hayne: Louise Litterick, 'Hayne van Ghizeghem', *New Grove*, viii. 417–18, and Ghizeghem, *Opera omnia*, ed. Barton Hudson (CMM 74; [Rome], 1977), pp. xxi–xxix; for Isaac: Picker, *Henricus Isaac: A Guide to Research*, 99–123; for Josquin: Jeremy Noble, 'Josquin Desprez', *New Grove*, ix.

TABLE 18.2. *Combinative chansons by Busnoys and Japart (securely attributed)*

A. Busnoys

Amours nous traite honnestement/Je m'en vois aux vert boys
Corps digne/Dieu quel mariage
L'autrier la pieça/En l'ombre du buissonet au matinet/Trop suis jonette
Mon mignault musequin/Gracieuse, plaisante muniere
On a grant mal par trop amer/On est bien malade pour amer trop
Une filleresse d'estouppes/S'il y a compagnon en la compagnie/Vostre amour

B. Japart

Il est de bonne heure né/L'homme armé
Je cuide/De tous biens plaine
Pour passer temps/Plus ne chasceray sans gens
Vray Dieu d'amour/Sancte Johanne baptiste/Ora pro nobis

TABLE 18.3. *Combinative chansons (including French–Latin song-motets) by Agricola, Compère, Hayne, Isaac, Josquin, and Ockeghem*

Composer	Secular works	Combinative chansons	Approximate percentage
Agricola	66	1	1.5
Compère	50	5 (all song-motets)	10 (= 0 without song-motets)
Hayne	14	0	—
Isaac	106	6 (1 song-motet)	5.6 (= 4.7 without song-motets)
Josquin	78	5 (4 song-motets)	6.6 (= 1.4 without song-motets)
Ockeghem	19	2 (1 song-motet)	10.5 (= 5.5 without song-motets)

works by the composers of Table 18.3 belong to the genre of the song-motet, which differs from the combinative, all-vernacular chanson in terms of both style and function, it seems clear that Busnoys and Japart stand in something of a class by themselves in their fondness for the combinative chanson with popular elements.

Finally, as one would expect, both Busnoys and Japart tend to treat the popular tunes that they incorporate either canonically or at least imitatively. Of the six Busnoys chansons listed in Table 18.2, all but one—*Une filleresse d'estouppes*—are shot through with one or another of the techniques, while Japart employs them in both *Il est de bonne heure né* and *Pour passer temps*. In all, the relatively large numbers of combinative chansons in the *œuvre* of both Busnoys and Japart and the use of canon and imitation in the settings of each composer at least hints at a possible line of compositional influence from one to the other.

731–3, 736; for Ockeghem: Perkins, 'Ockeghem, Johannes', *New Grove*, xiii. 494–5, and Ockeghem, *Collected Works*, iii, ed. Richard Wexler with Dragan Plamenac (Boston, 1992). My thanks to Professor Wexler for information from his edition prior to its publication.

3. 'Serial' Procedures

The third and final internal intersection between the works of Busnoys and Japart concerns their shared predilection for such serial-like procedures as retrograde motion, inversion, and even retrograde-inversion, as well as erudite and enigmatic verbal canons to help in their realization.[26] Table 18.4 lists the securely attributed works by Busnoys and Japart that use such techniques.[27] As with the combinative chanson, we can place Busnoys's and Japart's use of these techniques in a more meaningful context by noting their frequency in the works of other composers:[28] Obrecht: six occurrences, Isaac: four, Josquin and Mouton: three each, and Dufay: two. No other composer of the period utilized such techniques more than once, and there were few, indeed, who used them at all.

Though not included in Table 18.4, the setting of *J'ay pris amours* attributed to Busnoys in the *Odhecaton* and Ramos's *Musica practica*, but to Martini in Segovia deserves special mention. As I noted above, if the piece is by Busnoys, its implications could be significant. First, it would join the *L'homme armé* melody in the

TABLE 18.4. *Serial-like procedures in the works of Busnoys and Japart* (I = inversion; R = retrograde; R-I = retrograde inversion)

Composer/piece	Procedure	Verbal canon
A. Busnoys		
In hydraulis	R	no
Maintes femmes	R	yes
Missa L'homme armé	I	yes
unknown[a]	R	yes
B. Japart		
De tous biens plaine	I	yes
J'ay pris amours	R	yes

[a] Ramos attributes to Busnoys the canonic inscription 'Ubi α ibi ω et ubi ω finis esto'; the piece to which it belongs is, however, unknown. My thanks to Bonnie Blackburn for the citation.

[26] On the recognition of Busnoys's tendencies in this respect by such theorists as Bartolomeo Ramos de Pareja, Pietro Aaron, and Adrian Petit Coclico, see Higgins, 'Antoine Busnois', 15–17.

[27] For Busnoys, I have drawn on the inventory in R. Larry Todd, 'Retrograde, Inversion, Retrograde-Inversion, and Related Techniques in the Masses of Jacobus Obrecht', *Musical Quarterly*, 64 (1978), 50–78 at 72–3. I have omitted three of Todd's Busnoys entries because of their uncertain authorship: *J'ay pris amours*, attributed to Busnoys and Martini (see above, n. 21 and below); *Je suis venue*, ascribed to Busnoys and Hayne, and the Naples *L'homme armé* masses, for which Busnoys's authorship can only be conjectured. On Busnoys's claim to these masses, see Taruskin, *Busnoys LTW*, Commentary, 22–7, and id., 'Antoine Busnoys and the *L'Homme armé* Tradition', 275–83; Cohen, *The Six L'Homme armé Masses*, 68–70. For a view—altogether less convincing—that favours Caron as their composer, see Don Giller, 'The Naples *L'Homme armé* Masses and Caron: A Study in Musical Relationships', *Current Musicology*, 32 (1981), 7–28, and his Communication in *JAMS* 40 (1987), 143–6. Further on the use of retrograde (though from an earlier period), see Virginia Newes, 'Writing, Reading and Memorizing: The Transmission and Resolution of Retrograde Canons from the 14th and Early 15th Centuries', *Early Music*, 18 (1989), 218–34.

[28] The following is based on Todd, 'Retrograde, Inversion, Retrograde-Inversion', 71–6.

intersection of shared tunes, and thus constitute a second pre-existent melody set by both Busnoys and Japart. Second, and of greater significance, both Busnoys and Japart would have subjected it to serial-like manipulation, but with complementary procedures: Busnoys with inversion, Japart with retrograde motion. And still more significantly, Busnoys and Japart would be the only two composers to have so treated the popular melody. One wonders if Busnoys, at a 'composition lesson' with Japart, might have shown his student how he had manipulated *J'ay pris amours* with inversion, and then have said to him: 'Now you try it backwards!' On the other hand, since Japart and Martini were colleagues at Ferrara (see below), it is just as plausible and certainly easier to sustain that the same conversation took place there between those two composers.

In all, however, the three internal intersections—especially the shared fondness both for combinative chansons and for serial-like procedures—could conceivably signal a line of compositional influence leading from Busnoys to Japart. Any such influence, assuming, of course, that it involved direct contact, would have had to occur prior to Busnoys's full-fledged entry into the Burgundian chapel in October 1470,[29] or shortly thereafter. After that time we can be fairly certain that the career paths of Busnoys and Japart did not cross; and even if they did, the pattern of dissemination of Japart's works would make any such biographical details chronologically irrelevant to our central hypothesis. Whether formal or informal, a teacher–student relationship between Busnoys and Japart in the 1460s (perhaps even earlier) appears to be the most promising—if completely hypothetical—point of contact between the two composers.

External Intersections

The above reference to the dissemination of Japart's chansons leads nicely to the two external intersections, both of which concern certain aspects of the transmission of the two composers' works.

4. *Conflicting Attributions*

Of the six Japart chansons with conflicting attributions listed in Table 18.1 (above), three of them involve Busnoys. In fact, none of the other six composers has more than a single conflict with Japart. Table 18.5 now tallies by composer all the conflicting attributions in which Busnoys is involved.[30]

Two pieces of information immediately relevant to our central hypothesis emerge from Table 18.5: (i) just as Busnoys stood as the composer with whom Japart most often conflicted (see Table 18.1), so Japart is the composer with

---

[29] On the date, see Higgins, '*In hydraulis* Revisited', 43 and n. 32.

[30] Based on Higgins, 'Antoine Busnois', 313–36; in addition see note *a* to Table 18.5.

TABLE 18.5. *Conflicting attributions involving Busnoys*

Composers/piece(s)	Attributions	
	Busnoys	Other composer
Japart (3)		
Amours, amours	Bol Q17	Fl 229, Odh
Amours fait molt/Tant que nostre argent/Il est de bonne heure né	Bol Q17	Cas, Fl 229
Et qui la dira	Bol Q17	Fl 107bis
Caron (2)[a]		
Cent mille escus	Pix, Fl 229	Cas, CG XIII.27
Se brief je puys ma dame veoir	Pix	Fl 229
Hayne (2)		
J'ay bien choisi	Pix	Cas
Je suis venu	Pix	Cas
Isaac (2)		
S'amour vous fui (= *Malagrotta*)	Per 431	Par 676
Vous marchez/Vostre beauté	Niv	Vienna 18810
Ockeghem (2)		
D'ung aultre amer	Pix	Bol Q17, Cas, Dij, FR 2794, Niv, Par 2245
Quant ce vendra	Dij, Lab	EscB
Compère (1)		
Je ne fay plus	Bol Q17, Fl 229	Seg
Martini (1)		
J'ay pris amours	Odh	Seg
Mureau (1)		
Je ne fay plus	Bol Q17, Fl 229	CG XIII.27, Fl 176, Par 2245
'Pirson' (1)		
Amours fait molt tant	Bol Q17	Bas F.X.1–4

[a] One must at least consider the possibility of a third Busnoys–Caron conflict. About the problem surrounding the song *Pourtant se mon voloir*, see Brown, *A Florentine Chansonnier*, text vol., 250. Higgins, 'Antoine Busnois', omits the work from her catalogue.

whom Busnoys most frequently clashes, though admittedly by a narrower margin; and (ii) at least three of the next four composers in line—Caron, Hayne, Isaac, and Ockeghem, each of whom conflicts with Busnoys twice—have known biographical connections with Busnoys, thereby corroborating an observation that I made in my earlier study on conflicting attributions: the tendency for the music of composers whose careers intersected both geographically and chronologically to bear conflicting attributions in the sources.[31] For example, Busnoys

[31] See Atlas, 'Conflicting Attributions', 253–5 and 275–6.

and Hayne share a Burgundian court connection, while Busnoys and Ockeghem were together at Tours.[32] Caron, of course, has long been a problem, since there were apparently a number of musicians with that name. Yet all the Carons, with the seeming exception of Tinctoris's Firmin who is documented at Amiens in the 1420s,[33] were contemporaries of Busnoys and worked mainly within the narrow geographical orbit that extended from Cambrai to the nearby Burgundian court. Thus Caron the composer—no matter which Caron he may be—would no doubt have touched Busnoys's circle.[34] In the end, then, only Isaac, among the two-conflict composers, cannot be directly associated with Busnoys, although, to be sure, nothing is known of Isaac's career before he passed through Innsbruck in September 1484.[35]

In all, the three conflicting attributions between Busnoys and Japart speak strongly, I believe, for some kind of association between the two composers, although this hypothesis may be weakened by the fact that all three of the Busnoys ascriptions are transmitted in a single manuscript: Bologna Q 17. The three pieces involving the Busnoys–Japart conflicts appear almost in direct succession in that manuscript, and the fourth Busnoys attribution in the same manuscript, *Je ne fay plus*, is also challenged elsewhere.[36] Did Bologna Q 17 suffer from a 'Busnoys virus' inflicted by an infected fascicle-manuscript? Or was the virus perhaps Japart's? In the end we do not—perhaps cannot—know.

In my earlier article on conflicting attributions I suggested that repeated conflicts between two composers could signal a biographical association between them. I also made a corollary observation that conflicting attributions for a piece often coincide with substantive variants in the readings with which the piece was transmitted, and that these 'compositional' variants, in turn, might indicate that one of the composers named in the conflict might actually have revised the work

---

[32] On the Busnoys–Ockeghem connection, see Higgins, '*In hydraulis* Revisited', 70–8, and 'Antoine Busnois', 125–60.

[33] See James Thomson, *An Introduction to Philippe(?) Caron* (Musicological Studies, 9; Brooklyn, 1964), 4.

[34] The most thoughtful attempt to untangle Caron the composer from his namesakes is the essay by Barbara Haggh, above, Ch. 12.

[35] On Isaac in Innsbruck in 1484, see Martin Staehelin, 'Isaac, Heinrich', *New Grove*, ix. 329; Picker, *Henricus Isaac*, 4.

[36] See Richard Wexler, 'Newly Identified Works by Bartolomeo degli Organi in the MS Bologna Q17', *JAMS* 23 (1970), 107–18 at 116–18. The disposition within Bol Q17 of all pieces ascribed to Busnoys or Japart in any source is as follows (listed with number in Wexler's inventory, foliation in manuscript, text incipit, and attribution(s):

33	37ᵛ–38ʳ	*Je ne fay plus*	A. Busnois [Mureau/Compère]
58	63ᵛ–64ʳ	*Amours fait molt tant*	A. Busnois [Japart/Pirson]
59	64ᵛ–65ʳ	*Fille vous*	Yzac
60	65ᵛ–66ʳ	*Vostre bregieronnette*	Loyset Compere
61	66ᵛ–67ʳ	*Et qui la dira*	A. Busnois [Japart]
62	67ᵛ–68ʳ	*Amours, amours*	A. Busnois [Japart]
63	68ᵛ–69ʳ	*De tusche in busche*	Anon. [Japart/Isaac/Obrecht]
71	78ᵛ	*Tam bien* (superius and tenor only)	Anon. [Japart]

of the other.[37] Seen in this light, the readings in the three Busnoys–Japart conflicts may also point to compositional contact between the two composers. While Bologna Q 17 and Florence 107bis differ hardly at all with respect to their readings for *Et qui la dira*, there are some notable compositional variants in the transmission of both *Amours, amours* and *Amours fait molt tant*.

I shall limit myself to the discussion of one such variant for each piece. In *Amours, amours*, *Odhecaton* offers a reading in the altus at measures 41–3 that differs from those in both Bologna Q 17 and Florence 229 (see Ex. 18.1). Clearly, the altus in Bologna Q 17 and Florence 229 (where it is partially botched)[38] more successfully realizes the imitation with the superius (and, in part, the tenor) than does the altus of *Odhecaton*, the rhythm of which is also unimaginatively square (and thus rather Japart-like) in measure 42. Perhaps Japart, having composed the piece as it appears in *Odhecaton*, showed it to Busnoys, and received the following response from his teacher: 'But look how the imitation can be extended and tightened and the rhythm enlivened!', and Busnoys's revisions then worked their way into the dissemination of the work.

Ex. 18.1. Busnoys/Japart, *Amours, amours*, mm. 40–4: (*a*) altus in Bologna Q 17 and Florence 229; (*b*) altus in *Odhecaton*

(1) Odh: 4 minims   (2) Bol Q17: semibreve   (3) Fl 229 and Odh: *f*

(4) Bol Q17 and Odh: semibreve-minim   (5) Odh: dotted breve   (6) Bol Q17: lacking

[37] Atlas, 'Conflicting Attributions', 256 ff.
[38] We may also note that the scribe of Bol Q 17 simply omitted the semiminim *d'* and the minim *f'* in measure 43.

In the triple chanson *Amours fait molt tant/Il est de bonne heure né/Tant que nostre argent*, there is a series of variants that clearly defines a sub-tradition that appears only in two sources of German origin: Regensburg C 120 and Basle F. X. 1–4, where the piece is ascribed to 'Pirson' (Pierre de la Rue?). And as such, the variants may, admittedly, say more about this third composer's contributions to the piece than about the Busnoys–Japart question. The most notable of the variants appears in measures 18–19 of the superius, setting up a snippet of imitation with the altus at measures 21–2 (see Ex. 18.2). Again, whether Busnoys is revising Japart or vice versa or Pirson is revising either one or both of them is not clear. And I offer the example not as evidence towards the central argument, but as an instructive instance in which a third—and seemingly most peripheral—attribution for a piece may well have a legitimate claim to at least a portion of it.

Ex. 18.2. Busnoys/Japart, *Amours fait molt tant*, mm. 18–22: (*a*) all sources—with minor variants among them—except (*b*) Basle F. X. 1–4 and Regensburg C 120

(1) Bas F.X.1-4 and Reg C120 stand together against all other sources on at least four other significant occasions (all in the superius).

5. *Back-to-back Transmission*

The final intersection concerns the instances in which pieces attributed to Japart in one source or another, now including those with conflicting attributions, stand back to back with pieces ascribed to Busnoys in still another source. I have used two somewhat arbitrary conditions to define the intersection: (i) I have considered Japart's works as they are transmitted in four sources only (see below), and (ii) while I have considered works with conflicting attributions, I account only for those of Japart's pieces in the four sources that are either directly attributed to him or transmitted without an attribution at all (but for which an ascription to Japart appears in another source). Thus I have discounted those Japart-associated pieces (i.e. pieces attributed to him in at least one source) with conflicting attributions that appear in the four sources with an ascription to another composer, since in those cases the scribe/editor at least thought that he was entering a piece by someone other than Japart.

The four sources considered include Florence 229, written at Florence in the early 1490s, and *Odhecaton*, which, with nine and ten Japart-associated pieces, respectively, stand as the two largest repositories of Japart's music; the Casanatense chansonnier, written at Ferrara in 1481–2, and thus the only manuscript with music by Japart known to have been compiled in a musical centre where Japart himself was working at the time; and the anonymous *Tractatus de musica figurata et de contrapuncto*, which is included in the composite manuscript Paris 16664 and which is the only theoretical work to transmit a Japart composition, even if as a possible afterthought.[39] Table 18.6 shows the disposition of those Japart-associated works that meet the conditions just described. Table 18.7 then sums things up composer-by-composer.

What immediately strikes the eye in Tables 18.6 and 18.7 is the tendency for pieces attributed to Japart to be copied next to other pieces ascribed to him, a result, no doubt, of the tendency of *Odhecaton* to transmit clusters of Japart pieces one after the other.[40] But more important for our hypothesis are the two other composers next to whose works Japart's compositions most frequently appear: Busnoys (seven instances) and Martini (five). At the very least, Japart and Martini

---

[39] On the provenance of Fl 229 and Cas, see respectively: Howard Mayer Brown, *A Florentine Chansonnier from the Time of Lorenzo the Magnificent: Florence, Biblioteca Nazionale Centrale, MS Banco Rari 229* (Monuments of Renaissance Music, 7; Chicago, 1983), i. 9 ff.; and Lockwood, *Music in Renaissance Ferrara*, 224–6. On Paris 16664, see Willem Hering, 'De polyfone composities in het manuscript no. 16664 uit het *Fonds Latin* van de Bibliothèque Nationale te Parijs', *TVNM* 39 (1989), 28–37; all the pieces are transcribed in Hering's similarly entitled dissertation, University of Amsterdam (1987), which, however, I have not been able to consult. See also Nanie Bridgman, 'Paroles et musique dans le manuscrit latin 16664 de la Bibliothèque Nationale de Paris', in Ursula Günther and Ludwig Finscher (eds.), *Musik und Text in der Mehrstimmigkeit des 14. und 15. Jahrhunderts* (Göttinger musikwissenschaftliche Arbeiten, 10; Kassel, 1984), 383–409.

[40] The Japart-next-to-Japart total would zoom upward if *Canti B* and *Canti C* were taken into account. *Canti C* offers two Japart chansons back to back on fos. 52ᵛ–54ʳ (*Fortuna d'un gran tempo* and *Loier mi fault ung carpentier*) and then three in a row on fos. 78ᵛ–81ʳ (*Il est de bonne heure né/L'homme armé*, *De tous biens plaine*, and *Pour passer temps/Plus ne chasceray sans gens*). The three remaining Japart pieces in *Canti C* appear singly, though in one instance two of them are separated by only one non-Japart composition. Finally, although *Canti B* has only two Japart chansons (*J'ay pris amours* and *Je cuide/De tous biens plaine*), they appear one after the other on fos. 33ᵛ–35ʳ. In all, the three Petrucci prints transmit twenty of the twenty-three chansons associated with Japart, with thirteen of those twenty being transmitted in Japart-next-to-Japart fashion. That Japart enjoyed more than a coincidental relationship either with Petrucci's firm itself or with (one of) the printer's source(s) is something that must seriously be considered.

TABLE 18.6. *Japart-associated pieces (with or without direct attributions) in Florence 229,* Odhecaton, *Casanatense 2856, and Paris 16664*
(attributions in inventoried source in capitals, those from other sources in square brackets)

Source/folios	Attributions	Pieces
Florence 229[a]		
44ᵛ–45ʳ	[Martini]	*Martinella*
45ᵛ–46ʳ	JAPART [Josquin/Joye]	*J'ay bien rise tant*
46ᵛ–47ʳ	Anon.	*En riens de remede*
104ᵛ–105ʳ	REGIS	*S'il vous plait*
105ᵛ–106ʳ	JAPART	*Nençiozza mia*
106ᵛ–107ʳ	[Hayne]	*A l'audience*
110ᵛ–111ʳ	RUBINET	[no text]
111ᵛ–112ʳ	JAPART	*Cela sans plus*
112ᵛ–113ʳ	[Busnoys/Hayne]	*J'ay bien choisi*
151ᵛ–152ʳ	[Busnoys]	*Je ne demande*
152ᵛ–153ʳ	[Japart]	*Helas, qu'il est*
153ᵛ–154ʳ	ISAAC	*Maudit soit*
156ᵛ–158ʳ	MARTINI	*Fortuna d'un gran tempo*
158ᵛ–159ʳ	JAPART	*J'ay pris amours* (II)
159ᵛ–160ʳ	STOCKEM	*Hellas dame*
161ᵛ–162ʳ	[Weerbeke]	*Anima mea*
162ᵛ–163ʳ	[Japart/Isaac/Obrecht]	*T'meiskin*
163ᵛ–164ʳ	JAPART/[Busnoys/Pirson]	*Amours fait molt tant*
164ᵛ–165ʳ	JOSQUIN	*Adieu mes amours*
170ᵛ–172ʳ	CARON	*Madame qui tant*
172ᵛ–173ʳ	[Japart/Busnoys]	*Amours, amours*
173ᵛ–174ʳ	MARTINI	[no text]
Odhecaton[b]		
3ᵛ–4ʳ	DE ORTO	*Ave Maria*
4ᵛ–5ʳ	[Japart/Congiet]	*Je cuide*
5ᵛ–6ʳ	Anon.	*Hor oïres une chanson*
8ᵛ–9ʳ	Anon.	*J'ay pris amours/De tous biens plaine*
9ᵛ–10ʳ	JAPART	*Nençiozza mia*
10ᵛ–11ʳ	[Busnoys/Mureau/Compère]	*Je ne fay plus*
22ᵛ–23ʳ	[Hayne]	*De tous biens plaine*
23ᵛ–24ʳ	JAPART	*J'ay pris amours* (I)
24ᵛ–25ʳ	JAPART	*Se congie pris*
25ᵛ–26ʳ	JAPART/[Busnoys]	*Amours, amours*
26ᵛ–27ʳ	JAPART	*Cela sans plus*
27ᵛ–28ʳ	[Obrecht]	*Rompeltier*
31ᵛ–32ʳ	Anon.	*Ne l'oseray je dire*
32ᵛ–33ʳ	JAPART	*Helas, qu'il est*
33ᵛ–34ʳ	[Japart/Busnoys/Pirson]	*Amours fait molt tant*
34ᵛ–35ʳ	NINOT LE PETIT	*Nostre chambriere*
35ᵛ–36ʳ	BUSNOYS	*Acordes moy*
36ᵛ–37ʳ	JAPART	*Tambien mi son pensada*
37ᵛ–38ʳ	BUSNOYS (1st edition only)	*Le serviteur*

Source/folios	Attributions	Pieces
Casanatense 2856		
107ᵛ–108ʳ	MARTINI	*Tousjours biens*
108ᵛ–109ʳ	JAPART	*Trois filles*
109ᵛ–110ʳ	BOSSRIN	*Et trop penser*
156ᵛ–157ʳ	MARTINI	*Non seul uno*
157ᵛ–159ʳ	JAPART/[Busnoys/Pirson]	*Amours fait molt tant*
159ᵛ–161ʳ	OBRECHT	*Se bien fait*
Paris 16664		
87ᵛ– 88ʳ	BUSNOYS	*Pucellotte*
88ᵛ– 89ʳ	JAPART	*Trois filles*
89ᵛ– 90ʳ	Anon.	*Au matin*

ᵃ Fl 229 also transmits *Je cuide* (fos. 95ᵛ–96ʳ), but with an attribution to Congiet and surrounded by two anonymous songs, *Vray Dieu d'amours* and *Faictes moy ung tout seul plaisir*.

ᵇ Odh also transmits *T'meiskin* (fos. 29ᵛ–30ʳ), but with an attribution to Isaac (first edition, later deleted) and surrounded by Compère's *Allons ferons barbe* and his *Ung franc archier*.

TABLE 18.7. *Frequency of appearance of Japart-associated pieces adjacent to other Japart-associated pieces and works by other composers in Florence 229,* Odhecaton, Casanatense 2856, *and Paris 16664*

Japart	10	De Orto	1
Busnoys	7	Isaac	1
Martini	5	Josquin	1
Anon.	5	Mureau	1
Hayne	3	Ninot le Petit	1
Obrecht	2	Regis	1
Bossrin	1	Rubinet	1
Caron	1	Stockem	1
Compère	1	Weerbeke	1

share a well-documented Ferrarese connection.[41] And if we even allow for the chance that Japart may have been at Milan as early as 1474,[42] perhaps the Japart–Martini relationship extends back to that year, as Martini spent a good portion of 1474 at Milan.[43]

If, then, there is a correlation between the tendency for Japart- and Martini-associated pieces to be transmitted back to back and the documented intersection

[41] On Martini at Ferrara, see Lockwood, *Music at Ferrara*, especially 167–72.

[42] See above and n. 9. To be sure, the name Japart does not appear on any of the three Milanese rosters dated 4 July 1474 (on which Martini is included), 30 Mar. 1475, and 4 Dec. 1475; the rosters are given in Claudio Sartori, 'Josquin des Prés cantore del duomo di Milano (1459–1472)', *Annales musicologiques*, 4 (1956), 64–5.

[43] Lockwood, *Music at Ferrara*, 168.

of their careers at Ferrara and if, as Paula Higgins and Peter Wright have noted, there are similar correlations in connection with both Busnoys–Ockeghem and — though certainly less pronounced — Brassart–de Sarto,[44] we must surely consider the possibility of such a correlation between Japart and Busnoys, especially in the light of the four other intersections discussed above. Indeed, I find the paired transmission of Busnoys's *Pucelotte* and Japart's *Trois filles estoient* in Paris 16664 (nos. 3 and 4, respectively)[45] particularly intriguing, since the music appended to the anonymous treatise in which they so appear consists of only thirteen pieces, and the composers of only two of them are known: Busnoys and Japart. If, as I believe we should, we read any significance at all into back-to-back transmission of pieces by different composers,[46] we must allow that at least some scribes and compilers of manuscripts/prints at least occasionally thought of pieces by Japart and Busnoys as belonging together.

To conclude: while I have clearly not demonstrated conclusively that the careers of Busnoys and Japart intersected, much less that there was 'compositional contact' between them, or that Japart studied with Busnoys, the intersections that I have identified seem compelling none the less. And if no one of the intersections is entirely convincing by itself, the number and variety of musical correspondences seem more than merely coincidental.

In the end, however, the more relevant question is not whether Japart did or did not study composition with Busnoys (though it would certainly be interesting to know just whom Busnoys might have taught), but rather the question of what criteria we may invoke to posit a teacher-student relationship when hard documentation is lacking. And if the intersections that point to a possible Busnoys–Japart relationship provide a sufficently sound foundation for these methodological questions and speculations, they may eventually prove useful in disentangling the knotty web of student–teacher relationships that must have obtained among other fifteenth-century composers as well.

[44] The Busnoys–Ockeghem and Brassart–de Sarto transmission patterns are discussed in Higgins, 'Antoine Busnois', 242, who notes the tendency for pieces by Busnoys and Ockeghem to stand next to one another in both Dijon and Nivelle, and Wright, 'Johannes Brassart and Johannes de Sarto', 57–8.

[45] We might note that there are two other manuscripts that include both of these pieces: Casanatense, which has the Busnoys piece on fos. 81v–82r and the Japart chanson on fos. 83v–84r (so that there is but one intervening piece between them), and Pixérécourt, where the pieces occupy fos. 186v–187r and 104v–105r, respectively, and are thus widely separated.

[46] I am currently preparing an article that correlates back-to-back transmission of the same pair of pieces in two or more sources with composer attributions and readings. Briefly, I offer the hypothesis that some pieces not only circulated as part of a pair in a 'fascicle-manuscript' of one type or another, but that the fascicle-manuscript itself contained notated variants for one or both of the pieces, a kind of miniature 'variorum edition', as it were.

19

Poliziano, *Primavera*, and Perugia 431: New Light on *Fortuna desperata*

💇✪💇

HONEY MECONI

ORTUNA DESPERATA was the most popular Italian song of the fifteenth century and one of the most frequently used of all polyphonic models of the Renaissance, inspiring more than forty derivative settings over a period of almost seventy-five years by masters such as Josquin, Obrecht, Isaac, and Senfl, as well as numerous lesser-known and anonymous composers.[1] Surviving today are five masses (by Josquin, Obrecht, 'Periquin', and two anonymous composers),[2] thirty-six ensemble settings,[3] and two intabulations that

A shorter version of this article was read at the Twenty-Second Conference on Medieval and Renaissance Music, The University of Glasgow, July 1994, as well as at the Sixtieth Annual Meeting of the American Musicological Society, Minneapolis, 1994. My work on *Fortuna desperata* and other art-song reworkings has been supported by a Fellowship at Villa I Tatti in 1986–7 (made possible by grants from the Leopold Schepp Foundation and Hanna Kiel Fund, for which I am very grateful) and by a Faculty Research Grant from Rice University in 1987–8. Among the many people with whom I have discussed *Fortuna desperata* I should especially like to acknowledge David Fallows, Paula Higgins, Joshua Rifkin, Patricia Rubin, and Reinhard Strohm.

[1] The most comprehensive listing of these works appears in Honey Meconi, 'Art-Song Reworkings: An Overview', *Journal of the Royal Musical Association*, 119 (1994), 1–42 at 31–3. To this can be added three other settings, the *Esurientes* section of an anonymous four-voice *Magnificat sexti toni* found in Wrocław, Biblioteka Uniwersytecka, Oddział Rękopisów, MS I-F-428, fos. 164(a)ᵛ–164(b)ʳ; an anonymous four-voice *Missa Fortuna* in Herdringen, Schloss Fürstenberg, Bibliothek, MS 9821 (*olim* Paderborn, Erzbischöfliche Akademische Bibliothek), fos. 228–34; and Cabbiliau's five-voice motet *Anima mea liquefacta est* from Susato's *Liber nonus ecclesiasticarum cantionum* (RISM 1554⁹). I am grateful to Barton Hudson and Bonnie Blackburn respectively for bringing the last two works to my attention.

[2] The best modern edition of Obrecht's mass can be found in Jacob Obrecht, *Collected Works* (New Obrecht Edition), iv, ed. Barton Hudson (Utrecht, 1986), 49–91. For Josquin see Josquin des Prez, *Werken, Missen*, Deel 1, ed. A. Smijers (Amsterdam and Leipzig, 1926–31), 81–104; the version for the *New Josquin Edition* is being prepared by Barton Hudson. The mass by Periquin, who might be Pierre de la Rue, is found in Tarazona 3, fos. 181ᵛ–191ʳ (114ᵛ–124ʳ). In addition to the anonymous mass mentioned above, another appears in Bologna, Archivio Musicale della Fabbriceria di San Petronio, MS A. XXXVIII (*olim* CC), fos. 114ᵛ–123ʳ. There are no modern editions of these last three works.

[3] The ensemble settings will appear in *Fortuna desperata: Thirty-Six Settings of an Italian Song*, ed. Honey Meconi (Recent Researches in the Music of the Middle Ages and Early Renaissance; Madison, forthcoming).

probably come from ensemble originals.[4] All three voices from the original composition were used in later pieces, which include secular cantus-firmus settings, *si
placet* versions, combinative works, replacement contratenor compositions, liturgical and quasi-liturgical pieces, and works with Italian, French, German, and
Latin texts. A partial listing of settings, providing a chronology of appearances of
the various versions up to *c*.1510, appears in Appendix A.[5]

Although these works have figured centrally in studies by Otto Gombosi,
Alfred Loeffler, Julie Cumming, and Martin Picker,[6] many basic questions about
Fortuna desperata and its progeny remain unanswered, including when, where,
why, and by whom the original three-voice song was written. Another significant
problem, why composers reworked this piece so frequently, similarly warrants
further attention. Surprisingly, an aspect of the work usually ignored, its text (see
Table 19.1), provides considerable illumination on this composition's history.[7]

The three-stanza text heretofore associated with the song appears in a single
manuscript, Perugia 431. Another manuscript, Paris 676, gives the first two stanzas of this text, and five more music manuscripts present the initial strophe.[8] But
there exists another text source, brought to the attention of musicologists in
1939 but unexplored until now.[9] This is the poetry collection London
16439, purchased by the British Museum from the book dealers Payne
and Foss on 7 January 1847,[10] and formerly in the Biblioteca Chigiana in

---

[4] An intabulation attributed to Othmar Luscinius, where the tenor of the original appears in the lowest
voice, is in Berlin 40026, fos. 133ᵛ–135ʳ. A setting ascribed to HB (Hans Buchner), likewise with the original tenor in the lowest voice, is in the same tablature, fos. 135ᵛ–136ᵛ. Modern editions of these can be
found in *Die Orgeltabulatur des Leonhard Kleber, Zweiter Teil*, ed. Karin Berg-Kotterba (Das Erbe deutscher
Musik, 92; Frankfurt, 1987), 64–7 and 67–70, respectively.

[5] One source for the original version of *Fortuna desperata*, Frankfurt am Main, Stadt- und
Universitätsbibliothek, Fragm. lat. VII 20, does not appear in App. A since its date remains uncertain. This
source, recently identified by David Fallows, was found in the binding of a copy of Thomas Aquinas's
Summa theologica (pt. 2, bk. 1) published in Venice by Theodorus de Ragazonibus on 31 Mar. 1490. It is
not clear whether the music folios, which apparently came from a German-speaking territory, were part of
the original binding or from a later rebinding. Only two voices (superius and tenor) of *Fortuna desperata* are
present. My thanks to David Fallows for generously sharing his discovery.

[6] Otto Johannes Gombosi, *Jacob Obrecht: Eine stilkritische Studie* (Leipzig, 1925), 99–116; Alfred
Loeffler, 'Fortuna Desperata: A Contribution to the Study of Musical Symbolism in the Renaissance',
Student Musicologists at Minnesota, 3 (1968–9), 1–30; Julie E. Cumming, 'The Goddess Fortuna Revisited',
Current Musicology, 30 (1980), 7–23; and Martin Picker, above, Ch. 17. I am grateful to Professor Picker
for providing a copy of his paper in advance of publication.

[7] My thanks to Massimo Ossi for assistance with translation.

[8] Paris 4379, Segovia, London 35087, Florence 167, and Cortona 96. The text appearing in Table 19.1
is a collation of the Perugia 431 and Paris 676 readings; variants for all textual sources are given in Meconi,
Fortuna desperata.

[9] Cited in Federico Ghisi, 'Poesie musicali italiane: Canzonette a ballo, strambotti, frottole, canti e
trionfi carnascialeschi', *Note d'archivio per la storia musicale*, 16 (1939), 72. I should like to thank David
Fallows for bringing the London collection to my attention.

[10] On fo. 1ʳ of the manuscript is the inscription 'Purchased of Payne and Foss Jan 7. 1847'. Payne & Foss
were major London booksellers who collected in Italy in the 1840s; see A. N. L. Munby, *The Formation of
the Phillipps Library up to the Year 1840* (Phillipps Studies, 3; Cambridge, 1954), 43–5; and id., *The
Formation of the Phillipps Library from 1841 to 1872* (Phillipps Studies, 4; Cambridge, 1956), 1–3. The manuscript was part of a lot (now catalogued as Add. 16406–16558) purchased on 10 Oct. 1846, for which payment was deferred for financial reasons until 7 Jan. The manuscript appears to have come to Payne and Foss,
with a number of others, from the Rezzi family of Rome. According to his diary, Sir Frederic Madden, then

TABLE 19.1. Fortuna desperata *texts*

Perugia 431/Paris 676 version:

Fortuna desperata,	Hopeless fortune,
Iniqua e maledecta,	Unjust and cursed,
Che, de tal dona electa,	Who has defamed the reputation
La fama hai denigrata.	Of so distinguished a lady.
Fortuna desperata	
O morte dispiatata,	O pitiless death,
Inimica e crudele,	Hostile and cruel,
Che, d'alto più che stelle,	Who has thus lowered one
Tu l'hai cusì abassata.	Who was higher than the stars.
F.d.	
Meschina e despietata,	Wretched and pitiless!
Ben piangere posso may,	Well can I cry now,
Et desiro finire	And I desire to end
Li mei guay.	My woes.

London 16439 version:

Canzonetta intonata antica[a]

Fortuna disperata,	Hopeless fortune,
Iniqua & maladecta,	Unjust and cursed,
Che di tal Donna electa	Who has denied [defamed] the reputation
La fama ha dineg[r]ata.[b]	Of so distinguished a lady.
Fortuna disperata,	
Iniqua & maladecta.	
Sempre sia bestemmiata,	May your treacherous faith
La tua perfida fede,	Always be cursed,
Che in te non ha merzede,	For there is no mercy in you,
Ne fermeza fondata.	Nor fixed constancy.
Fortuna disperata,	
Iniqua & maladecta.	
O morte dispietata,	O pitiless death,
Inimica & crudele,	Hostile and cruel,
Amara piu che fele,	More bitter than bile,
Di malitia fondata.	Founded in malice.
Fortunata disperata,	
Iniqua & maladecta.	

    Finis.
[Faxii Julii de Medicis de Florentia][c]
M.D.X X.

---

  [a] Scribe 4 (= 1?). Unless otherwise indicated, the remainder of the text was written by Scribe 3 (= 1 or 2?).

  [b] Correction by Scribe 4?

  [c] Inscription (erased) and date by Scribe X.

Rome.[11] Comparison between the Perugia/Paris text and the London 16439 text reveals significant differences. Although the first strophes are identical, and the first two lines of the third London 16439 stanza open the second Perugia/Paris stanza, the similarities cease there.

The superior technical construction of the London 16439 version—as well as its presence in a literary manuscript—argues for its being the original. Each stanza has four seven-syllable lines and the poem follows the overall rhyme scheme of abba acca adda. The Perugia/Paris version, on the other hand, comes apart technically in the final stanza. The first two stanzas are regular (abba acca), but the final one (aded) circumvents the anticipated rhyme scheme of the poem. Further, the three syllables of the last line ('li mei guay') fall far short of the seven that characterize the others. In addition, unlike the London 16439 version, both Perugia 431 and Paris 676 have problems in their readings.[12] The last line of stanza 1 in

Keeper of Manuscripts in the British Museum, visited Payne and Foss on 21 Sept. 1846 to inspect and make a selection from the Rezzi manuscripts; Madden's diary records several manuscripts among those now classified as Add. 16406–16441. Those he selected were sent to him on 26 Sept. for approval. I am greatly indebted to Dr Scot McKendrick, Curator in the British Library Department of Manuscripts, for this information regarding the British Museum's purchase of the manuscript (private comm., 9 Aug. 1994). For bibliography on the Rezzi library, see Carlo Frati, *Dizionario bio-bibliografico dei bibliotecari e bibliofili italiani dal sec. XIV al XIX* (Biblioteca di bibliografia italiana, 13; Florence, 1933), 492–3.

[11] According to Ms Philippa Marks and Dr Mirjam Foot, Collections and Preservation, The British Library (private comm., 3 Aug. 1994), the manuscript was probably both cropped and bound upon or shortly after its acquisition by the Museum, though no 19th-c. records exist to confirm this supposition. In the Museum it was also provided with foliation, numbering of the gatherings in the upper left-hand corner of the first folio of each, modern paper folios before and after the parchment, marbled end-leaves, and cloth strips. Some of these alterations may have occurred as late as 1987, when a box was made for the manuscript. The manuscript was apparently stolen from the Biblioteca Chigiana, where it had the shelf-mark 2333 (later M.IV.81); when Giosuè Carducci wished to consult it in 1858 for his Poliziano edition he was informed that it had been lost for about twenty years. See Angelo Ambrogini Poliziano, *Le stanze, l'Orfeo e le rime de messer Angelo Ambrogini Poliziano*, ed. Giosuè Carducci (Florence, 1863), p. lxxxi. For additional information on London 16439 see ibid., p. cxxxviii; *Catalogue of Additions to the Manuscripts in the British Musuem in the Years MDCCCXLVI–MDCCCXLVII* (n.p., 1864; repr. Norwich, 1964), 209; Angelo Poliziano, *Opere volgari di messer Angelo Ambrogini Poliziano*, ed. Tommaso Casini (Florence, 1885), pp. ix–xii; Alessandro Palma di Cesnola, *Catalogo di manoscritti italiani esistenti nel Museo britannico di Londra* (Turin, 1890), 41, nos. 531–533; Vincenzo Pernicone, 'Sul testo delle Stanze del Poliziano', *Giornale storica della letteratura italiana*, 129 (1952), 1–25; Angelo Poliziano, *Stanze cominciate per la giostra di Giuliano de' Medici*, ed. Vincenzo Pernicone (Biblioteca del 'Giornale Storico', Testi, 1; Turin, 1954), pp. xix–xxi; Domenico de Robertis, 'Censimento dei manoscritti di rime di Dante II', *Studi Danteschi*, 38 (1961), 243–4; Vincenzo Pernicone, 'La tradizione manoscritta dell' "Orfeo" del Poliziano', in *Studi di varia umanità in onore di Francesco Flora* (Milan, 1963), 362, 365–8; Ida Maïer, *Les Manuscrits d'Ange Politien: Catalogue descriptif* (Travaux d'humanisme et Renaissance, 70; Geneva, 1965), 171–7; Andrew G. Watson, *Catalogue of Dated and Datable Manuscripts c. 700–1600 in The Department of Manuscripts, The British Library*, 2 vols. (London, 1979), i. 165; Daniela Delcorno Branca, 'Per un catalogo delle "Rime" del Poliziano', *Lettere italiane*, 23 (1971), 226; ead., 'Note sulla tradizione delle "Rime" del Poliziano', *Rinascimento*, 15 (1975), 64–6, 69, 72; Guglielmo Gorni, 'Novità su testo e tradizione delle "Stanze" di Poliziano', *Studi di filologia Italiana*, 33 (1975), 242, 250, 253, 255–6, 259, 262, 264; Daniela Delcorno Branca, 'Il ms. Riccardiano 2723 e la formazione delle antiche sillogi di "Rime" del Poliziano', *Rinascimento*, 16 (1976), 76–9, 82–92, 95; ead., *Sulla tradizione delle rime del Poliziano* (Florence, 1979), 143–8 *et passim*; Angelo Poliziano, *Rime*, ed. Daniela Delcorno Branca (Florence, 1986), 55–60 *et passim* (here mistakenly identified as 16436); Lorenzo de' Medici, *Stanze*, ed. Raffaella Castagnola (Florence, 1986), p. xx; and Paul Oskar Kristeller, *Iter Italicum accedunt alia itinera: A Finding List of Uncatalogued or Incompletely Catalogued Humanistic Manuscripts of the Renaissance in Italian and Other Libraries*, iv: Great Britain to Spain (London and Leiden, 1989), 100–1.

[12] London 16439 has one minor error at the start of the the final refrain, where the scribe mistakenly wrote 'Fortunata' instead of 'Fortuna'. On the bracketed *r* in l. 14 see below, n. 28.

Paris 676 incorrectly reads 'La fama tua hai denigrata', while the final verse of stanza 2 in Perugia 431 is the metrically faulty 'Ma si abassata'. The Perugia/Paris text is clearly an inexpert—albeit powerful—revision of London's. With the deletion of the impersonal second stanza and the last two lines of the third, the new poet has intensified the spirit of the original. Now the reference to death is explicitly linked with the unfortunate *donna,* and the new final strophe permits the narrator to voice his pain directly and include a veiled threat of suicide. The resulting poem is far more personal and arguably more effective.

Significantly, neither Perugia 431 nor Paris 676 set the text to the original three-part version of the song, presenting instead the most popular *si placet* setting; in other words, they transmit *Fortuna desperata* in a slightly later stage of its musical life. The other five musical sources for the text—including all texted sources of the original version—present the first stanza only and could theoretically belong to either poetic version of *Fortuna desperata.*

Still, alterations to the original text apparently occurred not far into the song's history—Perugia 431 is one of the earlier sources for a *Fortuna desperata* setting— and possibly in Naples, for the Perugia manuscript is Neapolitan, as may be Paris 4379, the earliest surviving musical source. Curiously, Fausto Torrefranca, working with the Perugia/Paris text but apparently unaware of Perugia's provenance, suggested a southern, possibly Neapolitan, origin for the song.[13]

The lengthy refrain of London 16439—the first two lines of stanza 1 reappear after each stanza—initially appears to distance its text from the composition that we know, whose only musical repetition is stanzaic. But two circumstances permit us to link poem and music. First, the heading in London 16439 shows that the writer knew that 'Fortuna desperata' had a musical setting, for the text is entitled 'Canzonetta intonata antica' (old canzonetta set to music). Two other poems in the manuscript are also designated as 'canzonetta intonata'; one of these, *Questo mostrarsi adirata di fore* has three known polyphonic settings (by Isaac, Bartolomeo Fiorentino, and Pintelli).[14]

---

[13] Fausto Torrefranca, *Il segreto del quattrocento: musiche ariose e poesia popolaresca* (Milan, 1939), 297. Torrefranca did not supply his reasons for this assessment, although he did cite as 'obvious dialect' Perugia's reading of 'ma si abassata' for 'm'ha' si' abasatta' (me la *sei* abassatta).

[14] For bibliographic information on the *Questo mostrarsi adirata di fore* settings see Giulio Cattin, 'Le rime del Poliziano nelle fonti musicali', in *Umanesimo e rinascimento a Firenze e Venezia,* 2 vols. (Miscellanea di studi in onore di Vittore Branca, 3; Florence, 1983), i. 387. The other 'canzonetta intonata', *Io ti ringrazio, Amore,* has no surviving settings but is included by Cattin in his list of Poliziano poems set to music on the basis of the London designation; see ibid. 386. A polyphonic setting survives for a third Poliziano poem from London, *Contento in foco sto come fenice,* but it receives no special heading in the manuscript. The designation of canzonetta for these three poems suggests a revision of one modern scholarly use of this term. Frank D'Accone has proposed to separate canzonette from ballate on the basis of syllable count, with the former containing eight syllables per line and the latter seven or eleven; see *Music of the Florentine Renaissance,* 11 vols., ed. Frank A. D'Accone (CMM 32; Neuhausen-Stuttgart, 1969–85), i, p. iv; ii, p. xi. *Fortuna desperata,* however, would be a ballata by this reasoning, as would *Questo mostrarsi adirata di fore* and *Io ti ringrazio, Amore*—the three canzonette of London 16439. Moreover, each of these three poems features a completely different formal structure in terms of rhyme scheme, refrain pattern, and numbers of lines. It thus seems that, in contrast to other genres, the term was used extremely freely without connotation of any specific technical features.

Second, although usually overlooked, refrain structure of a kind is present in the song as it appears in Paris 4379, Perugia 431, and Segovia. Ex. 19.1 shows the song's underlay as given in Paris 4379; the superius concludes with the words 'fortuna desperata'.[15] Segovia presents the same concluding text in the same place. Perugia 431 makes no attempt to underlay the text but instead strings out all three stanzas sequentially through the superius and tenor parts; as seen in Table 19.1, the first stanza is followed by 'fortuna desperata' and the second by 'f.d.' Even Paris 676 hints at a similar textual refrain. Its final line of text, 'la fama tua hai denigrata', extends from measures 42 through 51 in the superius; yet the last note of the piece is texted with another 'ta'—possibly indicating a repetition of the preceding text but perhaps referring instead to a 'fortuna desperata' refrain.

In other words, *Fortuna desperata* uses a refrain that is textual only, not musical, a procedure extremely rare in fifteenth-century song. That this refrain appears solely in the three earliest texted musical sources—Paris 4379, Perugia 431, and Segovia—is not surprising. The song as given in Ex. 19.1 is drawn from the earliest surviving manuscript and very probably represents its original form. As the years progressed the work was transmitted with bass rather than tenor clef for the lowest part, with signature flats in all voices rather than partial signatures, with the final superius cadence changed to a leading-note rather than under-third cadence, with the concluding bassus note moved from c' to f to eliminate its octave-leap cadence, and with numerous other shifts. The disappearance of the textual refrain, an unusual feature of the song, fits with the predilection of later scribes and composers to make the piece more 'normal' in appearance.[16]

Given that London 16439 apparently presents the original version of the text, we are naturally eager to know more about the manuscript. A summary of its contents appears in Appendix B, on the right-hand side.[17] Except for *Fortuna desperata*, four poems by Dante,[18] and five by Lorenzo de'

---

[15] Although Reinhard Strohm, *The Rise of European Music 1380–1500* (Cambridge, 1993), 620, suggests that the words really only fit the tenor, none of the surviving sources shows this texting pattern. Of the texted sources, Paris 4379, Segovia, and Paris 676 underlay superius only. London 35087 texts all voices, and a similar practice is implied for Perugia, which supplies but does not really underlay all three stanzas of text and then states 'In ciascum parte e data fortuna desperata etc' (in each part is given fortuna desperata etc). Florence 167 and Cortona 96 are cantus-firmus settings using the superius only of *Fortuna desperata*, each time fully texted. While the fit between text and music is admittedly weaker than with many contemporary Italian songs, it is still extremely unlikely that *Fortuna desperata* is a contrafact of a French chanson. First, stripped of all text, the work looks far more like an Italian song (because of its extensively homophonic texture) than a French chanson. Second, not all 15th-c. Italian songs are syllabic. Finally, the addition of the textual refrain makes the work considerably less melismatic. Concerning the appearance of the music itself, it is unclear from the manuscript whether the flat affecting the bottom voice's *e* in m. 27 should similarly govern the *e* in m. 35. For a discussion of the problems involved see Meconi, *Fortuna desperata*.

[16] For a full discussion of the song's evolution, see Meconi, *Fortuna desperata*.

[17] The Riccardiana manuscript, on the left-hand side, will be discussed below. For further information on London's contents see Maïer, *Les Manuscrits d'Ange Politien*, 171–7; and Poliziano, *Rime*, 55–60.

[18] His canzoni 'Così nel mio parlar voglio esser aspro', 'Amor che ne la mente mi ragiona', 'Amor, che movi tua vertù da cielo', and 'Io sento sì d'Amor la gran possanza'. Editions and translations may be found in *Dante's Lyric Poetry*, 2 vols., ed. K. Foster and P. Boyde (Oxford, 1967), i. 170–5, 106–11, 116–23, and 123–9, respectively.

Ex. 19.1. *Fortuna desperata* (Paris 4379, fos. 40ᵛ–41ʳ)

Ex. 19.1. *cont.*

Medici,[19] this substantial collection is otherwise exclusively dedicated to works from the pen of the famous humanist and poet Angelo Poliziano (1454–94), intimate of the Medici circle and one-time member of Lorenzo's household.[20] One of the two most important sources for Poliziano's Italian works, the manuscript contains his Latin elegy 'In violas a Venere mea dono acceptas', among his finest efforts in that genre, as well as the famous *Stanze cominciate per la Giostra del Magnifico Giuliano de' Medici*, an unquestionably great work of Italian literature and considered by many to be Poliziano's poetic masterpiece.[21] In addition to a large number of Poliziano's shorter Italian poems, the manuscript also contains his drama *Orfeo* and the letter from the author to Carlo Canale giving permission for publication of the drama.[22]

The manuscript currently consists of seventy-seven parchment folios flanked by modern paper ones.[23] The collection originally began with seven quinternions (fos. 3–67), copied by Scribe 1, who included guide-words at the end of each gathering.[24] The first folio (3ʳ) was attractively decorated with a professionally prepared illuminated spray initial; the other decoration in this first section,

---

[19] These include a fragment from his second *Selva* and four *canzoni a ballo*. The *Selva* fragment, Ottave 2–7, appears on fos. 31ʳ⁻ᵛ; the manuscript is missing one folio before fo. 31 and one after. For a critical edition of the text see Lorenzo de' Medici, *Stanze*, ed. Castagnola; the relevant lines are on pp. 3–6. Castagnola reverses the traditional ordering of the *Selve*; the London excerpt is from what she calls the first *Selva* and others call the second. The *canzoni a ballo* are 'I non mi vo scusar', 'Ben ch'io rida balli o conti', 'Donne belle i'ho cercato', and 'Ecci egli alcuna in questa compagnia'; for editions see Lorenzo de' Medici, *Tutti le opere*, 2 vols., ed. Paolo Orvieto (Rome, [1992]), ii. 732–3, 711, 724–5, and 723–4 respectively.

[20] That 'Fortuna desperata' is not Poliziano's is evident for several reasons. Even to a non-specialist it lacks that poet's customary elegance; moreover, it uses a formal structure unique in his output. Further, the work has been known to Poliziano scholars for more than two centuries without once appearing in an edition of his works. Only Casini (Poliziano, *Opere volgari*, xii) went so far as to say he was 'not certain' the work was by Poliziano, but he did not include it in either the 'incerte' or 'apocrife' sections of his edition. Most telling is the 15th-c. evidence. Except for London 16439, no manuscript or print of Poliziano's work contains this poem. Scribe 4, to be discussed below, added headings and attributions throughout London 16439, with copious ascriptions to Poliziano; 'Fortuna desperata' is merely called 'Canzonetta intonata antica'. In other words, Scribe 4, who was intimately acquainted with Poliziano's work, did not identify this as the poet's.

[21] 'In violas' (with Italian translation) appears in Angelo Ambrogini Poliziano, *Prose volgari inedite e poesie latine e greche edite e inedite*, ed. Isidoro del Lungo (Florence, 1867; repr. Hildesheim and New York, 1976), 233–6. For an edition of the *Stanze*, including English translation and commentary, see *The Stanze of Angelo Poliziano*, trans. by David Quint (University Park, Pa., 1993).

[22] For an edition of *Orfeo* and its accompanying letter see Poliziano, *Le stanze, l'Orfeo e le rime*, ed. Carducci, 93–112. An excellent treatment of both literary and musical aspects of *Orfeo* appears in Nino Pirrotta and Elena Povoledo, *Music and Theatre from Poliziano to Monteverdi*, trans. Karen Eales (Cambridge, 1982), 3–36; the book was first published in Italian as *Li due Orfei* (Turin, 1969). A recent edition of Poliziano's shorter Italian poems is Poliziano, *Rime*, ed. Delcorno Branca.

[23] Modern foliation of parchment folios (in pencil), 1–76, with one unnumbered folio between 75 and 76. The parchment folios are preceded by four modern paper ones; four more conclude the manuscript. Fos. 2ᵛ, 76ʳ and both sides of the unnumbered folio preceding 76 are blank. Fo. 1ʳ is blank except for the Payne and Foss inscription indicated above. The most detailed physical descriptions of London 16439 to date are those by Delcorno Branca in *Sulla tradizione*, 143–8; and Poliziano, *Rime*, 55–60; the following expands and, in a few instances, corrects her earlier work. I am indebted to Dr Scot McKendrick, Curator in the British Library Department of Manuscripts, for very helpful conversations regarding this manuscript.

[24] Folios are now missing between 30 and 31, 31 and 32, 39 and 40, and 47 and 48. An additional folio is missing between either 39 and 40 or 41 and 42; see Delcorno Branca, *Sulla tradizione*, 143–4; and Poliziano, *Rime*, 56.

modest pen-and-ink work, came from Scribe 1, as did the rubrification.[25] The guide-word at the end of the seventh gathering was the Greek letter omega, indicating the end of the manuscript as conceived in its earliest stages.

Scribe 2, writing in a slightly more formal hand than Scribe 1 but leaving out decoration and rubrification, then added another gathering, also a quinternion (fos. 68–76). The manuscript next received a formal frame with the addition of two poems by Scribe 3. The first, 'In violas a Venere' (fos. 1^v–2^r), appears on a bifolium of significantly different parchment added at the start of the manuscript.[26] The closing poem, 'Fortuna desperata', was written on fo. 75^v after the end of Scribe 2's work.

Several factors indicate that 'In violas a Venere' and 'Fortuna desperata' were not casual afterthoughts: the addition of new folios at the beginning; the use of a formal humanist book hand, the only one to appear in the collection; and a markedly higher degree of rubrification than anywhere else in the manuscript. 'In violas a Venere' starts at least every other line with a red initial and writes some interior words in red as well: 'Amor' once and 'Amoris' twice. 'Fortuna desperata' is even more lavish. Every line begins with a red initial, and the entire refrain is given in red at all three appearances. Indeed, once we exclude the illuminated initial that opens the *Stanze*, no poem in the collection has as colourful an appearance as 'Fortuna desperata'.

Despite its striking presentation, 'Fortuna desperata' is not out of place in its surroundings. After *Orfeo*, the collection concludes with works in forms typically associated with music and usually marked with their generic titles in the manuscript: *canzoni a ballo*, *ballatette*, *canzonette*, *canzoni*, *strambotti*; 'Fortuna desperata' obviously fits in well. Further, the 'musical' poems of the manuscript copied by Scribe 1 are presented in a similar, though not so lavish, manner.[27] Their refrains are also in red, the crucial difference being that the other poems' refrains are just a few words (or sometimes even a single word) rather than two entire lines. 'Fortuna desperata' ends with the indication *finis* given in red, standard procedure with the works in question. In other words, 'Fortuna desperata' forms a fitting conclusion to the collection, matching preceding works in genre and overall style of presentation while simultaneously providing a formal scribal frame to the manuscript in conjunction with the opening Latin elegy.

Yet another early hand appears in London 16439: Scribe 4 wrote Poliziano's 'Amor bandire e comandar vi fa' (at the bottom of fo. 71^v), added many of the poems' headings, including that for 'Fortuna desperata', and made various corrections throughout, including one in 'In violas a Venere' (making his work

---

[25] The decoration appears on fos. 24^r, 35^v, and 61^r.

[26] By beginning with this Latin elegy, this otherwise exclusively Italian collection bears some resemblance to contemporary chansonniers, which often opened with a short Latin work (albeit a sacred one).

[27] Scribe 2 uses no rubrification, as mentioned earlier, and omits refrains.

posterior to that of Scribe 3) and possibly one in 'Fortuna desperata'.[28] Delcorno Branca raises the possibility that Scribe 4 and Scribe 1 are equivalent; for that matter, Scribe 3 could be the same as 1 or 2, since the formal hand he uses would not readily betray identity with the more casual script of the others.[29]

The date 'M.D.XX' occurs at the bottom of the folio containing 'Fortuna desperata'; an inscription of ownership once appeared between the end of its text and the date. Although almost nothing is currently visible, even under ultraviolet light, references to the manuscript made before the eradication of this crucial text tell us what was originally there.[30] The first, a published citation from 1765, while the manuscript still resided in the Biblioteca Chigiana, asserts that the inscription read 'Faxii Julii de Medicis de Florentia. M.D.XXX.'[31] Two early nineteenth-century editions correct the date to 1520,[32] and Florence, Biblioteca Nazionale Centrale, MS II. iv. 590, a manuscript of Poliziano's poetry for which London 16439 served as exemplar, confirms the inscription.[33] Fo. 12[r] of the Florence manuscript contains a description of its origins: 'Ballate di M. Angelo Poliziano tratte da un ms. della Libreria Chisiana in pergamena segnato 2333 in 4°. Il d(ett)o codice ha scritto in fine d'altra mano "Faxii Julii de Medicis de Florentia MDXX".'[34]

In 1520, then, one of the Florentine Medici owned the manuscript, but which one remains unclear. Delcorno Branca, observing that the name 'Fazio' does not appear in the Medici family tree, noted also that the 'Faxii' in the Florence manuscript seemed a rewriting over something else, although this does not account for

---

[28] The manuscript was rebound at one point, with a consequent cropping of Scribe 4's addition on fol. 71[v]. Delcorno Branca calls Scribe 4 'L1' and lists his contributions in *Sulla tradizione*, 144–8. She does not include the heading for 'Fortuna desperata' in her list (her concern was with the Poliziano works), but the hand is clearly identical with the other *canzonetta intonata* indications. Similarly, the correction in 'Fortuna desperata' is not listed, but this is impossible to identify conclusively as it consists of a single letter.

[29] Delcorno Branca, *Sulla tradizione*, 144; and Poliziano, *Rime*, 56. Various small additions by much later (17th- and 18th-c.) hands appear on folios 25[v], 58[r], 70[v], 74[v], and 76[v]; see ibid. In addition, the black initials in the last gathering as well as those on fo. 41[v] date from this time.

[30] The inscription was evidently eradicated after the manuscript left the Biblioteca Chigiana and prior to its acquisition by the British Museum in 1847, doubtless to mask its identity and enable it to be sold. The parchment on fo. 1, which probably showed Chigiana shelf-marks, was also thoroughly scraped.

[31] Pierantonio Serassi, 'La Vita di M. Angelo Poliziano', in *L'Elegantissime Stanze di Messer Angelo Poliziano* (Padua, 1765), p. xxix n.: 'Questo Codice segnato num. 2333. è in pergamena, e contiene, oltre le Stanze per la Giostra, e l'Orfeo, tutte le Canzoni a ballo del nostro Poeta, alcuni Strambotti, ed altri graziosi componimenti. Nel fine v'è scritto d'altra mano: Faxii Julii de Medicis de Florentia M.D.XXX.'

[32] *Serie de' testi di lingua stampati, che si citano nel vocabolario degli Accademici della Crusca, posseduta da Gaetano Poggiali*, 2 vols. (Livorno, 1813), i. 266: 'un pregevolissimo Codice delle Rime del Poliziano membranaceo in 8.° scritto nel 1520. esistente nella Biblioteca Chigiana di Roma, segnato M IV 81'; and *Rime di M.[r] Angelo Poliziano*, 2 vols. in 1, with illustrations by Vincenzo Nannucci and Luigi Ciampolini (Florence, 1814), ii. 143 n. 183: 'un Codice membranaceo in 8°, scritto nel 1520, esistente nella Biblioteca Chigiana di Roma segnato M.4.81.'

[33] Poliziano, *Rime*, 38, 56, and 151; Delcorno Branca, *Sulla tradizione*, 12, 144. London 16439 was the exemplar for several manuscripts; see ibid. 127–8. The Florentine manuscript dates from the 17th-c.; see ibid. 38.

[34] Poliziano, *Rime*, 38. Delcorno Branca is somewhat inconsistent in her citation of this inscription; in *Sulla tradizione*, 12, the name is given as 'Faxii Iulii de Medici', while on p. 144, and in Poliziano, *Rime*, 151, she gives 'Faxii Iulii de Medicis'. I have not seen the manuscript in question.

the identical reading of the name provided in 1765.[35] She then suggested 'faxii' as a misreading for a title such as 'Magnifici', which would give the manuscript to Giulio de' Medici (1478–1534), the future Pope Clement VII and illegitimate son of the Giuliano who is the hero of Poliziano's *Stanze*, featured in this same manuscript.[36] This ownership would certainly account for the collection's presence in Rome prior to its nineteenth-century acquisition by the British Museum.

As noted above, the concluding date and the now-absent inscription were written in a different hand from the rest of the collection, and other factors point to a considerably earlier period of compilation. The inclusion of Lorenzo's second *Selva d'amore*, which dates from after 8 October 1486, provides a valuable *terminus post quem* overlooked by Poliziano scholars,[37] while comparison with other major Poliziano sources supplies further information on the period of compilation. The manuscript's contents, their ordering, and their textual readings connect it with a series of sources all originating close to Poliziano himself, either through his Medici contacts or the Florentine Studio where he lectured from 1480 on.[38] These sources come either from his lifetime or the period very shortly after his death in 1494. Nowhere is the connection closer than with Florence, Biblioteca Riccardiana, MS 2723; the contents of its original layer are compared

---

[35] Poliziano, *Rime*, 38, 56, 151. A dual misreading is certainly possible.

[36] Ibid. 151. Earlier, in Delcorno Branca, *Sulla tradizione*, 12, she suggested that the scribe might have erred in reading an abbreviation for 'Francisci', making the owner Francesco di Giuliano de' Medici. She changed her mind when noting that he was always referred to as Giuliano, never Giulio; see Poliziano, *Rime*, 151. As this article was going to press, Bonnie Blackburn suggested that the inscription refers to a member of Giulio's entourage, noting that (i) the reading 'Magnifici' proposed by Delcorno Branca could only refer to Giulio prior to his becoming a cardinal in 1513 and in any event would be an unlikely title for someone in holy orders; and (ii) including 'de Florentia' would be unusual for someone of Giulio's stature. This hypothesis, if correct, still places the manuscript in Medici circles if not precisely in Medici hands. I am grateful to Dr Blackburn for sharing her thoughts on this matter.

[37] Lorenzo's *Selve d'amore* are not included among his poems that appear in Poliziano's *Nutricia* of 1486, implying that they did not yet exist. Poliziano's poem, completed on 8 Oct. 1486, treats the history of poetry from Orpheus to Lorenzo, citing specific works; it is unlikely he would have omitted this major work (174 octave stanzas) by his patron, especially since it may have been the first classical *selva* in Italian. On Lorenzo's *Selve* see the introduction to Lorenzo de' Medici, *Stanze* as well as Sara Sturm, *Lorenzo de' Medici* (New York, 1974), 92, 109–15; and Lorenzo de' Medici, *Selected Poems and Prose*, ed. Jon Thiem (University Park, Pa., 1991), 154–5. For an edition of *Nutricia*, see Poliziano, *Prose volgari*, 369–427. Other datable works are included in London 16439; as stated above, the collection also contains Poliziano's letter to Carlo Canale giving permission for the publication of *Orfeo*. The letter was written before 21 Oct. 1483 (the date of death of Cardinal Francesco Gonzaga, referred to in the letter in a way suggesting he was still alive), and obviously after *Orfeo* (1480), but cannot be dated more precisely than that. See Ida Maïer, *Ange Politien: La formation d'un poète humaniste (1469–1480)* (Travaux d'humanisme et Renaissance, 81; Geneva, 1966), 391. Other datable works by Poliziano in the London manuscript include 'In violas a Venere', probably from 1473 (see ibid. 155), and *Le stanze*, left unfinished after the death of Giuliano de' Medici, the protagonist, in the Pazzi Conspiracy of 1478; see Quint, *The Stanze of Angelo Poliziano*, pp. x–xi. The 'canzonetta intonata' *Questo mostrarsi adirata di fore* is of little help in dating the manuscript; the ascription was added by Scribe 4, and the piece to which he referred might have been that of Giovanni Pintelli, whose precise date of arrival in Florence is unknown but could well have been before 1480. On Pintelli, see Frank A. D'Accone, 'Some Neglected Composers in the Florentine Chapels, ca. 1475–1525', *Viator: Medieval and Renaissance Studies*, 1 (1970), 263–88 at 274–8.

[38] See Delcorno Branca, *Sulla tradizione*, esp. 81–108; as well as Poliziano, *Rime*, 144–260.

with those of London 16439 in Appendix B.[39] The striking similarity between the two, extending even to the Lorenzo and Dante inclusions, leaps immediately to the eye. Indeed, a mere four pieces in London 16439 are absent from Riccardiana 2723, and of these, two are the ones Scribe 3 added, the opening Latin elegy and 'Fortuna desperata', while the other two appear almost at the very end of the collection. The missing folios probably provided still more concordances, for the gaps fall in highly suggestive places. Readings frequently drawn from the same exemplars underscore the coincidence of material.[40]

The Riccardiana manuscript has three layers, all of which can be dated.[41] The initial layer, the one so akin to London, contains both the extract from Lorenzo's *Selva*, already mentioned as no earlier than 1486, and the Latin ode Poliziano wrote for the 1487 autumn term of the Florentine Studio. Because the signature of the manuscript's early owner, Francesco di Lorenzo di Bernardo Medici, is dated 1487, the first layer of Riccardiana must have been completed sometime between autumn 1487 and 25 March 1488 (the date on which the Florentine calendar changed); the copyist may have been connected with the Studio.[42] London 16439 might date from the same time; in any event, Delcorno Branca connects it with the rapid diffusion of Poliziano's *Rime* in the period before 1500, and it may precede the Medici expulsion from Florence in 1494.[43]

Clearly, then, with the original text of *Fortuna desperata*, all roads lead to Florence. The London collection is one of the best and most important sources for Poliziano's Italian poetry. Ultimately owned by a Florentine Medici, it bears an extreme similarity to Riccardiana 2723 (itself originally from the Medici circle), whose initial layer was written sometime between 1486 and early 1488. Scribe 4 of London 16439, possibly identical with the manuscript's main scribe,

[39] Similar tables may be found in Delcorno Branca, *Sulla tradizione*, 72–3; and Poliziano, *Rime*, 154–5, which extend the comparison to other sources close to Poliziano. For information on the Riccardiana manuscript and inventories of its contents see Delcorno Branca, *Sulla tradizione*, 31–63; and Poliziano, *Rime*, 48–54.

[40] Clearly demonstrated in Delcorno Branca, *Sulla tradizione*, 81–108 and Poliziano, *Rime*, 184–246.

[41] On its dating, see Delcorno Branca, *Sulla tradizione*, 48–50; she was evidently unaware of the 1486 *terminus post quem* for Lorenzo's *Selva*.

[42] See Delcorno Branca, *Sulla tradizione*, 52; and Poliziano, *Rime*, 150 on the copyist. Scholars of Lorenzo de' Medici's poetry have overlooked the dates for Riccardiana's compilation, which narrow considerably the time-frame for the composition of his *Selve*.

[43] Delcorno Branca, *Sulla tradizione*, 126; reaffirmed in Poliziano, *Rime*, 146. Inexplicable is her dating of 'beginning sixteenth century' ('sec. XVI in.') given in *Rime*, 55. Delcorno Branca also notes that one of the headings added by Scribe 4 (her 'L1') in London 16439 suggests the atmosphere of mocking students, another possible connection with Riccardiana; see ibid., 147, and Delcorno Branca, *Sulla tradizione*, 128–32, where she notes that a number of early copyists of Poliziano were connected with the Studio. Scribes 1–3 of London 16439 were nevertheless professionals, and the opening illuminated initial of this manuscript likewise rules out casual compilation. On the question of dating, Dr Scot McKendrick has kindly informed me that the script of London 16439 is cumulatively more 15th- than 16th-c. A 16th-c. compilation would fit only if older scribes, trained and persisting in an earlier tradition, were at work, a circumstance unlikely in highly fashionable Florence. Scribe 4's designation of 'Fortuna desperata' as 'antica' presents no particular problems; ten years would suffice to warrant that adjective. Scribe 4, though working with the manuscript somewhat later than Scribes 1–3, is still part of the local Florentine Poliziano tradition described in Delcorno Branca, *Sulla tradizione*, 81–108 and Poliziano, *Rime*, 144–260.

knew of one or more musical settings of Poliziano's *Questo mostrarsi*; the three surviving today are all by composers who worked extensively or exclusively in Florence. The other poetry in the manuscript comes from two of Florence's most famous figures, Lorenzo de' Medici and Dante. The gathering structure is compatible with contemporary Florentine practice, and the spray initial fits best with this provenance. Certainly the place likeliest to retain the original poem is the city where it first appeared, and the idea of an exclusively Florentine anthology accords completely with a civic chauvinism fueled by Lorenzo de' Medici's documented interest in local literature.[44] It seems virtually certain, then, that the London manuscript presents a Florentine poem.

While it would be foolhardy to associate interest in the workings of Fortuna exclusively with Florence, the Medici circle was at least as concerned with the subject as other courts. Various poems of Lorenzo's deal specifically with the topic,[45] and references to fortune are scattered throughout Poliziano's works, including the *Stanze* featured in London 16439.[46] In 1479 Lorenzo, Poliziano, and two other poets even took part in a poetic exchange involving the struggle between Fortune and Love.[47]

Significantly, the very earliest conclusive date we have for any musical setting of *Fortuna desperata* also connects the work with Florence. This concerns the replacement contratenor setting written by Ser Felice di Giovanni Martini, transmitted in the Florentine manuscript Cappella Giulia XIII.27. Although this collection was compiled for Lorenzo de' Medici's son Piero between 1492 and 1494, the piece dates from more than a decade before. Active in Florence from at least July 1469, Ser Felice died there between 26 June and 14 August 1478,

---

[44] Virtually all writings on Lorenzo as poet attest to his triple role as author, theorist, and patron; a useful summary is found in Sturm, *Lorenzo de' Medici*, especially 25–34. Among other contributions, Lorenzo was responsible for the *Raccolta aragonese* of *c.*1476, a collection of Tuscan verse widely considered the first anthology of Italian poetry, while his *Commento* vigorously defends the use of the vernacular in literature. Curiously, musicologists searching for reasons behind the relative paucity of Italian song in the first seventy-five years of the 15th c. have neglected to note that far less Italian poetry (and certainly less poetry of the first rank) was written during that period than in the 14th c. Indeed, Benedetto Croce referred to the period 1375–1475 as 'the century without poetry' (Benedetto Croce, *La letteratura italiana*, 4 vols., ed. Mario Sansone (Bari, 1956–60), i. *Dal duecento al cinquecento*, 179–92). The *volgare* waged a protracted struggle during this time against the newly dominant classical Latin, and Florentine poets in the last portion of the century, including Lorenzo, were vital for the re-establishment of Italian as a respected literary language. Indeed, as Quint, *The Stanze of Angelo Poliziano*, p. ix, puts it, 'in the 1470s [Lorenzo] *presided* over a revival of Italian verse' (my emphasis). It is not surprising for 'Fortuna desperata' to come from this new cradle of vernacular literature.

[45] Including 'Crudel Fortuna, a che condotto m'hai', given in Lorenzo de' Medici, *Tutte le opere*, ii. 721–2; 'Fortuna, come suol pur mi dileggia', given with translation in Charles Dempsey, *The Portrayal of Love: Botticelli's Primavera and Humanist Culture at the Time of Lorenzo the Magnificent* (Princeton, 1992), 104; and 'Canzona fatto sendo malata una donna', given with translation ibid. 105–11.

[46] For lists of appearances of Fortuna in Poliziano's Italian poetry, see Diego Rossi (ed.), *Concordanza delle 'Stanze' di Angelo Poliziano* (Hildesheim, 1983), 160, and Jürgen Rolshoven and Alessio Fontana, *Concordanze delle poesie italiane di Angelo Poliziano* (Florence, 1986), 160.

[47] The series consisted of four sonnets composed in the following order: 'S'entr' agli altri sospir ch'escon di fore' by Lorenzo, 'Qual di aconito venenoso ardore' by Pandolfo Collenuccio, 'Non pure avvien che tanto dolce Amore' by Poliziano, and 'Se 'n fra l'altre tue pene avvien che Amore' by Girolamo Benivieni. The poems and a discussion are found in Maïer, *Ange Politien*, 247–51.

providing a valuable *terminus ante quem* for this work.[48] We have no evidence of *Fortuna desperata*'s being an international hit in the 1470s; the next decade sent it on its way to fame. It thus appears extremely likely that Felice dealt with a purely local piece.[49]

If *Fortuna desperata* is Florentine, for whom and when was it written? Hardly a typical courtly love complaint, the text apparently deals with the change in fortune of a high-ranking woman, with the implication that not only has her reputation been (unjustly) damaged, but that she is no longer alive. The text describes circumstances just specific enough to raise the possibility that it concerns a real event, a matter so far completely uninvestigated.

Far and away the most notorious and widely publicized death of a fifteenth-century Italian noblewoman was that in 1425 of Parisina Malatesta d'Este, young second wife of Niccolò III.[50] Observed *in flagrante delicto* with her stepson, Ugo d'Este (Niccolò's eldest son and presumed heir, even though of illegitimate birth), she and her lover were put to death by her husband. Although urged against this punishment by his advisors, Niccolò remained inflexible until receiving notification of his son's death, at which point he immediately regretted his

---

[48] On Ser Felice, see D'Accone, 'Some Neglected Composers', 280–1.

[49] Another early sighting of *Fortuna desperata* also provides a Florentine connection. *Fortuna desperata* furnishes the melody for the lauda 'Po chi tebbi nel core' by Florentine author Francesco d'Albizo (Franceschino degli Albizi) published in Florence in 1486; see *Iesus. Laude Facte & composte da piu persone spirituali* (Florence, 1486 n.s.), fo. 39ᵛ. On the lauda's author see *Laude spirituali di Feo Belcari di Lorenzo de' Medici, di Francesco d'Albizzo, di Castellano Castellani e di altri comprese nelle quattro più antiche raccolte con alcune inedite e con nuove illustrazioni* ed. [G. C. Galletti] (Florence, 1863), p. xii. Perhaps significantly, Pietro Aaron (*Libri tres de institutione harmonica*, fo. 39ᵛ) states that while in Florence he knew Josquin, Obrecht, Isaac, and Agricola—all composers who used *Fortuna desperata*; for the latest on Aaron's biography, see *A Correspondence of Renaissance Musicians*, ed. Bonnie J. Blackburn, Edward E. Lowinsky, and Clement A. Miller (Oxford, 1991), 74–100. Finally, Bonnie Blackburn has kindly informed me (private comm., 6 Aug. 1994) that Perugia 431 contains a heretofore unnoticed setting of a Poliziano poem, *Tu sei de' tuo belli anni ora in sul fiore* (presented as *Tu sei nel toi bel anni* on fo. 112ᵛ); the poem itself appears in London 16439 (App. 2, no. 122). Since Perugia 431 is one of the earliest musical sources to contain *Fortuna desperata*, the presence of Poliziano's poem as well is intriguing; perhaps the two works travelled from Florence at the same time. Although it might seem that *Fortuna desperata*'s absence from three major Florentine chansonniers—Florence 176, Florence 2356, and Pixérécourt—argues against the work's being Florentine, the reasons for the manuscripts' current datings (see Allan Atlas, *The Cappella Giulia Chansonnier (Rome, Biblioteca Apostolica Vaticana, C.G.XIII.27)*, 2 vols. (Musicological Studies, 27; Brooklyn, 1975), i. 246–7, 256, and 254–5 respectively) are repertorial and do not preclude earlier compilations prior to *Fortuna desperata*'s composition. Florence 176 is dated *c.*1475–80 for its restriction to music exclusively from the Ockeghem/Busnoys generation and could thus be somewhat earlier. Florence 2356 is dated *c.*1480–5 because it includes only two works from the Josquin generation, yet these two pieces, by Agricola, could come from Agricola's Italian sojourn that began in the early 1470s. Pixérécourt, currently considered from *c.*1480–4 and similarly with almost nothing from Josquin's contemporaries, could derive its sole Compère work from the composer's presence in Italy in the early 1470s.

[50] For Parisina's story see Antonio Frizzi, *Memorie per la storia di Ferrara*, 2nd edn., 5 vols., ed. Camillo Laderchi (Ferrara, 1847–50), iii. 450–3; Edmund G. Gardner, *Dukes and Poets in Ferrara: A Study in Poetry, Religion,and Politics of the Fifteenth and Early Sixteenth Centuries* (London, 1904; repr. New York, 1968), 34–9 and 49–50; Alfonzo Lazzari, *Ugo e Parisina nella realtà storica* (Florence, 1915); id., *Parisina* (Biblioteca dell'archivio storico italiano, 2; Florence, 1949); *Diario Ferrarese dall'anno 1409 sino al 1502*, ed. Giuseppe Pardi (Rerum Italicarum Scriptores: Raccolta degli storici italiani dal cinquecento al millecinquecento, 24, Pt. 7; Bologna, 1928), 17; and Werner L. Gundersheimer, *Ferrara: The Style of a Renaissance Despotism* (Princeton, 1973). I am grateful to Lewis Lockwood and Jane Bestor for sharing their voluminous knowledge of Ferrarese history.

decision and remained awake the rest of the night, sobbing, sighing, crying his son's name and calling for his own death.[51] The following day, seeking to justify his actions, he sent documents describing the events to all the courts of Italy, a highly unusual step. Many felt the punishment allotted Parisina and Ugo to be extreme, especially in the light of Niccolò's own notorious adulteries.

Such spectacular events were scarcely forgettable, and the tragedy served as impetus for numerous literary and artistic endeavours from the fifteenth into the twentieth century.[52] Pope Pius II wrote of it in the fifteenth century,[53] and the story figured as Novella XLIV in Matteo Bandello's famous collection of the following century.[54] In later times it served as subject of a poem by Lord Byron (*Parisina*, 1816),[55] and several operas, including ones by Donizetti[56] and Mascagni,[57] the latter based on a libretto by Gabriele D'Annunzio. The tragedy is even referred to in Pound's Canto XXIV,[58] and there are numerous other treatments by lesser talents. However, despite the fact that no other deaths of fifteenth-century Italian noblewomen achieved the notoriety that Parisina's did, the very early date of the tragedy, the strong Florentine associations of London 16439, and the presence of promising local candidates for *Fortuna desperata*'s subject make the unlucky Ferrarese duchess a less likely prospect as the song's *donna*.

The deaths of two noblewomen in the 1470s particularly affected Florentines. The earlier was that of Albiera degli Albizzi on 14 July 1473, struck down by pneumonia at the young age of 15.[59] Poets and humanists of the Medici circle joined in an outpouring of literary grief collected in an elaborate manuscript put together by the young woman's fiancé, Sigismondo Stufa (a close friend of Lorenzo de' Medici's), and sent to Annalena Malatesta, who had brought up Albiera.[60] Of the forty-two pieces, Poliziano contributed six Latin epitaphs; other authors include Marsilio Ficino and Alessandro Braccesi. 'Fortuna desperata' is nowhere to be found in this manuscript, but its Italian text would have

---

[51] Niccolò supposedly remained inconsolable for months, crazed with grief; see Lazzari, *Ugo e Parisina*, 59.

[52] For discussion of some of these see Lazzari, *Parisina*, 6–19.

[53] *Aeneae Sylvii episcopi Senensis, postea, Pii Papae II Historia rerum Friderici III Imperatoris* (Helmstedt, 1700), 180–1.

[54] Found in Matteo Bandello, *Tutte le opere di Matteo Bandello*, 2 vols., ed. Francesco Flora (Milan, 1934–43), i. 516–24; English translation in id., *The Novels of Matteo Bandello, Bishop of Agen*, 6 vols., trans. John Payne (London, 1890), ii. 242–52.

[55] Lord Byron, *The Complete Poetical Works*, ed. Jerome J. McGann, 7 vols. (Oxford, 1980–93), iii. 358–75.

[56] *Parisina* (1833), based on Byron's poem. Other operas based on Byron were those of Giribaldi (1878), Keurvels (1890), and Veneziani (1901).

[57] *Parisina* (1913).					[58] See Ezra Pound, *The Cantos of Ezra Pound* (New York, 1970), 112.

[59] On Albiera degli Albizzi, see Maïer, *Ange Politien*, 169–71.

[60] Stufa is sometimes referred to as Albiera's husband. The manuscript is Turin, Biblioteca dell'Accademia delle scienze, MS. N.V.T.7. See Federico Patetta, 'Una raccolta manoscritta di versi e prose in morte d'Albiera degli Albizzi', *Atti della R. Accademia delle Scienze di Torino*, 53 (1917–18), 290–4 and 310–28.

fitted poorly with this exclusively Latin and Greek collection. Curiously, a member of Albiera's family was later to write a contrafact lauda text for *Fortuna desperata.*[61]

Another local candidate for the subject of the poem is Simonetta Cattaneo, wife of Marco Vespucci (cousin to the famous explorer) and renowned beauty said to have been the model for some of Botticelli's most famous paintings, including *Primavera* and *The Birth of Venus.*[62] Despite her considerable posthumous fame, surprisingly little is known of her life. Born in Genoa in 1453, she moved to Florence on her marriage in 1469. On 28 January 1475 Florence held a joust to celebrate its peace treaty with Venice; Giuliano de' Medici, the winner, dedicated his tournament to Simonetta. This event was subsequently immortalized in Poliziano's most famous poem, *Le stanze per la Giostra,* where the love between Simonetta and Giuliano plays a major role.[63] In the year following the tournament, on 26 April, she died from consumption; Lorenzo de' Medici was kept informed of the progress of her illness and even sent his personal physician to care for her.[64]

Simonetta's death occasioned widespread mourning as well as another flood of commemorative poems. As Lorenzo de' Medici said, 'With the death of this woman, and as was fitting for such a public misfortune, all the best minds of Florence grieved in different ways—some in verse, some in prose—over the bitterness of this death.'[65] Poliziano wrote four Latin epitaphs for her;[66] other authors included Girolamo Benivieni in two sonnets,[67] Francesco Nursio Timideo da Verona in the Latin poem 'Carmen austerum in funere Simonettae Vespucciae Florentinae ad illustrissimum Alfonsum Calabriae ducem',[68] Piero Dovizi da Bibbiena in the elegy 'Heulogium in Simonettam puellam formosissimam morientem, cum qua Sponsus suus conqueritur',[69] Naldo Naldi in two Latin epigrams, 'Ad Laurentium Medicen carmen de laudibus Simonettae

---

[61] See above, n. 49.

[62] On Simonetta, see Achille Neri, 'La Simonetta', *Giornale storico della letteratura italiana,* 5 (1885), 131–47; Attilio Simioni, 'Donne ed amori Medicei: La Simonetta', *Nuova antologia di lettere, scienze ed arti,* ser. 5, vol. 135, Raccolta 219 (May–June 1908), 684–95; and Dempsey, *The Portrayal of Love,* 114–39 *et passim,* who provides an excellent summary of her art historical treatment. For a highly romanticized biography see Germán Arciniegas, *El mundo de la bella Simonetta* (Buenos Aires, 1962; Bogotá, 1990).

[63] Poliziano's *Stanze* have often been considered the inspiration for Botticelli's *Primavera, The Birth of Venus,* and *Venus and Mars;* see Quint, *The Stanze of Angelo Poliziano,* p. viii and the bibliography given on 104, esp. Dempsey, *The Portrayal of Love.* Lorenzo may also have been in love with Simonetta; see André Rochon, *La Jeunesse de Laurent de Médicis (1449–1478)* (Paris, 1963), 246–8.

[64] See ibid. 248.   [65] Translation from Lorenzo de' Medici, *Selected Poems and Prose,* 114–15.

[66] Numbers LXXV–LXXVIII in Poliziano, *Prose volgari,* 149–50.

[67] According to Maïer, *Ange Politien,* 283. According to Caterina Re, *Girolamo Benivieni Fiorentino: Cenni sulla vita e sulle opere* (Castello, 1906), 182, one of these, his sixth sonnet, is titled 'Sparito occhi miei lassi è ilchiaro sole'.

[68] The first tercet is given in Scipione Maffei, *Verona illustra,* 5 vols. (Milan, 1825–6), iii. 252; longer excerpts appear in Neri, 'La Simonetta', 139–40. The Medici family owned a copy of this poem; see Enea Piccolomini, 'Inventario della libreria Medicea privata compilato nel 1495', *Archivio storico italiano,* 3rd ser., 20 (1874), 76.

[69] Cited in Arnaldo Della Torre, *Storia dell'Accademia Platonica di Firenze* (Florence, 1902), 715.

morientis scribentem' and 'In Simonettam morientem puellam pulcherrimam',[70] and Bernardo Pulci in his sonnet 'La diva Simonetta a Julian de' Medici' and the elegy 'De obitu divae Simonettae'.[71] Lorenzo himself wrote four sonnets on her death; they take pride of place among the poems in his famous *Commento*, a series of poems and accompanying prose commentaries.[72]

Clearly Simonetta is a strong candidate for being the *donna* of 'Fortuna desperata'. Yet the defamation cited in the first stanza of the poem remains unexplained. Was this owing to her relationship with Giuliano de' Medici, possibly an adulterous one? After her death the unhappy Giuliano received Simonetta's portrait and clothes as gifts from her husband, hardly the act of a jealous man.[73] Lorenzo even said that no one, man or woman, envied her, although that statement surely falls in the realm of poetic licence.[74]

Several possible explanations present themselves. First, as noted, remarkably little is actually known about Simonetta. Her life may really have been full of controversy and scandal, with contemporary writers simply following the maxim of saying nothing evil about the dead. 'Fortuna desperata' may refer to some incident of her life otherwise unknown.

Second, 'Fortuna desperata' may be in direct response to Poliziano's *Stanze*, which opened the original layer of London 16439. Simonetta's death occurred during the composition of *Le stanze*, so Poliziano resurrected her in Book ii as none other than *Fortuna*. She makes her final appearance in the poem in a dream of Giuliano's, ending in the five stanzas given in Appendix C.[75]

In this section Simonetta crowns Giuliano and then dies, reappearing immediately as Fortuna. At first presented positively, Fortuna then receives the traditional negative interpretation in the remaining three stanzas, with virtue alone proclaimed the proper defence against its vicissitudes. This is scarcely a complimentary portrait of Simonetta; indeed, as Charles Dempsey has said, in contrast to her depiction in Lorenzo's sonnets, 'In the *Stanze* she appears in a much darker and . . . even menacing guise, as a cold and unstable Fortune tempting Giuliano

[70] Texts given in Naldus Naldius, *Epigrammaton liber*, ed. Alexander Perosa (Budapest, 1943), 12–13.

[71] The sonnet is given in Neri, 'La Simonetta', 141–6; the elegy on 146–7. Arciniegas, *El mundo de la bella Simonetta*, [142], says that Giuliano de' Medici also wrote poetry in her memory (saying 'Todos tenían que hacerlo' [they all had to do it]), but gives no supporting information.

[72] Poems and accompanying commentary given in Lorenzo de' Medici, *Comento de' miei sonetti*, ed. Tiziano Zanato (Istituto Nazionale di Studi del Rinascimento, Studi e testi, 25; Florence, 1991), 153–70. A well-known study devoted to these four sonnets and *Comento*'s opening *proem* is Angelo Lipari, *The Dolce Stil Novo According to Lorenzo de' Medici: A Study of His Poetic Principio as an Interpretation of the Italian Literature of the Pre-Renaissance Period, Based on His Comento* (Yale Romantic Studies, 12; New Haven, 1936). In a striking parallel to the revised version of 'Fortuna desperata', Lorenzo in his fourth sonnet sees no refuge for his torment save death.

[73] Arciniegas, *El mundo de la bella Simonetta*, [142]. For a recent discussion of mistresses in Renaissance Italy, see Helen S. Ettlinger, 'Visibilis et Invisibilis: The Mistress in Italian Renaissance Court Society', *Renaissance Quarterly*, 47 (1994), 770–92.

[74] Lorenzo de' Medici, *Comento*, 155–6.

[75] Stanzas 33–7, from Quint, *The Stanze of Angelo Poliziano*, 84–7.

in a false dream of glory . . . that ends in his destruction, bringing with it the corresponding end to the ideal figured in Simonetta.'[76]

'Fortuna desperata' then, could be a reaction to Simonetta's ultimately negative appearance in Poliziano's *Stanze.* The equation of Simonetta with Fortuna is a defamation of the reputation of so distinguished a lady. Fortune is cursed for that portrayal; it is also cursed for its traditional attributes, and, by implication, for causing Simonetta's death. 'Fortuna desperata', of course, closes the collection that originally opened with Poliziano's *Stanze,* where this depiction of Simonetta appears.[77]

A third possibility comes from a significant rereading of the poem. In London 16439 the last word of the first stanza was originally written as 'dinegata', and then changed—whether by Scribe 3 or Scribe 4 is impossible to ascertain—to 'dinegrata'. Of the seven musical manuscripts containing this stanza, Perugia 431 presents the same scenario, an initial writing of 'denegata' changed to 'denegrata'. Five other music sources give the word as 'denegata', with Paris 676 the only manuscript out of eight sources with an unequivocal 'denigrata'.

If the text originally read 'denigata', the tone of the poem changes substantially. Now fortune has merely denied rather than defamed the reputation of the distinguished lady; the poem becomes a lament for one taken too young, before her real 'fama' can be known. This fits Simonetta, dead at 23; it fits Albiera degli Albizzi, a mere 15 years old at the time of her death, even better. In fact, this interpretation of the text opens the field to any Florentine noblewoman dead at an early age. The widely eulogized Simonetta and Albiera may be the most likely candidates for being the *donna* of 'Fortuna desperata', but we cannot offer definitive proof for either one.

With the question of where answered and with some ideas provided as to when and why, we turn to the problem of musical authorship. Certainly one of the most important questions concerning *Fortuna desperata* is whether this famous work was composed by one of the greatest masters of the fifteenth century, Antoine Busnoys. Determining the composer of a piece obviously has no effect on its inherent quality (although scholars tend to ignore anonymous compositions). It does, however, have considerable ramifications for questions of authority, reputation, individual stylistic development, and other matters of concern in the study of fifteenth-century music, and the more significant the presumed composer, the greater our interest. Hence the authorship of *Fortuna desperata* elicits more than the usual attention.

[76] Dempsey, *The Portrayal of Love,* 145.
[77] The dating of Poliziano's *Stanze,* while more precise than for many poems, still presents problems. Obviously begun after the tournament (28 Jan. 1475) and clearly still being written after Simonetta's death (26 Apr. 1476), the poem received no further work after the death of Giuliano in the Pazzi conspiracy on 26 Apr. 1478. The exact date that Poliziano stopped writing the poem is unknown, but even Apr. 1478 leaves enough time for the composition of Felice's setting of the work.

A single source attributes the piece to Busnoys—the famous Segovia Cathedral manuscript, discovered in 1922 by Higinio Anglés.[78] At first generally accepted, this attribution came under attack in 1980 by Julie Cumming, who noted that the song does not appear in the principal northern sources for Busnoys's work and that his secular compositions are mostly *forme-fixe* chansons.[79] Paula Higgins effectively countered Cumming's arguments, pointing out that half the composer's chansons survive solely in Italian sources and that a preference for *forme-fixe* chansons by no means precludes setting an Italian poem.[80] More recently, other points against Busnoys's authorship have been raised by Barton Hudson, Joshua Rifkin, and Reinhard Strohm.[81] Summarized, the arguments are: (i) Italian songs are generally thought to originate in Italy, and we have no evidence of an Italian journey for Busnoys;[82] (ii) The ascription to Busnoys appears just once, in a source not especially reliable for the composer, since it is posthumous, originates far from his centres of activity, and contains only one other work by him; (iii) The work has a transmission pattern atypical of Busnoys; (iv) The composition is stylistically dissimilar to Busnoys's accepted works owing to its restriction of imitation to one brief passage, the choice of a fifth rather than octave or unison as the interval for imitation, the predominance of homorhythm and of what Rifkin calls unadorned discant (mm. 25–31, 32–6, 41–52), the frequent use of breves in all voices, and the appearance of two or more breves in a row; (v) The piece displays contrapuntal errors that a composer of Busnoys's stature would have avoided.

This critique, damning on first hearing, is entirely irrelevant. Its premisses can be refuted as follows.

First, substantial lacunae exist in Busnoys's biography. In the 1470s, for example, we have no information at all between July 1471 and June 1472, nothing from March through June 1473, nothing from March through June 1474, and nothing from July through September 1475.[83] For 1476 Busnoys can be pinpointed only once, in Margaret of York's chapel in Ghent on 7 December.[84] Gaps from January to June and October through December exist for 1477, and nothing

[78] Higini Anglès, 'Un manuscrit inconnu avec polyphonie du xvᵉ siècle conservé à la cathedrale de Ségovie (Espagne)', *Acta musicologica*, 8 (1936), 7.
[79] Cumming, 'The Goddess Fortuna Revisited', 7–8.
[80] Paula Higgins, 'Antoine Busnois and Musical Culture in Late Fifteenth-Century France and Burgundy' (Ph.D. diss., Princeton University, 1987), 22–5.
[81] Barton Hudson, 'Two Ferrarese Masses by Jacob Obrecht', *Journal of Musicology*, 4 (1985–6), 276–302 at 290–6; Joshua Rifkin, below, Ch. 20; and Strohm, *The Rise of European Music*, 620. I am grateful to Mr Rifkin for kindly providing an early version of his paper before its publication.
[82] With one exception, all surviving 15th-c. Italian compositions by northern composers are by musicians with documented visits to Italy. The exception is a work by Gilles Joye, a composer with considerable gaps in his biography.
[83] On Busnoys's biography see Paula Higgins, '*In hydraulis* Revisited: New Light on the Career of Antoine Busnois', *JAMS* 39 (1986), 36–86, especially 55–9 with its surviving paylists from Charles the Bold's chapel.
[84] Ibid. 61.

at all is known of his whereabouts in 1478.[85] There is plenty of time for a trip to Italy, even an extended one.[86]

Second, while Segovia is a manuscript about which many questions remain, including its precise connection with Italy, it is not necessarily a bad source for Busnoys. The northern repertory contained in the manuscript probably dates from before 1497, a mere five years after the composer's death.[87] Busnoys died in Bruges in November 1492, and some of Segovia's contents came from Flanders. Although certain of the manuscript's attributions are incorrect, others are accurate (including the sole other work attributed to Busnoys, his *Je ne demande autre de gré*), so a Busnoys ascription cannot be dismissed out of hand. Hence, Segovia is a manuscript containing a repertoire coming from an area of Busnoys's activity not long after his death, and it is accurate in its other Busnoys attribution—at worst a neutral witness to Busnoys's authorship, and possibly a good one.

Third, the transmission pattern of this work is unusual in comparison with that of chansons, but *Fortuna desperata* is not a chanson. Music in the fifteenth century tended to circulate by type more than by composer, and to find an Italian work by a northern composer treated differently from a French work scarcely proves inauthenticity. Certainly works somewhat unusual for a composer sometimes have unusual transmission patterns.[88] But we can make a more significant point. *Fortuna desperata* is truly *sui generis* and as such fits no expected distribution pattern. It stands out because of its position in contemporary music: one of the most popular pieces of the day, confirmed by its widespread transmission in its original form, in *si placet* versions, and in intabulations, it is also a favourite model for art-song reworkings. But *Fortuna desperata* is the only Italian song that matches this description; it both belongs with other big hits such as *Fors seulement* and *De tous biens plaine*[89] and stands apart from them because of its different genre.[90] In terms of transmission, then, *Fortuna desperata* would be a unique work for any composer, not just Busnoys.

---

[85] Ibid. 63.

[86] While lost pay records from the chapel for these times may have contained Busnoys's name, there is no guarantee that they did. Pierre de la Rue, for example, appears on every surviving Habsburg-Burgundian chapel paylist in the period 1492–1516, yet his presence is documented elsewhere during certain gaps in the records. For details see Honey Meconi, *The Secular Music of Pierre de la Rue* (forthcoming, Oxford University Press).

[87] Meconi, 'Art-Song Reworkings', 15–16.

[88] La Rue's *Requiem*, for example, appears in a series of sources not normally featuring his work.

[89] In Bologna Q 16, for example, it is not with the other Busnoys works, as Rifkin, below. Ch. 20, has noted. Here the song appears as part of a later addition where it follows another Fortuna work, *Fortune par ta cruaulté*, and precedes *De tous biens plaine*, matching the former in subject-matter and the latter in being a big hit. Several other later additions in this section were also extremely popular works, e.g. *Si dedero* and *Nunca fue pena maior*. In Florence 121 *Fortuna desperata* is again adjacent to *De tous biens plaine*, this time following it.

[90] In an earlier generation *O rosa bella* was a favourite for reworkings, but compositional activity with this model (and its transmission) seem to have ended about 1480. See Meconi, 'Art-Song Reworkings', 12–14 for more on this model.

Fourth, in terms of style, the use of a fifth as the interval for imitation is less common for Busnoys than the octave (or unison) but not unknown, and hence not a valid criterion for rejection from his works (see Ex. 19.2).[91] The relative lack of imitation, the predominant homorhythm, and the appearance of simultaneous and successive breves raise a point about generic style. *Fortuna desperata* is certainly dissimilar in general style to Busnoys's unquestioned secular works.[92] Again, however, those works are French *forme-fixe* chansons, and *Fortuna desperata* is an Italian song. Would Busnoys have applied the style he used for the former to the latter? Although the question of style transference between disparate vernacular genres remains unexplored, the odds are against ignoring the overall conventions of a given genre, and for Italian secular song of this time that means above all homophonic, homorhythmic texture. For some reason scholars have assumed that were Busnoys to compose a three-voice Italian work, he would do it in the style of a three-voice chanson, yet Italian songs by northern composers normally look more like Italian songs than French chansons. If Busnoys did compose *Fortuna desperata*, he (like other Franco-Flemish composers making a foray into the field) succeeded in meeting the most obvious stylistic criterion for contemporary Italian secular song.

Fifth, the perceived contrapuntal errors can all be found in undisputed works

Ex. 19.2. Busnoys, *C'est vous en qui j'ay esperance*, mm. 33–5

[91] A modern edition of *C'est vous en qui j'ay esperance* appears in Eugénie Droz, Geneviève Thibault, and Yvonne Rokseth (eds.), *Trois chansonniers français du XVᵉ siècle* (Documents artistiques du XVᶜ siècle, 4; Paris, 1927; repr. New York, 1978), 78–81. Paula Higgins has kindly supplied a list of additional examples of imitation not at the unison or octave: *Pucellotte que dieu vous guart, Vous marchez du bout du pié/Vostre beauté, On a grant mal par trop amer/On est bien malade pour amer trop* (imitation at the fifth); *Mon mignault musequin/Gracieuse, plaisante muniere, L'autrier qui passa, In myne zynn, Amours nous traite honnestement/Je m'en vois aux vert boys,* and *On a grant mal par trop amer/On est bien malade pour amer trop* (imitation at the fourth).

[92] An intriguing statement in Paula Higgins's dissertation suggests that even this sentence may come into question. According to Higgins, *Fortuna desperata* 'is entirely within the stylistic tradition of Busnoys's chansons transmitted in later sources of Italian provenance dating from the last decades of the fifteenth century', and 'Busnoys's later style, like that of Josquin, becomes markedly less imitative, less rhythmically rambunctious, and even more harmonically conceived than his earlier works'. See Higgins, 'Antoine Busnois and Musical Culture', 25.

of Busnoys.[93] These problematic procedures in *Fortuna desperata* include unavoidable diminished fifths, such as the one in measure 55, parallel fifths between superius and bassus in measures 12–13,[94] and, not previously mentioned in discussions of this work but jarring none the less, the accented double dissonance in measure 45, where the bassus *d* conflicts with both the superius and tenor.[95] Unavoidable diminished fifths appear in *C'est bien maleur* and other compositions (see Ex. 19.3).[96] Accented double dissonances, though extremely rare in Busnoys's works, do occur in his *O Fortune, trop tu es dure* (see Ex. 19.4);[97] while a comprehensive search of the composer's works reveals several instances of parallel perfect intervals.[98] These occur in their clearest form twice in three-voice texture (see Ex. 19.5).[99] Several other examples of parallel fifths do not articulate

[93] I use the term perceived since a number of scholars have argued that supposed contrapuntal infractions are at times characteristic stylistic features; parallel fifths, for example, are scarcely unknown for either Josquin or La Rue, to name but two major pre-Palestrina composers. See Peter Urquhart, above, Ch. 14, n. 2, for a bibliography on contrapuntal infractions and style. I should like to thank Professor Urquhart for kindly providing a copy of his paper before its publication.

[94] *Fortuna desperata* itself is transmitted in some sources with the offending superius *c'* altered to an innocuous *f'* that effectively renders the melodic line insipid. App. A shows whether each piece that uses the superius has C or F at this point; Frankfurt 20, mentioned above, n. 5, contains an F. The C is clearly the original pitch, creating a superior melodic line (of considerable significance in this extremely well-crafted voice). It also appears in more sources of the work than F, including some of the earliest reworkings (e.g. Martini's cantus-firmus setting as well as the Josquin and Obrecht masses). Unfortunately, because the melody was known with both pitches, we cannot always use the presence of one pitch or another as a reliable separable variant in attempting to establish relationships among sources and settings. A scribe confronted with a C reading might easily change it to F to avoid the fifths (as did Segovia's scribe with Martini's work, which appears earlier in Casanatense with a C), whereas a scribe copying a version with F may have changed it back to the stronger melodic motion of the C.

[95] The offending passage was altered in Zwickau 78/2 to avoid the dissonance.

[96] Modern edition in Droz, Thibault, and Rokseth, *Trois chansonniers,* 40–1. The diminished fifths in *Fortuna desperata* received varying contemporary treatment. In m. 55 the bassus must create either a harmonic diminished fifth with the tenor or a melodic tritone in its own line. Strohm, *The Rise of European Music,* 620, cites the tritone leap as 'unthinkable' in Busnoys, but the bassus accidental is absent in most sources, including all the earliest ones. In only three manuscripts, all from the early 16th c., is the *e* specifically flatted in m. 55: Paris 676, London 35087 (the source for Strohm's transcription), and Augsburg 142a. In an earlier passage, m. 35, the bassus *e* is securely flatted in ten sources, all but the first of which likewise date from the 16th c.: Bologna Q 16, Florence 27, Paris 676, *Canti C,* Augsburg 142a, Cape, London 35087, Florence 121, London 31922, and Zwickau 78/2; this last source (the only one not included in App. 1) was compiled in 1531, probably in Zwickau; it contains yet another copy of *Fortuna desperata* 2a. For the possibility that the *e* is also flatted in Paris 4379, see Meconi, *Fortuna desperata.* An extensive listing of diminished fifths in Busnoys's music is found in Urquhart, above, Ch. 14. I have intentionally refrained from providing any suggestions for *musica ficta* in Ex. 19.1.

[97] They appear on the third beat of m. 23 in *The Mellon Chansonnier,* 2 vols., ed. Leeman L. Perkins and Howard Garey (New Haven and London, 1979), i. 133. Casual dissonance is far more common in Busnoys than one might expect, but almost all other instances of double dissonance occurring on the tactus involve the suspension of one of the dissonant voices from the previous beat. Another example of double dissonance (without suspensions) occurs in *En tous les lieux,* m. 12, final beat (for a modern edition see Catherine Brooks, 'Antoine Busnois, Chanson Composer', *JAMS* 6 (1953), 111–35 at 134–5.

[98] My thanks to Paula Higgins, who prompted my perusal of Busnoys's works by alerting me to the presence of parallel fifths. I should also like to thank Dana Dalton for kindly providing transcriptions of Busnoys chansons not available in modern edition.

[99] Ex. 19.5(*b*) involves parallel triads. For a modern edition of *Quant j'ay au cueur,* see *Van Ockeghem tot Sweelinck: Nederlandsche Muziekgeschiedenis in Voorbeelden,* ed. A. Smijers (Amsterdam, 1939–56), 185–6; for *Missa L'homme armé,* see *Busnoys LTW,* Music, 1–48.

Ex. 19.3. Busnoys, *C'est bien maleur*, mm. 13–14

Ex. 19.4. Busnoys, *O Fortune, trop tu es dure*, m. 23

the initial fifth simultaneously (see Ex. 19.6).[100] In addition, several chansons with parallel fifths in one source have readings in other sources that avoid those fifths (see Ex. 19.7).[101] Since the same is true of *Fortuna desperata*, it is possible that the sources containing the fifths have the original version and the other sources were altered to eliminate the fifths.

Parallel fifths occur more often in four-voice texture, whether the initial fifth is

---

[100] Ex. 19.6(*b*) involves parallel triads; 19.6(*c*) has parallel first-inversion triads. 19.6(*d*) might be avoided by cadential *ficta*. For a modern edition of *Faulx mesdisans*, see *A Florentine Chansonnier from the Time of Lorenzo the Magnificent: Florence, Biblioteca Nazionale Centrale MS Banco Rari 229*, 2 vols., ed. Howard Mayer Brown (Monuments of Renaissance Music, 7; Chicago and London, 1983), music volume, 115–17; for *Chi dit on benedicite* see ibid. 111–12; for *Missa O crux lignum triumphale* see *Busnoys LTW*, 49–93; for *Anima mea liquefacta est/Stirps Jesse* see ibid. 132–7.

[101] Ex. 19.7(*a*) presents parallel fifths twice in a row, the upper note of the first fifth sounding earlier than the lower. Exs. 19.7(*b*) and (*c*) each involve parallel triads. Ex. 19.7(*d*) has a variety of different readings; its fifths might be avoided by cadential *ficta*. For a modern edition of *Seule à par moy* see *A Florentine Chansonnier*, 121–3; for *Ha, que ville est abominable* see ibid. 457–8. Paula Higgins has kindly informed me that *O Fortune, trop tu es dure* contains parallel fifths in m. 15 in all sources except Mellon. The critical edition of Busnoys's chansons, in preparation by Leeman L. Perkins, may ultimately reveal additional instances of parallel fifths.

Ex. 19.5. Parallel perfect intervals in three-voice texture in Busnoys: (*a*) *Quant j'ay au cueur*, m. 4; (*b*) *Missa L'homme armé*, Osanna, m. 8

articulated simultaneously or not (see Ex. 19.8).[102] Parallel octaves also occur (see Ex. 19.8(*d*) and Ex. 19.9).[103] Clearly, parallel perfect intervals are not unknown in Busnoys.

While the arguments and examples given above show that Busnoys *may* have written *Fortuna desperata*, we cannot show that Busnoys *must* have written this work. Because the song is his only extant Italian work,[104] and because the attribution comes from a source that may or may not be a good one for the composer, we are left, for now at least, in limbo.[105] More sophisticated understanding of Busnoys's compositional process may ultimately lead to a resolution of this problem.[106]

Turning to other possible composers in hopes of finding close stylistic kinship is also problematic. Of composers definitely or probably active in Florence in the 1470s we have the northerner Giovanni Pintelli (he is called 'francioso' in one

---

[102] Ex. 19.8(*b*) includes three consecutive fifths, the first of which is not articulated simultaneously. Ex. 19.8(*d*) includes parallel triads and parallel octaves as well as parallel fifths. For a modern edition of *Resjois toi terre de France* see *The Musical Manuscript Montecassino 871: A Neapolitan Repertory of Sacred and Secular Music of the Late Fifteenth Century*, ed. Isabel Pope and Masakata Kanazawa (Oxford, 1978), 391–4, and above, Ch. 11, Ex. 11.1; for *L'autrier la pieça* see Alice Anne Moerk, 'The Seville Chansonnier: An Edition of Sevilla 5-1-43 & Paris N.A. Fr. 4379 (Pt. 1)', 2 vols. (Ph.D. diss., West Virginia University, 1971), ii. 328–30. Other examples of parallel fifths (some involving parallel triads) appear in *Missa O crux lignum triumphale*, Patrem omnipotentem, mm. 56–7; *Alleluia verbum caro factum est*, mm. 7–8 and 19 (for a modern edition see *Busnoys LTW*, 129–31); and *En tous les lieux*, m. 35. Parallel fifths the notes of whose initial fifth are not articulated simultaneously occur in *Missa O crux lignum triumphale*, Kyrie II, mm. 2–3, 5–6; Patrem omnipotentem, mm. 49–50, 68; Et incarnatus est, m. 14; Osanna, mm. 8–9; Agnus I, mm. 19, 26–7; Agnus III, mm. 8–9; *Ad cenam agni providi*, m. 3 (this would be avoided by the use of *ficta*; for a modern edition see *Busnoys LTW*, 125–8); *Corps digne/Dieu quel mariage*, mm. 60–1 (for a modern edition see *A Florentine Chansonnier*, 417–19); and *En tous les lieux*, m. 1 (Brooks mistranscribed the second note of the contratenor line, which should be G) and 23 (this last could be avoided by the use of *ficta*).

[103] The first octave in Ex. 19.9 is not articulated simultaneously.

[104] Rifkin, below, Ch. 20, has argued convincingly that *Con tutta gentileça* is a contrafact.

[105] Both Hudson, 'Two Ferrarese Masses', 295 and Rifkin, below, Ch. 20, suggested that Segovia's scribe confused *Fortuna desperata* with the Busnoys chanson *O Fortune, trop tu es dure*, which lacks the initial word in some sources.

[106] Despite fine work by many scholars, we still lack an authoritative study of his secular compositions, owing in part to the absence of a critical edition of these works.

Ex. 19.6. Staggered parallel fifths in Busnoys: (*a*) *Faulx mesdisans*, mm. 37–8; (*b*) *Chi dit on benedicite*, m. 48; (*c*) *Missa O crux lignum*, Et in terra, mm. 49–50; (*d*) *Anima mea liquefacta est/Stirps Jesse*, m. 19

document), author of a setting of Poliziano's *Questo mostrarsi*, and Ser Arnolfo Giliardi, composer of two Italian songs, one of which, *O invida fortuna*, is another Florentine song about Fortune.[107] Other possibilities include Ser Matteo, a composer for whom no compositions survive, and Alexander Agricola, with two Italian pieces to his credit (one on a text by Lorenzo de' Medici).[108] The

[107] On Pintelli see D'Accone, 'Some Neglected Composers', 274–8; *Questo mostrarsi* is given as Ex. 3. For Giliardi, see ibid. 264–71; his two compositions are given as Exs. 1 and 2.

[108] On Ser Matteo, see ibid. 278–80. As a boy chorister in 1478 and an adult singer the following year, Matteo would have a youthful masterpiece in *Fortuna desperata* were he its composer. Agricola is in Florence in 1474, in Cambrai in March 1476, and then missing again until he reappears in Florence in Oct. 1491; see *New Grove*, s.v. 'Agricola, Alexander'. Agricola's Italian works (the carnival song to Lorenzo's text, *Donne, noi siam dell'olio facitori*, for which only the superius survives, and the strophic song *Amor, che sospirar mi fai*) are published in Alexander Agricola, *Collected Works*, 5 vols., ed. Edward R. Lerner (CMM 22; n.p., 1961–70), v. 66–8.

Ex. 19.7. Parallel fifths in Busnoys avoided in some sources: (*a*) *Seule a par moy,* m. 45; (*b*) *Chi dit on benedicite,* m. 35; (*c*) *Chi dit on benedicite,* m. 40; (*d*) *Ha que ville est abominable,* mm. 29–30

latter composer presents an interesting case because of the triple *si placet* setting in Augsburg 142a attributed to him (*Fortuna desperata* 2d). Scholars have always assumed that the attribution refers to the three new voices added to those of the original song, and indeed the new parts are typically Agricolesque in style. But an analogy may exist between this work and the triple *si placet* setting of *O rosa bella*.[109] That work survives in a single source (Trent 89), and it is unclear whether the attribution to Bedyngham refers to the three new voices or to those

---

[109] For Agricola's work see his *Collected Works,* v. 68–70; for a modern edition of the six-voice *O rosa bella* see John Dunstable, *Complete Works,* 2nd rev. edn., ed. Margaret Bent, Ian Bent, and Brian Trowell (Musica Britannica, 8; London, 1970), 133–4.

Ex. 19.8. Parallel perfect intervals in four-voice texture in Busnoys: (*a*) *Resjois toi terre de France*, mm. 33–4; (*b*) *Missa O crux lignum*, Confiteor, mm. 5–6; (*c*) *Missa L'homme armé*, Agnus III, m. 17; (*d*) *Lautrier la pieça*, m. 4

Ex. 19.9. Parallel octaves in Busnoys: *Missa O crux lignum,* Et incarnatus est, m. 14

of the original song, which is probably by Bedyngham.[110] Similar ambiguity may be at play in Agricola's setting.[111]

Following this line of reasoning, perhaps Ser Felice wrote the work. The ascription over *Fortuna desperata* in the Cappella Giulia chansonnier has been assumed to refer to the replacement contratenor voice only, but there is no guarantee that it does. Felice could easily be the author of the original three-voice setting, written prior to his death in 1478, to which the *si placet* altus and the new replacement contratenor, written by someone else, were added in the Cappella Giulia manuscript copied fourteen or more years later.

Further, Florentine archival records have numerous gaps throughout the 1470s; many composers for whom no local documentation remains (including Busnoys) may have visited the city.[112] Gilles Joye, for example, has no recorded presence in Italy, yet his *Poy che crudel Fortuna* (yet another local *Fortuna*) is a setting of a text by the Florentine poet Rosello Rosselli.[113]

[110] The original three-voice version receives its attribution to Bedyngham in Porto 714; Urb 1411 ascribes the work to Dunstable. For the most recent discussion of this attribution question, see David Fallows, 'Dunstable, Bedyngham and *O rosa bella*', *Journal of Musicology,* 12 (1994), 287–305.

[111] The reference in *O rosa bella* is admittedly a complex one: 'concordantie o rosa bella cum aliis tribus ut posuit bedingham et sine hys non concordant'; the reference to Agricola is straightforward.

[112] On Florentine musical life at this time see Albert Seay, 'The 15th-Century Cappella at Santa Maria del Fiore in Florence', *JAMS* 11 (1958), 45–55; Frank A. D'Accone, 'The Singers of San Giovanni in Florence during the 15th Century', *JAMS* 14 (1961), 307–58; id., 'Some Neglected Composers', 263–88; and the papers in *La musica a Firenze al tempo di Lorenzo il Magnifico: Congresso internazionale di studi, Firenze, 15–17 giugno 1992,* ed. Piero Gargiulo (Quaderni della *Rivista italiana di musicologia,* Società italiana di musicologia, 30; Florence, 1993).

[113] I should like to thank David Fallows for bringing the identification of this poet to my attention. There is no modern edition of the music, which is found in Porto 714, fos. 65ᵛ–67ʳ (no. 11). A modern edition of the text is in *Lirici toscani del Quattrocento,* 2 vols., ed. Andrea Lanza (Biblioteca di Cultura, 37; Rome, 1975), ii. 433–4.

The difficulty with these newly suggested composers, however, is the same as with Busnoys: we have no unshakable attributions and too little (in some cases no) comparable musical material by which to evaluate *Fortuna desperata*. Opening the field to a new composer provides no more certainty than before. We can confirm neither Busnoys nor any other author in his place; we may never be able to state definitively who wrote *Fortuna desperata*.

The problem of divining *Fortuna desperata*'s composer raises significant questions about its use as a model, as does the tracing of the song to Florence and the discovery of its potential identification with a famous noblewoman. To date, scholars investigating the Fortuna family have discussed two factors behind the song's reuse. The first factor is the symbolic function of the work, richly explored by several writers (especially Edward Lowinsky and Julie Cumming) who relate the treatment of *Fortuna desperata*'s borrowed material to representations of the power of Fortune.[114] Yet Fortune governs everything; therefore, every possible compositional permutation can be linked to Fortune's influence, making this a rather facile explanation for compositional choices. The ease with which Fortune is accorded responsibility has already been questioned by at least one scholar in connection with the first Agnus of Josquin's *Missa Fortuna desperata*. Here the composer inverts, transposes, and augments the original superius; Lowinsky sees this as a symbolic representation of the turning of Fortune's wheel.[115] Commenting on this interpretation, Jeremy Noble remarks, 'It may be so, but in the second section it is the tenor's turn to be pushed to the bottom of the texture, and it is not inverted, which seems to weaken the force of the symbolism.'[116]

Another example of the problem of assigning symbolic representation exclusive hold over *Fortuna desperata*'s reworkings is found in the anonymous five-voice chanson *Consideres mes incessantes plaintes/Fortuna desperata*.[117] This piece uses the first phrase of the borrowed tenor (moved down to Phrygian) and presents it twice as a cantus firmus, the second time in shorter note-values. Cumming relates this to the representation of Fortuna in the *Roman de Fauvel*, where good and bad fortune are symbolized by two wheels, one fast and one slow.[118]

---

[114] Edward E. Lowinsky, 'The Goddess Fortuna in Music with a Special Study of Josquin's *Fortuna dun gran tempo*', *Musical Quarterly*, 29 (1943), 45–77; and id., 'Matthaeus Greiter's *Fortuna*: An Experiment in Chromaticism and in Musical Iconography', *Musical Quarterly*, 42 (1956), 500–19, and 43 (1957), 68–85. Both essays by Lowinsky have been reprinted with revisions in id., *Music in the Culture of the Renaissance and Other Essays*, ed. Bonnie J. Blackburn (Chicago and London, 1989), i. 221–39 and 240–61 respectively. References are to the revised versions. For Cumming, see 'The Goddess Fortuna Revisited'.

[115] Lowinsky, 'The Goddess Fortuna', 239.

[116] Gustave Reese and Jeremy Noble, 'Josquin Desprez', in *New Grove*, ix. 724–5.

[117] *Fortuna desperata* 6i in Meconi, 'Art-Song Reworkings', 32. Jaap van Benthem, 'Einige wiedererkannte Josquin-Chansons im Codex 18746 der Österreichischen Nationalbibliothek', *TVNM* 22 (1971), 32–6, argues that this is by Josquin, a suggestion not widely accepted.

[118] Cumming, 'The Goddess Fortuna Revisited', 13. The *Roman de Fauvel* presentation is discussed in Howard R. Patch, *The Goddess Fortuna in Medieval Literature* (Cambridge, Mass., 1927), 170. For Lowinsky this same version of Fortuna required a considerably more complex musical realization: 'To reproduce this in music, one voice would have to give the *Fortuna* melody at a fast pace, another at a slow pace

Curiously, the work immediately preceding *Consideres mes incessantes plaintes* in its sole source, Vienna 18746, has a strikingly similar structure. This is another anonymous five-voice chanson, *A moy seulle*, which is based on *Comme femme*, another frequently used fifteenth-century model. *A moy seulle* likewise transposes the first phrase of its model's tenor (now down a minor third) and presents it twice as a cantus firmus, the second time in shorter note-values. This resemblance may be coincidental, or *Consideres mes incessantes plaintes* may have inspired *A moy seulle*, but there may also be compositional interaction between the two pieces entirely unrelated to *Roman de Fauvel*.

The two examples presented above scarcely invalidate the potential suitability of symbolic representation in *Fortuna desperata*'s reworkings; indeed, some interpretations are extremely convincing.[119] Rather, they caution against a too-ready acceptance of this single explanation.[120] Further, the re-examination of the text undertaken here opens a new realm of symbolic reference. While it is highly unlikely that all reworkings refer to the original lady (whoever she was), later treatments of *Fortuna desperata* could appropriately use this song to evoke connotations of any *donna* either unfairly treated in terms of her reputation or dead before her time (or both).

A second factor cited behind the song's reuse is the homage that later composers paid Busnoys. No one would argue that Busnoys was unworthy of homage; indeed, he might seem a logical choice for a composer such as Josquin, whose style was prefigured in many important ways by that of the older composer. Certainly many derivative compositions by a variety of composers use a work by Busnoys as a starting-point.[121] But Busnoys may not be the composer of *Fortuna desperata*, and other potential authors are of dramatically lesser stature, making them considerably less likely as objects of veneration. Further, homage to the original composer would have been tempered in certain cases by interrelationships with other composers and their *Fortuna desperata* reworkings. Senfl's extensive interest in *Fortuna desperata* surely grew from his close relationship with Isaac, author of five separate reworkings, while Obrecht's mass setting owes much to Josquin's (or vice versa).[122]

Finally, those who reworked the composition did not necessarily know whose piece they were using since, apparently, *Fortuna desperata* normally circulated

... a third voice would have to accompany the first melody at its own brisk rate but in contrary movement, while a fourth voice would move slowly but again in contrary movement' (Lowinsky, 'The Goddess Fortuna', 238). He sees these requirements met in De Vigne's setting of *Fortuna d'un gran tempo* (ibid. 229 and 238).

[119] Lowinsky's view of Greiter's work in 'Matthaeus Greiter's *Fortuna*', for example.

[120] See Meconi, *Fortuna desperata*, for further discussion of the various symbolic interpretations accorded the song's reworkings.

[121] For a summary see Higgins, 'Antoine Busnois and Musical Culture', 21–2.

[122] See Hudson, 'Two Ferrarese Masses', 298–9 for Josquin's primacy; Strohm, *The Rise of European Music*, 626–33, and Rob C. Wegman, *Born for the Muses: The Life and Masses of Jacob Obrecht* (Oxford, 1994), 220, for Obrecht's. Either scenario acknowledges influence beyond that of the original setting.

anonymously. The original song and its four-voice *si placet* versions appear twenty-nine times (including eight intabulations) in surviving manuscripts and prints; twenty-eight of these presentations are anonymous.[123] Indeed, the idea of Josquin's working with an anonymous piece as model for his mass fits rather well with his compositional proclivities. For a composer who borrowed as frequently as he did, remarkably few of his models come from named composers, for his sacred music draws far more often on chant while his secular music makes extensive use of anonymous popular melodies. His attributed polyphonic models are usually the big hits of the day—*De tous biens plaine* (Hayne), *D'ung aultre amer* (Ockeghem), *Comme femme* (Binchois?), *Tout a par moy* (Frye?); other borrowed pieces include *N'aray-je jamais mieulx* (Robert Morton) and *Malheur me bat* (Malcort?). This short list largely exhausts his models from known composers; note that authors of three pieces are uncertain.[124] In other words, Josquin rather rarely made overt gestures to the work of other composers, and his one work explicitly in honour of another, his *Nymphes des bois* for Ockeghem, quotes nothing from the earlier master.

Fortuna desperata may have been chosen as a model for its symbolic value (either representing Fortuna itself or an individual *donna*) or for purposes of homage, either to the original composer (if known) or to the author of a later reworking. Numerous other reasons could be added, including the desire of composers to take part in this specific compositional tradition as well as individual requests by patrons.[125] But arguably the single most important factor behind *Fortuna desperata*'s popularity is its musical quality.[126] If composers wished a symbolic representation of Fortuna, why this piece rather than the many other compositions dealing with Fortuna? More than forty works come from *Fortuna desperata*; the closest competitor is *Fortuna d'un gran tempo*, generating a mere seven derived pieces. If composers wished to pay homage to Busnoys, why this work more than any other of his eighty-odd compositions? If the original author were a nonentity or later composers had no idea who wrote *Fortuna desperata*,

[123] For full details see Meconi, *Fortuna desperata*.

[124] *Fors seulement* (Ockeghem) might be a possible addition to Josquin's group of borrowed polyphonic models, though both the possible Josquin settings are problematic; see the list in Meconi, 'Art-Song Reworkings', 30. Lawrence Bernstein, 'The Chanson at the Court of Louis XII: A Reevaluation', paper presented at XVIIIth Medieval and Renaissance Music Conference, Royal Holloway and Bedford New College, University of London, July 1990 has argued that Févin modelled his *Faulte d'argent* on Josquin rather than the other way around, removing that as a polyphonic model for Josquin. Bernstein has also made a convincing case for the inauthenticity of the setting of *Ma bouche rit* attributed to Josquin; see '*Ma bouche rit et mon cueur pleure*: A Chanson *a 5* Attributed to Josquin des Prez', *Journal of Musicology*, 12 (1994), 253–86. Finally, *Missa Mater patris* seems unlikely as an authentic mass, given its general stiffness and unimaginative use of material, an opinion shared (though not yet in print) by other scholars.

[125] I have examined reasons behind polyphonic borrowing in general and art-song reworkings in particular in Honey Meconi, 'Does *Imitatio* Exist?', *Journal of Musicology*, 12 (1994), 152–78; and 'Art-Song Reworkings', 16–25, respectively.

[126] I have raised this point before, ibid. 6. Strohm, *The Rise of European Music*, 620, likewise recognizes the importance of *Fortuna desperata*'s music.

why rework this piece more than virtually any other fifteenth-century polyphonic model?

Contrapuntal clashes notwithstanding, the work is a brilliantly paced, cumulatively powerful piece with extremely well-written, easily singable, and highly memorable superius and tenor lines. Conceived in Florence, possibly about the beautiful and unfortunate Simonetta Cattaneo, and possibly by master composer Antoine Busnoys, *Fortuna desperata* surely captivated later composers with its beguiling simplicity. For the dozens of later reworkings of this famous song, the factors of symbolism, homage, and other intellectual promptings may ultimately have been of only secondary importance to the sound of the music itself.

Appendix A
Chronology of *Fortuna desperata* to *c*.1510

Date	Source and provenance[1]	Composition
between 26 June and 14 Aug. 1478		death of Ser Felice di Giovanni Martini in Florence; *terminus ante quem* for original composition
c.1470–85	Par 4379 (prob. Naples)	original plus *si placet* altus (F)[2] [FD 1/2a][3]
c.1479–81	Cas (Ferrara)	Martini superius c.f. setting (C) [FD 6a]
prob. *c*.1485	Per 431 (Naples)	original, crossed out (F) [FD 1]* *si placet* setting (F) [FD 2a]*
1486	*Laude Facte* (Florence)	lauda *Poi chi tebbi nel core* 'Cantasi come Fortuna disperata'
pre-1487/8?	(Naples? Ferrara?)[4]	Josquin mass (C) [FD 12a]
1487–8?	(Ferrara?)	Obrecht mass (C) [FD 12b]
1490s	Bol Q16 (prob. Naples or Rome)	*si placet* setting (C) [FD 2b]
c.1490–1504	Leipzig 1494 (Leipzig?)	*si placet* setting (C) [FD 2a]* *si placet* setting (F) [FD 2a]*
1492–4	CG XIII.27 (Florence)	*si placet* setting with additional replacement contratenor; attr. to 'felice' (F) [FD 2a*/3a]
		Isaac tenor c.f. setting [FD 6b]
pre-1497 repertory[5]	Segovia (Spain)	original; attr. to 'Anthonius busnoys' (F) [FD 1]*
		replacement contratenor setting; attr. to 'Josquin du pres' (F) [FD 3b]
		Martini superius c.f. setting; here attr. to 'ysaac' (F) [FD 6a]*
		Isaac motet *Fortuna disperata/Sancte Petre/Ora pro nobis* (F) [FD 10a]
post-1497; post-1501?[6]	Bol Q17 (prob. Florence or nearby)	Isaac Sanctus [FD 11]

* = second or later source

[1] Manuscript dates and provenances are from *Census-Catalogue* unless otherwise noted.

[2] (F) or (C) indicates the pitch of the first note of the superius in m. 13 of the original setting.

[3] FD numbers refer to Meconi, 'Art-Song Reworkings', 31–3.

[4] The dating and provenance of Josquin's and Obrecht's masses remain uncertain; see Hudson, 'Two Ferrarese Masses', 289–98 and Wegman, *Born for the Muses*, 219–21. Josquin may have been in both Ferrara and Naples in the early 1480s; see Edward E. Lowinsky, 'Ascanio Sforza's Life: A Key to Josquin's Biography and an Aid to the Chronology of his Works', in id. (ed.), *Josquin des Prez: Proceedings of the International Josquin Festival Conference* (London, 1976), 31–75; repr. in *Music in the Culture of the Renaissance and Other Essays*, ed. Bonnie J. Blackburn (Chicago and London, 1989), 541–64. Sources for Josquin's and Obrecht's masses have not been included here, nor have later editions of the *Laude Facte*.

[5] Meconi, 'Art-Song Reworkings', 15–16.

[6] Meconi, 'The Manuscript Basevi 2439 and Chanson Transmission in Italy', in *Atti del XIV congresso della Società Internazionale di Musicologia (Bologna 1987)*, 3 vols., ed. Angelo Pompilio, Donatella Restani, Lorenzo Bianconi, and F. Alberto Gallo (Turin, 1990), iii. 171.

Date	Source and provenance	Composition
pre-1500?	Pesaro 1144 (Venice?)[7]	very free lute intabulation of S? (C) [FD 1]*
		free lute intabulation (C) [FD 1]*
early 16th c.	Fl 27 (prob. Mantua)	*si placet* setting (C) [FD 2c]
early 16th c.	Tarazona 3 (prob. Seville)	Periquin mass [FD 12c]
c.1500–10	Bas F.X.10 (Basle)	*si placet* setting; only bassus survives [FD 2a?]*
1502	Par 676 (Mantua)	*si placet* setting (C) [FD 2a]*
c.1502–6	Bol Q18 (Bologna)	superius c.f. setting (C) [FD 6c]
1504	*Canti C* (Venice)	*si placet* setting (F) [FD 2a]*
		Pinarol superius c.f. setting (C) [FD 6d]
c.1505	Wolf 78 (prob. S. Germany)	original (F) [FD 1]*
c.1505	Paris 27 (Venice?)[8]	lute intabulation of lower voices of original [FD 1]*
1505–14	Aug 142a (Augsburg)	triple *si placet* setting; attr. to 'Allexannderr A' = Agricola (d. 1506) (C) [FD 2d]
pre-1506	Cape (N. Italy)	*si placet* setting (F) [FD 2a]*
1507	Spinacino ii (Venice)	free intabulation of original, for two lutes (C) [FD 1]*
pre-1509[9]	Lo 35087 (Bruges?)	original (C) [FD 1]*
c.1510	Fl 121 (Florence)	original (C) [FD 1]*
		Isaac tenor c.f. setting [FD 6b]*
1510+	SG 462 (Paris and Glarus)	*si placet* setting (C) [FD 2a]*
		paraphrased tenor setting [FD 8a]
c.1510–20	Lo 31922 (prob. London)	*si placet* setting (C) [FD 2e]

---

[7] Pesaro, Biblioteca Oliveriana, MS 1144. See Walter H. Rubsamen, 'The Earliest French Lute Tablature', *JAMS* 21 (1968), 286–99; and David Fallows, '15th-Century Tablatures for Plucked Instruments: A Summary, A Revision, and A Suggestion', *Lute Society Journal*, 19 (1977), 10–18.

[8] Paris, Bibliothèque nationale, Département de la Musique, MS Rés. Vmc. 27. See François Lesure, introduction to *Tablature de luth italienne: Cent six pièces d'œuvres vocales pour luth seul et accompagnement pour luth* (Geneva, 1981) [unpaginated].

[9] The *terminus ante quem* for Lo 35087 is the death date of the original owner.

Appendix B
Comparison of London 16439 and
Original Layer of Riccardiana 2723

The following comparison is intended to show the similarities between the two manu-scripts; each piece in London 16439 and the original layer of Riccardiana is represented either by title (orthography does not necessarily match that of the manuscripts) or by number. The numbers refer to shorter works of Poliziano as given in Delcorno Branca, *Sulla tradizione*, 33–9; all works are by Poliziano (except 'Fortuna desperata') unless other-wise indicated. Boldface items appear in London but not Riccardiana, italic items in Riccardiana but not London. Nos. 2, 14, 47, 52, 60, 62, 69, 70, 73, 74, and 143 are unique to Riccardiana (which is missing its first folio and one folio between poems 60 and 61). Unless otherwise indicated, all poems were entered in London by Scribe 1.

RICCARDIANA 2723 (original layer = Scribe A)	LONDON 16439
	In violas a Venere mea dono acceptas (Scribe 3)[1]
Stanze Cominciate per la Giostra del Magnifico Giuliano de' Medici	Stanze Cominciate per la Giostra del Magnifico Giuliano de' Medici
Letter to Canale	
Orfeo	
1, 2, 3–13	
Lorenzo: 2nd Selva 1	missing folio [= end of Stanze & Lorenzo 2nd Selva 1?]
Lorenzo: 2nd Selva 2–7	Lorenzo: 2nd Selva 2–7
Lorenzo: 2nd Selva 8–12	missing folio [= Lorenzo 2nd Selva 8–12 and Pol. 14?][2]
14, 15–36	15–18, 22, 19–21, 23–36
	3–13
	78
37–43	37–43
	79
44	44
	83
45–6	45–6
47–52	missing folio or folios [= 47–52?]
53–8, *59–62*, 63–8	53–8, 63–8
69–74	missing folio? [= 69–74?]
75–7	75–7
78	
	Letter to Canale
	Orfeo (one folio missing within poem)

---

[1] Possibly the same as Scribe 1 or 2; the formal hand makes it difficult to tell.

[2] The missing folio was the first one of the next gathering. The guide words at the end of the previous gathering are the first words for Stanza 8 of Lorenzo's *Selva*. Assuming three stanzas per page, a spacing the scribe has been following, the missing folio would hold precisely the material suggested here.

79, *80–2,* 83, *84–91*
Lorenzo: I non mi vo scusar
100–8
Lorenzo: Ben ch'io rida balli o canti
   Donne belle i'ho cercato
   Écci egli alcuna in questa compagnia
109–11, *112–13,* 114–15
Lorenzo: In mezo d'una valle
Dante: Così nel mio parlar voglio
   esser aspro
   Amor, che ne la mente mi ragiona
   Amor, che movi tua vertù da cielo
   Io sento sì d'Amor la gran possanza
117–40

141

142

143
Jam cornu gravidus
Epistola . . . al S. Federigo
De laudibus artium liberalium verba

Lorenzo: I non mi vo scusar
100–8
Lorenzo: Ben ch'io rida balli o canti
   Donne belle i'ho cercato
   Écci egli alcuna in questa compagnia
109, 111, 114, 115, 110

Dante: Così nel mio parlar voglio
   esser aspro
   Amor, che ne la mente mi ragiona
   Amor, che movi tua vertù da cielo
   Io sento sì d'Amor la gran possanza
117–40 (Scribe 2)
1 (inserted by Scribe 4)
141 (Scribe 2)
Canti ognun ch'io chanterò (Scribe 2)
Donne mie, voi non sapete (Scribe 2)
142 (Scribe 2)
Fortuna desperata (Scribe 3)

Appendix C
Stanze 33–37 of Poliziano, *Stanze cominciate per la Giostra del Magnifico Giuliano de' Medici*[1]XXXVI

XXXIII

Poi Iulio di suo spoglie armava tutto,
e tutto fiammeggiar lo facea d'auro;
quando era al fin del guerreggiar condutto,
al capo gl'intrecciava oliva e lauro.
Ivi tornar parea suo gioia in lutto:
vedeasi tolto il suo dolce tesauro,
vedea suo ninfa in trista nube avolta,
dagli occhi crudelmente esserli tolta.

33

Then she armed Julio with her spoils, and made him blaze with gold; when he had reached the end of his battle, she entwined the olive and laurel around his head. There his joy seemed to turn into mourning: he saw his sweet treasure taken from him, he saw his nymph, enveloped in a sad cloud, cruelly taken from before his eyes.

XXXIV

L'aier tutta parea divenir bruna,
e tremar tutto dello abisso il fondo;
parea sanguigno el cel farsi e la luna,
e cader giú le stelle nel profondo.
Poi vede lieta in forma di Fortuna
surger suo ninfa e rabbellirsi il mondo,
e prender lei di sua vita governo,
e lui con seco far per fama eterno.

34

The air seemed to turn dark and the depths of the abyss to tremble; the heavens and the moon seemed to turn bloody, and the stars seemed to fall into the deep. Then he sees his nymph rise again, happy in the form of Fortune, and the world grows beautiful again: he sees her govern his life, and make them both eternal through fame.

XXXV

Sotto cotali ambagi al giovinetto
fu mostro de' suo' fati il leggier corso:
troppo felice, se nel suo diletto
non mettea morte acerba il crudel morso.
Ma che puote a Fortuna esser disdetto,
ch'a nostre cose allenta e stringe il morso?
Né val perch'altri la lusinghi o morda,
ch'a suo modo ne guida e sta pur sorda.

35

In these confused signs the youth was shown the changing course of his fate: too happy, if early death were not placing its cruel bit on his delight. But what can be gainsaid to Fortune who slackens and pulls the reins of our affairs? The flattery and curses of others do not prevail, for she remains deaf and rules us as she pleases.

---

[1] Translation by David Quint, *The Stanze of Angelo Poliziano* (University Park, Pa., 1993), 84–7.

XXXVI

Adunque il tanto lamentar che giova?
A che di pianto pur bagnar le gote?
Se pur convien che lei ne guidi e muova,
se mortal forza contro a lei non puote,
se con sue penne il nostro mondo cova,
e tempra e volge, come vuol, le rote?
Beato qual da lei suo' pensier solve,
e tutto drento alla virtú s'involve!

36

Therefore what can so much lamentation avail? Why do we still bathe our cheeks in tears? If need be that she must govern and move us, if mortal force can do nothing against her, if she broods over our world with her wings, and turns and tempers her wheel as she wishes. Blessed is he who frees his thoughts from her and encloses himself completely within his own virtue!

XXXVII

O felice colui che lei non cura
e che a' suoi gravi assalti non si arrende,
ma come scoglio che incontro al mar dura,
o torre che da Borea si difende,
suo' colpi aspetta con fronte sicura,
e sta sempre provisto a sua vicende!
Da sé sol pende, e 'n se stesso si fida,
né guidato è dal caso, anzi lui guida.

37

Happy he who pays no heed to her nor gives in to her heavy assaults, but like a rock that stands against the sea, or a tower that resists the north wind, awaits her blows with an unconcerned brow, always prepared for her changes! He depends only on himself, he trusts himself alone: not governed by chance, he governs chance.

20

Busnoys and Italy: The Evidence of Two Songs

꙳❦꙳

JOSHUA RIFKIN

For David Fallows at 50

SCHOLARSHIP loves a vacuum; and the life of Antoine Busnoys provides an irresistible one. Between 17 April 1483, when he last appears in the household records of Maximilian of Austria, and 6 November 1492, when a notice from the church of Saint-Sauveur at Bruges records his presumably recent death, Busnoys drops completely out of sight.[1] As with Shakespeare, more than a few scholars—myself hardly excluded—have felt inclined to wonder if he didn't spend at least some of the missing years in Italy.[2] Three points have encouraged speculation in this regard: theorists in Italy refer to Busnoys with some frequency; the music attributed to him in sources of the late fifteenth and early sixteenth centuries includes two songs with Italian texts; and the transmission of his secular works in particular shows a striking bifurcation—roughly half

My thanks to David Fallows for providing valuable information without which I could scarcely have prepared this contribution; to Bonnie Blackburn, for encouragement at crucial moments and kindnesses too numerous to mention; and to Paula Higgins, not only for sending me hard-to-find sources and information when I needed them most, but for reactivating a long-dormant passion for Busnoys.

[1] For the documents, see Paula Higgins, '*In hydraulis* Revisited: New Light on the Career of Antoine Busnois', *JAMS* 39 (1986), 36–86 at 53 n. 74, 62, and 67, as well as Reinhard Strohm, *Music in Late Medieval Bruges* (Oxford, 1985), 54–5 and 158. On p. 62 Higgins points to biographical *lacunae* in the years immediately preceding 1483 as well: 'During the years of his service with Maximilian, Busnois seems to have been a more fluctuating element in the chapel, with frequent absences over several months' time'; on p. 69 she speaks of 'Busnois's lengthy absences during what appear to have been his final years of service in Maximilian's domestic chapel'. Yet in so far as they survive, the documents for this period—all cited on pp. 63–7 and 85–6 of Higgins's article—show only brief interruptions in his service: between 19 May and 23 June 1479; from Feb. to Mar. or Apr. 1481; at the very end of 1482; and in Mar. 1483.

[2] See the comments in Paula Marie Higgins, 'Antoine Busnois and Musical Culture in Late Fifteenth-Century France and Burgundy' (Ph.D. diss., Princeton University, 1987), 104 and 114, or Howard Mayer Brown, *A Florentine Chansonnier from the Time of Lorenzo the Magnificent: Florence, Biblioteca Nazionale Centrale, MS Banco Rari 229* (Monuments of Renaissance Music, 7; Chicago, 1983), Text vol., 130, as well as the earlier references assembled in Higgins, '*In hydraulis* Revisited', 41 n. 22, and Barton Hudson, 'Two Ferrarese Masses by Jacob Obrecht', *Journal of Musicology*, 4 (1985–6), 276–302 at 295 n. 63, to which I would add the remarks cited in the following note. For a recent dissenting voice, see Gerald Montagna, 'Caron, Hayne, Compère: A Transmission Reassessment', *EMH* 7 (1987), 107–57 at 118–19 and 131.

his songs appear solely in French manuscripts of the 1460s and 1470s, the other half in Italian sources of the 1470s and later.[3]

While the picture that these different strands of evidence combine to weave certainly looks attractive, it has remained essentially unexamined, as much by its proponents as by those less inclined to accept it.[4] Nor will this occasion provide the chance to present anything like the comprehensive appraisal that what we might call the Italian hypothesis so plainly demands. But I shall take a fairly intensive look at one of the component parts of the hypothesis: the two Italian-texted songs, *Con tutta gentileça* and *Fortuna desperata*. Both pieces have already attracted a fair share of attention, especially in the last few years. As I hope the following investigation will show, however, they demand even more than they have yet received.

I

The belief that *Con tutta gentileça* and *Fortuna desperata* might have something to tell us about the geography of Busnoys's career rests on an assumption that itself requires examination: that a Northern composer would not have set a text in the Italian language without first having set foot on Italian soil. Barton Hudson has, in fact, gone some way towards substantiating this assumption, not least in respect to Busnoys.[5] Covering the ground again, in closer focus and from a slightly different perspective, only strengthens his findings.[6] Between Gilles Joye's *Poy che crudel* at the middle of the fifteenth century and the setting of *Consumo la mia vita* attributed to Johannes Prioris at its close, I cannot locate a single piece composed to Italian words by a musician whom we do not at some point find south

---

[3] On this last point, see my notes to the recording of Busnoys chansons on Nonesuch H-71247 as well as the more extended discussion in Higgins, 'Antoine Busnois and Musical Culture', 98–101. As many readers will by now recognize, my reference to 'French' manuscripts in fact means those sources of secular music long referred to as Burgundian. For the most comprehensive statement on the origin of the supposedly Burgundian chansonniers, see ibid. 234–96; see also, for additional evidence, Martella Gutiérrez-Denhoff, *Der Wolfenbütteler Chansonnier: Wolfenbüttel, Herzog August Bibliothek Codex Guelf. 287 Extrav.: Untersuchungen zu Repertoire und Überlieferung einer Musikhandschrift des 15. Jahrhunderts und ihres Umkreises* (Wolfenbütteler Forschungen, 29; Wiesbaden, 1985), 22–3; Louise Litterick, 'The Manuscript Royal 20.A.XVI of the British Library' (Ph.D. diss., New York University, 1976), 66–71, esp. 67 n. 78; and Joshua Rifkin, 'Scribal Concordances for Some Renaissance Manuscripts in Florentine Libraries', *JAMS* 26 (1973), 305–26 at 318–19 and 322–6—the objections to which in Gutiérrez-Denhoff, *Der Wolfenbütteler Chansonnier*, 101–2, as well as ead., 'Untersuchungen zu Gestalt, Entstehung and Repertoire des Chansonniers Laborde', *Archiv für Musikwissenschaft*, 41 (1984), 113–46 at 123, strike me as wholly unfounded.

[4] Montagna, 'Caron, Hayne, Compère', 118–19, implies that an unpublished study entitled 'The Chanson Repertory at the Northern Courts: France and Burgundy during the Era of Ockeghem' (cf. 109 n. 7) will provide a closer examination of the transmission and its implications; but this has yet to appear.

[5] See Hudson, 'Two Ferrarese Masses', 290–4; I must thank Martin Picker for alerting me to the importance of this article for the subject at hand.

[6] The survey that follows depends principally on Knud Jeppesen, *La frottola*, ii: *Zur Bibliographie der handschriftlichen musikalischen Überlieferung des weltlichen italienischen Lieds um 1500* (Acta Jutlandica, 41/1; Copenhagen, 1969), 265–92 in particular, with additional information from David Fallows's unpublished master list of pre-frottolesque Italian song.

of the Alps.[7] In only a handful of pieces—two by Robert Morton, two by the biographically frustrating Caron, and one credited to both Morton and his Burgundian colleague Adrian Basin—might we even think to encounter an exception; and with each of these, concordant sources or other evidence exposes the Italian version as a contrafact.[8] By the same token, Italian songs remain all but totally excluded from Northern manuscripts until the final years of the century—a time of sustained French presence in Italy.[9] Apart from the internationally

[7] *Poy che crudel*—on which see also below, n. 24—survives in Porto 714, fos. 65ᵛ–67ʳ, with the attribution 'Joye'; David Fallows assures me that a concordance in Florence 176 signalled in his article 'Robertus de Anglia and the Oporto Song Collection', in Ian Bent (ed.), *Source Materials and the Interpretation of Music: A Memorial Volume to Thurston Dart* (London, 1981), 99–128 at 121, does not in fact exist. For the sources of *Consumo la mia vita*, see below, n. 10, and the concordances listed in Lawrence F. Bernstein, 'A Florentine Chansonnier of the Early Sixteenth Century: Florence, Biblioteca Nazionale Centrale, MS Magliabechi xix 117', *EMH* 6 (1986), 1–107 at 103; on the possibility that Prioris may in fact have worked in Italy, see Richard Wexler, 'Prioris, Johannes', *New Grove*, xv. 275, and Christopher Reynolds, 'Musical Careers, Ecclesiastical Benefices, and the Example of Johannes Brunet', *JAMS* 37 (1984), 49–97 at 55–6 and 72. For the period under discussion, I find pieces with Italian texts or incipits attributed to the following composers of French or Netherlandish origin: Alexander Agricola, Adrian Basin, Caron, Compère, Ghiselin, Arnolfo Giliardi, Isaac, Japart, Josquin d'Ascanio, Josquin des Prez, Le petit Basque, Martini, Morton, Obrecht, Pintello, Crispinus de Stappen, Tinctoris, and Vincenet. For most of these, I would take the Italian connections as too well known to require commentary here. On the nationality of Arnolfo Giliardi and Pintello, see Frank A. D'Accone, 'Some Neglected Composers in the Florentine Chapels, ca. 1475–1525', *Viator: Medieval and Renaissance Studies*, 1 (1970), 263–88 at 264–7 and 274–7. On the pieces by Basin, Caron, and Morton, see the main text immediately following. The name 'Le petit Basque' occurs as an apparent scribal explicit on fo. 185ʳ (186ʳ) of Oxford, Bodleian Library, MS Canonici miscellany 42, a manuscript whose contents, script, and decoration leave no doubt of its Italian origin. Cf. *The Theory of Music*, iv: *Manuscripts from the Carolingian Era up to c. 1500 in Great Britain and in the United States of America*, ed. Christian Meyer, Michel Huglo, and Nancy C. Phillips (Répertoire international des sources musicales, B iii⁴; Munich, 1992), 117, as well as *Census-Catalogue* ii. 274–5, as well as Manfred Bukofzer, 'Three Unknown Italian Chansons of the Fifteenth Century', *Collectanea Historiae Musicae*, 2 (Florence, 1957), 107–9, esp. 109; unlike the *Census-Catalogue*, ii. 274, I see no evidence of 'three or four scribes' in the source—the entries look to me all like variations of a single hand.

[8] For Morton's *La perontina* and *Madonna bella*—actually *Paracheve ton entreprise* and *Plus j'ay le monde regardé*, respectively—and on *Vien avante morte dolente*, by Morton or Basin, see Robert Morton, *The Collected Works*, ed. Allan Atlas (Masters and Monuments of the Renaissance, 2; New York, 1981), 85, 88–9, and 93. On Caron's *Tanto l'afanno*, see Walter H. Rubsamen, 'From Frottola to Madrigal: The Changing Pattern of Secular Italian Vocal Music', in James Haar (ed.), *Chanson and Madrigal 1480–1530: Studies in Comparison and Contrast* (Isham Library Papers, 2; Cambridge, Mass., 1964), 51–72 at 52 and 172–242; for his *Fuggir non posso*, see below, pp. 511–12 and n. 34. Busnoys, whom I have left out of this list for obvious reasons, has a similar contrafact among his chansons: Bologna Q 16 transmits *M'a vostre cueur* with the incipit 'Terribile fortuna' (cf. Table 20.2). As a possible setting of an Italian text by a Northern composer I should perhaps also mention Ockeghem's duo on *O rosa bella* in Trent 90, fo. 445ʳ, although this represents a chronological—and generic—borderline case; cf. Johannes Ockeghem, *Collected Works*, iii, ed. Richard Wexler with Dragan Plamenac (American Musicological Society: Studies and Documents, 7; Boston, 1992), pp. lxxxvi–lxxxvii and 79.

[9] For a convenient overview of the sources involved, see Louise Litterick, 'Performing Franco-Netherlandish Secular Music of the Late 15th Century: Texted and Untexted Parts', *Early Music*, 8 (1980), 474–89 at 484. As Paula Higgins kindly reminds me, the Savoyard manuscript Cordiforme, absent from Litterick's conspectus, demands consideration here, as it prefaces its otherwise French repertory with fourteen songs in Italian. But even if, as seems probable, Cordiforme originated in the Francophone portion of Savoy, it clearly reflects the mixed French-Italian culture of the duchy, not to mention the career of its first owner, Jean de Montchenu: documents from 1460 place him in Rome, and from at most ten years later he headed the monastery of Sant' Antonio di Ranverso near Rivoli. The shield enclosing Montchenu's arms on fo. [D]ʳ, moreover, shows a typically Italian design. His manuscript thus stands at considerable remove from sources written in the Loire valley and further north; nor do we have any reason to imagine that its Italian pieces originated anywhere near its place of copying. Cf. *Chansonnier de Jean de Montchenu (Bibliothèque nationale, Rothschild 2973 [I.5.13])*, ed. Geneviève Thibault and David Fallows (Publications de la Société française de musicologie, 1/23; Paris, 1991), esp. pp. xv–xvii and lviii.

ubiquitous and much older *O rosa bella*, the sources contain no music whatever
with Italian text before the appearance of *Consumo la mia vita* and the anonymous
La gran pena che io sento on successive openings in the final layer of Laborde.[10]

Obviously, we cannot ignore the possibility that the sources and the biographical evidence tell less than the whole story. More than one scholar has drawn
attention to the presence of a strong Italian community in Bruges, where
Busnoys often stayed with the Burgundian court even before his period of service
at Saint-Sauveur.[11] Hudson has reminded us that Charles the Bold himself had a
fondness for things Italian, spoke the language, and had a sizeable group of
Italians at his court, some of whom numbered among his closest intimates.[12] Yet
the consequences of all this would seem anything but self-evident—as Richard
Vaughan has put it, 'It is easy enough to identify and enumerate Italian influx at
Charles's court, but difficult to show how it bore fruit'.[13] In this connection, a
sideways glance at another foreign element in Busnoys's milieu may prove
enlightening. Bruges, we might recall, supported a sizeable English contingent
alongside its Italians and clearly served as an important conduit for English
music.[14] Charles, if perhaps not the Anglophile that some writers have tended to
make of him, certainly had his own English connections, both musical and otherwise.[15] While he maintained an at best distant relationship to his wife, Margaret

[10] *O rosa bella* makes two appearances in the great Northern chansonniers of the 1460s and 1470s:
Wolfenbüttel 287, fos. 34ᵛ–36ʳ, transmits it in its original form, while an arrangement in Dijon 517, fos.
iiijˣˣxᵛ–iiijˣˣxiiʳ (93ᵛ–95ʳ), retains the superius, transposes the tenor up an octave, and provides a new contra; for the music of the original, see John Dunstable, *Complete Works*, ed. Manfred F. Bukofzer (Musica
Britannica, 8; London, 1953), or the rev. edn. by Margaret Bent, Ian Bent, and Brian Trowell (London,
1970), pp. 133–4 in both volumes. *Consumo la mia vita* and *La gran pena che io sento* appear in Laborde, fos.
136ᵛ–137ʳ and 137ᵛ–138ʳ, respectively. Gutiérrez-Denhoff, 'Untersuchungen', 118, 122–5, and 136, has
recently proposed dating these and other scribally related entries in Laborde as late as *c*.1500–20; none of
her observations, however, persuades me of the need to push this material much beyond the start of the 16th
c. As I shall try to show elsewhere, *Consumo la mia vita* probably represents a keepsake of sorts from the meeting between its poet, Serafino dall'Aquila, and Charles VIII of France at Novara in May 1495.

[11] See particularly Strohm, *Music in Late Medieval Bruges*, 56–7, 63–4, 72, and 138–9, and Hudson,
'Two Ferrarese Masses', 292, as well as Richard Vaughan, *Charles the Bold: The Last Valois Duke of Burgundy*
(London, 1973), 258–60. For Busnoys's documented stays at Bruges between 1472 and 1483, see Higgins,
'*In hydraulis* Revisited', 56 and 63–7; see also the more general remarks at 59 n. 81. In her review of
Strohm's book, Higgins has emphasized that several of the Italian families in Bruges had prominent repre-
sentation in Paris as well—a point of some potential interest in regard to Busnoys, given his evident ties with
that city; see *JAMS* 42 (1989), 150–61 at 159–60, and, for Busnoys's Parisian affiliations, Leeman L.
Perkins, 'Antoine Busnois and the d'Hacqueville Connection', in Mary Beth Winn (ed.), *Musique naturelle
et musique artificielle: In memoriam Gustav Reese* (= *Le Moyen français*, 5; Montreal, 1979), 49–64, and Paula
Higgins, 'Parisian Nobles, a Scottish Princess, and the Woman's Voice in Late Medieval Song', *EMH* 10
(1991), 145–200 at 153–8 and 190–2 in particular.

[12] See Hudson, 'Two Ferrarese Masses', 292, drawing on Vaughan, *Charles the Bold*, 164–6, and id.,
Valois Burgundy (London, 1975), 187–9; see also *Charles the Bold*, 162 and 258–60. Hudson errs, however,
in writing that Charles 'treasured his collection of books' in Italian ('Two Ferrarese Masses', 292); Vaughan
(*Charles the Bold*, 164) identifies only a single Italian book in the duke's possession, a volume that Charles
did not even commission but received as a gift from Louis XI.

[13] Vaughan, *Valois Burgundy*, 189.

[14] On the English, and English music, at Bruges, see particularly Strohm, *Music in Late Medieval Bruges*,
63–4, 66, 120, 123–7, and 131–3.

[15] The portrayal of Charles's relationship to the English and English music in Sylvia W. Kenney, *Walter
Frye and the Contenance Angloise* (New Haven, 1964), 13–17, which has had considerable influence on musicological studies, would seem overdrawn; in particular, statements like 'Charles . . . took more personal

of York, their marriage clearly brought a notable amount of English music to the court.[16] He spoke the English language well enough to converse with his brother-in-law, Edward IV, and to pacify a troop of mutinous English soldiers.[17] Charles could even appear to have valued settings of English poetry: if no such pieces occur in any of the Northern chansonniers once thought to hail from his court, Mellon, a collection whose repertory shows a pronounced Burgundian flavour despite its Neapolitan origin, contains three of them.[18] Nevertheless, we do not have a single English song by a composer not of English birth.[19] Nor, to the best of our knowledge, did the most prominent musical Englishman in Charles's service, Robert Morton, write any music in the language.[20]

Clearly, then, we can hardly take it for granted that Charles's Italian leanings would have had any measurable effect on musical productivity at his court. The same surely applies to the Italians in Bruges and elsewhere in the North. Hudson, indeed, suggests that 'it would be strange for an expatriate Italian to commission a French-speaking composer in the Netherlands to compose music to an Italian text during a period when even in Italy French music was preferred over Italian'.[21] This view requires some qualification. It overlooks the enormous prestige in Italy of native poetic-musical traditions that lay essentially outside the sphere of notation, as well as the receptivity of peninsular manuscripts both to written reflections of those traditions and to pieces that set Italian lyrics in a more elaborate polyphonic style reminiscent of the Northern chanson.[22] But on the

interest in the musical activities of his English allies' (p. 14), or 'Charles also seems to have exhibited some predilection for English musicians' (p. 16) go largely unsubstantiated.

[16] On Charles and Margaret, see principally Vaughan, *Charles the Bold*, 158–9; on the immediate musical consequences of their marriage, see particularly Rob C. Wegman, 'New Data Concerning the Origins and Chronology of Brussels, Koninklijke Bibliotheek, Manuscript 5557', *TVNM* 36 (1986), 5–25, esp. 10–11.

[17] For Charles and Edward, see bk. iv, ch. 8, of Commynes's memoirs, as printed in Philippe de Commynes, *Mémoires*, ed. Joseph Calmette and G. Durville (Les Classiques de l'histoire de France au Moyen Age, 3, 5, and 6; Paris, 1924–5), ii. 53, or, in translation, *The Memoirs of Philippe de Commynes*, ed. Samuel Kinser, trans. Isabelle Cazeaux (Columbia, SC, 1969–73), i. 275; for the episode with the English troops, see Vaughan, *Charles the Bold*, 384. Given these pieces of testimony, I find it puzzling that Vaughan downgrades the extent of Charles's English to '[s]ome scraps' (ibid. 163). Whether Charles needed English to converse with his wife would seem moot.

[18] On the origins of Mellon, see *The Mellon Chansonnier*, ed. Leeman L. Perkins and Howard Garey (New Haven, 1979), i. 17–28, as well as Ronald Woodley, 'Tinctoris's Italian Translation of the Golden Fleece Statutes: A Text and a (Possible) Context', *EMH* 8 (1988), 173–244 at 188; on its Burgundian affiliations, see Perkins and Garey, i. 4–8; on the possible association of the English songs with Charles's court, see ibid. 7–8 and Woodley, 'Tinctoris's Italian Translation', 188–9, many observations in which remain pertinent even if one does not accept the hypothesis of which they form part. I should note that Strohm, *Music in Late Medieval Bruges*, 129, describes the portion of Mellon in which all three English pieces appear as a 'somewhat self-contained . . . section', whose 'repertory is older than that in the rest of the manuscript' and 'came from Bruges'. Rather than seek to argue the pros and cons of this hypothesis, I should simply point out that it does not materially affect the argument set forth here.

[19] Cf. David Fallows, 'English Song Repertories of the Mid-fifteenth Century', *Proceedings of the Royal Musical Association*, 103 (1976–7), 61–79.

[20] Cf. Morton, *The Collected Works.*   [21] Hudson, 'Two Ferrarese Masses', 292.

[22] On the place of unwritten traditions in the Italian musical landscape of the 15th c., the essential statement remains Nino Pirrotta, 'Music and Cultural Tendencies in 15th-Century Italy', *JAMS* 19 (1966), 127–61, repr. in id., *Music and Culture in Italy from the Middle Ages to the Baroque* (Harvard Studies in the History of Music, 1; Cambridge, Mass., 1984), 80–112. The principal concentrations of pre-frottolesque

whole, Hudson's point seems well taken: certainly, the dominance of French texts in Italian secular repositories before the advent of the *frottola* remains incontestable.[23] In any event, speculation about what Italian patrons in the Low Countries might have commissioned from composers in Bruges or elsewhere does not alter the fact that we lack any tangible evidence for the use of Italian as a musical language north of the Alps in Busnoys's time.[24]

II

Against this background, the two Italian songs credited to Busnoys would thus indeed seem to provide strong *prima facie* evidence of a visit to Italy. We might feel particularly confident about this in the case of *Con tutta gentileça*. The piece comes down to us in the two closely related Florentine manuscripts Pixérécourt and Florence 229, lacking attribution in the first and under the name 'Antonius Busnois' in the second.[25] Its text, however, already appears some two generations earlier: the so-called Lucca, or Mancini, codex from the early fifteenth century

---

Italian song appear in the Neapolitan manuscript Montecassino 871 and in Escorial IV.a.24, all but the latest portions of which would seem now to come from northern Italy; Escorial IV.a.24 in particular stands out for its high proportion of chanson-like pieces. See *The Musical Manuscript Montecassino 871: A Neapolitan Repertory of Sacred and Secular Music of the Late Fifteenth Century*, ed. Isabel Pope and Masakata Kanazawa (Oxford, 1978); *The Chansonnier El Escorial IV.a.24: Commentary and Edition*, ed. Martha Hanen (Musicological Studies, 36; Henryville, 1983); Dennis Slavin, 'On the Origin of Escorial IV.a.24 (*EscB*)', *Studi musicali*, 19 (1990), 259–303; and David Fallows, 'Polyphonic Song in the Florence of Lorenzo's Youth *ossia*: The Provenance of the Manuscript Berlin 78.C.28: Naples or Florence?', in Piero Gargiulo (ed.), *La musica a Firenze al tempo di Lorenzo il Magnifico: Congresso internazionale di studi, Firenze, 15–17 giugno 1992* (Quaderni della Rivista italiana di musicologia, 30; Florence, 1993), 47–61 at 54.

   [23] For an overview of the relevant manuscripts, see Allan Atlas, *The Cappella Giulia Chansonnier (Rome, Biblioteca Apostolica Vaticana, C. G. XIII.27)* (Musicological Studies, 27; Brooklyn, 1975–6), i. 233–58; in all of them, Italian-texted pieces form at best a significant minority.

   [24] In the light of this conclusion, we may well speculate about the origins of Joye's *Poy che crudel*. Documents cited by Strohm, *Music in Late Medieval Bruges*, 27–8, place the composer at Bruges from 1451 onwards, although the record does show gaps; in particular, we seem to have no indication of him there between 1454 and 1462. To imagine *Poy che crudel* written in the North would presuppose that the text— which David Fallows has identified as the work of the Florentine Rosello Roselli—travelled all the way from Tuscany to Bruges and from there, in a setting by a composer relatively young and clearly little known, found entry into a repertory so closely identified with Ferrara as that of Porto 714; cf. Lewis Lockwood, *Music in Renaissance Ferrara 1450–1505: The Creation of a Musical Centre in the Fifteenth Century* (Oxford, 1984), 107–18. I think we might more reasonably conclude that Joye made an otherwise undocumented trip to Italy, or that *Poy che crudel*, as Strohm has already surmised (*Music in Late Medieval Bruges*, 126), represents yet another contrafact—although, for reasons suggested immediately above, hardly of an English setting.

   [25] Pixérécourt, fos. 13ᵛ–14ʳ; Florence 229, fos. 52ᵛ–53ʳ. On the provenance and relationship of the two manuscripts, see particularly Brown, *A Florentine Chansonnier*, Text vol., 9–15; see also the new information on the chief scribe of Florence 229 in Flynn Warmington, 'The Missing Link: The Scribe of the Berlin Chansonnier in Florence', *La musica a Firenze al tempo di Lorenzo il Magnifico*, 63–8 at 67. The combined evidence of repertory and heraldry indicates that the production of Florence 229 must have fallen between Sept. 1491 and Jan. 1493; cf. Brown, *A Florentine Chansonnier*, Text vol., 25; Louise Litterick in her review of Brown's edition, *EMH* 6 (1986), 303–17 at 307–8; and Joshua Rifkin, 'Pietrequin Bonnel and Ms. 2794 of the Biblioteca Riccardiana', *JAMS* 29 (1976), 284–96 at 295 n. 33. Allan Atlas infers a *terminus ante quem* for Pixérécourt from the absence in it of any music by Isaac, who arrived at Florence some time between 15 Sept. 1484 and 1 July 1485; see *The Cappella Giulia Chansonnier*, i. 255, as well as below, n. 202, and also the biographical evidence surveyed in Martin Picker, *Henricus Isaac: A Guide to Research* (Garland Composer

preserves it in a setting by the Florentine composer Andrea Stephani.[26] The version in Lucca enables us to recognize the poem as a *ballata*, something hardly possible on the basis of the rather fragmentary redaction in Pixérécourt and Florence 229. Perhaps more important, the presence of *Con tutta gentileça* in this early repertory would appear to have significant repercussions for Busnoys. Given the lack of any known concordances for either Stephani's piece or the verses on their own, it seems clear that this text neither travelled widely nor enjoyed prolonged currency. If Busnoys set it, therefore, he could scarcely have done so very far from Florence.[27]

But did he set it? I have no real inclination to question the attribution in Florence 229.[28] Howard Brown, however, has pointed to a problem of a different sort. 'It is not clear', he observes, 'how the poem was intended to be set to the music . . . The . . . phrase divisions found in both Florence 229 and Paris 15123 [= Pixérécourt] . . . make nonsense of the *ballata* form; the second line of the *ripresa* is divided by a full stop with coronas in all voices (m. 12) and the music for the first *piede* (beginning in m. 30) is not obviously distinct from what immediately precedes it'.[29] No fewer than three practised hands—Brown himself, Nino Pirrotta, and Walter Rubsamen—have tried fitting the text to the superius, with results about which they themselves can hardly have felt very easy.[30] Not surprisingly, Brown found himself moved to suspect 'that the poem was added as an Italian contrafactum to a preexisting piece by Busnois', and David Fallows has put it even more strongly: 'musical and poetic form match so poorly in Busnoys's setting that it is difficult to believe that he had anything to do with their assembly'.[31] These doubts receive a dramatic boost from a discovery made recently by Stephen Rees: another poem from the Lucca codex—*Fuggir non posso*, which even occupies part of the same bifolio as *Con tutta gentileça*—also made its way into Pixérécourt; provocatively, it serves there as the text for a piece of Caron's

Resource Manuals, 35; New York, 1991), 4–5, or Martin Staehelin, *Die Messen Heinrich Isaacs* (Publikationen der Schweizerischen musikforschenden Gesellschaft, ser. 2, vol. 28; Berne, 1977), ii. 19–20.

[26] Lucca 184, fo. [XCVIII]ʳ (p. 67, fo. 18bʳ); see *The Lucca Codex: Codice Mancini. Lucca, Archivio di Stato, MS 184 · Perugia, Biblioteca Comunale 'Augusta', MS 3065*, Introductory Study and Facsimile Edition by John Nádas and Agostino Ziino (Ars Nova, 1; Lucca, 1990), as well as the edition of Stephani's piece in *The Music of Fourteenth-Century Italy*, ed. Nino Pirrotta (CMM 8, vol. v; n.p., 1964), 38 (complete text on p. xv). The poem as found in Lucca carries the notice 'mancaci due stanze'.

[27] Nádas and Ziino have argued that the Lucca codex resided in Florence between '*ca*. 1410' and 'nearly two centuries later'; see *The Lucca Codex*, 47–9 (the quotations from p. 49). See also below, n. 34.

[28] Cf., however, below, pp. 518–19.

[29] Brown, *A Florentine Chansonnier*, Text vol., 228.

[30] For Brown's underlay, see ibid.; for Pirrotta's, see ibid., Music vol., no. 53; for Rubsamen's—which achieves partially better declamation at the cost of ignoring virtually all the ligatures—see 'From Frottola to Madrigal', 177–9.

[31] See *A Florentine Chansonnier*, Text vol., 228, and David Fallows, 'Busnoys and the Early Fifteenth Century: A Note on "L'ardant desir" and "Faictes de moy" ', *ML* 71 (1990), 20–4 at 24 n. 10.

that a local predecessor of Pixérécourt, Florence 2356, provides with the French incipit *Cui diem vous*.[32]

Thanks in part to this information, we can in fact raise Brown's conjecture to the level of certainty. Fig. 20.1 shows Stephani's setting of *Con tutta gentileça* as it appears in the Lucca codex, Fig. 20.2 Busnoys's superius in the version of Pixérécourt. Even a cursory glance cannot fail to reveal a striking congruence in textual disposition between the two manuscripts: both set the *ripresa* and the first of the two *piedi* beneath the notes of the superius, then accommodate the second *piede* and the *volta* on the final stave of that voice to the right of the concluding double-bar—with the difference, of course, that the layout in the Lucca manuscript makes perfect sense given the structure of the music, quite in contrast to what we have already observed with Pixérécourt. Several smaller details, too, reinforce the impression of uncommon closeness. In the third line of the poem, Lucca, Pixérécourt, and Florence 229 all share the doubtful word 'sparita' where, as Brown points out, we might better read 'aparita'.[33] An even more provocative example occurs in line 1. Pixérécourt and, again, Florence 229 mangle the obviously correct reading of Lucca, 'veçose ssi pulita', to 'se si pulita', which they then repeat in an apparent attempt to fill out the metre. In Lucca, as a glance at Fig. 20.1 will show, the course of the melody forces the first two syllables of 'veçose' beneath the level of the surrounding text, rendering them an easy candidate for omission. All these observations lead to a single inescapable conclusion: the scribe of Pixérécourt—or, more likely, whoever wrote the exemplar from which he worked—drew the text of *Con tutta gentileça* from the Lucca codex itself.[34]

We may thus definitively eliminate *Con tutta gentileça* from the list of Italian works by Franco-Netherlandish composers and add it to the tally of contrafacts. But if doing so would appear to remove it from the arena of biographical significance, it leaves an unanswered question about the music that we might pause to consider. As Brown has observed, 'neither the phrase structure, the tonal plan, nor the harmonic style [of *Con tutta gentileça*] correspond[s] closely with Busnois's French *formes fixes*'.[35] Indeed, we need not limit ourselves to the *formes fixes* to find a paucity of analogues for this piece. No other vocal genre either seems to offer a ready model, and the possibility of instrumental origin would appear even more remote: whether or not we have any reason to suppose that Busnoys wrote instrumental music in the first place, nothing about *Con tutta*

---

[32] My thanks to David Fallows for communicating the information on *Fuggir non posso*. Cf. Lucca 184, fos. [lxxxix]ᵛ–[xc]ʳ (pp. 54–5, fos. 18aᵛ–19aʳ), and Pixérécourt, fos. 36ᵛ–37ʳ, 'Caron'. Caron's piece appears with the incipit 'Cui diem vous' in Florence 2356, fos. 9ᵛ–10ʳ (13ᵛ–14ʳ), and—in a musically variant form—as 'Enquuque lentor' in Bologna Q 16, fos. cxiiiiᵛ–cxvʳ (130ᵛ–131ʳ); neither source provides an attribution.
[33] See *A Florentine Chansonnier*, Text vol., 227.
[34] The same would appear to hold true for *Fuggir non posso*. I might note that these observations provide concrete evidence for Nádas's and Ziino's suppositions about the whereabouts of Lucca in the 15th c. (see above, n. 27).
[35] *A Florentine Chansonnier*, Text vol., 228.

gentileça recalls even the least idiomatically conceived instrumental repertory of the period.[36]

Another observation of Brown's may, however, point to a way out of our quandary. Elsewhere in his edition of Florence 229, he notes that the manuscript contains at least two bergerettes shorn of their couplets and represented by their refrain alone.[37] As Brown recognizes, the unsuspecting eye could easily take these pieces for rondeaux—although rather odd rondeaux in some instances, as many bergerette refrains lack the medial cadence on a non-tonic degree so characteristic of rondeaux settings.[38] As it happens, the truncated bergerettes in Florence 229 include one by Busnoys, *J'ay mains de biens*, which has this incomplete form in both Florence 229 and Pixérécourt.[39] Indeed, as we see from Ex. 20.1, the opening of *J'ay mains de biens* looks strikingly similar to that of *Con tutta gentileça*.[40] Both pieces, moreover, share the same cleffing and mode, have approximately the same length—48 bars for *Con tutta gentileça*, 49 for the refrain of *J'ay mains de biens*—and lack a strong non-tonic cadence at mid-point. We might thus wonder if *Con tutta gentileça* does not present the disguised remains of a bergerette.[41] Ex. 20.2 presents an impression of how the putative original might have worked. I shall presuppose the most common sort of refrain, four lines in either octosyllables or decasyllables.[42] By analogy with Busnoys's rondeau *Chi dit on benedicite*, the cadence at measure 12 would mark the end of the first line.[43] The next phrase,

---

[36] For fundamental background on this point, see Litterick, 'Performing Franco-Netherlandish Secular Music', and ead., 'On Italian Instrumental Ensemble Music in the Late Fifteenth Century', in Iain Fenlon (ed.), *Music in Medieval and Early Modern Europe: Patronage, Sources and Texts* (Cambridge, 1981), 117–30.

[37] *A Florentine Chansonnier*, Text vol., 62. [38] See ibid. and 77–8.

[39] Cf. ibid. 231. Montagna, 'Caron, Hayne, Compère', 128, questions Busnoys's authorship of *J'ay mains de biens* and, for that matter, *Chi dit on benedicite*, which we shall encounter shortly. I cannot take this occasion to consider his arguments, nor to explore whether, and to what degree, the observations presented here might impinge on them.

[40] In saying this, I do not wish to claim any great distinctiveness for the starting gambit of either piece; see e.g. the juxtaposition of Busnoys's *Ung plus que tous* and Basin's *Madame faites moy savoir* in *A Florentine Chansonnier*, Text vol., 75.

[41] Unfortunately, the hope that the piece that follows *Con tutta gentileça* in Pixérécourt might turn out to represent the missing portion of the bergerette has proved illusory: the work, the anonymous *Chiamo merçe* (fos. 14ᵛ–15ʳ), itself falls into two parts and differs in cleffing, metre, and mode; cf. the transcription in Edward Pease, 'An Edition of the Pixérécourt Manuscript: Paris, Bibliothèque nationale, Fond fr. 15123' (Ph.D. diss., Indiana University, 1959), ii. 44–6.

[42] Busnoys's surviving bergerettes show no identifiable tendency to octosyllabic over decasyllabic lines or *vice versa*. Verses of both types, of course, may in fact contain an additional declaimed syllable, as formal versification does not count the final 'e' of a 'feminine' line; cf. the discussion of French metrics by Howard Garey in *The Mellon Chansonnier*, ii. 79–81. While my hypothetical underlay allows for this possibility with octosyllabics, experimentation has dissuaded me from attempting a similar accommodation with decasyllabics—even though lines 2 and 3 would in fact accommodate eleven declaimed syllables quite comfortably, producing a decasyllabic strophe akin to that of *J'ay mains de biens* (cf. Brown, *A Florentine Chansonnier*, Text vol., 231). The ligated notation of m. 2 might not correspond to Busnoys's original; in *J'ay mains de biens*, for example (cf. Ex. 20.1(*a*)), both Dijon and Seville–Paris present the semibreves in m. 2 as separate notes, producing a far more idiomatic declamation.

[43] For *Chi dit on benedicite*, see *A Florentine Chansonnier*, Music vol., no. 56; Busnoys's *M'a vostre cueur* (ibid., no. 228) also seems worthy of note in this connection for its inclusion of a medial fermata (after line 2) at m. 23. In a number of contemporary *formes fixes* settings, a similar cadence marks the end of the first hemistich; for examples in Florence 229, see nos. 64 (Agricola, *C'est mal cherché*), 77 (anon., *En effait*), 122 (Agricola, *En attendant*), and—a related if not perfectly analogous case—125 (Fresneau, *Ha qu'il m'ennuye*).

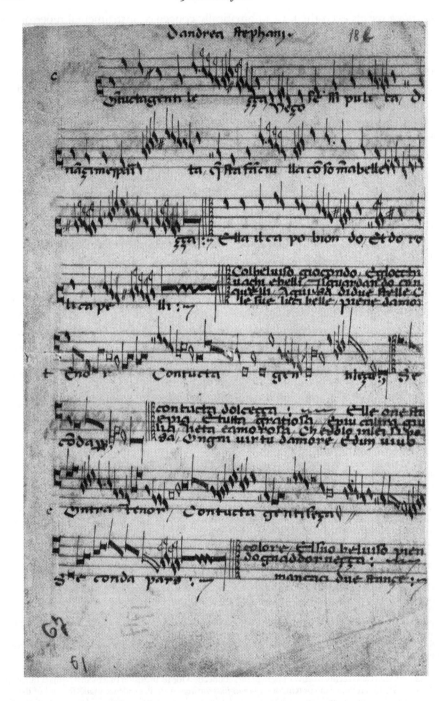

FIG. 20.1. Andrea Stephani, *Con tutta gentileça* (Lucca 184, fo. XCVIIIʳ)

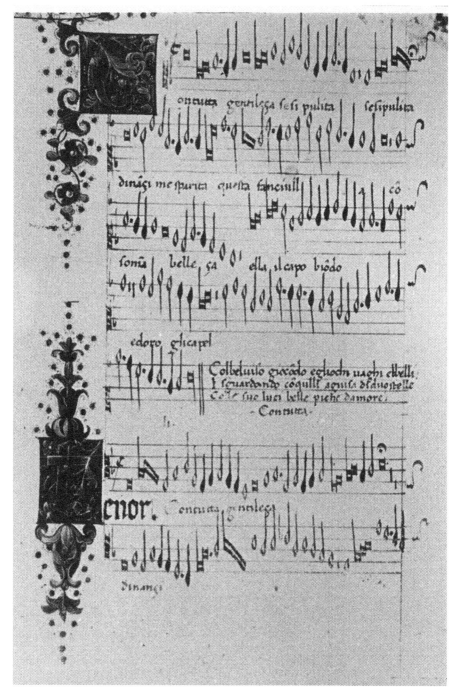

FIG. 20.2. Busnoys, *Con tutta gentileça* (Pixérécourt, fos. 13ᵛ–14ʳ)

Ex. 20.1. Busnoys, opening of (*a*) *J'ay mains de biens*; (*b*) *Con tutta gentileça*

Ex. 20.2. Busnoys, *Con tutta gentileça* as a hypothetical bergerette refrain
(x = text syllable)

measures 13–23, would set line 2, while the short phrases occupying measures 24–9 and 30–6 divide line 3 between them. The refrain would then conclude with the fourth line covering measures 38–48.[44]

Before leaving *Con tutta gentileça*, we should consider briefly some further implications that it might have. David Fallows has recently called attention to another Busnoys piece with a text of significantly earlier date, *Faites de moy tout ce*

Reading *Con tutta gentileça* in this fashion, however, would both stretch the hemistich virtually to the breaking point and, by deferring the completion of the first line to m. 23, result in an implausible formal imbalance.

[44] Reading *Con tutta gentileça* as a bergerette not only makes it more comprehensible musically but could also explain why the Florentines chose this particular poem to replace its French text: the Italian ballata, after all, has essentially the same form as the virelai, the extended sibling of the bergerette. On the other hand, both the omission of the presumed second part as well as the evident lack of concern for any sort of fit between words and music makes one wonder if any of the parties involved really cared much about issues of textual appropriateness in the first place; on this point, see also below, n. 52.

qu'il vous plaira.[45] Provocatively, the music appears with this text in only two sources—Pixérécourt and Florence 229.[46] If, after our experience with *Con tutta gentileça*, this raises our suspicions, a look at the composition itself only intensifies them. The five lines of verse set under the superius in both manuscripts do not, as Brown has suggested, constitute the refrain of a *rondeau cinquain*; as the rhyme scheme alone makes plain, they present the refrain of a four-line rondeau plus the first line of the following demistrophe.[47] Significantly, a third manuscript, the large chansonnier now divided between Seville and Paris, transmits Busnoys's chanson with an—unfortunately incomplete—poem beginning 'Amours me tient en son demaine'.[48] It would seem more than likely that this represents the text Busnoys actually set.[49]

These findings open something of a Pandora's box. Although—or perhaps because—Florence 229 and Pixérécourt preserve by far the largest concentration of Busnoys's work outside the great Northern chansonniers, their reliability as sources for his music has not really come under scrutiny.[50] Only Gerald Montagna has even broached the question; and as he did little to back up his misgivings with hard evidence or rigorous argument, they have remained largely without resonance.[51] Yet on reflection, it seems clear that he has struck a sore point. In the two pieces we have just examined, the decision to dress the music in stolen verbal plumage can only mean that the Florentine scribes lacked access to sources containing the right text.[52] We have seen, too, that *J'ay mains de biens* lost half its music in both Florentine chansonniers.[53] Pixérécourt names Busnoys as the author of Ockeghem's *D'ung aultre amer*, and Florence 229 credits him with

[45] See Fallows, 'Busnoys and the Early Fifteenth Century', 23; for the music of *Faites de moy*, see *A Florentine Chansonnier*, Music vol., no. 221.

[46] Pixérécourt, fos. 132ᵛ–133ʳ, anon.; Florence 229, fos. 238ᵛ–239ʳ, 'Antonius busnois'.

[47] See *A Florentine Chansonnier*, Text vol., 294, but also the qualifications expressed on 79–80; for the remainder of the text, see the transcription of an earlier setting in Mᵃ Carmen Gómez, 'El manuscrito 823 de Montserrat (Biblioteca del Monasterio)', *Musica disciplina*, 36 (1982), 39–93 at 85–7.

[48] Seville–Paris, fos. *m*11ᵛ–*m*12ʳ (Seville 5-I-43, fos. 97ᵛ–98ʳ), anon.; the piece also appears in Verona 757, fos. 38ᵛ–39ʳ, anonymously and without any text.

[49] Ironically, Howard Brown chose *Faites de moy* as his specimen piece for a pioneering article on issues of performance—including texting—in the 15th-c. chanson; see Howard Mayer Brown, 'On the Performance of Fifteenth-Century Chansons', *Early Music*, 1 (1973), 3–10 and esp. 4–5.

[50] Brown, for example, does not directly address the issue in his chapter on the Busnoys pieces in Florence 229; see *A Florentine Chansonnier*, Text vol., 72–82, esp. 72–3 and 80–1.

[51] See Montagna, 'Caron, Hayne, Compère', 127–8.

[52] We may also, I would suggest, read the addition of inappropriate text both to the works of Busnoys discussed here and to the Caron piece identified earlier (see above, and esp. n. 34) as a sign that at least the particular scribal circle responsible for Pixérécourt and Florence 229 regarded text underlay as somehow integral to a work's graphic appearance, even if it in fact had no utility for performance. For a further example in Florence 229, see *A Florentine Chansonnier*, Text vol., 269 (no. 152), and the remarks in Litterick's review, 315–16 n. 18. It would take us too far afield to consider the implications of such cases for the dispute over texting practice and performance in Italian manuscripts of the period—see, for example, the divergent views expressed in Litterick, 'Performing Franco-Netherlandish Secular Music', 478–84, and Brown, *A Florentine Chansonnier*, Text vol., 168.

[53] See above, p. 513.

Cent mille escus, which surely belongs to Caron.[54] Four more works assigned to Busnoys in one or the other of the two manuscripts have conflicting attributions as well—some of these, it would seem, of greater plausibility.[55] This does not mean to say that Florence 229 and Pixérécourt never reflect authoritative models; anyone with doubts on that count need only compare their version of *Seule a par moy* with the one in Casanatense 2856.[56] But scepticism would seem in order. Whether or not we should go so far as Montagna and regard 'the lone Busnois attributions [in Pixérécourt and Florence 229] not as "undisputed" but rather as "unconfirmed" ', we surely have no reason to think that the number of works by or attributed to him in Florence betokens any special connection with the composer.[57] Not only, therefore, does *Con tutta gentileça* fail to provide evidence of Busnoys in Italy; it also casts a dubious light on other supposed indications for his having gone there.

III

With *Con tutta gentileça* restored to the world of the French chanson, Busnoys's putative Italian output dwindles down to *Fortuna desperata*. Here, I think, we may safely accept the authenticity of the Italian text: the form of the music provides a satisfactory, if hardly intimate, fit to the strophic poem associated with it and certainly does not offer even the remotest suggestion of any known French genre.[58] Yet *Fortuna desperata* raises worries of a different sort; for if its connection to Italy would seem transparent enough, that to Busnoys has become increasingly less so.

---

[54] *D'ung aultre amer* bears the ascription 'busnoys' in Pixérécourt, fos. 189ᵛ–190ʳ; cf. Ockeghem, *Collected Works*, iii, p. lxiii. On *Cent mille escus*, see James Thomson, *An Introduction to Philippe(?) Caron* (Musicological Studies, 9; Brooklyn, 1964), 15–16 and 25; Brown, *A Florentine Chansonnier*, Text vol., 81; and below, n. 214 and p. 561. Without exception, the literature claims that Pixérécourt also ascribes this piece to Busnoys. But while the first letter of the heavily trimmed attribution on fo. 10ᵛ clearly reads 'b', the descender at the end of the name bears no resemblance whatever to the scribe's distinctive—and highly uniform—'y'; indeed, it comes much closer to his terminal 'n' as seen on fo. 106ᵛ ('Caron') or 133ᵛ ('Ochgen'). Cf. the reproductions in Andrea Lindmayr, *Quellenstudien zu den Motetten von Johannes Ockeghem* (Neue Heidelberger Studien zur Musikwissenschaft, 16; Laaber, 1990), 70, or above, Fig. 11.3, in her contribution to this volume. Could the scribe have written 'Basiron'?

[55] Cf. Montagna, 'Caron, Hayne, Compère', 127. Florence 229 and Pixérécourt conflict with one another on *Se brief je puis*, the former giving it to Caron, the latter to Busnoys (cf., most conveniently, Brown, *A Florentine Chansonnier*, Text vol., 242); Pixérécourt names Busnoys as the composer of *Je suis venue* and *J'ay bien choisi*, both of which Casanatense 2856 assigns to Hayne (cf. ibid. 217 and 254). On the remaining conflict, *Je ne fay plus*, see below, pp. 522–3 and esp. n. 72.

[56] See *A Florentine Chansonnier*, Music vol., no. 60, and Catherine Brooks, 'Antoine Busnois, Chanson Composer', *JAMS* 6 (1953), 111–35 at 129–30.

[57] See Montagna, 'Caron, Hayne, Compère', 127–8; for more on some of these 'unconfirmed attributions', see below, nn. 170 and 213, and pp. 561–2.

[58] On the text of *Fortuna desperata*, see Honey Meconi's contribution to this volume, Ch. 19. The phrase divisions of the superius would seem to force the singer to break the metrically necessary elisions at 'iniqua e' and 'fama ay' (cf. below, Ex. 20.6).

The first signs of unease manifested themselves in an article published by Julie Cumming in 1980. According to Cumming, certain features both of the transmission and in the piece itself made Busnoys's authorship look decidedly questionable.[59] These reservations did not go unchallenged; in her dissertation of 1987, Paula Higgins countered them at some length.[60] Yet at virtually the same moment as she came to the defence of *Fortuna desperata*, an article by Barton Hudson brought up new considerations militating against its attribution to Busnoys.[61] Given the timing of their contributions, neither Higgins nor Hudson could address the other's arguments. For Hudson and Cumming, moreover, the authorship of *Fortuna desperata* represented more or less a side-issue in articles primarily concerned with other things, while Higgins restricted her discussion largely to the specific points advanced by Cumming.[62] The matter has thus remained unresolved; and given the importance of the piece—not just for the biographical issues of primary concern here, but for other questions as well—a fresh examination would seem in order.[63]

We might best start with the transmission. As readers can see from Table 20.1, *Fortuna desperata* survives in a large and, indeed, growing number of sources.[64] Almost without exception, however, the many manuscripts and single printed edition remain silent about its composer: the only attribution that scholars have located thus far occurs in the extensive collection of polyphony housed without

---

[59] See Julie E. Cumming, 'The Goddess Fortuna Revisited', *Current Musicology*, 30 (1980), 7–23 at 7–8.

[60] See Higgins, 'Antoine Busnois and Musical Culture', 22–5.

[61] See Hudson, 'Two Ferrarese Masses', 290–6.

[62] The most recent published comment on *Fortuna desperata*, in Reinhard Strohm's *The Rise of European Music, 1380–1500* (Cambridge, 1993), 620, takes notice of Cumming and Higgins but seems to have missed Hudson's article; Strohm suggests that the piece 'originated in Italy, perhaps in Naples, *c*.1480, and that its supposed connection with Busnois is an error'.

[63] Of these questions, I might single out that of Busnoys's reputation and his impact on other composers. The circulation of *Fortuna desperata* vastly exceeds that of any other work attributed to him (cf. Leeman Perkins's catalogue, above, Ch. 13, App. D); and with the exception of *Je ne demande autre de gré*, no other secular piece of his served as a model for more than a single new composition. Readers can gain some impression of the stakes involved by trying to imagine the discussion of 'Busnois's Emulators' in Higgins, 'Antoine Busnois and Musical Culture', 21–2, with all references to *Fortuna desperata* removed, and with the remarks on Obrecht's *Missa Diversorum tenorum*—now known under the title *Plurimorum carminum I*—qualified by reference to Jacob Obrecht, *New Edition of the Collected Works (New Obrecht Edition)* (Amsterdam, 1983–), x, pp. xiii–xiv. They might also, I should note, remove the five-voice *Missus est angelus* from the list of 'Josquin's pieces based on Busnois models' (21 n. 31); cf. particularly Tom Braas, 'The Five-Part Motet *Missus est angelus Gabriel* and its Conflicting Attributions', in Willem Elders and Frits de Haen (eds.), *Proceedings of the International Josquin Symposium Utrecht 1986* (Utrecht, 1991), 171–83. Obviously, I mean none of this to minimize Busnoys's significance for his contemporaries and successors, let alone to suggest even remotely that his artistic stature in any way depends on the degree of influence he wielded; but statistical problems like these alert us to the need for more subtle, and ultimately more illuminating, measures of the effect that one composer might have on the work of another. For a valuable example involving Busnoys, see Rob C. Wegman, *Born for the Muses: The Life and Masses of Jacob Obrecht* (Oxford, 1994), 86–100, esp. 95–8.

[64] The previously unknown manuscript Frankfurt VII 20—more fully Frankfurt am Main, Stadt- und Universitätsbibliothek, Fragm. lat. VII 20—consists of three parchment leaves used as binding in a book of 1490; for a brief description, see Gerhardt Powitz, *Mittelalterliche Handschriftenfragmente der Stadt- und Universitätsbibliothek Frankfurt am Main* (Frankfurt, 1994), 93. I wish to thank David Fallows for sharing his discovery of this source and placing photocopies at my disposal.

TABLE 20.1. *Sources of* Fortuna desperata

1. Three voices
    Florence 121, fos. 25^v–26^r
    London 35087, fos. xi^v–xii^r
    Perugia 431, fos. 93^v–94^r (83^v–84^r)
    Segovia, fo. clxxiiii^r (167^r), 'Anthonius busnoys'
    Seville–Paris, fos. *n*11^v–*n*12^r (Paris 4379, fos. 40^v–41^r) (originally for three voices; altus added
        by a different scribe)
    Wolfenbüttel 78, fo. 2^v

2. Three voices plus altus 1
    Cape, fos. 78^v–79^r (79^v–80^r) ('Poi che t'hebi nel core')
    Leipzig 1494, fo. 62^r ('Virginis alma parens')
    Paris 676, fos. 24^v–25^r
    Perugia 431, fos. 94^v–95^r (84^v–85^r)
    St Gallen 462, fos. 6^v–7^r
    St Gallen 463, no. 144 (S and T only; but cf. below, n. 115)
    Seville–Paris, fos. *n*11^v–*n*12^r (Paris 4379, fos. 40^v–41^r) (cf. version 1)
    Zwickau 78/2, superius, fos. 42^r–43^r
    Canti C, fos. 126^v–127^r

3. Three voices plus altus 1a
    Florence 27, fos. 22^v–23^r ('Poi che te hebi nel core')

4. Three voices plus altus 2
    Bologna Q 16, fos. cxvii^v–cxviii^r (133^v–134^r)

5. Three voices plus altus 3
    London 31922, fos. 4^v–5^r ('Fortune esperee')

6. Three voices (version 1); four voices (version 2); 3 voices with substitute contra
    Cappella Giulia XIII. 27, fos. 56^v–57^r (63^v–64^r), 'Felice' (see below, Sect. VI)

Version not certain
    Basle F. X. 10, no. 17 (fo. 8^r) (four voices; B only)
    Frankfurt VII 20, fo. 1^r (S and T only)

call number at the cathedral of Segovia, which presents the music under the heading 'Anthonius busnoys'.[65] Like *Fortuna desperata* itself, Segovia's ascriptions
have occasioned a considerable measure of discussion. Long regarded as almost a
watchword for unreliability, they have recently undergone a notable rehabilita-
tion in Norma Klein Baker's dissertation on the manuscript.[66] Yet even if we

[65] For this and much of what follows, the reader may usefully consult the facsimile *Cancionero de la
Catedral de Segovia*, ed. Ramon Perales de la Cal (Segovia, 1977). A thorough inventory of Segovia appears
in Norma Klein Baker, 'An Unnumbered Manuscript of Polyphony in the Archives of the Cathedral of
Segovia: Its Provenance and History' (Ph.D. diss., University of Maryland, 1978), i. 242–559; readers without access to this work may consult the list of contents in Higinio Anglés, *La música en la Corte de los Reyes
Católicos*, i. *Polifonía religiosa* (Monumentos de la Música Española, 1; Madrid, 1941), 106–12, or its slightly
less detailed predecessor, Higini Anglès, 'Un manuscrit inconnu avec polyphonie du xve siècle conservé à la
cathédrale de Ségovie (Espagne)', *Acta musicologica*, 8 (1936), 6–17 at 8–17. As both authors number the
pieces identically, references to Baker's inventory will serve for Anglés's lists as well.
[66] See Baker, 'An Unnumbered Manuscript', i. 19–25, 34–62, and especially the conclusions on 60–2.
Higgins, 'Antoine Busnois and Musical Culture', 22–3 n. 34, emphasizes the significance of Baker's findings.

should accept Baker's conclusions in general, we can hardly regard Segovia as a source of proven credibility for every composer in particular. It remains, for example, especially problematic in regard to Compère.[67] At least on external evidence, there would seem no reason to accord it any special trust in regard to Busnoys either. Although the details of its creation remain obscure, the combined evidence of script, paper, and repertory show clearly that it originated in Spain at a date no earlier than 1495, and very likely some years after that.[68] This puts it at more than a little remove from Busnoys and the disputed song: roughly half a continent away from anywhere we know him to have set foot, and at least three years after his death, ten years after he had essentially completed his musical output as we know it, and, as we shall see, a minimum of fifteen years after the composition of *Fortuna desperata* itself.[69] Nothing that we can even surmise about the manuscript does much to close the gap.

To begin with, Segovia does not include a very large stock of Busnoys's work. Apart from *Fortuna desperata*, it attributes only a single piece to him, *Je ne demande autre de gré*, and contains just two more found under his name elsewhere, *Je ne fay plus* and *J'ay pris amours*.[70] Considering the size of the volume, this hardly speaks for either an overriding interest in his music or access to any

[67] Of the fifteen pieces that Segovia ascribes to Compère, only three bear his name in concordant sources as well, while five have conflicting attributions—which, in every instance but at most one, plainly have greater credibility than those in Segovia. For a statistical overview, see *Census-Catalogue*, iii. 137. Readers wanting to find their way to the individual pieces might consult the lists in Baker, 'An Unnumbered Manuscript', i. 578 (although omitting *Sancte Michael ora*, which Segovia in fact leaves anonymous), or Amanda Zuckerman Wesner, 'The Chansons of Loyset Compère: Authenticity and Stylistic Development' (Ph.D. diss., Harvard University, 1992), 26; failing this, they can piece together the titles from Ludwig Finscher, *Loyset Compère (c. 1450–1518): Life and Works* (MSD 12; n.p., 1964), 47–54, or Anglés, *La música en la Corte de los Reyes Católicos*, i. 106–12. On the disputed pieces, see Baker, i. 46–7, and the remarks below on *Je ne fay plus* (n. 72), *Helas* (n. 135), and *J'ay bieau huewer* and *Je ne puis plus* (n. 132).

[68] For the physical evidence, see Baker, 'An Unnumbered Manuscript', i. 63–108; on the precise *terminus post quem*—established by the topical chanson *Vive le noble rey de france* (fo. clxxxʳ [173ʳ], 'loysette compère') among the entries of the principal scribe—see ibid. 220–2, but in the light of Mary Beth Winn, 'Some Texts for Chansons by Loyset Compère', *Musica disciplina*, 33 (1979), 43–54 at 48–50. I should note, however, that Winn's argument relating *Vive le noble rey* uniquely to the battle of Fornovo, which took place in July 1495, does not strike me as ironclad, and I adopt it as a *terminus* for Segovia solely out of caution; the somewhat later date for the song accepted by Baker could in fact come closer to the mark. Whatever the case, anyone inclined to push the date of Segovia as early as possible should not forget that the composition of the chanson need hardly have followed directly on the heels of the battle, and that it would have taken a certain measure of time—weeks, perhaps, but also conceivably months or years—for the piece itself to have made its way into the manuscript. See also my remarks on the composer 'Adam', below, n. 140. The *terminus ante quem* remains open: while Baker ('An Unnumbered Manuscript', i. 195–218) has sought to link Segovia to Queen Isabella of Castile, who died in November 1504, and more specifically to the library that she deposited at the Alcázar, next to the cathedral of Segovia, in 1503, Emilio Ros-Fábregas has persuasively challenged the evidence on which these assertions rest; see 'The Manuscript Barcelona, Biblioteca de Catalunya, M454: Study and Edition in the Context of the Iberian and Continental Manuscript Traditions' (Ph.D. diss., City University of New York, 1992), i. 206–23.

[69] On the date of *Fortuna desperata*, see below, Sect. VI. If we accept Atlas's *terminus ante quem* for Pixérécourt (cf. above, n. 25), then virtually the entire body of music attributed without conflict to Busnoys would appear to have entered circulation before 1485; as exceptions I could list only five works, all for four voices: *Corps digne/Dieu quel mariage*, *In myne zynn*, *L'autrier qui passa*, *Une filleresse d'estouppes*, and the *Patrem vilayge*.

[70] *Je ne demande autre de gré* appears in Segovia on fos. cxiiᵛ–cxiiiʳ (105ᵛ–106ʳ), *J'ay pris amours* on fo. cxᵛ (104ᵛ), and *Je ne fay plus* on fo. clxxxiᵛ (175ᵛ); for the ascriptions, see further in the main text.

significant channels for it. A closer look, moreover, uncovers some critical problems even among these few pieces. The attribution of *Je ne demande*—again, to 'Anthonius busnoys'—receives ample confirmation elsewhere, both in musical sources and in Tinctoris's *Liber de arte contrapuncti*.[71] But *Je ne fay plus* surely belongs to Mureau rather than Busnoys; and Segovia attributes the piece to neither composer but to 'loysette compere'.[72] *J'ay pris amours*, while a better candidate for Busnoys's authorship, presents a similar situation. The *Odhecaton* assigns the piece to Busnoys.[73] So, too, by implication, does Bartolomé Ramos de Pareja: as Bonnie Blackburn has recognized, the theorist's *Musica practica* of 1482 credits Busnoys with a canonic inscription found also in the Segovia copy of *J'ay pris amours*.[74] This copy, however, bears the name 'Joha*n*nes Martini'. As with *Je ne fay plus*, therefore, we face two choices, neither of them favourable to our estimate of Segovia as a source for Busnoys. If we accept his authorship of the piece, then the manuscript or its antecedents stand guilty of failing to recognize authentic Busnoys when they saw it; if we opt for the contending ascription, then Busnoys's presence in the collection grows weaker still.[75]

[71] Copies of *Je ne demande* with attribution appear in Casanatense 2856, no. 104 (fos. 151ᵛ–153ʳ; 'Busnoys'); Pixérécourt, fos. 153ᵛ–155ʳ ('busnoys'); and *Odhecaton*, fos. 47ᵛ–48ʳ ('Busnoys'). For Tinctoris and *Je ne demande*, see below, pp. 538–40.

[72] For the complete sources of *Je ne fay plus*, see Atlas, *The Cappella Giulia Chansonnier*, i. 73–4, or Brown, *A Florentine Chansonnier*, Text vol., 229; the ascriptions to Busnoys—reading 'A. busnois' and 'Antonius busnoys', respectively—occur in Bologna Q 17 (fos. 37ᵛ–38ʳ) and Florence 229 (fos. 54ᵛ–55ʳ). For transcriptions of the music, see, among other places, *A Florentine Chansonnier*, Music vol., no. 55, and *Harmonice Musices Odhecaton A*, ed. Helen Hewitt and Isabel Pope (The Medieval Academy of America: Studies and Documents, 5; Cambridge, Mass, 1942, repr. New York, 1978), 235–6. On the authorship, see particularly Atlas, i. 74. While Brown (*A Florentine Chansonnier*, Text vol., 81) defends the attribution to Busnoys on musical grounds, his arguments do not strike me as persuasive. The absence of imitation, already noted by Atlas (cf. also below, n. 213), surely weighs more heavily against Busnoys than the more subtle aspects of phrase structure emphasized by Brown weigh against Mureau—especially as a further chanson by this composer, *Tant fort me tarde ta venue* (Florence 176, fos. 71ᵛ–73ʳ, 'G. muream'), displays precisely the clear structural articulation that Brown misses in the one piece of Mureau's on which he bases his comparison. The sources, too, strike me as favouring Mureau to a greater degree than even Atlas has stressed, not only because of their geographic distribution but on grounds of chronology as well: with Florence 176—which, incidentally, presents *Tant fort* and *Je ne fay plus* one after another (cf. below, n. 205)—Mureau's name makes its way into the transmission considerably earlier than does that of Busnoys (cf. Atlas, *The Cappella Giulia Chansonnier*, i. 247). Against this, Bologna Q 17 can claim no particular authority for its Busnoys attributions (see Atlas, i. 59 and 74), and the status of Florence 229, as we have already implied, would seem problematic (see above, Sect. II). On the ascription to Compère—the one composer who does not come seriously into contention—see, particularly, Baker, 'An Unnumbered Manuscript', i. 57–8, and Wesner, 'The Chansons of Loyset Compère', 216–18.

[73] *Odhecaton*, fos. 44ᵛ–45ʳ, 'Busnoys'; for a transcription from this source, see Hewitt, *Odhecaton*, 305–6.

[74] See Bonnie J. Blackburn, 'Obrecht's *Missa Je ne demande* and Busnoys's Chanson: An Essay in Reconstructing Lost Canons', *TVNM* 45 (1995), 18–32 at 32 n. 25; I wish to thank Dr Blackburn for sharing with me both her original discovery and her article in advance of its publication. For a transcription of *J'ay pris amours* from Segovia, see Johannes Martini, *Secular Pieces*, ed. Edward G. Evans, Jr. (Recent Researches in the Music of the Middle Ages and Early Renaissance, 1; Madison, 1975), 38–40.

[75] Determining the true author of *J'ay pris amours* presents some difficulty. The piece belongs to the genre that Honey Meconi has recently defined as the 'art-song reworking'; see her 'Art-Song Reworkings: An Overview', *Journal of the Royal Musical Association*, 119 (1994), 1–42, which Prof. Meconi generously shared with me before publication. Busnoys's known output includes no further compositions of this type, while Martini's includes several—among them, a further setting of *J'ay pris amours* (see Martini, *Secular Pieces*, 35–7, and *A Florentine Chansonnier*, Music vol., no. 179). The attribution in Petrucci, moreover, might not represent independent testimony but derive ultimately from Ramos. On the other hand, Martini's

Nor can we bring Segovia much closer to Busnoys by other means. The music in the choirbook covers a broad geographic span—broad enough, indeed, to have impelled more than a little speculation in recent years as to how most if it got to Spain. Some of the paths opened up in the course of this speculation would even seem to hold promising implications for Busnoys. Yet without exception, the promise fails to materialize. Baker, for instance, has proposed that the non-Spanish contents of the manuscript reflect the visit of the Habsburg-Burgundian chapel to the court of Castile in 1502; but as Reinhard Strohm and Honey Meconi have both observed, the absence of any music by Pierre de la Rue seriously undermines this hypothesis.[76] The absence of La Rue also weakens Meconi's case for associating the collection with an earlier Spanish-Habsburg encounter, the arrival on the Iberian peninsula of Marguerite of Austria in March 1497 and her wedding to Juan of Castile at Burgos the following month.[77] La Rue, after all, had sung in the Habsburg-Burgundian chapel since 1492; there seems no reason to think that the court would have propagated his music less energetically in 1497 than five years later.[78] With the single, and perhaps idiosyncratic, exception of the Chigi Codex, the earliest manuscripts in the great Habsburg-Burgundy complex already accord him a dominant position in their repertory; and while none of these sources would appear to go back as far as 1497–indeed, none of them demonstrably predates 1505–their repertorial profile surely reflects preferences established over more than a handful of years.[79] As Martin Picker has noted, too, the 'heavy representation' of La Rue in the

remaining secular output includes no canons even remotely like that of the disputed *J'ay pris amours*. Nor would Ramos, writing at Bologna contemporaneously with Martini's activity in nearby Ferrara—cf. Claude Palisca, 'Ramos', *Die Musik in Geschichte und Gegenwart* (Kassel, 1949–79), x, col. 1909—seem an easy witness to shake; and Blackburn, 'Obrecht's *Missa Je ne demande*', 32 at n. 25, has plausibly suggested that the attribution in Segovia could have arisen through a confusion with the 'other' Martini setting. Further indirect evidence for Busnoys's authorship of *J'ay pris amours* could come from the four-voice setting of Japart (*A Florentine Chansonnier*, Music vol., no. 152); this piece clearly emulates the disputed composition by transforming the original superius into a bass line through transposition and retrograde motion, all indicated by means of a canon whose wording shows the unmistakable inspiration of the inscription quoted by Ramos (cf. ibid., Text vol., 269)—and as Allan Atlas demonstrates in this volume (Ch. 18), Japart often took Busnoys's compositions as a model.

[76] See Baker, 'An Unnumbered Manuscript', i. 192–239, and esp. 226–39; Strohm, *Music in Late Medieval Bruges*, 143; and Meconi, 'Art-Song Reworkings', 15.   [77] See ibid. 16.

[78] For La Rue's early service in the chapel, see Walter Rubsamen, 'La Rue', *Die Musik in Geschichte und Gegenwart*, viii, cols. 225–6, as well as the important comments in Honey Meconi, 'Sacred Tricinia and Basevi 2439', *I Tatti Studies: Essays in the Renaissance*, 4 (1991), 151–99 at 156–7.

[79] Apart from Chigi, I refer here to Brussels, Bibliothèque royale, MS 9126; Jena, Universitätsbibliothek, MS 22; and Vienna, Österreichische Nationalbibliothek, MS 1783, all of which originated before the death of Philip the Fair in 1506. For general background on these sources, and La Rue's position in them, see Herbert Kellman, 'Josquin and the Courts of the Netherlands and France: The Evidence of the Sources', in Edward E. Lowinsky (ed.), *Josquin des Prez: Proceedings of the International Josquin Festival-Conference* (London, 1976), 181–216 at 192–4 and 209–11, as well as the relevant entries in the *Census-Catalogue*.The common assignment of Chigi to the late 15th c. rests more on hunches derived from the nature of its repertory than on concrete diplomatic or heraldic evidence; in terms of script, decoration, and layout, in fact, it would seem a direct predecessor to Brussels 9126, which dates from 1505 (cf. Kellman, 'Josquin and the Courts', 210). On the possibility that Vienna 1783—and with it, therefore, its scribal companion Jena 22—originated as early as 1500, see Walter H. Rubsamen, 'Unifying Techniques in Selected Masses of Josquin and La Rue: A Stylistic Comparison', in Lowinsky (ed.), *Josquin des Prez*, 369–400 at 370 n. 4.

Savoyard chansonnier Brussels 11239 surely reflects the influence of Marguerite, who lived in Savoy for more than five years after her marriage to Duke Philibert II in December 1501.[80]

In any event, the difficulties with both Meconi's and Baker's hypotheses hardly stop with La Rue. The wedding of April 1497, for example, cannot very well account for the prominent representation of Isaac and Agricola.[81] Agricola did not enter the Habsburg-Burgundian chapel until August 1500; and Isaac's Habsburg employment—with Marguerite's father, the emperor Maximilian, rather than the princess herself or her brother, Philip the Fair—began only in mid-November 1496 and may not formally have taken effect until a month after Marguerite arrived in Spain.[82] Beyond these two composers, moreover, it proves hard to find anything in Segovia that we can trace with confidence to either Burgundy or the Habsburgs, whether in 1497 or in 1502. Baker's claim that 'many of Segovia's composers had direct contact with the chapels of the Burgundian-Hapsburg courts' demands considerable qualification.[83] Apart from Agricola and Isaac, she cites Barbireau, Brumel, Busnoys, Caron, Compère, Hayne, Josquin, and Obrecht.[84] Busnoys, of course, we must leave aside as a moot point. Hayne's Burgundian service surely lies too far in the past to have

[80] See Picker's introduction to the facsimile edition *Chansonnier of Marguerite of Austria: Brussel, Koninklijke Bibliotheek, MS. 11239* (Peer, 1988), 8, as well as the fuller exposition of his views in 'A New Look at the "Little" Chansonnier of Margaret of Austria', in *Muziek aan het hof van Margaretha van Oostenrijk* (Jaarboek van het Vlaamse Centrum voor Oude Muziek, 3; Peer, 1987), 27–31, esp. 28–9. Despite the cautions advanced by Honey Meconi, 'Pierre de la Rue and Secular Music at the Court of Marguerite of Austria', ibid. 49–58 at 50, I find it hard to account for the combined evidence of the manuscript's repertory, heraldry, and later presence in Marguerite's library other than to assume that it originated at Savoy during her years of residence there. Unlike Picker, however, I cannot easily imagine Brussels 11239 as a wedding present for Marguerite, or even think of her as its first owner. In either instance, it would surely have borne the combined Savoyard and Habsburg-Burgundian arms visible, among other places, on the first opening of her later chansonnier, Brussels 228; see the pertinent remarks on heraldic usage in Warmington, 'The Missing Link', 66, as well as the reproductions in Martin Picker, *The Chanson Albums of Marguerite of Austria: MSS 228 and 11239 of the Bibliothèque Royale de Belgique, Brussels* (Berkeley and Los Angeles, 1965), frontispiece, pl. 2, and pl. 3, or the facsimile *Album de Marguerite d'Autriche: Brussel, Koninklijke Bibliotheek, MS. 228*, ed. Martin Picker (Peer, 1986). A manuscript starting with seven pieces on the theme of *regretz*, moreover, hardly seems a likely gift for even the most sombre bride. Perhaps the string of *regretz* pieces means that we should situate the chansonnier between Philibert's death in 1504 and Marguerite's subsequent return to the Netherlands.

[81] Segovia attributes eighteen or, more likely, nineteen pieces to Isaac—the very first piece, Isaac's *Missa Wohlauf Gesell von hinnen*, lacks its opening pages, which would presumably have contained an attribution—and nineteen to Agricola; only Obrecht, with thirty-one attributed compositions, exceeds these totals. Cf. Baker, 'An Unnumbered Manuscript', i. 576–83 (but note that *J'ay pris amours*, listed under the Isaac works on p. 579, does not bear an attribution in the manuscript; on a further piece in the list, *Moyses*, see below, n. 150), or the more easily accessible tally in *Census-Catalogue*, iii. 137; see also below, pp. 536 and 542.

[82] For Agricola's entry into the Habsburg-Burgundian chapel, see William F. Prizer, 'Music and Ceremonial in the Low Countries: Philip the Fair and the Order of the Golden Fleece', *EMH* 5 (1985), 113–53 at 126–7; for Isaac, see Staehelin, *Die Messen Heinrich Isaacs*, ii. 43–5, or Picker, *Henricus Isaac*, 7–8.

[83] See Baker, 'An Unnumbered Manuscript', i. 191.

[84] Ibid. 190–1. If, as seems probable, the inscription 'ferdinandus & frater eius' over the trio *Cecus non judicat de coloribus* represents an ascription to the brothers Johannes and Carolus Fernandes (see below, pp. 534–5), then we could add them to the list of composers affiliated with the Burgundian court, as Higgins has found them there in 1468 and 1470; see her review of Strohm, *Music in Late Medieval Bruges*, 159 n. 20. On the other hand, the qualifications we raise about Hayne would surely apply to them as well. See also below, n. 96.

significant implications, especially considering the wide circulation of his music; and the same consideration applies to Caron as well, assuming that we can affiliate him with Burgundy in the first place.[85] Barbireau had contacts with Maximilian, and his music survives largely in Habsburg-Burgundian manuscripts; but he appears in Segovia with only one composition, and his most widely circulated one at that.[86] Josquin had no recorded dealings with any of the Habsburgs before his famous encounter with Philip the Fair in 1501—which in any event probably never took place.[87] For Brumel and Compère, Baker can say only that they 'may have met the Burgundian chapel on its journey to Spain in 1501'.[88]

This leaves Obrecht, by far the dominant composer in Segovia.[89] While Obrecht grew up in the direct shadow of Philip the Good and Charles the Bold, he appears to have had at best glancing contacts with their Habsburg successors; and those for which we have documentation fall just after Marguerite's wedding or Philip's visit of 1502—too late, in either instance, to have had the impact on Segovia imagined by Meconi or Baker.[90] Martin Staehelin has observed as well that the Habsburg-Burgundy manuscripts contain strikingly few works of Obrecht.[91] Among these, moreover, only one, *Mille quingentis*, also appears in

[85] For Hayne and Burgundy, see Louise Litterick, 'Hayne van Ghizeghem', *New Grove*, viii. 417, and Higgins, '*In hydraulis* Revisited', 40 n. 17; for Caron, see Barbara Haggh's contribution to this volume (Ch. 12).

[86] On Barbireau, see most recently Elly Kooiman, 'The Biography of Jacob Barbireau (1455–1491) Reviewed', *TVNM* 38 (1988), 36–58, esp. 38–9 and 50–1, as well as Wegman, *Born for the Muses*, 292–3 n. 10. For another path by which Barbireau's music could have reached Segovia, see below, n. 110.

[87] On the meeting of Josquin and Philip the Fair, see Joshua Rifkin, 'A Singer named Josquin and Josquin d'Ascanio: Some Problems in the Biography of Josquin des Prez', forthcoming in the *Journal of the Royal Musical Association*.

[88] Baker, 'An Unnumbered Manuscript', i. 191.

[89] On Obrecht's representation in Segovia, see above, n. 81, as well as the discussion below, pp. 528–30.

[90] For Obrecht's youth, see Wegman, *Born for the Muses*, chs. 1 and 2, and esp. 34–5, 47–50, 56–8, and 62–9. Obrecht came into direct contact with the Habsburg courts on only two known occasions: in July 1497, when Philip the Fair visited Bergen op Zoom, and in Oct. 1503, when the composer received a payment from the Imperial court at Innsbruck for a mass on *Regina caeli*. Both occasions offered possibilities for musical exchanges with Philip's chapel: in 1497, the archduke's singers joined those of Bergen op Zoom for services, and the payment of Oct. 1503 came a day after Philip had concluded a visit to Innsbruck with his full entourage. On these events see, most recently, ibid. 303 and 342, respectively. The suggestion in Baker, 'An Unnumbered Manuscript', i. 123, that Obrecht 'participated in the musical activities' in March 1497 when Philip the Fair and his bride, Juana of Castile, 'were the focus of a triumphal entrance and reception at Antwerp' rests on a misreading of L. G. van Hoorn, *Jacob Obrecht* (The Hague, 1968), 58.

[91] See Staehelin, 'Obrechtiana', 19, as well as the overviews of manuscript sources in Chris Maas, 'Towards a New Obrecht Edition: A Preliminary Worklist', *TVNM* 26 (1976), 84–108 at 86–94, or Martin Picker, *Johannes Ockeghem and Jacob Obrecht: A Guide to Research* (Garland Composer Resource Manuals, 13; New York, 1988), 89–106, under Florence 2439, Jena 22, Rome 160, Vienna 15495, and Vienna 18832 (the Obrecht works in Vienna 11883 do not belong to the Habsburg-Burgundy portions of that manuscript); to the listings for Rome 160, however, readers should add the anonymous *Missa de Sancto Johanne Baptista* identified as a work of Obrecht by Mary Jennifer Bloxam, 'A Survey of Late Medieval Service Books from the Low Countries: Implications for Sacred Polyphony, 1460–1520' (Ph.D. diss., Yale University, 1987), 438–51, and Rob C. Wegman, 'Another "Imitation" of Busnoys's *Missa L'Homme armé*—and Some Observations on *Imitatio* in Renaissance Music', *Journal of the Royal Musical Association*, 114 (1989), 189–202 at 190–5. Admittedly, possible signs of a connection to the orbit of Emperor Maximilian come from the more substantial representation of Obrecht in Munich 3154, a source very likely compiled in the Imperial chapel, and from his presence as well in Jena 31 and 32, for which Jürgen Heidrich

Segovia; and here the Habsburg-Burgundy source, Florence 2439, stands notably closer in its readings to the one further concordance, Petrucci's *Motetti C*, than it does to the Spanish manuscript.[92] This lack of any significant intersection between Segovia and the Habsburg-Burgundy codices in fact goes well beyond Obrecht alone. Among works by other composers, I find exactly five items in Segovia that have concordances in manuscripts written at the court.[93] One of the five, Wrede's *Nunca fue pena mayor*, hardly required Netherlands mediation to find its way into a Spanish choirbook; and the remaining four—Josquin's *Missa L'homme armé sexti toni*, Pipelare's *Fors seulement*, and Agricola's *Je n'ay deuil* and *Oublier veuil*—all appear in a substantial number of sources beyond the Habsburg-Burgundian group.[94] Even if we extend the net to include Brussels 11239, the catch does not become significantly larger: Segovia and Marguerite's 'little' chansonnier have only three pieces in common, all of them works that circulated widely.[95]

We may thus regard the associations between Segovia and the Habsburg-Burgundian court discerned by Baker and Meconi as chimerical at best.[96] The

has recently proposed a similar origin; see Thomas Noblitt, 'Die Datierung der Handschrift Mus. ms. 3154 der Staatsbibliothek München', *Musikforschung*, 27 (1974), 36–56 at 47–8, and Jürgen Heidrich, *Die deutschen Chorbücher aus der Hofkapelle Friedrichs des Weisen: Ein Beitrag zur mitteldeutschen geistlichen Musikpraxis um 1500* (Collection d'études musicologiques/Sammlung musikwissenschaftlicher Arbeiten, 84; Baden-Baden, 1993), 2–3, 11, 15, 38–9, 101–15, 129–42, and 263–71.

[92] Cf. Segovia, fos. lxxxi^v–lxxxiii^r (81^v–83^r); *Motetti C*, superius, fos. 9^r–10^r ('Requiem'); and Florence 2439, fos. xlvii^v–xlviii^r ('Requiem')—this last easily consulted in the facs. edn. *Basevi Codex: Florence, Biblioteca del Conservatorio, MS 2439*, ed. Honey Meconi (Peer, 1990). I suspect, in fact, that the copy of *Mille quingentis* in Florence 2439 does not properly belong to the Habsburg-Burgundy complex at all. Not only does it use the frequent Italian spelling of the composer's name, 'Obreht', in place of the Flemish 'Hobrecht' found elsewhere in the manuscript (cf. below, at n. 101), but the scribe makes no further appearance in either Florence 2439 or the entire complex. In all likelihood, the addition post-dates the transfer of the manuscript to its Italian owners; cf. Meconi, 'Sacred Tricinia', 151–5.

[93] Compare nos. 2, 22, 42, 83, and 167 of Baker's inventory ('An Unnumbered Manuscript', i. 242–559) with the overview of the Habsburg-Burgundy manuscripts in Kellmann, 'Josquin and the Courts', 209. We can increase the total—though not significantly—if we add the three sections from Obrecht's *Missa Fortuna desperata* transmitted as a succession of textless pieces in Florence 2439, fos. xxxiii^v–xxxvi^r; cf. Baker, nos. 6a, 6f, and 6g (with Florence 2439 reinstated as a concordance for 6g).

[94] See the preceding note; Segovia transmits Pipelare's *Fors seulement* in a contrafacted version ('Exortum est in tenebris') not found anywhere else.

[95] Cf. Baker, 'An Unnumbered Manuscript', i. 242–559, under nos. 89 (Hayne, *Allez regretz*), 103 (Agricola, *Si dedero*), and 105 (Josquin, *In pace*). The readings of *Allez regretz* do in fact show an interesting, if hardly conclusive, stemmatic relationship between Segovia and Brussels 11239; cf. Picker, *The Chanson Albums of Marguerite of Austria*, 150. The other two pieces, however, reveal no special closeness. See also the following note.

[96] Some remarks in Wesner, 'The Chansons of Loyset Compère', 39–40, open up the possibility that Marguerite of Austria would have assembled much of the Segovia repertory during her childhood years at the French royal court. This could perhaps meet the reservations expressed earlier concerning some of the composers in the manuscript—Agricola, Compère, the Fernandes brothers (cf. Strohm, *Music in Late Medieval Bruges*, 88), Hayne (cf. Litterick, 'The Manuscript Royal 20.A.XVI', 69 n. 82, and 'Hayne van Ghizeghem', 417), and, just possibly, Josquin and Brumel. It could also help explain the reading of *Allez regretz* referred to in the previous note, as the further manuscripts involved, Florence 2794 and Laborde, would seem both to come from the French court (cf. above, n. 3, as well as Litterick, 'The Manuscript Royal 20.A.XVI', 66–71). Nevertheless, shifting the repertorial centre of gravity to France would still fail utterly to account for Isaac and Obrecht; nor does it explain why so little of this music appears in the later manuscripts from Marguerite's court—including the highly retrospective collection Brussels 228. Segovia and Brussels 11239, moreover, both transmit versions of Josquin's *Que vous madame/In pace* that lie at some

situation becomes more complicated, however, if we widen our view from the court in particular to the Habsburg Netherlands as a whole; for Segovia, as no one can fail to notice, displays a provocatively Flemish tinge.[97] Its cast of minor composers includes such characters as Petrus Elinc, *zangmeester* at the Nieuwe Kerk of Delft in the years 1504–6, and the unmistakably Flemish Roelkin, presumably identical with the 'Raulequin' documented as a *petit vicaire* at Cambrai in 1495.[98] At a time when songs in the Flemish language enjoyed limited currency beyond their native realm, no fewer than forty-one pieces in the manuscript—nearly half the non-Latin secular works in its principal layer—have Flemish incipits, even when concordant versions have text in French or Italian.[99] As both Albert Smijers and Rob Wegman have observed, moreover, the orthography of the Netherlandish texts remains all but flawless throughout.[100] Indeed, the chief scribe of Segovia, while unquestionably Castilian in his script and in some of his French misspellings, shows a decided predilection for Flemishisms, writing 'helaes' for 'helas', calling Hayne van Ghizeghem 'Scoen Hayne', and referring to Obrecht in the distinctively Flemish—and apparently authentic—fashion 'Hobrecht'.[101]

Obrecht himself may provide a geographic indicator. Despite his international reputation, his music does not really appear to have circulated in great quantity,

distance from the French tradition (cf. Atlas, *The Cappella Giulia Chansonnier*, i. 72); and while they both fall on the same side of the stemmatic divide in regard to their third concordance, Agricola's *Si dedero*, the large overall number of sources surely minimizes any significance this may have—not to mention that the sole French-court manuscript, Florence 2794, belongs in the opposite stemmatic camp (ibid. 79). Finally, since Marguerite returned to the Netherlands in 1493 (cf. Picker, *The Chanson Albums of Marguerite of Austria*, 10), the French-court hypothesis cannot account for *Vive le noble rey de france* (cf. above, n. 68).

[97] The Flemish characteristics of the manuscript, I might add, drive yet another wedge between it and Marguerite of Austria; cf. Meconi, 'Pierre de la Rue and Secular Music at the Court of Marguerite of Austria', 52.

[98] Previous commentators have read the attribution to Elinc as 'Eline', or even 'Elive'; I owe the correction to Rob Wegman, who refers me for biographical information to M. A. Vente (ed.), *Bouwsteenen voor een geschiedenis der toonkunst in de Nederlanden*, iii (Amsterdam, 1980), 87. Roelkin, too, has hidden under garbled renderings of his name—'Xoelrin', 'Roelrin'. I owe the correct reading to Bonnie J. Blackburn, 'A Lost Guide to Tinctoris's Teachings Recovered', *EMH* 1 (1981), 29–116 at 31 n. 7 and 35; my thanks to Dr Blackburn as well for steering me to Raulequin, on whom see Craig Wright, 'Musiciens à la cathédrale de Cambrai', *Revue de musicologie*, 62 (1976), 204–29 at 212.

[99] On the dissemination of Flemish songs in the period and territories of interest to us here, see, most recently, the handy overview in Eugeen Schreurs, *Het Nederlandse polyphone lied* (Peer, 1986), 21–30; on the number of Flemish-texted pieces, their place in the manuscript, and the relationship between Segovia's incipits and those in other sources, see Baker, 'An Unnumbered Manuscript', i. 223–4.

[100] See Albert Smijers, 'Twee onbekende motetteksten van Jacob Hobrecht', *TVNM* 16 (1941), 129–34 at 129–30 n. 1, and Wegman, *Born for the Muses*, 22.

[101] For the identification of the scribe as Castilian, see Baker, 'An Unnumbered Manuscript', i. 95–9, which confirms the earlier observation of Anglés, *La música en la Corte de los Reyes Católicos*, i. 106; on 'helaes' and other Flemish tendencies, see Baker, i. 99 and 225–6; on 'Scoen Hayne', see *Facsimile Reproduction of the Manuscripts Sevilla 5-I-43 & Paris N. A. Fr. 4379 (Pt. 1)*, ed. Dragan Plamenac (Publications of Mediaeval Musical Manuscripts, 8; Brooklyn, 1962), 5, or Baker, i. 164–5 n. 171; on 'Hobrecht', see Wegman, 'Music and Musicians', 199–200, and id., 'Het "Jacob Hobrecht" portret: Enkele biografische observaties', *Musica antiqua*, 8 (1991), 152–4 at 153. This unexpected linguistic propensity on the part of someone who plainly learned to write in Castile prompts speculation about the scribe's identity: we may surely regard him as either a Netherlander who emigrated early to Spain or as the Castilian-born child of a Flemish parent. Could Johannes Wrede have had a son? Cf. also Baker, 'An Unnumbered Manuscript', i. 206 n. 20.

and certainly no other source of mixed repertory accords him anything like the commanding position he enjoys here.[102] Segovia alone transmits the autobiographical motet *Inter praeclarissimas virtutes* and the deeply personal text of *Mille quingentis*; indeed, as Rob Wegman has emphasized, it even presents the two pieces in direct succession.[103] Under these circumstances, the high percentage of *unica* among the works ascribed to Obrecht surely denotes a more than ordinary degree of familiarity with the composer as well.[104] Significantly, only three of the works found in other sources have conflicting attributions; and in two of these instances, the weight of the evidence either comes down squarely on the side of Segovia or leans in its favour.[105] The third conflict proves more refractory; but even here, the precedence of the contending transmission over Segovia would hardly seem a foregone conclusion.[106] In all probability, then, the scribe of the

[102] For listings of Obrecht's works in Segovia, see Maas, 'Towards a New Obrecht Edition', 92–3; Picker, *Johannes Ockeghem and Jacob Obrecht*, 102; or Baker, 'An Unnumbered Manuscript', i. 580–1. Especially if we omit posthumous German sources or 'bleeding chunks' from the masses, only a handful of Obrecht's compositions survive in more than two or three copies, and only two works, *Parce Domine* and *Si sumpsero*, have the status of genuine 'hits'; similarly, the only serious concentrations of his music occur in the single-composer mass volumes issued by Petrucci and Mewes, and in the Ferrarese mass manuscript Modena, Biblioteca Estense e Universitaria, MS α M.1.2, very likely intended as a memorial. One can only surmise that Staehelin ('Obrechtiana', 19) momentarily let Segovia out of view when he describes the transmission of Obrecht's work in Spain as 'not . . . unusual'. For the background, see Maas and Picker as cited in n. 91; specifically on Modena α M.1.2, see Lockwood, *Music in Renaissance Ferrara*, 208 and 226–7.

[103] Cf. Wegman, 'Music and Musicians', 210, esp. n. 87; *Inter praeclarissimas virtutes* and *Mille quingentis* occupy fos. lxxviii^v–lxxxi^r (78^v–81^r) and lxxxi^v–lxxxiii^r (81^v–83^r), respectively.

[104] For the Obrecht *unica* in Segovia, see Baker, 'An Unnumbered Manuscript', i. 242–559, under nos. 12, 15, 20, 21, 23, 37, 49, 52, 55, 57, 60, 61, 62, 63, 79, 92, 96, 153; readers can also assemble the information from Maas, 'Towards a New Obrecht Edition', 98–105, or Picker, *Johannes Ockeghem and Jacob Obrecht*, 58–87. Three further pieces, the *Missa Adieu mes amours*, *Missa Libenter gloriabor*, and *Lacen adieu*, appear elsewhere without attribution; on the second and third of these, still without concordances in Baker, see, respectively, Maas, 'Towards a New Obrecht Edition', 99 (or Picker, *Johannes Ockeghem and Jacob Obrecht*, 65), and David Fallows's review of Picker's volume, *ML* 70 (1989), 247–9 at 249.

[105] Nos. 5, 6, 16, 50, 51, 65, and 104 in Baker's inventory all have their attributions confirmed in other sources — implicitly in the case of no. 5, the *Missa Rose playsante*, which appears in the 'Obrecht series' of Modena α M.1.2; cf. Martin Staehelin, 'Möglichkeiten und praktische Anwendung der Verfasserbestimmung an anonym überlieferten Kompositionen der Josquin-Zeit', *TVNM* 23 (1973), 79–91 at 85. We might recall as well that *Inter praeclarissimas virtutes*, although unique, affirms Obrecht's authorship through the appearance of his name in the text (cf. Wegman, *Born for the Muses*, 288–9 and 370–1). Among the conflicts, we can safely dismiss the attribution of *Ic weinsche alle scoene vrauwen eere* (fos. cxxxiiii^v–cxxxiiii^r [127^v (*sic*)–127^r]) to Stoltzer in Ott's *Liederbuch* of 1544; and the claims of Isaac and Japart to *T'meiskin was jonc* (fo. ciii^r [103^r]), while contemporary with Segovia, would not appear significantly better founded. See Baker, i. 43–4 and 47–8. On the third conflict, see the following note. Segovia also transmits the instrumental piece *La stangetta*, attributed to Obrecht in Zwickau 78/3, with the Latin incipit 'Ortus de celo flos est' and the attribution 'ysaac' (fo. clxxii^r [165^r]); whether or not Isaac composed this work (cf. below, n. 157), Obrecht clearly did not — cf. Dietrich Kämper, 'La stangetta — eine Instrumentalkomposition Gaspars van Weerbeke?', in Detlef Altenburg (ed.), *Ars musica, musica scientia: Festschrift Heinrich Hüschen zum fünfundsechzigsten Geburtstag am 2. März 1980* (Beiträge zur rheinischen Musikgeschichte, 126; Cologne, 1980), 277–88, esp. 278.

[106] The three-voice *Nec michi nec tibi* credited to Obrecht in Segovia, fos. clxxxvii^v–clxxxviii^r (181^v–182^r), appears in the Florentine manuscript Cappella Giulia XIII. 27, fos. 55^v–56^r (62^v–63^r), with the ascription 'virgilius' (for the music, see Atlas, *The Cappella Giulia Chansonnier*, ii, no. 50, or Brown, *A Florentine Chansonnier*, Music vol., no. 267; on the origins of Cappella Giulia XIII. 27, see Atlas, i. 24–8). If, as Frank D'Accone has suggested ('Some Neglected Composers', 281–2), 'Virgilius' refers to Ser Vergilio, a singer documented in Florence in the early 16th c., then the attribution in Cappella Giulia XIII. 27 might seem particularly credible; but the identification would appear open to question, as Cappella Giulia XIII. 27 dates from roughly a decade before the first recorded traces of Ser Vergilio on the Florentine scene. The piece

manuscript could draw on the resources, if not of Obrecht himself, then of someone fairly close to him.[107]

This, of course, opens up the possibility of a link to Bruges—a link in fact already suspected by Reinhard Strohm, and one that some may wish to see reinforced by the occurrence of *Fortuna desperata* in London 35087, a collection most likely written in Bruges.[108] But caution would seem in order. For one thing, we

itself, moreover, clearly goes back earlier still. Apart from Cappella Giulia and Segovia, it survives—always without attribution—in Florence 229 (fos. 288ᵛ–290ᵛ) and Speciálník (pp. 384–5), and, as a duo, in Perugia 431 (fos. 100ᵛ–101ʳ [90ᵛ–91ʳ], 'Helas') and Turin I. 27 (fos. 43ᵛ–44ʳ [45ᵛ–46ʳ]). The transmission falls essentially into two layers, the first represented in Perugia and Turin, the second in Speciálník and Florence 229; since this last manuscript appears to date from 1492 (see above, n. 25), the music must already have entered circulation by the late 1480s. The readings in Segovia and Cappella Giulia XIII. 27 form independent offshoots from the second layer: Cappella Giulia introduces a contrapuntally inadmissible variant in the lowest part at mm. 12–13 and adds a minim to the polyphony in mm. 72–3 and 88–9, probably as a consequence of errors in a parent source (against the implication to the contrary in Atlas, *The Cappella Giulia Chansonnier*, i. 133, readers should note the variant in the contra for Florence 229, m. 85, recorded in *A Florentine Chansonnier*, Music vol., 642); Segovia adds a concluding flourish in the lowest part (cf. ibid.). The two attributions, therefore, each stand at the end of a stemmatic line. As Baker has shown ('An Unnumbered Manuscript', i. 53–4), the rather ingenious explanation through which D'Accone ('Some Neglected Composers', 283-4) and, especially, Atlas (*The Cappella Giulia Chansonnier*, i. 131–2) have sought to defuse the conflict between them will not work: the inscription 'Nec michi nec tibi sed dividatur', found in Turin I. 27 (contrary to ibid. 132, the manuscript presents this correctly), can scarcely mean that one composer wrote the superius and tenor, the other the contra, as Turin I. 27 contains only the two presumably original voices and explicitly labels the piece 'Duo'; as Helen Palmer suggests to me, the motto would seem rather to characterize the motivic equality of the two voices. In any event, if the contra does represent the work of a different composer, then the geography and chronology of the transmission would seem to argue against Atlas's surmise that Obrecht wrote the original piece and Virgilius—however we identify him—added the third part; surely we may better assume the reverse. See also below, Sect. VI, esp. n. 261.

107 As Rob Wegman reminds me, the editors of the *New Obrecht Edition* incline to a rather low estimate of Segovia's value as a textual witness for the four Obrecht masses it contains; see the critical notes to vols. i (pp. xvi–xxi), iv (pp. xxxv–liii) , vi (pp. xxiii–xxix), and ix (pp. xxiv–xxxiii). But while Segovia certainly includes its share of copying errors and omits the final sections—at least part of the Agnus, and in one instance the Sanctus as well—of all four masses, none of this necessarily reflects on the quality of its exemplars. For one thing, virtually all the mass settings in Segovia lack their final sections, which means that we should perhaps ascribe their omission more to considerations of local usage than to defective sources. A careful examination of the variants, moreover, does not suggest that Segovia's readings for the Obrecht masses derive from models notably inferior—if at all—to those standing behind other sources; this would appear especially the case with the masses *Adieu mes amours* (vol. i), *Libenter gloriabor* (vol. vi), and *Rose playsante* (vol. ix).

108 For Strohm's speculations on Bruges and Segovia, see further in the main text. On the provenance of London 35087, see the facsimile *Chansonnier of Hieronymus Lauweryn van Watervliet: London, British Library Ms. Add. 35.087*, ed. William McMurtry (Peer, 1989), 5–6, but with reference to the scribal information communicated in *Census-Catalogue*, ii. 72, and to Leon Kessels, 'The Brussels/Tournai-Partbooks: Structure, Illumination, and Flemish Repertory', *TVNM* 37 (1987), 82–110 at 82 and 84–5, as well as below, n. 113. For Obrecht at Bruges, see Strohm, *Music in Late Medieval Bruges*, 38–40, and Wegman, *Born for the Muses*, 133–8, 156–60, and 303–8. If, as the art historian Dirk de Vos has proposed, the portrait of Obrecht dated 1496 originated in the workshop of Hans Memling, then Obrecht would presumably have visited Bruges for sittings after he moved to Antwerp in 1491; cf. Dirk de Vos, 'Een belangrijk portret van Jacob Obrecht ontdekt: Een werk uit de nalatenschap van het atelier van Hans Memling?', *Jaarboek 1989–90 Stad Brugge, Stedelijke Musea* (Bruges, 1991), 192–209, as well as id., *Hans Memling: The Complete Works* (Ghent, 1994), 336–8. But the connection to Memling seems problematic at best. De Vos suggests that the painter left the portrait incomplete on his death in 1494; if so, the elements added in the following two years must include not only such apparently anomalous features as the hands (cf. 'Een belangrijk portret', although also *The Complete Works*, 336), but more likely than not Obrecht's black gown and grey fur *aumusse*, which seemingly depict the garb he wore at Antwerp from the middle of 1494 to the middle of 1496; cf. Wegman, *Born for the Muses*, 296–7, and Kristine K. Forney, 'Music, Ritual and Patronage at the Church of Our Lady, Antwerp', *EMH* 7 (1987), 1–57 at 43. In the face of the complications to which all this leads, both for the internal history of the painting and for its relationship to Obrecht's biography, we must surely begin to wonder how well the attribution to Memling holds water. Did Antwerp truly have no painter skilful enough to execute this portrait?

cannot say how much time Busnoys himself spent in Bruges during the last years of his life.[109] Obrecht's peripatetic career means that his music could easily have reached Spain from other venues; he spent the greater part of the 1490s, for instance, in Antwerp, a city that Busnoys would seem hardly ever to have visited.[110] Not a single one of the major works that Obrecht supposedly composed for Bruges makes its way into Segovia.[111] Indeed, Strohm finds only two pieces in the entire manuscript—an anonymous hymn setting and a chanson of uncertain authorship—that he feels 'could have come directly from Bruges'; and for the second of these at least, his case plainly does not withstand examination.[112] London 35087, meanwhile, surely originated too late to have more than a very tenuous bearing on the matter: the inclusion of a work attributed to 'benedict*us*

---

[109] Cf. Strohm, *Music in Late Medieval Bruges*, 55, as well as Higgins's review (see above, n. 11), 153–4.

[110] For Obrecht at Antwerp, see Forney, 'Music, Ritual and Patronage', 38 and 42–4, and Wegman, *Born for the Muses*, 292–9 and 308–10; as Wegman writes on p. 293, Antwerp in the late 15th c. had surpassed Bruges to become effectively 'the great port of northern Europe'—a consideration not at all irrelevant in trying to retrace the lines of musical commerce so clearly implied by Segovia's repertory. Indeed, Segovia betrays possible ties to Antwerp beyond Obrecht: it provides by far the earliest attribution for one of the most famous works of an Antwerp composer, Barbireau's *Een vroylic wesen* (cf. the lists of sources cited below, n. 239), and it counts as one of the very few sources to contain more than two pieces by Matthaeus Pipelare, who evidently worked in Antwerp before his recruitment to 's-Hertogenbosch early in 1498; cf. Albert Smijers, 'De Illustre Lieve Vrouwe Broederschap te 's-Hertogenbosch', *TVNM* 13 (1932), 213–14, and Ronald Cross, 'The Life and Works of Matthaeus Pipelare', *Musica disciplina*, 17 (1963), 97–144 at 107–9. While Busnoys could well have visited Antwerp on occasions unknown to us, Forney makes no mention of his presence there, and Higgins finds him at Antwerp only on 27 Feb. 1473, 25 June 1477, and 29 Sept. and 13 Oct. 1481; see '*In hydraulis* Revisited', 56, 63, and 66.

[111] I have in mind the masses *De Sancto Donatiano* and *De Sancto Martino* as well as the motets *Homo quidam*, *O beate Basili*, *O preciosissime sanguis*, and *Salve crux arbor vitae*; see Strohm, *Music in Late Medieval Bruges*, 40–1 and 145–6; M. Jennifer Bloxam, 'Sacred Polyphony and Local Traditions of Liturgy and Plainsong: Reflections on Music by Jacob Obrecht', in Thomas Forrest Kelly (ed.), *Plainsong in the Age of Polyphony* (Cambridge Studies in Performance Practice, 2; Cambridge, 1992), 140–77, esp. 147–69; ead., 'A Survey of Late Medieval Service Books', 314–26 and 335–44; and Wegman, *Born for the Muses*, 165 n. 7. Wegman (ibid. 191) assigns four of the Obrecht masses in Segovia—*Fortuna desperata*, *Libenter gloriabor*, and *Rose playsante*—to 'the Bruges years 1485–91'; but the works display none of the specific liturgical elements that so compellingly locate *De Sancto Donatiano* and *De Sancto Martino*, nor does the manuscript evidence for their dating exclude other possibilities. Strohm (*Music in Late Medieval Bruges*, 144–5) does propose a possible association of two pieces in Segovia, the three-voice *Ave maris stella* (fo. clviii^v [152^v]) and the proportional duo *Regina coeli* (fo. cc^v [193^v]), with so-called *Salve* concerts given by the choirboys at Bruges. But the duo surely had no practical purpose beyond that of instruction (cf. below, at n. 136); and while we could imagine the high-cleffed *Ave maris stella* sung by choirboys, Strohm himself observes (p. 145) that '*Salve* concerts seem to have existed in Antwerp and Bergen-op-Zoom as well as in Bruges'. Similar cautions, I would suggest, apply as well to the speculations in Wegman, 156–7, on Obrecht's Netherlandish songs and Bruges theatrical representations. See also Higgins's remarks in her review of Strohm, 159 n. 22.

[112] See Strohm, *Music in Late Medieval Bruges*, 143; on possible indirect ties between Segovia and Bruges, see below, pp. 536 and 537 (esp. n. 134). Strohm connects the anonymous *Salve sancta facies* (fo. cxlviii^r [141^r]) to Bruges because it sets 'the hymn to St Veronica which is prominent in almost all Books of Hours from Bruges at the time'; while this overlooks the possibility that the text had equal prominence in other centres, the observation remains plausible. I have more serious problems with Strohm's remarks about *J'ay bien nourri*, a three-voice chanson that Segovia (fo. clxxxix^r [183^r]) attributes to 'Johannes joye'. According to Strohm, this piece 'also exists in different versions attributed to Johannes Japart and Josquin, but could be by Gilles Joye'. Not only does the wording make it less than wholly clear that 'different versions' means simply different sources for one and the same composition, but the style of the music, as Atlas has already pointed out, utterly excludes Gilles Joye as author; see Atlas, *The Cappella Giulia Chansonnier*, i. 79, and, for the music, ibid. ii, no. 18, or *A Florentine Chansonnier*, Music vol., no. 46. Transmission and stemmatic ties, moreover, reinforce Atlas's suspicion (i. 79) that the Segovia attribution may represent a corruption of 'Johannes japart'; see below, nn. 150 and 151.

appescelders' means that it cannot have reached completion very much before the death of its first owner, Hieronymus Lauweryn van Watervliet, in 1509.[113] Perhaps more important, its version of *Fortuna desperata* belongs to an entirely different branch of the transmission from that in Segovia. Roughly half the sources show measure 13 of the superius as it appears in Ex. 20.3(*a*); the rest present the reading seen in Ex. 20.3(*b*). London 35087 has the first variant; as David Fallows reminds me, this represents the form in which Obrecht knew *Fortuna desperata*, as he quotes it thus in his mass on the song.[114] But Segovia has the version reproduced in Ex. 20.3(*b*). Not only that, but it introduces three decorative variants shown in Ex. 20.4; these appear neither in London 30587 nor, for that matter, virtually anyplace else—apart from scattered instances of the second and third variants in polyphonic settings and late non-Italian manuscripts, we find them only in St Gallen 462 and 463.[115] The conclusion would thus

[113] Cf. the account Appenzeller's life in Glenda Goss Thompson, 'Appenzeller, Benedictus', *New Grove*, i. 507 (although the dating here of London 35087 specifically to 1506 does not rest on any independent evidence); the attribution, in the same hand as the music and text, appears over the chanson *Buvons ma commère* on fos. lxxviii^v–lxxviiii^r. For the date of Lauweryn's death, see William M. McMurtry, 'The British Museum Manuscript Additional 35087: A Transcription of the French, Italian, and Latin Compositions with Concordance and Commentary' (Ph.D. diss., North Texas State University, 1967), 11–12. London 35087 does, however, pose a chronological puzzle. As both Leon Kessels and I have reported (see above, n. 108), its chief scribe also wrote the first section of the Brussels–Tournai partbooks. In Brussels–Tournai and most of London 35087, the scribe's *custodes* show a form much like a tick-mark; but from fo. lxx^v of the London manuscript onward, the lower end of the symbol increasingly takes on the zigzag shape of a mordent, and this form soon dominates all but completely. This development surely places the scribe's work on London 35087 later than his contributions to Brussels–Tournai. An illumination on fo. 21^r of the Tournai partbook, however, bears the date 1511 (cf. Kessels, 'The Brussels/Tournai-Partbooks', 85). As the *terminus ante quem* of London 35087 appears secure, the answer to the problem may lie in Brussels–Tournai. Consideration of such physical details as gathering size (cf. ibid., 82 and 84), staff-ruling, and the rather odd distribution of *Een vraulic wesen* (ibid. 92)—which the first scribe clearly left incomplete, as his failure to enter an incipit reveals—suggests that a certain gap of time separated the two sections, and suggests as well that the scribe of the second section began copying with the intention of producing an independent manuscript, deciding only in the course of work to join his newly written pieces to the gatherings written by his predecessor; still more time may have elapsed, moreover, before the decorator and binder of the partbooks gave them their final shape. The dated illumination—which in any event occurs in the portion of the manuscript not written by the scribe of London 35087—could thus lie some years later than the actual copying.

[114] See below, n. 217. The congruence between London 35087 and Obrecht's mass could prompt us to ask if Obrecht himself might not have brought *Fortuna desperata* to the North after his Italian sojourn of 1477–8; this, incidentally, raises questions about Hudson's contention ('Two Ferrarese Masses', 289–98) that Obrecht must have composed his *Missa Fortuna desperata* during that visit. Reinhard Strohm has already shown that the second mass associated by Hudson with Italy, *Malheur me bat* (see ibid. 277–89), more likely originated in the Netherlands; see his review of *New Obrecht Edition*, vii, in *Notes*, 47 (1990–1), 552–4 at 553–4.

[115] Segovia's readings for mm. 20 and 35 recur together in London 31922 (with a rhythmic variant in m. 20) as well as in Josquin's *Missa Fortuna desperata* and the three-voice *Fortuna* attributed to him in Segovia (cf. below, nn. 217 and 258); that for m. 20 alone appears, sometimes with rhythmic modifications, in Obrecht's *Fortuna* mass (cf. below, n. 217) and in the settings attributed to 'Jo.pinarol' (*Canti C*, fos. 68^v–69^r) and 'Robert*us* Fabri' (St Gallen 463, no. 214), while the cadential decoration at m. 35 appears further in Zwickau 78/2 and an anonymous *zibaldone* in Florence 164–7, no. xxxix. The variant in mm. 9–10 occurs only in Segovia and the St Gallen manuscripts. Curiously, St Gallen 462 and 463 have the variant of Ex. 20.3(*a*) at m. 13. The scribe of St Gallen 462, the Swiss student Johannes Heer, began the manuscript while a student at Paris in 1510; on his death, if not earlier, it came into the possession of his friend Aegidius Tschudi, who copied a good number of pieces from it—including, obviously, *Fortuna desperata*—into St Gallen 463. Cf. Arnold Geering and Hans Trümpy, *Das Liederbuch des Johannes Heer von Glarus: Ein Musikheft aus der Zeit des Humanismus (Codex 462 der Stiftsbibliothek St Gallen)* (Schweizerische Musikdenkmäler, 5; Basle, 1967), vii–viii and xi–xii; and Donald Glenn Loach, 'Aegidius Tschudi's

Ex. 20.3. *Fortuna desperata*, superius, mm. 12–15: (*a*) Bol Q 16, Fl 27, Fl 121, Leipzig 1494, Lo 31922, Lo 35087, Par 676, SG 462, SG 463, Zwi 78/2; arrangements by Agricola, Fabri, Isaac (*Fortuna desperata/Sancte Petre*), Martini (Cas 2856; cf. nn. 157 and 220), Pinarol, anon. (Bol Q 18, fos. 28ᵛ–29ʳ); masses by Josquin and Obrecht; (*b*) Cape, CG XIII.27, Frankfurt VII 20, Per 431 (both versions), Seg, Seville–Paris, Wolf, *Canti C*; arrangements by 'Isaac' (*recte* Martini; cf. nn. 157 and 220) and anon. (Fl. 164–7, no. xxxix)

Ex. 20.4. *Fortuna desperata*: (*a*) decorative variants in Segovia, SG 462, and SG 463; (*b*) 'standard' readings

appear self-evident: even if other music entered the Segovia repertory by way of Bruges, we have not the slightest reason to think that *Fortuna desperata*—and its attribution to Busnoys—followed the same route.[116]

Another possibility mentioned in discussions of Segovia draws us in a very different direction. As Barton Hudson has noted, Segovia has a large number of concordances with Italian sources—enough, indeed, for Hudson to suggest that

Songbook (St Gall MS 463): A Humanistic Document from the Circle of Heinrich Glarean' (Ph.D. diss., University of California at Berkeley, 1969), 68–9. Given both the late date of St Gallen 462 and its curious mixture of readings, its significance for Segovia and *Fortuna desperata* would appear all but hopeless to assess; cf. also below, n. 164.

[116] Of course, multiple source traditions could coexist within the same city, even within a single scriptorium. Indeed, Kessels has demonstrated this for Bruges with pieces copied by the same scribe in London 35087 and Brussels–Tournai; see 'The Brussels/Tournai-Partbooks', 101 n. 13. But the point concerns not what could or could not possibly have happened, but what we have evidence for. Before leaving the Netherlands, I might make a final observation. Richard Taruskin has proposed that Juan de Anchieta collected more or less the entire contents of Segovia on a visit to the Low Countries before 1489; see *Een vrolic wesen*, ed. Richard Taruskin (Coconut Grove, Fla., 1982), 5. Not only, as Meconi has already has observed ('Art-Song Reworkings', 16 n. 55), does this date obviously lie too early for the repertory, but we have no evidence for the visit itself: while a codicil to Anchieta's will speaks of money lent someone 'in Flanders', this clearly relates to the years 1504–5, when Anchieta belonged to the retinue of Joanna of Castile in Brussels. See Robert Stevenson, *Spanish Music in the Age of Columbus* (The Hague, 1960), 131, and Mary Kay Duggan, 'Queen Joanna and her Musicians', *Musica disciplina*, 30 (1976), 73–92 at 84–5; I wish to thank Tess Knighton for alerting me to the latter reference.

'a sizable portion of its repertory must have been imported directly from Italy'.[117] Narrowing the focus, he cites observations by Allan Atlas that could indicate a special affinity between Segovia's readings and those of manuscripts originating in Naples.[118] 'While the details remain to be worked out', he concludes, 'it seems clear that the repertory of *Segovia* owes a substantial debt to that of southern Italy.'[119] Naples, in fact, looks attractive for other reasons as well. Dynastic affiliations would have created an obvious path for the transfer of music to Spain.[120] Agricola, the most heavily represented composer after Obrecht and Isaac, visited the Neapolitan court in the spring of 1492 and returned—perhaps for a longer stay—in the early months of 1494.[121] While at Naples, Strohm suggests, Agricola 'may have met' Tinctoris;[122] and Tinctoris himself maintains what looks like a very significant presence in Segovia. Although his music enjoys at best limited currency in surviving sources, he has some eight pieces in the manuscript, most of them unique.[123] According to Strohm, moreover, two works in Segovia echo musical experiences at Bruges and Chartres that the theorist described in *De inventione et usu musicae*. The curiously titled *Cecus non judicat de coloribus*, with its equally curious heading 'ferdina*n*dus & frat*er* eius', might have come 'from the repertory of the blind brothers Johannes and Carolus Fernandes, who astonished Tinctoris in Bruges in 1482 . . . with their instrumental duos'; and Tinctoris's own duo on *Tout a par moy* might recall the way one Gherardus of Brabant sang Frye's chanson 'in two parts on his own' at Chartres.[124] 'Could it be', Strohm asks, 'that this whole repertory was collected by Tinctoris, partly on his travels in the North . . .?'[125] Even allowing for the hyperbole of 'this whole repertory', the

[117] Hudson, 'Two Ferrarese Masses', 293.

[118] Cf. Atlas, *The Cappella Giulia Chansonnier*, i. 235–6 (note, however, that on p. 236 the reference to 'no. 18' should read '20') and 257; see also ibid. 79, 84, and 212–13, and the study cited below, n. 128.

[119] Hudson, 'Two Ferrarese Masses', 293.

[120] Cf. Atlas, *The Cappella Giulia Chansonnier*, i. 213, as well as the fuller background provided in id., *Music at the Aragonese Court of Naples* (Cambridge, 1985), 1–6.

[121] For Agricola's representation in Segovia, see above, n. 81, as well as the following paragraph in the main text; on his visits to Naples in the 1490s, see Allan W. Atlas, 'Alexander Agricola and Ferrante I of Naples', *JAMS* 30 (1977), 313–19, and id. and Anthony M. Cummings, 'Agricola, Ghiselin, and Alfonso II of Naples', *Journal of Musicology*, 7 (1989), 540–8. Gregory Lubkin, *A Renaissance Court: Milan under Galeazzo Maria Sforza* (Berkeley, 1994), 103, has recently stated that Agricola worked at Naples before coming to Milan in 1469; the assertion must rest on the archival documents cited at 313 n. 97, as none of the published literature to which Lubkin refers bears out the claim. For apparent written contacts between Agricola and Ferrante I of Naples during the 1470s, see ibid. 188 and 344 n. 15 (referring to 188 n. 16).

[122] For Agricola and Tinctoris, see Strohm, *Music in Late Medieval Bruges*, 143.

[123] For details on these works, and their exact number, see the next paragraph but one in the main text.

[124] Strohm, *Music in Late Medieval Bruges*, 143; cf. also ibid. 88 and 165 n. 38, as well as below, n. 134. *Cecus*—which has less credible attributions to Isaac and Agricola in later sources—appears in Segovia on fos. clcv^v–clcvii^r (189^v–190^r), *Tout a par moy* on fo. cciv^v (196^v). Strohm dates Tinctoris's encounter with the Fernandes brothers through a typically astute deduction that—just as typically—he does not make fully explicit: Tinctoris names the place where he heard them, and Strohm can document them at Bruges from Jan. to Mar. 1482 (ibid. 32).

[125] Strohm, *Music in Late Medieval Bruges*, 143. In seeking to establish a nexus around Tinctoris, incidentally, Strohm writes that Compère 'worked for some time' at the Aragonese court of Naples. But although Compère may well have spent time at Naples during the French occupation early in 1495, he never served the Aragonese court, and in any event Tinctoris would appear to have left Naples long before the

question certainly raises tantalizing prospects with regard to Busnoys—especially since he and Tinctoris might well have renewed their acquaintance at the very time the theorist encountered the Fernandes brothers.[126] Tinctoris, we might think, would hardly have had to travel north to obtain *Fortuna desperata*. But if he in any way stood behind its transmission in Segovia, then the credibility of the attribution would receive a major boost.

Yet once again, the prospects diminish on closer inspection. Segovia shares at best a slender portion of its contents—fourteen works in all—with Neapolitan sources.[127] The readings do little to tighten the links. As Norma Baker has already emphasized, Atlas finds significantly close agreement only for two pieces; and one of these, *Nunca fue pena mayor*, hardly presupposes dependency on Neapolitan models.[128] With the second piece, Hayne's *Amours amours*, Atlas

French arrived; cf. Joshua Rifkin and Barton Hudson, 'Compère, Loyset', *New Grove*, iv. 596, and Atlas, *Music at the Aragonese Court of Naples*, 5, as well as below, esp. n. 133. Further speculations on Compère, Naples, and Segovia appear in Montagna, 'Caron, Hayne, Compère', 152; as these rest on the very assumption that the present discussion seeks to question, they do not require comment here.

[126] Higgins, '*In hydraulis* Revisited', 66, documents Busnoys at Bruges in Dec. 1481 and Jan. 1482. For a more general consideration of Busnoys's relationship to Tinctoris, see ead., 'Antoine Busnois and Musical Culture', 247–50; Higgins shows that the two musicians presumably knew one another since the 1460s, when both resided in the Loire Valley. In the light of some recent speculations by Rob Wegman, the possibility of a tie between Tinctoris, Naples, and Segovia could appear to have ramifications for Obrecht as well; for Wegman suggests that Obrecht pursued university studies at Naples in the late 1470s (*Born for the Muses*, 73–6). The idea, however, lacks a very credible foundation. Wegman takes Obrecht's presence among the celebrated composers listed in Tinctoris's *Complexus effectuum musices* as a sign that Tinctoris knew of Obrecht and his music by about 1480—an improbable circumstance given Obrecht's youth unless the two had come into some sort of direct contact. But not only does this ignore the possibility that Tinctoris could have encountered the rising young star or at least his reputation while visiting the North in 1482, but it surely puts too much weight on a narrowly literal reading of the source evidence. The list appears solely in Ghent, Rijksuniversiteit, Centrale Bibliotheek, MS 70, a volume copied at Ghent in 1503–4; cf. Ronald Woodley, 'The Printing and Scope of Tinctoris's Fragmentary Treatise *De inuentione et usu musice*', *EMH* 5 (1985), 239–68 at 251–4, and id., 'Tinctoris's Italian Translation', 191–3. Since Obrecht himself hailed from Ghent (cf. Wegman, *Born for the Muses*, 21), it would seem hard to escape the inference that the scribe of Ghent 70 or its immediate exemplar simply added the name of the city's most celebrated musical native to Tinctoris's list; certainly, the qualifications registered by Wegman (ibid. 73 n. 10) and Woodley ('Tinctoris's Italian Translation', 192–3)—the latter of whom, in any event, wrote at a time when the place and date of Obrecht's birth had not yet come to light—do not strike me as providing a very consequential obstacle. See also below, n. 140.

[127] A maximally inclusive list of Neapolitan manuscripts of secular polyphony would include the following sources, none of which—at least in its principal body—dates from after the 1480s: Bologna Q 16, Escorial IV.a.24, Mellon, Montecassino 871, Perugia 431, and Seville–Paris; cf. Atlas, *Music at the Aragonese Court*, 118–23, and the literature cited there, but in the light of Fallows, 'Polyphonic Song in the Florence of Lorenzo's Youth', and Warmington, 'The Missing Link'. Not surprisingly, Segovia shares no repertory with the earliest of these manuscripts, Mellon and—in so far as it comes from Naples at all—Escorial IV.a.24. Apart from *Fortuna desperata*, it has a total of only thirteen concordances with one or more of the rest; cf. Baker, 'An Unnumbered Manuscript', i. 242–559, under nos. 41, 43, 103, 125, 126, 129, 130, 131, 137, 147, 151, and 167, to which readers should add *Sancta Maria ora pro nobis*, fo. clxviii[r] (161[r]), found also in Perugia 431, fo. 58[r] (48[r]).

[128] See Baker, 'An Unnumbered Manuscript', i. 27–8, esp. n. 73. In a study evidently not available to Baker, Atlas describes a third composition, the anonymous *Sancta Maria ora pro nobis* cited in the preceding note, as a 'significant concordance'—by which he means, in this instance, that the piece survives nowhere but in Segovia and Perugia 431; see Allan W. Atlas, 'On the Neapolitan Provenance of the Manuscript Perugia, Biblioteca Comunale Augusta, 431 (G 20)', *Musica disciplina*, 31 (1977), 45–105 at 49. But the extent of the significance would seem open to question: not only do minor variants separate the two versions, but Segovia transmits the piece with three voices, Perugia with four.

does indeed demonstrate convincingly that the version transmitted in Segovia could only have originated in Naples. But on his own evidence, the same version also travelled to Florence—from where, we shall see, it could also have reached Segovia.[129] Agricola's visit to Naples in 1492 lasted only a few weeks; and while he may have spent more time there in 1494, the documents found thus far cover only February and March.[130] Of the nineteen pieces credited to him in Segovia, moreover, a significant portion would seem open to question: only seven works have their attributions confirmed elsewhere, while as many as four have conflicting attributions—all of them at least as credible as those in Segovia.[131] At the same time, two undoubtedly genuine pieces of Agricola's land in the manuscript as works of Compère.[132]

Nor does the Tinctoris connection fare much better. As Atlas has already observed, the theorist had all but certainly left Naples by the time Agricola arrived there in 1492; the chance that he played a hand in the transmission of at least Agricola's music, therefore, would appear slender in the extreme.[133] The supposed correspondences with *De inventione et usu musicae* prove at best inconclusive: whatever the relationship between *Cecus* and the Fernandes brothers, its three-voice texture means that Tinctoris must have had other music in mind when he described their performance at Bruges; and the wording of the reference to Gherardus of Brabant makes it quite clear that his rendition of *Tout a par moy* comprised the superius and tenor of the original chanson rather than, as in Tinctoris's own version, the tenor and an extravagantly florid upper part.[134] Even

---

[129] See Atlas, *The Cappella Giulia Chansonnier*, i. 212–13, or the more elegant presentation in id., 'Aragonese Naples and Medicean Florence: Musical Interrelationships and Influence in the Late Fifteenth Century', in *La musica a Firenze al tempo di Lorenzo il Magnifico*, 15–45 at 26–7; also below, pp. 540–2.

[130] Cf. Atlas and Cummings, 'Agricola, Ghiselin, and Alfonso II of Naples', 540–2.

[131] For the pieces with further attributions to Agricola—among them several of his most widely circulated compositions—see Baker, 'An Unnumbered Manuscript', i. 242–559, under nos. 42, 81, 83, 86, 87, 103, 111. The *Odhecaton* (fos. 79ᵛ–80ʳ) assigns *De tous biens plaine* (Segovia, fo. clxxiiiiᵛ [167ᵛ]) to 'Pe. bourdon' (on whom see now Wegman, *Born for the Muses*, 70–2; contrary to Hewitt, *Odhecaton*, 211 n. 2, and various other sources, the attribution does appear over the music—at least in the Bologna exemplar); *Elaes* (fo. cxciiiiᵛ–cxciiiiʳ [187ᵛ–188ʳ]) appears in Seville-Paris, fos. *q*5ᵛ–*q*7ʳ (Seville 5-I-43, fos. 125ᵛ–127ʳ), with a now fragmentary attribution that most likely read 'Pietrequin' (cf. Plamenac, as in below, n. 175, 1952, p. 271); the Magnificat setting on fos. lxxiiiᵛ–lxxviʳ (73ᵛ–76ʳ) occurs in Rome, Biblioteca Apostolica Vaticana, Cappella Sistina 63, fos. lxxvᵛ–lxxxiiiʳ (77ᵛ–85ʳ), under the name Brumel; and the untitled mass on fos. cxxxvʳ–cxliiʳ (128ʳ–135ʳ) appears in four German manuscripts with an attribution to the mysterious Aulen. Cf. Baker, 'An Unnumbered Manuscript', i. 25, 44–5, 48–9, and 55–6.

[132] For these pieces—*J'ay bieau huewer* (fo. clxxxiiʳ [175ʳ]) and *Je ne puis plus* (fo. cxciiʳ [186ʳ])—cf. ibid. 58–9 and Wesner, 'The Chansons of Loyset Compère', 218–20 and 225–6. In two instances, however, Segovia supplies the correct, or presumably correct, attribution for pieces attributed to Agricola in other sources; see Baker, 'An Unnumbered Manuscript', i. 52–3, 56–7.

[133] See Atlas, 'Aragonese Naples and Medicean Florence', 19, as well as *Music at the Aragonese Court*, 52. The last record of Tinctoris in Naples dates from 27 Feb. 1491; on this, and on the general question of Tinctoris's whereabouts in the early 1490s, see Ronald Woodley, 'Iohannes Tinctoris: A Review of the Documentary Biographical Evidence', *JAMS* 34 (1981), 217–48 at 236–9.

[134] For the music of *Cecus*, see Geering and Trümpy, *Das Liederbuch des Johannes Heer*, 125–30 (with attribution to Agricola), or Alexander Agricola, *Opera omnia*, ed. Edward R. Lerner (CMM 22; n.p., 1961–70), v. 102–5; the third voice functions as an integral part of the texture and thus could not constitute a later addition. For *Tout a par moy*, see Baker, 'An Unnumbered Manuscript', ii. 1012–18, or, more

the number of Tinctoris's compositions in Segovia offers little reason to tie the manuscript to him. One item credited to the total, the chanson *Hellas le bon temps que j'avoie*, appears under the name 'loysette *com*pere'.[135] Of the seven pieces that Segovia does ascribe to Tinctoris, moreover, only one—a four-voice setting of *Le souvenir*—has a place in the main body of the volume; the remaining six all form part of a special fascicle consisting solely of duos, most of them proportional exercises like *Tout a par moy*.[136] As Bonnie Blackburn has observed, pieces of this sort typically appear 'not in a source of practical music but in a collection of didactic music examples, either forming a whole or scattered in a manuscript containing several treatises'.[137] Indeed, Segovia's concentration of duos has no real parallel in any other practical manuscript; not surprisingly, virtually all its few concordances occur in didactic collections of the kind Blackburn describes, and one of the Tinctoris pieces figures as well in the *Liber de arte contrapuncti*.[138] Baker would

handily, Johannes Tinctoris, *Opera omnia*, ed. William Melin (CMM 18; n.p., 1976), 138–40. The passage on Gherardus reads, 'Gerardus etenim Brabantinus conterraneus meus: illustrissimi ducis Borbonii aulicus (me presente: vidente: et audiente) sub porticu dextra insignis ecclesiae Carnotensis: cujus pueros musicam tunc docebam: supremam partem simul cum tenore: non voces alternando: illius cantilene: Tout aparmoy: perfectissime cecinit'; see Karl Weinmann, *Johannes Tinctoris (1445–1511) und sein unbekannter Traktat "De inventione et usu musicae": Historisch-kritische Untersuchung*, ed. Wilhelm Fischer (Tutzing, 1961), 34.

[135] Segovia, fo. clxxxiiiiˣ (177ʳ), with the incipit 'Elacs abraham'; for the other sources, see Hewitt, *Odhecaton*, 152; Brown, *A Florentine Chansonnier*, Text vol., 289; or Tinctoris, *Opera omnia*, pp. xiii–xiv. Admittedly, Tinctoris's claim to this piece seems to rest solely on the *Odhecaton*: to judge from the minimal variants, Florence 27, the only other source with the attribution, probably took the piece directly from Petrucci (cf. ibid. xiii). See also the comments in Baker, 'An Unnumbered Manuscript', i. 59–60—although the special connection between Tinctoris and Segovia that she infers would seem, particularly in light of the present discussion, circular. But whether or not Tinctoris composed *Hellas*, Wesner, 'The Chansons of Loyset Compère', 231–3, offers telling musical arguments to show that Compère did not.

[136] The four-voice *Le souvenir* appears on fos. cxviᵛ–cxviiʳ (109ᵛ–110ʳ); for a transcription, see Baker, 'An Unnumbered Manuscript', ii. 834–9, or Tinctoris, *Opera omnia*, 135–6. See also ibid. 128–9 and 137–46 for the six duos attributed to Tinctoris as well as an anonymous *Fecit potentiam* (fo. ccvʳ [197ʳ]) found on the same opening as one of them and tentatively—but not very credibly—assigned to the theorist by Anglés, *La música en la corte de los Reyes Católicos*, i. 111. The duo fascicle of Segovia occupies fos. ccʳ–ccvᵛ (192ᵛ–197ᵛ), a gathering now lacking its outermost bifolio; in its present form, it comprises twelve pieces, all but *Fecit potentiam* florid cantus-firmus settings, and all but one of these, the *De tous biens playne* of Roelkin, exercises in proportional complications. Lawrence F. Bernstein, 'French Duos in the First Half of the Sixteenth Century', in John Walter Hill (ed.), *Studies in Musicology in Honor of Otto E. Albrecht* (Kassel, 1980), 43–87 at 53–7, offers a useful discussion of Segovia's duos. The reader should note, however, that the list of them on p. 55 includes one piece of a different nature found elsewhere in the manuscript, Isaac's quodlibet on *De tous biens plaine* (fo. clxxviᵛ [170ᵛ]), and requires correction on several points: the folio references mix original and modern numberings without distinction; the *De tous biens plaine* ascribed to Agricola (fos. cxciiiiᵛ–cxcvʳ [188ᵛ–189ʳ]) in fact has three voices; and three genuine duos—Agricola's *Gaudeamus omnes* (fo. ccʳ [192ʳ]), Obrecht's *Regina coeli* (cf. above, n. 111), and *Fecit potentiam*—fail to appear.

[137] Blackburn, 'A Lost Guide', 31.

[138] Cf. ibid. n. 7. Two pieces by Tinctoris on fo. cciiiiʳ (196ʳ), *D'ung aultre amer* and a textless duo found in the *Liber de arte contrapuncti* as an Alleluia, recur in both Perugia, Biblioteca Comunale Augusta, MS 1013 (fos. 89ᵛ and 82ᵛ, respectively), and Bologna, Civico Museo Bibliografico Musicale, MS A 71 (pp. 297 and 290), while Roelkin's *De tous biens playne* (fos. cciiᵛ–cciiiʳ [195ᵛ (*sic*)–195ʳ]) appears on fo. 139ʳ of the Perugia manuscript; for the concordances, see Blackburn, 35–7 and 48–9 (Baker, 'An Unnumbered Manuscript', i. 513–14, lacks those with Bologna). Roelkin's florid but non-proportional duo also occurs in Warsaw, Biblioteka Uniwersytecka, MS Mf. 2016, fo. 25ʳ—significantly, the only one of these pieces to appear in a 'musical' source; cf. Blackburn, 35, as well as Fritz Feldmann, 'Zwei weltliche Stücke des Breslauer Codex Mf. 2016 (Aus der Zeit um 1500)', *Zeitschrift für Musikwissenschaft*, 13 (1930–1), 252–66 at 257–60 and 263–6 (including a facsimile of the Warsaw manuscript on p. 258). Both the florid and the proportional duo, I should emphasize, belong to another class of piece than quodlibet duos such as

thus seem on the right track when she writes, 'The homogeneity of this gathering . . . suggests that it was copied from an intermediary source which either was, or was copied from, a pedagogical source dealing with proportions'.[139] If such an intermediary source existed, the inclusion of Obrecht and Roelkin among the composers surely means that it came not from Italy but from somewhere much to the north—where, as manuscripts from Ghent and the region of Cambrai remind us, Tinctoris's theoretical writings remained far from unknown.[140]

Turning specifically to Busnoys, any hopes of tracing an association either to Tinctoris or to Naples in general also come up short. As already indicated, Tinctoris cites *Je ne demande autre de gré* as a work of Busnoys in his *Liber de arte contrapuncti*.[141] Ex. 20.5(*a*) shows the musical extract accompanying the theorist's remarks, which illustrates how the superius and the first of the work's two contratenors create what he clearly regarded as an irremediable diminished fifth.[142] Segovia falls into the trap against which Tinctoris sought to warn: as we see from Ex. 20.5(*b*), it adds a flat to the second contratenor—and thus, while removing the offending simultaneity, forces a linear tritone in the contratenor primus. It would not seem easy to posit anything but a distant relationship

---

Isaac's *De tous biens plaine* (cf. above, n. 136) or those found in the Seville–Paris manuscript; on these last, see Dragan Plamenac, 'The Two-Part Quodlibets in the Seville Chansonnier', in Gustave Reese and Rose Brandel (eds.), *The Commonwealth of Music: In Honor of Curt Sachs* (New York, 1965), 163–81.

[139] Baker, 'An Unnumbered Manuscript', i. 91.

[140] See the discussion of Cambrai, Bibliothèque municipale, MS A 416, in Woodley, 'The Printing and Scope of Tinctoris's *De inuentione et usu musice*', 246 and 258, and the remarks on Ghent 70 above, n. 126; Northern transmission of this sort, I might note, would explain the awareness of Tinctoris's proportional system demonstrated in Obrecht's *Regina coeli* (cf. Wegman, *Born for the Muses*, 74, as well as above, n. 111). One other composer represented in the duo fascicle of Segovia could also hint at a tie to the North. Bernstein, 'French Duos in the First Half of the Sixteenth Century', 53 n. 21, suggests identifying the 'Adam' named as the author of a *De tous biens playne* setting on fo. cci^r (193^r) as Adam von Fulda. As Segovia also credits its Adam with a French chanson, *Adieu commant joye y bon tamps* (fo. clxxviii^v [172^v]), this would appear unlikely. But—especially as the name Adam does not seem to have enjoyed much currency in the late 15th c., at least in the Netherlands (cf., for example, the lists of singers in Strohm, *Music in Late Medieval Bruges*, 181–91, and Wegman, 'Music and Musicians', 246–7)—we should perhaps give serious consideration to Adam Rener, or Adam of Liège. A document from the Imperial chapel lists Rener in July 1498 as one of six 'Mutanten Knaben'; since boys' voices tended to break later in those days than now, his birth date could well lie some three or four years earlier than *c*.1485, the figure conventionally given in the literature (see e.g. Martin Staehelin, 'Rener, Adam', *New Grove*, xv. 472). This revised estimate would also accord with the further evidence: in June 1500, her received leave to pursue studies 'In Burgundi', and in Dec. 1503, the first record marking his return to the Imperial court calls him 'Componisten'—a title hardly imaginable for an 18-year-old. For the documents, see Hertha Schweiger, 'Archivalische Notizen zur Hofkantorei Maximilians I.', *Zeitschrift für Musikwissenschaft*, 14 (1931–2), 363–74 at 365, 367, and 373, or, more recently, Heidrich, *Die deutschen Chorbücher*, 302–3.

[141] See Johannes Tinctoris, *Opera theoretica*, ed. Albert Seay (CSM 22; n.p., 1975–8), ii. 144 (bk. ii, ch. 33).

[142] On this passage, see Karol Berger, *Musica ficta: Theories of Accidental Inflections in Vocal Polyphony from Marchetto da Padova to Gioseffo Zarlino* (Cambridge, 1987), 95–9, and Peter Urquhart's contribution to this volume (above, Ch. 14). The sources show some disagreement over the nomenclature and relative position of the contras. Most of the sources label both voices either 'contra' or 'bassus' without further distinction; and while most place the lower of the two on the bottom half of the recto page—the usual location for a bass voice—Pixérécourt and the *Odhecaton* have the upper contra here instead. Only Florence 229 (fos. 151^v–152^r) presents the composition in a fashion competely unambiguous as regards both terminology and layout; cf. the transcription in Brown, *A Florentine Chansonnier*, Music vol., no. 147.

Ex. 20.5. Busnoys, *Je ne demande*, mm. 19–23: (*a*) quotation by Tinctoris; (*b*) version in Segovia

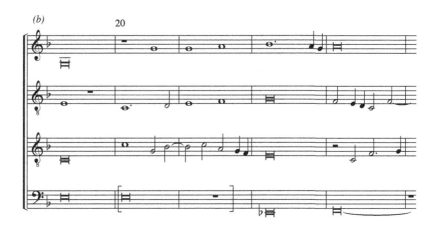

between Tinctoris and this version of *Je ne demande*. Nor do the chances improve very much if we choose to regard the flat as simply a piece of misguided scribal initiative with no real stemmatic significance.[143] *Je ne demande* survives in only a single manuscript of possible Neapolitan origin, the Seville–Paris chansonnier; and while the readings in Segovia certainly lie close to those in Seville–Paris, they lie equally close, if not closer still, to the readings in Pixérécourt.[144] Indeed, Segovia represents something of a stemmatic bridge between the two manuscripts.[145] This strongly implies, of course, that the scribe of Segovia obtained his

[143] The flat also appears in Casanatense 2856 (cf. above, n. 71), whose readings otherwise have no perceptible relationship to those of Segovia; cf. below, n. 145.

[144] *Je ne demande* appears in Seville–Paris, without attribution, on fos. *o7*ᵛ–*o9*ʳ (Seville 5-I-43, fos. 105ᵛ–107ʳ); on the provenance of the manuscript, cf. above, n. 127. For *Je ne demande* in Pixérécourt, see above, n. 71; for details of the readings, see the following note.

[145] The seven sources that transmit *Je ne demande* in its entirety—I have not had access to the fragmentary manuscript Cambridge R.2.71—fall into two groups. The first consists of Bologna Q 18 (fos. 39ᵛ–40ʳ) and Casanatense 2856; using Brown's transcription (cf. above, n. 142) as a point of reference, these manuscripts stand apart by virtue of shared variants in mm. 30₂ (superius: *c* minim), 33 (superius: 2 semibreves), 54₂ (superius: *g′–f′*), 57₄ (bassus: *d* minim), 60₂ (tenor: *f* minim), and 62₄–63₃ (superius: *a′–g′–f′* dotted minim–semiminim–semibreve). The five sources of the second group themselves divide into further

exemplar for *Je ne demande* through Italian contacts rather than from sources more obviously proximate to Busnoys; but at the same time it means that, as with *Amours amours*, we could just as readily situate those contacts in Florence as in Naples—assuming even that Seville–Paris comes from Naples in the first place.

We have still less reason to imagine a Neapolitan conduit behind *Fortuna desperata*. Segovia's reading of measure 13 does place it on the same broad line of transmission as both Seville–Paris and Perugia 431, a manuscript more certainly from the Neapolitan orbit.[146] Yet the sources that make up this side of the *stemma* cover a territorial span ranging from southern Italy to Germany.[147] More important, the variants shown in Ex. 20.4 preclude any assumption of a special association between the Spanish manuscript and at least any visible representatives of a Neapolitan tradition that we may have. In other words, just as Obrecht and Bruges fail to provide any explanation for Segovia's attribution of *Fortuna desperata*, so, too, do Tinctoris and Naples.

One final lead deserves consideration. In his remarks on Segovia's Italian connections, Hudson notes that it shares over thirty pieces with Florence 229.[148] In the light of our observations about *Je ne demande* and *Amours amours*, this statistic cannot help but arouse curiosity. Apart from *Fortuna desperata*, in fact, Segovia has no fewer than forty-one concordances with Florentine manuscripts of the late fifteenth or very early sixteenth century.[149] Given the size of Segovia

subgroups. The *Odhecaton* (cf. above, n. 71) has a number of unique readings that put it at some distance from the rest, displaying most notably a different cadential figure in the superius at m. 15 and an error in the tenor at the very end (cf. the transcription in Hewitt, *Odhecaton*, 311–12; note, however, that Hewitt presents the two lower voices in reversed position *vis-à-vis* Brown and that her measure numbers read one higher from 31 onwards). Of the four remaining manuscripts—Florence 229, Pixérécourt, Segovia, and Seville–Paris—the last clearly preserves the earliest readings, both in all but three local details presumably attributable to scribal intervention or error (m. 10$_2$, bassus: 3rd filled in; m. 37, superius: 3rd note *a*; m. 61, bassus: last two notes reversed) and, as Bonnie Blackburn has persuasively demonstrated, in its treatment of the problematic mid-point cadence (see 'Obrecht's *Missa Je ne demande*', 28–9, and esp. Ex. 4 on p. 27). Pixérécourt and Florence 229 would appear to derive from a common parent that both reworked the mid-point (cf. ibid.) and introduced two new readings: a dotted semibreve in place of the syncopated repetition semibreve–minim in the upper contra at m. 28, and an anticipation *f′* in place of the passing note *g′* found in all other sources at m. 52, superius; each manuscript also shows further individual variants that need not concern us here. Segovia occupies a middle position between Seville–Paris and the Florentine manuscripts: like Seville–Paris, it has the standard reading for m. 52, but it already has the Florentine reading at m. 28, and its version of the middle cadence, while singular, seems most closely related to that in Pixérécourt.

[146] On the origins of Perugia 431, see particularly Atlas, 'On the Neapolitan Provenance', 46–56, and Giulio Cattin, 'Il repertorio polifonico sacro nelle fonti napoletane del Quattrocento', in Lorenzo Bianconi and Renato Bossa (eds.), *Musica e cultura a Napoli dal XV al XIX secolo* (Florence, 1983), 29–45 at 34–40.

[147] The script and contents of Frankfurt VII 20 leave no doubt of its German origin, and the same applies to Wolfenbüttel 78; on this manuscript, see Martin Staehelin *et al.*, *Musikalischer Lustgarten: Kostbare Zeugnisse der Musikgeschichte* (Wolfenbüttel, 1985), 70–1. Zwickau 78/2, probably copied in the city where it still resides, belonged to the local rector Stephan Roth and bears the date 1531; see, most conveniently, *Census-Catalogue*, iv. 197.

[148] See Hudson, 'Two Ferrarese Masses', 293, with reference to the list in Brown, *A Florentine Chansonnier*, Text vol., 194. For present purposes, I would reduce Hudson's and Brown's tally—thirty-three pieces—by two: nos. 10 and 252 in Florence 229 represent free-standing excerpts from sacred works transmitted complete in Segovia and thus hardly count as genuine concordances.

[149] Cf. Baker, 'An Unnumbered Manuscript', i. 242–559, under nos. 36, 41, 42, 43, 47, 50, 56, 59, 65, 80, 81, 83, 87, 88, 89, 90, 94, 103, 104, 105, 107, 110, 113, 116, 120, 121, 125, 126, 128, 129, 130, 133, 134, 136, 137, 138, 139, 140, 141, 142, 143, 145, 149, 167; readers without access to Baker can trace the

and Florence 229 in particular, this in itself may not seem very remarkable, especially since many of the compositions involved—including the seemingly unavoidable *Nunca fue pena major*—belong among the more widely circulated pieces of the time. But the concordances make up close to a third of Segovia's non-Spanish secular repertory. Several of the pieces, moreover, appear to have remained confined to fairly limited circles; indeed, ten have no known transmission at all beyond Segovia and the Florentine manuscripts, and three of these ten even occur as a series in Florence 229.[150] At least on preliminary examination, too, a number of compositions beyond *Amours amours* and *Je ne demande* show significantly close relationships in their readings.[151] In these circumstances, the prominence of Agricola and Isaac might also seem to take on new significance: Isaac's ties to Florence hardly need elaboration, and Agricola fits within a Florentine context at least as well as in a Neapolitan one.[152]

Yet despite all this, a number of obstacles stand in the way of thinking that the compiler or compilers of Segovia could have indulged in something like a large-scale importation of music from Florence. The concordant pieces include several of obvious Flemish origin, which would hardly have come to Spain by way of

majority of the concordances through Brown, *A Florentine Chansonnier*, as cited in the previous note, as well as Atlas, *The Cappella Giulia Chansonnier*, i, under nos. 9, 24, 40, 91, and 167. Apart from Florence 229, the concordances involve the following sources: Bologna Q 17; Florence 107bis, 176, 178, and 2356; Pixérécourt; and Cappella Giulia XIII. 27. My total for the sources as a whole follows the same principles as those for Florence 229 spelt out in the preceding note.

[150] For the pieces in series—Isaac or Barle, *Het es al ghedaen*; Compère, *Beaulté d'amours* (or *Seraige*); and Barle, *Moyses*—cf. Brown, *A Florentine Chansonnier*, Text vol., 263; *Beaulté d'amours* and *Moyses* occur in close proximity in Segovia as well. For the remaining seven pieces, the list, alphabetically according to incipit, reads: *Dat ic my lijden* (Elinc or Johannes Agricola; cf. ibid. 215); *J'ay bien nourri* (Johannes Joye, Japart, or Josquin; ibid. 223); *J'ay pris amours* (Segovia, fo. cxviii^v [112^v], and Florence 178, fos. 2^v–3^r, 'YSAC'—although Segovia contains only the superius and tenor, which match the standard chanson, their level of transposition verifies the concordance indicated in Baker, 'An Unnumbered Manuscript', i. 373); *My my* (Isaac; *A Florentine Chansonnier*, Text vol., 212); *O venus bant* (Agricola; ibid. 239); *Pour vostre amour* (*Digau a les donzelles*, Brumel or Isaac; cf. Atlas, *The Cappella Giulia Chansonnier*, i. 227—who, however, overlooks the concordance with Segovia, fo. clxxxvii^r [180^r], 'Anthonius brumel'—as well as below, at n. 158); and *Vostre amour* (Isaac; *A Florentine Chansonnier*, Text vol., 212–13). According to both Anglés ('Un manuscrit inconnu', 14; *La música en la corte de los Reyes Católicos*, i. 110) and Baker ('An Unnumbered Manuscript', i. 36–7, 496, and 579), Segovia credits *Moyses* to Isaac (fo. cxci^r [185^r]); while I have not seen the manuscript itself, in neither of the reproductions available to me—an older microfilm as well as the facsimile—does the name appear.

[151] Brown has called attention to stemmatic ties between Segovia and Florence 229 in the case of Agricola's *J'ay bien huer*, and Atlas has done the same for the disputed *J'ay bien nourri*; see *A Florentine Chansonnier*, Text vol., 146–8, and Atlas, *The Cappella Giulia Chansonnier*, i. 81. In Compère's *Beaulté d'amours*, Segovia and Florence 229—the sole extant sources—appear to agree in every significant regard, even sharing a common error; cf. *A Florentine Chansonnier*, Music vol., no. 133, especially the note to m. 30, superius.

[152] For Isaac, see particularly Frank A. D'Accone, 'Heinrich Isaac in Florence: New and Unpublished Documents', *Musical Quarterly*, 49 (1963), 464–83. Agricola worked in Florence from Sept. 1491 to early May 1492 and returned there at least briefly in the late summer of 1492 and, it would appear, at the end of 1493 or the beginning of 1494; he also enjoys a commanding position in the Florentine manuscripts of the early 1490s. Cf. Frank A. D'Accone, 'The Singers of San Giovanni in Florence during the 15th Century', *JAMS* 14 (1961), 307–58 at 344–5; Rifkin, 'Pietrequin Bonnel and Ms. 2794', 289–91; Atlas and Cummings, 'Agricola, Ghiselin, and Alfonso II of Naples', 540–1 n. 1, 544–6 and 548; and Litterick's review of Brown, *A Florentine Chansonnier*, 307–8.

Tuscany.[153] More than a few works—even those stemmatically close, or unique to
Segovia and Florentine sources—have variant attributions or text incipits and
would thus seem to diminish the chances of immediate dependency.[154] Agricola's
representation, as we have seen, shows considerably more problems than we should
expect if it drew directly on sources close to the composer.[155] The same applies to
Isaac. Thomas Noblitt has shown that Segovia transmits an unauthorized version
of the *Missa Wohlauf Gesell von hinnen*.[156] Of the ten further pieces attributed here
to Isaac found as well with ascription elsewhere, no fewer than four occur under different names in sources plainly more authoritative either for Isaac himself or for the
alternate party.[157] A fifth piece, unique to Segovia, would seem doubtful for other
reasons; and a work credited to Isaac in the Florentine manuscript Cappella Giulia
XIII. 27 appears here with an attribution to Brumel.[158] All in all, then, we might
hesitate before reading even the most striking of the connections enumerated in the
last paragraph as indicating a direct line of transmission between Florence and
Spain. Perhaps we can best account for the evidence in all its contradictions if we
imagine Segovia and the Florentine manuscripts as the outer points of a triangle
with a third location—probably a Flemish urban centre—at its apex.[159]

[153] I assume Flemish provenance for Obrecht's *Meiskin es u* (cf. Brown, *A Florentine Chansonnier*, Text
vol., 278) and *Wat willen wij* (*Maule met*; cf. Atlas, *The Cappella Giulia Chansonnier*, i. 87–8); the disputed
Tmeiskin was jonck (*De tusch en busch*; cf. Brown, Text vol., 271, and above, n 105); Barbireau's *Een vroylic
wesen* (cf. Atlas, i. 65); the anonymous *Dat ic my lijden* and *Het es al ghedaen* (cf. above, n. 150, but also the
qualifications—not wholly persuasive, in my view—in Brown, Text vol., 126–7); and perhaps *Nec michi nec
tibi* (see above, n. 106). Cf. also below, n. 159.
[154] Those with differing attributions include *J'ay bien huer*, *Dat ic my lijden*, and *Het es al ghedaen* (cf.
above, nn. 150 and 151, and below, n. 157); for those with variant text incipits, see above, nn. 150 and 153.
[155] See above, p. 536.
[156] See Thomas Noblitt, 'Contrafacta in Isaac's *Missae* "Wohlauf, Gesell, von hinnen" ', *Acta musicologica*, 46 (1974), 208–16, esp. 213.
[157] Two pieces—*Comt hier* and *Het es*—have cross-attributions in Florence 229 (cf. Brown, *A Florentine
Chansonnier*, Text vol., 254; above, n. 150; and Baker, 'An Unnumbered Manuscript', i. 36–40), while a
third, *Fortuna desperata* (fos. cxvᵛ–cxviʳ [108ᵛ–109ʳ]), appears in the Ferrarese manuscript Casanatense 2856
(no. 102, fos. 147ᵛ–149ʳ) with an attribution to Martini (cf. ibid. 42–3, and, on Casanatense 2856, below,
n. 245). As Dietrich Kämper has shown, the fourth piece, *Ortus de celo flos est* (cf. above, n. 105), all but certainly belongs to Gaspar van Weerbeke; see 'La stangetta—eine Instrumentalkomposition Gaspars van
Weerbeke?'. Cf. also above, n. 150.
[158] Martin Just, 'Studien zu Heinrich Isaacs Motetten' (Ph.D. diss., Tübingen, 1960), i. 167–8, has
questioned the authenticity of the *Fortuna desperata/Sancte Petre* credited to 'ysaac' in Segovia, fos. clviiᵛ–clvi-
iiʳ (110ᵛ–111ʳ). In his contribution to the present volume—which he kindly made available to me as early
as Nov. 1992—Martin Picker defends the attribution, regarding the 'structural and stylistic anomalies' of the
piece 'as evidence more of immaturity than inauthenticity' (see above, Ch. 17 n. 33). Given the date of
Segovia, however (cf. above, n. 68), the transmission hardly offers compelling support for this position; and
the use of the *Fortuna* superius here in a form different from that employed in Isaac's better-accredited
Fortuna/Bruder Conrat (cf. Picker, n. 34) would seem to point against common authorship (although cf.
below, n. 220). On the piece attributed to Brumel, *Pour vostre amours* (cf. above, n. 150), see Baker, 'An
Unnumbered Manuscript', i. 41–2.
[159] An incident in Obrecht's biography raises the possibility of a slightly different configuration. In
1494/5 the composer played host at Antwerp to Bartholomaeus Martini, bishop of Segorbe in Spain and
master of the papal chapel (cf. Wegman, *Born for the Muses*, 295). Perhaps, then, we could envisage Rome
as the nodal point through which music flowed not only to and from Florence and the Netherlands, but also
from both places to Spain. Yet this seems needlessly complex, not to say geographically extravagant; and it
becomes even more implausible if we recall how easily Flemish texts deteriorated in any path of transmission
involving non-native speakers.

In any event, we must bear in mind that while Florentine ties may help clarify the history of Segovia, they do not necessarily shore up its credentials for Busnoys. As we have seen, the Florentine Busnoys tradition, for all its unquestioned importance, cannot claim anything like absolute authority in matters of transmission or attribution.[160] Whether or not, moreover, Segovia obtained its version of *Je ne demande* from Florence, the derivation of this version from the one represented in Seville–Paris offers tangible evidence of at least one intermediary lying between it and the composer or his immediate circle.[161] As for *Fortuna desperata*, discovery of Segovia's Florentine affiliations may at first seem to have positive repercussions for the question of authorship; for evidence we have yet to consider will show that the piece all but certainly originated on Florentine soil.[162] Yet precisely in this instance, the stemmatic relationship between Segovia and Florence fails to hold: although the two Florentine sources Cappella Giulia XIII.27 and Florence 121 stand on opposite sides of the fence with regard to measure 13, they retain the standard readings at the places shown in Ex. 20.4.[163] Segovia's readings for these measures, in fact, not only isolate it from every other source of *Fortuna desperata* but the two St Gallen manuscripts, but also consign it to the farthest reaches of the transmission. In each instance, the variant constitutes a decorative elaboration of the plainer form seen in the majority of sources; significantly, too, the only further occurrence of all three readings comes at an even later date than Segovia—1510 or not long afterwards.[164] Hence the attribution of *Fortuna desperata* to Busnoys enters the scene only at a terminal point in the stemma—further cause to regard it with extreme circumspection.

IV

But worries about the transmission of *Fortuna desperata* do not rest on Segovia alone. Cumming found herself troubled by the absence of the piece from what she called 'the central Burgundian sources where many of Busnois' chansons are found'.[165] Higgins dismissed this point with the observation that some 'half of Busnois's songs survive only in Italian sources, that is, in sources outside of the

---

[160] Cf. above, pp. 518–19.   [161] Cf. above, n. 145.

[162] See below, Sect. VI.

[163] Cf. above, Ex. 20.4; on Florence 121, see Bonnie J. Blackburn, 'Two "Carnival Songs" Unmasked: A Commentary on MS Florence Magl. XIX. 121', *Musica disciplina*, 35 (1981), 121–78, esp. 121–3, 149–50, and 178.

[164] See above, n. 115. In view of the apparent stemmatic affinity between Segovia and St Gallen 462, those who uphold Busnoys's authorship of *Fortuna desperata* may wish to argue for some sort of a link between the origin of the latter manuscript and Busnoys's known Parisian ties (cf. above, n. 11). Given both the nature of the stemmatic evidence and the chronological distances involved, however, I would hardly think this very plausible.

[165] Cumming, 'The Goddess Fortuna Revisited', 8.

"Burgundian" tradition to which Cumming alludes'.[166] Yet the riposte overlooks an important grain of truth in Cumming's argument. For if *Fortuna desperata* fails to appear in the great Northern manuscripts that play such an important role in the dissemination of Busnoys's music, it remains absent from almost any other significant source of his music as well.[167] Among the sources in which *Fortuna desperata* does make an appearance, only four—Segovia, Bologna Q 16, the Seville–Paris chansonnier, and *Canti C*—contain so much as a single further item by Busnoys.[168] Of these, moreover, *Canti C* yields only four more Busnoys pieces; and we have already observed how minimal a part Busnoys plays in Segovia.[169]

Yet before consigning *Fortuna desperata* to the outer limits of Busnoys transmission, we must consider Bologna Q 16 and Seville–Paris; for as we see from Tables 20.2 and 20.3, both these manuscripts include a substantial number of items credited in one source or another to Busnoys. Apart from *Fortuna desperata*, Bologna Q 16—which transmits almost all its contents without attribution—has eight pieces found elsewhere under his name alone and two that have conflicting attributions.[170] For Seville–Paris, the totals read fifteen—with one

---

[166] Higgins, 'Antoine Busnois and Musical Culture', 23; on the provenance of 'the central Burgundian sources' see above, n. 3. I cannot share Higgins's concern when she goes on to write, 'If transmission in the "central Burgundian sources" is the criterion by which the authenticity of Busnois's works is to be established, we would consequently have to reject the greatest part of his compositional output as *opera dubia*'— why should we worry about rejecting even 'the greatest part' of the works attributed to him? Cf., on this score, Giuseppina La Face Bianconi and Antonio Rossi, '"Soffrir *non* son disposto ogni tormento." Serafino Aquilano: figura letteraria, fantasma musicologico', in *Atti del XIV Congresso della Società Internazionale di Musicologia: Trasmissione e recezione delle forme di cultura musicale*, ed. Angelo Pompilio *et al.* (Turin, 1990), ii. 240–54 at 242–3.

[167] See also below, p. 555.

[168] Higgins recognizes that *Fortuna desperata* does not fit into the general pattern of Busnoys transmission (cf. 'Antoine Busnois and Musical Culture', 100), but she does not consider this in connection with the question of its authorship.

[169] *Canti C* contains *Corps digne* (fos. 105ᵛ–106ʳ) and *Maintes femmes* (fos. 1017ᵛ–1018ʳ [*recte* 117ᵛ–118ʳ]), both with the attribution 'Busnoys', as well as unattributed versions of *In myne zynn* ('Le second jour d'avril, fos. 55ᵛ–56ʳ) and *Une filleresse d'estouppes* (fos. 91ᵛ–92ʳ).

[170] I might take this opportunity to raise a question about *Je ne demande lialté*, found anonymously in Bologna Q 16, fos. xxxxvᵛ–xxxxviiʳ (60ᵛ–62ʳ), but with the attribution 'A. Busnoys' in its only other source, Florence 229, fos. 59ᵛ–61ʳ; for a transcription, see Brown, *A Florentine Chansonnier*, Music vol., no. 59. As a comparison of their opening measures suggests, the scribe of Florence 229 could well have confused this piece with the better-known *Je ne demande autre de gré*, which also occurs in Florence 229 (cf. above, n. 142) but lacks attribution there. A further look at the music reinforces this suspicion: both the hints of minim canon at mm. 30–1, 36–7, and 46–7 (although cf. *Je ne demande autre de gré*, mm. 23–4), and the imitation at the fifth and fourth in mm. 43–4 and 54–60, respectively, do not sit comfortably within the stylistic parameters of Busnoys's three-voice secular compositions (cf. below, n. 214; for another disquieting feature, see n. 215). Measures 54–60, indeed, appear worrisome not merely for the interval of imitation but for another reason as well: with a single exception—and for reasons readily understandable given Busnoys's prevailing compositional procedure (cf. Litterick, 'The Manuscript Royal 20.A.XVI', 89–91)—three-voice imitation initiated by the contratenor occurs nowhere but at the beginning of an entire composition or the ouvert of a bergerette. Provocatively, the exception involves the very composition that precedes *Je ne demande lialté* in Florence 229, *Faulx mesdisans* (fos. 57ᵛ–59ʳ, 'Busnoys'; *A Florentine Chansonnier*, Music vol., no. 58), which again has no attribution anyplace else. Since *Faulx mesdisans* stands apart from the normal run of Busnoys's secular works in other ways as well (cf. ibid., Text vol., 76 n. 19), we should perhaps regard its authorship, too, with reserve.

TABLE 20.2. *Busnoys in Bologna Q 16 (all anon.)*

Scribe I

A une dame j'ay fait veu (fos. xvii^v–xviii^r [31^v–32^r])
Advegne qu'advenir pourra (fos. xxxiii[bis]^v–xxxiiii^r [48^v–49^r])
Ce n'est pas moy (fos. lvii^v–lviii^r [72^v–73^r])
En voyant sa dame au matin (fos. cx^v–cxi^r [125^v–126^r])
Je ne demande lialté (fos. xxxxv^v–xxxxvii^r [60^v–62^r])
Laissez dangier ('Laisies moy') (fos. cviii^v–cviiii^r [123^v–124^r])
M'a vostre cueur ('Terribile fortuna') (fos. xxvii^v–xxviiii^r [41^v–43^r])
Ma tres souveraine princesse (fos. xlviiii^v–l^r [64^v–65^r])
S'amour vous fui ('Sans avoir', Isaac?) (fos. lxxxxvii^v–lxxxxviii^r [112^v–113^r])

Scribe II

Cent mille escus (Caron?) (fos. cxxviiii^v–cxxx^r [147^v–148^r])
Fortuna desperata (fos. cxvii^v–cxviii^r [133^v–134^r])

TABLE 20.3. *Busnoys in Seville–Paris (anon. except when marked *; attributions read 'Busnois')*

First layer

Scribe II

Je ne demande autre de gré (fos. *o*7^v–*o*9^r [Seville 5-1-43, fos. 105^v–107^r])
L'autrier la pieça/En l'ombre du buissonet/Trop suis jonette* (fos. *o*5^v–*o*7^r [Seville, fos. 103^v–105^r])
Maintes femmes m'ont dit souvent (fos. *o*9^v–*o*11^r [Seville, fos. 107^v–109^r])

Scribe IIa

Cy dit on benedicite (fos. *k*8^v–*k*9^r [Seville, fos. 70^v–71^r])
Ma tressouveraine princesse (fos. *l*10^v–*l*11^r [Seville, fos. 84^v–85^r])
O fortune tu es trop dure (second copy) (fos. *l*4^v–*l*5^r [Seville, fos. 78^v–79^r])
Povre pour necessité (Au povre par necessité) (fos. *l*5^v–*l*6^r [Seville, fos. 79^v–80^r])
Quelque povre homme que je soye (fos. *k*12^v–*l*1^r [Seville, fos. 74^v–75^r])
Un grand pons (Ung grand povre homme insane) (fos. *l*3^v–*l*4^r [Seville, fos. 77^v–78^r])

Scribe IIIa

Amours me tient en son demaine (Faites de moy) (fos. *m*11^v–*m*12^r [Seville, fos. 97^v–98^r])
J'ay mains de bien que s'il n'en estoit (fos. *m*4^v–*m*5^r [Seville, fos. 90^v–91^r])
Que ville (Ha que ville et abominable)* (fos. *m*12^v–*n*1^r [Seville, fos. 98^v–99^r])
Se brief puys madame voir (Caron?) (fos. *n*9^v–*n*10^r [Paris 4379, fos. 38^v–39^r])

Second layer and additions

Scribe I

Cent mille escus (Caron?) (fos.*g*9^v–*g*10^r [Seville, fos. 45^v–46^r])
Fortuna desperata (altus only) (fo. *n*11^v [Paris, fo. 40^v])
Fortune trop tu es dure (first copy) (fos. *d*7^v–*d*8^r [Seville, fos. 31^v–32^r])
Jaquelinne (si attende) (fos. *j*7^v–*j*8^r [Seville, fos. 57^v–58^r])
Je ne fay plus (Mureau, Compère?) (fos. *d*1^v–*d*2^r [Seville, fos. 25^v–26^r])
M'a vostre coer mis en oubli (fos. *j*5–*j*6^r [Seville, fos. 55^v–56^r])
Un plus que tous est (fos. *c*3^v–*c*4^r [Seville, fos. 17^v–18^r])

Scribe III

Fortuna desperata (fos. *n*11^v–*n*12^r [Paris, fos. 40^v–41^r])

piece appearing twice—and three.[171] On closer inspection, however, even these sources do not really bring *Fortuna desperata* closer into the fold. In Bologna Q 16, the eight uncontested Busnoys pieces, as well as one of the items with conflicting attribution, all occur in the main body of the manuscript, a corpus signed and dated 1487.[172] *Fortuna desperata*, on the other hand, belongs to a group of works added at a later time—possibly, as Allan Atlas has suggested, not until after 1492.[173] While this later material includes music of Busnoys's generation, it contains nothing attributed anywhere to Busnoys himself beyond *Fortuna desperata* and the disputed—and dubious—*Cent mille escus*.[174]

In Seville–Paris, too, *Fortuna desperata* seems at best to hover on the edge of the Busnoys repertory—although in this instance, it will take a bit more effort to demonstrate the point.[175] The 'Cancionero de canto d'organo' that Ferdinand Columbus purchased at Rome in 1515 betrays all the earmarks of a highly complex genesis.[176] For the present discussion, we can divide this into three layers, two principal ones and a handful of later additions; the second principal layer itself has an intricate internal structure that would seem to reveal a series of

---

[171] My talley does not include *Pour tant se mon voloir s'est mis* (fos. *112*ᵛ–*m*1ʳ [Seville 5-I-43, fos. 84ᵛ–85ʳ]), which Brown (*A Florentine Chansonnier*, Music vol., no. 96) prints as a work with conflicting attributions to Busnoys and Caron. On this piece, see ibid., Text vol., 250; *A Correspondence of Renaissance Musicians*, ed. Bonnie J. Blackburn *et al.* (Oxford, 1991), Letter 18, 350–2 n. 1; and Barbara Haggh's contribution to this volume (Ch. 12), n. 3.

[172] Cf. Edward Pease, 'A Report on Codex Q16 of the Civico Museo Bibliografico Musicale (formerly of the Conservatorio Statale di Musica "G. B. Martini"), Bologna', *Musica disciplina*, 20 (1966), 57–94 at 60.

[173] See Atlas, *Music at the Aragonese Court*, 121, but with reference as well to Sarah Fuller, 'Additional Notes on the 15th-Century Chansonnier Bologna Q16', *Musica disciplina*, 23 (1969), 81–103 at 84. I wonder, by the way, if the additions to the manuscript come from as many scribes as Fuller suggests (pp. 84–5); in particular, it seems to me that her Hands B and C more probably represent different phases of the same copyist.

[174] On *Cent mille escus*, cf. the references given above, n. 54.

[175] For background to what follows, see Dragan Plamenac, 'A Reconstruction of the French Chansonnier in the Biblioteca Colombina, Seville', *Musical Quarterly*, 37 (1951), 501–42, and 38 (1952), 85–117 and 245–77; Alice Anne Moerk, 'The Seville Chansonnier: An Edition of Sevilla 5-I-43 and Paris N.A. Fr. 4379 (Pt. 1)' (Ph.D. diss., University of West Virginia, 1971); Stanley Boorman, 'Limitations and Extensions of Filiation Technique', in Fenlon (ed.), *Music in Medieval and Early Modern Europe*, 319–46 at 326–39 and esp. the table on 327; and the facsimile cited above, n. 101. To spare the reader a hopeless tangle of parentheses, references in the following discussion to locations within the manuscript will rely on the original alphabetic foliation alone. In order, too, not to overload the literature with a new set of scribal designations, I shall retain the nomenclature introduced by Boorman, although it does little to make the copying history of Seville–Paris easier to grasp. I should, however, correct one misleading point. As both his labels and other clues reveal—on p. 326, for example, he credits the entire Seville–Paris manuscript to 'three scribes'—Boorman regards the hands he calls Scribe II and IIa as variant forms of a single copyist, and takes the same view of Scribe III and IIIa; but although II and IIa could conceivably—if not very probably—represent different stages in the work of the same individual, Scribe IIIa clearly has nothing whatever to do with Scribe III. Information on paper in the following notes relies on three sources: a breakdown of the gatherings in Seville made—rather hastily, as he emphasizes to me—by David Fallows and very kindly placed at my disposal; my own old notes on the gatherings in Paris; and Henrietta Schavran, 'The Manuscript Pavia, Biblioteca Universitaria, Codice Aldini 362: A Study of Song Tradition in Italy circa 1440–1480' (Ph.D. diss., New York University, 1978), 54–7. My findings on Seville–Paris derive in large measure from a seminar on the manuscript held at the University of Basle in the spring of 1993.

[176] For Columbus's purchase, see Plamenac, 'A Reconstruction' (1951), 504–5. As Plamenac notes, Columbus's description of the volume calls it 'viejo y mutilado'—old and mutilated.

identifiable subphases.[177] Table 20.4 provides an overview of the entire process. The first of the two main layers appears to form the remains of a chansonnier left essentially, if not absolutely, complete by the team that produced it. The surviving material covers all or most of gatherings *e, f, h,* and *k–o* as well as the start of gathering *p*; it represents the work of three scribes—labelled II, IIa, and IIIa in Stanley Boorman's conspectus of the manuscript—plus an initialer and what look like two different rubricators.[178] The second layer belongs almost entirely to

TABLE 20.4. *Layers in Seville–Paris*

Layer I

Scribes: II, IIa, IIIa
Gatherings: *e* (–*e*1ʳ), *f, h, k, l, m, n* (–*n*11ᵛ–*n*12ʳ), *o*, and fo. *p*1ʳ

Layer II

(*a*) Scribe: I
Gatherings: *b, c, d* (–*d*8ᵛ–*d*10ᵛ)
(*b*) Scribe: I
Gatherings: *a* (fos. 1–5, –*a*2ʳ), *j*
(*c*) Scribes: I, III
Gatherings: *g* (–*g*1ʳ–*g*4ʳ, *g*10ᵛ, *g*12ʳ?), *n*11ᵛ–12ᵛ (?); *p* (–*p*1ʳ, –*p*1ᵛ–*p*3ʳ, *p*10ᵛ?)

Layer III

Scribes: III, I (in gathering *q* only), others
Gatherings: *d*8ᵛ–*d*10ᵛ, *q, r*

---

[177] The unmistakable division between the first and second layers in terms of scribal hands and every other visible feature does not necessarily imply the 'material lapse of time' between the two imagined by Boorman ('Limitations and Extensions', 337 n. 43). Not only will our analysis suggest that at least the earliest stages of the second layer could have overlapped chronologically with the production of the first, but David Fallows's descriptions of the watermarks in the Seville portions of the manuscript indicate that both layers drew at least in some measure on a common stock of paper. A fuller attempt to grapple with the issues this raises must, however, await a future occasion.

[178] Cf. Boorman, 'Limitations and Extensions', 327; the first rubricator did most of the voice designations, the second, those in gathering *k*. Boorman errs in crediting Scribe II with fos. *o*11ᵛ–*p*1ʳ and *r*5ᵛ–*r*6ʳ: the former openings belong to Scribe IIIa, the latter very likely to none other than Ferdinand Columbus—the script seems to match some late additions to the index on fos. *a*1ᵛ and *a*2ʳ, which in turn match the alphabetical foliation that Plamenac has already attributed to Columbus; cf. Plamenac, 'A Reconstruction', (1951), 511, as well as the reproduction from Columbus's *Registrum A* in Catherine Weeks Chapman, 'Printed Collections of Polyphonic Music Owned by Ferdinand Columbus', *JAMS* 21 (1968), 34–84, pl. v (before p. 39). In addition, fos. *n*7ᵛ–*n*8ʳ show a text hand found nowhere else in the manuscript, but strikingly similar to that of the scribe who wrote most of Florence 176; cf. the reproduction in Jeppesen, *La frottola*, ii, p. xxiii. The scribes probably worked in the sequence II, IIa, and IIIa—certainly, IIIa comes latest, as his work succeeds that of both II and IIa on gatherings they initiated. On the other hand, the presence of what looks like a different rubricator in gathering *k* could mean that the decoration, at least, began at this point. Whatever the order of production, I suspect that the chansonnier as originally planned would have started with the present gathering *f*: not only did the initialer leave the first piece blank, as if expecting an illuminator to provide an especially elaborate decoration, but the composition, Walter Frye's *Ave regina caelorum*, opens at least two other manuscripts of the period, Laborde and Wolfenbüttel 287; cf. Plamenac, 'A Reconstruction' (1952), 103. The collection must also have contained at least five more gatherings than now survive; these would have occurred after both *e* and *f*, before and after *h*, before *k* (possibly one gathering between *h* and *k*; see further in the main text), and before *o*. Most if not all these would seem already to

Boorman's Scribe I, who both copied most of its contents and undertook the assembly of the manuscript as a whole.[179] As part of the latter operation, he furnished the volume with an index and a prefatory treatise on the rudiments of solmization; his chief musical contributions appear in gatherings *b–d* and *j*.[180] Of these gatherings, *b–d*—or more precisely, everything in them up to fo. *d*8ʳ—may predate the decision to combine his work with the surviving gatherings of the decorated chansonnier, as they include one composition, Busnoys's *O fortune tu es trop dure*, already present in that collection.[181] Gathering *j*, on the other hand, clearly served from the outset to link two portions of the chansonnier, possibly even to replace a gathering still extant but no longer usable.[182] Indeed, gathering *j* and the prefatory material on fos. *a*1–*a*5 together may pinpoint the moment when Scribe I moved to combine the previously independent gatherings *b–d* with the gatherings prepared by Scribes II, IIa, and IIIa. Both have the same six-stave

have vanished before the final assembly of Seville–Paris, as the surviving portions of the index list only two items not still present—cf. Plamenac, 'A Reconstruction' (1951), 514—and at least one of these, an Italian-texted composition, presumably belonged to one of the subsequent layers. The other missing piece, [O] *pulcerrima*, fell between nos. 27 and 57 of Plamenac's inventory (1952); if it did not occupy one of the pages evidently missing near the end of the later gathering *g* (see below), then it would have appeared in a gathering that followed directly after *e* or *f*.

[179] Cf. Boorman, 'Limitations and Extensions', 327. Contrary to Boorman, however, Scribe I did not write fo. *a*2ʳ (cf. the preceding note); Boorman also errs in crediting him with fos. *d*8ᵛ (see below, n. 185), *d*9ᵛ, and—at least in part—fos. *d*9ʳ, *d*10ʳ–*e*1ʳ, *g*10ᵛ, *g*12ʳ, and *q*1ᵛ–*q*2ʳ: if Scribe I wrote any of these last-named pages, they represent a very different stage in his development from that seen in the work securely attributable to him.

[180] The index as copied by Scribe I now breaks off, at the end of fo. *a*1ᵛ, after just under half the pieces beginning with the letter *S*; fo. *a*2ʳ contains a handful of entries, by Ferdinand Columbus, for the letter *V*. At first sight, it could look as if Scribe I simply abandoned the index. I think it more likely, however, that he in fact completed it on a leaf now missing, just as we may also assume that he had entered the letters *A–I* and most of *L*—he would presumably not have had *K*—on one or two leaves preceding the existing fo. *a*1ʳ. In any event, what we now know as gathering *a* clearly conceals a structure originally of greater complexity: David Fallows informs me that fos. *a*2–*a*3 form a bifolio, and that fos. *a*2–*a*5 show a different paper from fos. *a*6–*a*9.

[181] On fos. *d*8ᵛ–*d*10ᵛ, see above, n. 179, as well as further in the main text. For more on *O fortune*, see below, p. 561; as Scribe I's incipit, however, differs from that found in the copy of Scribe IIa, the duplication could have arisen through an oversight.

[182] The possibility of regarding *j* as a substitute gathering arises from two principal considerations: Scribe I does not generally seek to link gatherings from the earlier layer either to one another or to new material—the only comparable instance occurs at the boundaries of *n* and *o* (see below); and while he otherwise writes exclusively on quinternions (cf. Boorman, 'Limitations and Extensions', 335–6 n. 40; on a possible exception represented by gathering *g*, see below, n. 183), here he adopts the sextern structure used throughout the earlier layer. Against this, however, I should note that *j* contains a repertory noticeably more modern than that of *h*—though not entirely. Perhaps more important, Boorman has argued that the copy of Joye's *Ce qu'on fait* that straddles gatherings *j* and *k* divides into two different stemmatic traditions, with the superius, copied by Scribe I, uniquely related to Pixérécourt while Scribe II's tenor and contra correspond to the other sources; see 'Limitations and Extensions', 330–5. But the evidence—a variant beginning at breve 21 (cf. Brown, *A Florentine Chansonnier*, Music vol., no. 261, m. 21; Perkins and Garey, *The Mellon Chansonnier*, i, no. 9, m. 11)—strikes me as less than unequivocal. As the superius of Seville–Paris neither precisely matches that of any other source nor fits the lower voices in any extant version—it fills two breves where the tenor and contra in all the sources but Pixérécourt take only one—we may view it as a singular error, created perhaps by a doubling of note-values (with the present values halved, it fits the lower voices perfectly); it could well stand as parent, rather than sibling, to the three-semibreve reading in Pixérécourt, which, as Leeman Perkins has already stressed (*The Mellon Chansonnier*, ii. 218), transmits the lower voices in a reworked form plainly designed to accommodate the extra length of the superius. In any event, the composition at the border between *h* and *j*, the anonymous *Puis que je vis le regart*, sheds no significant light on the matter in one direction or the other (cf. ibid. 410–11), nor do any of the remaining pieces within *j* itself.

ruling in distinction to the seven-stave ruling of gatherings *b–d*; but the leaves in gathering *a* show the same watermark as *b–d*, whereas gathering *j* shows a different watermark not previously encountered.

Two further gatherings written in part by Scribe I, *g* and *p*, would seem roughly contemporary with *j*: the bulk of their leaves show the same six-stave paper, and their contents, so far as the initial letters allow us to determine, all made their way into Scribe I's index.[183] But the appearance in both gatherings of a hand not previously encountered—Scribe III, of whom we shall see more momentarily—could well mean that their copying followed that of *j* by at least some small margin. The final gatherings of Seville–Paris, *q* and *r*, definitely originated at a later point: not only does Scribe I appear only minimally in *q*, and not at all in *r*, but he registered none of their contents in the index. Scribal connections reveal further that the layer of additions represented by *q* and *r* extends as well to a handful of pages at the end of *d* and the first recto of *e*.[184]

With Scribe III, who appears in gatherings *q* and *r* as well as *g* and *p*, we come to the last significant copyist of Seville–Paris; and with him, we come as well to *Fortuna desperata*, the three original voices of which he added to an unfilled opening at the end of the older gathering *n*.[185] By all indications, Scribe III entered the history of Seville–Paris at the time Scribe I began to assemble the older and newer portions of the volume. Gathering *p*, in which Scribe III wrote fos. 1^v–3^r, starts with a bifolio evidently abandoned by Scribe IIIa; and *Fortuna desperata*, as we have seen, appears in a gathering also left unfinished by Scribe IIIa.[186] Scribe III would seem at first to have worked more or less concurrently with Scribe I, then assumed the leading position in the last phase of the manuscript's production. Within gatherings *g* and *p*, his pieces directly precede those copied by Scribe I; and as Boorman and others have recognized, *Fortuna desperata* shows the same sequence—while Scribe III wrote the piece in its three-part form, Scribe I subsequently added the alto voice.[187] In gatherings *q* and *r*, however, Scribe III dominates after Scribe I has all but vanished from the scene.

[183] The six-stave ruling appears in all but the two outermost bifolios of *g*—which have a paper found nowhere else in the manuscript—and in the outermost bifolio of *p*, a remnant from the first layer. *Salvator mundi* (fos. *g*4^v–*g*5^r), *Lo giorno mi consumo* (fo. *p*7^r), and *La morte che spavento* (fo. *p*9^v)—all copied by Scribe I—occur in the index; *Salvator mundi*, for reasons not yet clear, appears twice, once in Scribe I's hand, once as one of the later additions referred to above, n. 178.

[184] Cf. the following note and above, n. 179.

[185] Cf. Boorman, 'Limitations and Extensions', 327. Again, some of Boorman's attributions demand correction: fos. *q*3^v–*q*4^r and *r*6^v–*r*8^v all come from the hand that also wrote *d*8^v, while fos. *q*4^v–*q*5^r belong to an evidently singular hand.

[186] On the basis of this observation alone, it could look as if Scribe III himself belonged to the earliest layers of the manuscript. But apart from the evidence of gatherings *q* and *r* mentioned further in the main text, we must note that in both *g* and *p*, Scribe III continues writing on the six-stave paper that would seem to lie at the later end of the second principal layer; and in any event, the absence of any decoration removes any doubt on the matter.

[187] Cf. Boorman, 'Limitations and Extensions', 327; Plamenac, 'A Reconstruction', iii. 263; and Meconi, 'Art-Song Reworkings', 12–13 n. 40. On the script of fo. *p*1^r, see above, n. 178; the outer bifolio, although it lacks a watermark, shows the ruling—seven staves with the uppermost staff indented—used throughout gatherings *k–n*.

Given the participation of both Scribe I and Scribe III in the copying of
Fortuna desperata, it would seem most likely that both the entry of the three-voice
version and its subsequent expansion coincide with, or fall not long after, the
overall assembly of Seville–Paris. Unfortunately, we have no sure means of deciding more closely just where *Fortuna desperata* belongs. As we see from Table 20.5,
the end of gathering *n* presents an ambiguous situation. In addition to inserting
the altus for *Fortuna desperata* on fo. *n*11^v, Scribe I copied the superius of the next
piece, *Esprouver my fault elamy*, on the final verso of the gathering, thus joining it
to gathering *o*, another survivor from the first layer. Did Scribe III make his copy
of *Fortuna desperata* before Scribe I joined gatherings *n* and *o*—in which case we
might imagine that the inscription of the altus directly preceded that of the
superius to *Esprouver my fault*? Or did the insertion of *Fortuna desperata*, in both
its phases, follow the adjoining of the two gatherings? The index does not help:
not only did both scribes work on the manuscript after the compilation of the
index as well as before it, but *Fortuna desperata* does not begin with one of the letters represented in what survives of the register. Similarly, the temporal overlap
between Scribes I and III, as well as the prevailing stability of their hands, renders
the script all but useless for making the fine distinctions needed here.

TABLE 20.5. *Seville–Paris, fos. n11^r–o1^r (after Boorman)*

Folio	Scribe	Piece
. . . –*n*11^r	IIIa	*Du bon du cuer* (T and C, continued from *n*10^v)
*n*11^v–*n*12^r	III + I	*Fortuna desperata*, S, T, B + A
*n*12^v	I	*Esprouvez my fault* (S)
*o*1^r– . . .	II	*Esprouvez my fault* (T and C)

Nevertheless, any small uncertainties about the precise location of *Fortuna desperata* in the copying history of Seville–Paris that remain should not blind us to
the very clear lineaments of the larger picture. As Table 20.3 makes plain, all the
Busnoys repertory in Seville–Paris except *Cent mille escus* and *Fortuna desperata*—
and hence all the pieces for which Busnoys's authorship does not stand at issue—
occurs either in the first layer or in the principal gatherings of the second layer,
b–d and *j*.[188] By the same token, even if Scribe III should have begun copying

---

[188] Readers may notice, incidentally, that some of the Busnoys pieces in the first layer tend to fall in clusters: hence Scribe II copied the three four-voice songs that constitute his total contribution to the Busnoys
repertory on successive openings, and Scribe IIa similarly copied *Un grand pons, O fortune tu es trop dure*, and
Povre pour necessité one after the other. This latter group appears particularly interesting, as it follows another
work attributed elsewhere to Busnoys, the second setting of *Quelque povre homme que je soye*, with only a
single composition in between—an otherwise unknown bergerette with the text *Quant viendra la foy desiree*
(fos. *l*1^v–*l*3^r). We might thus wish to ask if the scribe had not intended to write a series of five Busnoys
pieces. But the music of *Quant viendra* (transcribed in Moerk, 'The Seville Chansonnier', ii. 229–31) can

TABLE 20.6. *Seville–Paris: music copied by Scribe III*

Vostre bruit (Dufay) (fo. *g*1^v)
De tous biens plaine (Hayne) (fo. *g*3^r)
Helas que pourra devenir (Caron) (fos. *g*3^v–*g*4^r)
Fortuna desperata (fos. *n*11^v–*n*12^r)
Fatti bene asto meschino (fos. *p*1^v–*p*3^r)
J'ay a mon cuer (fos. *q*7^v–*q*8^r)
Italian pieces, duos, etc. (fos. *q*8^v–*r*5^r; *r*3^v–*r*4^r variant form)

earlier in the overall process than we have so far assumed, we can see—with reference again to Table 20.3, as well as to Table 20.6—that none of his activities intersects with the core Busnoys repertory. Hence even granted the most liberal interpretation of his connection with Scribe I, we cannot assume he would have drawn on a stock of music that overlapped in any significant way with the music accessible to his colleague.[189] However complex the evidence, the result proves straightforward: in Seville–Paris no less than in the larger pattern of transmission, *Fortuna desperata* remains very much on the periphery of the Busnoys corpus.

V

The sources, then, do little to compel belief in Busnoys's authorship of *Fortuna desperata*. But they also have furnished nothing positive to disprove it. It would thus seem necessary to turn our attention elsewhere: to the question of how successfully we can place the song against the larger background of Busnoys's life and work as we know them.

Here I would start by taking up a thread first brought into play by Hudson. At the beginning of this article, we observed that speculation about Busnoys and Italy focused above all on the years 1483–92, the period of his life for which no documentation survives. But as Hudson pointed out, *Fortuna desperata* had already entered circulation by the late 1470s—before the summer of 1478, to put it exactly.[190] Not only does this deprive us of one more potential witness to Busnoys's whereabouts in his 'missing years', but it opens up an entirely new problem. Given our initial findings about Italian texts and Northern composers,

hardly sustain an attribution to Busnoys; if nothing else, the prevailing motion of the contra above rather than below the tenor—even in the final cadences of both *partes*—surely excludes his authorship. It would also seem far from certain that Scribe IIa regarded *Quelque povre homme* as a work of Busnoys; see below, at n. 226.

[189] The two copies of *O fortune tu es trop dure* reinforce the idea, already explored by Boorman, that the various scribes of Seville–Paris could have drawn on disparate parent sources (although see also above, n. 182): as the text incipits already suggest, they derive from very different models. Cf. Boorman, 'Limitations and Extensions', 326–39, as well as Perkins and Garey, *The Mellon Chansonnier*, ii. 347.

[190] See Hudson, 'Two Ferrarese Masses', 295–6, as well as below, Sect. VI.

the assumption that Busnoys wrote *Fortuna desperata* would now seem to pre-suppose a journey south of the Alps well before anyone had previously imagined. Indeed, considerations more specific to the piece itself allow us to drop the con-junctive hedge. In her contribution to this volume, Honey Meconi makes a per-suasive argument for associating the text of *Fortuna desperata* with Florence.[191] The evidence that provides the *terminus ante quem* for the music situates it, too, in Florence.[192] We thus find ourselves confronting virtually the same implica-tions that faced us with *Con tutta gentileça*: if Busnoys composed *Fortuna desper-ata*, he can only have done so not just in Italy, but in Florence or someplace very close to it. Yet getting Busnoys to Florence before 1478, even in our imagination, proves no easy task.

The earliest indications of Busnoys's activity, dating from February 1461 and April 1465, all place him at Tours.[193] From September 1465 until at least July 1466, he served as master of the choirboys at the church of Saint-Hilaire-le-Grand in Poitiers;[194] and between the latter date and the spring of 1467, he established an affiliation with the court of Charles the Bold. According to Higgins, 'the available evidence gives us every reason to suppose that, until his formal installation in the ducal chapel, some three years later, Busnois served Charles in an intermittent, free-lance capacity, accommodating his requests for musical service as the occasion arose'.[195] Yet even during this period of appar-ently loose connections, the pattern of the surviving documents does not suggest great leeway for a foreign voyage. We find Busnoys in Charles's service in March, late August, and October 1467; from December 1467 to July 1468; again in September 1468; and in August and September 1469.[196] Through calculations based on his apparent rate of payment, moreover, Rob Wegman suggests that these entries would in fact 'cover approximately the periods February to mid-March 1467, and late May 1467 until October or November 1468'; and Higgins has shown that the references from August and September 1469 clearly suggest further collaboration with the ducal chapel during the months that followed.[197]

Busnoys seems formally to have entered the Burgundian chapel in November 1470, after receiving an allocation for his livery the month before.[198] For the next five years, he clearly maintained a continual presence in the ducal household. Again, not every relevant document has survived; but as Higgins has emphasized,

---

[191] See Meconi's contribution to this volume, Ch. 19.
[192] See below, Sect. VI, and esp. the first paragraph.
[193] For Busnoys at Tours in 1461, see Pamela F. Starr, 'Rome as the Centre of the Universe: Papal Grace and Music Patronage', *EMH* 11 (1992), 223–62 at 249–51 and 260; for his presence there in 1465, see Higgins, '*In hydraulis* Revisited', 69–76, and esp. 70–1.
[194] See Paula Higgins's contribution to this volume, Ch. 7.
[195] Higgins, '*In hydraulis* Revisited', 48.   [196] See ibid. 42–7 (esp. 46) and 83–4.
[197] See Wegman, *Born for the Muses*, 64–5 (the quoted passage p. 65), and Higgins, '*In hydraulis* Revisited', 44; Higgins's findings, incidentally, effectively defuse the speculation on a possible diplomatic mission in Hudson, 'Two Ferrarese Masses', 296 n. 66.
[198] See Higgins, '*In hydraulis* Revisited', 43 and 84.

'it is statistically significant that Busnois's name appears on every known *escroe*', or daily expense record, 'from 1471 to 1475 on which the duke's domestic chapel is listed'.[199] After 1475 the record grows sketchier, as Charles reduced the size of the chapel that accompanied him on his military campaigns—and, it would appear, excused Busnoys from this arduous duty. Nevertheless, the composer appears in an isolated daily roll for the household of Margaret of York from 7 December 1476, and a reference found in the older literature may place him in Maastricht on 4 May of that same year.[200] What relevant documents have come to light for 1477 seem all to include him as well: he attended the funeral of Charles the Bold some time after 5 January; appears on what looks like every surviving *escroe* to record the chapel of Charles's daughter, Marie of Burgundy; and received an isolated payment in December.[201]

Obviously, the record has its gaps. But few of these amount to more than a handful of months; and the interruptions seem to occur so randomly—and so often together with identifiable losses in the underlying documentation—as to cut a large swatch of ground from under any speculation about travel to far-flung places. Only the discovery of new documents, of course, will make it possible either to push the windows of opportunity open still further or close them definitively. Yet at least on the Florentine side of the equation, we can get a step further even without archival finds.

If Busnoys visited Florence in the 1460s or 1470s and stayed there long enough to compose *Fortuna desperata*, we might reasonably expect to encounter traces of his presence in musical manuscripts copied in the city. Isaac's arrival in Florence some years later, after all, led to a dramatic upsurge in the representation of his music there, and the same appears to have occurred with Agricola.[202] Yet Busnoys remains strangely absent from any Florentine source before Pixérécourt.[203] Berlin 78. C. 28, by all indications the earliest of the surviving

[199] Ibid. 53–9 and 84; the quoted passage from 54.

[200] For the household roll, see Higgins, '*In hydraulis* Revisited', 61 and 84–5; contrary, however, to 61 n. 86, Geneviève Thibault, 'Busnois', *Die Musik in Geschichte und Gegenwart*, ii, cols. 515–20 at 515, does not say that Busnoys 'was exclusively in [Margaret's] service for all of 1476'—the phrase '1476 stand er im Dienste von Margarete' neither connotes exclusivity nor refers necessarily to the entire year. For Maastricht, see ibid.; I would regard this with caution, however, as the event described looks suspiciously like one recorded in a document bearing the date 4 June 1473 that Higgins has recently rediscovered; cf. '*In hydraulis* Revisited', 51–2 and 84. Nevertheless, if this would leave us without evidence for Busnoys's whereabouts in May 1476, it would help fill in a gap between 27 Feb. and 1 July 1473; cf. ibid. 56.

[201] See Higgins, '*In hydraulis* Revisited', 61, 63, and 85.

[202] Isaac does not have a single composition in any Florentine manuscript that does not demonstrably post-date his arrival there; compare Atlas's overview cited in following note with the list of sources in Picker, *Henricus Isaac*, 132–58. On Agricola, cf. Rifkin, 'Pietrequin Bonnel and Ms. 2794', 289 n. 13, and Litterick's review of Brown, *A Florentine Chansonnier*, 307–8.

[203] The overview of Florentine manuscripts in Atlas, *The Cappella Giulia Chansonnier*, i. 258, remains essentially valid, although it now requires the addition of Berlin 78. C. 28, as demonstrated in the articles cited in the following note, and the transfer of Bologna Q 17 to the 'post-1500' group; on this last point, cf. Craig Wright, 'Antoine Brumel and Patronage at Paris', in Fenlon (ed.), *Music in Medieval and Early Modern Europe*, 37–60 at 51–3, esp. 52 n. 38.

secular manuscripts from his generation, contains not a single composition of his.[204] Florence 176 and Florence 2356, which would seem to come next, have little more: the first transmits five compositions of assured authorship and _Je ne fay plus_—for which it in fact provides the earliest attribution to Mureau—while the second also preserves _Je ne fay plus_ and once contained _En soustenant vostre querelle_.[205] Even at a time when the topography of chanson transmission in Italy had not yet come into clear focus, Dragan Plamenac could find it 'surprising that Busnois, the chanson composer _par excellence_ of this generation . . . was included in Codex 2356 through only one chanson'.[206] Indeed, the surprise turns to something like stupefaction if we contrast this situation with the generosity of Busnoys's representation in Mellon: out of fifty-one pieces in this manuscript, no fewer than fifteen—well over a quarter of the total—bear attributions to Busnoys in one source or another.[207]

Against this background, it becomes clear that Pixérécourt does not merely contain a remarkable number of compositions by Busnoys, but also documents an extraordinary—and extraordinarily sudden—influx of his music into the Florentine repertory: with some twenty-five pieces by Busnoys, it more than quadruples his total in Florence 176, to say nothing of Florence 2356.[208] As Plamenac observed, the contrast 'is the more striking since there is great similarity between the repertoires of the Riccardiana codex [Florence 2356] and the Pixérécourt MS'—a similarity 'illustrated by the fact that of the eighty pieces originally present in the Florence codex (72 preserved and 8 missing but listed in the old Index) as many as thirty-five (31 preserved and 4 in the old Index) are found

---

[204] On the provenance and date of Berlin 78. C. 28, see Fallows, 'Polyphonic Song in the Florence of Lorenzo's Youth', and Warmington, 'The Missing Link'. If, as commonly assumed, Berlin 78. C. 28 dates from 1466, then its compilation could well have preceded Busnoys's hypothetical pre-1478 journey to Florence; but as Warmington demonstrates (ibid. 65–6), 1466 represents only a _terminus post quem_. Indeed, Warmington further acknowledges that the 'main reason to posit a date before ca. 1470 (or perhaps a few years later) is the nature of the repertory: the absence of any chansons by Antoine Busnoys, for instance, that we might expect to make an appearance in Florence around that time'. In the present context, of course, we must discard precisely this argument—the highly contingent nature of which Warmington in any event carefully acknowledges.

[205] The list of secure Busnoys chansons in Florence 176 comprises _A une dame j'ay fait veu_ (fos. 6ᵛ–8ʳ), _Fortune trop tu es dure_ (fos. 15ᵛ–17ʳ, 'Busnois'), _Joye me fuit_ (fos. 13ᵛ–15ʳ), _Mon seul et celé souvenir_ (fos. 17ᵛ–19ʳ), and _Quant ce viendra_ (fos. 69ᵛ–71ʳ). _Je ne fay plus_ (cf. above, n. 72) appears on fos. 73ᵛ–75ʳ with the attribution 'G. muream'; in Florence 2356, it occupies fos. 2ᵛ–3ʳ (6ᵛ–7ʳ). For _En soustenant_, recorded in the index of Florence 2356 but now missing, see Dragan Plamenac, 'The "Second" Chansonnier of the Biblioteca Riccardiana (Codex 2356)', _Annales musicologiques_, 2 (1954), 105–87 at 112–13. On the relative chronology of the two manuscripts, see particularly the observations in Atlas, _The Cappella Giulia Chansonnier_, i. 247 and 256, and Rifkin, 'Scribal Concordances', 313, 318, and 320–1.

[206] Plamenac, 'The "Second" Chansonnier', 113.

[207] Cf. Perkins, _The Mellon Chansonnier_, i. 4–5 and ii, _passim_. I have not drawn any comparisons with the other great Italian Busnoys repository of the period, Seville–Paris, because of the uncertainty over both its provenance and its date.

[208] Leaving questions of authenticity aside, Pixérécourt includes between twenty-one and twenty-three pieces with attribution to Busnoys plus a further seven ascribed to him in other sources; cf. the catalogue of his chansons by Leeman Perkins elsewhere in this volume (Ch. 13, App. D) as well as Lindmayr, _Quellenstudien zu den Motetten von Johannes Ockeghem_, 69–72, and above, n. 54.

also in the Paris source.'[209] The reasons for Busnoys's dramatic emergence on the Florentine scene, and the mechanism by which it came about, remain obscure. For present purposes, however, it will suffice to note that the moment of change all but certainly lies in the 1480s rather than the 1470s. Admittedly, we lack precise dates for any of the manuscripts involved. But given its close relationship in decoration, repertory, and readings to Florence 229, we surely cannot move Pixérécourt back much beyond its probable *terminus ante quem* of 1485; and this, in turn, would suggest that Florence 176 and Florence 2356 cannot much have predated 1480.[210] To fit Busnoys into this picture, we would have to have him in Florence no earlier than 1476, and at the same time assume that both Florence 176 and Florence 2356 originated by this date or at best not long afterwards. Once again, in other words, we face at best a narrow window of opportunity. To this point we may add one more. If *Fortuna desperata* circulated in Florence before 1478, then the scribes of Pixérécourt and Florence 229 would all but certainly have had access to it; if so, given their evident zeal for Busnoys, their failure to include it in either manuscript surely encourages the suspicion that it did not circulate in Florence under his name. All in all, it would take some rather fancy footwork with both biographical data and manuscript evidence to turn Busnoys into the author of *Fortuna desperata*.

It would take some fancy musical footwork as well. A transcription of *Fortuna desperata*, after Seville–Paris, appears as Ex. 20.6. To anyone with even a glancing knowledge of the seventy-odd other secular pieces ascribed to Busnoys, *Fortuna desperata* must look—to put it mildly—rather unlikely for even such a protean composer as him.[211] In saying this, I do not have in mind either the Italian text or the non-standardized formal structure that follows all but inevitably from it.[212] But I do find it hard to recognize Busnoys's hand in the utter simplicity, not to say outright plainness, with which the composer of *Fortuna desperata* realizes this framework. Rarely, for instance, does Busnoys show such a complete lack of imitative writing as we encounter here.[213] Not only that, but the one flash of

[209] Plamenac, 'The "Second" Chansonnier', 113.

[210] On the date of Florence 229, the *terminus ante quem* of Pixérécourt, and the relationship between the two manuscripts, see above, n. 25. I should note that my reasoning here merely affirms widely shared perceptions about the dates of all these manuscripts; but in the present context, we may think it necessary to make the foundations of our assumptions absolutely explicit. For the chronology of Berlin 78. C. 28, see above, n. 204.

[211] Higgins, 'Antoine Busnois and Musical Culture', 313–36, and Brooks, 'Anthoine Busnois, Chanson Composer', 124–7, both list seventy-one extant secular works with attributions to Busnoys; to these we may add *D'ung aultre amer* (cf. above, end of Sect. II) and, perhaps, *Resjois toi terre de France*, possibly ascribed to Busnoys in Pixérécourt, fos. 43ᵛ–44ʳ (cf. Lindmayr, *Quellenstudien zu den Motetten von Johannes Ockeghem*, 69–72, or her contribution to the present volume, Ch. 11). Cf. also above, n. 171.

[212] Cf. Cumming, 'The Goddess Fortuna', 8, and the response in Higgins, 'Antoine Busnois and Musical Culture', 23–4.

[213] Of the forty-six three-voice secular pieces other than *Fortuna desperata* that bear an uncontested attribution to Busnoys, only four—*Au povre par necessité, Ja que li ne s'i attende, Quant j'ay au cueur*, and the second setting of *Quelque povre homme*—have no imitation whatever or at best a scant hint of it (I do not count the non-canonic version of *Ha que ville* for obvious reasons); to these we may perhaps add *Au gré de*

Ex. 20.6. *Fortuna desperata* (Seville–Paris)

imitation that we do find, at measures 17–25, stands apart from his normal usage: as with most of his contemporaries, Busnoys's three-part secular music scarcely ever shows imitation between structural upper voices at any interval but the unison or octave.[214] I also cannot think of any instance in which Busnoys joins his superius and tenor in such extensive stretches of unadorned discant as we see in measures 25–31, again at 32–6, and in 41–52;[215] nor does he tend to move his total complex of voices more than fleetingly in the near or absolute homorhythm displayed not only in the passages just cited but in measures 1–4 and 9–15 as well. The rhythmic values themselves mark *Fortuna desperata* as uncharacteristic of Busnoys: in no piece known to me does the uppermost voice in particular proceed so determinedly in breves and semibreves, with only the slightest leavening of minims and anything smaller. Except, moreover, at the beginnings and ends of sections or, even more occasionally, of phrases, Busnoys virtually never lets the aggregate rhythm of his voices congeal into a simple breve, as happens here in measures 3, 11, 17, 19, 21, 25, 27, 30, and 46; and nowhere, to my knowledge, does he slow the momentum down so far as to present two or more breves in succession, as occurs here in measures 39–40 and 49–51.[216]

mes ieulx, which lacks any imitation in its refrain. A further six or seven pieces restrict imitation to one phrase alone: *Advegne qu'advenir pourra*, *Amours me tient* (*Faites de moy*), *C'est bien maleur*, *Chi dit on benedicite*, *J'ay mains de biens*, *Ma tres souveraine princesse*, and—if we count only the refrain—*Soudainement mon cueur a pris*. Interestingly, all but four of the items listed here (*Au gré de mes ieulx*, *C'est bien maleur*, *Ja que li ne*, and *Soudainement*) have attributions to Busnoys solely in Florence 229 and Pixérécourt; cf. above, end of Sect. II, and also below, pp. 561–2.

[214] *O fortune trop tu es dure* has a single phrase imitated at the fifth, and *C'est vous en qui j'ay esperance* and *Le monde est tel pour le present* have lines restated a fifth apart without polyphonic overlapping of the same motivic material; cf., respectively, Perkins and Garey, *The Mellon Chansonnier*, i, no. 37; *Trois chansonniers français du XVe siècle*, i, ed. Eugénie Droz, Yvonne Rokseth, and Geneviève Thibault (Documents artistiques du XVe siècle, 4; Paris, 1927, repr. New York, 1978), no. 39; and Catherine V. Brooks, 'Antoine Busnois as a Composer of Chansons' (Ph.D. diss., New York University, 1951), iii. 234–6. Among *formes fixes* or analogous settings of uncontested attribution, the only further exception to imitation at the unison or octave occurs in *Je ne demande lialté*, which I have already identified as suspect for other reasons (see above, n. 170, and below, at n. 227). In other uncontested three-voice pieces, imitation between superius and tenor at intervals other than the unison or octave occurs solely in the popular setting *Pucellotte que Dieu te gard* (Brooks, 'Antoine Busnois as a Composer of Chansons', iii. 237–8). The prevalence of imitation at the fifth in *Cent mille escus* greatly underscores the claim to this piece of Caron, whose fondness for this imitative disposition has gone largely unremarked—although cf. Montagna, 'Caron, Hayne, Compère', 122.

[215] Occasional moments of discant such as that—between tenor and contra, not between superius and tenor—which begins the second half of *Seule a par moy* (cf. Brooks, 'Antoine Busnois, Chanson Composer', 129, or Brown, *A Florentine Chansonnier*, Music vol., no. 60) do not really present analogues, not least because of their more florid rhythmic character. The closest approach to the kind of simple discant texture discussed here occurs in the problematic *Je ne demande lialté* (bars 23–5; cf. above, n. 170).

[216] In only a handful of songs—notably *J'ay mains de biens* (cf. Ex. 20.1), *Le monde est tel* (cf. above, n. 214), and the second setting of *Quelque povre homme que je soie* (Brooks, 'Antoine Busnois as a Composer of Chansons', ii. 106–9; see also below, at n. 226)—does more than a single measure within a phrase show the aggregate rhythm of a breve, and even here, no more than two such instances occur within an entire piece; *Soudainement mon cueur a pris* (ibid. iii. 174–7) has three such bars, but they occur in different *partes* of a bergerette. The *secunda pars* of *Ja que li ne s'i attende* (Perkins and Garey, *The Mellon Chansonnier*, i, no. 14) begins with a succession of four homophonic breves; but as the start of a section, this does not really count in the present context. We may also disregard a similar moment of stasis in the version of *Seule a par moy* transmitted in Casanatense 2856: this clearly represents a reworking, no doubt undertaken for reasons of instrumental limitations, of the obviously more credible reading preserved in Florence 229 and Pixérécourt; cf. Brooks, 'Antoine Busnois, Chanson Composer', 129, m. 5, and Brown, *A Florentine Chansonnier*, Music vol., no. 60, note to mm. 10–14. These points all neatly bear out the broader observation made more than

Ex. 20.7. *Fortuna desperata* altus, mm. 11–15, with (*a*) Seville–Paris version; (*b*) London 35087 version

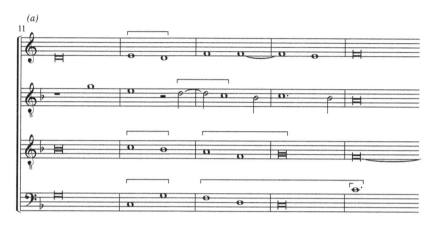

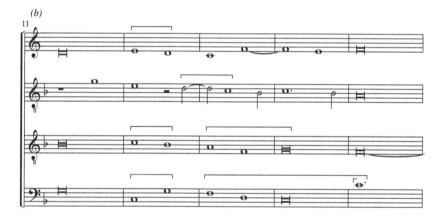

A last consideration returns us to the domain of pitch. As we have seen earlier, the sources show two different readings in the superius at measure 13: either the one shown in Exs. 20.3(*a*) or 20.7(*b*), or the more angular line present in Exs. 20.3(*b*), 20.6, or 20.7(*a*). Both Josquin and, as already noted, Obrecht preserve the first reading in their masses on *Fortuna desperata*.[217] In part on that basis,

forty years ago in Brooks, 'Antoine Busnois as a Composer of Chansons', i. 106: 'One of the most notice-able features in Busnois's contrapuntal style is the continuity of the polyphony . . . rarely[,] if ever, except at medial cadences, is there a break in the flow of the polyphonic writing; phrases are constructed so that they overlap constantly in the several voices, and there are very few holes in the texture'.

[217] Cf. *Werken van Josquin des Prés*, ed. Albert Smijers, Myroslaw Antonowycz, and Willem Elders (Amsterdam, 1921–66), Missen, no. 4; *Josquin des Prez: New Edition of the Collected Works (New Josquin Edition)* (Utrecht, 1987–), viii, 31–69, and xxvii, Critical Commentary, 77–8; and *New Obrecht Edition*, iv. 49–91. Josquin uses the superius melody in the Credo and (in inversion) in Agnus I, Obrecht in the Sanctus and in Agnus I.

there seems a case for considering this the original form of the line. If so, the blatant parallel fifths that it produces with the lowest voice would certainly render the *coup de grâce* to Busnoys's authorship. Like most composers of his generation, Busnoys writes his share of what we might call incidental parallels—fifths, unisons, or octaves moving in minims or faster, involving at least one inner voice, and occurring on unaccented beats.[218] But nowhere else that I know does he produce anything like these outer-voice fifths moving into a strong beat.[219] Nevertheless, caution would seem in order. Seville–Paris, surely the earliest source of all, already has the alternative reading, which avoids the fifths. The most widely disseminated altus—also present in Seville–Paris and perhaps transmitted there for the first time—clearly presupposes this form of the top voice: as Ex. 20.7 makes plain, combining it with the superius in the other form would add parallel unisons to the fifths already present.[220] Yet even if the superius seen in Exs. 20.3(*b*) and 20.7(*a*) should represent the original, it does not make the music significantly more plausible for Busnoys; for while it achieves contrapuntal acceptability, it does so at the cost of an awkward cadential formulation all but impossible to associate with so elegant a melodist.

At this point, we might well take stock. Any attempt to maintain Busnoys's authorship of *Fortuna desperata* has more than a few hurdles to overcome. The piece makes a near-total detour around all the major sources of his music and

---

[218] For examples, see Honey Meconi's contribution to this volume (Ch. 19).

[219] The two closest examples I can find—outer-voice fifths in *Chi dit on benedicite*, m. 48 (cf. Brown, *A Florentine Chansonnier*, Music vol., no. 56), fifths and octaves together in *L'autrier la pieça*, m. 7 (cf. Brooks, 'Antoine Busnois as a Composer of Chansons', iii. 210–13)—both involve smaller values and proceed to weak beats. The transmission of *Chi dit on benedicite*, moreover, shows more than a few problems of textual corruption, two of which also involve parallel fifths; cf. Brown's notes to mm. 35 and 40. Although *L'autrier la pieça* has only one source, Seville–Paris, we may suspect a flaw in the transmission here as well: when the music of m. 7 recurs at m. 44, the bassus has a different reading (*a*–*a* instead of *a*–*g*) that eliminates the parallels, although the dissonance treatment might seem less than suave; perhaps the bassus at both mm. 7–8 and 44–5 should read *a*–*b*–*c'*–*f*. The possibility of error would seem all the stronger in view of another demonstrable mistake in the source: at mm. 27–9, the rhythm of the altus should read dotted breve–minim–minim–breve.

[220] This does not prevent three sources—Leipzig 1494, Paris 676, and Zwickau 78/2—from combining the standard altus with the 'wrong' superius in just this fashion. St Gallen 462, which has the same configuration of voices, presents the altus at mm. 12–13 in a revised form that avoids the parallels; cf. Geering and Trümpy, *Das Liederbuch des Johannes Heer*, 17–18. The conflations in the Leipzig, Paris, and Zwickau manuscripts possibly indicate that the altus or even the superius sometimes travelled separately from the other voices, or that scribes might have notated the superius from memory. Indeed, the transmission of the *Fortuna desperata* attributed to both Martini and Isaac (cf. above, n. 157) all but compels us to assume one of these explanations: while the superius in Casanatense 2856 shows the reading of Exs. 20.3(*a*) and 20.7(*b*) at m. 13 (cf. the transcription in Martini, *Secular Works*, 19–21), Segovia has the alternate version. Mixed transmission of cantus firmus and polyphony, I might note, would seem to occur elsewhere as well: in Josquin's four-voice *De tous biens plaine* (cf. Hewitt, *Odhecaton*, 418–20, or *Werken van Josquin des Prés*, Wereldlijke Werken, no. 49b), the lower parts in mm. 50–1 would fit better with the reading of Hayne's chanson printed, among other places, in Knud Jeppesen, *Der Kopenhagener Chansonnier: Das Manuskript 291⁸ der Königlichen Bibliothek Kopenhagen* (Copenhagen, 1927, rev. repr. New York, 1965), 7–8; and in Isaac's *Le serviteur* (cf. Brown, *A Florentine Chansonnier*, Music vol., no. 257), mm. 65–6 of the superius should clearly have the reading—suggested by Brown as an emendation (ibid. n. 3)—found in many manuscript sources for the model composition. I wish to thank Honey Meconi for some stimulating conversations on this subject.

stands apart from his securely attributed compositions in virtually every musical dimension—texture, rhythmic language, and even, perhaps, basic technical competence. Its attribution to Busnoys would force us either to assume that he composed it in the North—and thus fly in the face of everything we know concerning Northern musicians and Italian texts, let alone more specific evidence about the song itself—or else to posit a journey to Florence in the face of both a documentary record more consistent with continuous residence in Burgundy and the neglect of his music in Florentine manuscripts until well after the time of the supposed visit. None of these considerations by itself, of course, can prove conclusive; and even taken together, they would surely have to yield in the face of a truly authoritative attribution. But no amount of wishful thinking will make the ascription in Segovia fit that bill. While our lengthy excursion into the manuscript and its repertory may have helped clarify some matters long shrouded in mystery, it has scarcely enhanced its credibility for Busnoys in general and *Fortuna desperata* in particular; and with such a slender reed to hang on, the claim of *Fortuna desperata* to a place in his canon simply cannot surmount all the other things stacked against it.

Before closing the book on the issue of Busnoys and *Fortuna desperata*, we might ask briefly how the piece acquired an attribution to him in the first place. Hudson, again, has already drawn attention to a plausible answer.[221] Mellon and the earliest layer of Seville–Paris both contain a rondeau of Busnoys's with a text beginning *O fortune trop tu es*—or *tu es trop—dure*.[222] Although the metre of the poem confirms this as the proper incipit, the three remaining sources for the work—none of which provides more than the first few words—drop the opening exclamation and present it as *Fortune trop tu es dure*.[223] It does not take a great leap of the imagination to get from here to *Fortuna desperata*. Confusions of this sort, in fact, seem to dog the Busnoys canon with particular frequency. More than thirty years ago, James Thomson suggested that Busnoys's name got attached to *Cent mille escus* through a confusion with his lost bergerette *Cent mille fois le jour*— a possibility that becomes all the stronger when one imagines the words *escus* and *fois* as they would appear in a fifteenth-century hand.[224] The scribe of Bologna Q 17 may well have had Busnoys's combinative chanson *Amours nous traite honnestement/Je m'en vois aux vert boys* in mind when he credited him with another combinative chanson surely by Japart, *Amours fait moult/Il est de bonne heure né/Tant*

[221] See Hudson, 'Two Ferrarese Masses', 295 n. 61. My own exposition of the evidence varies somewhat from Hudson's.

[222] Cf. Perkins and Garey, *The Mellon Chansonnier*, i, no. 37; Mellon has the first reading, Seville–Paris the second.

[223] Apart from the copy in the second layer of Seville–Paris, *O fortune* survives with incipits alone, and without the *O*, in Florence 176 (cf. above, n. 205) and Pixérécourt (fos. 126ᵛ–127ʳ, 'busnoys').

[224] See Thomson, *An Introduction to . . . Caron*, 15–16. The text of *Cent mille fois le jour* survives in Pierre Fabri, *Le grand et vrai art de pleine rhétorique*, ed. Alexandre Héron (Rouen, 1890, repr. Geneva, 1969), ii. 73, with the heading 'Aultre exemple [de bergerette]: busnoys'.

que nostre argent dura.[225] I wonder, too, if the setting of *Quelque povre homme que je soie* in Pixérécourt does not carry Busnoys's name only because of a failure to distinguish this piece from the version of the same text more reliably ascribed to him in Dijon.[226] Finally, as I have already suggested, the close resemblance in both textual and musical incipit between Busnoys's well-accredited *Je ne demande autre de gré* and the otherwise unattributed and stylistically anomalous *Je ne demande lialté* could easily have led the scribe of Florence 229 to assign the second to Busnoys while leaving the first anonymous.[227] That all these examples lend added credibility to Hudson's speculations about *O fortune trop tu es dure* needs no special emphasis.

But we might consider one other possible avenue of confusion as well. Entering the ascription for a short piece in Segovia with the incipit *Jamays*, the main scribe began to write 'Anthonius bus[noys]', only to break off and change the second name to 'brumel'.[228] It seems irresistible to ask whether he, or the source from which he copied *Fortuna desperata*, could have fallen prey to a similar confusion between Busnoys and another 'Anthonius', perhaps even another 'Anthonius B'. Among the various singers named Anthonius whom we can find in Italy during the third quarter of the fifteenth century, one looks especially appealing: Anthoine Baneston, or Antonio de Cambrai, who sang from at least 1474 to 1477 in the ducal chapel at Milan; from 1478 to 1481 at Ferrara; and, in a period too late to concern us, in the papal chapel.[229] Lewis Lockwood has

---

[225] For the sources and the question of authorship, see particularly Atlas, *The Cappella Giulia Chansonnier*, i. 58–9, as well as his contribution to the present volume (Ch. 18). On the other hand, as Bologna Q 17 also credits Busnoys with *Je ne fais plus* (cf. above, n. 72) and two further Japart pieces—among them another 'amours' composition—the resemblance between the two combinative chansons may not have played a decisive role in this particular misattribution. Cf. Atlas, *The Cappella Giulia Chansonnier*, i. 59 n. 2, and in this volume.

[226] Pixérécourt, fos. 164ᵛ–165ʳ, 'busnoys'; Dijon, fos. lxviiᵛ–lxviiiʳ (65ᵛ–66ʳ), 'Busnoys'. So far as I know, no other *forme fixe* poem of the 15th c. exists in two settings ascribed to a single composer. The music of the Pixérécourt *Quelque povre homme*, too, shows some disquieting features; cf. above, nn. 213 and 216. On the question of whether Seville–Paris might have supplied an implicit attribution for the piece, see above, n. 188.

[227] See above, n. 170.

[228] Segovia, fo. clxxixᵛ (173ᵛ); cf. Baker, 'An Unnumbered Manuscript', i. 473.

[229] For Antonio de Cambrai at Milan, see, most conveniently, Claudio Sartori, 'Josquin des Prés cantore del Duomo di Milano (1459–1472)', *Annales musicologiques*, 4 (1956), 55–83 at 64–5 n. 1, and Lora Matthews and Paul Merkeley, 'Josquin Desprez and his Milanese Patrons', *Journal of Musicology*, 12 (1994), 434–63 at 449–51. Antonio's name does not appear among the singers listed in a recently published court register of 1476; cf. Lubkin, *A Renaissance Court*, 266–7, and Evelyn S. Welch, 'Sight, Sound and Ceremony in the Chapel of Galeazzo Maria Sforza', *EMH* 12 (1993), 151–90 at 182. Nevertheless, Matthews and Merkeley would appear hasty in concluding that he did not belong to the chapel at all that year ('Josquin Desprez and his Milanese Patrons', 450), as he figures in a list from April 1476 that they themselves reproduce (ibid. 451); the discrepancy will no doubt require further consideration. On Antonio's service at Ferrara, see Lewis Lockwood, 'Music at Ferrara in the Period of Ercole I d'Este', *Studi musicali*, 1 (1972), 101–31 at 118–19, and id., *Music in Renaissance Ferrara*, 321–2 in particular. According to Lockwood (ibid. 160), a notarial document of 12 Feb. 1479 calls the singer 'Antonio Baneston of Cambrai'. This would seem to establish his identity with the papal singer Antonio Baneston, recorded in Rome from 1484 into the 16th c.; cf. Richard Jonathan Sherr, 'The Papal Chapel ca. 1492–1513 and its Polyphonic Sources' (Ph.D. diss., Princeton University, 1975), 26–38 and 50–1. Admittedly, Lockwood's enumeration of the Ferrarese chapel for 1487 (*Music in Renaissance Ferrara*, 323) includes an 'Antonio da Cambrai cantadore'. But I

proposed identifying Baneston as the 'Anthonius Piccardus' credited with a hymn setting in Montecassino 871.[230] This strikes me as unlikely, as the rare text of the hymn seems to hint at a special relationship to the monastery of S. Angelo at Gaeta, near Naples; we might sooner connect the attribution to the 'Antonio Pons franzese' cited as a singer at the Aragonese court in 1469 and 1476 and active during the intervening years in Milan.[231] Nevertheless, whichever Anthonius wrote this piece, I feel little inclination to pursue him very energetically as a possible author of *Fortuna desperata*; for here, as I shall now attempt to show, we have a much better option.

VI

The attribution of *Fortuna desperata* to Busnoys effectively surfaced in 1952 with Dragan Plamenac's inventory of the Seville–Paris manuscript.[232] Along with concordances for the piece itself, Plamenac listed a large number of settings; among these, he cited a five-voice version found in the Florentine manuscript Cappella Giulia XIII. 27 under the name 'Felice'.[233] Felice, as Frank D'Accone subsequently demonstrated, all but certainly meant Ser Felice di Giovanni, a contratenor who served at the cathedral of Santa Maria del Fiore in Florence from 1469 until his death some time between 26 June and 14 August 1478.[234] D'Accone and, shortly afterwards, Allan Atlas also took the first close look at the music bearing Felice's name. It turned out that four of the five voices in Cappella Giulia XIII. 27 correspond to the most widely disseminated four-voice version of the song; Atlas recognized the fifth voice as a bassus designed to substitute for the

---

suspect some sort of error here: the singer in question occurs in no other register for the surrounding years; his name does not appear among the Ferrarese singers listed in a papal indult of 1487 (ibid.); and not only does Lockwood always describe Antonio's service at Ferrara as lasting from 1478 to 1481 (cf. ibid. 152, 155), but a remark on p. 171 explicitly places him at Rome in 1487.

[230] See Lockwood, *Music in Renaissance Ferrara*, 152 and 155, and also the review by William F. Prizer, *JAMS* 40 (1987), 95–105 at 103; for the composition, see Pope and Kanazawa, *The Musical Manuscript Montecassino 871*, 270–1.

[231] On the text and its apparent significance, cf. ibid. 20–1 and 598. On Pons—or Ponzo, as Italian documents often call him—see Atlas, *Music at the Aragonese Court*, 95; Sartori, 'Josquin des Prés cantore del Duomo di Milano', 64–6 n. 1; Lubkin, *A Renaissance Court*, 266 and 334 n. 15; and Welch, 'Sight, Sound and Ceremony', 182. As Bonnie Blackburn informs me, Milanese documents often refer to Pons as Spanish ('Antonio spagnolo', 'Antonio hispano'); perhaps, given the unambiguous description of him as French in a Neapolitan document (see Atlas, 95), this has more to do with his Aragonese affiliations than with his nationality.

[232] See Plamenac, 'A Reconstruction' (1952), 262–3. Catherine Brooks had already noted the Segovia attribution in her dissertation, which bears the date April 1951; see 'Antoine Busnois as a Composer of Chansons', i. 15 and 37, and also her subsequent article 'Antoine Busnois, Chanson Composer', 111. Presumably, she and Plamenac found the attribution independently—but working from the same microfilms: Brooks wrote her dissertation under Gustave Reese, a close friend of Plamenac, and thanked Plamenac in her Preface 'for access to his microfilm collection'.

[233] See Plamenac, 'A Reconstruction' (1952), 263; for the music, see Cappella Giulia XIII. 27, fos. 56ᵛ–57ʳ (63ᵛ–64ʳ), and the transcription in Atlas, *The Cappella Giulia Chansonnier*, ii. 38–42.

[234] See D'Accone, 'Some Neglected Composers', 280, especially the document quoted there in n. 73.

original one.[235] On still closer inspection, however, it became clear that even this did not get the whole story right: as Cynthia Cyrus seems first to have observed, the second bass part not only clashes unconscionably with the original bassus but creates a series of clumsy parallels and dissonances with the altus. The new bassus in Cappella Giulia XIII. 27, therefore, can function solely with the two original upper voices.[236]

This finding puts the transmission of *Fortuna desperata* in Cappella Giulia XIII. 27 in an unexpected light. The manuscript presents not a single version, or even two alternate versions, of *Fortuna desperata* but rather a kind of assembly kit allowing no fewer than three different possibilities: the original three voices; the 'standard' four-voice version with contratenor altus; and a three-part arrangement combining the original superius and tenor with a new contratenor bassus. Perhaps not coincidentally, Cappella Giulia XIII. 27 offers a further compendium of this sort on the very next opening: a five-voice redaction of *De tous biens plaine* that divides into Hayne's original and a three-voice arrangement with the superius notated once between them.[237] The five voices notated for *De tous biens plaine* obviously involve not only two pieces, but two composers—neither of which, unfortunately, the manuscript names. *Fortuna desperata* clearly involves multiple talents as well; and in this instance, the source identifies one of them for us. But just what did Felice do?

Both D'Accone and Atlas had no doubt on this score: Felice composed the new bassus.[238] Their interpretation reflects a scholarly tradition that goes back at least as far as Otto Gombosi's influential monograph on Obrecht. Seeking to explain what he regarded as a conflict between Isaac and Obrecht over the authorship of *Een vroylic wesen*—the attribution to Barbireau had not yet come to light— Gombosi observed that Obrecht's name appeared only in the two St Gallen man-

---

[235] See D'Accone, 'Some Neglected Composers', 280, and Atlas, *The Cappella Giulia Chansonnier*, i. 135–6.

[236] See Cynthia J. Cyrus, 'Polyphonic Borrowings and the Florentine Chanson Reworking, 1475–1515' (Ph.D. diss., University of North Carolina at Chapel Hill, 1990), 14–15 n. 1 and 91–2. Independently of Cyrus, it would appear, Honey Meconi and Martin Picker made the same discovery not long afterwards; see Meconi, 'Art-Song Reworkings', 12 n. 40, and Martin Picker's contribution to this volume, Ch. 17 n. 16 (cf. above, n. 158).

[237] Cf. Atlas, *The Cappella Giulia Chansonnier*, i. 137–9 and ii. 43–5, as well as Cyrus, 'Polyphonic Borrowings',14–15 n. 1 and 93. This version of *De tous biens plaine*, incidentally, adds another member to a small family of pieces, otherwise including two anonymous duos on *D'ung aultre amer* in Seville–Paris and Marbriano de Orto's setting of the same tune in *Canti B*, that combine a pre-existent voice with a series of repeated melodic snippets; cf. Meconi, 'Art-Song Reworkings', 28–9, as well as *D'ung aultre amer*, ed. Richard Taruskin (Coconut Grove, Fla., 1983), 8–9, and *Ottaviano Petrucci: Canti B numero cinquanta, Venice, 1502*, ed. Helen Hewitt (Monuments of Renaissance Music, 2; Chicago, 1967), 52–5 and 159–61. The technique marks these compositions as important early contributions to the development of what I have termed 'motivicity'. Cf. Joshua Rifkin, 'Motivik – Konstruktion – Humanismus: Zur Motette *Huc me sydereo* von Josquin des Prez', in Herbert Schneider (ed.), *Die Motette: Beiträge zu ihrer Gattungsgeschichte* (Neue Studien zur Musikwissenschaft, 5; Mainz, 1992), 105–34, esp. 117–18; and id., 'Miracles, Motivicity, and Mannerism: Adrian Willaert's *Videns Dominus flentes sorores Lazari* and Some Aspects of Motet Composition in the 1520s', in Dolores Pesce (ed.), *Hearing the Motet: Essays on the Motet of the Middle Ages and Renaissance* (New York, 1997), 243–64.

[238] See D'Accone, 'Some Neglected Composers', 280; Atlas, *The Cappella Giulia Chansonnier*, i. 135.

uscripts 462 and 463, both of which transmit the piece with an altus found nowhere else; he thus suggested that Obrecht had in fact added the altus to Isaac's three-voice original.[239] More recently, Helmuth Osthoff and Martin Picker both proposed that the clear misattribution of Josquin's motet-chanson *Que vous madame/In pace* to Agricola in *Canti C* meant that Agricola composed the *ad placitum* altus transmitted in that source.[240] Especially in a context where Busnoys's authorship of *Fortuna desperata* remained unquestioned, the reading of the ascription in Cappella Giulia XIII. 27 proposed by D'Accone and Atlas would have appeared so obvious as to require no further elaboration. Not surprisingly, the subsequent literature has followed their lead.[241]

Yet if the explanatory model underlying the consensus on Felice and *Fortuna desperata* has impeccable scholarly credentials, it has a less than impeccable foundation in the sources.[242] Let us start with the question of added voices. As virtually everyone knows, Casanatense 2856 presents Colinet de Lannoy's *Cela sans plus* in a version that carefully distinguishes between the three voices of Colinet's original and a bass part added by Johannes Martini: while the ascription in the upper margin of the verso page reads 'Cosinet de janoy [*sic*]', the bass part shows the name 'Jo. martinj' just above the system and the label 'si placet' just below it.[243] But this represents the exception rather than the rule; indeed, I have yet to find a directly comparable example in the second half of the fifteenth century.[244]

[239] See Otto Johannes Gombosi, *Jacob Obrecht: Eine stilkritische Studie* (Sammlung musikwissenschaftlicher Einzeldarstellungen, 4; Leipzig, 1925, repr. Walluf bei Wiesbaden, 1972), 126, as well as Charles Warren Fox, 'Ein fröhlich Wesen: The Career of a German Song in the Sixteenth Century', *Papers of the American Musicological Society* (1937), 56–74 at 62; id., 'Barbireau and Barbingant: A Review', *JAMS* 13 (1960), 79–101 at 91–2 n. 55; and Ludwig Finscher, 'Obrecht', *Die Musik in Geschichte und Gegenwart*, ix, cols. 1814–22 at 1817 (with the original still ascribed to Isaac). For the sources, see the mutually supplementary listings and commentary in Atlas, *The Cappella Giulia Chansonnier*, i. 65–9; Baker, 'An Unnumbered Manuscript', i. 438; and Peter Woetmann Christoffersen, *French Music in the Early Sixteenth Century. Studies in the Music Collection of a Copyist of Lyons: The Manuscript Ny kgl. Samling 1848 2° in the Royal Library, Copenhagen* (Copenhagen, 1994), ii. 142–3.

[240] See Helmuth Osthoff, *Josquin Desprez*, ii (Tutzing, 1965), 162, and Picker, *The Chanson Albums of Marguerite of Austria*, 110 n. 47.

[241] See, for instance, Hudson, 'Two Ferrarese Masses', 295; Cyrus, 'Polyphonic Borrowings and the Florentine Chanson Reworking' 14–15 n. 1 and 91–2; and Meconi, 'Art-Song Reworkings', 12 n. 40 and 32. But see also below, n. 264.

[242] The observations that follow clearly bring me into conflict with the position advanced by Allan Atlas in his 'Conflicting Attributions in Italian Sources of the Franco-Netherlandish Chanson, *c.* 1465–*c.* 1505: A Progress Report on a New Hypothesis', in Fenlon (ed.), *Music in Medieval and Early Modern Europe*, 249–93; but note his own qualification on p. 273.

[243] See Casanatense 2856, no. 105 (fos. 152ᵛ–153ʳ).

[244] For some earlier and later examples, see further in the main text. The closest parallel in the period under consideration involves substitution rather than addition; I refer to the well-known copy of Cornago's *Qu'es mi vida preguntays* in Montecassino 871, pp. 256–7, which ascribes the original superius and tenor to 'Cornago' and two voices that replace Cornago's single contra to 'Oquegan'. Cf. the facsimile in Pope and Kanazawa, *The Musical Manuscript Montecassino 871*, pls. II and IIa; for discussions of the piece, see ibid. 564, and the literature cited there, as well as Louise Litterick, 'The Revision of Ockeghem's *Je n'ay deuil*', in Winn (ed.), *Musique naturelle et musique artificielle*, 29–48, and also below, n. 260. A second familiar example, the presentation of *O rosa bella* in Trent 89, fos. 119ᵛ–120ʳ, with three added voices and the notice 'Concordancie O rosa bella cum aliis tribus ut posuit bedingham et sine hiis non concordant', long counted as a further instance of at least implicit dual attribution; cf. Dunstable, *Complete Works*, 186 (rev. edn., 200). But as Trent 89 only mentions a single name, it does not in reality ascribe the 'concordancie' to someone

Given the Ferrarese origin of Casanatense 2856, we may surely suspect that the compilers went to such pains over the bass voice less out of a concern for truth in attribution *per se* than to highlight the contribution of the local *maestro*.[245] When Petrucci published the same four-voice version of *Cela sans plus* in *Canti B*, all mention of Martini vanished; the sole attribution—found, admittedly, in the index and not over the music itself—reads 'Lannoy'.[246] For Petrucci's editor, in other words, the presence of an extra part did not fundamentally affect the authorship of the piece; and this would in fact seem the universal pattern. In the overwhelming majority of cases, a work found with attribution in both three- and four-part versions carries the same attribution without regard to the number of voices.[247] Even in those rare instances where more than one author comes into contention, the idea that the cross-attribution applies to the added voice fails to withstand scrutiny. In the case of *Que vous madame/In pace*, for example, the interpretation advanced by Osthoff and Picker falters on two points. As we have seen with *Cela sans plus*, Petrucci's attributions for pieces with *si placet* parts clearly refer to the piece as a whole.[248] Perhaps more important, the ascription to Agricola occurs elsewhere independently of Petrucci—associated with the three-voice original.[249] There would also seem little chance of resolving the claims of Busnoys and Ockeghem to the rondeau *Quant ce viendra* by crediting one with the three-voice original, the other with the four-voice expansion found in Mellon and, in contrafacted form, Trent 91: the attributions, in Dijon, Laborde, and Escorial IV.a.24 appear over the three-voice version alone, while the version with an added altus remains anonymous.[250] As for *Een vroylic wesen*, Leon Kessels has pointed out that the technical standard of the altus in the St Gallen manuscripts rules out any realistic possibility that Obrecht wrote it; and in any event, the explanation advanced by Gombosi seems needlessly sophisticated given the well-known readi-

---

other than the composer of the 'aliis tribus'. Both Reinhard Strohm and David Fallows, moreover, have argued cogently that the notice in fact labels Bedyngham as the original composer—exactly in line with the practice that I seek to elucidate in the discussion immediately following. See Strohm, *The Rise of European Music*, 393 n. 71, and David Fallows, 'Dunstable, Bedyngham and *O rosa bella*', *The Journal of Musicology*, 12 (1994), 287–305, esp. 290–1. For a further instance of supposed dual attribution, see below, n. 262.

[245] On the origin of Casanatense 2856, see principally Arthur S. Wolff, 'The Chansonnier Biblioteca Casanatense 2856: Its History, Purpose, and Music' (Ph.D. diss., North Texas State University, 1970), 16–32, and Lockwood, *Music in Renaissance Ferrara*, 224–6.   [246] Cf. Hewitt, *Canti B*, 42.

[247] Compositions that maintain the same attribution whether *a 3* or *a 4* include: Agricola, *C'est mal cherché* and *Si dedero*; Caron, *Accueilles moy* and *Helas, que pourra devenir*; Hayne, *Amours amours*; Isaac, *La morra* and *Benedictus* (from *Missa Quant j'ay au cuer*); Molinet, *Tart ara mon cuer*; Obrecht, *Va uilment*; and Pietrequin, *Mais que ce fust*. Readers can piece together the details from Brown, *A Florentine Chansonnier*, Text vol.; Atlas, *The Cappella Giulia Chansonnier*, i; Hewitt, *Odhecaton*; Perkins and Garey, *The Mellon Chansonnier*, ii; Plamenac, 'A Reconstruction' (1952); and id., 'The "Second" Chansonnier', 128–69.

[248] Of the pieces mentioned in the preceding note, *Amours amours*, *C'est mal cherché*, and *Helas que pourra devenir* appear in the *Odhecaton*, *Tart ara mon cuer* in *Canti C*—all with ascriptions to their correct authors.

[249] See Atlas, *The Cappella Giulia Chansonnier*, i. 71–2.

[250] Dijon (fos. ii[v]–iii[r] [7[v]–8[r]]) and Laborde (fos. 27[v]–28[r]) both read 'Busnoys', Escorial (fos. 93[v]–94[r] [121[v]–122[r]]) reads 'hockenghem'. Cf. Atlas, 'Conflicting Attributions', 279; Hanen, *The Chansonnier El Escorial IV.a.24*, i. 169; and Perkins and Garey, *The Mellon Chansonnier*, ii. 248–51 (which overlooks the concordance in Trent 91, fos. 70[v]–71[r]).

ness of scribes and printers in the German-language world to credit Obrecht with pieces not at all his.[251] Moreover, it runs up against the treatment of a supposedly similar case in one of the two manuscripts where the attribution appears: St Gallen 463 transmits Josquin's *Miserere* with a sixth part carefully attributed to Bidone.[252] The very fastidiousness of the labelling, of course, recalls the similarly delimited attribution of Martini's bassus to *Cela sans plus* in Casanatense 2856 — and, for that matter, a telling earlier instance in Oxford 213, as well as yet another well-known later one, Verdelot's fifth voice to Janequin's *La bataille*.[253]

In pieces with an added voice-part, then, ascriptions not specifically attached to that voice clearly refer in the first instance to the original composition — even if, in so doing, they implicitly stretch the definition of that work to incorporate an unauthorized accretion.[254] In so far as they allow us any basis of comparison,

[251] On the altus, see Kessels, 'The Brussels/Tournai-Partbooks', 92–4. Among late German Obrecht attributions, I need mention here only the *Passio Domini Jesu Christi* of Longueval or Johannes a la Venture; Ninot le Petit's *Si oblitus fuero*; and Willaert's *Pater noster*. Cf. Maas, 'Towards a New Obrecht Edition', 84 and 103–5, and Picker, *Johannes Ockeghem and Jacob Obrecht*, 80–1.

[252] St Gallen 463, no. 213 (Discantus): 'Sexta vox si placet quam De Bidon composuit'; cf. *Werken van Josquin des Prés*, Motetten, Bundel 8, p. v. Ironically, Osthoff draws on the supposed parallel with St Gallen 463 in his argument about the *ad placitum* voice in *Que vous madame*; see above, n. 240.

[253] Oxford 213, fo. 31ʳ, carefully attaches the attribution 'G. dufay' to the middle voice alone of *La belle se siet*, which appears elsewhere anonymously and in two parts; cf. Charles Hamm, *A Chronology of the Works of Guillaume Dufay Based on a Study of Mensural Practice* (Princeton Studies in Music, 1; Princeton, 1964), 32–3 and also the facsimile reproduction *Oxford, Bodleian Library MS. Canon. Misc. 213*, ed. David Fallows (Late Medieval and Early Renaissance Music in Facsimile, 1; Chicago, 1995); for two other examples in Dufay, cf. Fallows, *Dufay*, 242. For *La bataille*, see Clément Janequin, *Chansons polyphoniques*, ed. A. Tillman Merritt and François Lesure (Monaco, 1965–71), i. 181.

[254] I can think of at most three exceptions to this rule. The first involves another version of *Fortuna desperata* — the six-part setting ascribed to Agricola in Augsburg 142a, fos. 46ᵛ–47ʳ (cf. also below, n. 263), which augments the three voices of the original with an equal number of added parts; for the music, see Agricola, *Opera omnia*, v. 68–70, or Luise Jonas, *Das Augsburger Liederbuch: Die Musikhandschrift 2° Codex 142a der Staats- und Stadtbibliothek Augsburg* (Berliner musikwissenschaftliche Arbeiten, 21; Munich, 1983), i. 127–31. Presumably, relative numbers play a deciding hand here; with three parts added to three, Agricola achieves sufficient parity with the composer of the borrowed voices to rank as the author of the entire setting. A possible second exception concerns *Nec michi nec tibi* (see above, n. 106). Here, however, we do not know for sure that one composer augmented the work of another; see also below, n. 261. As a final possible exception I would cite the four-voice *Gentyl prince de renom* ascribed to 'The kynge H. viij' in London 31922, fos. xxxixᵛ–xlʳ (49ᵛ–50ʳ). As scholars have long known, this consists of three voices already transmitted, without attribution, in the *Odhecaton* (fo. 95ʳ; transcription in Hewitt, 404) plus an altus of mind-boggling ineptitude; cf. *Music at the Court of Henry VIII*, ed. John Stevens (Musica Britannica, 18; London, 1962, and subsequent revised printings), pp. xx, 36, and 105; and David Fallows, 'Henry VIII as a Composer', in Chris Banks, Arthur Searle, and Malcom Turner (eds.), *Sundry Sorts of Music Books: Essays on the British Library Collections, Presented to O. W. Neighbour on his 70th Birthday* (London, 1993), 27–39 at 29–31. I very much doubt that the scribe of London 31922 meant the attribution to draw attention specifically to the altus; if, as generally assumed, this voice represents Henry's contribution to *Gentyl prince*, then he or the copyist must have felt that the addition alone gave him rights of domain not vouchsafed less exalted musicians. But I must admit to wondering about the king's role in the story. The problems of the altus surely go beyond questions of technical competence; it seems hard to imagine how anyone with even a glimmering of musicality — which Henry surely had — could ever have conceived this. Perhaps something got botched in the transmission. Perhaps, too, the three original voices have more to do with Henry than previously suspected. The title, or incipit, sounds very much like a dedication; or could it in fact represent an attribution of sorts? The three main voices of *Gentyl prince* certainly abound in the 'rough contrapuntal clashes' that Fallows ('Henry VIII as a Composer', 27) finds so typical of Henry's compositions. We do not know for sure when Henry began to invent music of his own; but it surely doesn't turn him into another Mozart to think that he could have created this 'exercise in minimalist chanson writing', with its narrow voice ranges and restricted harmonic palette (cf. ibid. 30–1), at the age of 8 or 9.

moreover, Florentine manuscripts fall into line with the prevailing usage. Cappella Giulia XIII. 27 contains a four-voice version of Pietrequin's *Mais que ce fust secretement*, which it supplies with an alien text incipit but still attributes to Pietrequin.[255] Florence 229 presents Caron's *Madame qui tant* with an added altus; and while all the remaining sources, which transmit the piece in three parts, leave the music anonymous, it hardly seems possible that the scribe of Florence 229 would have meant to identify Caron solely as the creator of the not very skil-ful altus — especially if, as Atlas has argued, that voice only entered the Florentine tradition after the original version had already appeared there in at least two manuscripts.[256]

Yet if all this would seem to cast doubt on what has become the standard read-ing for the ascription of *Fortuna desperata* in Cappella Giulia XIII. 27, we must recall that the second bassus transmitted here does not merely supplement the original work but supplants one of its parts. In matters of authorship, in fact, it would have done more than that. By all available evidence, musicians of the fifteenth century understood newly created voices — especially voices of a notably active character — that displaced one or more parts of a model composition as lit-erally wresting ownership of the resulting polyphony from the composer of the appropriated material. Hence the duos in Segovia based on the tenors of *Tout a par moy* or *D'ung aultre amer* carry attributions to Tinctoris rather than to Frye or Ockeghem; similarly, the canonic lower parts with which Josquin replaced the original contra of *De tous biens plaine* mean that the composition now belongs to him, and no longer to Hayne.[257] Although I know of only two three-voice pieces of this type that survive with attribution, both follow the same principle even though the ratio of old voices to new would appear on the surface to favour the original composer. Segovia transmits arrangements of *Fortuna desperata* and *La Martinella* in which an athletic, highly 'instrumental' contra replaces the original lowest voice; it ascribes the first to Isaac, the second to Josquin.[258] While the scribe may conceivably have thought Isaac the composer of the original *Martinella* and thus regarded the bassus in a manner somewhat akin to a *si placet* part, he surely did not believe that Josquin had written the original *Fortuna des-perata*.[259] The upshot of all this would appear obvious: if Felice created the second bassus for *Fortuna desperata* in Cappella Giulia XIII. 27 — a bassus very

---

[255] Cf. Atlas, *The Cappella Giulia Chansonnier*, i. 113–20.

[256] Cf. ibid. 205–7.

[257] For Tinctoris's *Tout a par moy* and *D'ung aultre amer*, cf. above, nn. 124 and 138, respectively; for Josquin's *De tous biens plaine*, cf. n. 220.

[258] See Segovia, fos. cxcvii^v–cxcviii^r (191^v [*sic*]–191^r), 'ysaac', and clxxxii^v (176^v), 'Josquin du pres', as well as the transcriptions in Baker, 'An Unnumbered Manuscript', ii. 990–7, and *New Josquin Edition*, xxvii. 16–17; on the Josquin attribution, which looks particularly implausible, cf. ibid., Critical Commentary, 77–8. Atlas, 'Conflicting Attributions', 261, seems to describe the Isaac piece as a kind of variant concord-ance, with conflicting attribution, for the Martini work from which its two upper voices come.

[259] An intabulation of *La martinella* in Basle, Universitätsbibliothek, F. IX. 22, fos. 27^v–30^r, ascribes the music to 'Isacio compositore'; cf. Martini, *Secular Pieces*, p. xix.

much like those of two Segovia pieces—an independent copy of the resulting three-voice setting would surely have borne his name and no other.[260]

Nevertheless, the matter cannot rest even here; for the new three-voice version of *Fortuna desperata* in Cappella Giulia XIII. 27 does not survive on its own but forms a subset of a larger modular complex. Hence while we cannot prove without doubt that the scribe of Cappella Giulia XIII. 27 would have shown the same measure of solicitude towards a fellow Florentine that the Ferrarese scribe of Casanatense 2856 did towards Martini, we would still think that an attribution restricted in essence to the second bassus would have appeared in direct proximity to that voice—especially since, in this context, the scribe would have had no other practical means of singling out the setting that it created. Admittedly, the sources fail to provide a direct parallel that could either corroborate or refute this supposition. As we have seen, the interlocking versions of *De tous plaine* on the following pages of Cappella Giulia XIII. 27 have no attribution.[261] Neither does the copy of *D'ung aultre amer* in Seville–Paris that presents a 'Bassus ab[s]que alio' on the same page as Ockeghem's original contra.[262] But the general pattern that we have observed surely leaves no real ground for thinking that the attribution placed over the full array of voices for *Fortuna desperata* refers to anything less than the fundamental component of that array—the original three-part song.[263] Read against the practice of the time, Cappella Giulia XIII. 27 does not call Felice the composer of a substitute bassus for *Fortuna desperata*. It calls him the composer of *Fortuna desperata* itself.[264]

[260] The dual ascription of *Qu'es mi vida preguntays* (see above, n. 244) clearly does not fit the pattern described here; the explanation probably lies both in chronology—the setting belongs to an earlier generation than the music considered in this paragraph—and in the character of Ockeghem's substitute contras, which, unlike the examples just mentioned, do not distinguish themselves in any significant respect from the original voices and thus amplify rather than transform the original composition.

[261] By coincidence or not, Cappella Giulia XIII.27 presents *Nec michi nec tibi* with its puzzling attribution to Virgilius on the opening immediately preceding *Fortuna desperata*. But if this has any bearing on the question of *Fortuna desperata*, then it more likely than not reinforces the assumption that the 'Felice' attribution refers to the original piece rather than an arrangement or any portion thereof; see the discussion of authorship above, n. 106.

[262] Seville–Paris, fos. *j*1ᵛ–*j*2ʳ (Seville 5-I-43, fos. 51ᵛ–52ʳ); cf. Ockeghem, *Collected Works*, iii, p. lxiii. In a rare slip, Plamenac ('A Reconstruction', 1952, 249–51) misread the rubric as 'Bassus ab alio' and took this to mean that 'the name of the original composer was probably given in this source but was cut off later'. The error has continued through the literature, most consequentially in Taruskin, *D'ung aultre amer*, 2, who makes explicit what Plamenac implies: 'In the manuscript all three original parts as Ockeghem conceived them are given, plus the "bassus ab alio"—or "bass by someone else."'

[263] At first sight, it could appear that the layout of the music itself reinforces this conclusion: the manuscript groups the three original voices together on the verso page, the two additional voices on the recto, thus setting Felice's name, in the upper margin of the verso, directly above the three-voice *Fortuna desperata*. But the arrangement would seem fortuitous, as the copy of *De tous biens plaine* mixes Hayne's voices and those of the arrangement in an apparently meaningless order. In Augsburg 142a, moreover, Agricola's *Fortuna desperata* shows the three original voices on the left, Agricola's new voices on the right; but the attribution, spread across both pages—'Allexander' on the verso, 'A' on the recto—leaves no doubt that it refers to the whole.

[264] As I only learned after I had come to the conclusion argued in the preceding paragraphs, Honey Meconi has independently explored a similar line of reasoning in her contribution to this volume. Nevertheless, if I arrived at my ideas without knowledge of hers—as she certainly arrived at hers without knowledge of mine—I may never even have started down the path to these ideas without her. Late in my

Assuming that we have understood the attribution in Cappella Giulia XIII. 27 correctly, the question then arises of whether we should believe it. Here, I see no room for doubt. Felice may have died some fifteen years before the creation of Cappella Giulia XIII. 27.[265] But even at this distance, the Florentine scribes would surely have had reliable sources for the work of a compatriot. Still more to the point, we must recall that *Fortuna desperata* itself clearly originated in Florence.[266] In other words, the attribution in Cappella Giulia XIII. 27 presents us with a Florentine source ascribing a Florentine piece to a Florentine composer. Or to put it yet another way: if we cannot depend on Cappella Giulia XIII. 27 to tell us the author of *Fortuna desperata*, what can we depend on? Some, perhaps, might argue that the absence of an attribution in Florence 121 betrays a measure of uncertainty in the local tradition; but Florence 121 contains no attributions whatever, leaving the point moot.[267] Some, too, might think it unlikely for such an obscure figure to have created such a celebrated work in his only identified composition. But *Fortuna desperata*, for all its touching eloquence, hardly presupposes the skills and sophistication of a major composer—quite the contrary; and in any event, as the creator of one great success and, so far as we know, nothing else, Felice does not stand alone. We might, for example, usefully remember Malcort, whose one surviving composition, *Malheur me bat*, enjoyed sufficient esteem to serve as the basis of masses by Josquin, Obrecht, and Agricola—and attract attributions to Martini and Ockeghem.[268] Malcort, we might also note, had to wait a long time for modern research to give him his due: not until Rob Wegman and Barbara Haggh uncovered singers to whom we could put his name did scholars acknowledge what simple logic could have told them long before.[269]

preparation of this article, the scholarly grapevine brought me rumours of her arguments about the text of *Fortuna desperata*. My own thoughts about the origin of the piece had focused, like those of Strohm (cf. above, n. 62), on Naples, and word of a Florentine connection surely helped open my eyes to other possibilities—and precisely this, I suspect, enabled me to recognize what I, like so many others, had so long failed to see even when staring it right in the face.

[265] Cf. Atlas, *The Cappella Giulia Chansonnier*, i. 26–8.   [266] See above, beginning of Sect. V.
[267] Cf. Blackburn, 'Two "Carnival Songs" Unmasked', 170–7.
[268] On the sources and attributions, cf. particularly Atlas, *The Cappella Giulia Chansonnier*, i. 149–55; Brown, *A Florentine Chansonnier*, Text vol., 88–9; and Hudson, 'Two Ferrarese Masses', 279–83, but in the light of Wegman, 'Music and Musicians at the Guild of Our Lady in Bergen op Zoom', 240, and Strohm as cited above, n. 114.
[269] See Wegman, 'Music and Musicians at the Guild of Our Lady in Bergen op Zoom', 221–30 and 240, and the following works by Haggh: 'Music, Liturgy, and Ceremony in Brussels, 1350–1500' (Ph.D. diss., University of Illinois at Urbana-Champaign, 1988), 627; 'Itinerancy to Residency: Professional Careers and Performance Practices in 15th-Century Sacred Music', *Early Music*, 17 (1989), 359–66 at 366 n. 39; and 'Crispijne and Abertijne: Two Tenors at the Church of St Niklaas, Brussels', *Music & Letters*, 76 (1995), 325–44, at 338–9. Prior to these discoveries, Atlas (*The Cappella Giulia Chansonnier*, i. 149–55, and esp. 153) had irrefutably removed Martini from contention but did not attempt to resolve the claims of Ockeghem and Malcort; and while Brown (*A Florentine Chansonnier*, Text vol., 88–9) recognized the weakness of the ascription to Ockeghem, he sought to restore the credibility of that to Martini—not least because '[a] composer named Malcort, otherwise completely unknown, is not apt to have written so fine a composition' (88). Hudson ('Two Ferrarese Masses', 279–82) subsequently completed the elimination of Ockeghem, but he, too, found it 'difficult to believe that one who could compose a piece of the popularity and sophistication of *Malheur me bat* would not have left further evidence of his existence' (283)—and so opted for Martini.

The composer of *Fortuna desperata* has also had a long wait for recognition; in so far as his name has gained any posthumous currency at all, it has done so through a dubious gloss on his own creation. Only now can he enjoy the honour to which authorship of perhaps the most famous Italian song of the later fifteenth century entitles him—a belated, but still gratifying, *fortuna felice*.

VII

We can conclude simply. If Italian songs by Busnoys existed, they would offer a powerful reason for thinking that he spent a portion of his career in Italy. But we have no Italian songs by Busnoys. While he may well have composed *Con tutta gentileça*, he did not do so to an Italian text; and while *Fortuna desperata* has an Italian text, he did not compose it. What I described at the outset as the 'Italian hypothesis' thus comes to rest solely on the theorists and on the dissemination of the secular music. The theorists, however, do not really yield much grist for biographical inference. Apart from Tinctoris, who had a documented personal acquaintance with Busnoys, few writers mention him more than once.[270] As Paula Higgins has shown, moreover, several of the theoretical references to Busnoys seem beholden more to discussions in earlier treatises than to first-hand knowledge of the man or his music.[271] In any event, theorists do not write solely about composers in their own back yard—even Tinctoris, who knew Busnoys in the 1460s, surely did not require continued personal contacts to write about his works.[272] As for the sources, the rather sobering findings that we have made about Pixérécourt and Florence 229 leave no doubt that the scribes or patrons behind these manuscripts pursued their enthusiasm for Busnoys at more than a little distance from the composer. Clearly, whatever explains the dramatic shift in the transmission of his work from France to Italy, it does not presuppose his presence on the Italian scene.

Busnoys may, of course, have visited Italy in the 1480s nevertheless. But on the evidence presently available, we really do not have any reason to think he did. More likely than not, he remained in the North, on those same Habsburg-Burgundian territories in which he had moved since the 1460s. Musicological studies, especially in the English language, have tended to neglect this part of the world; only recently have we begun to recover a sense of the rich musical life that flourished there in the later part of the fifteenth century.[273] In this respect, the career of Antoine Busnoys proves exemplary. Not every great master needed to venture beyond the Alps.

---

[270] Cf. the overviews in Brooks, 'Antoine Busnois as a Composer of Chansons', i. 7–8, and Higgins, 'Antoine Busnois and Musical Culture', 13–21.

[271] Ibid., esp. 15–16 and 20.   [272] Cf. above, n. 126.

[273] Obviously, I have in mind above all Strohm's *Music in Late Medieval Bruges* and the various works of Rob Wegman cited in the course of this study, not to mention Higgins, '*In hydraulis* Revisited'.

Notes on Contributors

ALLAN W. ATLAS is Distinguished Professor of Music at Brooklyn College and the Graduate School of the City University of New York. In addition to interests in the Renaissance, he has written extensively on Puccini and has recently published a book entitled *The Wheatstone English Concertina in Victorian England* (Oxford, 1996).

JAAP VAN BENTHEM teaches at the Rijksuniversiteit Utrecht and is author of numerous studies on the music of Josquin and his contemporaries. He is currently producing a new critical edition of the works of Johannes Ockeghem.

ALEXANDER BLACHLY is Associate Professor and Director of Choral Music at the University of Notre Dame. The 1992 recipient of the Noah Greenberg Award of the American Musicological Society, he is founding director of Pomerium, with whom he has produced seven commercial recordings, including *Antoine Busnoys: In hydraulis and Other Works* (Dorian 90184, 1993).

M. JENNIFER BLOXAM is Associate Professor of Music at Williams College. She is the author of articles in *JAMS*, *Early Music History*, *Journal of Musicology*, and numerous anthologies and dictionaries. Her areas of special interest include fifteenth- and sixteenth-century masses and motets, and especially their relationship to late medieval liturgy and chant, religious art, and literature.

HOWARD MAYER BROWN (d. 20 February 1993), was Ferdinand Schevill Distinguished Service Professor at the University of Chicago. The author of numerous books, articles, and editions of Renaissance music, he is widely regarded as one of the greatest musicologists of the century.

DAVID FALLOWS is Professor of Music at the University of Manchester. He is the author of *Dufay* (rev. edn., London, 1987), editor of *Chansonnier de Jean de Montchenu* (Paris, 1991), and *Oxford, Bodleian Library, MS. Canon. Misc. 213* (Chicago, 1995), and has written extensively on fifteenth-century songs.

BARBARA HAGGH is Associate Professor of Music at the University of North Texas. She has edited the book *Musicology and Archival Research* (Brussels, 1994), as well as *Two Offices for St Elizabeth of Hungary* (Ottawa, 1995), and has also published articles on Dufay, the Order of the Golden Fleece, and music in late medieval Brussels.

PAULA HIGGINS is Associate Professor of Music at the University of Notre Dame and currently Editor-in-Chief of *JAMS*. The 1987 recipient of the Alfred Einstein Award of the American Musicological Society, she has published numerous articles on Busnoys and his contemporaries and is currently at work on a book about Fanny Mendelssohn Hensel. Her forthcoming monograph *Parents and Preceptors: Authority, Lineage, and the Conception of the Composer in Early Modern Europe* will be published by Oxford University Press.

ANDREA LINDMAYR-BRANDL is Assistant Professor in the Department of Music at the University of Salzburg and editor of the *Mozart Jahrbuch*. Author of *Quellenstudien zu den Motetten von Johannes Ockeghem* (1990), she is working on an edition of the works of Gaspar van Weerbeke.

MICHAEL LONG is Professor of Music at the State University of New York, Buffalo. The 1990 recipient of the Einstein Award of the American Musicological Society, he has published articles on the musical culture of the fourteenth and fifteenth centuries and is completing a book on fourteenth-century Italian secular song.

HONEY MECONI is Associate Professor of Music at Rice University. Her research interests include borrowing in Renaissance music as well as the music of the Habsburg-Burgundian court. Her book on Pierre de la Rue will be published by Oxford University Press. She is currently at work on a monograph about Hildegard of Bingen.

MARY NATVIG is Associate Professor at the College of Musical Arts, Bowling Green State University, where she directs the Early Music Ensemble, plays in the Balinese gamalan, and performs regularly on violin, viola da gamba, and rebab. She is author of a number of studies on Busnoys and late fifteenth-century Burgundian musical culture.

LEEMAN L. PERKINS is Professor of Music at Columbia University, editor of *The Mellon Chansonnier* (New Haven, 1979), and author of numerous articles on Busnoys, Okeghem, and their contemporaries. General Editor of the Masters and Monuments of the Renaissance series published by the Broude Trust, for which he is completing an edition of Busnoys's chansons, he will soon embark on the edition of a volume of motets for the New Josquin Edition. His forthcoming history of Renaissance music will be published by W. W. Norton.

MARTIN PICKER is Professor Emeritus of Music at Rutgers, The State University of New Jersey. A specialist in Franco-Flemish music of the late fifteenth and early sixteenth centuries, his main publications in this area include *The Chanson Albums of Marguerite of Austria*; *Fors Seulement: Thirty Compositions*; *The Motet Books of Andrea Antico*; and the Garland Composer Resource Manuals *Ockeghem and Obrecht* and *Henricus Isaac*.

JOSHUA RIFKIN is conductor of the Bach Ensemble and author of numerous articles on fifteenth-century manuscripts, Schütz, Bach, and Schubert. His recording *Antoine Busnois: Chansons* (Nonesuch: H-71247) with the Nonesuch Consort was the first devoted exclusively to Busnoys's music.

PETER URQUHART is Associate Professor of Music at the University of New Hampshire. His research centres on problems of pitch and structure in Franco-Flemish music of the fifteenth and sixteenth centuries. An editor of the New Josquin Edition, he is also director of the ensemble Capella Alamire, which has released four recordings of Franco-Flemish music by Josquin, Ockeghem, Busnoys, and Gombert.

FLYNN WARMINGTON, an independent scholar working in Cambridge, Massachusetts, is the author of numerous studies of fifteenth-century manuscripts.

Rob C. Wegman is Assistant Professor of Music at Princeton University. A former British Academy Postdoctoral Research Fellow at Corpus Christi College, Oxford, he is author of *Born for the Muses: The Life and Masses of Jacob Obrecht* (Oxford, 1994) as well as a number of pioneering articles on the musical culture of Busnoys and his contemporaries.

Richard Wexler is Associate Professor of Music at the University of Maryland, College Park. He is the editor, with Dragan Plamenac, of *Johannes Ockeghem: Collected Works, Volume III*, and is currently at work on a complete edition of the works of Antoine Bruhier for the Broude Trust. He has been appointed by the Library of Congress to be the general editor of the projected edition and facsimile publication of the Laborde chansonnier.

Index of Manuscripts and Early Printed Books

The index is mainly limited to discussions of sources *per se*, but under each source reference is made to works listed in the Index of Compositions by or Attributed to Busnoys. Catalogues of Busnoys's chansons, with concordances, may be found in Chapters 2 and 13.

Index of Compositions by
or Ascribed to Busnoys

The index includes works ascribed to Busnoys in at least one source, as well as works attributed to him by modern scholars.

General Index